A HISTORY OF WALES

A HISTORY OF WALES

From the Norman Invasion to the
Edwardian Conquest

John Edward Lloyd, M.A.

PROFESSOR OF HISTORY IN THE UNIVERSITY
COLLEGE OF NORTH WALES, BANGOR

Introduction by Jessica Jahiel, Ph.D.

BARNES
&NOBLE
BOOKS
NEW YORK

Introduction Copyright © 2004 by Barnes & Noble Books

First Published in 1911 as Volume 2 of J.E. Lloyd's *A History of Wales*

This edition published by Barnes & Noble Publishing, Inc.

Cover Design by Pronto Design, Inc.

2004 Barnes & Noble Publishing, Inc.

ISBN 0-7607-5241-9

Printed and bound in the United States of America

1 3 5 7 9 10 8 6 4 2

CONTENTS

INTRODUCTION

WALES, the "land of song," has a unique language and a complex history. The Romans tried and failed to conquer Wales; centuries later, the Normans who took England in 1066 tried—and had to persist for more than two hundred years before they finally succeeded. When King Edward I of England at last vanquished Llywelyn and achieved his goal of ruling Wales, he was able to control it only by constructing a series of costly castles, almost bankrupting his government in the process. What was it about the land and people of Wales that made it so difficult for a wealthier, more centralized, more organized, and better-equipped power to subdue and hold them—and what made it possible for Edward to prevail at last in 1282?

A History of Wales: From the Norman Invasion to the Edwardian Conquest, is actually volume II of Lloyd's work, *A History of Wales: From the Earliest Times to the Edwardian Conquest,* first published in 1911. This work covers the centuries from the Norman invasion to the point at which Wales came under English rule following the death of David ap Llywelyn in 1282. The story told in this volume is a fascinating and detailed account of those years of conflict during which a geographically and politically fragmented Wales fought to preserve its independence and then to maintain its very identity. During those centuries, changes in the social structure, religion, and economic base of Wales strengthened the Welsh desire for independence. At the same time, paradoxically, those very changes may have enabled the English to achieve what the Romans had been unable to accomplish: the conquest of Wales.

A well-written historical account should be as enthralling as an adventure recounted by the campfire and should present a good story of the people, geography, weather, and events that shape a nation. Lloyd's work does all that and more. Even readers with only a casual interest in the history of Wales, perhaps intrigued by reading or watching a work of fiction such as the popular *Brother Cadfael* books and television dramas, will quickly find themselves caught up by the story and carried along by the flow of Lloyd's enjoyable and easy-to-read narrative style.

For many years, J.E. Lloyd's *A History of Wales: From the Earliest Times to the Edwardian Conquest* was the standard history for early Wales; the authoritative source for information about Wales before the year 1282. Almost a hundred years after its first publication, it remains an important resource for scholars and historians and is used as a reference work by researchers around the world. First published in 1911, Lloyd's monumental work was the first serious attempt to create a compilation of the early history of Wales. Its importance to Wales and to the study of Welsh history cannot be overstated. Working from manuscript sources, many of them incomplete and most written in Latin or Welsh, Lloyd set out to sort and sift through the writings for genuine, verifiable information. His goal was to set down the truth in as objective a manner as possible, his focus was on facts, but his writing is anything but dry—his *History of Wales* tells a captivating, compelling story.

John Edward Lloyd, born in England in 1861, was Welsh by parentage. He began his academic career by attending the University of Wales at Aberysthwyth, which opened in 1872. After studying at Lincoln College, Oxford, he returned to Aberysthwyth and became a lecturer of Welsh history at the University, gaining recognition for the quality of his research and publications in Medieval Welsh history. Later, he became the first Professor of History at the University College of North Wales, Bangor (1895-1930). He was the first Chairman of the Board of Celtic Studies and the editor of its *Bulletin*; he also served as editor of the first edition of the *Dictionary of Welsh Biography*. R.T. Jenkins, the first Professor of Welsh History at the University of Wales, Bangor (1930-1948), and a later editor of the *Dictionary of Welsh Biography* (1941-70), made the statement that Lloyd had "created Welsh history." In 1934, Lloyd was knighted in recognition of his contribution to Welsh scholarship.

Whether or not it is true that J.E Lloyd, in the words of R.T. Jenkins, "created Welsh history," in writing *A History of Wales: From the Earliest Times to the Edwardian Conquests* he certainly provided the Welsh with both a coherent history and a way to study history. The monumental work was an authoritative source and a basis for the work of future scholars; the methods of painstaking and critical analysis employed by Lloyd set the standards for Welsh historiography.

The study of written history and of the process of writing history is becoming steadily more complex as scholars delve deeper into the study of the methods and approaches of historians. There are trends and fashions in the study and writing of history, as there are in everything else, but historiography demands a critical approach—it is essential to consider the source, even when that means looking into the mirror. In order to understand history as written by any individual author, it is important to know something of the author himself—not only his intellectual and cultural environment and influences, but also, if possible, his ambitions and motivations. Today's historiographers must look analytically at the works and the historians who are their subjects, and ask 'How good were their sources, what were their assumptions, and why?" as well as "What points were they trying to make, what agendas were they attempting to follow?"

Lloyd's impact on the study and writing of Welsh history is both vast and profound. In a real sense, he created Welsh history as an academic discipline and set the standards for the critical examination of sources. The scope of his scholarship and influence is a subject of great interest to current students of both history and historiography. This is perhaps best reflected by the title of a current project being developed by the Board of Celtic Studies of the University of Wales at Bangor: an in-depth examination of "J.E. Lloyd and the development of Welsh historiography."

Since Lloyd's *History* was first published in 1911, many scholarly and popular works by more recent historians have followed the path established by Lloyd's efforts. Inevitably, criticisms have flared and faded along with the trends in the writing of history. Nonetheless, even today his *History* remains an authoritative source and the basis for other scholars' research. Lloyd's dedication to research and accurate reporting, together with his enjoyable writing style, are still an extremely appealing combination. From the historian's and scientist's perspective, perhaps the greatest value derives from the huge scope of this authoritative work together with Lloyd's own, very realistic assessment of the function and usefulness of *any* historical work. No author can ever claim that his work, however brilliant and however significant, is the final word on the subject. There is no doubt that Lloyd understood and accepted this. In his own words, from the author's preface to the first edition: "In a field where so much is matter of conjecture, it has not been possible altogether to avoid speculation and hypothesis, but I can honestly say that I have not written in support of any special theory or to urge any preconceived opinion upon the reader. My purpose has been to map out, in this difficult region of study, what is already known and established, and thus to define more clearly the limits of that "terra incognita" which still awaits discovery."

The years during which Lloyd was studying, then teaching, doing research, and writing the *History* were also the years during which a strong nationalist movement was developing in Wales. Scholars were an essential part of this movement. Just as Lloyd's work was providing new depth and legitimacy to the study of Welsh history, the work of John Morris-Jones (1864-1929), Professor of Welsh at Bangor University, was providing the same depth and legitimacy to the study of Welsh language and literature. And just as Lloyd's efforts resulted in the publication in 1911 of a monumental work that would stand as a lasting contribution to the history and national identity of Wales and to the way in which history was studied, Morris-Jones' scientific approach resulted in the publication in 1913 of a similarly seminal work on Welsh language and literature.

The major influences on J.E. Lloyd's life were Wales itself, its people and language and politics, and the steady growth of the Welsh national revival. Lloyd was a founding member of the Cymru Fydd (Young Wales) movement in 1886, together with Owen Edwards and others. The objective of this movement was to gain self-government for Wales. Some individuals and groups went further, seeking complete independence for Wales and official status for the Welsh language, but all were agreed on the importance of developing a system of education. This in itself was nothing new—higher education in Wales had been the dream of many Welshmen over many centuries—but in the late nineteenth century, the dream was becoming a reality.

The University College of Wales at Aberystwyth was founded in 1872 and was maintained for ten years by support from the people of Wales. With eventual assistance from the government, two additional colleges were created: The University College of South Wales at Cardiff in 1883 and the University College of North Wales at Bangor in 1884. The University of Wales, consisting of these three colleges, was established by royal charter in 1893. History was taught at Bangor from the University's founding in 1884. Two more royal charters established the National Library and the National Museum in 1907.

Thus, the context of Lloyd's *History of Wales: From the Earliest Times to the Edwardian Conquest* is one of Welsh national revival. Lloyd's achievements and those of other scholars of the period reflected the new possibilities provided by a system of Welsh higher education.

They also represented a new beginning in Welsh literature, and contributed immensely to the development of a strong sense of Welsh national identity. The new surge in Welsh scholarship had begun in 1900 when John Rhys and Brynmor Jones published *The Welsh People,* and in 1902 and 1906 when Owen Edwards published *Wales* and *A Short History of Wales.* When these works were followed in 1911 by Lloyd's *History of Wales from the Earliest Times to the Edwardian Conquest,* and, two years later, by *A Welsh Grammar, Historical and Comparative* by John Morris-Jones, Wales had, at last, the solid foundations for a national identity: a separate history and culture, scholarship, the beginnings of a Welsh historiography, and a separate language.

Lloyd's observations of Welsh language use and grammar led him to postulate a connection between the early Welsh, the Irish, and the early peoples of Europe. He believed that the earliest Welsh people and language were not, in fact, Celtic, but predated the arrival of the Celts; he suggested that the earliest Welsh may have had an Iberian origin.

It appears that he was correct. Recent genetic research at University College, London, has established that the Welsh, genetically speaking, have little in common with "Celts," but everything in common with the Basques who live on the French-Spanish border. The study revealed that a particular Y chromosome, common in Ireland and Wales, and especially common in north-west Wales, the more rural and traditionally more isolated part of the country, is also common in the Basque population though not at all common in England or indeed in the rest of Europe. This makes it probable that the early Welsh, like the Basques, came from the earliest (Paleolithic) inhabitants of Europe. It seems likely that these pre-Celtic people were the first modern inhabitants of Britain. These "first Britons" owe their genetic survival to the fact that Wales was relatively unaffected by the large-scale Anglo-Saxon invasion that devastated the population of England.

The notion of the existence, let alone the development, of a "national character" was out of fashion for some time, but is enjoying a mild resurgence now that some theories based primarily on linguistics and anthropology are being given some support and legitimacy by the results of genetic studies. The Welsh border does seem to have functioned as a sort of "genetic barrier", blocking the advance and influence of the Anglo-Saxons; that said, there is still no clear answer to the question of whether genetics may have played a more important role than, say, geography and climate in the development of the Welsh national character.

Certainly by Lloyd's time, something had changed in the Welsh body politic. The new nationalism was bringing the Welsh together in a new way. The Wales about which Lloyd wrote in *A History* was tribal and disunited, divided, even subdivided—at worst, a group of small principalities dedicated to fighting one another; at best, a temporary, loose confederation of princelings temporarily united as a response to actual or threatened invasion. The Welsh in 1282 were united in defeat; by Lloyd's time, they were united in the common cause of restoring national awareness, pride, and a strong national identity. Lloyd, Morris-Jones, and others thus helped achieve what Llywelyn could not: They unified the country and gave a history and a voice to Wales, reminding the Welsh that Welsh independence was a goal that should and would be met.

No more than 150 years ago, the entry under "Wales" in early editions of the Encyclopaedia Britannica read "for Wales, see England." Today's entry under "Wales" is lengthy, complex, and detailed, as befits any description or discussion of a nation that can claim one of the oldest living cultures in Europe. This is due in no small part to the work of Sir John Edward Lloyd, the historian whose seminal book gave Wales a history, helped create and promote a sense of national identity, and still stands as an authoritative source and unmatched resource for researchers, historians, and, indeed, anyone with an interest in the history of Wales.

Jessica Jahiel, Ph.D., is an author and editor with more than thirty years experience in the publishing industry. She lives in Illinois.

CHAPTER I

THE NORMAN CONQUEST. — FIRST STAGE

(In a paper on "Wales and the Coming of the Normans," included in the Transactions of the Honourable Society of Cymmrodorion for 1899–1900, I have discussed in some detail the events of the period 1039–93, and I may perhaps be pardoned if I refer the reader to this essay for a full account of the evidence on which I have relied in writing this chapter. As an appendix to the paper, Ann. C. MSS. B. and C. for this period are printed in parallel columns from the original MSS.)

I. GRUFFYDD AP LLYWELYN.

BOTH in England and in Wales events were ripening in the middle of the eleventh century for the revolution known as the Norman Conquest. Instead of the ruin and devastation caused by the attacks of a savage enemy who could not be overthrown and yet knew not how to turn his victories to any beneficent purpose, there was to be submission to a foreign foe who with the yoke imposed order and civilisation. But, notwithstanding the likeness of their fortunes in this respect, the two countries were governed during the years which preceded the coming of Duke William by men of a very different temper, and the difference affected vitally the course of the ensuing struggle. England had as king the half-Norman Edward, a foreigner by breeding and in sympathies, who familiarised the English with Norman ideas and institutions; when the combat came, it was fierce, but short and decisive, and the Norman invaders soon became absolute masters of the country. Wales was during the same period under the sway of as striking a personality as any to be encountered in Welsh history—a strong and passionate ruler of men, who struck boldly for the national cause and rekindled the dying fires of patriotic enthusiasm.

1

In Wales, therefore, the battle between the new-comer and the native raged obstinately and long and left the Norman in possession of a portion only of the field for which it had been fought. The Norman Conquest of Wales was not, indeed, completed until long after the name of Norman had been merged, so far as Britain was concerned, in that of Englishman.

After the meteoric careers of Llywelyn ap Seisyll and Rhydderch ab Iestyn, there was a return, both in North and South Wales, to the ancient dynasties; Iago ab Idwal, a great grandson of Idwal the Bald, was chosen to rule over Gwynedd, while Deheubarth acknowledged the lordship of Hywel and Maredudd, grandsons of the Einon ab Owain who fell in 984. This was, however, but a brief triumph for legitimacy, for in 1039, after a reign of six years, Iago was slain by his own men, and the only son of Llywelyn ap Seisyll,[1] who bore the name Gruffydd, stepped into the position which his father had once filled with such distinction.[2]

Border traditions, preserved by the facile pen of Walter Map, have handed down a vivid portrait of Gruffydd ap Llywelyn, of which the clear-cut outlines in nowise run counter to the facts recorded of him in history, but rather derive confirmation from them. As a youth he was, we are told, sluggish and unadventurous, given to loafing around the paternal hearth and insensible to the charm of a dangerous enterprise—a lad whose want of spirit seemed disgraceful to the kinsfolk who saw in him the natural successor of his father as king of Gwynedd. But one New Year's Eve,[3] driven out of doors by the reproaches of his sister, he had an experience which wrought his conversion into a bold and strenuous warrior. The night was a night of signs and omens; in many ways might a man learn on this last evening of the year what should befall him in the coming twelvemonth, and Gruffydd chose the least perilous, that of eaves-dropping. He planted himself against the wall of a house where a company were intent upon the process of boiling large pieces of beef in the family "callor" or cauldron. "Strange," said the cook, "but here is one piece which, however firmly I drive it down with my fork, always persists in coming to the top." Gruffydd drank in the words, convinced that they were prophetic of his own future, and from that moment was another man; what taunt and reproach could not do was brought about by the spur of ambition and the vision of coming greatness. The man who thus attained the full measure of manhood in a moment of transformation was cast in a large mould. He had courage, persistence, a quick imagination, the tyrannous, masterful spirit, impatient of all rivalry, and—

what is often found in conjunction with this last—a cordial and easy manner, the expression of a nature at ease in the confidence of its own strength. Neither in love nor in war would he brook any effort to supplant him, and young men who might grow to be a menace to his power were marked for destruction. But his wit played like a lambent name around the darker aspects of his career. "Speak not of killing," said he, "I do but blunt the horns of the offspring of Wales, lest they should wound their dam." Nor was he without those generous impulses which often redeem the violence and cruelty of passionate, forceful men. Map tells the tale how, on the occasion when Gruffydd and Edward came together to negotiate a treaty of peace, neither would at first cross the Severn to meet the other, lest this should be construed as an admission of inferiority, until at last Edward threw dignity to the winds and entered the ferry-boat, whereupon Gruffydd, completely won over by this humility, plunged into the waters to meet the boat, embraced it fervently as it came up and carried the king ashore on his shoulders. One whose better nature could be thus aroused by the sight of virtue in others was clearly not altogether the tyrant and man of blood.

In 1039 Gruffydd became king not only of Gwynedd, but also of Powys (unless, indeed, he was already possessed of this region), and he was thus enabled at the outset of his reign to strike a blow at Mercia which by its boldness and vigour drew attention at once to the rise of a new power in Wales. At Rhyd y Groes on the Severn, a ford in the neighbourhood of Welshpool, the situation of which cannot be more precisely indicated, he suddenly fell upon a Mercian army which had no warning of his approach and inflicted upon it a crushing defeat.[4] Its leader Edwin, brother of Earl Leofric of Mercia, and other men of note were slain, and so complete was the victory that Gruffydd had no need to guard its fruits by assuming the defensive, but was able to pass on to other designs. The stroke was such as to raise the Welsh king forthwith to the position he occupied in regard to England until the year of his death—to make him the terror of the border, portentous and invincible, against whom reprisals were of little avail.

For the next few years Gruffydd's chief concern was to make himself master of Deheubarth. Maredudd ab Edwin had been slain in 1035, and it was, therefore, with Hywel ab Edwin he had to contend, a prince who, as representative of the ancestral line of the district, was by no means easy to dislodge. Gruffydd attacked his territories in the year of Rhyd y Groes, invading Ceredigion and ravaging the lands of the church of Llanbadarn Fawr, and the sudden onslaught was for the moment successful. But Hywel was soon able to recover his position, as may be seen from the fact that he met Gruffydd in battle in 1041[5] at Pencader, near the spot where Dyfed, Ceredigion and Ystrad Tywi meet. The king of Gwynedd was the victor and carried off his defeated rival's wife — a deed which, though duly apologised for by the author of the "Gwentian Brut,"[6] is quite in keeping with Map's portrait of Gruffydd as the fiercely jealous husband of a very beautiful bride. Notwithstanding this defeat, Hywel was still lord of Dyfed and Ystrad Tywi, in 1042, for in that year he met a host of Danish marauders at Pwll Dyfach, some 5 miles northwest of Carmarthen, and signally overthrew them. An unrecorded reverse followed, so that in 1044 he is found returning to Deheubarth as an exile and entering the mouth of the Towy with the aid of a Danish fleet. It was his last enterprise; Gruffydd offered a stout resistance to the invaders, and the death of Hywel in the fray at last gave him the crown for which he had so long striven.

The line of Hywel the Good had at this time no candidate to offer in the room of Hywel ab Edwin, and it might have been supposed, therefore, that Gruffydd had a clear course before him. But in the year following the victory of Aber Tywi a new rival showed himself, in the person of another Gruffydd, son of Rhydderch ab Iestyn, and thus able, equally with the king of Gwynedd, to appeal to the memory of a father who had ruled gloriously. The local associations of this family were with the regions of Erging and Gwent Uchaf,[7] but Gruffydd ap Rhydderch nevertheless found means of stirring up on his behalf the provincial feeling of Deheubarth, and organised a formidable movement against the intruder from North Wales. So threatening was it that in 1046 Gruffydd ap Llywelyn had recourse to English help; the intervention of Earl Swegen, son of Godwine, whose earldom included Herefordshire and Gloucestershire, was secured, and king and earl went together through South Wales, hoping no doubt to crush the movement in favour of the son of Rhydderch.[8] The peace which followed was but the treacherous lull before a storm; next year the "uchelwyr" [9] of Ystrad Tywi, now as ever untamable in their independence, suddenly fell upon the "teulu," the household guard,[10] of the northern leader, and slew 140 of their number. Gruffydd can scarcely have been far away, and probably escaped with difficulty from the trap which had been laid for him. It was in vain that he punished the daring attempt by a general devastation of Dyfed and Ystrad Tywi: his authority in South Wales was for the time being shattered, and for the next eight years it is Gruffydd ap Rhydderch who appears as king of Deheubarth.

If he had not been overshadowed and ultimately overwhelmed by a prince of the calibre of Gruffydd ap Llywelyn, Gruffydd of South Wales might have played no mean part in the history of his country. He showed in his brief reign an abundant energy and something of the daring of his greater namesake. In 1049 he was confronted with the peril of a Danish invasion; the heroic remedy was adopted of removing all available plunder from the coast region to the inaccessible woods of the interior.[11] Not content with this, Gruffydd resolved to make common cause with the pirates and to divert their operations from his own shores to those of his neighbours in Gwent and the Forest of Dean.[12] Gwent Iscoed had been seized about 1040 by the house of Morgannwg; Meurig ap Hywel ab Owain, who, owing to his father's advanced age, had assumed the sovereignty some years before the death of the latter in 1043, had possessed himself of the region by force and now ruled it through his son Cadwgan.[13] Gruffydd, therefore, led with alacrity the thirty-six ships of the pirate fleet to the mouth of the Usk, and, when they had done sufficient mischief there, passed with them across the Wye to the great English manor of Tidenham, which was also ravaged without mercy. Bishop Ealdred of Worcester summoned the shire forces of Herefordshire and Gloucestershire to meet the invasion, but the response was feeble and the Welsh of the border included in the levy played their comrades false and gave information to the foe. The result was that Gruffydd was able to surprise the English camp, in the early dawn of a summer's day, and to scatter with great slaughter the force assembled for his discomfiture. This victory, it is certain, was turned to good account by the southern king in the next few years; it was no doubt with his support and encouragement that the ravages were committed for which in the first week of 1053 his brother Rhys ap Rhydderch suffered death at the bidding of Edward,[14] and it is difficult not to trace the hand of Gruffydd in the sudden raid of the same year upon Westbury on Severn, a little to the west of Gloucester, when the Welsh slew a number of the "wardmen" who guarded the city against surprise on the side of the Forest of Dean.[15]

There is little to indicate how Gruffydd ap Llywelyn was in the meantime employed. During the reign of Gruffydd ap Rhydderch he appears but once upon the stage, in an attack upon Herefordshire, delivered in the early summer of 1052.[16] It may well be believed that the occasion for the striking of this blow was the rise in this part of the border of a new and formidable force in the Norman settlement which for some reason or other found Herefordshire specially congenial soil. Earl Swegen, Gruffydd's former ally, had been forced to abandon the realm, with all his kin; his place at Hereford was filled by Ralph, son of the count of the Vexin and King Edward's sister, and with this Norman kinsman of the king's had come others of the same alert and daring race, Richard son of Scrob, who built himself a castle a little south of Ludlow, Osbern, surnamed Pentecost, who may have been the first builder of Ewias Harold Castle, and a Robert who has not been identified. Gruffydd was keen enough to discern that neighbours of this type were far more to be dreaded than the thegns and ceorls of Mercia, and his foray was probably quite as much defensive as offensive in its purpose. He had almost reached Leominster when a mixed force of Normans and English gave him battle, only to suffer a crushing defeat, which enabled Gruffydd to return triumphantly with his spoil, his renown not a whit abated, but rather enhanced by his victory over this new foe. As men told the story with trembling lips, it was not forgotten that the fatal day was the thirteenth anniversary of Rhyd y Groes.

The culminating period of Gruffydd's reign is now approached, during which he was master of the whole of Wales, as well as of much which until his appearance had been English soil. In 1055 [17] he compassed and brought about the death of his rival, Gruffydd ap Rhydderch, and thus was enabled to add Deheubarth once more to his dominions. He had not been many weeks in the enjoyment of his new position ere the vicissitudes of English party politics gave him an ally from an unexpected quarter. At the time of the expulsion in 1051 of Godwine and his sons, Ælfgar, son of the great Earl Leofric of Mercia, had received Harold's earldom of East Anglia; this he had been forced to resign on Harold's return with the rest of the family in 1052, but it had again been bestowed upon him when Harold succeeded his father as Earl of Wessex in 1053. At a council held at London on 20th March, 1055, charges of treason were brought against Ælfgar which there are no means of testing, but which, whether well founded or not, were but weapons in the party strife between the house of Leofric and Godwine. [18] Deprived of his earldom and outlawed, the baffled noble sought help in the first instance, as Harold had done under similar circumstances in 1051, from the Danes of Ireland; he soon had at his command a fleet of eighteen ships, conveying a considerable body of hired troops. Something suggested to him at this point an alliance with Gruffydd ap Llywelyn; [19] the bargain was soon struck, and the united force of Welshmen, Irish mercenaries and followers of Ælfgar made a most formidable combination. It was agreed by the conspirators that no more damaging attack could be made upon Edward and his realm than one which should shake to its foundations the Norman settlement at Hereford. They marched, therefore, on 24th October upon this city; the troop of defenders which Earl Ralph put into the field a couple of miles from the place was soon scattered in flight, with the maladroit earl at their head, the castle was taken with a rush ere its terrified inmates had time to rise from their meal,[20] and Hereford was given up to fire and plunder. Not even the new cathedral, which Bishop Athelstan had recently built on a spot overlooking the full-flowing Wye, was spared from pillage; seven of its canons were killed as they strove to bar the doors against sacrilegious attack; its rich vessels and furniture were carried off, and all that did not tempt the spoiler perished in the general conflagration. The city itself fared no better; booty and captives in abundance loaded the train of Gruffydd and Ælfgar, as they made their way back to Wales.

This bold defiance of the power of the English king did not fail to evoke a speedy answer. Earl Harold, now the chief figure at Edward's court, was commissioned to avenge the insult, and gathered a force at Gloucester for the purpose. But he was not able to penetrate further into the enemy's country than a few miles beyond the valley of the Dore;[21] the secret of Welsh campaigning had not yet been revealed to him, and his final resource was to fortify Hereford against future raids of the kind, leaving Gruffydd untouched in his mountain stronghold. It was clear that peace must be concluded with Ælfgar, whose help made the Welsh chieftain doubly dangerous; after much parleying, an agreement embracing all parties was drawn up at Billingsley, near Boulston in Archenfield,[22] which for the moment restored peace. It was altogether to the advantage of Ælfgar, who regained his earldom and his former position, nor is it to be supposed that Gruffydd's interests were ignored in a settlement so favourable to his ally,—he, too, was no doubt allowed to retain the conquests he had won along the border. How considerable these were will appear from a brief survey of the state of affairs in the march during the latter part of Gruffydd's reign.

Rhuddlan on the Clwyd, which had once been held by the Earls of Mercia, was in 1063 a royal seat of Gruffydd's, where his ships could lie safely in the mouth of the river, ready to bear the king to whatsoever port of his dominions he might choose.[23] The whole country from here to the vale of Maelor, as far as Wat's Dyke to the east, had been cleared by Gruffydd of its English settlers, who no longer tilled the fields of Preston (Prestatyn), Merton (Mertyn), Whitford, Bruncot (Broncoed) and Hope. At Bishopstree (Bistre) he had another residence, to which his vassals in the region of the Alun brought their dues of beer, butter and the like. The Maelor district had for many years formed the English hundred of Exestan, and in 958 King Edgar of Mercia is recorded to have bestowed upon St. Werburgh's Abbey, Chester, the hamlet of Hodeshlith (Hoseley) within its bounds.[24] But under Edward the Confessor the whole of this fertile plain, in which "ham" and "ford" and "stock" bear witness to an English settlement of long standing, was in the hands of Gruffydd; it had, indeed, been formally bestowed upon him by Edward, it maybe in 1055, but in any case, as the recognition of an accomplished fact. Almost the whole hundred of Mersete, lying around Oswestry, was in the like case, and one learns that the English loss was recent from the statement made in Domesday that Whittington, Maesbury and Chirbury, which in 1066 yielded no revenue whatever to the crown, had between them furnished half a night's ferm in the days of Ethelred. The Severn was still the boundary between the two races from Melverley to Leighton, but further south evidence of the aggression of Gruffydd is again forthcoming. Not only Chirbury, but a score of villages round about, where the English system of hidage had been in full force, had been rendered uninhabitable, and, instead of fifty hides paying the king's taxes, there was nothing but a great forest. Along the Herefordshire border, signs of the activity of Gruffydd are, as might be expected, everywhere visible. A line drawn from Brampton Bryan on the Teme to Willersley on the Wye would roughly indicate the western limit of English occupation at this time; all the English villages between this and Radnor Forest—Knighton, Radnor, Kington, Huntington and a score of others—had been abandoned to the Welsh, largely, no doubt, as the result of the raid of 1052. South of the Wye, again, the country bore vivid witness to the work of 1055; only a few villages lining the south bank of the river are entered in Domesday as yielding an income to English lords under the Confessor, and of Archenfield or Erging as a whole it is said that, though at one time paying rent and service to the English king, it had been so devastated by Gruffydd and his successor Bleddyn as to be of no value to the crown in 1066. This remarkable tale of border conquest may fitly close with a reference to Gruffydd's position in Gwent, where he drove out, not the English, but the local dynasty, represented either by Meurig ap

Hywel or by his son Cadwgan.[25] No precise date can be fixed for this event, but the Domesday notices of Nether Went show that the Welsh leader was firmly established in this region at the time of his death; they speak of certain Welshmen, among them Abraham, Archdeacon of Gwent, and Berddig, the king's poet, whose lands had been granted to them by King Gruffydd free from the payment of dues.[26] Thus Gruffydd ruled from sea to sea, king of the four realms of Gwynedd, Powys, Deheubarth and Morgannwg, and master of many a mile to the east of Offa's Dyke.

The peace of Billingsley was of little avail in ending the border warfare between English and Welsh, for in a few months the conflict was renewed.[27] There is good reason for supposing, however, that on this occasion the English were the aggressors. In the February following the sack of Hereford, Bishop Athelstan died, after forty-four years' tenure of the see; a chaplain of Harold's named Leofgar was appointed in his stead, who was very loth, despite his promotion to high ecclesiastical office, to abandon the secular habits he had followed as a priest. He gave great offence by refusing to shave his moustache,[28] and further scandalised the devout by leading in full military array an army against the Welsh, with the sheriff Ælfnoth and the priests of his cathedral. A fighting prelate of this pattern, with the injuries of his see to avenge, was not likely to wait for an attack before taking up arms, and the impression that it was he and not Gruffydd who threw down the gage of battle is confirmed by the fact that the two armies met in the valley of the Machawy, some distance above Glasbury, and many miles to the west of the line which then parted Welsh and English.[29] The day was the 16th of June,[30] and once again Gruffydd won a brilliant victory; bishop and sheriff were among the slain, and those of the host who escaped slaughter were scattered in flight. An attempt was made, as in the previous year, to wipe out the stain of this defeat by a regular campaign against the ever-victorious Welshman, but the marching and encamping had no result save the loss of men and horses, and in the end it was resolved to try the effect of negotiation. So serious had the situation become that the greatest men in the land concerned themselves in the pacification, Earl Harold, the old Earl Leofric of Mercia, and Ealdred of Worcester, soon to become Archbishop of York. By their joint efforts a settlement was arrived at; Gruffydd swore to be faithful as an underking to King Edward and in return was no doubt suffered to retain his conquests. If the meeting between the two rulers described by Map is a historical incident, this was in all likelihood the occasion when it took place; as lord of Gwent, Gruffydd had easy access to Beachley, near Chepstow, where he is said to have awaited Edward, and Aust, just across the channel, whence the English king sailed, was within easy reach of Gloucester.

By the death of Earl Leofric, husband of the renowned Godgifu or Godiva, and himself one of the commanding figures of this period, Ælfgar became in 1057 Earl of Mercia. Gruffydd's ally was thus brought into close neighbourhood with him, for their territories now marched from Hawarden to Ludlow. A still closer tie was formed by the marriage about this time of Gruffydd and Ælfgar's beautiful daughter, Ealdgyth,[31] and the birth of a daughter Nest, to be a fresh pledge of amity between the houses of Gwynedd and of Mercia. Thus when once again, in 1058, the enemies of Ælfgar procured his banishment, he was once more, as in 1055, reinstated with the aid of Gruffydd; some help was also given on this occasion by the fleet which Magnus, son of Harold Hardrada of Norway, brought into the Irish Sea with a vague idea of conquering England; the major purpose was not achieved, but incidentally Magnus weakened Edward's position by contributing to the triumph of the two allied powers of the West.[32]

Ælfgar and Gruffydd as confederate neighbours were fortified against all attack, and accordingly nothing is heard of any further movement against Wales until the end of the year 1062. It is in this year, about Easter, that the last reference occurs to the earl,[33] and, in the absence of any record of the date of his death, he may safely be assumed to have died not many months later. His young son Edwin succeeded to the earldom, and Gruffydd was at once made to feel how momentous for him was the removal of the strong hand, of his friend. Earl Harold obtained the king's leave to try what could be effected by one bold stroke, a bolt from the blue launched at the Welsh chief in the ease of his palace, ere he had time to plan means of escape.[34] The plot was all but successful; directly after the Christmas festivities of the court at Gloucester, at a season when campaigning in Wales was most unusual, Harold rode with a small force of huscarls to Chester, where Ælfgar could no longer bar his progress, and thence made a dash for Rhuddlan, hoping that the suddenness of the onslaught and the swiftness of his movements would enable him to swoop upon his prey ere it was startled into flight. But Gruffydd received timely warning of the approach of the foe, and, hastily boarding one of the vessels that floated with the tide beneath the ramparts of his castle, slipped through the

"Forryd," the "seaward ford" of the Clwyd, into the open sea ere his pursuers were upon him. The smoke of his burning ships and houses and halls curling up into heaven told him afar the story of Harold's disappointed rage.

But the respite which Gruffydd won by his promptitude was brief. His overthrow was now a prime object of the English government, and, as soon as the returning spring made operations in Wales practicable, an expedition was organised against him. Tostig, Earl of Northumberland, brought a force of cavalry into the country, probably skirting the northern coast, with Anglesey as his goal, while his famous brother led a body of light armed troops, specially fitted to traverse the rough Welsh mountains, from Oxford to Bristol, and there at the end of May embarked with his men in a fleet which carried him round the greater part of Wales to meet the northern contingent. The course of the campaign cannot be outlined with any certainty, but it would seem likely that, in the first place, the appearance of Harold's armada in the Bristol Channel deprived Gruffydd of such support as he had in South Wales; at the touch of the foreigner, provincial jealousy awoke in full vigour; the men of Deheubarth gave hostages to Harold and threw off the yoke of Gwynedd. In the second place, there are evidences of a struggle in North Wales, in which the light infantry of Harold no doubt did great execution. The fastnesses of Snowdon were penetrated, the Welsh king was driven from one hiding-place to another, and his subjects were sore beset on every hand. In this extremity Gruffydd, who must have had enemies in abundance, was deserted by those nearest to him; he fell on 5th August, 1063,[35] as the result of a plot, and his head was forthwith sent to Harold as the price of peace.

Such was the tragic end of a career recognised alike by English and Welsh as one of exceptional brilliancy. "He was king," says the English annalist, "over all the Welsh race." The Welsh chronicle styles him "head and shield and defender of the Britons," and expatiates, with unaccustomed rhetoric, upon his melancholy fate; "and now was left in solitary glens the man erst deemed invincible, the winner of countless spoils and immeasurable victories, endlessly rich in gold and silver and precious stones and purple apparel".[36] He founded no dynasty, but he bequeathed to the Welsh people the priceless legacy of a revived national spirit; in his vigour and daring the nation felt its youth renewed and no longer harboured the hidden fear that it had grown old and effete among the peoples of the earth.

II. THE NORMANS AND THE WELSH MARCH.

The overthrow of Gruffydd and the subjugation of Wales must be regarded as a military triumph of the first order. Futile as the previous attempts of Harold had been to curb the power which threatened the peace and good order of the whole English realm, he had at last succeeded in putting an end to the Welsh peril; in the phrase of the Anglo-Norman poet Gaimar, "there was no more heed paid to the Welsh".[37] So deep was the impression made upon the English by the achievements of the earl and his light armed infantry that in the next century the incidents of the campaign, passed on as they were from lip to lip, became involved in a mist of legend, such as ever gathers around the telling of deeds which nourish a nation's pride. Gerald of Wales speaks of pillar-stones, almost certainly mythical, which were erected by Harold to mark the scenes of his victories, each one bearing upon it the inscription: "Hic fuit victor Haroldus".[38] John of Salisbury depicts a slaughter which swept away nearly the whole of the male population of the country, so that the women had to beg the special permission of the king to marry Englishmen.[39] Exaggerations such as these serve to show how vividly Harold's successes appealed to the imagination of his fellow-countrymen and how they recognised in him the saviour to whom it was but meet to offer the crown he had so manfully defended.

Nevertheless, Harold did not conquer Wales in the sense in which this was done by Edward I., or even obtain the hold upon the country which was acquired by Henry I. What he achieved was the reduction of the Welsh question from one of national importance to its old status as a mere border difficulty. New rulers were placed in power; Bleddyn and Rhiwallon, the sons of an unknown Cynfyn ap Gwerstan by his wife Angharad, the widow of Llywelyn ap Seisyll, submitted to Harold and from him received Gwynedd and Powys, swearing to be faithful to King Edward in all things and to pay all renders which in the past had been yielded to the English crown.[40] At the same time, or, it may be, somewhat later, the line of Hywel the Good was reinstated in Deheubarth in the person of Maredudd ab Owain ab Edwin, a nephew of the Hywel ab Edwin whom Gruffydd had crushed in 1044.[41] Cadwgan ap Meurig came to his own again in Morgannwg,[42] while the line of Rhydderch ab Iestyn, though excluded from Deheubarth, put forth a vigorous shoot in Caradog ap Gruffydd ap Rhydderch, who held Gwynllwg and Upper Gwent.[43] From none of these new men was there reason to fear attacks on the grand scale, such as had made the late leader so formidable, but they were under no greater restrictions than the predecessors of Gruffydd ap Llywelyn, and had it in their power to harass the marches no less persistently than in the days of yore. One incident of the border strife which an English chronicler has recorded may be cited to illustrate the position.[44] It would appear that in 1065, two years after the fall of Gruffydd, Harold led an expedition into Nether Went and, having subdued it, ordered the building of a royal residence for the Confessor at Portskewet. So confident was he of the successful accomplishment of his work that he arranged that Edward should pay a visit that summer to his new hunting-lodge, and saw to it that the place was fully provisioned. But on the 24th of August, as the builders were still at their task, Caradog ap Gruffydd made a sudden descent from the hills, slew the workmen and their few defenders and carried off with much glee the stores of food and drink which had been got together for the use of the royal household. The chronicler does not suggest that any vengeance was taken or found possible; notwithstanding the great campaign of 1063, the spirit of the Welsh was still unbroken and their independence was scarcely less ample than before.

Such was the footing on which relations between England and Wales stood when the events of 1066 brought about a complete change of scene, and in the space of a few short months radically altered the situation with which Welshmen had to deal. The conquest of England by Duke William of Normandy meant far more for the Welsh than the substitution of a strong for a weak king of England; accompanied as it was by a great influx into the island of the duke's adventurous subjects and neighbours, it meant that, instead of a sluggish, home-keeping race, who had for ages given up colonisation, Wales must now face the onset of a crowd of busy pioneers, the flower of a people pre-eminently gifted as colonists, men not in the least afraid of the difficulties and dangers of Welsh campaigning. The struggle with the Norman began almost immediately, and for the next thirty-five years it is the topic of primary interest in Welsh history. At one period, the centre of the movement is to be found in North Wales; later on, it is in South Wales that the foreigner makes most headway, but alike in North and South the presence of the Norman is the dominant factor in the situation, and all is confusion and disorder until a rough equilibrium is established between the two contending races.

It has been shown that the Normans had already obtained under the Confessor a firm foothold in Herefordshire. One of the earliest steps of King William was to make sure of this valuable starting-point for further operations by bestowing the earldom of Hereford upon one of his ablest and most trusty lieutenants, William fitz Osbern, lord of Breteuil, his second cousin and hereditary steward of Normandy.[45] The new earl lost no time in bringing home to the Welsh the fact that an era of conquest had begun, and, short as was his tenure of the earldom and important as were his responsibilities in other parts of the kingdom, effected so much in four years as to show that with longer life he might have anticipated by a couple of decades the winning of South Wales. This is the more remarkable in that all this time a bitter struggle was going on to the north of Hereford for the possession of the border. William's first measures excited a revolt, wherein was witnessed for the first time that co-operation between the Mercians and the Welsh which is an outstanding feature of the next few years; Bleddyn and Rhiwallon joined the great Mercian landowner, Eadric the Wild, who had broad estates on the borders of Wales, in an attack upon Herefordshire and Hereford Castle which did serious damage to William and his followers in the summer of 1067.[46] In the following year there was still a more formidable combination; Earl Edwin of Mercia, who had submitted to the king and accompanied him upon the visit to Normandy which occupied most of the year 1067, broke out into revolt with his brother, Earl Morcar of Northumbria, enlisted Bleddyn in his cause, and made ready for a great effort on the part of North and West to shake off the Norman yoke.[47] But Edwin, though an attractive and popular leader, was weak and irresolute; he had scarcely entered upon the struggle ere he laid down his arms and made his peace with the king. Others were not so easily daunted; Eadric, in particular, carried on the war, with the aid of his Welsh allies, into the year 1069, when from north, south and west a combined onslaught was made upon the royal garrison at Shrewsbury. Earl William was able to bring reinforcements upon the scene which saved the castle,[48] but the situation was still precarious until, at the beginning of 1070, the king, after his famous mid-winter march across the bleak and rain-swept Pennines, made his appearance for the first time at Chester, the centre of the Mercian resistance, and took measures to place his supremacy both here and at Shrewsbury upon a firm and settled foundation. When Eadric a few months later, recognising the futility of further conflict, made his final submission to the Conqueror,[49] the subjection of the border was at last complete, and Wales was thrown, in its opposition to Norman rule, henceforth entirely upon its own resources.

Fitz Osbern's busy career was now almost at an end, yet, notwith-standing the difficulties of what may be called the aftermath of Hastings, he had achieved great things as Earl of Hereford. His dash-ing leadership drew around him a great number of adventurous knights, whom he lavishly rewarded out of the royal coffers, not alto-gether to the satisfaction of the careful king.[50] With their aid he pro-tected the earldom from the ravages of the Welsh by building strong castles along the border, at Wigmore, Clifford, Ewias Harold, Monmouth and Chepstow, each becoming the centre of a Norman settlement.[51] In the case of Wigmore and of Clifford he is known to have provided for the economic needs of the castle by establishing beneath its shadow a chartered borough, to which he no doubt granted those liberal "customs of Breteuil" already conceded to the Norman burgesses of Hereford.[52] Nor was he content with a purely defensive policy; a vigorous attack was made upon Maredudd ab Owain of Deheubarth, his brother Rhys ab Owain and Cadwgan ap Meurig of Morgannwg.[53] As a result, the whole region of Gwent fell into William's hands;[54] from his two bases at Monmouth and Chepstow he pushed forward as far as the Usk, and finally destroyed Welsh independence in this ancient border realm. The inhabitants were treated with some consideration; many of them were allowed to retain their lands on the easy terms which had been conceded to them by Gruffydd ap Llywelyn, and the Welsh "praepositi" or maers were left undisturbed in their offices.[55] While Gwent was thus annexed, William seems a little time before his death to have come to terms with Maredudd and to have adopted, with the sanction of the king, the policy of protecting the marches from the rapine of the Welsh chief by giving him lawful possession of certain English manors. Three hides at Ley, on the river Lugg, were granted to Maredudd free from the payment of geld with this end in view,[56] nor was this an isolated gift, for lands at Kenchester[57] and elsewhere are known to have been conferred upon him as part of the same policy.

At the end of the year 1070 Fitz Osbern left England, and on 20th February, 1071, was slain in battle near Cassel in Flanders. His earl-dom and his English possessions passed to his second son Roger, who had neither the ability nor the fidelity of his father; in 1075 he plot-ted unsuccessfully against King William and brought down with a crash the edifice of power so skilfully raised by the first earl. Lifelong imprisonment and forfeiture of all his lands and dignities were the penalties paid by Earl Roger for his rash enterprise, and many of his father's knights who had joined in the conspiracy were involved in the ruin which befell him.[58] A catastrophe of these dimensions must have had a chilling effect upon the ardour of the colonisers of the South Welsh border; the king marked his distrust of the situation by creating no new Earl of Hereford, and it may be conjectured that the sudden fall of the house of Breteuil was in a large measure responsible for the arrest at this point of the advance upon South Wales which had promised so well under Earl William.

The figures of Maredudd, Cadwgan, and Bleddyn disappear from the stage shortly after that of William fitz Osbern and thus the men who were concerned in the early struggle for ascendancy along the march give place to a new generation. Maredudd was attacked in 1072 by Caradog ap Gruffydd of Gwynllwg, who brought the Normans, no doubt from Gwent, to his assistance and slew his rival in a battle on the banks of the Rhymni.[59] The realm of Deheubarth then passed to Maredudd's brother Rhys, who was too weak to defend it from Norman raids; twice, in 1073 and 1074, Ceredigion was ravaged by the men of the Earl of Shrewsbury, who descended upon it from the mountains of Arwystli.[60] About the same time Cadwgan ap Meurig, the last of the old dynasty of Morgannwg, slips out of sight,[61] his place being taken, it would seem, by the irrepressible Caradog ap Gruffydd.[62] The last of the three to quit the scene was Bleddyn, who was slain in 1075 by Rhys ab Owain and the "uchelwyr" of Ystrad Tywi, perhaps in an attempt to make himself master of Deheubarth. Bleddyn had ruled for twelve years not ingloriously. He had defended his crown in the battle of Mechain in 1070, and, though he had lost his brother Rhiwallon in the fray, had then rid himself of two dangerous rivals in the sons of Gruffydd ap Llywelyn, who had perished, the one in the battle and the other of exposure not long afterwards. His efforts to check the growth of the Norman power in the West have already been recorded. But more than this; he belonged, it is clear, to the gentle and high-minded type of ruler so signally illustrated by Hywel the Good. "He was the mildest and most clement of kings," says *The Chronicle of the Princes*, preserving, no doubt, a contemporary Llanbadarn record, "and did injury to none, save when insulted, nor loved to avenge the insult when it came; to his kinsmen he was gentle; widows and orphans and the weak he defended; he was the support of the wise, the glory and corner-stone of the Church, the delight of all lands, open-handed to all, terrible in war, but in peace beloved." [63] If this eulogy should seem overstrained, it is to be remembered that Bleddyn ap Cynfyn is one of the very few Welsh princes who are known to have introduced amendments into the law of Hywel[64] and that there is, therefore, solid evidence of his interest in the welfare of his people. His spirit of charity and benevolence supplies the best explanation of the fact that his murder was regarded as an outrage, and that, though he had no claim to rule on the score of birth,[65] he established a dynasty in Powys which lasted until the fourteenth century.

III. THE NORMANS IN NORTH WALES.

The year 1075 maybe regarded as marking an epoch in the progress of the Norman Conquest alike in North and in South Wales. In South Wales the fall of Earl Roger and the decision of the crown to appoint no successor to the earldom helped to bring about a halt in the victorious progress of the Normans along the South Welsh border which lasted for many years. In North Wales the death of Bleddyn encouraged a competitor for the crown of Gwynedd to assert his claims, who, though at first dogged by ill-fortune, finally triumphed over all difficulties and not only ousted his rival but won successes against the Norman invaders which for ever defeated their ambitions in this part of the country.

Although Bleddyn left a numerous family, it would appear that no son of his was old enough at the time of his death to be put forward as a claimant for the crown, and Gwynedd was therefore seized by one Trahaearn ap Caradog, who claimed as Bleddyn's first cousin,[66] and whose original seat of power was the cantref of Arwystli. Although the connection between Arwystli and Gwynedd was close,[67] it was locally a part of Powys, and thus the accession of Trahaearn was not cordially welcomed by the sensitive provincial feeling of Mon and Arfon, especially as he brought in his train another chieftain from Powys, namely, Cynwrig ap Rhiwallon of Maelor,[68] who lorded it over the men of Lleyn. At this opportune moment Gruffydd ap Cynan, the representative of the ancient line of Gwynedd, stepped upon the scene to claim the inheritance from which his family had for so many years been excluded. Not since 1039, when his grandfather Iago ab Idwal had been assassinated, had any member of this house borne rule in North Wales, and so little was it known in the country that at his first appearance Gruffydd was styled, not "son of Cynan," but, after a fashion most unusual among the Welsh, "grandson of Iago".[69]

Gruffydd has the unique distinction among Welsh princes of being the subject of a biography, which, though it is not the work of a contemporary, for it was composed during the reign of his son Owain, was written sufficiently near his time to be a valuable historical authority.[70] Despite some inaccuracies and the inevitable disposition to magnify the deeds of its hero, the *Ancient History of Gruffydd ap Cynan ap Iago* tells a story which is in general conformity with what is known of the history of the time, and in the following pages the evidence yielded by it is used without hesitation. According to the life, Iago's son Cynan had found during the ascendancy of Gruffydd ap Llywelyn a safe retreat in the Danish kingdom of Dublin, and had married Ragnhildr, a grand-daughter of King Sitric of the Silken Beard.[71] Gruffydd was born in 1054 or 1055 in the city of Dublin;[72] under the system of fosterage, which prevailed among the Irish no less than the Welsh, he was brought up under the care of a family who lived at Swords, some miles to the north of the city, but within the limits of the Scandinavian settlement.[73] As Gruffydd grew to manhood and learnt the history of his house, his eyes turned more and more to Wales and to the kingdom of which he was the rightful heir. No great career was open to him in Ireland; his grandfather Olaf had long been dead, and the family of Sitric had by this time ceased to hold power in Dublin,[74] while the death of his father Cynan, of whom he was probably bereft at a tender age, left it to him to prosecute the claim to the throne of Gwynedd. When the news was brought him of the death of Bleddyn, he deemed that the hour had come to strike a blow for legitimacy and ancient blood.

Recognising that the chief force in his favour would be the tribal spirit of independence which made Mon and Arfon and Lleyn disdain to take orders from Powys, he landed at Aber Menai, the port and ferry at the western mouth of the Menai Straits, which gave ready access to the first two of these regions.[75] He was gladly welcomed by the leading men of the district, and preparations were made for a determined attack upon Trahaearn and his ally Cynwrig. Help from any and every quarter was acceptable in such a conflict, and Gruffydd did not hesitate to take ship to Rhuddlan, where Robert of that ilk was already established, and beg the aid of the foreign invader, which was most cheerfully accorded, against the holder of the crown of Gwynedd. On his return to Aber Menai, a small but carefully chosen band of warriors, sixty men from Robert's lordship of Tegeingl and eighty from Anglesey, was rapidly despatched to Lleyn under the guidance of the three sons of Merwydd, notable gentlemen of that cantref who had sought shelter from the oppression of Cynwrig's followers in the sanctuary of Beuno at Clynnog Fawr. The onslaught was so sudden that Cynwrig was without difficulty surprised and slain, and the sons of Merwydd regained their old position and authority. It was now resolved to press home the advantage which had been thus gained and to march upon the second and more formidable of the usurpers who held Gwynedd captive. With a large force Gruffydd made his way south, and in the cantref of Meirionydd came upon Trahaearn, who was no doubt advancing to meet his rival from Arwystli. The battle was fought in Glyn Cyfing, perhaps the narrow glen now known as Dyffryn Glyncul,[76] and at a spot known to posterity as Gwaeterw, or the "Bloody Acre," a victory was won by Gruffydd which for the moment gave him all he desired and drove Trahaearn in headlong flight to his native Arwystli.

Seated on his ancestral throne, the new ruler of Gwynedd inaugurated his reign by an attack upon the Norman settlement at Rhuddlan, holding himself in nowise bound to friendship with Robert because of the help he had a little earlier received from him. In truth, the activity of the Normans along the northern coast of Wales was at this time a most dangerous menace to Welsh independence. Since the beginning of 1070 Chester, no longer held by the friendly Earls of Mercia, had been the centre of a power which knew no rest in its strenuous efforts to win territory from the Welsh. William I. had in the first instance given the city and county, with the title of earl, to Gherbod of Flanders, but after a brief tenure of power he had been succeeded by Hugh of Avranches, one of the most powerful of the barons in the royal train.[77] For thirty years the figure of Earl Hugh dominated the northern march of Wales; his gross, unwieldy bulk, whence he derived the nickname of "Hugh the Fat," [78] did not more surely fix the beholder's gaze than did his restless activity make itself felt from Snowdon to the Peak. He was devoted to sensual pleasures, and ever had those around him who could minister to them, yet, despite his corpulence and love of ease, he was no sluggish idler, but shared to the full the energetic Norman temper. Formidable in war, liberal to his followers, beset by a crowd of eager young retainers, he was well fitted to carry on an active crusade against the Welsh, and it was no fault of his or of his lieutenants that Gwynedd and the Middle Country did not fall permanently under Norman rule. Of these lieutenants the chief was the Robert of Rhuddlan already mentioned, a cousin of his, who had been trained in arms at the court of the Confessor, and after the victory of Hastings had attached himself to the service of Earl Hugh.[79] His merits as a soldier secured for him the post of danger, which was also that of greatness and power for the successful holder; at King William's command a castle was built on the site of the stronghold of Gruffydd ap Llywelyn at Rhuddlan, and Robert was placed in charge, with instructions to use it and the adjoining cantref of Tegeingl as a base of operations, first against Rhos and Rhufoniog, and later against Anglesey and Snowdonia. This was in 1073;[80] it must have been very shortly afterwards that Robert entered upon his obstinate warfare with the North Welsh princes, attempting to capture Bleddyn by surprise and narrowly missing complete success; the king escaped, but Robert's little band carried off much booty.[81] Thus the war between Robert and the Welsh had just begun when in 1075 Gruffydd ap Cynan made a raid upon the new castle at Rhuddlan, destroyed its outworks and slew many of the defenders, and returned home with valuable spoil, but without having captured the solid keep which was the nucleus of the fortress.[82]

It soon appeared that Gruffydd, remarkable as his first successes had been, had not really won a lasting victory, and he returned from Rhuddlan to find disaffection seething in his realm. This was largely due to his retention among his "teulu" or household troops of many of his Irish followers and companions, whose alien speech, dress, equipment and manners were a constant offence to the people among whom they lived, superadded to the unpopularity of the turbulent class to which they belonged. The grievance was especially felt by the men of Lleyn and Eifionydd, who were not attached to Gruffydd's house by the same long tradition of obedience and respect as bound to him the islanders of Môn,[83] and the murder of fifty-two Irishmen of the royal warband, as they slept unsuspectingly in their quarters in the villages of Lleyn, was the signal for a revolt which threw the king on the defensive in the cantref of Arfon. Trahaearn awoke to his opportunity, secured the aid of his neighbour, Gwrgeneu ap Seisyll of Powys,[84] and appeared with an army in the revolted cantrefs. The insurgents were met by Gruffydd, who had, save his Danish henchmen, only the dwellers of Môn and Arfon to support him, at Bron yr Erw, above Clynnog,[85] just as they were descending from the border pass of Bwlch Derwin into the low-lying plain of Arfon. Gruffydd's valour, which is duly set forth by his zealous biographer, availed him nothing; his troops were overwhelmed and he himself fled to Aber Menai, whence he was borne across the sea to the Skerries and finally to Wexford. Thus within the limits of this eventful year he had won, enjoyed and lost a kingdom.

For the next six years (1075–1081) Trahaearn was the chief ruler of Gwynedd. But, though he was strong enough to lead in 1078 an expedition into Dyfed, of which more will be said anon, his power rested on most insecure foundations, and was constantly menaced, on the one hand by Gruffydd, who did not cease harassing him by sea, and on the other hand by the Normans, who saw in the divided state of the country the best of reasons for pushing on their schemes of conquest. The Life of Gruffydd speaks of a great Norman raid upon Lleyn, in which Earl Hugh, Robert of Rhuddlan, Warm of Shrewsbury, and a certain Walter, perhaps Walter de Lacy, were at this time concerned; with Gwrgeneu and the men of Powys as their guides, a host of knights and foot soldiers crossed the passes of Eryri and encamped for a week in the hapless can tref.[86] But ravages of this kind, blighting as they were in their immediate effects, were less dangerous to the freedom of the Welsh than the slow but continuous progress of the foreigner along the northern coast. To this neither Trahaearn nor Hywel ab Ithel was able to oppose any effectual resistance; Robert from his base at Rhuddlan seized the latter's territories of Rhos and Rhufoniog, and, having imprisoned him, built at Degannwy on the site of an ancient British fortress, a new castle which was to serve as the starting-point of the conquest of Gwynedd above Conway.[87] It would, no doubt, have fallen to the lot of Trahaearn to be the next victim of Norman aggression, had not Gruffydd ap Cynan cut short his career and forestalled the invader in 1081.

This was the year of the memorable battle of Mynydd Cam, in which all the leading figures of the period took part, and which left its impress permanently on the history of Gwynedd and of Deheubarth.[88] On the one side the combatants were Gruffydd ap Cynan, seeking the crown which had slipped from his grasp, and Rhys ap Tewdwr, king of Deheubarth, over whom ill-fortune had also for the moment triumphed. On the other were Trahaearn, Meilyr, son of Rhiwallon ap Cynfyn, and Caradog ap Gruffydd, now lord of Morgannwg, and probably bent upon adding the rest of South Wales to his realm. Gruffydd joined his ally at Porth Clais, near St. David's, where Rhys had been compelled to seek sanctuary; he brought to his aid a valuable contingent of troops from Ireland, with whom he had sailed from Waterford harbour, Danes wielding two-edged axes, Irish footmen with darts and war-flails (which flourished spiked balls of iron), his own warriors with shield and glaive. The host marched out from St. David's with the solemn blessing of Bishop Sulien and his clergy, and at the close of the day came upon the enemy's camp at Mynydd Cam, a spot which unhappily has not been identified, though it cannot have been far from the borders of Dyfed. Rhys, if one is to believe the Life (none too impartial a witness), was not willing to engage that night, but Gruffydd's impetuous passion would brook no delay, and he rushed in the fading light upon his foes. They were soon broken and scattered; Trahaearn, Meilyr and Caradog all fell in the fray, and Gruffydd had a clear course before him. He made haste to ravage Arwystli and thereafter, Powys, the lands which had sent oppressors to Gwynedd, and then entered triumphantly into possession of his own. It was, perhaps, a secondary result of the victory that Gwrgeneu of Powys was slain by the sons of Rhys Sais.

Notwithstanding this signal victory, the hour of Gruffydd's final triumph had not yet come. He had disposed of his rival, but he had still to contend with the tide of Norman invasion, which was now reaching its high-water mark in North Wales and threatening to engulf the whole region. Earl Hugh had no intention of recognising Gruffydd as prince of a country which he hoped soon, through his cousin Robert, to hold in the hollow of his hand, and, with the help of Earl Roger of Montgomery, he contrived to inveigle him to Rhug in Edeyrnion, where he was taken prisoner and his Irish bodyguard broken up.[89] It was not the Norman custom to shed the blood of a captured enemy; the humane teaching of the Church had to this extent borne fruit. But life-long imprisonment was the common lot of the man who had fallen into the power of his foe, and it is no matter of surprise that Gruffydd was carried off to the earl's castle at Chester, there to spend many a year in close confinement.

Little is recorded of the movements of the principal men in North Wales during the next few years. But at this point a most valuable witness as to the precise position of affairs on the border appears in the Domesday survey, or "description of all England," compiled, as is well known, in the year 1086, While a detailed discussion of the notices in this record bearing upon Wales would carry us beyond the scope of the present work, it will be of great assistance to collect at this point the evidence which it affords as to the progress of the conflict between Norman and Welshman in North Wales, and, later on, to deal similarly with its testimony as to the South. The first point to which attention may be directed is the strong position held by Earl Hugh. "In Cheshire," runs the record, "the bishop of the city holds of the king all that pertains to his bishopric. All other land in the shire is held of the king by Earl Hugh and his men." [90] Thus the great men of the shire, Robert of Rhuddlan, Robert fitz Hugh of Malpas, William Malbanc of Nantwich, and others, were tenants of the earl and bound to serve him in his enterprises. His resources are thus seen to have been such as to make him a most formidable antagonist. From his central stronghold of Chester, his power radiated in all directions. Not only the whole of our Cheshire, but also the modern county of Flint, both east and west of the Dee, with the intervening portion of Denbighshire, was under the authority of Earl Hugh. The northern part of this region formed the ancient English hundred of Atiscross,[91] so called from an ancient cross near Flint which no doubt marked the meeting-place of the men of the hundred. The heart of the hundred, namely, the strip of coast from Basingwerk to Hawarden, which was guarded on the west by a great forest, had never ceased, since its first occupation by the Mercians, to be tilled by English farmers, and what is witnessed here is the transference of manors, after the fashion which prevailed throughout England, from English to Norman lords. Earl Hugh came into Earl Edwin's demesne of Hawarden; Robert of Rhuddlan succeeded two English landowners at Leadbrook. But the outlying portions of the hundred, as has been shown above, had been annexed by Gruffydd ap Llywelyn, and the next point which deserves notice in the Domesday evidence is the extent to which the work of Gruffydd had in the twenty years following his death been undone.

Rhuddlan, where Gruffydd had held court, was now the centre of the movement of aggression against the Welsh of Gwynedd.[92] Around Robert's castle was a little borough, in which eighteen burgesses, brought thither for the comfort and convenience of the garrison, had trading privileges such as those which were enjoyed in the boroughs founded by William fitz Osbern in Herefordshire.[93] They had their church, their mint, their mills and fisheries in the Clwyd; trade was again springing up in the district, and its mineral wealth was not neglected. Of the surrounding agricultural region part was held by the Earl and part by Robert, but everywhere, at Prestatyn, Halkin, Whitford, Bodffari and Caerwys, the plough was at work and a servile population was paying its dues to Norman superiors. Such was also the case in the valley of the Alun, where Gruffydd's manor of Bistre had been parcelled out among various lords.[94] The hundred of Exestan, held by Gruffydd under a formal grant from the Confessor, had in like manner been recovered from the Welsh; Gilbert de Venables was lord of Hope,[95] and three Norman tenants of Earl Hugh divided between them the extensive lands of the manor of Gresford.[96]

The losses of the Welsh were, however, not to be measured merely by the gains of Earl Hugh. Beyond the river Clwyd, the limit of the old English settlement, the authority of the Earl of Chester did not extend, and all that was conquered to the westward of this river fell directly to Robert of Rhuddlan, whose aim was to make himself lord of Gwynedd, with no homage to render save to the crown. The two cantrefs of Rhos and Rhufoniog were already in his possession, and, though the fact does not appear from the survey, the new castle of Degannwy was, no doubt, complete. The rest was in process of being absorbed, and Robert had taken the precaution to secure a legal title by obtaining from the king a grant of the whole of "Nortwales," *i.e.*, Gwynedd, in consideration of an annual rent of £40. Only the lands of the see of Bangor, for which it was no doubt hoped to provide a Norman occupant, were exempted from this grant.[97] After the fall of Trahaearn and the capture of Gruffydd, the English government clearly regarded the crown of Gwynedd as having escheated to the feudal overlord, and, passing over all Welsh claims, bestowed the dignity upon Robert, who thus succeeded to all its pretensions. He made haste to enforce them to the full, and in the survey itself he is found registering a claim to the cantref of Arwystli, which was then in the occupation of Earl Roger of Shrewsbury, but which Robert's Welsh tenants averred was a member of the realm of Gwynedd.

It now remains to speak of the second great lord of the North-Welsh march, Roger Montgomery, the friend and counsellor of the Conqueror, who bestowed many lands and privileges upon him, and finally, about 1071, made him Earl of Shrewsbury. Earl Roger's lordship of the lands of Shropshire was not quite so absolute as that of his neighbour in the adjoining county of Chester. In addition to the bishops of Chester and of Hereford, there were other magnates who held Shropshire manors directly of the king, notably Ralph Mortimer, whose broad lands in the valley of the Teme were partly within the county, but were not held of the earl.[98] Nevertheless, the position of Earl Roger was little removed from that of a palatine earl, ruling the shire as freely as the king his kingdom.[99] Nearly all the leading men of the shire were his vassals, ably seconding him in his warfare with the Welsh. Such was the position of Warin the Bald, to whom he gave the office of sheriff and the hand of his niece Amieria, of William Pantulf, of Corbet, and of Robert of Sai, commonly known as Picot.[100] In the fifteen years which elapsed between Earl Roger's establishment in the shire and the compilation of Domesday some changes, as was but natural, took place; Warin was succeeded on his death by Rainald of Bailleui, who married his predecessor's widow,[101] while Roger and Robert fitz Corbet appear in 1086 in their father's stead. But the system remained the same; the earl had everything in the shire which had been King Edward's,[102] and, while retaining for himself some royal manors, such as Whittington and Chirbury, granted others to his lieutenants to be the foundation-stones of new depenent baronies. It was thus that Rainald was enabled in Maesbury to build the new castle of L'Œuvre and lay the foundations of the lordship of Oswestry,[103] and that Roger fitz Corbet obtained "Alretone " as the basis of the lordship of Cause.[104]

A force so well equipped for attack was hardly likely to leave the Welsh of Powys undisturbed. The name of Montgomery became, indeed, one of mournful import throughout the whole of Mid Wales, and at one time it seemed impossible to say to what heights of greatness it might not attain in the country. Already in 1086 there had been considerable encroachments upon Welsh territory. The commote of Ial had been seized; this Earl Roger had granted to Earl Hugh, no doubt because it marched with the hundred of Exestan.[105] Edeyrnion, the scene of the capture of King Gruffydd, and Cynllaith had been subdued and annexed to the Oswestry fief of Rainald the sheriff. A certain "Tuder Wallensis" held a Welsh district as the vassal of the earl; he has been identified, on good grounds, with Tudur ap Rhys Sais and his territory was probably Nanheudwy.[106] In the hundred of Mersete, which had been almost wholly lost to the English under the Confessor, Rainald was lord of a compact group of manors, in which the immigrant Welsh were retained as tillers of the soil. Along the Severn there had been little change; Roger fitz Corbet was powerful around the Breiddin, but had not crossed the river into Powys. The Chirbury district was, however, one of the areas recaptured by the Normans; Earl Roger restored the place, which was the ecclesiastical centre of a wide region,[107] to something of its old importance, and not far off, in the border forest which three English thegns had used as a great chase, built a castle to which he gave the name of the family seat in Normandy. The new Montgomery was destined to have a history no less famous than that of the old, and it became at once the starting-point of organised attacks upon Welsh territory. Ceri and Cydewain were at the mercy of Earl Roger, and, after the fall of Trahaearn at Mynydd Carn, Arwystli, too, could offer no resistance to his victorious progress. The year of the survey found him posted on the borders of Ceredigion, ready for the Montgomery invasion of Deheubarth for which seven years afterwards the way was opened.

The historian is fortunate in being able to use the evidence of Domesday to illustrate the power of Robert of Rhuddlan, for in two years after the date of the survey he disappears from the scene, and this without transmitting his great authority to any bearer of his name. Serious disorders broke out in England soon after the death of the

Conqueror in September, 1087; the Norman magnates, for the most part, resented the arrangement which he had made for separating the duchy from the crown and flouted the authority of the new king. The malcontents included nearly all the great men of the Welsh border; only Earl Hugh was sincerely loyal to the cause of William Rufus. Earl Roger had three sons among the rebellious company who held out in Rochester Castle,[108] and, though he joined the king in the siege, clearly did so as much in the interests of the besieged as of the leader whose banner he professed to follow. Such, too, was the attitude of Robert of Rhuddlan, who returned to the Vale of Clwyd in the early summer of 1088, after the complete triumph of the king, to find out that the Welsh had taken advantage, as was ever their wont, of the quarrels of their oppressors to ravage and plunder the conquered territories.[109] Rhuddlan had suffered severely, and the mortified Robert, his spirit embittered by the failure of the baronial movement, laid his plans for a ruthless revenge. But all his threats came to nought. On the 3rd of July he was taking his midday sleep in the castle of Degannwy, with no thought of danger or of warlike alarms, when news was hurriedly brought him that three Welsh ships had been beached at the foot of the Great Orme's Head, and that their crews were scouring the tableland above and carrying off cattle, with women and children, as plunder to their vessels. His first step was to send out messengers to call together the armed forces of the district to repel this daring raid. But he soon perceived that they would come too late; the marauders had already got their booty aboard and only waited the rising of the tide to float their vessels from the position in which they had grounded them earlier in the day. From those towering limestone cliffs he could watch them at their work, and the spectacle filled him with dire indignation. He refused to regard the situation as hopeless, begged the few unarmed retainers he had around him to join him in attacking the plunderers, and, when they declined the desperate enterprise, threw prudence to the winds, and, attended by a single knight, himself made his way down the steep mountain path towards the shore. Instantly the darts and arrows of the whole troop of Welshmen were directed against him, and, as he wore no armour, his shield soon fell from his nerveless hands and he sank to the ground in death. The enemy were upon him in a moment; his head was cut off, and in barbaric triumph fixed as a trophy to the mast of the leading ship. By this time the tide was beginning to set the vessels free for their voyage home; they were already afloat and speeding westward when Robert's men began to assemble on the shore of the Conway, filled with grief at the sudden loss of their lord. The sight of his bleeding head spurred them at first to attempt pursuit, but the Welsh had gained a good start, and, when the head was by a counsel of prudence thrown into the sea, the men of Degannwy desisted from a chase which had but a bare chance of success.

Notwithstanding this achievement of the Welsh, the progress of the Normans in Gwynedd was in no degree checked. Earl Hugh forthwith stepped into the place of his relative, receiving, it may be, a formal grant from the crown of the independent lordship which had been held by Robert.[110] He it is, at any rate, who during the next few years is found actively engaged in the conquest of Môn and Arfon. According to the life of Gruffydd ap Cynan, castles were built by Earl Hugh at this time in Meirionydd, in Arfon—the one at Carnarvon and the other at Bangor—and in Anglesey, the last being, no doubt, the castle at Aber Lleiniog mentioned elsewhere in the life.[111] This evidence is amply confirmed by other sources. It is known that a Breton named Hervé, who must have owed his elevation entirely to Norman influence, was consecrated bishop of Bangor in 1092.[112] In the following year the earl refounded St. Werburgh's house at Chester as a Benedictine abbey; among the grants which he makes to the monks are two manors in Anglesey and one in Rhos, the tithe of the fisheries of Rhuddlan and of Anglesey, and the right to have engaged in the latter a ship carrying ten nets.[113] At the beginning of the year 1094 the Norman Conquest of North Wales appeared almost complete, and the observer who did not look below the surface might well have supposed that the days of Welsh independence were numbered in this, its ancient and impregnable stronghold. But, in point of fact, the Normans had reached the zenith of their success in Gwynedd; in the years that followed, their forces were, first, challenged and attacked, and, finally, driven altogether out of this region.

IV. RHYS AP TEWDWR.

While North Wales was in the grip of the invader, South Wales was ruled by a Welsh prince who had considerable success in the difficult task of holding the Normans at arm's length. Until his fall in 1093 Rhys ap Tewdwr was as fortunate as his fellow-ruler Gruffydd ap Cynan was unlucky. Deheubarth, it has been shown, was in 1075 in the possession of Rhys ab Owain, who was responsible in that year for the much lamented death of Bleddyn. Retribution followed with no halting foot; in 1078 Trahaearn of North Wales invaded Dyfed, defeated Rhys in the battle of Goodwick, not far from Fishguard,[114] and, having put all his "teulu" to the sword, drove him, as the "Chronicle of the Princes" puts it, "o'er rocks and through brakes, like a frightened stag before the deerhounds".[115] At the end of the year he and his brother Hywel were killed by Caradog ap Gruffydd, and the throne of Deheubarth was vacant. It was claimed by Rhys ap Tewdwr, a great-grandson of the Einon ab Owain ap Hywel Dda who fell in 984,[116] and for a year or two this claim seems not to have been seriously contested.[117] In 1081, however, the ambition of Caradog ap Gruffydd impelled him to attempt the conquest of Deheubarth, and Rhys was so hard pressed as to be forced to take refuge in the church of St. David's. Here he was joined by Gruffydd ap Cynan, with whose aid he won the historic victory of Mynydd Carn—a victory which not only disposed of Caradog, but also firmly established Rhys upon his throne.

The year of Mynydd Cam witnessed another event which, whatever its precise occasion, was undoubtedly of great importance for South Wales. It was in 1081 that William the Conqueror paid his one visit to Wales, which he penetrated as far as St. David's. The Welsh and the English accounts of this expedition do not depict it in quite the same light; according to the monks of St. David's, the king's journey was a pilgrimage, undertaken out of respect for the memory of their saint;[118] according to the English chronicle which records the visit, it was made at the head of an armed force and it resulted in the "freeing" of many hundred men.[119] There can be little doubt that the second is the more reasonable presentment of William's purpose; devout as he was, he had other work to do than pay his court to remote and unfriendly sanctuaries, and his real motive was, no doubt, to impress the chieftains of South Wales with a due sense of his power and to relieve the small bands of Normans which were shut up in isolated castles, out of reach of the border. But he did not omit to pay reverence to the shrine of the great Dewi, and, what is more, it is most likely that he met in this neighbourhood the new ruler of Deheubarth and concluded with him a peace which lasted during William's lifetime. In the survey of 1086, it is said that "Riset" of Wales renders to the king an annual ferm or rent of £40.[120] Now it will be noticed that this is the precise sum paid by Robert of Rhuddlan as lord of Gwynedd, and it is, therefore, an almost certain conclusion that the item represents the rent of Deheubarth, paid by Rhys ap Tewdwr under a compact which protected him in the enjoyment of his ancestral possessions. That he was so protected is suggested by many facts in the history of the period, and, if a formal agreement be presumed, no time is so likely to have produced it as the year of this expedition undertaken by the Conqueror to the uttermost parts of Dyfed.

Five years after the journey to St. David's the Domesday survey shows the position of affairs on the South Welsh border, and demonstrates that there had been little advance on the part of the Normans since the death of William fitz Osbern. There had been no effective occupation of any spot within the modern counties of Radnor, Brecknock and Glamorgan. Certain Norman lords laid claim in virtue of royal grants to Radnor, Knighton, Norton, Cascob and the surrounding districts, but the region had not yet recovered from the ravages of Gruffydd ap Llywelyn, and there were no Norman settlements in these villages.[121] Matters had apparently stood still for some ten or fifteen years, except for certain conquests in Ewias and Gwynllwg which may have been of later date. Wigmore, Clifford, Ewias Harold and Caerleon were the westernmost outposts of Norman rule, and the conquest of Brycheiniog and of Morgannwg had not yet been seriously undertaken.

This halt in the process of conquest was more probably the result of want of royal encouragement than of any lack of enterprise in the marcher lords. Powerful barons were seated on the Herefordshire and Gloucestershire border. Osbern fitz Richard was lord of Richard's Castle and Byton, and claimed many vills on the confines of Maelienydd which at the time yielded him nothing but the game he hunted in their wooded glades.[122] He had succeeded his father, Richard fitz Scrop, in the time of the Confessor, and had married a daughter of Gruffydd ap Llywelyn.[123] At Wigmore was Ralph Mortimer, first of that famous English house; the Conqueror had about 1075 established him as a great border magnate by bestowing upon him a number of Shropshire and Herefordshire manors set free by the treason of Earl Roger and the death of the Confessor's widow.[124] Cleobury and Leintwardine were his, and he had claims, not yet substantiated, upon vills like Pilleth and Waterdine which bordered upon Maelienydd.[125] The valley of the Clun was the domain of Picot of Sai.[126] The castle and lordship of Clifford had been given to Ralph of Toeni,[127] whose principal interests lay elsewhere and who does not, therefore, play a conspicuous part in the doings of the march. Not so was it with Roger de Lacy; he had just succeeded in 1086 to the lands bestowed upon his father Walter for gallant service against the Welsh[128] and was himself an active marcher lord; his chief seat was at Weobley and the

Welsh commote of Ewias was in his hands.[129] The castle of Ewias was the centre of a separate lordship, held in the year of the survey by Alfred of Marlborough, in succession to his uncle Osbern Pentecost.[130] The valley of the Dore and most of Archenfield were parcelled out among various holders, who received from the Welsh inhabitants the old honey renders which had formerly been paid to Welsh princes. But in the angle formed by the meeting of the Monnow and the Wye a Norman settlement had taken root, with Earl William's castle of Monmouth as its centre. After the catastrophe of 1075, the king had put the place in charge of the Breton Wihenoc, who, on becoming a monk, had transmitted his position to his brother's son, William fitz Baderon, ancestor of the later lords of Monmouth.[131]

If it be added that Earl William's conquest of Gwent had been fully utilised, but that further progress in this quarter is at most represented by Turstin fitz Rolfs castle at Caerleon, with a little tilled land around it,[132] it will be seen that there is ample warrant for the view that at the death of William I. the South Welsh border stood much as it did in 1071, and that the conquest of South Wales had not begun. It can scarcely be a coincidence that immediately on the accession of William Rufus a change of attitude is to be observed. There is no reason to think that the new king refused to recognise the position of Rhys ap Tewdwr and repudiated the arrangement made by his father; indeed, the contrary is suggested by the fact that the wholesale conquest of Deheubarth did not begin until after the Welsh leader's death. But Rufus could not hold the reins of discipline with the firm hand of his predecessor. In the outbreak which followed his accession, nearly all the powerful men of the march, as has been pointed out above, were ranged against him. The barons of Herefordshire and Shropshire, including Roger de Lacy, Ralph Mortimer, Osbern fitz Richard and his son-in-law, Bernard of Neufmarché, made a determined attack upon the city of Worcester and brought their Welsh tenants in great force into the fray; only the constancy and high spirit of the saintly Bishop Wulfstan saved the place from the violence of this motley company of rebels.[133] One need not be surprised, therefore, to find evidence in this year 1088 that a beginning is being made of the conquest of Brycheiniog. The records of the abbey of St. Peter's, Gloucester, assign to this year the gift to the abbey by Bernard of the vill and church of Glasbury, a place which lies well within the border of Brycheiniog, being about 4 miles south-west of Hay.[134] Bernard was the son of

Geoffrey of Neufmarché and first appears in England at the end of the Conqueror's reign. By his marriage with Nest, a daughter of Osbern fitz Richard, he obtained a footing on the Welsh border and was enabled to undertake the conquest of the ancient realm of Brychan.[135] Entering the country at its most vulnerable point, where between the Black Mountains and the Wye a passage lies open to the Llyfni valley and thence to the vale of Usk, he had already made considerable progress and probably occupied Talgarth, the Welsh capital of the district, at the time that the death of Rhys ap Tewdwr in 1093 gave him the opportunity of winning a completer triumph.

While Brycheiniog was thus feeling the first edge of the Norman Conquest of South Wales, the greater part of Deheubarth continued, even under Rufus, to acknowledge the authority of Rhys. He had on two occasions to do battle for his crown, but on both his antagonists were Welshmen and not Normans. In 1088 he was attacked by the sons of Bleddyn, who now ruled over Powys; at first defeated and forced to take refuge in Ireland, he speedily returned with the aid of a Danish fleet and overthrew his rivals in a battle in which Madog and Rhiryd ap Bleddyn fell, their brother Cadwgan escaping with his life.[136] In 1091, on the death of Cydifor ap Gollwyn, a powerful magnate of Dyfed, his sons threw off their allegiance to Rhys and offered the crown to Gruffydd ap Maredudd, who since his father's death in 1072 had been an exile in England, in occupation of the Herefordshire manors bestowed upon Maredudd by Earl William.[137] Once again Rhys was triumphant; in the battle of Llandudoch, fought near the mouth of the Teifi, Gruffydd was defeated and slain.

But in the Easter week (17th–23rd April) of 1093, Rhys at last met his fate. He was killed by the Norman invaders of Brycheiniog, not far, it would seem, from the new castle they were attempting to build at Aberhonddu.[138] Whether he fell in fair fight or by treachery is uncertain;[139] all that is clear is that his death opened the flood-gates of Norman rapacity in South Wales, and that its many trickling rills now united in one great deluge which swept the country from end to end. The idea that with him had disappeared such legal right as had any claim to respect from the dwellers on the march finds expression in the Welsh as well as in the English chronicles. If Florence of Worcester tells us that "from that day kings ceased to bear rule in Wales," it is in the chronicle of the Princes (Brut y Tywysogion) that the statement is made that with Rhys "the kingdom of Wales was overthrown".[140] Neither assertion has any point for the observer who can take a wide view of Welsh history, but they signify that in the eyes of contemporaries the death of Rhys put an end to a period of orderly, legitimate rule; there was no one who had a rightful claim to the position which he held, and force was to be henceforth the sole arbiter of the affairs of the distracted and unhappy country.

CHAPTER II

THE NORMAN CONQUEST. — SECOND STAGE

(For the history of the period 1093–1135 I have used Annales
Cambriæ and the Bruts, the life of Gruffydd ap Cynan, and the usual
English sources. I may express here my general obligations to the work of
Mr. J. Horace Round, whose minute and accurate knowledge of this
period is so well known.)

I. THE STRUGGLE AT ITS HEIGHT.

THE years 1093–1099 may be regarded as the crisis of the Norman
attempt to subjugate Wales. Now that the obstacle had been removed
which was created by the position of Rhys ap Tewdwr, a united effort
was made to carry the whole country by storm, and scarcely any part
of it escaped invasion. On the other hand, the Welsh were now fully
alive to the danger which threatened their existence as a nation, and
the national resistance was as general in extent and as resolute in
spirit as the occasion demanded. At the beginning of the twelfth century the struggle had been fought out and its broad issues decided,
however much it might rest with later generations to settle matters of
detail; North Wales, it was decreed, was to retain substantially its
Welsh rulers and its independence, while most of what was best worth
having in the South was to fall into the hands of the invader.

In little more than a week after the fall of Rhys,[1] Cadwgan ap
Bleddyn took advantage of the situation to ravage Dyfed, hoping that
the overthrow of his rival might serve to aggrandise his own power
and that of the kingdom of Powys. But it was reserved for a greater
than Cadwgan to reap the benefit of the new turn of affairs. Earl
Roger now moved from his base in Arwystli and at the beginning of
July occupied Ceredigion, in which he built the first Norman castle,

near the mouth of the Teifi, at a spot then known as Din Geraint (Geraint's fastness), but in later times as Aberteifi and Cardigan.[2] Thence the Montgomery hosts poured into Dyfed, which was soon in their power from sea to sea; the land was conferred by the king upon a younger son of Earl Roger's, named Arnulf, who fixed his capital at the place ever since known as Pembroke, a name which, like Builth and Kidwelly, transfers to the Norman castle the ancient appellation of the surrounding district.[3] The first Pembroke castle, which Arnulf entrusted to the custody of his chief follower, Gerald of Windsor, was hastily and roughly constructed in the form of a stockade,[4] but it was erected on a position of great natural strength, and it was partly to this that Pembroke owed its singular fortune among Welsh castles, in that it never fell, even temporarily, into the hands of the Welsh. In the eastern end of Dyfed, William fitz Baldwin, sheriff of Devon and a mighty man in that county, was commissioned by Rufus to plant another Norman post, which he established at Rhydygors, a ford on the Towy a mile south of the old Roman fort of Carmarthen and the church of Llandeulyddog.[5] In all this no regard was paid to the claims of the two young sons of Rhys ap Tewdwr; Gruffydd, the elder, was carried off by his friends in alarm to Ireland, while Hywel, less fortunate, was seized by Arnulf and kept in close confinement.[6]

Deheubarth having thus become altogether the prey of the invader, it was not to be expected that the regions lying between it and the English border should escape. Rhys was slain, it has been seen, in a conflict with the Normans of Brycheiniog, and it cannot be doubted that one of the earliest results of his death was the occupation by Bernard of Neufmarché of the whole of the three cantrefs of that district. The date of the conquest of Glamorgan is not known, but, while there is no reason to think that the task had been commenced under the Conqueror,[7] it was in all probability not long delayed after the accession of Rufus and may have been well advanced by the year 1093. The last Welsh ruler of the country was Iestyn ap Gwrgant, who represented no ancient claims, but had seized power on the fall of Caradog ap Gruffydd in 1081.[8] In spite of the laborious particularity with which tradition tells the story of Iestyn's defeat and overthrow, it still remains a subject upon which history is perforce silent.[9] All that can be said with any confidence is that the Norman leader was Robert fitz Hamon, a scion of a noble house who won the special favour of Rufus and by him was enriched with valuable possessions in Gloucestershire.[10] Starting from this base, he no doubt began operations by building a castle at Cardiff, which became the capital and centre of his lordship; from the banks of the Taff he and his attendant knights swept the whole country as far as the Tawe, and the history of the Welsh principality of Morgannwg was for ever closed. It was probably about the same time that the Norman Conquest of the cantref of Buellt, or Builth, was achieved. About 1095, Philip of Briouze, who had just succeeded to the lands of his father, the great Sussex magnate, William of Briouze, is found established at Radnor, which was no longer debatable border land, but the centre of a Norman lordship.[11] It is known that the lords of Radnor held Builth from the first years of Norman predominance in South Wales,[12] and thus one is prepared to find Philip addressed about 1100 as one of the principal holders of land in the diocese of St. David's.[13]

The subjugation of Wales had thus made very substantial progress when in the spring of 1094 Rufus left England for Normandy.[14] At once the Welsh, driven to despair by the rapidity with which their enemies were sweeping all before them, resolved to rise in revolt. The movement began in Gwynedd,[15] where in a short space of time all the castles built by Earl Hugh to the west of the Conway were carried by assault, the island of Anglesey was recovered, and a Norman army which was despatched to retrieve these losses was defeated at Coed Yspwys by Cadwgan ap Bleddyn.[16] The Earl of Chester appears to have been engaged at this time in continental affairs[17] and the defence of the northern march devolved upon another Earl Hugh, namely, the second son of Roger Montgomery, who had just succeeded his father in the earldom of Shrewsbury;[18] a victory won by him over one body of insurgents[19] was small amends for the loss of Gwynedd and the ravaging of many villages on the Cheshire and Shropshire border. Of the Welsh leaders, Cadwgan was certainly the most prominent and perhaps did most to animate his countrymen to resistance.[20] But it is just to observe that this is the year in which Gruffydd ap Cynan reappears upon the stage, and one cannot doubt that the presence among them of their hereditary chief was a special encouragement to the men of Môn and Arfon. It is not possible to say how long he had been a prisoner,[21] nor can absolute confidence be placed in the romantic story which tells us how Gruffydd escaped through the daring of young Cynwrig the Tall of Edeyrnion, who carried him off in his fetters from Chester market-place, while the burgesses were at dinner, and bore him on his shoulders to a safe retreat without the city. But the account of his later wanderings in Ireland, in Ceredigion, in Ardudwy and in Lleyn, a homeless and hunted, but not friendless man, is probably trustworthy, and from it one learns that the help of Godred Crowan, king of Man,[22] was first invoked by Gruffydd against the Norman garrison of Aber Lleiniog, and that, when this plan failed, he landed at Nevin, gathered a great host of the men of Gwynedd and took the castle with the slaughter of its custodian and a hundred and twenty other knights. Thus Gruffydd played an honourable and strenuous part in this conflict, which ended so signally in favour of Gwynedd as to give that region immunity from further attack for rather more than twelve months.[23]

The example of revolt was speedily followed by the men of South Wales, who fell with such fury upon the castles lately planted in their midst in Dyfed and Ceredigion as to destroyall save Pembroke and Rhydygors. Even the return of the king to England at the close of the year[24] had no effect upon the movement, for there was disaffection among the Norman magnates, and in 1095 Earl Robert of Northumberland took up arms against Rufus and sought to place Stephen of Aumale upon the throne. The greater part of the year was devoted to the suppression of this rebellion, which had in another respect a bearing upon Welsh history, in that it brought about the fall of Roger de Lacy; for his share in this conspiracy he was disinherited and driven from England, while his possessions were given to his brother Hugh.[25] Thus it was not until the end of the year that the king was free to undertake operations against the Welsh. Little had been done meanwhile by the barons of the march; Glamorgan and Brecknock were still firmly held, and from these lordships attacks were directed upon Gower, Kidwelly and Ystrad Tywi, but the ardour of the insurgents was in no way abated and the capture of the border castle of Montgomery, to the imminent danger of South-western Shropshire, was the deed of daring which convinced Rufus that he must throw the power of the crown into the quivering balance.[26]

The expedition which followed was in no way remarkable, and belonged, indeed, to a type of which the next two centuries were to furnish many examples.[27] It entered North Wales in the month of October in formidable strength, divided among a number of detachments, which were to move along various roads converging upon Snowdon. Woodcutters cleared the tangled thickets and clumps of woodland which not only hindered the progress of the English, but provided excellent cover for their foes. About 1st November the whole force assembled at Mur y Castell in northern Ardudwy. It was then realised that the campaign, instead of being closed, according to anticipation, in time for a retreat before the rigours of winter, was merely beginning; the Welsh, with the mobility characteristic of a people having little but portable property, had deserted their homesteads before the advance of William's troops, carrying off their cattle and household goods, and, having transferred these belongings to safer quarters in Môn and in Eryri, were now harassing the invaders by a succession of ambushes. Rufus resolved to rest content with the display of power which he had made, and returned to Chester without having checked in any degree the violence of the storm which was raging in the country.

Throughout the year 1096 the tide of revolt ran high. On the death of William fitz Baldwin, the garrison he had placed in Rhydygors abandoned the castle, and thus another Norman outpost, the last except Pembroke in this region, was swept away. Emboldened by the success of their comrades in the north and the west, the Welsh of Brycheiniog, Gwynllwg and Gwent threw off the yoke and won victories which at the moment made no small stir, though their ultimate effect was small, owing to the failure to capture the castles in these districts.[28] The men of Gwent repelled an army which had marched upon them from Glamorgan[29] and inflicted great slaughter upon it at Celli Carnant.[30] The men of Brycheiniog, led by Gruffydd and Ifor, sons of Idnerth ap Cadwgan,[31] fell upon another host which had issued from the same region and totally routed it at Aber Llech, about three miles north-east of Ystrad Gynlais.[32] It seemed possible that even Pembroke, stoutly as it was defended by Gerald, might fall into Welsh hands; Uchtryd ab Edwin and Hywel ap Gronw,[33] with the aid of the "teulu " of Cadwgan ap Bleddyn, invaded the peninsula and closely beset the castle, while the country around was ravaged far and wide. The siege was a notable one and many tales were told in later years of the skill and courage of the castellan.[34] So dark was the outlook that a number of knights made ready to escape from the fortress in a little vessel while the seaward passage was still open; Gerald frustrated their purpose and punished them by investing their squires with their lands and dignities. The last four flitches of bacon which the garrison possessed were cut into pieces and flung from the battlements into the midst of the besieging army, in order to give the impression that food was abundant within and that it was, therefore, useless to expect to starve the men of the castle into surrender. A more subtle device was the plan adopted by Gerald of writing a letter to his superior Arnulf, to the effect that he need not trouble to relieve him for four months, and then contriving that the bearer of this missive should lose it at Lamphey, some two miles away, where Bishop

Wilfrid, then in residence at the place, was soon put in possession of it and did not fail to communicate its tenor to the Welsh leaders. Whether as a result of this manoeuvre or not, the siege was unsuccessful; Uchtryd and Hywel, having amassed a great quantity of booty, gave up the more important task of reducing their enemies' stronghold and retired with their plunder, leaving Gerald once more master of the shores of Mil-ford Haven. This failure to capture Pembroke was a turning-point in the history of the South Welsh revolt. It left to the Normans a most important base of operations, from which the process of reconquest might be carried on. At the beginning of 1097 Gerald was sufficiently secure of his position to venture upon a raid into Pebidiog, intended, no doubt, as an act of retaliation for the favour shown by Bishop Wilfrid towards the insurgents. The spring saw Rufus once more in Wales.[35] Though the Welsh and the English chroniclers agree that the expedition was as barren of results as that of 1095, the castles which the king ordered to be built must have had some effect upon the situation, and all the signs henceforward point to a gradual subsidence of the revolt in the South, leaving the Welsh at the end of the reign in possession of Ceredigion and Ystrad Tywi only.

But in the North the issue of the conflict was very different. In the summer of 1098 Earl Hugh of Chester resolved to make a serious effort to repair the losses he had sustained at the hands of the Welsh in the region of Môn and Arfon.[36] He obtained the service as guides of Owain and Uchtryd ab Edwin, men who in all probability were tenants of his in Tegeingl and whose ambition was no doubt tempted by the hope of large rewards. Earl Hugh of Shrewsbury joined forces with his brother earl and the army made for the shores of the Menai Straits. Gruffydd ap Cynan and Cadwgan ap Bleddyn, as leaders of the Welsh resistance, adopted the policy of withdrawing, with all their people, into the isle of Anglesey, and there, with the help of a hired fleet from across the Irish Channel, defending themselves, in the expressive language of Gruffydd's biographer, "as in a fortress girt by the ocean". It was a wise movement, had the honour and good faith of the Danish mercenaries been proof against corruption, but, when the two earls encamped on the coast of Arllechwedd, it soon appeared that the foreign fleet was open to consider a higher offer, and ere long Gruffydd found his allies turned against him and the Normans pouring into the island. Thinking that all was lost, he and Cadwgan fled in a panic to Ireland, and the triumph of the invaders was for the moment complete. There followed a week, perhaps more,[37] of rapine and carnage, when even the protection of religion was of no avail. Men especially remembered, in the light of his tragic fall so soon afterwards, the impious violence of the Earl of Shrewsbury, how he had made the church of Llandyfrydog a kennel for his dogs and had cruelly mutilated an aged priest who had given counsel to the Welsh. When the riotous fury of the victors was at its height, a sudden change was wrought by the appearance off Priestholm of a strange flotilla. It was that of Magnus Barefoot, king of Norway, who in the course of a great raid upon the islands of the West had reached Man and was now making for the sister isle of Anglesey. He had no special quarrel with the Welsh or their oppressors, but in the true pirate spirit at once attacked the force which he found in possession, and the "battle of Anglesey Sound" began. It is described in lively terms by the king's poet, Gisl Illugisson, who tells how "the men of Magnus scored many a target with their bright spear points," and how "the king shot with both hands. . . the white arrowheads sped from the bow he drew". The Earl of Shrewsbury, known to the Norsemen as "Hugh the Proud," was a conspicuous figure on the Anglesey shore, clad in full armour and riding hither and thither in the swirling shallows. In the midst of the conflict he fell, pierced through the eye by an arrow which was universally believed to have been aimed by Magnus himself; the sea closed over his body, which was not recovered until the retreating tide left it where it sank. This disaster spread consternation through the ranks of the invaders, but the king took no advantage of his success; the fleet sailed away as suddenly and with as little purpose as it came, and the Normans were once more in control of the island.

Yet it would seem that their position had been seriously imperilled, and that the attempt to convert Anglesey into a Norman settlement was now to be finally abandoned. The captives, young and old, whom they had gathered together in the course of the expedition, were carried off across the Conway, but it does not appear that any substantial body of troops was left to occupy the conquered districts, and, if there was any representative of Earl Hugh's authority in Mon and Arfon at the end of the year, it can only have been the Welshman Owain ab Edwin, whose resistance to any movement in favour of independence was not a thing to be reckoned upon.[38] Most truly is it said by Giraldus Cambrensis that the power of the English in Anglesey ceased from the hour of the death of Earl Hugh. If at first sight the event appears too casual to have brought about so complete a change in the position of affairs, one must take into account the importance of sea power as a necessary element in every scheme for the conquest of the lands lying west of the Conway. Without control of the sea passage to Chester, Rhuddlan and Degannwy, the Norman holder of Anglesey was in a helpless plight, at the mercy of countless foes who could bar every road whence he might expect supplies and reinforcements. The attack of King Magnus, though the danger in this case had so suddenly passed away, showed how a real and formidable peril might arise, and it was decided that the risks of campaigning in Gwynedd were too great to warrant any further attempts at conquest.

The fruit of this decision is seen in the following year, when Gruffydd and Cadwgan, learning that the skies had cleared, returned to Wales. Gruffydd recovered Mon, most probably with the consent of the Earl of Chester; Cadwgan was invested by Robert of Bellême, the new Earl of Shrewsbury, with Ceredigion and his share of the family inheritance of Powys. While the Normans showed no disposition to relax their hold upon such regions as Glamorgan, Brecknock, Dyfed, Tegeingl and Rhos, the years of the revolt had taught them that there were others, such as Anglesey, Powys and Ceredigion, which they could not retain in their own hands without serious risk of disaster.

II. THE PREDOMINANCE OF POWYS.

The salient feature of Welsh history during the first half of the reign of Henry I. is the prominence of Powys and its ruling family, the house of Bleddyn ap Cynfyn. Exposing to England a long frontier, which was pierced by valleys giving access to its inmost recesses, the realm of Powys was not fitted by nature to play a heroic part in the conflict between Welsh and English; its chieftains had no Eryri in which to entrench themselves in the hour of danger, and they usually appear, therefore, as allies of the foreigner, or, at the best, as vassals of the stronger state of Gwynedd. During the opening years of the twelfth century, however, Powys, under the guidance of the sons and grandsons of Bleddyn, enjoyed a brief predominance, and the deeds of its rulers furnish for a time the central point of interest in the history both of North and South Wales. At first sight this may be supposed to be due to the fact that the house of Bleddyn had a chronicler, the cleric of Llanbadarn Fawr who, kept the record now embodied in "Brut y Tywysogion,"[39] a man who had a particular kindness for the family and a special pride in its achievements. But this fact is an index merely to one of wider significance; the church of Llanbadarn did but honour the dynasty which was supreme in its own land of Ceredigion, and this position, an altogether exceptional one for Powys, well illustrates how in this age that kingdom was extending its influence in all directions. Fortune for a few years favoured the land of Cadell and Tysilio; the temporary suspension of the line of Deheubarth, the ruin, which Gruffydd ap Cynan was slowly and painfully repairing, of the realm of Gwynedd, and the fall, in the height of its power and glory, of the house of Montgomery, all gave for the time being an advantage to the rulers of Powys which they did not enjoy under ordinary conditions.

In 1098 Robert of Bellême had succeeded his brother as Earl of Shrewsbury, and thus the eldest and, by general admission, the most bloodthirsty and tyrannical of the sons of Earl Roger was brought into close relations with the Welsh. His four years' rule of the border was no doubt marked by violence and oppression,[40] but the building of a new castle at Carreghofa, intended to command the valleys of the Tanat and Vyrnwy, is the only measure undertaken by him against the Welsh of which there is specific record.[41] On the other hand, his cession of Ceredigion to Cadwgan has already been mentioned, and his relations with the sons of Bleddyn were on such a footing as to make it possible for him to win their support in the hour of need. His ruin was in truth wrought, not by his cruelty and misgovernment, but by his overweening ambition, which from the first months of the new reign attracted the jealous eye of the king, a monarch who would tolerate no rival in his dominions. The crash came in the summer of 1102, when the earl, having been summoned to Henry's court to answer charges which he could not meet, resolved to appeal to arms and put all the castles of his various lordships in a state of defence.[42] Henry first took measures for the reduction of Arundel in Sussex and Tickhill in Yorkshire; he had then before him the more difficult task of breaking down the strong position which Robert had made for himself in his earldom of Shropshire. Not only was Shrewsbury strongly fortified and the new castle of Bridgenorth made almost impregnable, but the Welsh vassals of the earldom, Cadwgan, Iorwerth and Maredudd ap Bleddyn, were induced by gifts and promises of freedom to throw in their lot with their feudal lord. Robert led them to the pillage of Staffordshire and encouraged them to carry off their booty to the Welsh hills, where there was small chance of its being recovered. As Robert's brother Arnulf was a confederate with him in his rebellion and could command Dyfed and assistance from Ireland, the king was confronted by a serious situation; for the first (but by no means the last) time in the history of the border, baronial pride had come to terms with patriotic enthusiasm, and the combination threatened to leave him little he could call his own in the western parts of his realm. During the siege of Bridgenorth the position was anxiously reviewed; it was finally resolved to endeavour to detach the Welsh from a cause which could ensure them no lasting advantage, and William Pantulf, a large holder of land in North-east Shropshire,[43] whom Robert had dispossessed, was deputed to win over Iorwerth, deemed the most influential of the three brothers. The plan was completely successful; before Earl Robert, or, indeed, the other two leaders of the men of Powys, who were still working in his interest, had time to realise that a change of front had taken place, a great Welsh host was ravaging Shropshire at the bidding of Iorwerth, and the earl's Welsh alliances had become a rope of sand. After this, the surrender of Bridgenorth was not long delayed, and when Henry marched upon Shrewsbury, Robert accepted defeat as inevitable, resigned himself to the king's mercy, and was allowed to leave England, shorn of all his possessions on this side of the Channel and under sentence of perpetual banishment from the realm.

The fall of Robert involved all the members of his house who held English land in the like doom, and Arnulf had soon to abandon Dyfed. During the struggle he had not only fortified Pembroke, but had also entered into an alliance with Murkertagh O'Brien, the powerful ruler of Dublin and of a great part of Ireland, whose daughter he married.[44] But he had reaped no advantage from the Irish connection, for the reappearance in the Irish Sea of the great Magnus Barefoot had raised for Murkertagh a problem far more urgent than was presented by the difficulties of his son-in-law. The King of Norway spent the winter of 1102–3 in the Isle of Man, building castles for which the material was partly obtained from the forests of Anglesey,[45] nor was it until he fell in August, 1103, in the course of a raid upon Ulster, that Murkertagh once more breathed freely. Meanwhile the house of Montgomery had been overthrown, and, though Murkertagh wrote to Archbishop Anselm to thank him for his kindly intervention on behalf of Arnulf,[46] he took no active steps to aid his son-in-law in his resistance to Henry. Pembroke was resigned to the king, and its first Norman lord spent the rest of his days in comparative obscurity among his own people, his unconsidered old age a pathetic contrast to the splendour and ambition of his prime.[47]

Many changes resulted from this uprooting of the most powerful family in Wales and its borders. Following the example of the Conqueror in 1075, Henry refrained from filling the vacant earldom, and, while still treating Shropshire as a marcher lordship rather than as an ordinary shire, governed it through ministers of his own. It was probably not long after 1102 that he set over it as viceroy or justiciar one Richard of Beaumais, a clerical retainer of the Montgomery family who had given proof of business aptitude.[48] In 1108 Richard was raised to the see of London and for the next fifteen years he exercised with vigour and success the not very consonant functions of bishop and warden of the march. As for the Welsh lands of Robert and Arnulf, it had been part of the bargain with Iorwerth that these should be conferred upon him; Powys, Ceredigion, Ystrad Tywi, Gower, Kidwelly and Arnulf's half of Dyfed (the other was vested in the Fitz Baldwin family) had all been promised to him. He was soon to learn that he had been duped and that Henry had quite other plans for most of these districts. About Powys and Ceredigion no difficulty was made, and the arrangement under which Cadwgan took from his brother the latter region, with a share of the family realm, was confirmed. But when Iorwerth, having handed Maredudd, as a dangerous disturber of the peace, to the royal custody, appeared to claim the rest of the expected reward, he found that Pembroke was to be given to a Norman knight named Saer,[49] while Hywel ap Gronw was to be lord of Ystrad Tywi, Gower and Kidwelly. Such treatment of a man who knew well how valuable the service he had just rendered to the king was not likely to quicken his loyalty to the crown, and it is only what one would expect that in 1103 Iorwerth should be arraigned at Shrewsbury before a royal tribunal and on conviction thrown into prison.

Yet, if Iorwerth and Maredudd failed personally to profit by the revolution which had come about, Cadwgan was able to take full advantage of it and held for some years a very strong position. Hywel ap Gronw did not live long to enjoy the broad lands Henry had bestowed upon him in Deheubarth; in 1105[50] Richard fitz Baldwin took steps to reassert his rights in Eastern Dyfed and rebuilt and replenished the castle at Rhydygors which had been destroyed on the death of his brother William in 1096.[51] Only the river Towy parted the castle from Hywel's domains in Kidwelly, and hostilities between him and the garrison were inevitable. By the foul treachery of Gwgon ap Meurig, who was foster-father to his son and in whose house he was sleeping in all confidence, he was in the following year done to death, and thus one possible rival to Cadwgan was removed by Norman violence. In 1105 Saer was also dispossessed of Pembroke, and the custody of the castle and the surrounding region was given by the king to Arnulf's old castellan, Gerald of Windsor.

Gerald had about 1100 married Nest, a daughter of Rhys ap Tewdwr, in order to buttress his position as officer by means of something like a territorial claim,[52] but he had not the prestige of the name of Montgomery to support him in his difficult position, so that he was not at first a serious check upon the power of Cadwgan. In North Wales that prince was even more securely established. Owain ab Edwin had died in 1105, having profited nothing by his adhesion to the foreign cause in 1098. His brother Uchtryd became Cadwgan's vassal, receiving from him Meirionydd and Cyfeiliog on the purely feudal condition, of which this is the first example in Welsh history, that he would be faithful to his lord and render him succour against all his enemies.[53] Hywel ab Ithel, the hereditary lord of Rhos and Rhufoniog, who had been forced to flee to Ireland in 1099,[54] was established on his return in so much of these cantrefs as was not actually held by the Normans, and the power behind his little throne was that of Powys and the sons of Bleddyn.[55] Gruffydd ap Cynan, under whom Gwynedd was after the lapse of many years to regain her ancient predominance, is admitted by his panegyrist to have held during this period a quite modest position as the lord of the seven cantrefs west of the Conway and north of the Mawddach.[56] Only in Arwystli, where the sons of Trahaearn ap Caradog were now beginning to assert themselves, was there dangerous opposition to the influence of Powys, and the slaughter of Meurig and Griffri, sons of Trahaearn, in 1106 by Cadwgan's son Owain was the first incident in a long feud between the two houses.

In spite of the favours heaped by fortune for a time upon him, it cannot be said that Cadwgan showed himself the man to profit by his good luck and to wrest still further advantages from the capricious hand of fate. His was a weak character, amiable, no doubt, but wanting in the sterner qualities which were demanded by the problems of statecraft in that turbulent age. The very vigour and energy of the house of Bleddyn, which might have proved so serviceable under the control of a recognised head, was under the lax rule of Cadwgan turned suicidally against itself, and the violent family quarrels of the next thirty years supply the readiest explanation of the speedy decline of Powys as the dominant power in Wales. Besides Iorwerth, who was still a prisoner of the king's, and Maredudd, who escaped from captivity in 1107, there were the numerous sons of Cadwgan, led by Owain his heir,[57] and two sons, Madog and Ithel, of the Rhiryd ap Bleddyn who had fallen in 1088 in battle with Rhys ap Tewdwr. It was no light task to check the warring ambitions of this group of kinsmen, and Cadwgan's failure to achieve it brought its certain penalty with it in loss of territory and finally of life itself. The first disturber of the peace was Cadwgan's own son Owain, whose bold and romantic abduction of Nest in 1109 was an act of reckless defiance to the English king; fascinating as is this story of passion and daring, which breathes the spirit of the early heroic age, and which Homer might well have told, its other aspect is not to be forgotten, as a reckless escapade which was fraught with misfortune for Owain's father and for his fellow-countrymen of Powys. At a great feast which Cadwgan gave this year in one of the courts of his land of Ceredigion,[58] Owain heard much of the beauty of Nest, the wife of Gerald of Pembroke, and, as the lady was his own second cousin, he resolved to pay a visit to the castle of Cenarth Bychan,[59] where she was at the time in residence with her husband, and see with his own eyes the graces of form and feature which were the occasion of so much eloquence. He found them not a whit less marvellous than they were reported, and left the castle with the determination, in spite of all laws and regardless of risk, to become possessor of the fair one who has been not inaptly styled the "Helen of Wales". One dark night he and some fifteen companions stealthily worked their way into the stronghold by burrowing under the threshold of the gate; directly they were within the wall they rushed with wild cries upon the sleeping inmates and added to the alarm and confusion by setting fire to the buildings. By the advice of his wife, Gerald attempted no resistance, but made a hurried escape through a garderobe; thus the raiders found their task an easy one, and, having burnt and dismantled the castle, Owain carried off Nest and her children to Ceredigion. The story suggests that the heroine did not play an altogether unwilling part in the affair; at any rate, she did not disdain afterwards to use her influence over her lover to bring about the return of Gerald's children to their father's roof. None the less, the outrage was a challenge to the king, of which Henry did not fail to take prompt notice.

It was to no purpose that Cadwgan, fully alive to the danger of the situation, sought to induce his son to abandon his unlawful prize. In his infatuation Owain was blind, and soon the blow fell. Bishop Richard turned to another branch of the family of Powys, to Ithel and Madog ap Rhiryd, and promised them a large increase of territory if, with Llywarch ap Trahaearn of Arwystli and Uchtryd ab Edwin of Meirionydd, they would undertake a crusade against Cadwgan and his guilty son. The result was an invasion of Ceredigion which scattered its terrified folk in all directions; some fled south to Dyfed and barely escaped the vengeance of Gerald, others found shelter in Ystrad Tywi and in Meirionydd, others met their death in battle with the men of Maelienydd. Even the churchmen of Llanbadarn and of Llanddewi Brefi learnt that the sanctity of their ancient fanes was poor protection against robbery and outrage. Owain and Cadwgan found a hiding-place from the storm in an Irish merchant-vessel which was anchored in the estuary of the Dovey and at the first opportunity Owain made his escape across the channel to the hospitable court of King Murkertagh, while Cadwgan, having no sins of his own for which to make amends, in a short while made his peace with the crown and was allowed to settle in the border vill which he had received as the dowry of his Norman wife, the daughter of Picot of Sai. In Powys, Madog and Ithel obtained Cadwgan's lands in return for the aid which they had given to the king.

Fortune, however, gave Cadwgan one more opportunity. The new rulers of Southern Powys were turbulent and quarrelsome, and Henry, having no desire to add to their scope for mischief, restored Ceredigion to its former lord, who compounded for the misdemeanours of his house by the payment of a fine of £100 and by a promise to have no dealings in future with the exiled Owain. The bargain was no sooner made by him than it was put in jeopardy by the return of his son, but as he came to Powys, and not to his father's territory, Cadwgan was not at first affected. It was to Madog ap Rhiryd that Owain joined himself, and, as that prince had already incurred by other acts the hostility of Bishop Richard, the first result was the release in 1110 of Iorwerth ap Bleddyn, after seven years' captivity, in the hope that he might prove a better ruler than the other members of his dynasty. Iorwerth so far justified the royal choice as, first, to appeal to Owain and Madog to desist from the border forays they undertook for their private benefit, and then, when this produced no effect, forcibly to drive them from his realm. Owain was now thrown back upon Ceredigion, and he did not hesitate to cast aside his father's interests once again, making the land a basis for incursions into Dyfed and. carrying thither the luckless captives whom he forthwith shipped as slaves for the Irish market. It was not long ere Owain's excesses reached a climax in the slaughter on the highway of a distinguished member of the Flemish colony, one William of Brabant.[60] Henry was now convinced that Cadwgan was incapable of keeping his son in check; he took Ceredigion from him and bestowed it upon Gilbert fitz Richard, whose family held it until the close of the reign. A daily allowance of twenty-four pence was assigned to Cadwgan, to enable him to live in England, but no land was given him, until he obtained in the following year his third and last chance of proving his capacity for rule. As for Owain, he deemed it wise again to seek refuge in Ireland.

Iorwerth had but a brief career as prince of Powys. The outlaw Madog contrived, after a short sojourn among the Irish, whose manners, we are drily informed, he found wanting in humanity,[61] again to secure a foothold in the territory of his uncle, who vainly strove to shake himself free from the compromising connection. The severity of Iorwerth hardened Madog's heart against him, and he resolved to achieve his freedom by a deed of blood. Besetting Iorwerth in 1111 in the house in which he was staying in the commote of Caereinion, he scattered the prince's bodyguard in flight and drove him back at the spear's point into the flames of the burning building. This murder was soon followed by another. The removal of Iorwerth again raised the problem, which the government found so perplexing, of the arrangements to be made for the rule of Powys, and no better solution presented itself than the reinstatement of Cadwgan and the pardon of Owain. Accordingly, Cadwgan was installed in the valley of the Severn, and it was signified to him that he might recall his son. But he had scarcely tasted the joys of recovered power and dominion ere he was struck down by Madog, into whose clutches he had foolishly allowed himself to fall, at Trallwng Llywelyn, the modern Welshpool,[62] where he closed ingloriously his chequered and stormy career.

Bishop Richard was cynically indifferent to the crimes of Welshmen against each other, and thus Madog profited by his deeds of treachery so far as to obtain a portion of Powys, which is described as including Caereinion, a third of the commote of Deuddwr, and the tref of Aberriw.[63] To the rest Owain succeeded, returning from his second exile in Ireland to wield an authority which was not impaired until his death in 1116. He was more successful as an independent prince than while subject to his father's tutelage. He appears to have taken his uncle Maredudd into his service as "penteulu," or captain of the guard,[64] and Maredudd in return, while engaged in 1113 upon one of the usual raids upon Arwystli, laid hands upon Madog and sent him in chains to Owain, who, after the barbarous manner of the age, avenged his father's death by blinding him. In 1114 his power was put to the severe and unusual test of a royal invasion of the country.

Henry's Welsh campaign of that year[65]—the first of his reign—was directed not merely against Gruffydd ap Cynan, though it will be seen in a later chapter that its chief object was to limit the Venedotian power, but also against Owain of Powys and his uncle Maredudd, who now held Caereinion.[66] Owain was obliged to retreat with his people and their movable goods into the fastnesses of Gwynedd, having no safe hiding-place in his own land, but, when Gruffydd came to terms with the king and so put an end to further resistance, he had no difficulty also in winning the royal favour. His Llanbadarn admirer and panegyrist treats it as a high compliment that Henry took the prince of Powys with him when he crossed over to Normandy in September, but one may be permitted to see also in the step a measure of precaution. Be this as it may, Owain received the honour of knighthood and returned to his dominions when the king came back to England in July, 1115. He met his death in the following year in the king's service. The rising of Gruffydd ap Rhys had thrown Deheubarth into a ferment, and the king resolved to make use, not only of the Norman garrison of the district, but also of the jealousy and rivalry of other Welshmen to crush a claimant who threatened to be a serious danger. Owain ap Cadwgan and Llywarch of Arwystli were induced to bring their forces into the field, and in the midst of the operation the former came suddenly into the grasp of the man he had so sorely wronged, namely, Gerald, the Constable of Pembroke. They were fighting on the same side, and Owain was retiring in leisurely fashion with but ninety men to defend him and the booty with which he was laden, when at Ystrad Rwnws, near the confluence of the Towy and the Cothi,[67] he was overtaken and beset by a great company, of Flemings, whose hostile purpose was not to be mistaken. The unsleeping vengeance of Gerald at last attained its end and his archers laid Owain low.

The death of Owain, whom Florence of Worcester dignifies with the title of "King of the Welsh," [68] may be regarded as closing the period of the supremacy of Powys. No other figure stands out, among the posterity of Bleddyn in this age, with the same air of distinction and power. His possessions were divided among his brothers, Einion, Morgan, and Maredudd, and Powys was thus greatly weakened and exposed more than ever to the evils of intestine strife. The future rested with Maredudd ap Bleddyn, who until now had held but a poor position in the matter of territory, but who henceforward profits by his policy of waiting, as his younger rivals gradually quit the stage.

III. SOUTH WALES UNDER HENRY I.

While the house of Bleddyn was working out its troublous destiny in Central Wales, the South was slowly but steadily being subjected to foreign rule. The conquests of the reign of Rufus were but the prelude to a thorough and systematic process of settlement and subjugation which went on throughout the reign of Henry and left South Wales at his death with scarcely a corner under the sway of a native prince. Except for the outburst of 1116, there is nothing to show that this onward movement was contested; under the firm and resolute guidance of Henry, it advanced with the calm and resistless might of an incoming tide. To fight it seemed almost as futile as to contend with a law of nature; for the average denizen of the South, as for the chronicler of Llanbadarn, Henry was "the man with whom none may strive, save God Himself, who hath given him the dominion"[69]

A general survey of the Norman colonies of this period will bring out clearly the extent to which they ultimately covered the ground, leaving hardly a single foothold for Welsh independence. It is natural to begin with Pembroke. Here Gerald of Windsor was in authority for the greater part of the reign, holding the castle for the king. The neighbouring fortress of Carew, or Caeriw, was apparently the family seat, for it was. from it they took their territorial name; as the reign advances, the sons of Gerald and Nest, William and Maurice, take their father's place as the defenders of Norman prestige.[70] Not far off was the castle of Manorbier, the home of Odo of Barry; about 1130 Odo was succeeded by his son William, who married Gerald's daughter Angharad and became the father of Giraldus Cambrensis.[71] Whether or not it was held as an earldom by Arnulf Montgomery, the whole region was certainly organised on the footing of a shire, of which one Hait was in 1130 sheriff, accountable for dues which reached the respectable figure of £60.[72] Not only the ancient cantref of Penfro was included in his jurisdiction, but also those of Rhos and Deugleddyf,[73] which were about 1108 converted into outworks of the royal stronghold at Pembroke by a remarkable piece of colonisation.[74] Large numbers of Flemings, who were apparently already in the country, were transported by King Henry into this corner of Wales and established as possessors of the soil. They formed no military aristocracy, content to be maintained and served by the native population, so long as power and wealth were exclusively theirs, but were an industrious community of farmers, traders and woollen manufacturers, whose settlement involved as thorough a displacement of the ancient inhabitants as did the English conquest of South-eastern Britain. It was thus that Southern Dyfed lost its Welsh character; the Welsh language ceased to be spoken there, and, English having gradually taken the place of Flemish, it became "Little England beyond Wales"; nearly all the Welsh placenames disappeared, and the vills took their names from their new settlers, a Lambert, a Hubert and a Jordan, for instance, giving new titles to Lambston, Hubberston and Jordanston respectively.[75]

The principal castle of Rhos was at Haverford,[76] at the head of the estuary of the Western Cleddau. During most of this reign, it was in the custody of a certain Tancard, who was powerful throughout the cantref and who died not long before 1130, leaving several sons, none of whom, except the youngest, Richard, survived their father for more than a few years.[77] Deugleddyf fell mainly into the hands of a Fleming named Wizo, who built the castle of Wiston, known to the Welsh as Castell Gwis, and was succeeded there by his son Walter.[78] According to tradition, the first Norman lord of the cantref of Cemais was one Martin of Tours,[79] but there is nothing to show that the district was conquered in his time rather than in that of his son Robert fitz Martin, who is found in possession about 1115. It is not, indeed, very likely that this region, which was separated from Southern Dyfed by a range of mountains, was permanently occupied by the Normans before its flanks had been secured by the seizure of Ceredigion in 1110 and the succession of a Norman bishop at St. David's in 1115. Its central stronghold was at Nanhyfer (or Nevern), where extensive earthworks are still to be seen on the hill above the venerable church of St. Brynach. Emlyn was probably seized about the same time by Gerald of Pembroke, whose heirs are found in possession of the lordship in the latter half of the century. The rock of Cilgerran, towering high above the wooded gorge of the Teifi, was the perch on which the lords of Emlyn fixed the keep designed by them to secure the humble obedience of their new subjects.[80]

The tale has already been told of the transference of Ceredigion from the weak hands of Cadwgan to the masterful control of Gilbert fitz Richard. The new ruler came of a notable Norman family; his grandfather, Count Gilbert of Brionne, had played a conspicuous part in the civil wars which raged during William the Conqueror's minority; his father, Richard of Bienfaite, had joined in the invasion of England and afterwards received many favours from the king. Among them had been the gift of the manor of Clare in Suffolk, and thus arose a family name which during many centuries was famous alike in England and in Wales. Gilbert succeeded to the English estates of his father about 1090, but his career was undistinguished until Henry gave him his opportunity in 1110.[81] He forthwith took possession of the whole of the four cantrefs and built two castles to secure his prize, "the one," as the local annalist tells us, "over against Llanbadarn, near the mouth of the river called the Ystwyth, and the other near the mouth of the Teifi, at the spot known as Din Geraint, where Earl Roger had formerly placed a castle".[82] The latter, it has been shown at the beginning of this chapter,[83] was the castle of Cardigan, posted on a little hill which commanded the tidal reach of the Teifi just where it was crossed by the bridge giving access to Cemais and the south.[84] The former was the first castle of Aberystwyth, but its site was clearly not that of the existing ruin, nor was it within the limits or in the outskirts of the town, which, though it has long been known by the name of Aberystwyth, is much more fitly described as Aberheidol. It can be inferred with certainty from the minute account of the attack upon it in 1116 given in the pages of the Llanbadarn chronicler that the original fortress of Aberystwyth crowned the slight eminence at the back of the farm of Tanycastell, which lies in the Ystwyth valley a mile and a half to the south of the town.[85] Aberystwyth and Cardigan were, however, far from being the only strong places erected in the district to ensure its thorough subjugation. Gilbert brought with him many followers, for whom he provided dependent lordships; thus at the end of the reign Walter de Bec had a castle in Geneu'r Glyn, near the church of Llanfihangel,[86] Richard de la Mare had another in the centre of the county, a certain Humphrey was established in the valley of the Cletwr,[87] and a certain Stephen had a fortress which may perhaps be connected with the bridge over the Teifi at Lampeter known as Pont Stephan.[88] Peithyll, Ystrad Meurig, Blaen Porth were also fortified places during this period; to no quarter of Wales did the title of "a land of castles" more truly appertain than to Ceredigion during the quarter of a century which followed its conquest by Gilbert. On the death of the first Norman lord in 1117,[89] it passed without question to his eldest son, Richard fitz Gilbert, and nothing seemed wanting to make it as Norman as Penfro or Morgannwg.

In the valley of the Towy the castle of Rhydygors and the claims of Richard fitz Baldwin disappear together in the year 1106, and, when light is next thrown upon the affairs of the district, in the year 1109, the local fortress is Carmarthen, and a representative of the king, Walter, the sheriff of Gloucester, is busying himself there in the royal interest.[90] The new stronghold was not built within the walls of the Roman fort, where stood the church of Llandeulyddog,[91] but on a height close by, which looked down upon the waterway of the Towy, here affording easy access to the sea for vessels of light burthen.[92] Henceforward, Carmarthen is always a royal fortress, and in 1130 it is disclosed by the one Exchequer record of the reign which has survived as an important, administrative centre, where a considerable revenue was collected for the crown. Thus Alfred son of Anschetil is returned as owing £3 for his father's lands, which were in the neighbourhood of Llangain;[93] the men of Cantref Mawr owe a fine of forty shillings for the slaughter of a vassal of Bishop Roger of Salisbury;[94] Bleddyn of Mabudryd, the country around Pencader, with his brothers, is mulcted in seven silver marks for the abduction of the daughter of Bledri.[95] This Bledri, in full Bledri ap Cydifor,[96] appears to have played the difficult part of intermediary between the two races; while he figures, ay "Bleheric the Welshman," among the knights of the "honour" of Carmarthen,[97] he is elsewhere styled Blederic Latimer, or the Interpreter, as though it were his special duty to convey the royal commands to his fellow-countrymen.[98] His lands lay in the neighbourhood of Newchurch, a little to the north of the town.

The reference above to Cantref Mawr may suggest, what was certainly the case, that it enjoyed during this period a greater amount of freedom than any other portion of South Wales. Its wooded glens and solitary moorlands alone gave scope under Henry's iron sway for the development in the region south of the Dovey of a life moulded in accordance with Welsh ideals. But even here the hand of the monarch was visible in the partition of authority between several chieftains. No one Welsh prince was allowed to tower above his fellows even on the narrow stage of Cantref Mawr; Rhydderch ap Tewdwr, a brother of the late king of Deheubarth, was allowed to hold a certain extent of land, but he was kept in check by one Owain ap Caradog, a member of another house, to whom Henry gave a portion of the Cantref.[99] In Cantref Bychan, on the other side of the river, Norman supremacy was undisguised; Richard fitz Pons, who had important interests in Brecknock, had crossed the mountains and received from the king the investiture of the district. This was before 1116, in which year mention is made of Richard's castle, which stood near the meeting ground of many streams, not far from the church of St. Dingad, and hence acquired its name of Llanamddyfri (now Llandovery), "the church amid the waters".[100] The settlement of Cantref Bychan was not as complete, however, as that of Southern

Dyfed and Ceredigion, for Richard is not known to have had any other castle in it, and he committed even this to the custody of a local chief, Maredudd ap Rhydderch ap Caradog. After the death of Hywel ap Gronw in 1106, the commote of Cydweli was bestowed by the king upon his trusty and powerful minister, Bishop Roger of Salisbury, justiciar of the realm, who built at the spot where the Lesser Gwendraeth falls into the sea a castle which guarded the road to Carmarthen. Around it soon sprang up the borough of Kidwelly, with Norman, English and Flemish burghers, who before 1115 had their own parish church of St. Mary's.[101] The bishop did not hold the commote until his death, for towards the end of the reign the lordship was transferred to Maurice of London, whose family had been for some time settled at Ogmore in Glamorgan.[102] Gower had also been vested in Hywel ap Gronw, and, upon his death, had been granted by Henry, like Cydweli, to a man in whom he had the fullest confidence, namely, Earl Henry of Warwick, his friend and companion, who fixed the centre of the lordship at the mouth of the Tawe and thus became the founder of Swansea.[103] Through the influx of English settlers the southern or peninsular half of the commote soon lost its Welsh features as thoroughly as Penfro and Rhos, and the distinction was set up, which has lasted to our own day, between Welsh and English Gower. Henry died in 1119[104] and was succeeded in his earldom and in the lordship of Gower by his son Roger.

It was not by arms alone, or the development of trade and industry, that the conquerors of Deheubarth secured their hold of the country which had fallen into their grasp. They called religion to their aid. The devotion of the Normans as a race to the interests of the Church, and their high respect for the monastic or "religious" life, is one of the most familiar features of their history, attested by a thousand acts of obsequious service. In Wales, it is true, they paid scant regard to the ecclesiastical foundations they found in possession, but from the first they followed the policy of making large grants from their conquered territories to houses of religion in England and in France, and this led in many cases to the establishment in Wales of "cells" or subordinate houses, under the rule of a prior, for the management of the property and the collection of its revenues. The cell was invariably placed under the shadow of a castle and, as the native element found no footing in it, it became an integral part of the Norman garrison, to the spiritual needs of which it ministered and with the fortunes of which it rose and fell. Monasteries of this type were to be found at the close of Henry's reign at Pembroke, St. Dogmael's, Carmarthen, Kidwelly, Llangenydd and Llanbadarn Fawr. The priory of Pembroke was founded by Arnulf Montgomery in 1098, when he gave to the abbey of St. Martin at Sees, established by his father, the church of St. Nicholas hard by his castle and a liberal provision of land.[105] This monastic settlement on the southern bank of the little stream which skirts the castle acquired the name of Monkton, and its church became the mother church of St. Mary's and St. Michael's within the walls of Pembroke town.[106] The nucleus of the abbey of St. Dogmael's was furnished by the ancient church of Llandudoch near the outlet of the Teifi. Though its real protector was the castle of Cardigan, it lay in the lordship of Cemais, and it owed its existence to Robert fitz Martin, who first gave the church, about 1115, to the new abbey of St. Saviour of Tiron, a reformed Benedictine house, and encouraged a few monks to settle there under a prior. In a few years he formed a larger design, provided a much ampler endowment, and persuaded the abbot of Tiron to raise the house to the dignity of an abbey. The first abbot, Fulchard, was installed not long after 1120.[107] At Carmarthen the first Norman foundation was a cell of Battle Abbey in Sussex, the great monastery reared by the Conqueror to commemorate his victory at Hastings. Henry I. gave his father's abbey the church of Llandeulyddog, with its venerable associations, the new church of St. Peter which had been built not far off, and land for the maintenance of a few monks. Thus matters stood when Bishop Bernard of St. David's, desiring to establish at Carmarthen a house of Augustinian canons, cast jealous eyes upon the possessions of Battle, and, after much negotiation, induced the monks in 1125 to abandon their claims and dissolve the cell in return for compensation elsewhere offered to them by the king. The priory thus became a convent of black canons and was enriched by gifts from Bernard, Bledri ap Cydifor, and other dwellers within the sphere of Norman influence in this region.[108] Kidwelly Priory was founded before 1115 by the builder of Kidwelly Castle, Bishop Roger of Salisbury, who made it a cell of Sherborne, a house for which he had a special affection as a former seat of the bishopric which he held. In this case, no existing church was chosen as the site of the monastery, probably because none was sufficiently near the castle, but a new church was consecrated, which served, as has already been indicated, for the needs of the burgesses.[109] Llangenydd Priory owed its origin to Earl Henry of Warwick, who gave the church, one of the older sanctuaries of Gower, to the abbey of St. Taurin at Euveux;[110] it was a little cell and never attained to any importance. It remains to speak of the cell of St. Peter's, Gloucester, formed by Gilbert fitz Richard at Llanbadarn Fawr. Owing to the reconquest of Ceredigion by the Welsh on the death of Henry I., its history soon comes to an end, but the evidence for its existence is clear and the monks of Gloucester lost no opportunity of reiterating their claim to hold this church and its extensive domains. The priory was probably founded in 1116 or 1117 and entered upon all the rights of the ancient "clas," including the lordship of the manor of "Y Faenor" between the Clarach and the Rheidol and the tithes of all Penweddig.[111] There must have been some disturbance of the clergy of the old order, and it is not without significance in this connection that the full Llanbadarn narrative embodied in "Brut y Tywysogion" does not extend beyond 1116.

By such means did Norman and Breton knights, English and Flemish traders, gradually secure a firm hold of Deheubarth, as though never to be dislodged. Only once was there a serious rising against them, and this was due to the bold bid for power made in 1116 by Gruffydd ap Rhys. The heir to the wide claims of Rhys ap Tewdwr had spent his childhood and early youth in exile in Ireland; about 1113 he returned, an ambitious young man, full of the restlessness of unsatisfied desire, to his native land of Deheubarth.[112] For some two years he lived a roving life, the guest at times of his brother-in-law, the castellan of Pembroke, and at others of his relatives in Cantref Mawr. The figure of the forlorn scion of an ancient race of kings, stripped of wealth and power and wandering from this to that hospitable roof-tree, touched the imagination of the men of South Wales, and Henry was warned that the homeless lad was beginning to be dangerous to his authority. Gruffydd did not wait to be seized by the king's officers, but, at the first suggestion of sinister designs, made off to Gwynedd, where he hoped for protection from the now powerful Gruffydd ap Cynan. But the northern prince had seen something in the previous year (1114) of the might of the king of England, and was not in the mood to court a second invasion by harbouring a fugitive who lay under the weight of Henry's displeasure. He promised to surrender the youth and proceeded to carry out the undertaking with little regard to the claims of patriotism or of hospitality. Gruffydd ap Rhys narrowly escaped capture, and, even when he had taken refuge with the "clas" of Aberdaron, was not much more secure, for the prince of Gwynedd, had he not been restrained by his counsellors, would have infringed the rights of sanctuary of the Church in order to prove his zeal in the royal service.

From Aberdaron the youthful outlaw crossed Cardigan Bay to his former haunts in South Wales and resolved in his despair to run amuck among the Norman castles of the district, in the hope that out of the confusion of a general rising he might pluck some advantage for himself. In the spring of 1116 he made an onslaught on the castle of Narberth, which he destroyed; next, he attacked Llandovery, which was stoutly defended for Richard fitz Pons by its Welsh castellan, Maredudd ap Rhydderch ap Caradog, so that only the outworks were taken, the keep remaining intact.[113] The same partial success followed the siege of the Earl of Warwick's castle at Swansea, nor did Gruffydd reflect how little his cause was helped by victories which left his enemies unharmed in impregnable retreats. Nevertheless, he had done enough to arouse the enthusiasm of his countrymen; crowds of young Welshmen gathered around him, and the authorities began to fear for the safety of Carmarthen. The plan was adopted of entrusting its defence to the neighbouring chiefs, who were out of sympathy with this ill-planned and ill-ordered revolt; Maredudd of Cantref Bychan, Gruffydd's uncle, Rhydderch,[114] and Owain ap Caradog each undertook to keep the castle for a fortnight. It chanced that the dreaded attack was made during Owain's term of service and that Owain himself fell in seeking to repel it; the result was that Gruffydd was able to set fire to the town and to carry off valuable booty to the woods. His prestige now rose higher than ever, and he soon found himself at the head of a very considerable force, which he forthwith led to the plunder of Ceredigion.[115] After some successes at Blaen Porth Hodnant,[116] which did not, however, include the taking of the castle, the host marched northwards to Penweddig and stormed the fortress which Razo, Gilbert's castellan at Aberystwyth, had built for himself in Ystrad Peithyll. They then addressed themselves to the capture of Aberystwyth itself. But the point had now been reached when the inherent weakness of the movement, the lack of generalship in its leader and of discipline among the rank and file, could no longer be masked under superficial triumphs. Gruffydd's negligence enabled Razo to draw reinforcements under cover of night from the neighbouring castle of Ystrad Meurig, and his irresolution wasted the best part of the day which he devoted to the siege. When, at last, the attack was delivered, there was confusion among the besieging troops, giving Razo an opportunity he did not neglect of scattering the loosely knit lines of his opponents in unexpected flight. Gruffydd's army melted away and he found shelter once again in the impenetrable woods of the Great Cantref.

The attempt of the king to use Owain ap Cadwgan and Llywarch ap Trahaearn for the overthrow of Gruffydd has been already mentioned.[117] It was unsuccessful; Owain was cut down in the midst of the expedition by his enemy Gerald and Llywarch then abandoned the enterprise and went home. Gruffydd's history during the rest of the reign cannot be traced in detail, but he is known to have so far broken down the king's hostility as to obtain from him a portion of Cantref Mawr. In 1127 he was obliged, as a result of the charges of his Norman neighbours, to seek refuge for a time in Ireland,[118] but he would seem to have soon recovered his position. During the closing years of Henry's reign his home was the commote of Caeo,[119] which occupied the upper valley of the river Cothi; here he settled with his wife Gwenllian, daughter of Gruffydd ap Cynan, and here were born to them four sons, Maredudd, Rhys, Morgan and Maelgwn,[120] of whom the second lived long and gloriously, while the other three were cut off in their youth.

Our survey of the conquest of South Wales under Henry I. may fitly close with some account of those lordships on the eastern march which had been conquered once for all under Rufus, and during this reign were being consolidated and developed. All that is known of Radnor and Builth is that they continued to be held by Philip of Briouze until the close of the reign,[121] while of the intervening region no more can safely be said than that Hugh Mortimer, who succeeded his father Ralph at Wigmore about 1104, appears to have acquired some hold upon the valleys of the Ithon and the Edw.[122] But no such obscurity rests during this period upon the history of Brecknock, Glamorgan and Gwent, which are shown by contemporary records, chiefly monastic charters, to have been parcelled out by their lords among a number of knights, who made haste to extract the full advantage of their position. Bernard of Neufmarché ruled Brycheiniog until about 1125.[123] His principal castle was built where the Honddu falls into the Usk, at a spot known to the Welsh from its situation as Aberhonddu, but called by the English Brecon, from the lordship of which it was the centre. As in the lordships of West Wales, the military station became also a civic and a monastic centre; before 1106 Bernard had founded a borough at Brecon and had bestowed upon Battle Abbey the means of establishing a cell there.[124] The narrative of the foundation of the priory contained in the Chronicle of Battle will show how such an institution might grow.[125] A monk of Battle named Roger is first found staying with Bernard and obtains from him a grant of the church of St. John the Evangelist standing near the castle, and, for his maintenance, the site of the old Roman fort at the confluence of the Ysgir and the Usk, known as "Vetus villa" or "Yr Hên Gaer"[126] With the help of a brother monk named Walter, Roger rebuilds the church, provides suitable monastic quarters, and gathers in further endowments. The lady of Brecon, Agnes or Nest, daughter of Osbern fitz Richard, in gratitude for a recovery from sickness, gives the manor of Berrington, near Tenbury, which she had no doubt received from her father as a marriage gift.[127] Monks assemble at the spot and finally, with the consent of Bernard and the king, a cell of Battle is constituted, with Walter as its prior.

From the roll of benefactions made to the priory[128] some information may be gleaned as to the principal vassals of the lord of Brecknock and the houses which drew their descent from them. The name of Picard is to be seen in the earliest of all the Brecon charters;[129] his portion of the lordship was the commote of Ystrad Yw Uchaf,[130] and he made his home at Tretower, in the vale of the Rhiangoll, building in all likelihood the four-square stone keep of which the lower courses still remain, and which gave its name to the "hamlet of the tower".[131] Picards or Pichards dwelt here for many generations, stout defenders of the English against the Welsh cause and generous patrons of the priory founded by their lord. Ystrad Yw Isaf would seem to have been allotted to Robert of Turbeville, whose stronghold was at Crughywel; Turbevilles were here in authority until the reign of Henry III.[132] La Haie Taillée, the "clipped hedge," a name which the Welsh rendered "Y Gelli Gandryll," [133] was the seat of another castle, which was held for Bernard by William Revel; in this case the fief reverted ere long to the chief lord and became a part of his demesne.[134] Talgarth, the ancient capital of Brycheiniog, was retained by Bernard in his own hands. Between Brecon and Talgarth, Roger of Baskerville held land and handed on his name to several generations of descendants.[135] It is not certain when the commote called "Cantref Selyf"[136] — it was but a part of the old cantref of that name[137] — came into the possession of the Clifford family, but about the middle of the twelfth century Walter, son of Richard fitz Rons, is in possession of it and rules it from his castle of Bronllys overhanging the Llynfi.[138] These were the knights who owed service to Bernard and who some ten years before the death of Henry saw a new lord take his place at Aberhonddu. By his wife Agnes, Bernard had a son Mahel and a daughter Sybil. But Mahel, after he had grown to manhood, had his inheritance snatched from him by what was believed to be the shameless perjury of his mother. Her anger having been stirred up against him by the vengeance he had taken upon a paramour of hers, she swore that he was himself the offspring of adultery and thus diverted the inheritance from him to his sister.[139] As Sybil was married in the spring of 1121 to one of the highly trusted ministers of the crown, namely, Miles of Gloucester, son of Walter the sheriff, this turn of affairs was not by any means disagreeable to the king, and he sanctioned an arrangement under which Miles was to come on his marriage into immediate possession of a part of the lordship and to obtain the whole on Bernard's death.[140] Miles held Brycheiniog with a firm grip until his death, nor was it of much account that, according to the well-known story told by Giraldus Cambrensis, the birds of Llangors lake would not tune their merry notes in recognition of his dominion, while they instantly obeyed the call of their true lord, Gruffydd ap Rhys.[141] It was the iron age, with no ear for the voice of sentiment.

The story of the lordship of Glamorgan is very similar to that of Brecknock. Here, too, while the chief lord retained a substantial part of the conquered region as his own demesne, much of the land went to form subordinate fiefs held by the knights in the conqueror's train. Here also the whole lordship was carried by a daughter, on the death of the first holder, to an outsider who was not concerned in the conquest, and in this case was no less a person than King Henry's natural son, Robert. Fixing upon the site of the Roman fortress at Caerdyf[142] as the centre of his new domain, Robert fitz Hamon raised there the moated mound which was the beginning of Cardiff Castle, and upon which was placed at a later date the many-sided keep of masonry still towering above it[143] — the visible sign for many generations of the authority of the lords of Glamorgan. Cardiff became a borough, the inhabitants of which had two churches, the parish church of St. Mary and the chapel of St. John;[144] it was also the administrative centre of the lordship, where the sheriff (for, like Pembroke, this marcher lordship was important enough to be treated as a shire)[145] held the county court of Glamorgan for the tenants of the lord's own demesne, and where the knights who held outlying districts as subordinate fiefs repaired to render such service as was due to their chief.[146] Broadly speaking, Robert retained in his own hands the fertile coast region from the Rhymney to the Afan, including the plain of Cibwyr around Cardiff, the lands of Llandaff, Llanilltud and Llancarfan and the region of Margan between the Ogwr and the sea.[147] The march between

Gower and Glamorgan, lying west of the river Neath, was given to Richard of Grainville, a Devonshire knight who raised his castle on the river bank.[148] The land between the Neath and the Afan was, with wise generosity, bestowed upon the dynasty which Robert had dispossessed. Iestyn ap Gwrgant, it is true, is represented by tradition to have sought consolation for his loss of a kingdom in religious seclusion, dying in the priory of Llangenydd in Gower,[149] but his son Caradog became lord of Rhwng Nedd ac Afan and was the first of a line who long held the district and its castle and borough of Aberafan.[150] Between the Ogwr and the Ewenni lay the lordship of Coety, where Payn of Turbeville founded the illustrious house which left its mark so deep in the annals of Glamorgan.[151] Another son of the unfortunate Iestyn, named Rhys, appears to have received the castle and lordship of Rhuthyn.[152] Powerful magnates in the low-lying lands were William of London at Ogmore Castle, Herbert of St. Quintin's at Llanblethian, near Cowbridge, Robert of Humfreville at Penmark, and Robert l Sor at Peterston on the Ely.[153] The regions of Meisgyn, Glyn Rhondda and Senghenydd were left in the hands of the Welsh, who ranged over the wide moorlands with their sheep and cattle and from time to time reminded their more prosperous neighbours of the plain by sudden raids upon them of the ancient and unforgotten claims of a conquered people.

Robert fitz Hamon, fighting on the king's side against Duke Robert in Normandy, was wounded in the head, and, after living for some months with beclouded brain, died in March, 1107.[154] He left as heiress a daughter, Mabel, who, with her great possessions in Glamorgan, Gloucestershire and elsewhere, passed into the king's guardianship, so that for many years the province was under Henry's direct rule.[155] Finally he gave her in marriage to his illegitimate son Robert, who, after the drowning of the heir to the crown in the shipwreck of 1120, assumed new importance in the royal circle and was created Earl of Gloucester.[156] For some twenty-five years Earl Robert bore rule at Bristol and at Cardiff as a great noble of the realm; it was at the latter place that he kept, within the strong walls of his castle, that illustrious prisoner of the king's, Duke Robert of Normandy, of whom he had charge from 1126 until death set the unhappy captive free in February, 1134.[157] No man was more trusted by Henry and no one more fully repaid his confidence by unswerving fidelity in later days to the cause of the Empress Matilda. His services to letters will be spoken of in a future chapter, and it would seem that in his dealings with the Welsh he showed a just and tolerant spirit; even his party opponent, the author of the *Deeds of King Stephen,* admits that peace and tranquillity prevailed in the region which during the civil war he brought for a time under his authority.[158]

The cantref of Gwynllwg, stretching from the Rhymney to the Usk, was a member of the lordship of Glamorgan, held under Robert fitz Hamon by Robert of Hay,[159] but afterwards vested in the chief lord. Below the height on which stands the ancient foundation of Gwynllyw or St. Woollo, the Usk winds its way in leisurely fashion through a broad tidal channel to the Severn estuary. Here was set up the principal castle of Gwynllwg, which the Welsh called "Y Castell (or, in shorter form, Y Cas) Newydd ar Wysg," but which the English styled, from the settlement at its foot, New Port or New Borough.[160] The broad lands of Gwent, on the other hand, formed no part of the territory bestowed upon Robert fitz Hamon and passed to other knights, who were of independent authority on this western march. Henry I., at some time prior to 1119, gave the forfeited lands of Earl Roger of Hereford in Gwent Iscoed or Netherwent to Walter fitz Richard, a brother of Gilbert fitz Richard, the winner of Ceredigion, and thus established the Clare family between the Usk and the Wye, where they long held in their hands the key of South Wales, the rock-built keep of Chepstow.[161] On the banks of the Usk two brothers from Ballon in Maine were settled by Rufus, Hamelin at Abergavenny, which became the centre of the lordship of Gwent Uchcoed or Overwent, and Winibald at Caerleon, where he was the successor of Turstin fitz Rolf. Hamelin disappears after 1106 and before 1119 Brian fitz Count, a natural son of Count Alan of Brittany, takes his place at Abergavenny. Winibald, on the other hand, seems to have held the legendary seat of King Arthur's rule throughout the reign of Henry I. and to have been succeeded there by his son Roger.[162] At Monmouth, the centre of an important marcher lordship, William fitz Baderon was succeeded about 1125 by his son Baderon.[163] Ewias passed through more than one vicissitude: its powerful lord, Roger de Lacy, was in 1095 disinherited and driven from England for his share in the Mowbray conspiracy against Rufus, and his lands were given to his brother Hugh.[164] Hugh, again, died without issue about 1115, and Ewias Lacy was bestowed by Henry I. upon Payn fitz John, one of the baronial officials upon whom he relied so much for the carrying out of his plans for the government of the country.[165] One notes with interest that at the end of Henry's reign the three contiguous lordships of

Brecknock, Ewias and Upper Gwent were held by three of his trusty counsellors and administrators, who formed in this district a solid nucleus of resistance to feudal unrest and disaffection.

It may be said of almost all these little kings of the southeast, as of their comrades further west, that they believed in the wisdom of allying their cause with that of religion by planting colonies of monks in the territories they had acquired. The reigns of Rufus and Henry I. saw the foundation of a number of religious houses in the region between the Tawe and the Wye. Robert fitz Hamon, while it was his special aim to enrich the abbeys of Tewkesbury and of St. Peter's, Gloucester, with the spoils of the older Welsh churches of his dominions, appears to have founded a cell of the former house at Cardiff, the now vanished St. Mary's serving, no doubt, as the priory church.[166] Richard of Grainville was more ambitious; in 1130 he gave the brethren of Savigny le Vieux, where a monastic reformation had been inaugurated, land between the Neath and the Tawe for the establishment of an abbey of the reformed type, which soon became an important institution.[167] Owing to the merging of the order of Savigny in 1147 in the more famous fraternity of Citeaux,[168] the later history of Neath Abbey belongs to the tale of Cistercian progress in Wales and it forms a substantial chapter in that interesting record. In Gwynllwg, Robert of Hay made the church of Basaleg a cell of the renowned abbey of Glastonbury,[169] while Winibald of Caerleon founded at Malpas, not far from his castle, a priory which was dependent upon Montacute in Somerset.[170] Goldcliff, set up in 1113 by Robert of Chandos, was an alien priory, subordinate to the great Norman house of Bec.[171] Chepstow was the oldest of all the Norman foundations, for it owed its origin to William fitz Osbern, who made it a cell of the abbey he had himself endowed at Cormeilles.[172] Abergavenny claimed Hamelin of Ballon as its founder, who, being a native of Maine, attached it to the abbey of St. Vincent at Le Mans.[173] Monmouth Priory was also of early origin and could boast of this distinction, that its founder Wihenoc, the Breton who held the castle for William I. after the fall of Earl Roger, not only gave the church and much property with it to the abbey of St. Florent at Saumur on the Loire, but proved at the same time the sincerity of his devotion by renouncing his worldly honours and entering St. Florent as a monk. With a simplicity which was rare in the high-born Norman devotee, he outran the lavish gifts of his neighbours by the bestowal of himself.[174]

There was one house of religion established by Normans upon Welsh soil during this period in the building of which policy had no part and which was the outcome of unalloyed religious fervour. In an age when it was as common to endow abbeys and priories as nowadays colleges and schools, the story of the foundation of Llanthony was told and retold as memorable and unique, and drew the sympathetic attention of the highest in the land.[175] Llanddewi Nant Honddu, "St. David's in the valley of the Honddu," [176] was a little mountain church in the wildest part of Ewias Lacy, at the bottom of a winding glen which was walled in on three sides by hills towering to the height of a thousand feet above the river below. Here came, in the time of Rufus, a knight William who, forswearing his military ambitions and laying aside for ever his blood-stained arms, devoted himself to the service of God as an anchorite, who should pray and fast in solitude in this forest hiding-place. His fame soon spread abroad, for nothing so quickly touched the imagination of that age as a life of exceptional austerity, and in 1103 he was joined by a companion, a priest named Ernisius, who was one of the chaplains of Queen Matilda. The next step was to rebuild the church; in 1108 the new building, erected in honour of St. John the Baptist, the pattern of all hermits, was conse-crated by Bishops Urban of Llandaff and Reinelm of Hereford.[177] And now the two solitaries were urged to extend to other souls the spiritual advantages of this holy retreat and to allow a convent of some kind to be formed there. They yielded, decided to join the order of Austin Canons, a body who combined the monastic life with the exercise of priestly functions, and soon had as many as forty canons around them in this remote wilderness. Hugh de Lacy gave with alacrity the necessary endowments, and would willingly have given mure had not the two founders dreaded the growth of riches and luxury, lest their house should degenerate and become no better than a common Benedictine abbey. During the lifetime of Henry I. neither the prosperity nor the reputation of Llanthony suffered eclipse; it became one of the most famous houses of Great Britain. Bishop Roger of Salisbury visited it, and, on his return, astonished his royal master by telling him that it had cloisters for the building of which the whole treasure of the realm would not suffice, thus speak-ing in a parable of its girdle of mountains. The queen's interest was aroused, and she also paid the place a visit; it was long remembered how the purse of gold which she had contrived to slip into the folds of Knight William's dress had been, not indeed discourteously rejected, but forthwith diverted to the adornment of the church. It was at Llanthony, rather than in any Gloucestershire abbey, that Walter of Gloucester, father of the famous Miles, chose to end his days,[178] and it was from Llanthony that Miles and Payn fitz John in 1129 desired the king to appoint a successor to Bishop Richard of Hereford. The prior, Robert of Béthune, selected for this honour, fought strenuously, as became the sincere recluse, against his promotion; he prevailed upon Urban of Llandaff, his diocesan, to refuse for a year and more the requisite assent. At last, Pope Innocent II. intervened, and in 1131 broke down the opposition of the bishop and the prior. But the parting of Robert from the loved scene of his early labours was a sore one. His biographer and companion, William of Wycombe, tells how, when they reached the summit of Hatteral Hill and cast a last look upon the homes of peace beneath, the troubled spirit of the prior found vent in sobs and tears, "for it seemed to him that, like Adam of old, he was being driven from Paradise into exile".

IV. THE SUBJUGATION OF THE WELSH CHURCH.

(The materials for the history of the Welsh Church under Rufus and Henry I. will be found in H. and St. i. 299–344, Lib. Land. and the contemporary chroniclers. Newell, History of the Welsh Church, and Jones and Freeman, History and Antiquities of St. David^s, may be used with advantage.)

It was a natural result of the triumph of the Norman arms that the Welsh should in a large measure lose control of the agencies which provided for their spiritual needs, for, though the Normans were devout and not divided from the vanquished race by any serious religious differences, yet they had their own ideas as to what was seemly and admirable in religious organisation and were by no means prepared to accept Welsh ecclesiastical institutions as they stood. While knight and monk and trader were parcelling out the land for their enjoyment, a process was going on which may be compendiously described as the subjection of the Welsh Church. For, although the term Church can hardly in strictness be applied to a body which had no constitutional unity, no recognised head and no synod for common action,[179] yet the four Welsh dioceses, while they had no machinery to enable them to act in concert, were closely knit together by community of sentiment and practice, and the policy of the conquerors towards them was in essence the same. If not formally, yet substantially, the measures of the Normans were directed against a national church.

Of these measures the first in order of importance was the filling of the Welsh sees with men, who, by making profession of canonical obedience to the Archbishop of Canterbury, put an end to the independence of their dioceses and brought them into the southern province of the English Church. While much of the evidence advanced at a later time in support of the claim of St. David's to be a metropolitan see was flimsy and unhistorical, this part of the case undoubtedly rested on a firm foundation, that the dioceses of Wales had not before the Norman Conquest generally recognised the authority of Canterbury.[180] The change which was now brought about was, therefore, fundamental; it proved irrevocable, and as decisively marks an epoch in the history of the Welsh Church as the submission to Rome in the eighth century or the Reformation in the sixteenth.

The first attempt to subject a Welsh bishopric to Norman control was made in connection with Earl Hugh of Chester's brief tenure of power in Anglesey and Snowdonia. The see of Bangor was at this time vacant, and in 1092 the earl procured the election as bishop of a Breton named Hervé,[181] who was, one of the favourite chaplains of Rufus.[182] Owing to the death of Lanfranc in 1089 and the king's delay in appointing a successor, there was at the time no Archbishop of Canterbury; Hervé was accordingly consecrated by Archbishop Thomas of York,[183] and the question of obedience to a metropolitan is not known to have arisen.[184] But in other ways national feeling was unmistakably flouted in the appointment; the election was probably a forced one, and ten years later Paschal II. does not scruple to describe the promotion as barbarously and absurdly carried out, in a way only half excused by the barbarity of the people over whom Hervé was set.[185] Bishop and flock never arrived at an understanding; the former adopted harsh measures and relied for protection upon the armed bands who surrounded him; the latter retaliated by killing his relatives and threatening his own life.[186] Finally, when the Norman power waned in the district, Hervé had to beat a retreat; the pitiful case of the Welsh bishop who could not live in his diocese engaged for many years the attention of king, pope and primate, until in 1109 he was translated to the newly established see of Ely.[187]

Thus the subjection of the see of Bangor under Hervé was only temporary, as was the Norman conquest of Gwynedd which made it possible. It was otherwise in Gwent and Morgannwg. Not only was the conquest of Robert fitz Hamon thorough and lasting, but, owing to its nearness to such active centres of English life as Bristol, Gloucester and Hereford, the see of Llandaff had for ages been in close touch with England. The cathedral clergy were largely of English upbringing,[188] and during the tenth and eleventh centuries the bishops had commonly been consecrated by the English primate.[189] During the

Norman invasion the bishopric was held by Herwald, a Welshman educated in England, who had been consecrated in 1036 by Archbishop Kinsige of York,[190] and who died at a great age on 6th March, 1104.[191] Thus there was little resistance to overcome in this region and nothing to do but await the death of Herwald, when his place might be filled by a prelate of a less provincial type. Meanwhile, the old man's weakness exposed the lands of the see to indiscriminate plunder and left the diocese without a real head.[192] He was suspended by Anselm for some fault,[193] but died nevertheless in possession of his bishopric. Owing to the quarrel between Henry I. and Anselm and, it may be, to the illness of Robert fitz Hamon, there was delay in appointing a successor, and it was not until 11th August, 1107, that a young cleric of the diocese, Urban, Archdeacon of Llandaff, was consecrated by the primate at Canterbury.[194] There is no evidence as to his origin and he may have been a Welshman,[195] but what is beyond doubt is that, before consecration, he promised canonical obedience to Anselm and his successors, and thus placed Llandaff in definite subordination to the English primate.[196] Little is known of the doings of Urban in the early years of his episcopate, but in the latter part of it he was a prominent prelate of the English Church and shared fully in its life. He attended the Council of Rheims in 1119,[197] the Council of Westminster in 1125,[198] and the second Council of Westminster in 1127,[199] besides taking part in the consecration of many bishops. There could be no greater contrast to the seclusion of Herwald. Nevertheless, he was far from neglecting the special interests of his see. His little cathedral was only some twenty-eight by fifteen feet, not reckoning the aisles and the porch, and he resolved, in accordance with the spirit of the time, to undertake a scheme of rebuilding. The work was commenced in 1120,[200] but proceeded slowly for lack of funds; it was in progress when John of Crema, the papal legate to England, visited Llandaff in 1125 and gave his benison to the enterprise.[201] Whether Urban had the satisfaction of seeing the building completed is not known, but to the movement initiated by him are no doubt to be attributed the earliest portions of the existing cathedral, and among them the beautiful presbytery arch, which is believed to have been the chancel arch of the structure of Urban's planning.[202] He was also a doughty combatant on behalf of the rights of his see. His differences with the chief lord, Earl Robert of Gloucester, were amicably adjusted, and a formal agreement drawn up at Woodstock in 1126,[203] but the struggle with the bishops of St. David's and Hereford, which involved the question of the limits of their dioceses, he carried on till the day of his death. Receiving no support in the matter from the English bishops, he took the case in person to Rome in 1128, and again in 1129, and was a third time in attendance at the papal court when death put an end to his efforts at Pisa in the autumn of 1133.[204]

The next see to fall under the yoke of Canterbury was St. David's, and this was a surrender of the highest significance. For St. David was the best-known saint in Wales, honoured by the largest number of churches; his episcopal seat had for ages been the chief ecclesiastical centre of the country, notwithstanding that the bishop seems to have had none of the privileges and to have exercised none of the rights of a metropolitan.[205] Such ecclesiastical culture as flourished in Whales reached its highest point at St. David's; at the end of the eleventh century, the tradition of learning represented earlier by Asser was still worthily carried on by Bishop Sulien, a native of Llanbadarn Fawr, who had spent many years in study in the chief monastic schools of the Celtic world.[206] Until 1093 the surroundings of St. David's were purely Welsh, and it was the fall of Rhys ap Tewdwr which exposed to Norman attack this ancient stronghold of Welsh religion and ultimately led to the loss of its independence.

The last of the independent line of bishops was Wilfrid, who, despite his name, was a Welshman,[207] elected in 1085 on the retirement of Sulien and consecrated, during the ascendancy of Rhys ap Tewdwr, without reference to Canterbury.[208] There is no need to ask, therefore, to which side he gave his sympathy and countenance in the struggle between Norman and Welshman for the possession of Dyfed. During the siege of Pembroke by the Welsh in 1096 he was, as has already been mentioned, in the counsels of the besieging host, and his cantref of Pebidiog was raided in the following year by Gerald of Windsor by way of retaliation.[209] He is said to have been seized on one occasion by the men of Arnulf Montgomery and held a prisoner for forty days.[210] His relations with Anselm are not easy to define with exactness; the primate at first asserted his authority by issuing against him a decree of suspension, but in the spring of 1095 the two came to an understanding and Wilfrid's position was recognised, with what sacrifice of liberty on his part it is impossible to say.[211] Anselm, at any rate, was so far his friend as to write about 1100 to the Norman magnates of Deheubarth, bidding them respect him as their bishop and, in particular, restore to him whatever they might have seized of the property of his see.[212] Under Henry I. he ruled St. David's for fifteen uneventful years, endeavouring, it would seem, to be at peace with all men. A letter has been preserved in which he thanks the abbot of

St. Peter's, Gloucester, for the gift of a pastoral staff, most opportunely made when he was in sore need of one, and promises in return to protect the rights acquired by the abbey in the church of Wiston, so long as the monks pay due regard to *his* rights as bishop.[213] Not long after this, in 1115, Wilfrid died, and at once the question of the future of the see became one of living and burning interest.

According to the Canterbury monk Eadmer, the clergy of St. David's asked Henry to nominate Wilfrid's successor,[214] but this must be regarded as the English official version of the affair, for there is good evidence that the majority of the "clas" resented and treated as an insult the appointment of an outsider.[215] There were among them men of learning and character whom they deemed suitable for the office, such as Daniel, son of Bishop Sulien, who as Archdeacon of Powys played for many years amid universal esteem the difficult yet honourable rôle of mediator between Gwynedd and his adopted province.[216] But the king was determined to make full use of this opportunity for completing the conquest of South Wales and to place in the see a man who could be trusted to come to the aid of Norman knight or prior or chaplain in any emergency calling for the intervention of the Church. The representatives of the "clas," summoned to the capital for the purpose, were told to elect one Bernard, a chaplain of Queen Matilda's, and on 18th September, 1115, the election took place, followed on the same day by the ordination of the bishop-elect as priest at Southwark. The consecration was pressed on with like expedition; Sunday, the 19th, saw the ceremony performed at Westminster, where it had been specially fixed in order to enable the queen to attend and witness the elevation of her old servant.[217] It is scarcely necessary to say that Bernard's profession of obedience to Canterbury was full and explicit.[218]

During the lifetime of Henry I. (whom he survived), Bernard did not fall short of the expectations formed of him as a royal nominee. He was a good scholar, of polished and easy manners and conversation,[219] and had no intention of treating his promotion to St. David's as a sentence of banishment. Like Urban he attended the Councils of Rheims (1119)[220] and Westminster (1127);[221] in 1121 he was sent across the Channel by the king to conduct the papal legate Peter to England;[222] in 1123, after attending the Easter court at Winchester,[223] he went to Rome with the new Archbishop of Canterbury;[224] in 1129 he was again at Rome in the spring,[225] and in August attended the Council of London.[226] His controversy with Bishop Urban took him to the second Council of Rheims in 1131,[227] and in each of the two following years he was in London upon the same business.[228] But, while his career as a courtier and high ecclesiastic of the English Church was a busy one, he found time, like Urban, to watch over the interests of his diocese. There is evidence that he, too, rebuilt his cathedral, though in this case the later work of Bishop Peter has swept away every vestige of the early Norman church.[229] He took in hand the reorganisation of the "clas" or cathedral chapter, which received as a body and consumed under no fixed rules the large revenues derived from the lands of the see, particularly in Pebidiog. It was wasteful and wrong from the Norman point of view that so much wealth should be lavished upon men who were under no monastic vows and whose manner of life was secular and not ascetic. Bernard made the "claswyr" canons, assigning to each a fixed portion of the somewhat slender endowment which was left after his extensive grants of land to the foreign knights settled in Pebidiog as his vassals.[230] In this as in other respects he was the enemy of the old order, bent upon introducing into West Wales the ideals now generally current in Europe. He gave his full support to the new monasteries founded by the Norman conquerors and was himself the real founder of the house of black canons at Carmarthen.[231]

After the expulsion of Hervé, there seems to have been a deadlock for about twenty years in regard to the bishopric of Bangor. The Welsh of Gwynedd were not able to put forward the name of any candidate acceptable to the king, and they were too securely entrenched in their mountains to allow Henry to force a bishop upon them. Whether during this period they dispensed altogether with episcopal authority, or actually had a bishop who had received consecration in Ireland, must remain an open question.[232] But early in 1120 the difficulty came to an end. Gruffydd ap Cynan procured the election of a certain David, and Henry assented to the choice, provided that the supremacy of Canterbury was fully recognised by the new prelate. According to William of Malmesbury, David was none other than the Irish cleric of that name who had accompanied the Emperor Henry V. on his famous journey to Italy in 1110 and had written an account of the expedition unduly favourable to his royal master.[233] If this was the case, it is not hard to see why the king of England should have so readily agreed to the election of his son-in-law's courtly chaplain. But the matter remains in some doubt,[234] and all that is clear is that David was of Celtic origin [235] and not, like his brother bishop of St. David's, of the dominant Norman race. Nevertheless, his consecration at Westminster by Archbishop Ralph on 4th April, 1120,[236] preceded as it was by a profession of obedience to the see of Canterbury,[237] marks the entry of the third Welsh diocese, the one best able to preserve its independence, into the position of a subordinate member of the English Church.

The fourth Welsh see, that of St. Asaph, was during the whole of this period in abeyance. The position of the cathedral, on the border between Wales and England, had always been unfavourable to the growth of this see, and from 1073 to 1145 St. Asaph itself was within the English sphere of influence, being included in the dominions of the Earl of Chester,[238] while the greater part by far of the diocese as since defined was in the possession of the Welsh. No bishop was, therefore, chosen during this time, and episcopal duties were performed in the district by the prelates of neighbouring sees.[239] Tegeingl was probably treated as a part of the diocese of Northwest Mercia (having its bishop's seat successively at Chester, Coventry, and Lichfield), and it is in keeping with this that here only in North Wales was a foreign monastery founded under Henry I., namely, the abbey of Basingwerk, set up as a house of the order of Savigny by Earl Ranulf II. of Chester in 1131.[240] Southern Powys, on the other hand, was probably attached for the time to the see of St. David's; it has already been shown that there was in this age a close political connection between Powys and Ceredigion,[241] and one may infer that this extended to church government from the fact that about 1125 the Archdeacon of Powys was a member of the notable family of scholars founded by Bishop Sulien of Llanbadarn and St. David's.[242] Yet, although this generation had never seen a bishop of St. Asaph, the memory of the former existence of the see had not died out. When in 1125 attempts were on foot to compose the eternal feud between the Archbishops of Canterbury and York, it was proposed to transfer from the former to the latter the bishoprics of Chester and Bangor and "a third which lies between these two, but is now vacant, owing to the desolation of the country and the rudeness of the inhabitants".[243] The proposal fell through, but it was seriously entertained, and it deserves notice as an indication of the complete indifference to national sentiment with which the authorities of the English Church at this time approached the consideration of Welsh ecclesiastical problems. North and South Wales were to be permanently sundered in all Church relations; thus does the history of even the dormant see of St. Asaph illustrate the success with which the Normans had imposed their yoke upon the Welsh in the religious no less than in the secular sphere.

The annexation of the bishoprics was historically the most important feature of the Norman policy of subjugation, and a few words will suffice in illustration of its other aspects. One result of Norman ascendancy was the breaking up, wherever it extended, of the old "clas" organisation. Where the "clas" had a bishop at its head, it continued to exist as the cathedral chapter. But elsewhere within the range of Norman influence, it was either displaced, as at Llanbadarn Fawr and Llandeulyddog, by a new monastic foundation,[244] or else reduced, as at Llancarfan and Llanilltud Fawr, to the level of an ordinary parish church. For the Norman the "clas" was a college of secular canons, a type of ecclesiastical institution which had been much discredited, especially in the Norman world, by the fierce austerity of the Hildebrandine movement, and he felt under no obligation to protect it. Robert fitz Hamon gave to the Benedictine abbey of Tewkesbury the revenues of Llanilltud Fawr[245] and to St. Peter's, Gloucester, those of Llancarfan.[246] Glasbury, the "clas" on the Wye, had been bestowed upon St. Peter's by Bernard of Neufmarché at the very beginning of his conquest of Brycheiniog.[247] It resulted from this action that the "clas" as an institution survived only in North Wales and its borders, in churches such as Holyhead, Aberdaron and Towyn, which were out of reach of the hand of the spoiler.

Another and more straightforward form of plunder was the seizure of Church property by individual knights and its devotion to their own uses. In the confusion of the conquest it was almost inevitable that the line of separation between secular and ecclesiastical property should often be overstepped and that estates in the hands of the Church should be seized no less than those yielding a revenue to civil superiors. This was a kind of encroachment against which even foreign prelates raised a vigorous protest,[248] but for the most part without effect. The see of St. David's lost, if our authorities are to be trusted, the wealthy manors of Cenarth Mawr, Lawrenny, Upton, Llanstadwell and St. Ishmael's, all seized by the conquerors of Dyfed.[249] Llandaff was so impoverished under the feeble Herwald that its twenty-four canons had been reduced in 1119 to two.[250] The domains of St. Asaph for a while totally disappeared, and in 1086 laymen held those lands at Meliden, Kelston, Bryngwyn, Cilowain and Bodeugan which seem to have been part of the ancient endowment of the "clas" of Llanelwy.[251]

The last mark of subjection to which reference will be made had no such practical bearing on the material life of Wales as those discussed above; it touched the realm of sentiment merely and yet was none the less keenly felt by a people so imaginative as the Welsh. This was the rededication of churches bearing the names of Welsh founders, unknown to the Christian world at large, to saints of wider reputation, commemorated throughout the length and breadth of Christendom. In the case of the Norman, the change was dictated by the requirements of fashion; it was the substitution of the modern and the civilised for the antique and the grotesque. But in the eyes of the Welshman, it was the displacement of the ancient presiding genius of the place; the new patron might be dignified and worthy of respect, but he was not, like the old, rooted in the soil and endeared by a thousand happy memories. Even the fame of Dewi did not protect him at first from being eclipsed in his peculiar shrine and habitation at Mynyw; his church was dedicated to St. Andrew and his own name placed second in its official title, as though his unaided merits were insufficient to secure honour and protection for the spot.[252] Similarly at Llandaff, St. Peter took precedence of the ancient patron of the place, St. Teilo,[253] and at Carmarthen, St. John the Evangelist was set before, and finally altogether ousted, the obscure Teulyddog.[254] Glasbury, passing under the control of St. Peter's, Gloucester, abandoned Cynidr for the apostle honoured by its masters, though Cynidr's Well is to this day pointed out in the parish.[255] In many cases an attempt was made to soften the harshness of the transition by choosing a new saint whose name would vaguely recall that of the old. Thus at Cilgerran, Llawddog was succeeded by St. Laurence;[256] at Rockfield, Cynfal made way for St. Kenelm (a Mercian saint, with no Welsh connections);[257] at Foy, Tyfoe became St. Faith.[258] In general, however, the effect was to add greatly to the number of St. Mary's, St. Nicholas's, St. Peter's, St. Thomas's and St. Andrew's in Wales, and to uproot many ancient ecclesiastical landmarks, which told of the heroic days, lying far back in the past, of the Church now fallen into weakness and bonds.

NOTE TO CHAPTER XII. § 4. — Bishop Sulien and his Family.

A twofold interest attaches to Sulien (Old Welsh Sulgen — *cf. Lib. Land.* 145, 154–6, etc.), the last but one of the independent bishops of St. David's; in the first place, the testimony of *B.T.* as to his eminence as a teacher is confirmed by the existence of MSS. written, as well as a work composed, under his guidance; secondly, he founded a family of scholars, known in Central Wales for nearly a century, and thus his career serves to remind us that the system of hereditary succession which had rooted itself so firmly among the Welsh clergy (see p. 215 above) had its merits as well as its defects.

According to *Ann. C.* and *B.T.* he was Bishop of St. David's from 1072 or 1073 to 1078, when he resigned and was succeeded by Abraham, and again, after the murder of Abraham by the Norsemen, from 1080 to 1085, when he resigned a second time. He died on 1st January, 1091, at the age of eighty (so the *Bruts*; the lxxv. of *Ann. C.* MS. C. is probably for Ixxx.), having won the highest repute for wisdom and given instruction to many scholars. From a Latin poem to which reference will shortly be made some further particulars of his life may be gleaned. He was a native of Llanbadarn Fawr, sprung, it may be, from a clerical family ("*sapientum. . . parentum*" suggests this), and early distinguished himself by a thirst and aptitude for learning. After some study in Welsh ("Britannas") schools, he sailed for Ireland, still famous for its teachers, but was driven by contrary winds to Scotland ("Albania"), where he studied for five years. He then carried out his purpose of visiting Ireland ("Scotorum arua") and remained in the island for thirteen (?) years. He returned to Ceredigion ("ad patriam remeans") and there earned great renown as a teacher; four sons, Rhygyfarch the Wise, Arthen, Daniel and John, were born to him, whose education he made his special care. In late life he was chosen Bishop of St. David's ("Uallis Rosinae") and held the office for twelve years, but not continuously, for "bis revocatus" confirms the statement of the chronicles that he was twice called to it, the second time after an interval of retirement. He resigned once more, but was still alive ("in senio") when the poem was written.

As to the poem itself, it was composed by Sulien's son John or Ieuan between 1085 and 1091, and written by him on the fly-leaves of a copy of the *De Trinitate* of St. Augustine which he was at the time transcribing. The MS. is now at Corpus Christi College, Cambridge (No. 199), and the full text of the poem may be seen in H. and St. i. 663–7. Ieuan copied the theological treatise at his father's request ("genitoris nota"), and the result is of interest, not only as evidence of the scope of the studies in Sulien's school, but also as a specimen of old Welsh handwriting just before it was profoundly modified by Norman influences (Rhys, quoting Bradshaw, in *W. Ph.* (2) p. 248). Another MS. written in the same hand and coming from the same school is the Psalter at Trinity College, Dublin (A. 4, 20), which contains Jerome's direct translation from the Hebrew. The scribe was apparently one "Ithael," but Ieuan ap Sulien was the illuminator, and certain Latin verses in the MS. are by Rhygyfarch, another son of the great doctor. See *Arch. Camb.* I. i. (1846), 117–25 (J. O. Westwood), H. and St. i. 189–90, Bradshaw, *Collected Papers,* p. 477.

Lastly, the well-known life of St. David in Vesp. A. xiv., though not preserved in an eleventh-century MS., purports to be the work of "Ricemarchus" and may safely be regarded as another product of the activity of the school of Sulien.

The chronicles enable us to follow the fortunes of Sulien's posterity until the middle of the twelfth century. Rhygyfarch (for his supposed episcopate see note 208 above) died in 1099 at the age of forty-two, having received no other instruction than his father's and yet having won wide repute as a man of learning. A poem of his, preserved in Cotton MS. Faustina C. i. (fo. 66a) records the tribulations which befell the Welsh of Deheubarth as the result of the Norman irruption of 1093 and reproaches them for their feeble resistance to the invader. His son Sulien, called after his grandfather, was left an orphan at a tender age and was brought up by the clergy of Hanbadarn ("mab maeth eglwys llan padarn," — B. Saes. s.a. 1145); he also cultivated learning and was much in request as a peacemaker and a judge. He died, probably at Llanbadarn, on 22nd September, 1147. Ieuan died on 30th March, 1137; though his father's name is not given the man who is described as "archpresbyter of Llanbadarn" and "wisest of the wise" can scarcely have been other than the son of Sulien. Of Arthen. ap Sulien nothing is known, but Henry ah Arthen, the "foremost scholar in Wales in his time" (B. Saes.), who died in 1163, was no doubt his son and a representative in the third generation of the traditions of his house. The fourth son of the bishop, named Daniel, became Archdeacon of Powys, in the days when there was close connection between that region and Ceredigion, and died at the end of 1127, having played an eminent part as intermediary between Gwynedd and Powys. His son, Cydifor ap Daniel, died Archdeacon of Cardigan in 1163 and thus the family kept up the tie with the land of their origin until their disappearance from the ken of the historian.

CHAPTER III

THE NATIONAL REVIVAL

(Ann. C., the Bruts and Buch. Gr. ap C. are the principal authorities for this section.)

I. THE RECOVERY OF GWYNEDD.

THE death of Henry I. on 1st December, 1135, brought about an immediate change in the position of affairs in Wales. Everywhere the foreign yoke was cast off, the power of the new settlers was dauntlessly challenged, and a new spirit of daring and independence seemed to have seized the whole Welsh race. It was not that advantage was taken of the succession of a weak ruler to the throne of the indomitable Henry, for the rising was instantaneous and it spread from end to end of Wales long before there was time to try the mettle of Stephen. It was not the outburst of the revolt, but its unchecked progress, which revealed the weakness of the king. Under any king, it would for a time have seriously taxed the resources of the crown, for in it forces found vent which had long been gathering strength, but had been hitherto repressed and restrained by the personal ascendancy of Henry.

The quarter of Wales which had least felt the weight of the late king's hand had been Gwynedd, and it was natural, therefore, that the new movement should find its centre and inspiration here. Throughout the reign of Henry, Gwynedd had been quietly winning back its old freedom and supremacy, which had been so shaken by the conquests of Robert of Rhuddlan and Earl Hugh of Chester. It will be well, before describing the dramatic crisis of 1135–37, briefly to trace the course of events in this part of the country, where the preparations for the change of scene had been slowly going on, out of ken of all but the acutest observers.

During the period 1100–14 Gruffydd ap Cynan, with no rival to disturb his peace of mind, had made himself master of the country west of the Conway.[1] By the death of Earl Hugh the Fat in 1101,[2] his most formidable adversary was removed from his path; the earldom of Chester underwent a long minority, for Richard was only seven at his father's death.[3] So substantial had the power of Gruffydd become that in 1114 Henry deemed it wise to lead an expedition against him.[4] There was no lack of pretexts for the attack; Earl Richard had serious complaints to make of the way in which the king of Gwynedd received fugitive vassals of his from Rhos, and at midsummer a large force moved upon Wales. The princes of Powys took fright at the invasion; Maredudd ap Bleddyn hastened to make his peace with the king, while Owain ap Cadwgan transferred himself and his belongings to the mountain fastnesses of the West, but the issue of the campaign shows that it was Gruffydd who had really to dread the king's coming. The army advanced in three detachments; from the south came the Normans of Deheubarth, aided by a contingent from Devon and Cornwall,[5] and at Mur y Castell, near Trawsfynydd, joined the king, who had travelled westward by the old Roman road across the Berwyn. The third detachment was led by King Alexander I. of Scotland and Earl Richard, and no doubt set out from Chester by the coast road leading to the mouth of the Conway.[6] Against so brave a muster of royal troops the Welsh could do little; there was no fighting and the campaign resolved itself into a matter of negotiations between Owain and the king and between Gruffydd and the leaders of the northern detachment. Owain regained the royal favour on comparatively easy terms, but Gruffydd, in addition to rendering homage and fealty, had to pay a heavy fine. He lost no territory or prestige, but it is easy to see that the expedition made a serious impression upon him, for in the following year he was ready to give up Gruffydd ap Rhys to Henry's vengeance and seven years later could not be persuaded again to take up arms against so mighty a king.

Gruffydd was, in fact, growing old; he was not far from sixty, and the blindness of his last years was probably already creeping upon him. It is not surprising, therefore, that he should begin to fall into the background of the story and play a somewhat passive part, while the forefront of the stage is occupied by his sons, now growing to vigorous manhood. By his wife Angharad, the flaxen-haired daughter of Owain ab Edwin, whom he married about 1095, he had three sons, Cadwallon, Owain, and Cadwaladr, and five daughters,[7] and about

1120 the two elder sons, it would seem, were old enough to take the field in place of their father. The task which was to engage them for the next fifteen years or so was the breaking up of the influence exercised by the house of Powys, both directly and through dependent chiefs, upon the lands which bordered their realm to the north-west, and the annexation of these to Gwynedd. In the furtherance of this scheme they were greatly helped by the weakness of the line of Bleddyn, which after the death of Owain ap Cadwgan in 1116 had no able representative and was much divided in its interests. Maredudd ap Bleddyn was the most notable figure in their midst, a man of the older generation who by escaping assassination outlived all the younger members of that turbulent clan and died in 1132 lord of the whole land of Powys.[8] But he was in no position to contend against the rising ambition of Gwynedd; when in 1121 King Henry led an expedition against him,[9] provoked by attacks which had been made upon the defenceless lands of Cheshire,[10] he was forced to retreat for protection to the Snowdonian wilds and to appeal to Gruffydd for support. The king of Gwynedd was not prepared to risk anything on behalf of the rival dynasty,[11] and Maredudd had to purchase peace by the payment of a fine of 10,000 cattle.

The first advances of Gwynedd to the east were made across the Conway, into the regions of Rhos and Rhufoniog, lying between that river and the Clwyd. In 1118 there had been an important change in the political situation in these cantrefs; Hywel ab Ithel, who had long ruled them under the protection of Powys,[12] made war upon his neighbours, the sons of Owain ab Edwin, who were lords of the cantref of Dyffryn Clwyd.[13] Hywel brought Maredudd ap Bleddyn, with 400 warriors from Powys, to his aid, while Gronw ab Owain and his brethren had the help of Norman knights from the lands of the Earl of Chester, which still extended as far as Rhuddlan, if not Degannwy. A bloody battle was fought at Maes Maen Cymro, a mile to the north-west of Ruthin,[14] in which Hywel and his forces won the day and Llywarch ab Owain was slain. But Hywel himself was severely wounded, and his death six weeks later turned the momentary victory into a real defeat. There would seem to have been no one of his line to take his place, and his overlord, the king of Powys, was not strong enough to annex the two cantrefs to his own realm. Accordingly, they fell into the grasp of the sons of Gruffydd ap Cynan, for, though this is not expressly stated in the chronicles, it is clearly implied in what is said of the further progress of Gwynedd to the east.[15]

The next region in which they showed their strength was Meirionydd. This cantref, it has been seen,[16] was bestowed by Cadwgan ap Bleddyn, in the heyday of his power, upon Uchtryd ab Edwin, to be held as a vassal state of Powys. Uchtryd had not served his masters with particular fidelity, and, on the death of Owain in 1116, he resolved to be free and began to build at Cymer, the "confluence" of the Wnion and the Mawddach,[17] a castle which was to guarantee him his independence. Einion ap Cadwgan and Gruffydd ap Maredudd at once took up the challenge, attacked Meirionydd, destroyed the new castle and drove Uchtryd into flight. So far as is known, he never regained the position of a lord of territory, but lived, a landless man, with his nephews in Dyffryn Clwyd.[18] Meirionydd was now made a part of the kingdom of Powys, and for seven years was governed by Einion ap Cadwgan. But on his death in 1123 quarrels arose among his kinsmen as to who should succeed him. Cadwallon and Owain,[19] the sons of Gruffydd ap Cynan, saw their opportunity and invaded the cantref in the interests of Gwynedd. Their first step was to carry off the inhabitants and their property into their own territories, but this can only have been a temporary measure and must ere long have been followed by their definite occupation of the district, from which Owain sallied forth in 1136, when he opened his campaign against the Normans of Ceredigion. The men of Powys were too weak to retaliate upon them and could only punish their ally, Llywarch ap Trahaearn of Arwystli, who, as usual, had taken the side of the enemies of the house of Bleddyn.

Dyffryn Clwyd next went the way of Rhos and Rhufoniog. In 1124 Cadwallon, who was clearly as unscrupulous as he was energetic, slew the three rulers of the cantref, Gronw, Rhiryd, and Meilyr ab Owain, notwithstanding that they were his mother's brothers. The annexation of this region to Gwynedd no doubt immediately followed, for only thus can we account for the presence of Cadwallon some years later in the valley of the Dee and for the appearance in the following reign of Owain's men before Mold. Thus ended the house of Edwin of Tegeingl as a ruling dynasty; it had striven to use its position in the border lands which parted Gwynedd from Powys so as to pit the one powerful neighbour against the other, and, like the Count of St. Pol, who played a similar part in the struggle between Louis XI. and Charles the Bold, had earned the distrust of both. Between the upper and the nether millstone, it had been ground to powder.

In 1132 the victorious career of Cadwallon came suddenly to a close. Still pressing eastward from the vantage-ground of his recent conquests, he was brought to a stand in the commote of Nanheudwy, not far from Llangollen,[20] and there defeated and slain by an army from Powys, in which his cousin, Cadwgan ap Gronw ab Owain, bore a part and thereby avenged his father's death. For a time a limit was set to the growth of Gwynedd and the men of Powys had a measure of relief. But the work had substantially been done which was to make Owain, when he succeeded to his father's throne, the most powerful of the Welsh princes and Gwynedd the chief state of Wales. The author of the *Life of Gruffydd ap Cynan,* at the close of his narrative, allows us to hear, above the clash of arms which fills the rest of his story, the piping notes of peace and of jocund plenty, as he tells of the prosperity of Gwynedd in these days of security from foreign alarms. No longer did men build and sow for the needs of a single year, with fear in their hearts that the raider from across the hills might at any moment give hut and harvest to the flames. They planted orchards and laid out gardens, set up fences and dug out ditches; they ventured to build in stone and, in particular, raised stone churches in place of the old timber oratories. Thus arose many an "Eglwys Wen" or "White Church," gleaming in its coat of limewash,[21] until, as the writer puts it, the face of Gwynedd was bespangled with them as is the firmament with stars! Gruffydd himself built great churches in the principal royal manors, and, though none of these have survived the rebuilding which was so general in the later Middle Ages, the Norman doorway of Aberffraw may well be a relic of his work.[22] It was possibly his example which stirred up the religious communities of Gwynedd to the renewing of their ancient sanctuaries and thus produced the Norman churches, still in a large measure intact, of Penmon, Aberdaron and Towyn.

When Gruffydd died in 1137,[23] he had thus the satisfaction of knowing that he bequeathed to his sons a wider and more prosperous realm than any it had been his lot to rule in earlier years. Old,[24] decrepit and blind, he had no personal share in the great upheaval which marked the last two years of his reign, but the successes of Owain and his young brother, Cadwaladr (who now appears upon the scene), were all the more grateful to him in that he knew them to rest for foundation upon his own labours in the day of small things. He made a pious and peaceful end, having around his death-bed Bishop David of Bangor, the archdeacon of the diocese, Simeon of Clynnog,[25] and the Prior of St. Werburgh's, Chester, and leaving sums of money for the good of his soul to many notable churches of his own and other lands.[26] Among these he did not forget the Danish foundation of Christ Church, Dublin,[27] where he had worshipped as a boy. He left to his wife, who survived him twenty-five years,[28] a suitable maintenance, including the profits of the port and ferry of Aber Menai, the scene of many of his youthful adventures. Welsh sentiment forbade him to bestow the whole of his kingdom upon his eldest son, Owain, and thus a division with Cadwaladr took place which sacrificed the unity of Gwynedd and gave rise in course of time to serious disputes. His remains were laid to rest in a tomb erected in the presbytery of Bangor Cathedral, to the left of the high altar. So rested at last a man whose life had been troubled and stormy in no common degree.

II. THE GREAT REVOLT.

The great revolution in Welsh affairs which now took place was long remembered by the foreign settlers as a turning-point in the history of their adopted country. The day of Henry's death was for them as fateful as was for another aristocracy in a later age the day of the capture of the Bastille. Portents were believed to have marked it, such as startled the people of Elfael, where a lake and a reservoir both burst their banks on this ill-omened night.[29] It was reckoned a striking proof of the powers of divination possessed by the Flemings of Dyfed that many of them, six and even twelve months previously, had read the signs of the coming storm, and had thereupon without hesitation sold all they had and quitted the doomed colonies, where as yet no cloud appeared above the horizon.[30]

It was immediately after the coronation of Stephen that the first outburst took place. Hywel ap Maredudd, a Welsh chief who had retained some authority in the western parts of Brycheiniog, gathered an army in this district and descended upon the plains of Gower, a region in which not only Norman, but also English colonists had settled in great numbers under the protection of the Earls of Warwick. Somewhere between Loughor and Swansea a battle was fought on the 1st of January, 1136, in which the Welsh had their first taste of victory, killing over 500 of their adversaries.[31] It was the signal for a general uprising throughout South Wales. Gruffydd ap Rhys now saw the opening for which he had long waited, and, realising that the crisis called for something more than local action, and was, in fact, a national opportunity, he made his way with all speed to Gwynedd and appealed to the sons of Gruffydd ap Cynan to help him in the endeavour to rid Deheubarth of its foreign oppressors. Meanwhile, his wife Gwenllian, who was a daughter of the king of Gwynedd, took the field against the foreigner and marched against the castle and town of Kidwelly. This romantic adventure had a tragic end; a little north of the town she was met by Maurice of London, now lord of the district, and totally routed; she herself was slain and with her her young son Morgan, while another, Maelgwn, was taken prisoner.[32] She had chosen to play a part which, in Wales, as in other Christian lands, was deemed unfitting to her sex, but patriotism has lovingly preserved her memory in the name, still borne by the battlefield, of Maes Gwenllian.[33]

The Kidwelly victory was, however, but a casual triumph for the Anglo-Norman forces, and soon there followed an event which had the most disastrous consequences for them.[34] Richard fitz Gilbert, the powerful lord of Ceredigion, was with King Stephen in the early part of the year, but, having failed to extort from him the concessions he desired, returned in anger to the marches of Wales. Upon reaching Abergavenny, on 15th April, he was warned by Brian fitz Count, ruler of Upper Gwent, of the dangerous state of the country, and offered an escort as far as Brecon. But Richard would have no help; long years of unquestioned supremacy had bred in him an overweening confidence, and when the thick woods of Coed Grwyne were reached, on the borders between Gwent and Brycheiniog, he dismissed Brian and his knights and rode unarmed with a few followers into the forest. The tale was even told that he bade a fiddler and a minstrel play and sing before him as he went, so that all might see with how light a heart he undertook this journey. He had not gone far ere he fell into an ambush set for him by the Welshmen of Gwent under Iorwerth ab Owain, grandson of the Caradog ap Gruffydd who was so powerful in this district in the days of the Conqueror. He and his company were soon cut down, and the tidings spread apace that the mightiest of the Norman magnates of Western Wales had been laid low by the prowess of the insurgents.

No sooner did the news reach Gwynedd than Owain and Cadwaladr prepared to invade Ceredigion, which had been thus bereft of its lord. They were already established in Meirionydd, on the northern side of the Dovey estuary,[35] and the fact that Ceredigion had formerly belonged, not to Gwynedd, but to Deheubarth, did not, it may be regarded as certain, delay their advance for a single moment. They entered the province from the north, and soon stormed and burnt the castles of Walter de Bee at Llanfihangel[36] and of the Clares at Aberystwyth. How they dealt with Llanbadarn is not on record, but the sudden change at this point in the attitude of the Llanbadarn chronicler is full of significance;

whereas under Henry I. he reserves his praises for the chieftains of Powys and towards the end of the reign grows perfunctory and lifeless in his notices, the entry of Owain and Cadwaladr is hailed by him with transports of delight and they are lauded to the skies as "two bold lions, virtuous, fearless and wise, who guard the churches and their indwellers, defend the poor and overcome their enemies, affording a safest retreat to all who seek their protection".[37] The two princes, it is clear, treated with respect the property of Llanbadarn, while at the same time restoring to its former position the Welsh element which had been dislodged to make room for the monks of Gloucester.[38] Marching southward, they were joined by Hywel ap Maredudd of Cantref Bychan and Madog ab Idnerth[39] of Rhwng Gwy a Hafren and took three more castles, that of Richard de la Mare, of unknown situation, that of Dineirth, possibly near Llanbadarn Trefeglwys,[40] and that of Caerwedros, at Llwyn Dafydd.[41] They had now collected an embarrassing amount of plunder and returned home to dispose of it before undertaking further operations.

It was not long, however, ere they reappeared upon the scene. About Michaelmas they again invaded the province, accompanied not only by the princes who had been with them in the earlier part of the year, but also by Gruffydd ap Rhys[42] All the Welshmen of Central Wales were in their train, including not only foot soldiers innumerable, but also many hundreds of well-armed horsemen, for the Welsh had now learnt the arts of knighthood from their Norman masters and could put heavy cavalry in the field as well as the old national infantry.[43] The host made straight for Cardigan, the principal castle of the province, hoping by its capture to complete the conquest of Ceredigion, but was confronted at Crug Mawr,[44] two miles out of the town, by an army gathered out of all parts of Norman South Wales. Stephen, the constable of the castle, Robert fitz Martin, lord of Cemais, William and Maurice, sons of Gerald of Windsor, were the leaders of the Norman array,[45] and an obstinate battle was fought, upon the issue of which hinged the fortunes of the foreigners in Deheubarth for many a long day. It was a signal victory for the Welsh, who drove their enemies from the field, pursued them to the river Teifi, and set fire to the town; the bridge across the river was broken, possibly by the weight of the fugitives who crowded in wildest terror across it in their efforts to gain a safe hiding-place in Cemais, and hundreds who escaped the sword met their death by drowning, until the stream was clogged with the bodies of men and of horses. Those who fled to the town were not more fortunate; they perished in the general conflagration, which swept away, among other buildings, the church of Holy Trinity founded by the colonists.[46] Only the castle stood intact [47] and afforded a refuge to a small company of Richard fitz Gilbert's people, including his widow, a sister of the Earl of Chester. Elsewhere, all was at the mercy of the Welsh, who pitilessly ravaged the country, carrying off to their homes, and especially to Gwynedd, at the close of the campaign captive women in great numbers and other spoil on which they set special value, in particular, arms and armour and costly apparel.

The failure to take the castle illustrates the strength in this age of defensive works and the advantage which in ordinary times the Normans had over their foes as the builders of massive keeps of stone. Under Henry I. the victory of Crug Mawr would have availed the Welsh but little, for the garrison of Cardigan would have held out until it was relieved by a royal force bent on summary vengeance. The new fact in the situation was the loss by the Crown of its hold over the great barons; suspicion and mistrust, though it had not yet broken out into open hostility, parted Stephen and the magnates of the West, so that joint action against the Welsh on anything like an effective scale was impossible for them. In the present case, the king, moved by the perilous plight of the lady of Ceredigion, besought Miles of Gloucester to strike across country from his castle of Brecon and bring her in safety to England, but, though this commission was duly executed, no further measures were taken by the rescuer than were necessary to his task, in spite of his very direct interest as a marcher lord in the restoration of the old order in Wales. It was much the same with the expedition fitted out by Stephen a little later for the reconquest of Ceredigion; he entrusted the matter to a deputy, who took it up without enthusiasm and abandoned it as soon as it began to present difficulties. Baldwin was Richard fitz Gilbert's brother[48] and had thus a family interest in winning back the derelict lordship; he was supplied with light-armed knights and with 500 archers at the royal expense. But he got no further than Brecon; here terrible accounts reached him of the fury and determination of the insurgents, who had by means of felled trees rendered impassable all the roads leading across the mountains to Cantref Bychan and were awaiting his approach. He dallied among the men of Miles of Gloucester in the vain hope that the obstacles before him would in time melt away, and then, having spent his allowance, returned ignobly to England. Robert fitz Harold of Ewias,[49] despatched to a different part of Wales, showed a bolder and more resolute spirit, but he achieved no permanent success, and Stephen in his discouragement abandoned the idea of further expeditions and left the Welsh to themselves, cherishing the comfortable hope that they would fall a prey to civil discord and the evils incident to a life of idleness and rapine.

With such a spirit prevailing- in the high counsels of the realm, it is not surprising that the Welsh revolt grew more formidable day by day. In 1137 Gruffydd ap Rhys turned his attention to Dyfed and swept across the cantref of Rhos, now largely occupied by Flemish settlers.[50] An incident of the campaign was the killing by Gruffydd's eldest son, Anarawd, of Letard Little King, a Fleming whose name is preserved in that of Letterston[51] and who was clearly a man of mark in the district. The deed was done without the sanction or knowledge of Gruffydd, but the St. David's chronicler approves it as having rid the world of an "enemy of God and St. David," who had no doubt earned the title by attacks upon the rights of the cathedral clergy in the cantref of Pebidiog. Very shortly afterwards Gruffydd himself died, at about the same time as his namesake of the North, but under very different circumstances. He was no veteran laying down his armour after a well-fought day and entrusting to other tried and seasoned warriors the standard he could no longer hold. He was cut off in the flower of life,[52] when fortune was but beginning to smile upon him and when as yet his young sons were unfit to bear the burden which fate thus thrust upon them. The eldest two, Anarawd and Cadell, were just of an age to take a part in the warlike activities of the time, but the sons of Gwenllian, Maredudd and Rhys, were children of tender years.[53]

Nevertheless, there was no pause in the South Welsh movement. Owain and Cadwaladr appeared in 1137 for the third time in Ceredigion, and, taking the eastern instead of the western route, destroyed in succession the castles of Ystrad Meurig, Lampeter (if this indeed was "Stephen's Castle")[54] and Castell Hywel, then known as Humphrey's Castle. Emboldened by their success, they crossed the Teifi and made for Carmarthen; the capture of this important royal stronghold was the climax of their victories and placed the whole valley of the Towy in their power. It is noteworthy, however, that no further advances were made in this direction; that prudent and cautious temper which governed all the enterprises of Owain was perhaps at work in this instance, leading to a concentration of effort upon the conquest of Ceredigion and its annexation to Gwynedd. In 1138 the two Northern princes, aided by Anarawd and Cadell ap Gruffydd, brought a Danish fleet of fifteen ships into the mouth of the Teifi, so as to besiege by land and sea the little force which still held out obstinately in Cardigan Castle.[55] It was not a successful expedient; the garrison were able to beat off the attack, and the Danes, who were no doubt from Dublin, indemnified themselves by sacking the monastic settlement at St. Dogmael's, on the other side of the river. The castle was not, in fact, captured for many years; in the meantime, Ceredigion was divided between the princes of Gwynedd. To Cadwaladr was assigned the northern half, from the Aeron to the Dovey, which he ruled from the castle of Aberystwyth; a natural son of Owain, named Hywel, who was of age to fend for himself, received the southern half and thus held a post of danger which was well fitted to put his valour to the proof. Owain himself, as the eldest son of the late king of Gwynedd, had now serious responsibilities at home and is heard of no more in immediate connection with the affairs of Ceredigion.

In consequence of the Llanbadarn origin of the only Welsh record of this period, the story of the conquest of Ceredigion is one which it is possible to tell with some fulness, but there is every reason to suppose that, far from standing alone, it is but typical of what was going on throughout Wales during this season of revolution. Scattered references to the revolt confirm the impression that it extended to almost every part of the country. The annals of Chester relate that on 3rd March, 1140, the castle of Bromfeld, which probably stood at Marford or Wrexham,[56] was burnt, as a result, it scarcely admits of doubt, of the activity of the men of Powys. Further to the south the castle of Cause was taken by the same agency,[57] and it was no doubt in this region that Payn fitz John, Sheriff of Shropshire and of Herefordshire, was on the 10th of July, 1137, pierced through the head and slaia as he was pursuing a band of Welshmen.[58] What is said by the chronicles as to the reconquest of Elfael and Maelienydd in 1144 by Hugh Mortimer implies that earlier in the reign the Welsh had been busy in this district also, where they were no doubt led by the local chieftain, Madog ab Idnerth, and his sons.[59] In Brycheiniog, though Miles of Gloucester kept his hold of the province, a great devastation by Hywel ap Maredudd is recorded.[60] In Cantref Bychan, the other magnate of that name, son of Maredudd ap Rhydderch, was in full revolt, and the Clifford family, now represented by Walter, son of Richard fitz Pons, lost all authority in the region of Llandovery.[61] Even in the valley of the lower Usk, lying in the midst of the sphere of influence of Earl Robert of Gloucester, Morgan ab Owain was bold and aggressive; he seized the castle of Usk[62] and contrived in the confusion of the time to make himself lord of Caerleon.[63]

As the tide of revolt rose, the intervention of the English crown, the only power able to cope with it, became less and less likely. The landing of the Empress Matilda, daughter of Henry I., on 30th September, 1139, at Arundel in Sussex,[64] opened an era of civil war, a time of strife during which the energies of the great men of the realm were almost fully occupied in their mutual hostilities, so that measures against the Welsh were only possible when a particular baron, having for the moment no domestic feud upon his hands, was able to devote a little individual attention to minor operations against them. The marcher lords were nearly all partisans of the Empress, following in this respect the example of their leader, Earl Robert of Gloucester, who was Matilda's half-brother. Miles of Gloucester was one of her most ardent supporters, and was rewarded in 1141 by the revival for his benefit of the Earldom of Hereford.[65] On the same side were Earl Roger of Warwick,[66] Brian fitz Count,[67] Robert fitz Martin,[68] and William fitz Alan,[69] while Bishop Bernard of St. David's was one of the few prelates in constant attendance upon Matilda.[70] These names account for Glamorgan, Brecknock, Gower, Ewias,[71] Upper Gwent, Cemais, Oswestry and Pebidiog, so that it is not surprising that, in the absence of any substantial support of Stephen in the West, Earl Robert should have been able, as an unfriendly chronicler admits, to preserve in this region a "semblance of peace"[72] Gilbert fitz Gilbert, brother of the late lord of Ceredigion, was at first attached to the cause of Stephen, who conferred upon him in 1138 the title of Earl of Pembroke.[73] But he did not appear in West Wales for many years after his elevation to this dignity, and in the meantime had ceased to be of the king's party.[74] Ranulf, Earl of Chester, who had succeeded to the lands and dignities of his father, Ranulf of Bayeux, on the death of the latter, in 1128,[75] played consistently for his own hand, but in doing so was more often found with Matilda than with Stephen. Thus the magnates who were concerned with Wales were substantially of one accord in their support of the Empress and were able to keep the war out of the Welsh borders. Nevertheless, its existence was an effectual bar to any scheme of reconquest; so far as can be seen, the first important successes against the Welsh were won in 1144, when Hugh Mortimer of Wigmore regained Maelienydd and Elfael, and in 1145, when Earl Gilbert came to Dyfed and rebuilt the castle of Carmarthen.

The year 1146 supplies a concrete instance of the mutual distrust which during this reign tied the hands of the English and gave the Welsh their opportunity. Earl Ranulf, hard pressed at this time by the vigorous onslaughts of the men of Gwynedd, appealed to Stephen for support, hoping that, as in 1114, a King of England and an Earl of Chester might again march together into the wilderness of Snowdon and bring the Welsh insurgents to their knees.[76] Stephen was at first disposed to accede to this request, but a hostile faction at his court at once raised a great outcry, alleging that the scheme was a traitorous plot on the earl's part to get the king into his power. Nothing, they asserted, could be more dangerous to the royal person than this madcap expedition into a land of forests and mountains, destitute of food and water for the needs of an army and inhabited by an enemy whose wiles none could foresee. Instead of receiving in his defence of the frontier the assistance of a royal army, the earl was decoyed to court and then thrown into prison; the sequel was the capture by Owain at the close of the year of the Cheshire fortress of Mold. While party spirit reigned through the length and breadth of England, the Welsh had nothing to fear, and they succeeded in winning during these years advantages which they did not again lose until the extinction of Welsh independence.

III. THE NATIONAL AWAKENING AND THE CHURCH.

The Welsh revolt naturally had its effect upon the Welsh Church. It is true that in this domain the results achieved were not so striking as in the secular sphere, but the new spirit of independence nevertheless made itself felt, leading to struggles which, though in the main fruitless, kept alive the tradition of freedom. The work of Henry I. was not undone, but claims were advanced and hotly defended which had the value of preserving the old conception of a Welsh national church.

It is uncertain when Bishop Bernard first put forward the claim of St. David's to be the metropolitan see of Wales, and his own right, in consequence, to rank as archbishop side by side with the prelates of Canterbury and York.[77] The oldest document bearing upon the subject is a letter addressed by the canons of St. David's to Honorius II. (1124–30),[78] in which the story is told which afterwards became so familiar, of the transference of the archiepiscopal pall held by St. David and his successors to Brittany by Archbishop Samson at the time of the Yellow Plague, whereby the Menevian Church lost this outward sign of its primacy among the churches of Wales.[79] It seems likely that this letter was written with the concurrence of Bernard, who may, therefore, be taken to have raised the matter during the lifetime of Henry I. On the other hand, it is scarcely probable that so assiduous a courtier pressed his claim with vigour while Henry was alive, and it was clearly the general upheaval in Wales after 1135 which encouraged him to embark, as he did, on a resolute campaign on behalf of the ecclesiastical independence of Wales. He commenced operations during the pontificate of Innocent II. (1130–43)[80] and had by the year 1140 won such a reputation as a patriot as induced Owain and Cadwaladr to appeal to him to support them in their opposition to the promotion of Meurig to the see of Bangor.[81] He carried on the war under Lucius II. (March, 1144, to February, 1145), who wrote from the Lateran on 14th May in a favourable strain and promised that papal legates about to visit England should go carefully into the case.[82] He continued it under Eugenius III. (1145–53), whom the cathedral chapter approached on the subject immediately after his election.[83] At one point in the struggle Bernard seems to have obtained the coveted dignity, but some flaw in procedure led to the immediate reversal of the decision in his favour.[84] The matter was finally fought out, so far as Bernard himself was concerned, in the year 1147, when Theobald of Canterbury and the bishop of St. David's argued their case in the presence of Eugenius at Meaux.[85] Bernard maintained not only the historic liberty of his see, but also his own freedom from any obligation to the English primate. This was a contention soon disposed of; Bishop Robert of Bath was able to testify that in 1115 there had been complete submission to the claims of Canterbury, and that Bernard's zeal on behalf of the rights of his church was a comparatively recent affair. On the 29th of June the Pope wrote to say that the appellant had lost his own case, but that it was still open to him to prosecute the claim of his see; 18th October, 1148, was assigned for the adjourned hearing of the suit.

For Bernard, however, the contest was at an end; in the summer or early autumn of 1148 he died,[86] and the dispute entered upon a new phase, it being now the object of the Canterbury party to obtain the election of a successor who would let the whole matter rest.[87] The Welsh canons, determined to use their advantage to the utmost, made choice of a man upon whom they could depend to keep the question of the metropolitanate well to the front. But the delegates whom they sent to England abandoned the cause and were induced to elect instead David fitz Gerald, son of the castellan of Pembroke, who was already a member of the chapter as archdeacon of Ceredigion. This was a clear victory for the English, for, though David was, on the mother's side, of Welsh descent,[88] and a partial concession was thus made to Welsh national feeling, he not only professed obedience in the fullest terms to the see of Canterbury, but took an oath specially tendered to him, engaging not to raise in any form the vexed question of the rights of St. David's. Thus secured against attack, Theobald consecrated him at Christ Church, Canterbury, on 19th December, 1148, and as he was easy-going and unadventurous, of a wholly different type to the restless, enterprising Bernard, the matter of the metropolitanate slumbered for many years. His nephew, Giraldus Cambrensis, makes the most of his freedom from greed and ambition, but has to admit that under his rule the spoliation of the lands of the bishopric still continued. The hostile critic, probably a Welshman, who has left a brief record of his impressions of this episcopate, is more severe;[89] he gives a long list of possessions alienated by David from the see and asserts that the doors of the cathedral were closed during the greater part of his period of office.

The spirit of the times manifested itself at Bangor also, where a vacancy arose on the death of Bishop David, who did not long survive his lord, Gruffydd ap Cynan.[90] A Welshman named Meurig, or Maurice,[91] was elected to the see, and early in December, 1139, was presented to King Stephen at Worcester by the bishops of Hereford and Chichester as the choice of the clergy and people of the diocese.[92] At this stage, however, a hitch arose; Meurig informed his introducers that he was not prepared to swear fealty to the king, having been forbidden to do so by a man for whom he had the profoundest veneration, his predecessor's archdeacon. It would appear that this cleric, Simeon of Clynnog,[93] was at Bangor the power behind the episcopal throne. Meurig possessed no great force of character and his scruples were soon overborne; he not only swore fealty to the king, but made a full submission to Canterbury,[94] and in 1140 was consecrated by Theobald.[95] In consequence of this surrender, or for some other reason, he incurred the displeasure of Owain and Cadwaladr, who wrote to Bishop Bernard alleging that he had entered the church of St. Daniel as a thief, and not by the door, and asking for a conference on the subject at Aberdovey on 1st November, to which the young Anarawd of South Wales should be invited.[96] Whether the conference met and with what result is unknown; the opposition would seem to have died down, leaving Meurig in possession. Here, again, the victory rested with Canterbury, but it was of some moment that the issue had been raised and that, at least, a Welshman had been elected.

In the diocese of Llandaff, Earl Robert of Gloucester was during this period in undisturbed possession, and one need not look for signs of the recovery of independence by the Welsh. Nevertheless, it is noteworthy that Urban was succeeded by a Welshman, a cleric of the diocese, who had been for many years Archdeacon of Llandaff.[97] Uchtryd was consecrated by Theobald in 1140,[98] at the same time as Meurig of Bangor, and made as full a profession of obedience to Canterbury;[99] he recognised the archbishop's authority without demur in matters of Church jurisdiction.[100] But he was not of the ordinary type of Norman prelate; his enemies called him illiterate and worse,[101] and he had a daughter, Angharad, whom he married to Iorwerth ab Owain of Gwynllwg,[102] so that it may be supposed that the Welshman in him overshadowed the ecclesiastic.[103] On his death in 1148,[104] he was succeeded by one Nicholas,[105] who was no doubt more after the regular pattern, since he had been for thirty years a monk of St. Peter's, Gloucester,[106] and was now specially chosen for the see by Theobald;[107] yet he too was of Welsh blood, the son of a certain Gwrgant,[108] and could not have been altogether out of sympathy with the Welshmen over whom he was set as shepherd.

It was in this age of unrest that the see of St. Asaph, which had for a long period been dormant, was revived and furnished with a bishop. The consecration of one Gilbert to this bishopric by Archbishop Theobald at Lambeth in 1143 is the earliest event in its history which is attested by contemporary evidence.[109] Why the step of creating what was practically a new diocese was taken at this time is not easy to determine. If any reliance could be placed upon the letter of the chapter of St. David's to Eugenius, with its tale of an intended consecration by Bernard, which Theobald was able to forestall,[110] one might suppose that the scheme was a part of the St. David's campaign, designed to add a third to the two suffragans of the would-be archbishop. It is more probable that the move was directed against the claims of Bangor, which no doubt followed closely in the wake of the conquests of the men of Gwynedd. Rhuddlan and its neighbourhood, where the cathedral stood, were still held by the men of the Earl of Chester, but Owain was in possession of the upper valley of the Clwyd, and it was perhaps deemed wise to anticipate the demands which might be made on behalf of Bishop Meurig by placing a bishop in the long-deserted throne of St. Kentigern. That Gilbert was of the Norman, not of the Welsh race, his name sufficiently shows; he was succeeded, moreover, in 1152 by another cleric of the immigrant race, the well-known Geoffrey of Monmouth.[111]

Thus in various ways did the Welsh uprising affect the fortunes of the Welsh Church, without at the same time breaking the fetters imposed upon it in the previous reign. It was an easier matter to shake off the yoke of the English crown than to escape from the control of the English primate, in this age when ecclesiastical power was at its height in England.

NOTE TO CHAPTER XIII., § 3. —
The Alleged Archbishopric of St. David's.

It is undoubtedly the case that Asser (cap. 79) styles Nobis, his relative and predecessor as Bishop of St. David's, "archiepiscopum"; but this title was merely used as an honourable designation and did not carry with it the powers of a metropolitan (see chapter vii. note 43). The British Church, in fact, inherited the traditions of a time when the system of subordination to the chief bishop of the province had not been developed. Consequently, no evidence exists, apart from the worthless testimony of the letter to Eugenius in Gir. Camb. iii. 56–8 (*Invect.* ii. 6). that the bishops of St. David's ever exercised any kind of authority over the other bishops of Wales. Though Rhygyfarch makes Dewi an archbishop, consecrated such by the patriarch of Jerusalem and recognised by all after the Synod of Brefi (*Cambro-Br. SS.* 135–6, 139), he clearly does not mean to invest him with anything more than mere precedence over his fellows, Padarn and Teilo. It was only when the question of subjection to Canterbury became a burning one that the clergy of St. David's felt the weakness of their case in having no Welsh provincial head whom they could set over against the successor of St. Augustine. The claim to be the seat of the Archbishop of Wales was then put forward on behalf of St. David's itself. Hereupon there arose a new difficulty; how was the undeniable fact to be got over that there was no record of the bestowal by the pope at any time of an archiepiscopal pall upon any occupant of this see? Some genius suggested that the pall worn at this time (though not without opposition from Tours—see H. and St. ii. 91–6) by the Brecon Archbishop of Dol was really that of the Menevian See. Samson, the founder of the church of Dol and popularly supposed to be its first archbishop ("sancti Samsonis Dolensis Archipraesulis" in *Hist. Reg.* ix. 15), was known to have come to Brittany from Dyfed (see page 145), and it would further appear that in the catalogue of bishops of St. David's the name Samson was to be found. In defiance of chronology, it was therefore assumed that the Samson of the list, though separated from

Dewi by some twenty names, was the Samson of saintly renown, who was, in fact, Dewi's contemporary and never ruled at Mynyw at all. Currency was first given to this story of the transference of the pall from St. David's to Dol about 1125; it appears in the letter of the chapter to Honorius II. (Gir. Camb. iii. 59–60 (*Invect.* ii. 10)), and is thenceforward a principal weapon in the St. David's armoury—see Gir. Camb. vi. 102–3 (*Itin.* ii. 1).

Geoffrey of Monmouth had no particular interest in pushing the St. David's claim, and in the text of the *Historia Regum* he is silent on the subject. According to his scheme, the three metropolitan sees were London, York and Caerleon, (ix. 12), and David, though he died in his favourite monastery of Menevia, was "archbishop of the City of the Legions," and was succeeded in that office by Cynog of Llanbadarn. In the *Prophecy of Merlin* (vii. 3), however, which was probably compiled from Welsh sources, a passage occurs to the effect that Menevia shall be clad in the "pallium" of the City of the Legions. This enabled the champions of the St. David's claim to reconcile their account of affairs (as they were compelled to do by the authority of the *History of the Kings of Britain*) with that given by the great romancer; St. David, it was held, transferred the archiepiscopal dignity from Caerleon to his solitary fane in the west of Dyfed. Eagerly accepted by Giraldus (vi. 56, 101 (*Itin.* i. 5; ii. 1); iii. 46 (*Invect.* ii. i)), this theory made for itself a secure place in later Welsh literature (*Iolo MSS.* 82–3; *Drych y Prif Oesoedd,* bk. ii. ch. 2) and is even allowed to figure as sober history in the learned and dignified pages of the author of the *Essay on the Welsh Saints* (p. 197).

CHAPTER IV

OWAIN GWYNEDD

(Ann. C. and the Bruts continue to be the primary authorities for this, as for previous chapters. The works of Gir. Camb. are full of allusions to the period. OF modern works which have been helpful, one may mention Eyton's Court, Household and Itinerary of Henry II. and J. H. Round's Feudal England.)

I. THE RIVALS OF OWAIN.

IT was fortunate for the Welsh people that after the emancipation at the beginning of the reign of Stephen they did not find themselves leaderless, a flock without a shepherd, but that a prince arose who was able to give them wise and enlightened guidance and to teach them how to harvest the gains they had won. Owain Gwynedd was the first of a succession of such leaders; his work was carried on, almost without a break, by Rhys ap Gruffydd, Llywelyn ab Iorwerth, and Llywelyn ap Gruffydd, to the latest years of Welsh independence — it was, in fact, under him that the Welsh nation attained the full measure of national consciousness which enabled it for a century and a half successfully to resist absorption in the English realm.

As the eldest son of Gruffydd ap Cynan, Owain succeeded in 1137 to the principal portion of his father's lordship of Gwynedd. He was not the only Owain ap Gruffydd among the princes of his day, for Gruffydd ap Maredudd of Powys had, on his death in 1128, left behind him a son Owain, who ultimately became the ruler of the southern part of his grandfather's dominions. In order to distinguish the two, a method not very usual in the naming of Welsh chieftains was adopted; territorial titles were given to them, and the one became Owain of Gwynedd, while the other was styled Owain of Cyfeiliog, from the commote in which he was settled by his uncle Madog in 1149.[1] Owain Gwynedd was also known as Owain Fawr, *i.e.*, "Owain the Great,"[2] a description he fully deserved. Welsh history can scarcely show a nobler or a better balanced character. His greatness was recognised alike by bard and by chronicler, by Welshman and Englishman, and among his eulogists are Archbishop Thomas of Canterbury[3] and Giraldus Cambrensis.[4] An outstanding feature of his character was his wisdom and prudence;[5] in him the native impetuosity and fire of the Celt were subjected to a perfect restraint, and, while he could lead against the foe with energy and decision, he was circumspect and cautious to a degree unusual among the high-spirited members of his class. The same self-restraint showed itself in his dealings with his own people; he is praised for justice and moderation,[6] and very few of his recorded actions seem to belong to that category of deeds of reckless violence which covers so much of the activity of his fellow-princes. His affections were strong, and a deep melancholy fell upon him when in 1146 he lost his young son Rhun, and again in 1162 upon the death of his mother;[7] moreover, it was probably his love for his second wife, Cristin, which made him oppose so resolutely the demand of the Church that he should put her away on the ground of consanguinity.[8] Altogether, the figure of Owain stands out with a clearness of outline not common in Welsh history and the picture is undeniably an attractive one.

A foil to the greatness of Owain was furnished by his younger brother Cadwaladr, who is first heard of in the Ceredigion campaigns and was a prominent personage throughout his brother's reign, surviving him some eighteen months. Cadwaladr was the ordinary, as Owain was the exceptional, Welsh prince. He was restless, impulsive, quick to suspect and hasty to strike —

> In power unpleased, impatient of disgrace.

He had to a conspicuous degree the open-handed liberality which was in popular estimation the prime virtue of a prince,[9] but, even if some allowance be made for the trying position of a younger son, he cannot be said to have played a patriotic or magnanimous part. After the unsuccessful attack upon Aberteifi in 1138, he is next heard of at the battle of Lincoln, fought on 2nd February, 1141, where to our surprise he appears, with Madog ap Maredudd of Powys, at the head of a great host of Welshmen brought into the English civil war by the Earl of Chester.[10] The rudely armed throng, despised as barbarians by their knightly opponents, had the satisfaction of joining in the rout which made King Stephen a prisoner, and in the subsequent sack of the city of Lincoln, but it may be doubted whether Owain approved of the adventure, which was all to the profit of the great border lords, followers of the Empress Matilda. Two years later Cadwaladr was concerned in something worse than an act of vainglorious folly. His retinue fell upon the young Anarawd ap Gruffydd of South Wales, who was in close alliance with him and was married to his daughter (or, it may be, his niece),[11] and treacherously put him to death. That Cadwaladr was privy to the deed may be judged from the righteous indignation of his brother Owain, who resolved to strip him of his territories and at once set his son Hywel to expel him from his possessions in the north of Ceredigion. Marching across the Aeron, Hywel soon carried out his orders and burnt the castle of Aberystwyth. Cadwaladr saw himself left without a foothold in the country, and in 1144 turned for assistance to the customary quarter, bringing to Abermenai a hired fleet from Dublin which was to compel his brother to reinstate him.[12] It would seem that Owain was not prepared to press matters to the furthest point on this occasion; the quarrel ended in a reconciliation and the restoration of Cadwaladr to his lands, after some difficulty had been experienced in getting rid of the foreign allies, who in vain demanded their stipulated reward.

Harmony prevailed between the two brothers for eight years after this encounter, though it may be conjectured that the elements of discord were meanwhile accumulating which were to find vent in the still more serious explosion of 1152. It is possible that Owain had a hand in the events of 1147, but this is uncertain; the attack upon Meirionydd in that year has rather the aspect of a private adventure on the part of his sons, Hywel and Cynan. Hywel came from the south, from his lands in Ceredigion, Cynan from the north, where he probably held Ardudwy, and between them they swept the cantref from end to end. Cadwaladr had, however, built himself a castle at Cynfael[13] and entrusted its defence to Morfran, abbot of the neighbouring "clas" of Towyn;[14] the capture of this was no easy task, for its works were strong and the keeper insensible alike to menaces and to bribes. At last, it was carried by storm, and Cadwaladr ceased to bear rule in Meirionydd. The real rupture with Owain was, however, five years later, when Cadwaladr was driven from the isle of Anglesey,[15] the cradle of the royal line of Gwynedd, and, this time fleeing east instead of west, found a refuge in England, where he lived for five years as an exile.

It would seem, indeed, that Cadwaladr had before his banishment formed an influential English connection which would make it natural for him to turn to England in the hour of his need. Tradition affirms that he married a lady of the house of Clare[16] and there is evidence in support of this view, showing also that "Alicia de Clara" was his wife before 1153.[17] It is obvious that the object of this marriage, at whatever time contracted, was to give Cadwaladr a better hold upon Ceredigion, and Alice was, therefore, in all probability a daughter of Richard fitz Gilbert.[18] In this case she was a sister of Earl Gilbert of Hertford and a niece of Earl Ranulf of Chester,[19] so that the exiled chief was not without powerful friends across the border. They availed him little, however, against the firmly established authority of his brother, which was daily extending over a wider area.

For, while Cadwaladr had been enduring those buffets of fortune which wait upon the path of the inconstant, Owain's career had been one of steady progress. Reference has already been made to the Earl of Chester's concern at the threatening state of affairs in 1146; his appeal to the king for support, whatever his enemies might say, was fully justified by the state of the border. No sooner was news brought to Wales of the earl's captivity in Northampton than the men of Powys crossed the Dee and began to ravage Maelor Saesneg. They were met at Wich on 3rd September by Robert of Mold, hereditary steward of the earldom, and defeated with great slaughter.[20] But meanwhile Robert's own frontier castle of Mold[21] was being closely besieged by the men of Gwynedd, and before the end of the year it fell into their hands. No more acceptable Christmas gift was it possible for them to bestow upon their lord. He had been overcome with grief at the death in this year of his young son Rhun, a comely, winsome lad, long of limb, fair of hue, with flashing blue eyes and curls of gold—a Prince Charming of the genuine high-born Celtic type.[22] There had been no consolation for the sorrowing father, cut to the heart by the bitter stroke, until the unexpected news of the capture of the long-coveted fortress awoke him from his stupor and reminded him that he had still a country for which to live.

By his conquest of Moldsdale or Ystrad Alun, Owain had Iâl within his grasp, and in 1149 he showed his determination to add this commote also to his dominions by building at Buddugre within its borders a castle which commanded the pass from Dyffryn Clwyd.[23] He thus returned to that policy of aggression against Powys which had been in suspense since the death of his brother Cadwallon in Nanheudwy in 1132 and aroused the enmity of his powerful neighbour, Madog ap

Maredudd. Madog had succeeded his father as the principal ruler of Powys in this year 1132; although Hywel ab Ieuaf, of the house of Trahaearn, was under-king in Arwystli,[24] and although Madog gave Cyfeiliog in 1149 to his nephews Owain and Meurig, sons of Gruffydd ap Maredudd, yet he was reckoned overlord of the whole, and his dominions were said to extend from Pulford (near Chester) to the extreme point of Arwystli,[25] or, as the poet Gwalchmai phrased it —

> From Plynlimmon's top to the gates of Chester,
> From the lights of high-roofed Bangor
> To the edge of Meirionydd's limit.[26]

Like other Welsh princes, Madog had profited by the disorders of the time. H is neighbour in the Oswestry district was William fitz Alan, son of a Breton knight who had received many favours from Henry I. and brother of the Walter fitz Alan who founded the Scottish and royal house of Stuart.[27] William's father had apparently succeeded to the position of Rainald of Bailleui on the Shropshire border,[28] and he himself entered upon it towards the end of the reign of Henry. At first, he was on good terms with Stephen, receiving from him in 1137 the office of sheriff of Shropshire, in succession to Payn fitz John. But he was married to a niece of Robert of Gloucester and this led him into rebellion; in August, 1138, he fortified Shrewsbury Castle against the king, and only escaped capture by a flight which left the garrison to bear the brunt of the royal vengeance.[29] Henceforward, he was attached to the cause of Matilda and her son, and it is not surprising that his hold upon Oswestry so slackened that in 1149 Madog ap Maredudd, descending from the hills of Cyrn y Bwch, was able to seize the place and repair the castle as a stronghold for his own use.[30] The district was for a few years completely in Madog's power; his natural son, Owain Brogyntyn, was brought up at Porkington, a little to the north of the town,[31] and the author of the tale of *The Dream of Rhonabwy* makes Madog[32] undisputed lord of Dudleston and all the land between the Ceiriog and the Vyrnwy.[33]

A prince who had won such successes was not likely to stand idly by while the men of Gwynedd poured into a commote which had for centuries been reckoned a part of Powys.[34] In the year following the invasion of Iâl, Owain Gwynedd and Madog came to blows. Though there is no record of the achievement, Owain seems about this time to have taken Rhuddlan Castle and made himself master of Tegeingl;[35] accordingly, he and Madog met at Coleshill, once a manor of the Earl of Chester[36] and miles away from the Welsh border, but now, as the star of Wales rose to the zenith, to be the battleground of the two Welsh leaders. The prince of Powys did not rely upon his own strength, but came into the field with the support of troops lent him by Earl Ranulf, who had good reasons of his own for wishing to check the progress of Owain. Nevertheless, it was Owain who won the day and thereby made sure of his hold, not only upon Ial, but also upon Tegeingl and Ystrad Alun. His position became still more secure in 1153, when Earl Ranulf died, leaving an heir only six years old,[37] who could not for many years take up the sword and defend his father's inheritance. On the eve of the accession of Henry II., Owain found himself possessed of almost everything for which he had toiled; he was freed from the rivalry of his brother Cadwaladr and of Madog ap Maredudd and had brought his men within sight of the red towers of the great city on the Dee.

The weakness of the central authority which had allowed the Welsh to reap advantages so extensive came at once to an end when Henry of Anjou obtained the crown at the close of 1154.[38] By the peace of Wallingford, arrived at in the previous year, the party strife of the past fifteen years had been ended; Matilda's followers and those of Stephen agreed to accept the former's young son, who already promised to be a ruler of vigour and decision, as unquestioned heir. Yet it is no matter for surprise that Henry should for some time have postponed action against the Welsh, leaving them in possession of their conquests. He had other work to do of a more urgent kind — order to evolve out of administrative chaos, rebellious barons to tame, private castles to dismantle and private armies to disband, not to speak of his important interests on the Continent, where he was lord of a domain which stretched from the English Channel to the Pyrenees. He devoted the first year of his reign to the restoration of the royal authority in England and among other recalcitrant lords brought into subjection two leading magnates of the Welsh march, Earl Roger of Hereford and Hugh Mortimer of Wigmore. Roger had succeeded to the earldom in 1143, when his father Miles, after enjoying the dignity but two years, had been accidentally shot by a companion while hunting in the Forest of Dean.[39] He was through his mother Sybil of Welsh descent,[40] and he now relied upon the Welshmen of his lordship of Brecknock to support him in his resistance to the new king. But his friends persuaded him to submit; at Easter he made his peace with Henry and had his earldom confirmed to him.[41] Hugh Mortimer gave more trouble; a set campaign was fought against him, and it was not until his castles of

Cleobury, Wigmore and Bridgenorth had been taken by the king that peace was secured, in July, 1155, along the western border.[42] The next year was devoted by Henry to his French possessions; he went thither in January and did not return until April, 1157.

It was probably at the Council of Northampton, held on the 17th of July, that measures against Owain Gwynedd were finally resolved upon.[43] Opposition to Henry from other quarters had now died down; in these very months the boy King Malcolm of Scotland met him in the Peak and resigned to him the counties in the north which had been seized by the Scotch during the turmoil of the previous reign. He had the support of the other princes of North Wales against Owain, of Cadwaladr, to whom he had given an estate worth £7 a year at Ness in Shropshire,[44] of Madog ap Maredudd, of Madog's brother, Iorwerth the Red, and of Hywel of Arwystli.[45] To reduce the prince of Gwynedd to obedience seemed, therefore, an easy task, and he set out from Chester in high hopes of a successful campaign. In summoning the feudal host for the expedition, he had greatly reduced the numbers of the levy in order to provide for a much longer term of service, so that he might not be hampered by its expiry before the work was half done.[46] The knights were reinforced by archers from the Shropshire borders, brought northward by William fitz Alan, the new sheriff of the county.[47] A fleet, moreover, was to second the efforts of the army by operations from the seaward side; it was apparently manned in Dyfed and sailed to meet Henry from the port of Pembroke.[48]

Meanwhile, Owain and his sons Dafydd and Cynan prepared to meet this formidable onset. Owain posted himself at Basingwerk, or Dinas Basing, as it was styled by the Welsh, the ancient stronghold which marked the northern end of Wat's Dyke and barred the road to Rhuddlan. The sons took up their position in the great wood which lay to the west, crowning the higher ground as far south as Hawarden, and thus opposed a barrier to the flanking of the main camp at Basingwerk.[49] Henry knew nothing of Welsh methods of warfare, and with youthful heedlessness walked into the trap which had thus been laid for him. He sent his main army by the direct road along the coast, but plunged himself, with a body of light armed troops, into the thick of the forest, whence he hoped to fall upon Owain unawares. He was not long in repenting of his folly; the skirmishers of Dafydd and Cynan immediately set upon him and for a little while the fate of king and kingdom trembled in the balance. Eustace fitz John, constable of Chester, and Robert of Courcy, another prominent baron, were slain;

it was only the coolness of Earl Roger of Hertford [50] which saved the king's life, and in the confusion the rumour ran wildly about that he was indeed among the dead—a rumour which caused Henry of Essex, hereditary constable of England, incontinently to throw down the royal standard and flee in the utmost dismay.[51] Little by little, however, the scattered company, and with them the king, made their way to the shore and safely rejoined the main body of the army. The day had been inglorious and disastrous for the English, but it was not a day of rout; for Owain, finding himself too weak to withstand the foe, left his station at Basingwerk and retreated to the neighbourhood of St. Asaph.[52] The Welsh had their losses also, and Giraldus tells a touching story of a greyhound which guarded faithfully for more than a week the body of its master, a young Welshman slain in this battle, and held at bay the ravenous beasts and birds of the forest.

The king's road was now clear to Rhuddlan, and, as he reached this gate of the Vale of Clwyd, Owain retreated still further west.[53] It was probably at this point that Henry was informed of the ill success of his naval expedition. Instead of meeting him at Rhuddlan or Degannwy, the ships had cast anchor in the harbour of Moelfre,[54] and the prospect of plunder had led to the landing of a number of knights, who had not spared in their ravages the churches of Llanbedr Goch and Llanfair Mathafarn Eithaf. During the night there was a mustering of the natives from all parts of the island, and on the following day a battle was fought which vindicated the outraged honour of the saints of Môn. The invaders were defeated: Henry fitz Henry,[55] a son of King Henry I. by Nest of Pembroke, fell beneath a shower of lances, and his half-brother, Robert fitz Stephen,[56] was seriously wounded and escaped with difficulty to the ships in the roadstead. This disaster, coupled with his own perilous experiences, no doubt convinced the king that he had gone as far as was practicable that year in the effort to subjugate the prince of Gwynedd and that it was time to offer terms. Owain, on his side, had received sufficient proof of the might of the English crown; ever prudent and sagacious, he saw the need of purchasing a peace which would give him time to consolidate his power, and thus an agreement was not long delayed.

The conditions included the tender of homage to Henry and the delivery of hostages for future good behaviour.[57] Owain was further required to restore Cadwaladr to his former possessions and to resign all claim to Tegeingl. This district reverted once more to English rule; Rhuddlan Castle again became a border fortress and was entrusted to

Hugh of Beauchamp;[58] Basingwerk was also fortified. Previous to the Welsh occupation of this region, there had been a Cistercian abbey at the latter place, originally founded by Earl Ranulf of Chester in 1131 as a house of the order of Savigny and transferred in 1147, with the other houses of that rule, to the more popular order of Citeaux.[59] The king, on his return to Chester, not only confirmed to the monks what they had previously held in Tegeingl, but gave them, out of the forfeited lands of William Peverel of Nottingham, the vill of Glossop in Derbyshire, as a thankoffering, it may be conjectured, for his providential escape from death in the woods of Coleshill.[60]

Thus Owain lost his recent acquisitions between the Clwyd and the Dee and was obliged again to give his protection to his restless and troublesome brother. It has to be added, also, ere the record of this year's transactions is complete, that, after Henry's departure, Iorwerth the Red of Powys attacked and destroyed the castle in Iâl which had been built in 1149 in token of the ascendancy of Gwynedd. Owain's sun, which had hitherto shone so resplendently and triumphantly, was now clouded over and its radiance dimmed. Yet it was but a temporary obscuration; in a few years the clouds which had gathered are seen slowly to disperse and his career ends as brilliantly as it had begun.

II. THE VICTORIES OF THE SONS OF GRUFFYDD AP RHYS.

While Owain was thus building up a stable realm in the north, the sons of Gruffydd ap Rhys had been no less busy and almost as successful in the south. The eldest of them, described by the "Chronicle of the Princes" as "the hope and stay and glory of the men of South Wales,"[61] had, indeed, been cut off by the crime of 1143, but, although this left the fortunes of the family for a few years in the sole charge of Cadell, the younger brothers, Maredudd and Rhys, were rapidly growing out of childhood, and as early as 1146, when the elder of the two was about sixteen, appear with their surviving brother at the head of the armies of Deheubarth. The activity of the three was confined to Deheubarth in the stricter sense, that is, to the three regions of Dyfed, Ceredigion and Ystrad Tywi; in eastern South Wales Hugh Mortimer had in 1144 recovered his authority in Elfael and Maelienydd, and the lords of Brecknock and Glamorgan maintained their position without interruption through the whole epoch of revolt. But, within the limits indicated, the sons of Gruffydd held the country at their command, as they swept down from the uplands of Cantref Mawr upon castle and town and drove the Normans who held them eastward to Swansea or westward to Pembroke and St. David's.

In 1145 Earl Gilbert came, it would seem for the first time, to visit his earldom and the adjacent lands of Dyfed. He determined to repair the breaches which had been made by the late war and set about rebuilding the castle of Carmarthen, taken by the Welsh in 1137. With a view to operations against Ceredigion, which he no doubt hoped to recover for the house of Clare, he built a castle also in the commote of Mabudryd, at Pencader or in its neighbourhood.[62] He was not long in learning how weak the once dreaded Norman power had become. Cadell was provoked by these measures into reprisals; with the aid of the youths, Maredudd and Rhys, he attacked in 1146 the new castle of Mabudryd,[63] took it by storm and slew the garrison. Hywel ab Owain, who held southern Ceredigion, came to his aid, and together they repeated the exploit of Hywel's father and captured the castle of Carmarthen. Llanstephan also fell into their victorious grasp. The Normans and Flemings of Dyfed, led by William and Maurice fitz Gerald and William fitz Hai,[64] did their best to recover Carmarthen, so important a link in the chain of South Welsh castles, but the new daring and self-confidence of the Welsh comes to light in the bold resistance offered by the young Maredudd, who held the place stoutly against a force far larger than his own and flung down into the fosse the scaling ladders up which the enemy sought to swarm into the beleaguered fortress. These events left the Welsh masters of Eastern Dyfed.

In the following year the unusual spectacle is presented of a quarrel among the foreign settlers turned by the Welsh to their own profit. Strife had arisen for some reason or other between William fitz Gerald and Walter fitz Wizo, the lord of Deugleddyf,[65] whereupon the former, half Welshman as he was, turned to Cadell and his brothers for aid against his fellow-baron. The opportunity was gladly seized; not only Cadell, Maredudd and Rhys, but Hywel ab Owain also came, and the destruction of Walter's castle of Wiston, or Castell Gwis, as it was called by the Welsh, removed one more obstacle to the spread of Welsh influence in Dyfed. Cadell resolved to make Carmarthen the capital of his rapidly growing realm, and, having put the castle into a state of thorough repair, in 1150 further protected himself by widespread devastation of the region of Cydweli. At this point, however, his career came suddenly to an end. While engaged in the warrior's favourite pastime of hunting, probably in Coed

Rhath, the great forest which then skirted Saundersfoot Bay,[66] he was set upon in 1151 by a party of knights and archers from the neighbouring town of Tenby, who reckoned when they left him they had finished their work. In this they were mistaken; Cadell still breathed and was in time cured of his wounds. But he never recovered his old position; the shock had robbed him of his vigour and his zest for battle, and all that is hereafter recorded of him is that in 1153 he went on pilgrimage to Rome[67] and in 1175 died in the abbey of Strata Florida. Young as they were, Maredudd and Rhys were now the sole leaders of the men of South Wales.

No slackening of effort was occasioned by the change of leadership. In the year of Cadell's eclipse as a ruler, his two brothers took advantage of their hold over Cydweli to carry their ravages yet further afield; crossing the Loughor, they entered Gower, and, having destroyed the castle which guarded the passage of the river, devastated the region without mercy. East and west their power was felt, and the year 1153 saw them triumph at points as far removed from each other as Tenby and Aberafan. The attack upon Cadell was avenged by the capture of the former of these two places, of which the gates were seized in a night surprise—a deed of daring well fitted to disturb and alarm the men of Penfro, who saw the Welsh almost at the portals of their great stronghold by the sea. It may well have been the occasion of the panic which Giraldus Cambrensis witnessed as a boy at Manorbier, a castle only five miles from that which was taken by Maredudd and Rhys.[68] He was but a child at the time, but he well remembered the sudden night alarm, the wild rush to arms and to the shelter of the castle, and his own singular persistency in regarding the church, standing lonely on the hillside, as the real place of security in this hour of peril. The excitement, he says, soon passed away; the Welsh princes were not able to press home their victory. In the month of May they were at the other end of the Severn Sea, attacking the outskirts of Glamorgan. Their conquest of Gower enabled them to threaten this lordship, which by the death of Earl Robert of Gloucester in 1147 had passed into the hands of his son William, and they destroyed the castle of Aberafan, held at this time, it seems likely, by Caradog ab Iestyn in feudal subjection to the earl.[69]

While the sons of Gruffydd ap Rhys had been thus winning triumphs at the expense of the Norman and the Fleming, they had been also engaged in another movement, no less profitable to the kingdom of Deheubarth. This was the expulsion of the men of Gwynedd from Ceredigion. The conquests of Owain and Cadwaladr had left this province in the possession of the northern dynasty; Cadwaladr held the portion between the Aeron and the Dovey, while Hywel ab Owain ruled between the Aeron and the Teifi. In Cardigan itself it would seem as if Robert fitz Stephen still held the castle for the Clares, for, though Hywel and his brother Cynan in 1145 raided the town and carried off much booty, they are not credited with the capture of the fortress which had so long resisted the onslaughts of the Welsh.[70] This was the state of affairs until 1149, when Cadwaladr, having built a castle at Llanrhystud, handed it over with his portion of Ceredigion to his son Cadfan. Hywel deemed the moment a suitable one for aggression, and, seizing his cousin, possessed himself in 1150 of his land and castle; he was now lord of the whole province. But the southern princes, who had long been watching for their opportunity, now intervened; Cadell, Maredudd and Rhys, vindicating the ancient territorial rights of their house, attacked Hywel and took from him all that he held to the south of the Aeron. In 1151 they pressed their advantage still further and won most of Northern Ceredigion, which they secured by rebuilding the Clare stronghold of Ystrad Meurig. They did not succeed at this time in capturing Hywel's chief castle at Llanfihangel[71] and their conquest of Llanrhystud was only temporary, for Hywel recovered it before the end of the year.[72] But two years later the reconquest was complete; Maredudd and Rhys, now deprived of the help of Cadell, gained entire possession of Penweddig, the northernmost of the four cantrefs of the province, and Ceredigion was once again attached to the crown of Deheubarth. No serious attempt was made to challenge the hard-won victory of the sons of Gruffydd ap Rhys; there was, indeed, some talk of an invasion by Owain Gwynedd in 1156, but Rhys forestalled matters by building a castle at the mouth of the Dovey, probably at Tomen Las (Green Mound), near Glandovey, where there is an ancient ford across the river, and thus warded off the threatened blow.

Meanwhile, he had been left sole ruler of Deheubarth. His brother Maredudd, who had lived long enough to earn a reputation not only for valour but also for wisdom, justice, and clemency,[73] died in 1155, at the early age of twenty-five. A strange fatality had pursued all the sons of Gruffydd of South Wales, with the exception of Rhys, who, though a mere youth, now bore, as the solitary representative of his house, the whole burden of the southern realm. But this single living shoot of an ancient and well-nigh blasted stock was full of vigour, and in time it became the sturdy trunk out of which there sprang a new and sprightly growth of branches.

III. THE TRIUMPH OF OWAIN.

The victory of Henry II. in 1157, though purchased at a heavy cost, was a clear and decisive one, and it was not unreasonable for the king of England to suppose he had broken down all that was formidable in the Welsh resistance. Owain of Gwynedd had accepted his terms; Madog of Powys was his close ally. It was true that Rhys of Deheubarth, not having yet experienced the weight of the royal arm, was still holding out in the south, but the course of events soon showed that he could not maintain a single-handed opposition. Thus not only Henry, but Owain also, came to the conclusion that the Welsh power of resistance was for the time being at an end; the unique opportunity of the anarchy had passed away, and every act of the king of Gwynedd during the next eight years reveals his conviction that nothing was to be gained, but on the other hand everything was in danger of being lost, by a continuance of the defiant attitude of the days of Stephen. Yet in truth the success of the English rested on no firm foundation; it had been brought about by exceptionally favourable circumstances, and, when affairs began to assume a more normal aspect, the natural strength of the Welsh became evident, and they achieved a triumph which had lasting results.

In the early part of 1158 Rhys ap Gruffydd, whose career had hitherto been one of unimpeded progress, found that the day of reckoning with the English king was no longer to be postponed. His first impulse was to resist, and he concentrated for the purpose all that he and his people had in the forest retreats of Ystrad Tywi. But the hot fit gave way to more sober counsels; he was persuaded to journey across the border and place himself in the hands of Henry. In doing so he had to make up his mind to even larger sacrifices of territory than had been wrung by war from Owain Gwynedd, for the restoration of royal authority in South Wales meant the re-establishment of the barons in the lordships from which they had been ejected during the revolt, and notably of the Clares in Ceredigion and of the Cliffords in Cantref Bychan. Thus it was with sadly shorn power that Rhys returned to Deheubarth, as the lord of Cantref Mawr and some other scattered territories lying in the midst of baronial lands, and soon after, at the beginning of June, the new era was marked by the appearance in Ceredigion of Earl Roger of Hertford,[74] who was come after twenty-two years to claim his father's inheritance, and who forthwith garrisoned the castles, so lately held by Rhys, at Ystrad Meurig, Castell Hywel,

Aberdyfi, Dineirth[75] and Llanrhystud. About the same time Walter Clifford recovered his hold upon Cantref Bychan and Llandovery.[76] The new order was not readily accepted by the Welsh; Rhys's nephew, Einon ab Anarawd, destroyed Castell Hywel and slew the garrison, and the southern prince himself reopened hostilities against Clifford and Earl Roger. But, when Henry came west with banners flying for a second Welsh expedition, Rhys again made a complete submission,[77] and the king crossed to the Continent in the middle of August,[78] no doubt believing that he had effectually disposed of the Welsh problem for many years.

A dramatic incident of the year 1158 deserves to be recorded, not only for its own sake, but also as an illustration of the irrepressible spirit of independence which still lived in districts supposed to be completely subjected to baronial power.[79] The hills of Senghenydd, between the Rhymney and the Taff, were at this time held, as a dependent barony of the lordship of Glamorgan, by one Ifor ap Meurig, whose wife, Nest, was a sister of Rhys ap Gruffydd. He was short of stature, and therefore known as "Ifor Bach," but no man excelled him in daring and resource. He first appears on the scene as the adversary of his next neighbour on the east, Morgan ab Owain of Gwynllwg and Caerleon, whom he waylaid and slew in this year 1158, with his chief bard, named Gwrgant ap Rhys.[80] No increase of territory accrued to him as the result of this deed, for Morgan was succeeded by his brother Iorwerth, who continued to hold Caerleon under the protection of the king. But Ifor now flew at larger game, and, having a quarrel with his overlord, Earl William, as to the extent of his holding, determined to carry his point by an expedient of surpassing boldness. His plan was to kidnap the earl, with the countess and the heir to the earldom, in their castle of Cardiff, carry them off to Senghenydd, and then make his own terms for their safe restitution. It was a scheme beset with enormous difficulties; the castle was strongly walled and well furnished with watchmen; the town at its foot was full of knights, archers and other troops—nothing could be done by mere force, and to attempt a capture by stealth was to run the gauntlet of a hundred accidents which could not be foreseen. Nevertheless, with the aid of ladders, and, probably, of secret allies within the castle, Ifor and his companions gained access to the earl's apartments, seized him, the Countess Hawise, and their young son Robert,[81] and were in their own inaccessible woods before a hand could be lifted against them. The exploit served its immediate purpose, for Ifor's demands were conceded, but it did still more in demonstrating that the Welsh of Glamorgan, though conquered, were not yet crushed, and that it was dangerous to drive them to the wall.

An important element in Henry's victory over Owain Gwynedd had been the support given him by Madog ap Maredudd, whose sway extended over the whole of Powys. Madog had lost something by the accession of a strong king to power, for Oswestry was now recovered by William fitz Alan, who in July, 1155, was received into Henry's favour and reinstated as sheriff of Shropshire.[82] But he had gained what was of more account—a protector against the aggression of Gwynedd, and he continued on the best of terms with the king until his death. This took place early in 1160, when Madog was laid to rest in the soil of the holiest sanctuary of his realm, the church of Tysilio in Meifod.[83] The passing of so notable a prince moved more than one bard of his time to vigorousverse: —

> If hearts can break for weight of sorrow,

sang Cynddelw the Great,

> Mine will be rent in twain.

Now that he was gone, men were bold against Powys, but

> While Madog lived, there was no man
> Durst ravage his fair borders.
> Yet nought of all he held
> Esteemed he his save by God's might.[84]

Gwalchmai, too, bemoaned the loss of "the roof timber of Powys, the mighty dragon of dragons".[85] The epoch was, indeed, a notable one, affecting both the internal history and the external policy of Powys. Madog's eldest son, Llywelyn, described as the "sole hope" of the realm, was killed very shortly after his father, and there resulted a division of the territory between Owain Cyfeiliog, Iorwerth the Red and Madog's other sons, Gruffydd, Owain Fychan and Owain Brogyntyn, which finally broke up the unity of Powys; never again was it under the rule of a single prince. The policy of consistent friendship with the English court also came to an end; though Owain Cyfeiliog and Iorwerth sometimes recurred to it, it was not even for them a uniform principle of action, and in any case it could not be, under the altered circumstances, the menace to Gwynedd it had been in the hands of Madog. When Owain Cyfeiliog and Owain Fychan are found joining in 1163 to assault and destroy the royal castle of Carreghofa, it is clear that one at least of the conditions which gave Henry his early advantage over the Welsh has disappeared.[86]

Owain Gwynedd was not at all slow to realise the importance of the death of Madog as affecting the balance of power between Powys and Gwynedd. The elegy of Cynddelw bears its testimony to his aggressions —

> If my noble master were alive,
> Gwynedd would not now be encamped in the heart of Edeyrnion.[87]

Moreover, it is on record that in 1162 Owain was in possession of Cyfeiliog and its castle of Tafolwern. Hywel ab Ieuaf, of the adjacent cantref of Arwystli, in that year took the castle by surprise, but was driven out by the prince of Gwynedd, who ravaged Hywel's lands as far as Llandinam, defeated him with great slaughter in a pitched battle, and refortified the captured stronghold.[88] But Owain did not allow the changed situation in Powys to modify in any way his attitude towards the English government. "Quieta non movere" was still his motto in this respect, and a diplomatic correctness the aim of his whole policy.

In flat contrast to the prudence of his northern comrade was the restless daring and unquenchable energy of Rhys ap Gruffydd. The peace which he made with the king on the eve of the latter's departure for France lasted but a few months; in 1159 the South Welsh prince was again in arms, attacking the castles of Dyfed. He laid siege, among others, to Carmarthen and put the place in such peril as to bring upon the scene a powerful relieving force, led by Earl Reginald of Cornwall.[89] This proved a momentary check to his progress; he was forced to retire to the wilds of Cantref Mawr and entrench himself in his castle of Dinweiler. But the attempt of the English to improve upon this victory and overwhelm Rhys himself was a notable fiasco, which only served to bring out the high courage of the prince and the defensive strength of his position. Five earls, namely, Reginald of Cornwall, William of Gloucester, Roger of Hertford, Richard of Pembroke and Patrick of Salisbury,[90] marched together to hunt Rhys out of his lair; they were accompanied by Cadwaladr of Gwynedd, with his nephews Hywel and Cynan, whose presence, no doubt, signified that their father wished to repudiate all sympathy with the rebellion. Yet, notwithstanding this imposing array of forces, Rhys held his ground; his enemies found him too strongly posted to venture upon an assault against him, and parted company without having effected anything. A little later he agreed to a truce which enabled him to dismiss his followers to their homes.

During the next two or three years Rhys kept comparatively quiet. Owain Gwynedd still pursued the policy of propitiating the supreme power; when in 1160 Cadwallon ap Madog of Maelienydd seized his brother Einion Clud [91] and made him over as a captive to the northern prince, Owain promptly handed him to the custody of the crown.[92] In 1162, however, Rhys once again raised the banner of revolt; he attacked and took the castle of Llandovery. For some years the government had recognised the insecurity of this stronghold and had disbursed large sums for its defence, as though it were one of the buttresses of the realm and more was involved in its maintenance than the private interest of Walter Clifford.[93] Nevertheless, it fell, and the name no longer appeared in the royal records. The time had now come, however, when the king, whose long absence abroad had been so favourable to the enterprises of Rhys,[94] was again to give his personal attention to the affairs of South Wales, and no sooner did he show himself on the scene of action than it was seen how accurately Owain Gwynedd had gauged the situation. Henry returned to England in January, 1163; a few months later he was on the way to Glamorgan, surrounded by a force which left no doubt as to his intention thoroughly to subdue the rebellious prince.[95] Superstition, no less than motives of a more ordinary kind, cleared the way before him; it was bruited abroad that he was the "freckled man of might" of a prophecy current among the Welsh,[96] whose crossing of the Ford of Pencarn,[97] not far from Newport on the Usk, would be of evil omen to the land. Hope clutched for a moment at the possibility that this man of fate might not cross by the ancient ford, which was now usually discarded for another, and that thus the spell might be broken. But, as ill-luck would have it, Henry's horse, startled by a blast of unaccustomed strength which was blown in honour of the king by the native trumpeters, shied at the usual crossing place and could not be persuaded to ford the stream, until, cantering along the bank, it reached the ancient point of passage and thus fulfilled the ominous prediction. Henry's progress was thereafter unopposed, not only in Glamorgan and in Gower, but even in Rhys's own sphere of influence. He passed through Carmarthen, and, crossing the defiles of the Gwili at last came upon his foe at Pencader, on the confines of Ceredigion.

All that is certainly known of the meeting is that Rhys, offering no resistance, surrendered himself to the king. It is suggested in one quarter that this was done by the advice of Owain Gwynedd,[98] but the same writer elsewhere speaks as if the submission had been obtained by a trick.[99] Be this as it may, Rhys was now a prisoner and accompanied the king on his return to England by way of Ceredigion, Maelienydd and Radnor.[100] The future of Cantref Mawr was in the balance; should the captive prince be reinstated at Dinefwr, or an attempt be made to reduce the district to subjection? If one were to believe the tale which passed from lip to lip in those days, it would be necessary to suppose that the decision in favour of Rhys was obtained by hoodwinking the king. He sent a Breton knight, we are told, to survey the country, and this man was taken by his guide, a priest of Cantref Mawr,[101] through the roughest and wildest parts of the cantref, until he was ready to swear that the king had nothing to gain by the annexation of such a desert, or by the conquest of a people so savage that at a pinch they could subsist on roots and herbs, as he had seen the priest do with his own eyes. A statesman like Henry, one may confidently aver, was not thus easily misled; his resolve to send Rhys back to Dinefwr was no doubt based upon the consideration that the Welsh were not to be dislodged from their last retreat, and, if deprived of their former leader, would merely set another in his place. Hence Rhys was allowed on 1st July to do homage at Woodstock to the king and to his heir, with Malcolm of Scotland and Owain of North Wales,[102] and soon afterwards reappeared at his ancestral home on the banks of the Towy.

His experiences had in no way blunted the edge of his appetite for war. Scarcely was he re-established as lord of Cantref Mawr ere he began to make preparations for resuming the conflict. It was easy to find good grounds for doing so; in 1163, probably during his enforced absence from South Wales,[103] his gallant nephew, Einon ab Anarawd, had been treacherously murdered as he slept by one of his own men, Walter ap Llywarch. When the murderer was sheltered from vengeance by the power of Earl Roger of Hertford,[104] Rhys had a substantial motive for attacking Ceredigion, and accordingly in 1164 he entered the province, destroyed the chief castle of the commote of Mabwnion,[105] and also a new one placed at the mouth of the Rheidol,[106] and ravaged far and wide, until little else but the town and castle of Cardigan remained in English hands. Henry saw that his campaign of the previous year had been labour lost and began to prepare for another which should do its work more thoroughly; at the Council of Northampton, held in October, 1164, he asked for and was promised a large levy of foot soldiers, suitable for Welsh warfare, wherewith to chastise the shameless breaker of treaties.[107]

But the patience of Owain and the persistence of Rhys were now alike to meet with their reward. Even more than the disunion of Wales, the solid unity of England under its vigorous and popular young king had been a stumbling-block in the path of the Welsh patriot. It was at the Council of Wood-stock in 1163 that the great quarrel between Henry and Archbishop Thomas took its rise; during the ensuing fifteen months it grew more and more formidable, and in the very Council of Northampton at which measures were devised for crushing Rhys, the archbishop was subjected to such persecution as to induce him not long afterwards to quit the realm. Although outwardly the king's power had suffered no diminution, the controversy caused an acute division of public opinion, and Henry had no longer the support of a united people. There can be no doubt that it was the commotion in England which emboldened Owain, after years of waiting, to join Rhys in throwing down the gage of battle, and, with two such leaders committed to an offensive policy, the lesser princes were not long in declaring their hostility also, so that at the end of the year, as the St. David's chronicle has it, "all the Welsh of Gwynedd, Deheubarth and Powys with one accord cast off the Norman yoke".[108] The decisive hour had come in the struggle for Welsh independence.

Henry perceived that it was now no mere question of putting down Rhys ap Gruffydd, but that he had to deal with a widespread movement of most formidable proportions. He prepared for the campaign, therefore, with all the care requisite for a great undertaking.[109] Troops were requisitioned from all parts of his wide empire, from Normandy, from Anjou, from Scotland, from Poitou and from Aquitaine.[110] Mercenaries came from Flanders and elsewhere, and in the records of the reign one may read how the sheriffs of London paid £30 for shields and nearly £140 for clothing for a group of these lawless adventurers.[111] The feudal host was summoned and the great magnates were pressed, not only to furnish their proper quota of heavy cavalry, but also, as had been settled at Northampton, to supply serving men who would fight on foot.[112] Lances, arrows and coats of mail were sent down to Shrewsbury,[113] where the host was to assemble. Messengers of the king treated with the Danes of Dublin for the services of a fleet to harass the coast of Gwynedd. In order that nothing should interfere with the task set for the summer, Henry devoted the spring to a short continental visit, during which he came to terms with the foreign powers most likely to disturb his plans, the king of France and the Count of Flanders.[114] When he returned, about the middle of May, he found the war already begun. Owain Gwynedd's son Dafydd had crossed the Clwydian range into Tegeingl and carried back much plunder into the cantref of Dyffryn Clwyd. The castles of Rhuddlan and Basingwerk were in serious danger, and the king's first step was to lead a hurried expedition to their relief, with such forces as chanced to be at hand.[115] He only spent three or four days in the district, for he did not wish to disarrange the elaborate preparations which had been made for an attack upon the grand scale. Accordingly, at the end of July he was in Shrewsbury at the head of a great host and shortly afterwards arrived at Oswestry,[116] whence it was his purpose, no doubt, to follow the old line of march across the mountains to Mur Castell.

The gravity of the crisis was by no means lost upon the Welsh. Menaced by a more powerful fighting force than had ever been got together for the subjugation of Wales, they drew to each other in a close union and confederacy of which earlier Welsh history can scarcely show an example. Gwynedd, Powys, Deheubarth, Rhwng Gwy a Hafren, presented a solid front. In this hour of trial, the proved worth of Owain Gwynedd won for him unquestioned leadership; with his brother Cadwaladr, he assembled the men of Gwynedd at Corwen, in the vale of Edeyrnion, where Henry's passage might be effectually resisted, and thither there came to his aid Rhys ap Gruffydd from the south, Owain Cyfeiliog, Iorwerth the Red, and the sons of Madog ap Maredudd from Powys, Cadwallon ap Madog and his brother Einion Clud from the lands between the upper waters of the Wye and the Severn. It was the crowning moment of Owain's career, and, though he did not actually engage the king's army at close quarters, the victory won was more truly his than that of any other chief in the great gathering of Edeyrnion.

The English army moved westward from Oswestry and soon found itself in the thick forest growth of the Ceiriog valley.[117] Here it was received by a band of skirmishers, who, although without regular leaders, boldly harassed the invaders from the shelter of the over-hanging woods and did no small execution. Henry ordered a general clearing of the timber, and, having thus secured an open space for his passage, began to ascend the bare slopes of the Berwyn range, which here rise to a height of nearly 2,000 feet. The road along which he and his troops made their laborious way is still known as "Ffordd y Saeson"—the English Road;[118] it leads across wild stretches of heath and bog to the pass from which one descends to the valley of the Dee. Here there was little to fear from the onslaughts of the enemy, but much from the unkindness of nature. In a reasonably dry August the transit across these inhospitable moors might have been easily accomplished, but on this occasion the skies put on their most wintry aspect; rain fell in torrents[119] and flooded the mountain meadows, until the English camp became a morass. The ample scale of the expedition now became its bane; the host was too unwieldy to transport across the heights in the teeth of a hurricane of wind and rain and under the vigilant eye of an unsleeping foe. Moreover, the problem of feeding it had become serious; the original store of provisions, diminished, it may be, by the ravages of the storm, was all but exhausted, and it was idle to hope to replenish it in the enemy's country. No step could have been more repugnant to the king than that which he now perceived to be inevitable — to return to his base of operations without having won even the semblance of a victory. Yet it was all he could do; wrathful and baffled, he led his weary troops back to the Shropshire plains, and, having failed to lay hands on the Welsh, vented his spleen upon their unhappy hostages. Twenty-two of these, including two sons of Owain Gwynedd and a son of Rhys ap Gruffydd, were cruelly mutilated to satiate the king's rage.[120] There was still one other weapon he could use, and he hastened to Chester[121] to meet the naval contingent from Dublin and other Danish ports which he had hired for the harrying of the coast of Gwynedd.[122] But here again it was his fate to encounter disappointment; the ships which found their way there were too few to effect his purpose, and he sent them back to Ireland without attempting this part of his programme.

Thus the great English armament had come to nought. Nor was its failure accidental; Henry showed that in his eyes the defeat was final by abandoning the idea of a conquest of Wales. He made no preparations during the following winter to wipe out the ignominy of his inglorious retreat, but contented himself with strengthening the border castles,[123] and, when the spring came, he turned, not to Wales, but to the Continent. He sailed from Southampton in March, 1166, and was absent from England for fully four years. Everything goes to show that he looked on the Berwyn disaster as the grave of his Welsh ambitions. It was true that he had not crossed swords with the leaders of the Welsh, but the elements had done their work for them; the stars in their courses had fought against the pride of England and humbled it to the very dust. To conquer a land which was defended, not merely by the arms of its valiant and audacious sons, but also by tangled woods and impassable bogs, by piercing winds and pitiless storms of rain, seemed a hopeless task, and Henry resolved no longer to attempt it.

The gathering of princes at Corwen broke up with the sense that the dark cloud which had overhung their land had passed away and that once again it was possible to breathe the air of freedom. There were some to whom the deliverance seemed to be the direct act of God, a manifestation of Divine displeasure against the English. For, the night before the catastrophe, the invaders had burnt several Welsh churches, an act which stirred up the younger Welshmen to thoughts of retaliation, until the wise Owain pointed out that it behoved them, as the weaker side, to make sure of Divine favour, and that the sacrilege of the foe was a certain presage of destruction.[124] Assured of the safety of their land, the princes went their several ways, and, with his usual impetuosity, Rhys ap Gruffydd took in hand without delay the completion of the conquest of Ceredigion. He had gained possession of almost the whole of the province, but the castle of Cardigan was still tenaciously held for Earl Roger by its castellan, Robert fitz Stephen. This last remnant of Norman power in a district in which it had once been supreme now passed into Welsh hands; about 1st November the castle was betrayed to Rhys by a Welsh cleric named Rhygyfarch and was forthwith razed to the ground. The garrison were allowed to retire from the place with the half of their goods, but the doughty Robert was cast into prison, where he remained for more than three years.[125] Soon afterwards Rhys captured the Carew stronghold of Cilgerran, and thus had Emlyn within his grasp; his territory now embraced Ceredigion, Ystrad Tywi and a large part of Dyfed. He had, in short, recovered the position which he held when Henry first encountered him, and, as the event proved, had finally disposed of the Clares in Ceredigion and the Cliffords in Cantref Bychan. Attempts made in 1166 to shake his position in the lower valley of the Teifi were fruitless; though a Norman and Flemish army devastated the commote of Iscoed and twice essayed the recapture of Cilgerran, he was not dislodged from his conquests. The defeat of the king had inspired the Welsh of all Wales with new hope and courage and in like measure had discouraged and depressed the foreign garrison.

Owain Gwynedd was more deliberate in his movements, but no less purposeful. He set himself to destroy the royal castles in Tegeingl which had been built in 1157 and which prevented the extension of his territory westward to the Dee. First, he attacked Basingwerk and in 1166 took it; the troops sent by the king in the autumn to rebuild it under the Earls of Leicester and Essex were scattered by a sudden onset of the Welsh,[126] and no fortress was ever again erected on the spot, which was left to the monks of the Cistercian abbey. In 1167 the more difficult problem of capturing Rhuddlan was taken up; the forces of Gwynedd were deemed scarcely equal to the enterprise, and Rhys ap Gruffydd was called in from the south to aid Owain and Cadwaladr in their undertaking. For three months the siege was carried on, months during which the garrison looked in vain for relief, for Henry was abroad and deeply immersed in his continental troubles. At last, at the end of the year, the resistance broke down and Owain won the castle. He destroyed it, together with the neighbouring stronghold of Prestatyn, and thus gained undisputed possession of Tegeingl.[127] The victory was one which worthily closed his military career, for it was the culminating triumph of a long series of successes won by him and by his father, which had extended the bounds of Gwynedd to the Dovey and the Dee.

It was not to be expected that the close union of all the Welsh princes which signalised the year of Henry's great attack would survive the removal of the danger which had brought it about. Owain and Rhys, indeed, remained firm friends and allies, but the princes of Powys were once again divided, some taking the Welsh and some the English side. The first to make his submission to the government was Iorwerth the Red. Iorwerth's adhesion to the patriotic cause was but a temporary aberration; he had been with the king in 1157 and had then received Sutton, near Wenlock, and other manors in Shropshire on condition of acting as the king's "latimer" or emissary to the Welsh.[128] He now returned to his former allegiance and seems to have been rewarded by being placed in possession, in April, 1166, of the border castle of Chirk.[129] His nephews, Owain ap Madog and Owain Cyfeiliog, resented his action, and in the same year drove him out of Mochnant, which they divided between them, making the Rhaeadr the line of separation. It is noteworthy that this division became a permanent one, dividing Northern and Southern Powys, and, in later times, the counties of Montgomery and Denbigh. Next year saw Owain Cyfeiliog also on the English side; he was attacked by Owain, Cadwaladr and Rhys in the interest of Owain ap Madog, upon whom was bestowed his commote of Caereinion, and in his extremity turned to his English neighbours, with whom he had probably already entered into relations.[130] Their aid soon re-established him in Caereinion, and henceforth he was generally on the king's side in the border conflicts.

These closing years of Owain's life were filled with conflict in another sphere than the military, namely, the ecclesiastical. In 1161 or 1162 Meurig, bishop of Bangor, died, and thus the old dispute was reopened as to the control of the English over the see.[131] Owain, it would seem, desired to promote to it one of the clergy of the diocese, named Arthur,[132] but was opposed by the king. When the Archbishop of Canterbury was forced to quit the realm in 1164, the prince of Gwynedd hoped to take advantage of the situation to checkmate Henry; he suggested to Thomas in 1165 that the new bishop should be consecrated by another prelate, since he was out of reach himself, but that he should nevertheless render canonical obedience to Canterbury. The archbishop was too astute to agree to what might prove to be a most dangerous precedent, and ordered that no election be for the present made. Owain paid no heed to this request, but, having exacted an oath from the chapter that they would elect no one save with his consent, obtained the election of Arthur and sent him to Ireland for consecration. The Archdeacon David, who had sworn fealty to the archbishop and had been entrusted by him with the custody of the see, deserted the cause of Canterbury and abetted these proceedings. It was in vain that Thomas, in the early part of 1166, summoned the archdeacon and other leading clergy of the diocese to meet him and elect in accordance with his wishes, in vain that Alexander III. added to his injunctions the weight of papal authority. Owain and the chapter remained obdurate, nor was any bishop elected so as to win recognition from Canterbury and Rome for many years.

The last two events of Owain's long and brilliant career were his dispatch of an embassy in 1168 to the court of Louis VII., offering him help in his war with Henry II. and hostages as a pledge of good faith,[133] and his steadfast refusal to put away his wife Cristin, or Christina, whom the archbishop and the pope required him to give up as being of kin to him within the prohibited degrees.[134] She was the daughter of Gronw ab Owain ab Edwin and thus was his first cousin.[135] Though the archbishop suggested that the lady might be honourably provided for out of Owain's ample possessions, if a separation were once brought about, he refused to listen to the proposal. Nor was he moved by the archbishop's flattering allusions to his triumphant issue out of the difficulties of earlier days, his discretion and wisdom, his love of pious meditation, his pre-eminence above all the other princes of Wales. He maintained his attitude of resistance until his death, which took place on 23rd November, 1170.[136] Though he had been excommunicated by the archbishop for his disobedience in this matter and the closely related affair of the vacant bishopric, the clergy of Bangor gave him honourable burial in their church, building him an arched tomb in the wall of the presbytery, close to the high altar.[137] Thus was laid to rest, after sixty[138] strenuous years of patriotic service, the trusty pilot, whose steady hand and watchful eye had guided the ship of state through foaming rapids and whirling eddies into the full, smooth current of freedom and prosperity.

IV. THE LITERARY REVIVAL.[139]

The struggle for independence which absorbed the energies of the Welsh in the middle of the twelfth century had one result which is often found to follow in the wake of a great patriotic movement—it led to a literary revival. To trace this revival in detail, to weigh the value of its contribution to Welsh literature, to analyse its forms, would carry us beyond the limits of the present work, and is a task best left to those who have made this field of study peculiarly their own. But no account of mediæval Wales would be adequate which did not take some cognisance of it, and an endeavour must therefore be made to outline its salient features.

In the first place, however, something must be said of the author who, though he did not write in Welsh and probably was not a Welshman by origin, gave world-wide currency in this age to the ancient traditions of Wales, and thereby nourished the pride of the Welsh race, secured it an honourable standing in the European community, and; enshrined its heroes among the valiant and worthy of all time. Geoffrey of Monmouth, it is more and more being recognised, was the real fount and source of the vogue of the Arthurian cycle of romance, the first populariser of the legends of early Britain; his *History of the Kings of Britain* broke absolutely new ground in literature and had an immeasurable influence upon the course of literary movements in Western Europe.[140] He claims attention, therefore, at this point as a cardinal instance of the new literary forces brought into play by the interaction of Welsh and Norman life and ideas. Of his early history nothing is certainly known, but it may be surmised from the name he usually bears[141] that he was a native of Monmouth and—for a Geoffrey at this time would scarcely be a Welshman—a member of the foreign settlement in that town.[142] Another name by which he was commonly known in his own day was Geoffrey Arthur (Gaufridus Artur),[143] a title understood, when he had become famous, to refer to the great hero of his tale. But there is evidence that he used it in the days of his obscurity, and reason, therefore, to suppose that his father's name was Arthur.[144] If this were indeed the case, then the presumption would be strong that Geoffrey was the son of one of the Breton followers of Wihenoc of Monmouth,[145] and the problem how a foreigner came to be so deeply interested in the legends of the old British time would be solved. It is not without significance in this connection that Geoffrey makes the insular often seek the aid of the Armorican Britons; indeed, he avers, through the mouth of King Salomon of Brittany, that it has never gone well with the island since the latter left it.[146]

Geoffrey first appears upon the scene in 1129, when he witnessed, with other clergy of Oxford, the foundation charter of Osney Abbey.[147] These clerical witnesses are headed by Walter, Archdeacon of Oxford, and it is, therefore, probable that Geoffrey had already attached himself to a man whom in the *History* he praises as an orator of repute and a student of history, and to whom, if we are to believe him, he was indebted for the "British book" forming the basis of his own work.[148] During the next ten years he was probably engaged in the compilation of the *History*; it is, at any rate, known that in 1139 there was a copy at the abbey of Bec in Normandy of what looks like a first edition, which was shown at that time by Robert of Torigni, a monk of the abbey, to Henry of Huntingdon, the historian, as he passed through on his way to Rome.[149] One MS. of the work, preserved at Berne in Switzerland, has a double dedication, to King Stephen and to Earl Robert of Gloucester, which suggests that an edition was issued in 1136–8, when these two potentates were on fairly friendly terms with each other.[150] In all other MSS. the dedication is to Robert alone, pointing to a time when Geoffrey had chosen his side in the great civil conflict, and, as was but natural in a man of the western march, had chosen that of the warlike earl who ruled both banks of the Severn.[151] Despite his fame as a man of letters, he had to wait long for his meed of recognition, and, when this came in 1152, it took the form of the bishopric of St. Asaph, an outpost of Anglo-Norman authority, rendered for the moment untenable by the aggressions of Owain Gwynedd. Geoffrey was ordained priest on 16th February, and on the 24th consecrated at Lambeth by Archbishop Theobald, after professing the fullest submission to Canterbury.[152] It is not likely that he ever saw his cathedral; in December, 1153, he was at Westminster in the great assembly which ratified the peace between Stephen and the young Henry,[153] and in 1155 he died,[154] at a time when the Welsh were still in possession of Tegeingl.

A keen controversy has been waged over the question of the sources of Geoffrey's work. What was the "very ancient volume in the British tongue," lent him by Archdeacon Walter, which he professed to have rendered into Latin? Did it come from Brittany, or from Wales?[155] Was it a copy of the *Historia Brittonum* of Nennius, done into the vernacular, or some other compilation of the kind no longer extant? The question has even been asked, had it any real existence? was not the whole business a bit of literary artifice? Into these matters it is impossible to enter here; they are topics for discussion by the historian of the romantic literature of Europe. But, in view of the respect with which the authority of Geoffrey soon came to be regarded by serious historical writers,[156] it may not be amiss to set down here two conclusions which are of cardinal importance in this connection. The first is, that no Welsh composition exists which can be reasonably looked upon as the original, or even the groundwork, of the *History of the Kings of Britain*. *Brut Tysilio* has been by some writers raised to this position of honour,[157] but, instead of being anterior to, it is of later date than the Welsh translation of Geoffrey's work known as *Brut y Brenhinoedd,* and no MS. of it is earlier than the sixteenth century.[158] Those who would fain believe that Geoffrey preserves for us valuable Welsh traditions are, therefore, confronted with this difficulty, that there is nothing to show he did not invent everything beyond what he got from the well-known sources, Gildas, Nennius, and Bede.[159] The second conclusion which affects the historical, as distinct from the literary, value of Geoffrey's work is that much of the detail which fills out his narrative is beyond doubt of his own invention. The process of elaboration can often be watched. Occasionally, it is true, he makes use of a genuine local tradition, as when, in opposition to Nennius, he links the death of Vortigern with the stronghold on the Little Doward, near his own home at Monmouth.[160] But more often he is the literary craftsman bending stubborn material into the shape that suits his purpose. Thus for his marvellous array of personal names he rifles the old tribal genealogies; this is the source of his "Dunvallo Molmutius," his "Gurguint barbtruc," his "Gorbonianus," "Cursalem," and many another sonorous title.[161] His handling of the fall of Allectus in A.D. 296 is very characteristic. This successor of Carausius as independent emperor in Britain was overwhelmed by Constantius, the founder of the Constantian dynasty, but he had sent before him with a part of his army the able general Asclepiodotus, who was praetorian prefect; and thus it comes about that in the chronicles which were current in the Middle Ages the latter has the sole credit of the achievement.[162] Geoffrey does not hesitate to style Asclepiodotus Duke of Cornwall and to transform him into a British patriot, who kills the Roman tyrant Allectus and shuts up the Roman garrison in London, reigning afterwards in peace for ten years.[163] He treats British authorities with the same irresponsible gaiety. The five kings attacked by Gildas, who ruled various parts of Western Britain when the *Ruin of Britain* was composed, supplied just the material which he needed; four of them are accordingly named by him, in the order followed by Gildas, as *successive* kings of the Britons, and, with a solemn particularity worthy of Swift or Defoe, Constantine, Conan and Wortipor are said to have ruled three, two, and four years respectively![164] It is idle to look for history, in any guise, from a writer who allowed himself such freedom and whose first and last thought was for literary effect.

One must also, on other grounds, deny the title of historian to Geoffrey's contemporary, Caradog of Llancarfan. In the epilogue of his work, the vivacious romancer, who has brought his story to the death of Cadwaladr, warns off all other writers from the special domain he has appropriated, but tells William of Malmesbury and Henry of Huntingdon that they may deal with the Saxon kings, and Caradog that he may continue the British narrative to modern times.[165] That Caradog ever did so there is not the slightest reason for thinking; a life of Gildas is attributed to him,[166] but nothing else on any ancient authority. In particular, it is highly improbable that he had any share in the compilation of the *Chronicle of the Princes*.[167] Both under Henry I. and later, the centre of interest in this chronicle is in South-west Wales, at Llanbadarn, St. David's, or Strata Florida; there is a complete silence as to the affairs of Glamorgan, and Llancarfan is scarcely once mentioned.

History, indeed, was not a specially remarkable feature of the literary revival now under consideration, if attention be confined to what was composed in Welsh.[168] Poetry, oratory and story-telling were the channels through which the newly awakened literary interest found expression in the vernacular. It was a popular literature which came into existence, not at first preserved in writing,[169] but orally transmitted, not developed under ecclesiastical or monastic influences, but springing up spontaneously in the courts of the princes and the homes of the wealthier tribesmen. At the same time, though it was meant to be heard and not read,[170] and though it appealed to the public—a leisured public, be it remembered, for the Welsh, like all warlike and pastoral peoples, found time hang heavy on their hands—

and not to a cultured class, yet it was not a literature of simple, unso-
phisticated forms, but elaborate and full of conventions; it was largely,
though not entirely, the concern of a special professional order, who
inherited the ancient bardic traditions.

Evidence has already been given of the persistence among the
Welsh from Druidic times of a class of skilled singers and poets.[171] It
was in honour and repute at the court of Maelgwn Gwynedd; it celebrated the fierce conflicts of Angle and Cymro in the sixth and seventh centuries. A few verses written in a copy of Juvencus which is now
in the Cambridge University Library show that Welsh poetry was
being composed in the ninth century.[172] In the age of Hywel Dda the
bardic order was of recognised standing and clearly denned privileges. Membership of it implied freedom of status; the "bardd" or
"cerddor" (the terms were interchangeable) might be a free landowner,
or a "treftadog," having landed expectations, or even an "alltud" or
stranger, but he could not be an "aillt" or villein, a bondsman of the
soil.[173] The craft seems, indeed, to have been a hereditary possession
of certain families,[174] and in the contest between Cynddelw the Great
and Seisyll Bryffwrch for the office of "pencerdd" to Madog ap
Maredudd it was reckoned an effective taunt to say —

> From yon stock no bards have sprung.[175]

Beyond birth, however, careful instruction was needed to make a
mature and accomplished bard; this was given by the "pencerdd," or
bardic president, to all the beginners of his district, who practised
upon harps strung with horsehair until they had thoroughly learnt
their business, when the "pencerdd" admitted them, on payment of a
fee of twenty-four pence, to the full privileges of the order.[176] They
still remained under his authority, but might now practise their craft
for the ordinary rewards of a fully fledged minstrel.

Both the "bardd teulu" and the "pencerdd" stood out from among
the common crowd of bards, but their position was very different. To
borrow an ecclesiastical analogy, one was the court chaplain, the
other the bishop of the diocese. The "bardd teulu" was the chief minstrel of the court, being reckoned among its twenty-four officers; he
had special duties towards the "teulu" or household troops, one of
which was to sing the ancient strain entitled "The Monarchy of
Pictland" in front of the ranks as they were arrayed for battle.[177] The
"pencerdd" or chief poet, on the other hand, filled no place in the
service of the crown; he was the head of the whole bardic community
within the limits of the kingdom,[178] taking precedence even of the

"bardd teulu".[179] The symbol of his authority was the chair in which he sat; this he won in a poetic competition, in which the award was apparently made by the judge of the court,[180] and accordingly the "pencerdd" is sometimes styled the "chaired bard".[181] Unlike his modern successor, who wins a chair in a National Eisteddfod, the "pencerdd," once successful, was secure against rivalry for the rest of his life; when the king gave him the harp which was the perquisite of his office,[182] he paid an "ebediw" or succession fee as though for an estate,[183] and entered into a lordship which was as solid and permanent in its way as that of any prince.[184]

With such an organisation it is not to be supposed that poetical composition was at a standstill among the Welsh bards until the revolt in the time of Stephen. Proof that the art had not been forgotten may, indeed, be found in the life of Gwynllyw written about 1100, where the story is told of a "Britannus versificator," who, while composing a Welsh ode in honour of the saint, was gravelled for lack of matter which would form an effective close. Gwynllyw obligingly sent a flood which swept the whole plain from St. Woollo's to the sea and spared only the poet's house; perched on its roof in a great waste of waters, the good man found the poetic climax he wanted in the story of his marvellous deliverance.[185] Yet, whatever may have been composed during this period, nothing has been handed down to our day which is indubitably older than 1135, except the little poem written by Meilyr on the battle of Mynydd Carn.[186] It may be fairly concluded that the court poetry of this age was too lifeless and conventional to survive; it was only in the white heat of the universal national uprising that the singers of Wales took fire and chanted deathless lays which their countrymen would not willingly let die. Meilyr himself, the harbinger of the new era, the earliest of the "Gogynfeirdd" of the Welsh poetic renascence, sang very differently of the vanquished of 1081 and of Gruffydd ap Cynan in 1137; in the interval he had learnt the art of a sustained and trumpet-like music of which there is no trace in his first poetic effort.

It is only possible to notice here in the briefest fashion the singers who, rising on the crest of the movement for independence, transferred the passion of the people into song and became the vanguard of a succession of Welsh poets which has continued to the present day. Meilyr was a man of Anglesey, from whom the hamlet of Trefeilyr, in the parish of Trefdraeth, took its name.[187] After serving Trahaearn ap Caradog in his youth, he attached himself to Gruffydd ap Cynan, becoming, it would seem, his "pencerdd," with a seat of privilege at the court of Aberffraw. His elegy upon Gruffydd is the first poem written under the influence of the triumphs over the English, and breathes a spirit of fierce daring: —

> The king of England came with his battalions —
> Though he came, he returned not with cattle.
>
> .   .   .   .
>
> Gruffydd hid himself not, but with open force
> Hotly did champion and protect his people.[188]

The "Deathbed of Meilyr the Poet" is in a more placid vein and well illustrates what was best in the religious feeling of the age:- —

> In my last home may I wait the call!
> My chosen sanctuary hath the sea beside it;
> 'Tis a solitary, untrodden refuge,
> And around the churchyard heaves the bosom of the deep.
> Fair island of Mary I white isle of the saints!
> How blest to lie there against the day of uprising!
>
> .   .   .   .
>
> The God who did make me will to himself receive me
> With the pure souled multitude of the dwellers in Enlli.[189]

Meilyr's son, Gwalchmai, was also a dweller in Anglesey, where Trefwalchmai preserves his name.[190] He belonged to the full tide of the poetic revival, celebrating with abundant vigour of diction and striking pictorial power the successes of Owain Gwynedd. He was a warrior-poet, handling the sword with the same impetuous passion as the harp: —

> Gwalchmai am I called, a foe to all English.
>
> .   .   .   .
>
> Bright is my sword and of dazzling fashion
> In the day of battle; my shield flashes gold.
> Multitudes praise me that have not seen me —
> Ladies of Gwent — I am reckoned all fury.[191]

Though the chief bard of Gwynedd, Gwalchmai sang on occasion in honour of Madog ap Maredudd and did not stint his eulogy: —

> No easier is it for thy foe to escape thy chastisement
> Than 'tis to find the sand-flat where no sand is.[192]

But the court poet of Powys in this age was Cynddelw Brydydd Mawr (*i.e.*, the Great Bard), who, while he addressed odes during his long life to many princes of North and South Wales, devoted his muse especially

to the service of the land of Tysilio, its warriors, its saints, its peculiar privileges. His contest with Seisyll Bryffwrch for the office of "pencerdd" in
Powys has been already mentioned; despite his lack of bardic ancestry,
he seems to have succeeded in the competition, nor will the modern
reader be disposed to quarrel with the verdict, if the poems of Seisyll
which have been preserved are fair specimens of his bardic talent.
Cynddelw was a prolific and versatile composer; the themes of love, war,
religion and death in turn engage his muse, and, though his power over
the Welsh language may have encouraged him to make undue use of
the poetic device of alliteration, there is much that is impressive in the
rapid, on-flowing current of his verse. Inferior to Gwalchmai in the gift
of vivid description, he has nevertheless many a graphic image, as in his
elegy on his first patron, Madog ap Maredudd: —

> Poet's friend, poet's bond, who spoke right well,
> He was a stedfast anchor in the waste of the wide sea — [193]

and in his verses to Owain Fychan of Powys: —

> Leading his host mid the uproar of battle —
> A roar as of torrents falling into the full sea.[194]

It is a proof of the force and vitality of this poetic movement that it
was not confined to those who made bardism their profession, but
influenced some of the men of action of the day. A certain degree of
skill in playing upon the harp was widely diffused in Wales at this
period; each "uchelwr" had a harp among his more valuable possessions,[195] and no accomplishment was more highly prized than ability
to play upon it.[196] One need not marvel, therefore, to find Hywel ab
Owain Gwynedd and Owain Cyfeiliog among the singers of this age,
nor will a close inspection of the poems they have left behind them be
necessary to convince us that it was true poetic talent, and not courtly
indulgence, which gained for them this distinction. Owain was a man
of keen intelligence and resourceful wit; it was but natural he should
turn his hand to the popular craft of minstrelsy, and his "Hirlas
Owain" (The Drinking-horn of Owain[197]) is well conceived and skilfully carried out. He bids his "menestr" [198] or cupbearer fill and carry
to each of his brave comrades in turn the royal drinking-horn —

> The long, blue buffalo-horn of high privilege, set with old silver.

As this is done, he recounts the deeds of each hero, and it is not until
he has said the words of praise in the case of Tudur and Moreiddig
that he remembers that they are no more: —

A deathstrain it must be, for I have lost them both.
O Christ! how I grieve for the heavy mischance,
For the loss of Moreiddig, so sorely needed.

Hywel's was a romantic and restless career and his life is reflected in
his verse, in which he pours a wealth of poetic fancy at the feet of his
twin goddesses — Nature and Woman. The man who took Meirionydd
by storm in 1147 and made the flames roar round its castle of
Cynfael[199] was himself taken captive by its delicate beauty: —

A wave of white foam sweeps hard by its hamlets,
And as it speeds it is likest the silvery rime.
I love that sea-strand of Meirionydd,
Where a snow white arm was my pillow,
I love to hear in the thickets of privet
The nightingale's note in the far famed Meeting of Waters.[200]

While it is chiefly the poetry of this age which has been preserved in
literary form, there is abundant evidence that this was but one of many
diverse kinds of mental discipline practised among the Welsh.
Giraldus speaks of their skill in vocal music, which they sang in parts,
and not, as elsewhere, in unison;[201] of their rhetorical powers as plead-
ers in their courts CHAP. of law;[202] of their story-tellers,[203] their geneal-
ogists,[204] their diviners.[205] In general, he says of them: "They are a race
of subtle and penetrating intellect. Whatever the subject of study to
which they may apply themselves, their rich natural endowment of
mind enables them to excel in it." Native gifts had been developed and
strengthened by the inspiration of the great national struggle; as in
England in the days of Elizabeth, proved ability to stand alone in the
face of formidable attacks from without had given the nation a new
spirit of boldness and self-reliance, and this found expression in a literature which, while not altogether independent of foreign influences,
was in the main a spontaneous outgrowth of the soil.

CHAPTER V

RHYS AP GRUFFYDD

I. THE GREATNESS OF THE LORD RHYS.

UPON the death of Owain Gwynedd, the leadership of the Welsh passed from north to south and fell into the hands of Rhys ap Gruffydd, who stood henceforth until the day of his death as the unquestioned head of the princes of Wales. This was a position which no other South-Welsh prince attained after the fall of Rhys ap Tewdwr; geographical conditions were unfavourable to the rise of an independent power in the south. The country was open to the invader; no such natural barriers as the wide marsh of Rhuddlan and the precipitous cliffs of Penmaenmawr barred the way of the foreign adventurer, and though in the heart of South Wales there was one dis-trict—the Great Cantref—which was wild enough to give the Welsh perpetual shelter and so keep alive the spirit of resistance, it was too much of a wilderness to be, under ordinary circumstances, the terri-torial basis of a formidable power. Snowdon, no doubt, could match it in rugged desolation, but Snowdon had behind it—not to speak of its own rich mountain-pastures—the sunny cornfields of Môn, an unfail-ing source of strength to the princes of Gwynedd. Thus the career of Rhys was exceptional; natural difficulties were overcome, in part by the virile energy and spirit of the man, but in part also through the operation of unusually favourable circumstances.

Among these was the quarrel between the king and Archbishop Thomas, which, as was pointed out in the last chapter, had much to do with the successful national outbreak in 1165. Its tragic and pitiful close on 29th December, 1170,[1] left Henry weaker than ever, a monarch so bereft of friends and of reputation that the Welsh had no reason henceforth to dread his vengeance. It was the good fortune of Rhys not only to benefit by this general improvement in the position of the Welsh cause, but also by another event which was of special advantage to himself, *viz.*, the Anglo-Norman conquest of Ireland. It would be no exaggeration to say that the exploits of Earl Richard and his followers were the making of Rhys as a prince of wide and firmly established authority. Since the days of Giraldus Cambrensis, keenly anxious for the credit of his family, attention has often been called to the predominant part played in this movement by the foreign colony of Dyfed, by the Normans and Flemings of South-western Wales. But no stress has been laid upon the fact, which is of the highest interest for the student of Welsh history, that this exodus brought immediate relief to Rhys by diverting into a new channel the energies of his ancient foes, nor has it been observed how the king, in his jealous suspicion of the new Anglo-Irish power, completely reversed his former policy in South Wales and set himself to favour and exalt Rhys as a counterpoise to the Pembrokeshire magnates.

King Dermot of Leinster,[2] casting about for aid in the recovery of his throne, turned in the first instance to Henry II., and in the winter of 1166–7 travelled to Aquitaine to engage his interest and support.[3] But he found that the courteous reception given him on his arrival was all he was to expect from the English king, and on the return journey through South Wales he made efforts to enlist others in his cause. Richard of Clare, who had succeeded his father Gilbert as Earl of Pembroke and lord of Nether Went,[4] was approached by him, at the time with no great success,[5] and he seems also to have appealed to Rhys ap Gruffydd to set free for an Irish expedition his prisoner, Robert fitz Stephen, who had been in the prince's hands since November, 1165.[6] When, however, he sailed from St. David's in the summer of 1167, he had in his train only one important recruit, namely, Richard fitz Godebert of Rhos,[7] with a small contingent of fighting men, and accordingly he sent over in the following year his "latimer" or interpreter, Morice Regan, with letters to divers great men in England and Wales, appealing for armed help. To this appeal there was a much better response; Robert fitz Stephen, after a three years' captivity,[8] was now released by the shrewd policy of Rhys, who foresaw that the Irish enterprise would keep him busily employed for the rest of his life, and early in May, 1169, he landed at Bannow Bay, not far from Waterford Haven, accompanied by his nephews, Meilyr fitz Henry,[9] Miles of St. David's,[10] and Robert of Barry,[11] together with one

Maurice of Prendergast[12] (near Haverfordwest) and a nephew of Earl Richard, Hervé of Montmorency,[13] sent by the earl in part redemption of his promise of assistance.

The invaders, though often in sore straits, had remarkable success in their enterprise. First, the Danish city of Wexford fell into the power of Robert fitz Stephen and was bestowed upon him by King Dermot. Next, the arrival of Maurice fitz Gerald, another of the descendants of Nest of South Wales, brought an accession of strength to the company and enabled Dermot to make a vigorous onslaught upon his enemies. In the spring of 1170 another of the great clan came over in the person of Raymond the Fat, son of William fitz Gerald of Carew, while the August of this year at last saw Earl Richard cross the Channel to render the long-promised assistance to the king of Leinster and to receive the reward for which he had bargained — the hand of Dermot's daughter and the reversion of his kingdom. The capture of Waterford by the earl broke the power of another Danish stronghold in Ireland, and it was then resolved to attack Dublin, the principal seat of the Ostmen, ruled at this time by Hasculf mac Torkil. At the end of September the city was taken, Hasculf finding safety in flight. The death of Dermot in the spring of 1171 completed the triumph of the earl by placing within his grasp the prize for which he had toiled — the crown of the fair province of Leinster.

His success brought the king of England upon the scene. Henry had apparently given no sanction to the earl's adventure at the time it had been undertaken, and had afterwards marked his displeasure at the whole affair.[14] When the news reached him of Richard's succession to the crown, he recognised that the matter had become serious and that he must act promptly, if Ireland was not to become independent. The moment, indeed, was not very propitious for an expedition, for Henry was still involved in the obloquy brought upon him by the archbishop's murder and had not yet been reconciled to the pope. Nevertheless, in Ireland he would be conveniently out of the way while the storm was subsiding, and accordingly, at a council held at Argentan in July,[15] he resolved to cross over, the fair words of Earl Richard's envoys nowise deterring him from his purpose.

Landing at Portsmouth at the beginning of August,[16] he collected a large army, and early in September was at Newnham, on the edge of the Forest of Dean, in readiness for the journey through South Wales which was to take him to the fleet assembled in Milford Haven. At this point he was met by Earl Richard, who had resolved to turn aside the king's wrath by a timely submission and who now made his peace with

Henry by the sacrifice of Dublin and other gains.[17] At the same time Rhys ap Gruffydd came into the royal presence, relying, no doubt, upon overtures which had already been made to him,[18] and was received into full favour on promising to deliver twenty-four hostages and to render a payment of 300 horses and 4,000 cattle.[19] The process had begun which was shortly to make Rhys the principal supporter of the crown in South Wales. A minor Welsh prince, Iorwerth ab Owain of Gwynllwg, had less reason to be grateful for the royal visit. For some fault which is not recorded, Henry deprived him of Caerleon, a possession of the family since the days of Stephen;[20] it may be that he thought it unfitting that a castle so near the high road into South Wales should be in the hands of a Welsh custodian. Iorwerth waited until the army was well on its way to Pembroke, and then, with the aid of his sons, Owain and Hywel, and his nephew, Morgan ap Seisyll ap Dyfnwal of Upper Gwent, took vengeance in a raid upon the town he had been forced to abandon to the king's men. The castle stood the siege and was by the king's orders specially provisioned in order to meet further attacks.[21] Meanwhile Henry had reached Pembroke, spreading panic as he went by threats of punishment for the neglect of the marchers to impede the progress of Earl Richard as he set out on his campaign [22] — threats which came to nothing, but which clearly reveal the suspicion and distrust now harboured by the king towards a class hitherto high in royal favour. Contrary winds kept the expedition from sailing for nearly a month after Henry's arrival[23] and enabled him to bestow some attention upon Wales. On Michaelmas Day he paid a state visit to the shrine of St. David, somewhat to the embarrassment of Bishop David fitz Gerald, whose resources were not quite equal to the demands of the occasion. But the king was gracious, made a suitable offering to the cathedral altar, limited the number of the bishop's guests to 300 men, and was careful to return to Pembroke the same night.[24] Although the day was wet and many had, for lack of room at the tables, to dine standing, the affair passed off agreeably, and no doubt the men of Dyfed, of all races, were flattered at the attention shown to their patron saint, whom Normans and Flemings called to their aid in their Irish warfare with as much assurance as though they were his undoubted fellow-countrymen.[25] More important, however, than this pious pilgrimage was the compact with Rhys ap Gruffydd which Henry now completed. On his arrival at Pembroke he formally recognised his old antagonist as rightful holder of the lands he had won; not only Cantref Mawr was to be his, but also Ceredigion and Cantref

Bychan, despite the respective claims of the houses of Clare[26] and Clifford; in addition he was to have Ystlwyf and Efelffre,[27] on the south bank of the western Taf. Emlyn, also, which Rhys had taken from William fitz Gerald in 1165, was left in his hands.[28] In further proof of his goodwill the king released Rhys's son Hywel, whose long residence in England as a hostage earned for him afterwards the epithet of "Sais," *i.e.*, Englishman. He also allowed the prince ample time to make up the amount of the promised tribute, contenting himself with a few horses in present satisfaction of what was due. Having thus unmistakably shown his intention to treat Rhys henceforth as a trusty friend and supporter, he sailed for Ireland on the 16th of October, and on the next day landed near Waterford.[29]

For the rest of his life Rhys held a position of unquestioned supremacy in South Wales. In the summer of 1171 he had resolved to make Aberteifi the chief stronghold of his dominions; on the ruins of the dismantled fortress of Robert fitz Stephen there arose ere long a brand new castle of stone and mortar, a visible emblem of the power of a prince who, with the keen insight into affairs which always distinguished him, was resolved henceforth to be recognised not only as a great Welsh chieftain but also as a great baron of the realm. Henry's return to England by way of St. David's and Cardiff in the spring of 1172 gave Rhys an opportunity of still further improving his relations with the English crown. The king was by this time impatient to be back in Normandy, where the pope's legates were ready to purge him from the stain of the archbishop's murder.[30] He landed at Porth Stinan [31] with a small following (the bulk of his train had sailed for Pembroke) on the morning of Easter Monday (17th April), was received by the canons at the White or Western Gate, heard mass in the cathedral, and having, in the absence of any other preparation, eaten the dinner (by an august providence saved for him, says the courtly Giraldus) of one of the minor clerics of the place, made off with all speed for Haverfordwest.[32] Yet he was not too busy to see Rhys at Talacharn (Laugharne) and to conclude with him an agreement which a little later led to the appointment of the prince of Deheubarth as "justice" of South Wales.[33] Interpreted in the light of subsequent events, this somewhat singular title may be taken to signify that Rhys was henceforth to have under his control the lesser chieftains of South Wales, in Gwynllwg, Gwent, Morgannwg, Elfael and Maelienydd, and to be responsible for their good behaviour. It is the position which seems to be set forth by another title peculiar to Rhys, who is constantly termed by poet and chronicler "yr Arglwydd Rhys" — the Lord Rhys.[34]

It was not many months ere Rhys had ample opportunity to show his gratitude and justify the confidence reposed in him. The king's difficulties, far from disappearing with his reconciliation to the pope, were about to enter upon their most acute stage. As he travelled home from Ireland he had received Divine warning—so the tale was afterwards told—of the storm which was soon to burst upon him and test to the foundations the stately fabric of his rule. As he lingered after mass on Low Sunday in St. Piran's Chapel within the walls of Cardiff Castle, he had been confronted by a strange, uncouth figure, who had ordered him to forbid Sunday markets throughout his realm.[35] His reply had been a jest, whereupon the unknown monitor had promised him, ere a twelvemonth had elapsed, such trouble as would last him to the end of his life. In the few moments which Henry took to digest this rebuke, the man vanished from the scene beyond recall. It was in fact at Eastertide, 1173, that the great revolt of Henry's sons began which combined all the king's enemies in France and Britain against him and which was not suppressed for a year and a half, leaving even then a legacy of bitterness and mistrust which darkened all the rest of the reign. In this crisis Rhys was not found wanting. At the first news of rebellion, he sent his son Hywel to Normandy to serve in the king's train.[36] In the following year, when the tumult had spread to England, he led a large force to the siege of Tutbury on the Dove, a castle which Earl Ferrers was holding against the royal officers.[37] When the king's arrival at Northampton brought about the submission of the earl at the end of July,[38] Rhys's troops, to the number of 1,000, were transferred to the immediate service of the king and crossed the Channel with him in August, to fight his battles against Louis of France.[39] Well might the chronicler say that at this time Rhys was the king's "right loving friend".[40]

In May, 1175, Henry returned to England. The skies were now serene, and the king began once more to hold councils for the settlement of public affairs. The assembly which met at Gloucester on 29th June was devoted to Welsh business and affords striking proof of the commanding position which Rhys had now attained.[41] He appeared at the head of all the minor princes of the South, most of them connected with him by ties of kinship or marriage, and all relying upon his influence and protection to keep them in good standing with the crown. Three of them came from the lands between Wye and Severn; Cadwallon ap Madog of Maelienydd was his first cousin,[42] Einion Clud of Elfael, a brother of Cadwallon, was his son-in-law,[43] and so too was Einion ap Rhys of Gwerthrynion.[44]

Two were from Morgannwg, namely, Morgan ap Caradog ab Iestyn, who had succeeded his father at Aberafan and was the son of Rhys's sister Gwladus,[45] and Gruffydd of Senghenydd, son of the redoubtable Ifor Bach, and another nephew, therefore, of the lord of Aberteifi.[46] From Upper Gwent came Seisyll ap Dyfnwal, who had married Gwladus after the death of her first husband,[47] while Gwynllwg was represented by Iorwerth ab Owain, the only one of the seven, it would seem, who was not allied by some family tie to their common lord and champion. Yet even for Iorwerth, Rhys was able to do something. Since the king had taken Caerleon from him in 1171, he had maintained a constant struggle against the royal power and had seen some changes of fortune. When Henry was passing through Newport in 1172, he had summoned Iorwerth to meet him and discuss his grievances with him, but the unfortunate murder at this moment of the young Owain ab Iorwerth by men of the Earl of Gloucester from Cardiff put an end at once to the negotiations and drove Iorwerth and his surviving son Hywel into the ways of rapine and outlawry once more.[48] In 1173 the outbreak of the revolt against Henry gave them an opportunity which they did not neglect; on 21st July Iorwerth regained possession of the keep of Caerleon, and this success was followed on 16th August by a great raid upon Nether Went which carried Hywel to the walls of Chepstow.[49] When the turn of the tide came in the summer of 1174, Hywel had good reason to fear the king's vengeance, but Henry's speedy return to Normandy [50] relieved his anxiety for the time. Soon after the castle of Usk which he held was betrayed into the hands of Earl Richard's men, while early in 1175 he and his father lost Caerleon once again. Hywel's cruel mutilation of a relative of whose rivalry he was afraid had perhaps weakened his hold upon the Welshmen of Gwynllwg, but, be this as it may, his father secured the good offices of Rhys, and, as the result of the conference at Gloucester, was reinstated in the much-coveted City of the Legion. Cadwallon and Einion Clud, who had also scores to settle with the king, purchased the enjoyment of their lands by promising each to pay a composition of 1,000 cattle.[51]

Notwithstanding the harmony which prevailed on this occasion, the year, ere it closed, was stained by a treacherous massacre which bred a long and obstinate feud between the Welsh and the English of Upper Gwent. It had no effect upon the fortunes of the Lord Rhys, but it well illustrates the difficult task he had in hand in endeavouring to secure peace between the two races. On the death of Earl Roger of Hereford in 1155,[52] the lordships of Brecknock and Upper Gwent had passed to his brother Walter, who succeeded to the family estates but not to the earldom. In a few years Walter's death without issue[53] caused the patrimony again to pass to a brother, Henry, and, by a strange fatality much commented upon at the time, Henry and a fourth brother, named Mahel, in turn came to these lands, only to lose them in a little while through a sudden stroke which carried them off while as yet they were without heirs.[54] Henry was slain in Gwent by Seisyll ap Dyfnwal on 12th April, 1175;[55] Mahel a few months later was killed in a fire which broke out at Walter Clifford's castle of Bronllys, when a stone from the summit of the keep fell on his head.[56] It was the death of Henry which led to the massacre of Abergavenny. Brecknock and Upper Gwent had now come into the possession of a new family, for when the catastrophe at Bronllys cut off the last of the male line of Earl Miles,[57] his inheritance had been divided, as was the rule in such cases, between his daughters, the sisters of Mahel, and the two Welsh lordships had been assigned to Bertha, the wife of William of Briouze, lord of Radnor and Builth.[58] Their son William, a man who was for thirty-five years to play a leading part in the history of South Wales, took over this great marcher inheritance at the end of 1175 and signalised the beginning of his rule by exacting a pitiless vengeance for the murder of his uncle Henry.[59] Shrewd contemporaries absolved him from some of the guilt of this bloodthirsty deed, blaming the elders who advised him, his uncle, Philip of Briouze and Ranulf Poer, a royal official of the borders, and even holding the king in a measure responsible. But the popular voice attributed to him the full infamy of a crime committed in his own castle and by his own men. Under pretext of hearing a royal ordinance as to the bearing of arms, Seisyll, his son, Geoffrey, and other leading Welshmen of Gwent were lured to Abergavenny and there set upon and slain without the slightest warning. Not content with this, the retainers of William had forthwith mounted their swiftest horses, and, before the tidings of their exploit had got abroad, had spread ruin far and wide in Seisyll's country, which was near at hand. Arrived at the court of the slain chieftain, they had carried his wife away as a captive and had slain in her arms his seven-year-old son, named Cadwaladr. The border warfare was at all times savage and unpitying, but it did not often witness perfidy and barbarity of this deep dye; small wonder was it, men thought, that misfortune should beset the path of the lord of Abergavenny.

With a rapid transition from grave to gay, one passes from this scene of blood to the great festival held by the Lord Rhys at Christmastide, 1176. It was celebrated in the new castle of Aberteifi, and is of special interest as the occasion of the first Eisteddfod of which there is trustworthy record.[60] True it is that the institution does not appear under this name, but its features are unmistakable. First of all, it was proclaimed twelve months in advance, in accordance with a custom which is still followed, and competitors were invited, not only from all parts of Wales, but also from England, Scotland[61] and Ireland. Next, one observes that a twofold competition was organised; the one was poetic and intended to test the mettle of bards from North and South Wales and their skill in the Welsh metres; the other was musical, open, it would seem, to the minstrels of any nation and to the player of any instrument, for mention is made not only of harpists, but also of crowders and pipers.[62] Lastly, the prize in each case was a chair, suggested, no doubt, by the chair which was won by the successful "pencerdd,"[63] and supplemented, as a mere honorary reward, by more satisfying gifts from the hand of the bounteous giver of the feast. The musical chair, it is recorded, was carried off by one of Rhys's own subjects, but the poetic honours fell to the men of Gwynedd; thus early did the South prove its aptitude for music and the North its skill in the weaving of Welsh verse. North and South joined to do honour in this memorable gathering to the prince whose gifts of leadership had made him the first Welshman of his time.

While Rhys was thus winning triumph upon triumph, Gwynedd had been distracted by the rivalries of the sons of Owain.[64] Civil war had broken out immediately upon the death of the Northern hero, and the first victim was the warrior-poet Hywel, who was overwhelmed in a battle fought near Pentraeth in Anglesey before the end of the year 1170.[65] His enemies were Owain's widow, Christina, and her sons, Dafydd and Rhodri, who thus got rid of a formidable competitor for the chief place in Gwynedd. The seven sons of Cadifor, his foster-father, bravely defended their lord: —

> The sons of Cadifor, a noble band of brothers,
>   In the hollow above Pentraeth,
> Were full of daring and of high purpose —
> They were cut down beside their foster-brother.

It would be difficult to find a more apt illustration of the way in which the custom of fosterage perverted the natural order of things, taking away the affection of brethren in blood for each other and substituting for it the attachment of foster-brethren brought up under the same roof.[66] After the battle of Pentraeth peace reigned in Gwynedd for a season; the remaining sons of Owain appear to have agreed upon a partition of their father's lands, and the death of their uncle Cadwaladr on the night of 29th February, 1172,[67] increased in a little while the divisible stock. It has, indeed, been very persistently asserted that Iorwerth, who bore the nickname "Trwyndwn," *i.e.*, Flat-nosed,[68] was excluded by his deformity from all share in the succession,[69] and, having been driven out of Gwynedd, came to an untimely end in Powys. But an elegy upon him by Seisyll Bryffwrch is extant, in which he is styled "ruler of Arfon," and his grave is said to be in Llandudclud, a church at the head of the Conway Valley, now known as Penmachno.[70] Hence it is certain that he was included in the general division, and there would seem to be good ground for the tradition that he held the commote of Nanconwy, with its castle of Dolwyddelan.[71] Another son of Owain, named Maelgwn, received Anglesey as his portion, while Cynan, it may be conjectured, was established in the regions afterwards held by his sons, namely, Ardudwy, Eifionydd and Meirionydd.

It was the ambition of Dafydd which first led to a renewal of strife. In 1173 he drove Maelgwn from Anglesey, and in the following year embarked upon a much larger scheme of aggression, involving the conquest of the whole of Gwynedd. The death of Cynan in this year removed one obstacle from his path, and the imprisonment of Maelgwn, who had returned from an exile in Ireland to renew his claims, disposed of another; Iorwerth was most probably dead, and thus Dafydd had only to deal with his brother Rhodri and his nephews,[72] Gruffydd and Maredudd, the sons of Cynan. He overcame them without difficulty and then bethought himself of a scheme for still further strengthening his position. In the upheaval of 1173-4 he had been no less loyal to Henry than had Rhys of South Wales,[73] and it seemed to him he might claim some reward. He despatched a special envoy, one Simon the Monk,[74] to ask from the king the hand of his half-sister Emma, who was a natural daughter of Geoffrey of Anjou,[75] famed for her beauty, and now, it would seem, a widow.[76] Henry did not regard the match with a very favourable eye,[77] but Dafydd was at the moment an important ally, and the marriage took place in the summer of 1174.[78] For a few months the star of the newly wedded prince was decidedly in the ascendant, and his poet, Gwilym Rhyfel, though he would do nothing so unbardic as congratulate his patron upon the foreign alliance, is reckless in the extravagance of his eulogy.[79] Dafydd has the three gifts—the strength of Hercules, the wisdom of Solomon, the comeliness of Adam. Next to the friendship of God, none is so greatly to be desired as that of the king of Cemais, whose hand replenishes the cups of yellow gold.

But in the following year Dafydd's greatness underwent a considerable eclipse. To make sure of his most dangerous rival, Rhodri, he had imprisoned him; the captive, however, soon made his escape, and appealed so successfully to the men of Anglesey and Eryri that Dafydd was dislodged from his newly won gains to the west of the Conway and forced to fall back upon the cantrefs to the east of the river, over which he had a stronger hold. At the same time the sons of Cynan recovered their father's lands. The point has now been reached at which the contending forces let loose by the removal of Owain Gwynedd attain an equilibrium. Dafydd finds himself unable to unite the whole of Gwynedd in subjection to him, and agrees to a partition with Rhodri, with the Conway as the line of division, while by common consent Meirionydd, Ardudwy, and Eifionydd are reserved for Gruffydd and Maredudd ap Cynan. These arrangements were not carried out without some heart-burnings among those whom they forced to a transfer of allegiance; the poet Gwalchmai bewails the loss of his liberal patron Dafydd:—[80]

> I shall be poorly bestead without it,
> The friendship of my renowned Dafydd.
> Rhodri will not keep me; he needs me not,
> He sets no price upon me.

He consoles himself by recalling the names of the great ones he has served, Owain, Cadwallon, Cadwaladr, the sons of Gruffydd, Madog, the son of Maredudd—true lovers of his art who knew his worth—

> Well earned were their praises.

But time soon healed these wounds, and in later years Gwalchmai sang with all his accustomed fire in praise of Rhodri, the "great rampart of his people".[81]

In 1177 there was another great gathering of Welsh princes for conference with their English overlord, representing, not South Wales alone, as at Gloucester in 1175, but the three provinces of Gwynedd, Powys, and Deheubarth. The first meeting was apparently at Geddington, in the Forest of Rockingham, where fealty was sworn to the king by a number of Welshmen in the early part of May;[82]

later in the month there assembled to meet the king at Oxford a company which included nearly every Welsh prince bearing rule at the time in the country.[83] Rhodri, indeed, was absent, and so, too, the sons of Cynan, the latter, as will be seen, to their cost, but Dafydd, the prince of Gwynedd whose conduct most nearly affected England, inasmuch as he held Tegeingl and Dyffryn Clwyd, was in attendance. From Powys came Owain Cyfeiliog, well known at the English court for his ready wit and his constant loyalty to Henry, and highly esteemed by his people as a just and enlightened ruler.[84] His cousin and namesake, Owain Fychan, lord of Mechain, Cynllaith, and Mochnant Is Rhaeadr,[85] was not at the council, but Northern Powys was represented by another of the sons of Madog ap Maredudd, Gruffydd of Bromfield, ruler of Maelor and of Ial. Madog ab Iorwerth Goch was also present, but rather in the capacity of "latimer" or king's interpreter, which he had inherited from his father, than as a territorial lord.[86] The Lord Rhys answered for Deheubarth and, as became the position he had now attained, takes the first place in the chronicler's list. Lastly, Cadwallon ap Madog of Maelienydd came from the region betwixt the Wye and the Severn; the death of his brother, Einion Clud, is recorded by the Welsh chronicles under this very year, so that perhaps he came to court with hopes of adding Elfael also to his possessions.[87] Other princes made their profit out of the conference. Dafydd prevailed on the king to grant him as a marriage gift the lordship of Ellesmere,[88] while Rhys set up a claim, which, in the absence of the sons of Cynan, was not contested, to the cantref of Meirionydd.

The spirit of concession shown by the crown at the Council of Oxford marks a definite stage in the long struggle between Wales and the English power. A period of truce has been reached, during which England abandons all attempts upon the independence of its ancient foe and is content to see Rhys ap Gruffydd and his lesser companions in arms grow strong and rich and influential. Henry had perhaps taken to heart the words of the wise old Welshman whom he had asked, on the expedition to Pencader in 1163, his opinion as to the effect of the royal campaign. "I doubt not," was the reply, "that now, as oftentimes of yore, this race of mine may be brought low and much broken by the might of English arms. Yet the wrath of man, if God's anger be not added, will never utterly destroy it. For I am persuaded that no other race than this and no other tongue than this of Wales, happen what may, will answer in the great Day of Judgment for this little corner of the earth." [89]

II. GIRALDUS CAMBRENSIS.

(The works of Gir., as edited in the Rolls Series, with the prefaces of Brewer, Dimock, and Warner, supply ample material for the subject of this chapter. Mention may also be made of Owen's Gerald the Welshman (second ed. 1904), Hoare's edition of the Itinerary, and the translation of the Irish and the Welsh treatises edited by T. Wright for Bohn's Series.)

Among the many figures which crowd the stage at this period of our narrative, none stands out more clearly than that of Gerald of Barry, long known to the world of letters by his scholastic name of Giraldus Cambrensis. In the eyes of the men of his own age he was not, indeed, a figure of the first rank,[90] and, did we depend upon his contemporaries for our knowledge of him, we should scarcely distinguish him among the many busy scholars and clerics of his day. But, with prodigal self-revelation, he has told us his own story, and, while that sure literary touch of his, inspired as it was by acute observation and keen interest in the common things of life, has made his epoch a living reality for us, in a way that is true of no other period of early Welsh history, it may be said that nothing is so lifelike in the picture as Giraldus himself. The portrait could not be improved; a duller soul would have painted himself in dull, conventional tones of the right clerical hue; a wiser one, less charmingly open and frank in his vanity, would have drawn a stately and impressive figure, clad in robes of dignity and uprightness, and would never have been betrayed into those disclosures of weakness and folly which make Giraldus one of the most amusing and at the same time one of the most lovable men of his age.

By birth and upbringing Giraldus was a member of the foreign colony settled in Southern Dyfed. His father was William of Barry, lord of Manorbier, where about 1146 Giraldus was born.[91] His mother was Angharad, daughter of Gerald of Windsor, the castellan of Pembroke. His brother Robert was one of the foremost of the Anglo-Norman invaders of Ireland,[92] and another brother Philip took a part somewhat later in the same great movement.[93] Notwithstanding all this, he had some Welsh blood in his veins; his grandmother on the maternal side was the famous Nest, daughter of Rhys ap Tewdwr, and what is remarkable is that from the first he made the utmost of this connection, never failing to emphasise his Welsh descent,[94] regarding Wales as his beloved fatherland,[95] and posing as a Welsh patriotic leader. For the English as a race he was full of contempt; they were born to slavery and in Wales were neatherds, shepherds, cobblers, craftsmen and what not, plebeians of the rankest kind;[96] the noble Norman first claimed his admiration, and, next in order, the freeborn, fearless Welshman, who spoke his mind unabashed in the presence of kings.[97] He was proud of his knowledge of Welsh, though at the same time far from proficient in the tongue, and he was always willing to try his hand at the interpretation of Welsh place-names, a pursuit as fascinating for him as for others in our own day no less slenderly equipped than he was.[98] Nevertheless, the Welsh themselves never recognised in this brilliant cosmopolitan scholar a genuine fellow-countryman; like some great comet in the sky, he startled and aroused them, extorted their admiration, and then disappeared, to be thought of no more.

The youngest of four brothers, Giraldus was from early youth designed for a clerical career. His uncle, David fitz Gerald, was bishop of St. David's,[99] and it was under his relative's guidance he commenced his studies. In course of time he found his way to Paris, then the goal of all ambitious young scholars in Northern Europe, and spent his early manhood, during three long terms of residence,[100] in the discipline of its schools, from which he emerged a skilled writer of Latin, thoroughly steeped in the classical learning (by no means contemptible) of the day, with a mind well stocked with the most diverse information and a fluent pen which could transmute into literature the most unpromising material. Thus equipped he returned to Dyfed about 1175,[101] in readiness for the part, for which his family influence predestined him, of the aristocratic secular clerk and pluralist, the man of many benefices, active in business, haughty in temper, of pronounced patrician sympathies. To the end of his life Giraldus hated all monks without distinction, and for them he reserved his choicest vials of invective.[102] Their ideal of seclusion from the world made no appeal to him;[103] their aggressive claims and lofty pretensions moved him to indignant ridicule. Nevertheless, he fully accepted the monastic ideal of celibacy and chastity as the rule for the whole clerical order and in this respect was a fierce reformer, ever thundering against the laxity which, in spite of the rule of the Church, had allowed the rise among secular priests of real though unacknowledged marriage.[104] It was, no doubt, the conviction of Giraldus that, unless the parish and the cathedral were above reproach in this respect, they would lose all spiritual influence, and the actual control of the Church would pass to the obnoxious monks, who, despite occasional grievous lapses, paid something more than lip-service to the celibate idea.

His first public appearance in Wales was as one of a commission of two appointed by Archbishop Richard to secure that throughout the diocese of St. David's the tithe of wool and of cheese should be paid, a custom to the contrary having taken root in the district. It was a task which well brought out the energy and courage of the young ecclesiastic, for though the Welsh, who were in those days careful tithepayers,[105] fell in at once with the new proposal, there was stout resistance from the Flemish flockmasters of Rhos, Deugleddyf, Angle, and Laugharne, and it was only with the help of his relatives, Philip of Barry, Odo of Carew,[106] and William fitz Hay,[107] that Giraldus succeeded in carrying through his task. Such zeal deserved promotion, and the Archdeaconry of Brecknock offered itself as a natural reward. It had long been held by one Jordan,[108] whose advanced age and possession of a wife afforded a double reason for depriving him; with the consent of the archbishop[109] Giraldus became, in 1175, archdeacon, with a residence at Llandduw, near Brecon,[110] and the "golden prebend" of Mathry in Pebidiog.[111] Other churches which he is known to have held are those of Llanwnda,[112] Angle,[113] and Tenby.[114]

Two incidents are recorded which illustrate the vigour of these early official days. He proposed, in the exercise of his functions, to visit the Welsh districts of Elfael and Maelienydd, but was informed that they were by custom outside his jurisdiction and only subject to the authority of their respective rural deans.[115] It was idle to oppose local usage in this way to the will of a man who deemed it his special mission to reduce Wales to ecclesiastical order, and Giraldus paid no heed to the remonstrance. He was not even daunted when other arts were employed and he was threatened with the consequences of a "galanas" or blood feud alleged to exist between his family and certain magnates of the district. Taking up his quarters in Llanbister, the principal church of Maelienydd,[116] he appealed for support to his kinsman, Cadwallon ap Madog,[117] and was rewarded for his boldness by a complete victory. Cadwallon came at once to his aid, forced the clergy of Llanbister to make amends for their discourtesy, and sent his son Hywel to escort the archdeacon during the rest of his tour. A little later he had to deal with a more formidable antagonist. At the Council of Westminster in May, 1175, the clergy of St. Asaph had asked that their bishop, Godfrey, who had been non-resident for ten years, should be compelled either to return to his see, or to resign it.[118] The king, in his new mood of friendliness towards the Welsh, not only obtained the resignation of Godfrey, but appointed in his stead a distinguished Welshman, named Adam, a canon of Paris and a well-known teacher in the university of that city.[119] No Welshman had hitherto occupied this see, and it would seem that Adam hoped his Welsh origin might be of service in pushing its interests. In particular, he hoped to establish its claim to include the lands between Wye and Severn as part of the ancient realm of Powys,[120] and, as a first step, he entered into relations with Cadwallon of Maelienydd with a view to the seizure of St. Michael's, the church of the commote of Kerry,[121] which was only separated by a low range of hills from the undisputed domain of St. Asaph in Southern Powys. The moment seemed especially favourable, inasmuch as Bishop David fitz Gerald had died in May, 1176,[122] and St. David's had just then no official head. But this was to ignore the zeal of the new Archdeacon of Brecknock, within whose sphere of authority Kerry lay.[123] Giraldus hurried to the spot, met the bishop face to face in the churchyard, threatened him, despite his high office, with excommunication, and remained master of the field. His promptitude and energy saved the church for the diocese of St. David's, to which, in spite of political changes severing it from Maelienydd,[124] it remained attached until the middle of the nineteenth century.[125]

Such a man might well seem to be marked out by destiny for the vacant bishopric. Birth, learning, and character alike appeared to qualify him for the post, and there was a general expectation in Dyfed that he would receive it. But at court different ideas prevailed. A little before the death of David, in March, 1176, the archdeacons and canons had formally revived, in the Council of Westminster, the long dormant question of the metropolitan rights of their Church.[126] Their claim was one which Henry, with all his readiness to make concessions to Wales, was not prepared for a moment to entertain, and he had, therefore, no intention of promoting to the see a man who was certain to make it a burning question and who had already shown that he could fight to good purpose. Moreover, Giraldus belonged to that great Pembrokeshire clan whose Irish achievements had aroused his distrust; whatever he might be willing to do for the Welsh, he had no wish to extend the power of the Normans of Dyfed. Thus the canons, who had tried to facilitate the election of the Archdeacon of Brecknock, were sharply brought to book, and at the Council of Winchester, held in August, 1176, required to choose Peter of Lee, prior of the Cluniac cell of Wenlock.[127] The election took place in the royal presence, and on 7th November, Peter was consecrated at Canterbury, having made the usual profession of canonical obedience to the representatives of Archbishop Richard.[128] Thus ended the first struggle of Giraldus for the bishopric of St. David's. His disappointment was great, but his youth—he was not thirty—and the hostility of the king had been greatly to his disadvantage; on a future occasion he might hope to be more fortunate.

During the next few years he led a somewhat restless existence, as though the defeat of his ambitions had left him with no clear purpose or vocation. For a time he went back to Paris, to take up once more the scholar's life;[129] next, he returned to Wales and accepted the post of administrator of the diocese of St. David's for Bishop Peter, who found residence there uncongenial. As was inevitable, quarrels arose; even had there been no question of animus against a successful rival, the fiery and implacable nature of Giraldus made him the worst possible intermediary between bishop and chapter, and accordingly he gave up the position in disgust and turned his eyes in other directions. In February, 1183, he went over to Ireland with his brother Philip,[130] but, greatly as the country engaged his interest, found there no opening to his mind. Not long afterwards he entered the royal service; the king was on the Welsh border in treaty with the Lord Rhys and other Welsh princes,[131] and, possibly on the recommendation of Bishop Baldwin of Worcester,[132] chose the Archdeacon of Brecknock as a suitable agent for business of this kind. In this occupation Giraldus remained much longer than might have been expected; he was for more than ten years a cleric of the court, engaged in various diplomatic and ceremonial missions, involved in a round of duties which kept him immersed in business to his heart's content, kept him, also, well to the front, and, at the same time, allowed him some leisure to cultivate his literary gifts. In 1185 he was sent to Ireland with the king's youngest son, John, in consideration, no doubt, of the prominent position held by his kinsfolk in the island. After a year's stay there he returned to England and began the first of his important literary works, that astonishing compound of shrewd and careful observation, miraculous fable and idle gossip which he called *The Topography of Ireland*.[133]

With the exception of his great struggle for St. David's in the reign of John, the best-known incident in the career of Giraldus is the mission which brought him to Wales in the spring of 1188.[134] The capture of Jerusalem by the Saracens in 1187 had rekindled throughout Europe the crusading spirit; the kings of England and France took the cross, and their example was soon followed by the Archbishop of Canterbury. Baldwin,[135] who had been translated to the primacy from Worcester in 1184, resolved to spend the coming Lent in an effort to raise a body of crusaders from Wales, a country which produced excellent foot-soldiers,[136] and was known for its devotion to religious causes. He chose as his companions Alexander, Archdeacon of Bangor, who interpreted in the Welsh-speaking districts,[137] and Giraldus, as a man familiar with the Norman lordships of South Wales. Baldwin had a second purpose in view, which he successfully accomplished; he wished, by celebrating mass at the high altar of each of the four Welsh cathedrals, to give visible proof of his authority as metropolitan in every quarter of the country.[138] The canons of St. David's saw clearly the danger ahead and tried to persuade the Lord Rhys to obstruct the archbishop's passage in the interests of the independence of their see.[139] But Rhys had, it would seem, no particular zeal for their cause; on the contrary, he smoothed the path of Baldwin in every possible way, met him with all respect and ceremony on his entry into South Wales, entertained him bountifully at his castle of Aberteifi and was all but persuaded to take the cross.[140] What is stranger still is that Giraldus, whose whole life was dedicated, broadly speaking, to the cause of the independence of St. David's, on this occasion was coldly indifferent to it, and, as far as in him lay, was an accomplice of the archbishop in his assertion of the Canterbury claim.

The tour occupied about five weeks, beginning at Hereford in the early part of March[141] and ending at Chester, in time for the celebration of Easter, on 14th April. Most of the time was spent in South Wales; a leisurely progress was made through Radnor, Elfael, Brecknock, Gwent, Gwynllwg, Glamorgan, Gower, Cydweli, and Dyfed. Four days were given to Ceredigion, and there then remained but a week for Gwynedd, which was rapidly traversed by way of Towyn, Nefyn, Bangor, Aberconwy, and Rhuddlan. Powys was left untouched, save for a visit to its outskirts at Oswestry; Bishop Reiner of St. Asaph had already done some work in this district, and Owain Cyfeiliog, alone of all the princes of Wales, was hostile to the primate's mission. Nevertheless, in spite of the pressure of time and other difficulties, the immediate results of the tour were remarkable. Three thousand well-armed warriors, if Giraldus is to be believed, donned the cross,[142] including Maelgwn ap Cadwallon of Maelienydd, Einion ab Einion Clud of Elfael, and a son of the Lord Rhys, named Maelgwn. Occasionally, the mission found itself in an unfriendly environment, as for instance at Bangor, where Bishop Gwion[143] took the cross under coercion and not a single recruit could be won from the "teulu" of Rhodri. Yet, in the main, the preaching of the crusade aroused genuine enthusiasm, and there was substance in the remark of John

Spang, court fool of the Lord Rhys, to his master, preserved, it is needless to say, by Giraldus himself, that, if the archdeacon had been able to preach in Welsh, not a man would have resisted the appeal and remained at home in his service.[144]

In the long run, however, the expedition bore little fruit. The quarrel between Henry and his sons delayed for many months the preparations for the Second Crusade, and when, on the death of his father, Richard took up the matter in earnest and set out for the East, the zeal of very many had grown cold, and, like Giraldus, they found excellent reasons for disregarding their vow. Even the diplomatic victory of Baldwin over the chapter of St. David's was of little avail to his successor, Hubert Walter, when fortune again made Giraldus the protagonist in a conflict on behalf of the rights of the see. The most lasting and valuable result of the tour was the book in which the archdeacon carefully recorded his impressions of it and which appeared in its earliest form in 1191.[145] The *Itinerary of Wales* is of high value for the study of Welsh history at the end of the twelfth century; accurate in its facts, genial in spirit and crowded with a wealth of gay and animated figures which move briskly across the scene, it pictures for us the Wales of Rhys ap Gruffydd, the native home of fierce but devout tribesmen, the adopted home of haughty knights and grasping clerics, with a vividness and force not easily to be matched. In the *Description of Wales* which followed the *Itinerary* in 1194,[146] there is a broader and more philosophical outlook, a completer survey, taken from the Olympian heights of a scholar's lofty seclusion, but in the earlier work Giraldus mingles in the crowd, catches its accents, is borne along by its changing passions, and thus becomes a very mirror of that fighting, chaffering, praying age.

III. WALES IN 1188; CLIMAX OF THE POWER OF RHYS.

The perambulation of Wales by Baldwin and Giraldus in 1188 affords the opportunity of a political survey of the country at this period, and it is especially convenient to be able to make such a survey in this year, the last but one of Henry's long reign, before the disturbance which was brought about by his death. It reveals a Wales very largely in Welsh hands, especially in the north, ruled over, indeed, for the most part, by a large number of chieftains of no great force or ability, but with one towering figure among them in the person of the Lord Rhys.

In Gwynedd there had been no change since 1175. Dafydd and Rhodri still held the bulk of the province, with the Conway as their boundary; Gruffydd ap Cynan was lord of Meirionydd and Ardudwy, his younger brother Maredudd, of Eifionydd.[147] The claim of the Lord Rhys to Meirionydd, though recognised by the king at the Council of Oxford in 1177, had been in the following year so hotly contested by the sons of Cynan[148] that the attempt to make it good and to enlarge Deheubarth in a northerly direction had been abandoned. A young son of Iorwerth ab Owain, named Llywelyn, had just attained his majority and was beginning to make himself troublesome to his uncles, but as yet he gave them no serious concern. Rhodri looked chiefly for support to the Lord Rhys, whose daughter he married;[149] Dafydd relied on the English alliance, and, ruling from his castle of Rhuddlan districts but newly wrested from a long English domination, strove with all his might to keep the peace between the two races.[150]

As the two missioners did not traverse Powys, the political divisions of this province are less clearly traced. But it is evident that Gruffydd ap Madog was still in power in Northern Powys and Owain Cyfeiliog in the south. A conquest of Maelor effected by Earl Hugh of Chester on 13th June, 1177, with the aid of Dafydd,[151] who was returning from the Council of Oxford, was not permanent, and thenceforward the right of the descendants of Madog ap Maredudd to bear rule in this district remained unchallenged. In 1187, a little before the visit of Giraldus, a third prince of Powys, who had long ruled territories midway between those of Gruffydd and Owain, namely, Owain Fychan, had been removed by death; he had perished at Gwern y Figyn, near his castle of Carreg Hofa,[152] in a treacherous night attack made upon him by Gwenwynwyn and Cadwallon, the sons of Owain Cyfeiliog.[153] It was not, however, the southern, but the northern prince, his brother, who chiefly profited by his removal; Gruffydd ap Madog appears in the following year as lord of the country west of Oswestry[154] and Cynllaith would seem to have been vested permanently in his descendants, until it was lost by the most famous of them all, the heroic Owain Glyn Dwr. As a prince, Gruffydd (who died in 1191)[155] was renowned for his profuse liberality;[156] he was also amenable to ecclesiastical influence, for Giraldus records with satisfaction that in 1188 he was persuaded by the archbishop to put away his wife, Angharad, who, as the daughter of Owain Gwynedd, his mother's brother, was his first cousin.[157] Two other sons of Madog ap Maredudd were still alive and possessed of some small share of their father's wide dominions; Owain Brogyntyn was lord of Penllyn and Edeyrnion,[158] and Elise ap Madog of lands in the same region.[159] In Arwystli, the house of Trahaearn ap Caradog had retained its ancient position, and the cantref was not yet absorbed in Powys; on the death of Hywel ab Ieuaf in 1185,[160] he was succeeded by his son Owain, known from one of the hamlets of Arwystli as "Owain o'r Brithdir".[161]

The pages of the *Itinerary* leave us in no doubt as to the continued ascendancy of Rhys ap Gruffydd in Deheubarth. He met the company as they entered South Wales at Radnor, thus asserting his authority over the lords of Elfael and Maelienydd. When they entered the territory under his direct rule, he was waiting to receive them at Aberteifi, and he went with them until at the passage of the Dovey they quitted his dominions. Ceredigion, Cantref Mawr, Cantref Bychan, Emlyn, with other regions in Dyfed, formed his principality, but his influence was felt far beyond this area. The lord of the cantref of Cemais, William fitz Martin, a son or grandson of the founder of St. Dogmael's, notwithstanding his Norman lineage, had deemed it prudent to take a daughter of the great chieftain to wife.[162] Elfael was ruled by Einion ab Einion Clud, also known as Einion o'r Porth, who had succeeded his father in 1177 and was also a son-in-law (or, it may be, a grandson) of the Lord Rhys.[163] A kinsman of Rhys ruled in Maelienydd, where in 1179 Cadwallon ap Madog had been succeeded by his son Maelgwn. Cadwallon's death, it may be remarked, had been the occasion of somewhat unusual measures of vengeance taken by the crown. He had been killed by certain followers of Roger, the heir to the Mortimer estates, as he was returning from the king's presence under the protection of a royal safe-conduct, and accordingly the matter was treated as something far more serious than a mere local feud; some of the offenders were put to death and others forced to seek refuge in the woods, while Roger himself was cast into prison. The incident showed that, where the king's honour was touched, Welshmen might hope for even-handed justice between them and the great ones of the march.[164]

The relentless border feuds, which centuries of reprisals had made incurable, were a great obstacle to the maintenance of peace between Rhys and the king, and constantly bade fair to engage them in a conflict which neither desired. The men of Gwent had never forgotten the massacre of 1175, and, after seven years of waiting, found in 1182 an opportunity of exacting a most ample vengeance. With the kinsfolk of the murdered Seisyll at their head they beset the castle of Abergavenny, the scene of the bloody deed; lurking in the overgrown brushwood of the ditches, they outwearied the vigilance of the constable, broke into the castle at early dawn, and, having gained possession of all save the keep, gave it to the flames.[165] Nor did this content them. A little later they found Ranulf Poer, sheriff of Herefordshire, who had borne a leading part in the ever memorable tragedy, assisting William of Briouze in the building of a fortress at Dingestow on the river Trothy. Their attack, delivered in this case also at dawn, proved irresistible; Ranulf was slain, William with difficulty escaped capture, and, though the arrival of Ranulf Glanville, the justiciar of the realm, with reinforcements restored the balance in favour of the English, the prestige and glory of the day remained with the Welsh.[166]

Another element of difficulty in the relations between the southern leader and the crown was created by the growth of the sons of Rhys into manhood and independence. Of these at least five had attained to maturity in 1188, namely, Gruffydd, Maelgwn, Cynwrig, Hywel Sais, and Rhys. Three of them listened to the preaching of the crusade in Ceredigion, and the tall, lithe figure of the fair-haired Cynwrig, wearing loosely the light costume of the country, seemed to Giraldus the very embodiment of native dignity.[167] It was hardly to be expected that these young men, full of energy and ambition, should quietly fall into the peaceful and cautious ways recommended by a ripe experience to their father. Accordingly, Rhys had laid upon him the burden of reconciling to the king, not only the borderers of Gwent and Morgannwg, but also his own restless offspring, and the task, in spite of goodwill on both sides, was one of no small difficulty. In July, 1184, after two years' absence on the Continent, Henry was at Worcester and was there met by Rhys, who promised the fullest amends for all the misdeeds of his underlings; he would deliver one of his sons, he said, as a hostage for the future tranquillity of the marchland and would bring his turbulent kinsmen to the royal presence to make their peace.[168] A little later he was again with the king at Gloucester, confessing his inability to carry out the terms agreed upon, as to which he had no doubt been overruled by the bolder counsels of the younger generation.[169]

Yet it is clear that Rhys retained the king's confidence to the end of the reign. Peace, rather than war, with Wales was still the royal policy, as it had been since 1170, and in 1186, when a struggle between England and France was believed to be impending, Henry took special pains to secure himself by negotiation against any outbreak of trouble on the Welsh border. Rhys was invited to Hereford to meet Archbishop Baldwin of Canterbury and Ranulf Glanville and was there treated as an honoured guest, whom it was important to gratify and win over.[170] At dinner he was seated between his host, William de Vere, who had just been raised to the see of Hereford, and another magnate of the realm, Walter fitz Robert of Dunmow, both connected with the great family of Clare.[171] How easy and genial were the relations of those who thus sat at the episcopal board may be inferred from the fact that, when the talk turned upon Rhys's possession of what had once been the Clare lordship of Ceredigion, the Welsh prince, with fine courtesy, expressed his pleasure that he had lost his inheritance in those bygone days to no base or laggard clan, but to a family of rare fame and distinction, whereupon the bishop, not to be outdone in graceful compliment, signified that their loss of those Welsh possessions had been made in turn almost acceptable to them by the thought of the noble and valiant prince who now enjoyed them. There was an element of business in these courtesies, for the king desired, not only the friendship and goodwill of Rhys, but also a supply of infantry from Wales for the French war which he expected shortly to be waging.[172]

It remains to speak briefly of the marcher lords who wielded authority in 1188. The earldom of Chester was held by the young Ranulf, who had succeeded his father, Earl Hugh, in 1181;[173] his marriage to Constance, widow of the king's son Geoffrey, added greatly to his importance, but as a French rather than an English potentate, and thus strengthened the growing tendency of this house to find the satisfaction of their ambition elsewhere than on the Welsh border. Mold was still held by the barons of Montalt, hereditary stewards of the Earls of Chester.[174] Ellesmere was in the hands of Dafydd ab Owain,[175] whose position thus made him an intermediary between the English and the Welsh. At Oswestry, the William fitz Alan of the days of Stephen had been followed by a second baron of that name, who also inherited from his mother, Isabella of Sai, the lordship of Clun.[176] Montgomery was not yet a royal fortress, but remained a fief of the house of Bollers, established there since the reign of Henry I.[177] Roger Mortimer, first of the many lords of Wigmore who bore that famous name, was supreme on the borders of Maelienydd. Brecknock, Builth, Radnor, and Upper Gwent formed the ample domain of William of Briouze or, as we may now style him with the English chroniclers, William de Breos. The events which placed William in this exalted position and made him the leading personage in South Wales on the English side at the close of the twelfth century have already been narrated;[178] it suffices to add that he was a typical Norman baron, as scrupulous in his attention to the forms of religion as he was ruthless and grasping in his dealings with his fellow-men. The author of the massacre of Abergavenny would not pass a church or a wayside cross without stopping in his talk to offer up a prayer, and he would speak to children in the street for the mere satisfaction of hearing them answer his greetings with the conventional words of blessing.[179]

The two great lordships of the southern coast were at this time in the custody of the crown, having both passed to heiresses who had not yet been provided with husbands. Earl Richard of Pembroke and Striguil, the conqueror of Leinster, had closed an adventurous career at Dublin in the summer of 1176, leaving his great possessions in England, Wales, Ireland, and Normandy to an infant daughter of three.[180] It was not until July, 1189, that Richard I., in fulfilment of a promise made by his father, bestowed the hand of Isabella upon that pattern of loyal knighthood, William Marshall, a famous crusader and a companion of Henry's last hours, so that thus there came to be once more an Earl of Pembroke and lord of Nether Went.[181] In like manner the lordship of Glamorgan and Gwynllwg was vested in a woman. The only son of Earl William of Gloucester had died in 1166;[182] three daughters were left to him, but from about 1176 it seems to have been understood that the youngest, Avice or Hawise, was to carry the inheritance by marriage to the king's son John.[183] The earl died in 1183;[184] nevertheless the marriage had not taken place when Henry died six years later, and meanwhile Glamorgan had been administered by officials of the crown. It was no easy task which fell upon their shoulders; in 1185 they had to cope with a great Welsh rising, in the course of which the towns of Cardiff and Kenfig were burnt and the castle of Neath was so closely beset that it was necessary to send a force of knights by sea to its relief.[185] The royal accounts further show that much money was expended in the maintenance of the fabric and the garrison of the castles of Newport, Rhymni, and Newcastle.[186] It is not apparent who led the insurgents, but Morgan ap Caradog ab Iestyn, who was lord of Rhwng Nedd ac Afan in 1188,[187] was most probably a prime mover in the affair, if one may judge from the critical position to which the castle of Neath was reduced. Hywel ab Iorwerth, now lord of Caerleon, gave his support to the English,[188] in pursuance of a policy of moderation which he seems to have consistently followed since the Council of Gloucester.[189]

It will thus appear, on a broad survey of the situation, that the Lord Rhys was at the close of this reign in a position of assured pre-eminence. His friendship with the king secured him from any attack on the part of the English government, and there was no marcher lord who could injure him, save perhaps William de Breos. Little wonder, then, that he encouraged his warriors to volunteer for the holy war in the East, and even seriously contemplated going on crusade himself.[190] At the age of fifty-six, with grown-up sons able to defend the liberties of Deheubarth, he might well suppose that he had completed his full tale of domestic warfare, and might now dedicate his battle-worn sword to the service of the Most High. Fate willed it otherwise; his wife dissuaded him from his pious intention, and his long life ended in a red and fiery sundown, in the midst of renewed civil conflicts and of struggles against the English such as those which had so busily employed his youth and early manhood.

CHAPTER VI

THE CLOSE OF THE TWELFTH CENTURY

I. OLD AND NEW LEADERS.

THE death of Henry II.[1] marks an epoch in the relations between England and Wales as surely as that of Henry I. In 1189, as in 1135, the removal of the strong hand led at once to disturbances across the border, and the want of effective control over Wales was almost as marked under Richard I. as under Stephen. It is true that the second Henry had maintained the peace rather by skilful diplomacy than by naked force, and that his son was not without real strength of character, so that the parallel is far from complete. But Richard's devotion to the crusade and to other interests remote from his duties as an English king had the same practical effect as the nerveless and vacillating rule of Stephen; Wales was again involved in turmoil and strife, war against the foreigner leading up to civil discord, as the various popular leaders jostled each other in the endeavour to prove themselves appointed of God to the headship of the Welsh race. The first in the field was, naturally, the Lord Rhys, who had been unquestioned leader for twenty years, and who now, like a seasoned war horse, smelling the battle afar off, boldly threw himself into the struggle. It was, however, only for a short time; death at last claimed his due from the hoary warrior, and the bitter feuds of his sons soon deprived Deheubarth of the predominant position it had enjoyed under his sagacious rule. Powys, under the young Gwenwynwyn, and Gwynedd, under the still younger Llywelyn ab Iorwerth, were the real rivals for supremacy, and the contest between them, ending in a complete victory for Llywelyn, is the salient feature of the new Wales ushered in by the thirteenth century.

Tumult always marked the interval between the lapse of royal authority through the death of a king and its revival when the heir was properly invested by coronation with the royal power, and among the measures taken by Richard and his advisers in July, 1189, to tide over this difficult period was the despatch of a special envoy to Wales, where trouble was particularly to be feared. At the suggestion of Archbishop Baldwin, Giraldus Cambrensis, who was then with the court in Normandy, was sent across the Channel to use his influence as peacemaker along the border.[2] When he arrived, after adventures which included the threatened loss of his way-money, his official papers, and—most important of all (he tells us)—his one copy of the as yet unpublished *Itinerary*,[3] war had already broken out. The Lord Rhys had shown that he recognised no obligation to the new ruler by a great raid upon the foreign colonies in South Wales. Rhos, Penfro, Gower, and Carnwyllion were overrun; the castles of Laugharne and Llanstephan were taken in the first wild onslaught, their garrisons offering no resistance, though the inexperience of the Welsh in castle-guard led to the loss of both fortresses later on; and the royal stronghold of Carmarthen was closely besieged.[4] If we may believe Giraldus, he did something to calm the storm which had arisen,[5] but he was not able to exercise much control over Rhys, who maintained his attitude of hostility. When Richard landed in England in the middle of August, he had some thoughts of marching immediately into Wales to chastise the audacious folk who thus boldly challenged his authority, but he was persuaded that the matter did not call for his personal intervention, and that Welsh affairs might well stand over until after the coronation.[6] The presence of Bishop Gwion of Bangor and Bishop Reiner of St. Asaph at this ceremony,[7] which was held on 3rd September, may be taken to show that Rhodri and Dafydd did not join in the revolt. As soon as the crowning had been accomplished, the new king sent his brother John to the West with an army capable of dealing with the rising, but the expedition led to no great change in the situation. Notwithstanding that John, by his marriage to Hawise of Gloucester on 29th August, had become lord of Glamorgan,[8] with a considerable stake in the Welsh border, he was more concerned to establish his position in England, in view of the early departure of his brother for the East, and his policy, therefore, was to make peace as speedily as might be and return to the centre of affairs. The minor princes met him at Worcester and made their submission;[9] he induced Rhys to abandon the siege of Carmarthen and accompany him to Oxford to meet the king, but it was in no suppliant mood, for the Welsh leader no sooner found that it was not Richard's intention to make a special journey west for the purpose of receiving his homage than he resolved upon an immediate return to Wales.[10] Thus the king and Rhys were still unreconciled when in December the former set out for the Holy Land.

A chronicler who tells of the indignant withdrawal of Rhys assigns as the reason the departure from the custom of the previous reign. Richard would not come to meet him, "as the king his father had been wont to do".[11] A new era had in fact set in, as was shown by the conduct of both sides. The English government was at no pains to conciliate; the Welsh put themselves under no restraint. As soon as Richard had quitted England, the Lord Rhys entered upon a prolonged campaign against the Norman castles of South Wales, in which he was remarkably successful. Before the end of the year he was master of the castle of St. dear's, which he gave with the surrounding district to his son, Hywel Sais.[12] In 1190 he strengthened his hold upon the region of Cydweli, which he had already taken from its Norman lord, William of London, by rebuilding the ruined fortress which was its centre.[13] Next year he attacked Nanhyfer, the principal castle of Cemais, which was held by his son-in-law, William fitz Martin, and, having captured it, made it over to his son Gruffydd.[14] In 1192 the special object of attack was Llawhaden, the residence of Bishop Peter of St. David's; it was taken by Gruffydd, and the way was thus thrown open for further incursions into Deugleddyf. A long siege was laid to the castle of Swansea; the fall of this fortress was almost brought about by famine, and would have given to the Welsh the whole commote of Gower, but discord arose among the sons of Rhys, and, after the loss of a number of his men by drowning, he retired from the enterprise. Nevertheless, the good fortune of his house did not desert him, and in 1193 yet another castle fell into Welsh hands. Hywel Sais surprised Wiston and with it its lord, Philip fitz Wizo,[15] with his family, thus adding Deugleddyf to the regions conquered from the foreigner. So rapidly and unexpectedly had the Welsh policy of general aggression borne fruit that the victors were now beginning to be embarrassed by their success; they had taken more castles than they could defend, and, as a measure of precaution, Hywel and Maelgwn destroyed Llawhaden, exposing themselves to a counter-attack within the broken defences in which their men severely suffered.

While thus successful against the foe, the house of Deheubarth was far from being a united and harmonious whole. It was divided against itself in flagrant hate and hostility. Two parties appear to have arisen among the sons of the Lord Rhys, due, perhaps, to the inferiority of certain of their number in birth and privilege. Gruffydd was evidently designed to be his father's heir; already in 1189 he was married to Matilda, daughter of William de Breos,[16] and upon the death of Rhys his claim to Dinefwr and the headship of Deheubarth was conceded. With him usually acted Rhys, distinguished from his father as "Rhys Fychan" (the Less), or, more commonly, "Rhys Gryg" (the Hoarse).[17] Maelgwn, on the other hand, was Gruffydd's bitter enemy,[18] and, as he was a man of courage and enterprise, having distinguished himself as early as 1187 by a successful raid upon Tenby,[19] the jealousy and enmity of the two perturbed the whole of South Wales. The struggle was partly one between the craft and cunning of the established royal favourite[20] and the boldness and dash of the popular hero; it was also in some measure a reflection of local feeling, for Maelgwn's home and the chief source of his support was Ceredigion,[21] while Gruffydd was strong in Ystrad Tywi. With the darling of the West, who, it may be observed in passing, was very far from being a Saul in stature,[22] went Hywel Sais, concerned chiefly in the affairs of Dyfed; the tall and handsome Cynwrig, singled out as a young man by Giraldus Cambrensis for special admiration,[23] played no part in the political strife of his day and carried his goodly presence to the grave without having in any way disturbed the tenor of his long life of dignified inaction.[24]

The contest began in 1189, when the Lord Rhys was persuaded to imprison Maelgwn, who had withdrawn from his crusading vow of the previous year, as a dangerous adventurer. The influences at work are readily discerned; it was Rhys Gryg who had made the suggestion and Maelgwn was sent to Dinefwr, where he was in the power of his rival Gruffydd. Fearful lest his father should relent the harsh treatment he had meted out to a not ignoble son, Gruffydd secured himself still further by handing the prisoner over to William de Breos, who was not likely to set a Welsh chief at liberty save for a substantial consideration. The captivity lasted until 1192, when the Lord Rhys succeeded in getting Maelgwn away from his prison in Brycheiniog;[25] the released prisoner joined in the siege of Swansea in that year, but, as may be supposed, the ill-feeling between him and Gruffydd was acute, and it has already been noticed as an important factor in the failure of the operations. In 1193 Maelgwn and Hywel Sais were working together in the defence of Welsh interests in Deugleddyf, but the year did not close without an act of civil war; on Christmas night the household troops of Maelgwn attacked with catapults and took by assault the castle of Ystrad Meurig, belonging either to the Lord Rhys or to one of his sons. The climax of this family bickering came in 1194, when, in a conflict between Hywel and Maelgwn and their father, the latter was defeated and captured, to find a prison in that castle of Nanhyfer, now held by Maelgwn, of which three years previously Rhys had deprived William fitz Martin.[26]

Meanwhile, the English government was in no position to intervene. During the absence of Richard on crusade and his subsequent imprisonment in Germany,[27] John was making as difficult as possible the task of those who wielded the royal authority at home, and the two parties thus formed were much more anxious to use the Welsh for their own interests than to repress and subdue them. It was, no doubt, made a charge against Roger Mortimer in 1191 that he was in league with the Welsh against the crown, but this was a mere party accusation, put forward by the justiciar, William Longchamp, to justify his banishment of this powerful marcher baron and his seizure of Wigmore and other castles.[28] When John, a little later in the year, was preparing to bring thousands of his Welsh tenants to a conference at Winchester, as a protection against possible treachery, the justiciar had no.scruple in hiring other Welshmen at the royal cost, so that in case of an encounter hillman might meet hillman and the battle be fought on something like equal terms.[29] Under his successor, the Archbishop of Rouen, the situation was hardly different; John had Welshmen at his back in the movement of 1193–4,[30] and the business which at this time often took Giraldus to Wales, as he tells us, in the service of the queen-mother and the justiciar was clearly to conciliate Rhys and prevent his throwing his weight into the scale in favour of the opposite party.[31]

When Richard was at last released by the emperor and appeared once more in England, it might have been expected that vigorous measures would have been taken by him to deal with the situation in Wales. But there is no evidence that it gave him any concern. He spent a couple of months in the island, was solemnly re-crowned, and then passed to the Continent, where he spent the remaining five years of his reign.[32] The greater energy which was undoubtedly shown by the English in their dealings with Wales during this period is to be attributed, not to him, but to the new justiciar. Hubert Walter succeeded to this office at the end of 1193, and, being already Archbishop of Canterbury, was able to exercise the powers both of church and state, in the king's absence, with decisive authority. He had been trained in business by Ranulf Glanville, and it was, therefore, a maxim for him that the Welsh must be kept under vigilant observation and control. Though he did not intervene in person in Wales until 1196, his influence may, perhaps, be traced in the bolder front shown by the foreigners in 1195, which made it a year of reaction and disaster for the men of Deheubarth. Roger Mortimer, returned from his exile, attacked Maelienydd and rebuilt the castle of Cymaron. On Whit Sunday a Flemish army recaptured Wiston and thus restored Deugleddyf to its former owners. Finally, William de Breos, now high in the confidence of the government and employed as sheriff and as travelling justice,[33] stormed St. dear's and captured within it a large number of the most trusty followers of Hywel Sais. So alarmed was Hywel at these reverses that he destroyed the fortifications of Nanhyfer, lest this castle also should slip from his hands and the enemy thus be enabled to reconquer Cemais.

It cannot be doubted that the continuance of domestic strife, no less than the greater vigour on the English side, was responsible for the arrest of the flowing current of Welsh success. The Lord Rhys had not long remained a prisoner in Nanhyfer; Hywel Sais, with a keener sense of filial duty than his brother, had released him in despite of Maelgwn. But in 1195 the old man had to face another conspiracy of the same type. Rhys Gryg, with a younger brother Maredudd, who was just emerging from boyhood,[34] entered into a secret understanding with the men of Cantref Mawr and Cantref Bychan and thereby obtained possession of Dinefwr and Llanymddyfri. This plain intimation that he was regarded as an extinct force, playing an idle part on a stage where he had outstayed his welcome, following as it did upon the ignominy of imprisonment, would seem to have spurred the Lord Rhys to one last effort, in which he showed all the fiery enthusiasm and reckless daring of his prime. The flame which had been burning low, flickering and visibly sinking into the grey dulness of ashes, suddenly blazed forth in one blinding sheet of light, ere it vanished for ever in the dying embers. By the exercise of stratagem, he laid hold of the two conspirators and imprisoned them in Ystrad Meurig Castle,[35] in a land where, it may be presumed, they had no following. Then, in the ensuing year, he unfurled his banner as of yore for a great campaign against the English, which would show that his eye was not dim nor his natural force abated. First, he attacked Carmarthen, the centre of royal power in South Wales, and burnt the whole town to the ground, leaving only the castle standing. Next, he gathered around him a great host from all parts of the South, and, crossing the highlands of

Builth, appeared before the castle of Colwyn, the principal fortress of Upper Elfael, a district which had been seized by William de Breos. It was taken and burnt—a triumph which emboldened Rhys to attempt still greater achievements. Pouring across the heights of Radnor Forest, his exultant army fell upon the border stronghold of Radnor itself, held by the house of Breos since the days of William Rufus. Its lord was at this time in the opposite quarter of South Wales, but two of his neighbours, Roger Mortimer of Wigmore and Hugh de Say of Richard's Castle,[36] brought their men into the field in its defence. They were utterly defeated by the victorious Rhys; forty of their knights and a multitude of foot-soldiers were cut down by the Welsh, and, after setting fire to the town, the invading host turned aside to a new field of activity, the castle lately erected by William de Breos in Lower Elfael. Here Rhys was no less successful than before; his catapults and siege engines forced the garrison to surrender, and Painscastle would have been razed to the foundations had not William at this juncture offered terms which the Welsh leader thought it prudent to accept. Their nature is not known, but they were no doubt connected with the counter-operations of William in Dyfed, in the course of which a good part of the town of Aberteifi had been destroyed.

Rhys had now fought his last fight, for on 28th April, 1197,[37] he died. At the age of sixty-five[38] his work as a warrior was done, and the stirring deeds of his last heroic effort at leadership were not likely to be repeated. His name will live in Welsh history as that of the greatest of the princes of Deheubarth, whose long and persistent struggle against the Anglo-Norman power was the chief means of keeping alive in South Wales the idea of Welsh nationality and independence. In the North, the Welsh principalities had now attained such a position that the continuance of Welsh institutions and traditions seemed fairly well assured; in the South, they maintained themselves with difficulty against large and powerful foreign colonies. Rhys was throughout his life the centre and rallying-point of the southern national resistance; while never the mere barbarian, bent on sheer destruction, insensible to the claims of an advancing civilisation, he was always the firm and immovable patriot. He was buried in St. David's cathedral;[39] owing to a quarrel with Bishop Peter, he was at the time of his death under excommunication, but this difficulty was overcome by the infliction of penitential discipline upon the unheeding corpse,[40] and Rhys at last rested worthily in the historic fane which was for him, as for his fathers, the holiest in all Wales.

The removal of Rhys, who had so long dominated Welsh life, was the opportunity of the princes of the younger generation who aspired to leadership, and it was for some years an open question which quarter of Wales would furnish his successor as head and champion of the Welsh race. Neither Gwynedd nor Deheubarth, as it chanced, supplied the first candidate for the position, but that region of Southern Powys hitherto remarkable for the strictly local and provincial temper of its patriotism. The cool, sagacious Owain Cyfeiliog, almost always in prudent alliance with the English, was succeeded by the fiery and headstrong leader of revolt, Gwenwynwyn. Owain would seem to have thrown off the cares of rule about 1195 and to have retired to the monastic peace of Ystrad Marchell—a Cistercian abbey of his own foundation—where he died and was buried in 1197.[41] The accession of Gwenwynwyn to power was immediately followed by attacks upon the English border, which were so formidable as in September, 1196, to bring the justiciar, Archbishop Hubert, upon the scene.[42] A considerable army laid siege to Gwenwynwyn's castle of Trallwng, known to the English as Pool,[43] and, after vain efforts to scale the walls, obtained an entrance by undermining them. With a clemency which was unusual on the border, the justiciar allowed the garrison to depart with the honours of war. But he lost nothing by his humanity, for before the end of the year Gwenwynwyn had recovered possession of his castle, and it was now his turn to show magnanimity and allow the foe to retire unscathed in battle array.

Having proved his ability to hold his own against the English, Gwenwynwyn next undertook the extension of his borders. It is remarkable that from the first he harboured no designs against his kinsmen in Northern Powys, but ever looked southward, his ambition being to reclaim for Powys her old predominance in Central Wales. On the death of Gruffydd Maelor in 1191, he had been succeeded by his sons, Madog and Owain;[44] the death of the latter in 1197 vested the whole of Northern Powys in Madog, who thereby became ruler of Welsh and English Maelor, Ial, Nanheudwy and Cynllaith.[45] It was thus that the twofold division of the province into Powys Fadog and Powys Wenwynwyn came about, the Rhaeadr and the Tanat forming the boundary,[46] and this division the southern prince, restless and enterprising as he was, made no attempt to disturb. He chose rather to attack Arwystli, which had for ages been within Powys, but not of it, ruled by a separate dynasty and a different ecclesiastical authority. Here his opportunity seems to have been afforded by the death in 1197 of the native chieftain, Owain o'r Brithdir;[47] he attached the cantref to his own dominions and thus brought its political isolation to an end, though it remained for centuries a part of the diocese of Bangor. In the same year, he found means to intervene, to his own profit, in the affairs of Deheubarth, which had been thrown into great confusion by the death of the Lord Rhys. After an interview with Archbishop Hubert on the borders, Gruffydd, the designated heir, had been recognised as his father's successor,[48] but had at once been confronted by the ever jealous Maelgwn, who had latterly been in banishment, but now appeared in Ceredigion to claim a share of the inheritance. Gwenwynwyn supplied the exile with troops and he was thus enabled to take the town and castle of Aberystwyth; what was even more gratifying to Maelgwn was that Gruffydd himself fell into his hands, whom with all haste he made over to his friend and patron in acknowledgment of his obligations. The prince of Powys had not only a dangerous neighbour and rival in his possession; he had a pawn which he could use in negotiations with the government, and the result was that ere long Gwenwynwyn received the border castle of Carreg Hofa from the English,[49] while Gruffydd found a prison in Corfe.[50]

By these early successes the prince of Powys was led to dream of still greater conquests. He aspired, the *Chronicle of the Princes* tells us, "to restore to the Welsh their ancient and due rights, possessions, and boundaries".[51] He entered upon a scheme of reconquest from the barons of the march. During the preceding ten years matters had, on the whole, gone badly with the Welsh in the region between Wye and Severn. In Maelienydd the seizure of the castle of Cymaron had deprived the sons of Cadwallon, Maelgwn, and Hywel, of a substantial part of their inheritance,[52] and the death of Maelgwn in 1197 was a further blow to Welsh power in this district.[53] In Elfael the way had been opened for the invader by the death of Einion o'r Porth in 1191;[54] William de Breos had thereupon taken possession of the cantref, in the two commotes of which he built two castles, one in the valley of the Colwyn for Upper Elfael, and another, styled by the Welsh Castell Paen, or "Payn's Castle," in the valley of the Machawy for Lower Elfael.[55] The latter was known to the English as "Castrum Matildis" or Castle Maud, no doubt because it had been stoutly defended against a Welsh attack in 1195 by Maud of St. Valery, the Amazonian wife of its builder and lord.[56] Now, although the Lord Rhys had destroyed the castle of Colwyn in his great raid of 1196, Painscastle had been restored by him intact to its master and still enabled William to link together his lands at Radnor and

Brecon. Gwenwynwyn singled it out as the most dangerous to the Welsh of the late encroachments upon their liberty, and in July, 1198, beset it with a great army, in which were very many of the men of Gwynedd, willing allies in this patriotic enterprise.[57] The gravity of the crisis was recognised by the English government, and Gruffydd ap Rhys was released from captivity and sent to the border to treat with his fellow-countrymen. But his mediation was of no avail, and Geoffrey fitz Peter, who had newly succeeded Archbishop Hubert as justiciar,[58] saw that nothing could save Painscastle and Elfael for the English but a victory in the open field. On 13th August[59] he attacked the Welsh host, which was marshalled in three divisions, one of infantry, one of cavalry, and one mixed, and at the first onset scattered it in flight. Many thousands of Gwenwynwyn's followers were slain, while the English boasted that they had scarcely lost a man. A decisive triumph was won for English ascendancy in Mid Wales, and the Prince of Powys saw the prize for which he had fought, the leadership of the Welsh people, pass beyond redemption from his grasp. It was reserved for the hands of the more wary and cautious Llywelyn of Gwynedd.

II. THE RISE OF LLYWELYN AB IORWERTH.

The only son of Iorwerth Drwyndwn, lord of Nant Conwy,[60] was born in the early part of 1173.[61] His mother was Margaret, daughter of Madog ap Maredudd,[62] and there is good reason for thinking that his father died while he was but an infant, and that he was taken for safety from his first home at Dolwyddelan[63] or its neighbourhood to his mother's land of Powys, where, as he grew from childhood into youth, he learnt that he had rights of inheritance of which he was being defrauded. In later years, when he had triumphed over all his rivals, his success was regarded by some as a Divine vindication of legitimacy, as expounded by the Church,[64] for Iorwerth was not the offspring of that marriage with Christina which the Church had so persistently condemned,[65] but of an earlier union with Gwladus, daughter of Llywarch ap Trahaearn of Arwystli.[66] It is not to be supposed, however, that considerations of this kind weighed much with the Welsh, whose ordinary law of inheritance took no count of the status of the mother of an heir,[67] and the young Llywelyn owed the lofty position which he attained to no other cause than his own fortitude and courage, which made light of difficulties that might have been for ever the prison of a less heroic soul.

The young prince had no sooner reached his majority at the age of fourteen than he began, probably with the aid of his mother's kinsfolk, to assert his claim to a share of Gwynedd. When Giraldus was passing through North Wales in 1188, he had already begun to harass his uncles, David and Rhodri, who between them held most of their father's realm.[68] The steps by which he rose to the height of his ambition and made himself chief ruler of Gwynedd are not easy to trace, but it is clear that in 1194 he took a long stride towards his goal. For some years previously there had been quarrels between Rhodri and his southern neighbours, the sons of Cynan. About 1190 the latter had driven Rhodri out of Anglesey,[69] whereupon he had sought the help of Reginald, king of Man, marrying his daughter as a pledge of alliance, and in 1193 he had with the aid of a Manx contingent expelled his rivals and again possessed himself of Aberffraw.[70] Thus passed the "Gaelic Summer," so called, no doubt, because of the influx of Gaelic-speaking allies from Man into Gwynedd;[71] before the year was out their work had been undone, and the sons of Cynan had again ejected Rhodri. It is in the following year that Llywelyn first appears on the stage of history. What is certain is that he had the friendly aid of Gruffydd and Maredudd ap Cynan, and that together they defeated David in a fiercely contested battle fought at the mouth of the Conway.[72] The poets are loud in their praise of the valour of Llywelyn on this day. "Many were the foes of my lord," sings Cynddelw, "but there fell of them in the fight seven times the number of the stars." Prydydd y Moch marks his early appearance in the warrior's garb —"at ten," he says with poetical exaggeration, "he was the bold darling of fortune — the terrible Llywelyn". What is obscure is the part played by Rhodri in the upheaval of this year; did he return from exile to join in the general movement against David or was he David's ally and involved in the ruin which befell his brother? After the victory of Aberconwy, Llywelyn won fresh triumphs at the passage of the Menai at Porthaethwy, where, says his poet with bated breath,

> Over the sounding surge we rode our steeds as they swam,

and again at Coedaneu, in the heart of Anglesey, but there is no clear indication of the foes whom he fought, and the story of his achievements, romantic as it certainly was, can only be told, therefore, in the barest outline.

Whether victory or defeat was his portion, Rhodri did not long survive it, for he died in 1195.[73] The political situation in Gwynedd during the ensuing five years is tolerably clear. Gruffydd, the elder of the two sons of Cynan, bore rule in Anglesey, Arfon, Arllechwedd and Lleyn, and thus excluded Llywelyn for the time being from the older Gwynedd and the ancestral seat of power at Aberffraw.[74] The younger brother, Maredudd, no doubt received Meirionydd and lands to the north as his share of the spoils of victory. Llywelyn's portion was east of the Conway, where David had formerly held sway; he had as neighbours his kinsmen the princes of Northern Powys. David had not at first been entirely dispossessed; three castles, no doubt on the English border, had been left to him, to enable him to play, though with sadly diminished state, the part of a prince.[75] In 1197, however, he was captured by Llywelyn,[76] and the rest of his days he spent in England, living with his wife, the royal Emma, and their son Owain in the manors of Ellesmere and Halesowen they had received from Henry II.[77]

Llywelyn was now fairly started upon his long and triumphant career. His first intervention in the border warfare between English and Welsh was unhappy; he sent a large number of his men to the assistance of Gwenwynwyn in the campaign of 1198 and very many of them fell at Painscastle.[78] But when he took action on his own account, there was a different tale to tell; on 6th January, 1199, he captured the castle of Mold,[79] which protected Hawarden and Chester from the onslaughts of the Welsh and was the seat of the seneschal of the earldom, Robert of Montalt.[80] The achievement recalled the glories of Owain Gwynedd,[81] and promised a speedy return of the days when Gwynedd took the foremost place in Wales. Llywelyn had still much to do to win for himself the proud position of his grandfather, but his power began to be felt from that winter day when, as Cynddelw rapturously sang, "Alun ran red" with the blood of the foes of the "terror and torment of England".[82]

III. THE MONASTIC REVIVAL.

(The early history of the Cistercians in England is told by Miss Cooke in the Eng. Hist. Rev. vol. viii. (1893), pp. 625–76. I have also made use of Janauschek, Origines Cistercienses, tom. i (Vienna, 1877), Dugdale's Monasticon. (new ed.), Birch's History of Margam Abbey, and dark's collection of Glamorganshire charters.)

While the process of the years was thus altering the political aspect of Wales, making the older heroic names but a memory and bringing new protagonists upon the stage, a change had also, silent and scarce perceived, come over the face of Welsh religion. The monastery was restored to its ancient place in Welsh religious life. In a former chapter[83] it was shown how the Norman conquest of South Wales was accompanied by the foundation of new monastic houses, Benedictine, Tironian, and Augustinian. But these houses were, without exception, founded by the invading race and added to the strength of the alien element in the land; castle and priory went closely together in a partnership not easily sundered. Some of the cells were small and merely served to collect from the neighbourhood dues which were sent to a rich abbey in England or in France.[84] Towards the end of the twelfth century all this came to be changed, and the principal agency at work was the influence of the monastic order of Citeaux.

Wales was not without monastic traditions; its monasteries had, indeed, been at one time famous, nor were the vestiges of that day entirely extinct. The ordinary "clas," or mother church, had, no doubt, lost much of its monastic character, but in such communities as those of Priestholm and Beddgelert the ideals of celibacy and retirement from the world were in a measure retained.[85] Asceticism was, however, represented for the ordinary Welshman of those days rather by the hermit or anchorite than by the monk. One may gather from the story of Caradog of Rhos how great the reverence with which this type of religious devotee was still regarded.[86] Caradog, a noble youth of Brycheiniog, well trained in many arts and, among them, in the playing of the harp, was a favourite courtier of Rhys ap Tewdwr.[87] But he was unlucky enough to lose two of his master's most valuable dogs[88] and the anger of Rhys drove him in disgust from the court, to seek admission into the clerical order at the hands of Bishop Herwald of Llandaff. From the first Caradog set the solitary life before him as his goal and he soon passed from Llandaff to the neglected shrine of St. Cenydd in Gower, which, when he had cleared it of bush and bramble, became his first oratory.[89] His next residence was at St. David's, where he was ordained priest; ever bent on seclusion, he withdrew ere long to the peninsula of Barry, on the coast of Pebidiog,[90] until the persistent attacks of the sea-rovers forced him to retire to a more sheltered home. About 1105 he settled in Rhos, probably at Haroldston, near Haverfordwest,[91] and here spent the remainder of his days. The Flemings, sent to this district as colonists by Henry I., tried to dislodge him, but in vain; he suffered much from the hostility also of Tancard, the castellan of Haverford,[92] but held his ground until his death on 13th April, 1124.[93] The learning of Caradog Fynach was renowned throughout Wales,[94] and so great was the repute of his sanctity that Tancard, for all his enmity, would not suffer the good man's corpse to be taken for burial to St. David's, lest relics of such virtue should be lost to the neighbourhood, and portents were needed to induce him to relax his hold. Caradog was finally buried in the north transept of the cathedral,[95] and seventy years later, when Giraldus Cambrensis wished to press upon the pope the claim to canonisation of a denizen of Dyfed, he could think of no worthier name to put forward than that of the hermit of Rhos.[96]

Such, then, was the type of holiness which appealed to the religious instinct of Welshmen at the end of the reign of Henry I.—a solitary warfare with the evil one, drawing no support from a common monastic life.[97] Nor was there any great change in this respect during the next thirty years, although the forces were slowly gathering which were to reconvert the Welsh to a belief in monasticism. The houses founded in the reign of Stephen, even those which were the result of the new Cistercian movement, were in their origin of the familiar alien type, foreign communities planted on the soil by the strong hand of the conqueror, and only Welsh in the source from which they drew their revenues. In 1141 Maurice of London, lord of Ogmore and Kidwelly, gave to St. Peter's, Gloucester, certain churches near the river Ewenny, with the result that the priory of that name was founded as a cell of the great western abbey.[98] A noble church was built on the spot, which still stands in its massive Norman strength, but the house was always small and overshadowed by its greater neighbours.[99] On 16th September, 1140, a community was formed which furnished Wales with its first Cistercian monastery.[100] An offshoot of the great abbey of Clairvaux, where St. Bernard was then at the zenith of his fame, its early history is obscure, but it is known that in 1144 it found a temporary home at Little Trefgarn, near Haverfordwest, where Bishop Bernard settled it on land belonging to the see of St. David's.[101] Some years later, probably in 1151,[102] it moved to the neighbourhood of Y Ty Gwyn ar Daf (The White House on the Taf), where Hywel the Good had held his famous council;[103] the abbey was not built on the banks of the Taf, but a mile away, on the river Gronw, and its true name is Blanchland, Whitland, or Alba Landa, "the White Moor".[104] The site was given, with other lands in the district, by one John of Torrington,[105] and it is sufficiently clear that, though this convent became the mother-house of all Cistercian foundations of Welsh origin, it owed its birth to no impulse of native devotion, but to the ordinary zeal of the foreigner for foreign conventual forms. If one could believe that the second Welsh Cistercian abbey, a colony of

Whitland, was actually established at Cwm Hir in Maelienydd as early as 1143 by one Maredudd ap Maelgwn,[106] an exception would have to be admitted to the general trend of affairs at the time; Maredudd, however, is otherwise unknown as a prince of this region,[107] and in any case the early foundation was an abortive one, the true birth-year of the abbey being that of its re-foundation in 1176.[108] The year 1147 saw a great accession to the strength of the Cistercian order in Wales; by the absorption of the order of Savigny, Neath and Basingwerk were transferred to it,[109] and in the same year Earl Robert of Gloucester founded Margam, soon to become one of the most famous seats of religion in Britain.[110] But even yet it could hardly be said that the movement had gained any hold upon the Welsh people.

Time, however, was all that was needed to enable the Cistercian ideal to win the affection of a folk for whom it had a natural affinity. It was gradually borne in upon the Welsh that these monks were of a very different type from the easy, luxurious Benedictines, comfortably quartered under the shadow of protecting castle walls, who had hitherto been in Wales the sole representatives of their class. "Our houses shall not be built," ran an early rule of the Cistercian order, "near cities, castles or villages, but in places far removed from the concourse of men."[111] No description could be truer of Blanchland, which Leland in the sixteenth century saw "standing in a vast wood as in a wilderness,"[112] or of Cwm Hir, hidden in a mountain glen in Maelienydd. These monks of Clairvaux, if strangers, were no allies of the Norman or Breton conqueror; they came from distant Champagne and sought the solitudes of Wales, not as auxiliaries of baronial power, but in order to save their own souls. Nor was it merely in their choice of a place to dwell in that the Cistercian brethren showed themselves to be unlike the monks with whom Welshmen had hitherto been familiar. Their distinguishing mark was a rigorous and exacting self-denial, a resolute return to the austerity of primitive times and a noble scorn of all compromise with the world.[113] At every point their system was a protest against the laxity which had crept into the monastic fold. They wore simple garments of undyed wool, and thus were "white monks" as distinguished from the "black monks" of the older pattern. They were abstemious in diet, eating no meat at any time and fasting for a great part of the year. Their churches were plain and unadorned, and at first they were loth to take tithes or other endowments of the kind and desired to live by the labour of their own hands. In all these respects the Cistercian practice was a return from degenerate Benedictine ways to the simplicity of the early ascetics, and as such it made a strong appeal to men who had not forgotten the traditions of Celtic monasticism in the days of its primal earnestness and warmth. The Cistercian abbot was a St. David or a St. Teilo restored to life.

It was soon after their great victory of 1165 that the Welsh began to regard the new movement with a kindly eye, and the evidence goes to show that the change of attitude was very largely due to the enlightened policy of the Lord Rhys. It is clear that, from the time when he recovered full ascendancy in South Wales, the prince of Deheubarth uniformly protected and honoured monastic institutions within the sphere of his influence. His favour even fell upon the older foundations, despite their foreign origin; he confirmed to the Benedictine abbey of Chertsey the cell of Cardigan which it had acquired from St. Peter's, Gloucester,[114] and for some years left undisturbed at Llandovery a cell which had been founded by the Cliffords as an offshoot of Great Malvern.[115] He was a donor to the commandery established by the Knights Hospitallers at Slebech in Deugleddyf.[116] It was but natural, therefore, that, when he came into possession of the country around Whitland, he should give his patronage to this house and confirm to it the gifts of John of Torrington. But he did much more. About 1165 it was ruled over by a Welshman named Cynan,[117] a fact which shows how soon the Welsh element had found its true place in the Cistercian world, and one may reasonably conclude that it was this circumstance that induced Rhys to become, not merely the protector of the abbey, but also a liberal benefactor to it.[118] He bestowed upon it lands in Ystlwyf and Efelffre, in Emlyn, in Cantref Mawr and in Ceredigion, and among them the rich meadows of Rhuddlan Teifi, for which the monks successfully contended with the canons of Tal y Llychau.[119] As a crowning mark of confidence, Rhys sent to Whitland, there to spend youth, manhood and old age as a melancholy, sightless recluse, his son Maredudd, who had been blinded by Henry II. after the repulse on the Berwyn mountains.[120]

A little earlier than that famous victory, Whitland had sent out a colony which was to become the foremost monastic community in Wales. On 1st June, 1164,[121] the monastery of Ystrad Fflur, a name soon Latinised into Strata Florida, was founded on the banks of the little river Fflur,[122] in the upper valley of the Teifi, the land being the gift of Robert fitz Stephen, who was at the time the chief personage in the Clare lordship of Ceredigion.[123] It was at first a house of quite modest proportions, and for a year or two its future must have seemed extremely doubtful, for in 1165 Robert fell into the grasp of the Lord Rhys and therewith English authority in Ceredigion came to an end. But it weathered the storm and not long after so recommended itself to the victorious prince as to receive from him a very ample extension of the original endowment.[124] Behind the monastery the endless hills of Plynlimon stretched in wave upon wave of grassy upland, affording pasture for sheep and cattle innumerable, and as the new order was much given to pastoral occupations, Rhys threw open this region to the monks of Strata Florida, until their boundaries reached the river Wye.[125] As a result, perhaps, of this change of fortune, the site of the abbey was moved a couple of miles away to the banks of the Teifi, and here building soon commenced on a large scale; the walls began to rise of one of the largest churches in Wales, over 200 feet long, in a style which was characteristic of that age of transition from Norman to Early English forms.[126] The abbots must have been Welsh almost from the beginning; one David was at the head of the house in 1185[127] and Abbot Seisyll took a conspicuous part in the preaching of the crusade in 1188.[128] It was a natural result that Welsh princes should desire to end their days and be buried in a sanctuary which they now regarded as wholly their own. In 1175 Cadell ap Gruffydd, who had for more than twenty years been lost to the active life of Wales, is recorded to have died as an inmate of the abbey;[129] ten years later, Hywel ab Ieuaf of Arwystli was laid to rest within its walls.[130] Strata Florida was well embarked upon its brilliant career as the premier abbey of Wales.

Under the powerful patronage of the Lord Rhys, the Cistercian movement made rapid headway in the later years of the twelfth century. On 22nd July, 1170,[131] a colony of Whitland was established in North Wales. The bounty of Owain Cyfeiliog provided a site in the commote of Ystrad Marchell[132] and the new abbey came to be known as that of Strata Marcella. It received grants of land in Penllyn, in Edeyrnion and Cyfeiliog, where the grange of Talerddig was set in the midst of the broad grazing-grounds which lie around the head waters of the Severn. A terrible scandal overshadowed its earliest years and almost blighted the hopes of those who looked to the Cistercian order to revive the monastic spirit in Wales.[133] Enoch, its first abbot, and, no doubt, a Welshman, was a zealous and earnest worker, who threw himself with energy into the task of establishing a Cistercian nunnery for Welshwomen at Llansantffraid in Elfael. The enterprise led him into temptation; he allowed himself to be carried away by a violent passion for one of the inmates, a lady of birth and beauty, and finally eloped with her, deserting his abbey and his order and exposing both to the ridicule and scorn of the whole country. Enoch repented of his sin and returned to the abbey, but Ystrad Marchell must have stood the strain of this catastrophe with difficulty, and nothing further is heard of the ill-starred nunnery. Nevertheless, the progress of the new movement was not seriously threatened. On 1st August, 1176,[134] the community of Cwm Hir, which had probably been out of possession for some thirty years, was restored to its former seat on the banks of the Clywedog. The refoundation may be taken to have been the work of Cadwallon ap Madog,[135] at this time prince of Ceri and Maelienydd, though some help was given by Einion Clud of Elfael.[136] The death of an abbot Meurig in 1184[137] shows that here, as elsewhere, the Welsh element was in the ascendant.

A few years later Strata Florida sent out its first colony, which settled at Nant Teyrnon, a couple of miles from Caerleon, and founded a house known indifferently as the abbey of Caerleon or that of Lantarnam.[138] The early history of the abbey is far from clear, but it would appear to have been set up in 1179 by the bounty of a Welsh prince, Hywel ab Iorwerth of Caerleon.[139] Its foundation is, therefore, a further witness to the popularity of the Cistercian movement among the Welsh, and by its means the white monks obtained a footing in the highland pastures of Gwynllwg and Miskin, around Mynydd Islwyn and Aberdare.[140] The second colony of Strata Florida travelled in the opposite direction and carried the new enthusiasm for the first time into Gwynedd. In July, 1186, they settled at Rhedynog Felen, not far from Carnarvon,[141] but ere long were removed to that site near the mouth of the Conway which was for a century to be the seat of the abbey of Aberconwy.[142] It is impossible to say to whose patronage they were indebted for their introduction into the country or whose liberality gave them their early endowments; only the name of Gruffydd ap Cynan ab Owain has been preserved as the donor of Gelliniog on the Menai Straits,[143] for when, after his accession to full power throughout Gwynedd, Llywelyn ab Iorwerth extended to Aberconwy his special favour and protection, the fame of all other benefactors was sunk in that of the mighty prince of North Wales. Lands in Creuddyn, Arfon, Eifionydd, Arllechwedd, Môn and Rhufoniog had by this time enriched the house, and all were confirmed to it by Llywelyn's charter.[144] It was characteristic of Cistercian ambition that the abbey, already in possession of pastures on the southern slopes of Snowdon which stretched to the topmost crag of that monarch of mountains, set itself, with the aid of Llywelyn, to break up the monastic community of Beddgelert, of immemorial standing in that vicinity, and to annex its lands. The attempt was only defeated by an appeal to the justice of the holy see.[145]

The expansion of the order in Wales continued until the very end of the thirteenth century. In 1198 or 1199 Cwm Hir sent out an offshoot to Meirionydd,[146] where land was provided, probably by Maredudd ap Cynan, at that "cymer" or confluence of the Mawddach and the Wnion where once had stood the castle of Uchtryd ab Edwin.[147] Meirionydd and Ardudwy were abundantly furnished with those upland grazing grounds especially coveted by Cistercian industry, and the liberality of Maredudd and his brother Gruffydd soon established the abbey of Cymer in possession of many a grassy vale between Trawsfynydd and Machynlleth, where little but the lowing of their herds and the bleating of their flocks broke the august silence of the mountains.[148] Soon afterwards Ystrad Marchell supplied a convent to the one quarter of Wales, viz., Northern Powys, which had not yet received one. On 28th January, 1201,[149] Madog ap Gruffydd, at the instance of the abbots of Whitland, Strata Florida, Ystrad Marchell and Cwm Hir, established Cistercian monks at Llyn Egwestl in Ial, in a valley known from the ancient pillar of King Elisedd as Glyn y Groes (The Vale of the Cross) and thus was founded the abbey of Valle Crucis.[150] He bestowed upon the monks lands in Ial and Glyndyfrdwy and in the neighbourhood of Wrexham and Chirk.[151] Ere long their beautiful church rose upon the spot, a building of which the tall lancet windows, severe yet well proportioned, are still mirrored in the depths of the monastic fishpond.

Nunneries would seem to have been no part of the old Welsh monastic system, and the issue of the experiment made in this direction at Llansantffraid was scarcely encouraging to those who wished to see houses of religion for women established in Wales. Nevertheless, two Cistercian nunneries came into existence at this period and retained their position until the general dissolution of monasteries in the reign of Henry VIII. Llanllyr, on the southern bank of the Aeron, was founded by Rhys ap Gruffydd as a daughter-house of Strata Florida; after the great prince's death, it was despoiled of some of its lands by the greed of the mother-abbey, but retained a tolerable endowment.[152] Llanllugan owed its origin to Maredudd ap Rhotpert, lord of Cydewain[153]; it was not rich in landed revenues, but drew the tithes of several important churches in Southern Powys.[154]

It has been already said that the new outburst of enthusiasm for the monastic life which marks the close of the twelfth century in Wales was due in the main to sympathy with Cistercian ideals, and thus the order came to be as familiarly known in Welsh valleys as in Yorkshire dales. But it is worthy of note that the monastic revival also benefited to some slight extent other religious orders, which shone in the reflected radiance of the holy brethren of Citeaux. Rhys ap Gruffydd, whose broad and catholic sympathy extended to the most diverse forms of religious effort, introduced into his dominions the Premonstratensian order, establishing a house of canons at Talyllychau (or Talley), not far from his royal seat of Dinefwr.[155] There can be no doubt that its inmates were Welshmen, and in 1215 the pure Welsh blood of its abbot, Iorwerth, was a main argument for his election to the vacant see of St. David's.[156] The Knights Hospitallers were another community who at this time gained the favour of the Welsh; mention has already been made of the gifts of the Lord Rhys to the commandery of Slebech, founded by Walter fitz Wizo on the banks of the eastern Cleddau,[157] and it can have been little, if any, later than the year 1200 when the knights obtained a footing in Gwynedd.[158] Their North Welsh home was at Dolgynwal, not far from the source of the Conway, and it was probably Llywelyn ab Iorwerth who gave them the spot known to-day by the appropriate name of Yspyty Ifan or the Hospital of St. John.

The warm zeal and devotion of these years transferred to the hands of the monks a very large part of the soil of Wales and perhaps doubled the amount of land under ecclesiastical control in the country. In time to come the monks were to repay the generosity of their countrymen, not merely in the regular way of spiritual sustenance and comfort, but also by their services as patrons and custodians of the national literature. In the age of Rhys ap Gruffydd, however, the appeal for support was a purely religious one, and no better proof can be supplied of the genuine earnestness of Welsh faith at this time than the ungrudging response which was accorded to it.

IV. WELSH SOCIETY IN 1200.

(A complete picture of Wales at the end of the twelfth century is given by Giraldus Cambrensis in his Descriptio; other valuable sources are the De Nugis Curialium of Walter Map and the Mabinogion.)

At the end of the twelfth century, during the whole of which the Welsh had been exposed to Norman aggression and to the subtler yet no less potent influence of Norman culture, it is natural to inquire what manner of men the course of their history had made them, how far they differed from and how far they resembled their ancestors of the pre-Norman days. There is, happily, no lack of material for an answer to this question; more than one shrewd observer of this period has placed on record his view of the Welsh character and his impressions of Welsh society, and the general effect of the testimony is to show that in essentials Wales still retained its ancient social structure, remaining a tribal and pastoral community in spite of the great wave of feudalism which beat upon its eastern flank and daily threatened to engulf the older social system.

The economic basis of society was still the pasturing of flocks and herds. Agriculture held, in the purely Welsh districts, a quite subordinate position. "Most of their land," says Giraldus, "serves for grazing; little of it is used for tillage, still less for gardens and scarcely any for orchards."[159] Their manner of life was reflected in the food they ate; milk, butter and cheese were staple articles in their diet, which also included abundance of meat, but no great quantity of bread.[160] Let the Cistercian boast, quoth the witty Walter Map, his abstinence from flesh; I pit against him the hardy Welshman, who eats no bread.[161] William of Newburgh speaks of the wooded glades of the country, where there was rich herbage for innumerable sheep and cattle, but remarks that there was little land suited for the raising of crops, and that, in consequence, corn was imported from the neighbouring English shires.[162] Low-lying Anglesey, with an average rainfall not much above that of south-eastern England,[163] was an exception, and owed to its fertility its title of "mam Cymru," *i.e.*, the nourisher of Wales,[164] but Eryri remained until the nineteenth century a land almost entirely innocent of the plough.[165]

Broadly speaking, therefore, Wales was at this time without that basis of agricultural industry which is the condition of a settled way of living and of all development in commerce, craftsmanship, navigation, and architecture. The life of the people was simple and its needs soon satisfied. In addition to corn, it was necessary to import iron and salt, two products which the country did not yield,[166] and most of the cloth used in Wales was of foreign manufacture, though the coarse kind of rug or blanket known as "brychan" was made at home.[167] There must also have been some little equivalent in the way of exports; Welsh timber is known to have been in request, and, during the progress of the new buildings at Abingdon, Abbot Faritius kept six wagons, each drawn by twelve oxen, which were constantly employed in the haulage of wood cut in the marches of Powys.[168] But, when these deductions have been made, there is full warrant for the statement of

Giraldus that the Welsh did not busy themselves with trade, with ship-ping, or with any kind of handicraft.[169] No Welsh prince of this period coined money, built ships, or granted trading privileges. No towns arose as the result of the action of any Welsh chief, though Rhys ap Gruffydd was enlightened enough to give his protection to the bor-oughs he found established at Cardigan and Llandovery.[170] Little communities might gather around the leading monasteries and royal strongholds, but of true urban life there was none in the districts under native rule; the Welshman's interests were entirely rural, while the country meant for him no rich succession of smiling, well-tilled fields, but Nature's profusion of rock, glen, moor, copse, lake, and meadow, in the midst of which he lived the blithe and careless life of the hunter, the fisher, and the herdsman.

It is the predominantly pastoral character of Welsh life which explains the mobility of the people and the ease with which they baf-fled their foes by transporting their chattels from a threatened dis-trict to one of greater security. They had no stake in the soil — no buildings they feared to sacrifice, no crops they would not readily abandon. Again and again the policy of retreat is followed, in 1095, on the occasion of the first invasion of Rufus, in 1114 and in 1121, when Henry I. attacked Wales, and in 1158, when Rhys ap Gruffydd was menaced by the power of Henry II.[171] It was resorted to in 1211 by Llewelyn ab Iorwerth, when John led an army against him.[172] Invasions had no terrors for men who could in a few hours pack up all their household goods in wagons or on the backs of sumpter-horses, drive their sheep and swine and cattle before them as they moved westward to the mountain passes, and cheerfully leave to the vengeance of the enemy the rudely-fashioned huts of lopped timber and wattle which had sheltered them and theirs for a season or two from the wind and rain of heaven.[173]

One is not surprised to find a race nurtured under such conditions described as hardy, energetic, and of great endurance. The Welsh, says Giraldus, are an active, restless people, temperate as to food and drink, and much employed in those pursuits which strengthen the body and train men to suffer all manner of hardships.[174] They pass the livelong day in these occupations — the reference is, no doubt, primarily to the young "boneddigion" — traversing woodlands, scaling mountain ridges, throwing the javelin, shooting arrows, and come back in the evening to a frugal, but well-earned meal at the family hearth. An adventurous boldness, for which no task was too heavy, no dangers too formidable, was the quality they especially strove to cultivate, and many a tale was told of the daring exploits by which they proved their mettle and their resource. Let the following, vouched for by Walter Map, serve as a sufficient illustration. Cadwallon ab Ifor, lord of Senghenydd, had a most valuable mare, the fame of which brought one Genillyn of North Wales to the South on a predatory errand.[175] Adventurous theft was in those days as honourable among the Welsh as piracy among the heroes of Homer, and it was no less honourable because the penalty of failure was instant execution. But Genillyn found the task he had set himself more difficult than he had expected, and one evening he unbosomed himself to his host Trahaearn, telling him how rigorously the noble animal was guarded against mishap. Trahaearn laughed him to scorn, called him a North-Welsh coward, and undertook the business himself. In the daytime the mare grazed in the midst of a crowd of retainers; at night she was tethered in the farthest end of the chieftain's hall at Gelligaer, with the banked-up fire on its open hearth between her and the only door, and around it the sleeping "teulu," while betwixt her and the fire four trusty slaves slept on a "brychan," so as to be ready instantly to defend their precious charge from any interference. Trahaearn was in nowise daunted by these obstacles. One dark, starless night, when all the inmates of the "neuadd" were in profoundest sleep, he cut a small hole in the door, deftly inserted his hand and shifted the bolt, and soon had the portal wide open. Next he unloosed the mare, slipped on her the bridle he carried with him, tied her tail to the rough selvage of the "brychan," and dragged the four slaves, as they slept, through the middle of the great fire. He was well on his way out ere they could realise what had happened to them; their cries, as they awoke to the situation, roused the remainder of the sleepers, but by this time Trahaearn, with the "brychan" behind him, was riding swiftly through the forest. For a while the stray sparks which clung to the surface of the blanket enabled his track to be followed, but, as these were gradually extinguished, he was lost in the impenetrable darkness.

Men bred in this austere school developed into well-knit and resourceful warriors, especially fitted for that guerrilla warfare which was constantly being waged between the English and the Welsh. War and preparation for war were indeed the normal occupation of the Welsh freeman. "The defence of their native land and of its liberty," says Giraldus,[176] "is their sole concern; they fight for fatherland and labour for liberty. . . . They deem it ignoble to die in their beds and an honour to fall in the field of battle.[177] . . . They will expose their defenceless bodies to the attacks of mail-clad knights, will engage without weapons fully armed men, and will rush on foot against masses of heavy cavalry. And often in such encounters their mere nimbleness of movement and their indomitable courage will win for them the victory." If their first wild onslaught was not successful, they were easily dispersed in flight, but their retreat was not a rout; their light equipment, which included a corslet, but as a rule no other defensive armour, enabled them as they fled to harass their pursuers with missile weapons, and so great was their elasticity that it was always unsafe to assume that a final and crushing defeat had been inflicted upon them.[178] The men of North Wales were especially skilful in the use of the lance; the South Welsh arm was pre-eminently the bow, a weapon drawn with remarkable effect by the warriors of Gwent, who could drive their arrows through thick oaken doors and even transfix knights to the saddles of their horses.[179] Giraldus did well to impress upon the English government the folly of sending heavy cavalry of the usual feudal pattern to contend against such enemies as these, who never opposed to it cavalry of their own or held their ground in a pitched battle, but trusted to the methods of surprise and panic, disconcerting, worrying and demoralising the foe.[180]

Yet, notwithstanding the stress laid upon military matters, Welsh life was not without a more kindly and genial aspect. In the home circle the Welshman was generous and open-handed, and prime importance was everywhere attached to the virtue of hospitality.[181] The stranger who in his journeyings reached a Welsh homestead of the better sort neither asked for nor was offered shelter and entertainment; they were his by unquestioned right. He gave up to his host the custody of his arms, and, by his refusal or acceptance of the water proffered for the washing of his feet, showed whether he was to be regarded as a visitor for the day or proposed to stay the night. But it was reckoned highly discourteous to question him as to his movements, until, at any rate, the third day of the visit had been reached, and meanwhile, he was free of the house and all it could afford. No greater insult could be offered to such a guest than to suggest to him that he was outstaying his welcome. Walter Map has a tragic tale to tell of a foolish wife who, in her husband's absence, upbraided a casual visitor, as he lay on his couch one morning, with his reluctance to face a snowstorm which he could see raging without, as he looked through the open door. Stung by her reproaches, the man had risen and made off into the forest, where he was soon beset by ferocious wolves. The husband, hearing on his return what had happened, was beside himself with rage, and avenged his tarnished honour by forthwith killing his hapless wife. He then set himself to trace the footprints of the stranger, whom he found at last sitting exhausted in the snow and watched by a great wolf, the last of a pack of ten of whom the traveller had despatched the remainder. When the wolf had been speared, he bore his guest back to the forlorn shelter of his home, but the man did not long survive, and his kin took up the feud on his behalf, treating the matter as one of "galanas," since the conduct of the wife amounted to nothing less than manslaughter.

The Welsh had the merits and the faults of a strenuous, impulsive, quick-witted and eager race. They roamed their hills barefoot and thinly clad, slept in their day clothes on the hardest of couches, and never bemoaned the loss of a dinner.[182] Norman luxury was not allowed to corrupt the Spartan simplicity of their daily life. Nor had they any touch of the servility of the English; from the highest to the lowest, they were unabashed in the presence of the great, and spoke their minds with delightful frankness of utterance.[183] They were firm in friendship, but implacable as foes. When their ire was roused they spilt blood like water, and shrank from no danger to themselves in the effort to avenge an injury or win a point in the great game of war. Oaths and promises were lightly broken; the keenly felt present wrong overshadowed and dwarfed the past engagement.[184] Yet it was only as representing the survival of tribal custom and morality that Welsh life could be termed barbarous. In intellectual ability and mental culture the race stood high, and its achievements in the sphere of letters have already been described.[185] Poets, chroniclers, musicians, and writers of romance appealed to a public of trained intelligence. In religious devotion, also, the Welsh were not inferior to any nation in Christendom.[186] Their hermits and recluses were of spotless purity of life, and universal reverence was rendered to them. Warlike as the people were, they scrupulously observed the peace of the Church, and the lands devoted to the service of religion were never disturbed by the clash of arms. Despite their failings, they would indeed be a happy and fortunate folk, thinks Giraldus, and sure of the blessings of this world and the next, if they had good pastors and bishops and were under the rule of one good prince.

CHAPTER VII

LLYWELYN THE GREAT: EARLY MANHOOD

(In the reign of John, the great series of English state records begins to be fairly complete, and light is thrown on the history of Wales by the Charter, Patent and Close Rolls. I have also used, in addition to the Welsh and English chroniclers for the period, the Rotulus Misae of 11 John and the Rotulus de Praestito of the following year, Rymer's Foedera, Dugdale's Monasticon, the works of Gir. Camb., and the poems in the Myv. Arch. Norgate's John Lackland and McKechnie's Magna Carta have also been of much service.)

I. THE RIVALRY OF LLYWELYN AND GWENWYNWVN.

THE thirteenth century may, in Welsh history, be appropriately described as the age of the two Llywelyns. During its first forty years the figure of the elder prince of that name mounts into ever greater prominence until it dominates, in unquestioned pre-eminence, the whole of Wales. At a later period the younger Llywelyn comes to the front as the one leader of the Welsh people, pursuing his grandfather's policy for many years with all his grandfather's success, until in the last quarter of this century, so fateful in the annals of the Welsh, his good fortune deserted him and he fell a victim to the power and skill of Edward I., bringing down with him in his ruin the edifice of Welsh independence.

Llywelyn ab Iorwerth had proved his capacity, not only by the vigour and spirit with which he had secured for himself a share in the realm of Gwynedd, but also by his victorious assault upon the border fortress of Mold at the beginning of 1199. During the next four years his progress was rapid. In 1200 his cousin Gruffydd ap Cynan died, having in his last hours, according to a fashion which was beginning to become popular, donned the habit of a monk in the new Cistercian abbey of Aberconwy.[1] Llywelyn at once entered into possession of Arfon, Anglesey, and Arllechwedd,[2] to the exclusion of Gruffydd's son Hywel, and thus became lord of almost the whole of Gwynedd, including Aberffraw, its "principal seat" and ancient centre, Bangor, the home of its bishop, and Degannwy, the cradle of its ruling house.[3] He was now indubitably the foremost prince of North Wales, though Gwenwynwyn of Powys was still, as the course of events was to make clear, a rival by no means to be despised. In the following year these conquests were rounded off by the acquisition of Lleyn.[4] This district was held by Maredudd ap Cynan, who had perhaps received it from Llywelyn on the death of Gruffydd on condition of faithful service;[5] be this as it may, Maredudd is accused of intriguing against his powerful cousin, who drives him out of the cantref to his southern lordship of Meirionydd. In 1202 he lost even this, being supplanted by his nephew, Hywel ap Gruffydd,[6] a young prince who made no difficulty about submitting himself entirely to Llywelyn and thus establishing the lord of Gwynedd in full authority from the Dovey to the Dee.

The inevitable struggle with Gwenwynwyn now began. In August, 1202, Llywelyn raised a force for the reduction of Southern Powys, calling to his aid the other princes of North Wales, who responded to the summons, with the exception of Elise ap Madog, lord of Penllyn.[7] But peace was brought about by the intervention of the clergy ere the two rivals came to blows on this occasion,[8] and the warlike fury of Llywelyn, diverted from its principal object, fell upon the hapless head of Elise. He dispossessed him of Penllyn and its castle of Bala,[9] treating him as a vassal who had fallen short of his obligations to his lord, and only allowed him, for his bare maintenance, the castle of Crogen [10] and a few trefs in a remote corner of the commote. By this measure of reprisal the prince of Gwynedd secured a firm foothold for the next attack upon Gwenwynwyn, which could not be long delayed.

In the struggle between the two princes, the decisive influence was to be the action of the English crown. The change which took place when by the death of Richard I. in April, 1199, the youngest of the sons of Henry II. became king of England was one of much importance for Wales. Richard knew nothing of the country and was content to leave its government to his ministers; John, on the other hand, was not only a lord of the Welsh march, but had also gained, as a rebel leader, some insight into Welsh politics and the Welsh character. In dealing with Wales, he had useful experience to guide him, and he pursued, on the whole, a settled and consistent policy. His aim was to divide and to disintegrate, to checkmate the designs of the more formidable chiefs by favouring their rivals, so that thus the land might be torn by the strife of opposing and not ill-balanced parties. It was a policy which for many years bade fair to be successful, and only failed because the statesmanship of Llywelyn enabled him to take advantage of the serious difficulties in which the king involved himself as his reign drew to a close.

John seems to have begun with the idea of giving his special favour to Llywelyn, and in September, 1199, took him under his protection and confirmed him in possession of all his lands.[11] But a fuller review of the situation led him to change his mind, and in December, not only did he secure to Gwenwynwyn all the territories he had, but promised him, in significant terms, what he might win from. the king's enemies.[12] As a similar grant was made at the same time to Gruffydd ap Cynan,[13] one may easily see that Llywelyn was for the time being the object of the royal suspicion and disfavour. When John came over to England for a short visit in the spring of 1200, his attitude was still the same; he gave Gwenwynwyn on 11th April the valuable royal manor of Ashford in Derbyshire for a render of one sparrowhawk each year, and therewith leave to hunt, with four greyhounds, in the king's forests as he journeyed to and from the court.[14] It was in this year that Llywelyn became master of the whole of Gwynedd; his sudden rise may perhaps have altered the opinion held of him by the English government, for towards the end of the year another change of policy is to be perceived; there is an evident desire not to drive so powerful a chieftain to extremities, but to come to a reasonable arrangement with him. First, a truce is made with him;[15] then he is invited by John to meet him and discuss terms of peace,[16] and, when this plan has broken down and the king has to return to France, the Archbishop of Canterbury and the justiciar, Geoffrey fitz Peter, Earl of Essex, are despatched to the border to arrive at an understanding with so troublesome a foe.[17] The result was the treaty of 11th July, 1201; Llywelyn swore fealty to John and promised to do homage as soon as the king was in England again; in return, he was recognised as the rightful possessor of all the lands he had acquired, subject only to any fair legal proceedings which might be brought against him under English or Welsh law.[18]

When Giraldus Cambrensis, in the course of his campaign on behalf of the rights of St. David's and his own, visited North Wales in the winter of 1201-2, the loyalty of Llywelyn was by no means assured, and the archdeacon laid himself open by his proceedings to the charge of stirring up the embers of a strife which had only just been composed.[19] Gwenwynwyn was still regarded as the friend of the English, too friendly to give much encouragement to Giraldus in his patriotic crusade.[20] But after the encounter of the two princes in the summer of 1202, the zeal of the prince of Powys visibly waxed fainter; under the influence, it may be, of the persuasion of Llywelyn, he inclined once more to the old role of firebrand of the marches, and at the end of the year attacked the lands of William de Breos.[21] In 1204 John was once more in England, after an absence of more than two years; the time had arrived when Llywelyn must make good his undertaking as to the render of homage. There was a little delay at first,[22] but in the course of the summer he seems not only to have discharged this obligation, but also to have formed a close tie with the king by obtaining a promise of the hand of his natural daughter Joan.[23] An alliance of this kind had been formed by his uncle David and had proved of very great service to him;[24] it chanced that by the death of David in 1203[25] the castle and manor of Ellesmere, given to him as a marriage gift by Henry II., had again come into the possession of the crown,[26] and nothing could be more natural than that in the spring of 1203, when this new marriage probably took place,[27] Llywelyn should receive from the king as a sign of goodwill these lands which had for so long been held by a scion of the house of Gwynedd.[28] It had seemed likely during the previous five or six years that the Northern prince would find a wife in a very different quarter, for he had been negotiating with Pope Innocent III. for leave to marry a daughter of Reginald, king of Man, wedded as a child to his uncle, Rhodri.[29] In April, 1203, the requisite papal authority had been obtained, but the Manx alliance was not concluded when the specially advantageous match with the daughter of his overlord presented itself to Llywelyn as the more attractive alternative.

While the king had thus been craftily balancing Llywelyn and Gwenwynwyn against each other in the North, his policy in South Wales was not dissimilar. Here his opportunity was provided for him by the incurable rivalries of the sons and grandsons of the Lord Rhys. It has already been shown that, on the death of the veteran leader of the South in 1197, Gruffydd was recognised as his father's heir in respect of Dinefwr and Cantref Mawr, but was soon afterwards captured by his brother Maelgwn, who was acting in concert with Gwenwynwyn. The defeat of the latter at Painscastle in 1198 brought about another turn of the wheel of fortune; Gruffydd was set free and restored to his lands, to embark upon a struggle with Maelgwn, in which for a while he was very successful. Before the end of the year, he had won from his rival all Ceredigion,[30] except the castles of Cardigan and Ystrad Meurig, and in 1199 he captured the castle of Cilgerran, commanding the cantref of Emlyn. Against this Maelgwn had nothing to set, save a solitary triumph at Dineirth in Ceredigion; he saw his power fast slipping from him, and in his extremity he turned to John. On 3rd December, 1199, the king by charter conferred upon him the four cantrefs of Ceredigion and that of Emlyn, on condition that he would resign to the crown the castle of Cardigan and the adjoining commote of Is Hirwen.[31] A few months later the transfer was effected;[32] thus did Maelgwn, in the language of the patriotic chronicler, "choose rather to share with the enemy than with his brother, and sell to the king the castle of Aberteifi for a little weight of gold and the curses of all the clergy and lay folk of Wales".[33] The "Key of Wales," as it is elsewhere termed,[34] was again placed in English hands, and the king, moreover, made a good friend upon whom he could rely for defence of the royal interests in Deheubarth.

During the next few years the hand of death fell heavily upon the sons of the Lord Rhys. On 2nd July, 1201, Maredudd ap Rhys, who was lord of Cantref Bychan and its castle of Llandovery, was killed in the commote of Carnwyllion by the followers of William of London, lord of Kidwelly.[35] His brother Gruffydd at once took possession of his lands, but in less than a month was seized with illness and on 25th July died, leaving by his wife Matilda two young sons, named Rhys and Owain.[36] In 1204 Hywel Sais was treacherously wounded in Cemais by the men of his brother Maelgwn, and not long afterwards found a grave in the quiet precincts of Strata Florida.[37] By these events Maelgwn was more than ever brought to the forefront of affairs; in 1201, on Gruffydd's. death, he recovered Cilgerran and now began to aspire to rule in Ystrad Tywi; in 1203 he invited the aid of his old ally, Gwenwynwyn, and with his help seized Dinefwr in Cantref Mawr and Llandovery and Llangadock in Cantref Bychan, to the exclusion of his nephews, Rhys and Owain ap Gruffydd.[38] This was the climax of his power; in the following year he was driven from Ystrad Tywi by a compact between his nephews and Rhys Gryg, under which the former took Cantref Bychan and the latter Cantref Mawr as their respective shares of the spoil won from him. He was beginning to suffer from the turn of events in the North, where his friend Gwenwynwyn was being eclipsed in the favour of both English and Welsh by Llywelyn.[39] It was another serious blow to Maelgwn when in this year

1204 William Marshall, Earl of Pembroke, paid a visit to his lands in Dyfed and vindicated his claim to the lordship of Emlyn by a successful assault upon Cilgerran.[40] Maelgwn was now reduced to the position of lord of Ceredigion once more.

The uneasy relations between John and Gwenwynwyn came to a head in 1208, when the prince of Powys felt the full weight of his sovereign's displeasure. Important events had paved the way for the rupture. The persistent refusal of the king to recognise Stephen Langton as Archbishop of Canterbury had at last drawn from the papal armoury the formidable weapon of an interdict; on Sunday, 23rd March, in this year,[41] all religious services throughout England and Wales were discontinued at the bidding of Innocent and no sacraments save baptism and extreme unction were allowed to be administered. John's reply was simple — to confiscate all clerical and monastic property as forfeited by the failure to perform the duties attached to it, and for the next five years he had wealth in abundance out of which to pay mercenary troops and keep his enemies in subjection. He struck without hesitation at all who had aroused his suspicion or dislike, and among the first singled out for attack was the great baron of the march, lord of Radnor, Builth, Brecknock, Upper Gwent and Gower, who had been for thirty years the leading figure in Norman South Wales. At the beginning of the reign William de Breos had received the king's license to conquer all he could from the Welsh;[42] in 1202 John had entrusted to him, with praise of his faithful service, the custody of his lands and castles in Glamorgan, Gwynllwg, and Gower.[43] In 1203 he had bestowed Gower upon him and his heirs, to be held by the service of one knight.[44] Matters now wore a very different aspect. Early in 1207 William was ordered to give up Glamorgan and Gwynllwg to Falkes of Breauté,[45] a foreign adventurer high in the king's favour, and in the spring of the following year John was so dissatisfied with his erstwhile honoured lieutenant as to require him to surrender all his lands in England and Wales in pledge for the payment of his heavy debts to the crown.[46] From this blow William never recovered; the efforts made by him and his sons William and Reginald to oppose force to the king's decree proved futile, and in their despair they fled to Ireland.

Among those who benefited by the fall of the great marcher lord was Peter fitz Herbert, a constant companion of the king, who now received a third part of the lordship of Brecknock, with the castle of Blaen Llyfni.[47] Gwenwynwyn deemed the opportunity a favourable one for reviving his old scheme of conquest in Mid Wales, and began to ravage the lands of the new lord. He soon discovered his mistake. John promptly took notice of the aggression, bade the marchers give their aid to Peter,[48] and when the prince of Powys, overawed by these measures, came to Shrewsbury on 8th October to sue for peace, refused to let him return. The price of Gwenwynwyn's liberty was to be the render of twenty hostages, and meanwhile all his lands were to be taken into the custody of the crown.[49]

There followed an unexpected result, though it might without difficulty have been foreseen. Llywelyn seized this favourable moment for the execution of the design from which he had turned aside in 1202. He marched upon Southern Powys and straightway took possession of the whole country. His sudden appearance in Arwystli and Cyfeiliog at once produced a commotion in South Wales. Maelgwn, whose line of action had always been to support the now vanquished Gwenwynwyn, saw himself seriously threatened in Ceredigion, and, as a measure of defence, dismantled the castles of Aberystwyth, Ystrad Meurig, and Dineirth, which if captured might enable an invader to hold the north of the province against him. Nevertheless, Llywelyn was not diverted from his purpose; he occupied the province as far as the Ystwyth, rebuilt the castle of Aberystwyth, and handed over the district between the Ystwyth and the Aeron to the sons of Gruffydd ap Rhys. The young Rhys and Owain, established since 1204 in Cantref Bychan, had of late been hard pressed by their neighbour, Rhys Gryg, who had just destroyed their castle of Llangadock,[50] but they had now a powerful patron and defender.

These proceedings were of a kind to excite some concern at the king's court, where it was not desired to make Llywelyn too powerful. But John still regarded him with a favourable eye, notwithstanding his bold and independent action. On Christmas Day he wrote, in answer to a letter from Llywelyn, to say he would overlook all that had been done to the injury of Gwenwynwyn and treat the prince as a good son once more, if he would perform certain promises made in the letter.[51] What these were can only be conjectured, but it is certain that during 1209 Llywelyn and the king continued to be on excellent terms. They may possibly have met in the spring;[52] later in the year the prince of Gwynedd gave the fullest proof of his loyalty to his father-in-law by joining, with a contingent of his men, the expedition led by John against William of Scotland.[53] Accompanied by Hywel ap Gruffydd who held Meirionydd as his vassal, Gwyn ab Ednywain, his "distain" or seneschal,[54] and Ystrwyth, his clerk and messenger,[55] he was at Newcastle at the end of July, and on 4th August took his place in the serried ranks of the host which at Norham forced the Scotch king to a peace. Gwenwynwyn was meanwhile living in pitiful dependence upon the royal bounty.[56] Llywelyn was no doubt one of the Welsh chiefs who did homage at Woodstock in October,[57] and in January, 1210, a gift of falcons sent to him by the king bore witness to the fact that he was still in the sunshine of the royal favour.[58]

Thus far Llywelyn had maintained himself in power by the skill and address with which he had steered his bark amid the troubled currents of his time. He had promptly seized every opportunity of extending the limits of his rule, while at the same time carefully watching the temper of John and guarding himself from any step which might permanently alienate him. He was now to be subjected to a severer test, to show how he could comport himself in adversity, when he had to bear the full force of the king's displeasure. A thundercloud was gathering overhead, which was soon to burst upon him in all its fury. The dexterous steersman was to appear in a new light and to prove his fortitude by weathering the blackest and most desperate of hurricanes.

II. THE FIGHT FOR THE FREEDOM OF ST. DAVID'S.

(Nearly all that is known of this subject comes from the works of Gir. himself and especially from De Rebus (which, however, breaks off, in the one extant MS., at the end of 1199) and Men. Eccl. The documents are conveniently arranged, with many notes, in H. and St. i. 394–452; for summaries of the course of the struggle see Jones and Freem. 286–94; Newell, History of the Welsh Church, chap. viii.; Owen, Gerald the Welshman, chap. iii.)

It was not only in the domain of civil life that the Welsh spirit of independence showed itself at this time; it found expression also, as had often been the case before, in ecclesiastical affairs. From 1198 to 1203 a determined battle was fought against the see of Canterbury, notwithstanding that it was backed by the power of the English crown, in order to win recognition of the metropolitan position of St. David's. The story has been told, with great particularity and no lack of pungent comment, by the principal actor in it, the unsuccessful aspirant to the vacant bishopric, Giraldus Cambrensis, and it may, on this account, fill a somewhat larger space in the history of the period than in a strict view of proportion rightfully belongs to it. But, though the struggle had no lasting results, and may even have been less interesting to Wales at large than Giraldus in his vanity would have us believe, yet it deserves notice as a remarkable attempt to realise a patriotic ideal, and one which, though it failed to achieve its immediate object, nevertheless bore fruit in other ways.

The archdeacon had, in 1196,[59] abandoned the service of the crown because he despaired of receiving any adequate reward,[60] and had betaken himself to Lincoln to study theology.[61] It was here he heard of the death of Bishop Peter on 16th July, 1198,[62] opening once more for him the door of hope which had been closed against him in 1176. His prospects were certainly better on this than on the previous occasion. He had with advancing years gained in experience and reputation; he might hope that his diplomatic labours would be remembered in his favour by the king and his advisers. There was a substantial Welsh majority in the chapter,[63] which was quite prepared to push the claims of a native candidate. But Giraldus had throughout to contend with two main difficulties of the most formidable kind, so serious, in fact, that nothing but his indomitable spirit and unquenchable energy could have prolonged the struggle for the five years during which it was kept alive. In the first place, there were among the Welsh canons two opposing parties, two family groups, in fact,[64] and, while the descendants of Jonas were supporters of Giraldus, the descendants of John had a candidate of their own in Abbot Peter of Whitland,[65] who was one of their number, born in the cathedral city itself. In the second place, Archbishop Hubert fully realised the danger of allowing the dispute as to the rights of the see to pass, by the election of Giraldus as bishop, into the hands of a man so able and determined, so well fitted by the extent of his family influence, also, to make it a really formidable question. With the rough persistence which was characteristic of him, he never rested until the archdeacon had been vanquished without hope of recovery.

The first stage through which the matter passed was one of negotiation between the chapter and the archbishop. The former resolved to submit four names for consideration; they would accept, they said, Giraldus, Abbot Peter, the Abbot of St. Dogmael's, or Reginald Foliot, a young relative of the last bishop. To none of these would Hubert agree; he was bent on the appointment of a man without local connections, and offered them their choice of a Cistercian abbot named Alexander and Geoffrey, prior of Llantony. This uncompromising attitude greatly helped the cause of Giraldus; in their determination to fight the archbishop the chapter turned to him as the man marked out by fortune to be the champion of their rights, summoned him to their aid from his studious retreat at Lincoln, and early in 1199 were encouraged by him to appeal from the archbishop and the justiciar to the king. Before this could be done Richard had died, and a further delay resulted from the necessity of submitting the matter afresh to a new king, at a time when he was engrossed in more weighty cares. Giraldus had at first some hope of gaining the goodwill of John, who had known him for years and had in 1192 offered him the bishopric of Llandaff.[66] But the influence of the archbishop was too powerful, and no declaration in favour of the archdeacon could be obtained from the king during his brief visit to England for the coronation. The chapter now made up their minds to act decisively, and on 29th June[67] Giraldus was elected at St. David's, in spite of the opposition of the government. It was in vain that the primate threatened to consecrate the prior of Llantony, whether he were elected or no; the canons were for the moment bent upon a course of defiance, and it was resolved that the bishop-elect should carry the case to the supreme tribunal of the church at Rome. At the end of November, Giraldus was in the holy city, ready to plead his cause before the pope of the day, the astute and masterful Innocent III.

It was inevitable that with the question of the claim of Giraldus to have been duly elected bishop the larger issue of the independence of the see should be brought to the front once more.[68] Indeed, it is doubtful whether the mere bishopric, shorn of the dignity with which it was sought to invest it, would have had much attraction for Giraldus; it was not well endowed[69] and the title of bishop had in itself no fascination for him.[70] The matter was, however, adroitly placed on the broadest national footing; stress was laid on the way in which the spiritual authority of Canterbury was used by primate after primate to further the merely temporal ends of the English crown. Welsh insurgents were liable not only to the ordinary penalties of defeat, but also to those of excommunication, while the Welsh Church was held in bondage, the free choice of its canonical electors overridden and unfit bishops forced upon it, as part of the purely political campaign against Welsh national aspirations.[71] Archbishop Hubert was, indeed, at no pains to throw a veil over this part of his case; it was precisely in order to keep the Welsh under control by ecclesiastical censures that he deemed it necessary, he told the pope, to resist with all his power the designs of the archdeacon.[72] Little wonder, then, that Giraldus was able to secure the countenance and support of the princes of Wales, even those who, like Llywelyn, had no interest in exalting the see of Deheubarth above the remaining three.[73] In nothing does the statesmanship of the prince of Gwynedd appear more strikingly than in this advocacy of the St. David's claim; he was well aware that, in view of the forces arrayed against it, it would probably fail, but as an experienced politician he knew the value of a strenuous protest and held that Giraldus had by his brave, though ineffectual, resistance done genuine service to the Welsh national cause.[74]

At Rome there was every disposition to listen to the Welsh case. The jurisdiction of the papal court as the highest tribunal in all church matters was a valuable asset for the papacy, and every encouragement was given to litigants to avail themselves of it. About the question of the status of the see there was, at first, some hesitation, but Giraldus was soon able to convince the pope that there was a case for discussion and that this was not by any means the first occasion on which it had been submitted to the arbitrament of the holy see. The archbishop's defence was hardly serious; to the election of Giraldus in June he opposed the election of Abbot Walter of St. Dogmael's in December, and thus laid himself open to the charge of having forced a second choice on the electors while the appeal to Rome was still pending as to the lawfulness of the first. Thus Giraldus was able to obtain some important concessions; in May, 1200, a commission of English bishops was appointed by the pope to report upon the question of status and that of the election, while the administration of the see was meanwhile committed to the indefatigable archdeacon.

When Giraldus returned to Wales, he found that what he had won at Rome was counterbalanced by what, during his absence, he had lost at St. David's. The archbishop had realised his mistake in peremptorily rejecting all the candidates of the chapter, and now saw that the right policy was to exploit the internal feuds of this body. For the moment his favourite was the abbot of St. Dogmael's, and, as Walter was notoriously illiterate and unfit for the episcopal dignity,[75] Peter of Whitland and his clan were won over by the prospect of an impasse which might finally turn out to their advantage.[76] Thus Giraldus had not only to cope with the continued hostility of the crown,[77] but also with that of a majority of the chapter; he was hampered in the exercise of his duties as administrator by Abbot Walter, who on his election in December, 1199, had been put into possession of the temporalities of the see.[78] There was nothing he could do but hunt up more documents in support of the primacy of St. David's and return to Rome for the formal hearing of the case, fixed for 4th March, 1201.

By this time the representative of the archbishop at the papal court had a more plausible tale to tell. Realising that Innocent meant business, he put forward the plea that the December election was merely a confirmation of one which had taken place as early as 7th January, 1199, when Hubert, having full authority for the act from the chapter, chose the abbot of St. Dogmael's. It was thus sought to deprive Giraldus of the important advantage he enjoyed in these proceedings as the candidate first elected. For so skilful a controversialist it was easy to pick holes in this argument, with which the whole action of the archbishop in the course of the year 1199 was inconsistent, but, instead of rejecting it, the court preferred delay and fixed 1st November, 1202, for the re-trial of the whole matter, the interval to be devoted to the collection of evidence. In the meantime, the pope continued to give his powerful protection to Giraldus, who was sent away at the end of July with letters confirming him in his office of administrator and requiring the archbishop to pay half the expenses of the suit. It was well that Innocent still befriended him, for on his re-appearance in this country he found the hostile forces arrayed against him more resolute than ever. The Welsh princes had not deserted his cause; Maelgwn and Rhys Gryg did what was possible for him in the south,[79] Llywelyn was a warm supporter in the north,[80] and even Gwenwynwyn hospitably received him, while unwilling to sanction a collection on his behalf.[81] At St. David's the Jonas party still upheld his claim,[82] but the rest of the chapter was unfriendly and would not even support him on the archbishopric question, so unwilling were they to yield him any assistance. Throughout England the power of the crown was used to the utmost against him, so that even sympathisers like the bishops of Ely and Worcester[83] and William fitz Alan[84] could do little for him. He spent the year 1202 in weary journeys to interview friends, to checkmate enemies and to satisfy commissions, and got out of the country, not without difficulty, in time to appear for the third time at Rome in January, 1203. On the way thither he called at Clairvaux and Citeaux and dealt retribution to a most persistent foe by procuring the deposition of Abbot Peter.

The long duel was now drawing to its inevitable close. During Lent the case was fully argued before the pope, and evidence adduced, which Giraldus held to be perjured and corrupt, in favour of the

January election of Walter. Innocent made no difficulty about accepting it; it was no part of his policy to offend so influential a prelate as
Hubert, and the right solution of the question appeared to him to be
the quashing of both elections, that of the abbot on the ground that
the archbishop was not properly authorised to elect, that of the
archdeacon on the ground that it took place while the legality of the
other was as yet undetermined. This decision, announced on 15th
April, was entirely satisfactory to the opposition, who cared nothing
for Walter and only desired to be rid of Giraldus. But, short of con-
ceding his claim, the pope was disposed to do much for the man who
had so valiantly fought the battle of his church and his own and
whose racy talk and naive egotism had interested and diverted him.
Papal letters were issued securing him against vindictive proceedings,
entrusting the control of the new election to his friends, the bishops
of Worcester and Ely,[85] and—best of all—appointing a commission
from the province of York to go into the still unsettled question of
subjection to Canterbury.[86]

Nevertheless, the cause for which Giraldus had done battle was
hopelessly lost. When he arrived in England in August he was able
to prevent the elevation to the vacant see of the young canon,
Reginald Foliot, who was next put forward by the archbishop, but,
deserted as he now was by almost the whole chapter,[87] he had himself no prospect of attaining the dignity which had been the dream
of his life. He decided to abandon a campaign which could lead to
no useful result and concurred in the election in November of the
prior of Llantony. Geoffrey was consecrated on 7th December,
1203, in St. Catherine's Chapel, Westminster,[88] having made the
usual profession of obedience to Canterbury, but having given no
pledge that he would refrain from raising the question of independence.[89] Giraldus, on his part, promised to let this question rest
during the lifetime of Hubert, made his peace with the archbishop
and the king,[90] resigned his archdeaconry to his namesake and
nephew,[91] and withdrew finally from St. David's affairs. The evening
of his stormy life was quiet and serene; he renewed his devotion to
study and to literature, and in these pursuits reached a hoary old
age under Henry III.[92] Famous fighter, ruthless critic, gifted wielder
of the pen though he was, no chronicler of the day thought fit to
record the year of his death.[93] But posterity has taken a juster measure of his deserts, and Llewelyn spoke with true foresight when he
declared that the fight for St. David's would be remembered "as
long as Wales should stand".[94]

III. LLYWELYN IN CONFLICT WITH JOHN:
PEACE OF WORCESTER.

Soon after the beginning of the year 1210, the friendly relations between Llywelyn and John, which had never been so marked as in the previous year, were suddenly broken off. The occasion of this rupture is not easy to determine. The year was that of the Irish expedition, undertaken by the king, with the help of the revenue he now derived from the bishops' lands, in order to assert his authority in the island against the more powerful barons, notably the Earl Marshall, Earl Hugh of Ulster, his brother Walter Lacy and the fugitive William de Breos. Now William was a good deal in Wales and its borders during the summer, endeavouring to regain his territories,[95] and it is possible that he persuaded the prince of Gwynedd to make common cause with him in a hostile movement which was to come to a head while John was embroiled in Irish affairs.[96] If this was so, Llywelyn showed something less than his usual foresight. For William proved but a broken reed, whose resistance to the power of John soon collapsed, leaving him no alternative but to flee as an outlaw to France and abandon his wife Matilda and his eldest son William to the pitiless vengeance of the hardest heart in Christendom.[97] It was probably no accidental coincidence that about the same time Gwynedd was invaded by forces under the command of the Earl of Chester, the justiciar, and the bishop of Winchester;[98] nor did it avail Llywelyn that in his alarm he destroyed his castle of Degannwy; it was rebuilt by the earl with timber which he found not far off, and another castle was constructed at Holywell to protect the march.[99]

Meanwhile John's Irish progress had been an uninterrupted triumph. He had travelled by the usual South-Welsh route, passing through Glamorgan,[100] where his trusty henchman, Falkes of Breauté, was governor for him,[101] and thence by way of Swansea and Haverford to Pembroke, which he reached about 3rd June.[102] Here he was detained, probably by contrary winds, for a fortnight; about the 17th he set sail from Milford Haven and landed near Waterford. He spent rather more than two months in Ireland, sweeping all before him, and arrived at Fishguard on the return journey on 26th August.[103] Thence he journeyed by way of Haverford, Kidwelly, Margam, and Newport to Bristol. This display of unquestioned power had, as was inevitable, a marked influence upon the affairs of South Wales. Not content with the overthrow of William de Breos, John had brought low during this expedition the greatness of another baron of the march, whom he had formerly delighted to honour. Robert fitz Richard of Haverford was the chief magnate of Rhos, having inherited a proud position from his father, Richard fitz Tancard.[104] Though reputed by Giraldus an enemy of the Church,[105] he had founded under the shadow of his castle a priory of Austin canons,[106] and only a year or two had passed since the king had entrusted to him the keeping of the castle of Cardigan.[107] Nevertheless, for some unknown offence he was now deprived of all he had, and in 1211 he died an exile in a foreign land.[108] Another result of the king's passage through Wales was to give fresh vigour to the enemies of Llywelyn, who were now, in the altered posture of affairs, in favour once more as the king's friends. On 8th September Rhys Gryg, with the help of royal troops, attacked Llandovery, which was held for his nephews, Rhys and Owain, the close allies of the prince of Gwynedd; the garrison capitulated on terms, and the castle, with a number of valuable horses, fell into his hands. About the end of November, John restored Gwenwynwyn to his dominions in Southern Powys; Maelgwn at once came to the conclusion that his day of recovery had also come, and, having come to terms with the king, prepared to eject Rhys and Owain from northern Ceredigion. The chronicler of Strata Florida,[109] who was friendly to Llywelyn, records the upshot with glee; the two young princes with 300 chosen warriors, made an onslaught by night upon Maelgwn's camp at Cilcennin, drove him ignominiously into hasty flight, and captured his nephew, Cynan ap Hywel, and his chief counsellor, Gruffydd ap Cadwgan. It was an indubitable victory, not without its element of comedy, but it had no great effect upon the general situation, and the fortification of Builth at the king's command by Engelard of Cigogné[110] threatened the sons of Gruffydd ap Rhys with danger from a new quarter.

Confident of his hold upon South and Mid Wales, the king now resolved that there must be a day of reckoning for the prince of Gwynedd, who, heedless of the gathering storm, was at this moment ravaging the border.[111] He summoned to meet him at Chester[112] all the other leaders of the Welsh, and almost all obeyed, not only Llywelyn's old enemies, Gwenwynwyn, Maelgwn and Rhys Gryg, but with them men like Hywel ap Gruffydd and Madog of Northern Powys, who had hitherto followed the banner of the son of Iorwerth.[113] That prince had for the nonce no allies but the sons of Gruffydd ap Rhys. At first, indeed, it did not seem as if the threatened onslaught would be very effective. The men of Gwynedd followed their oft-repeated tactics on such occasions, retreating from the lower lands with all their possessions to the fastnesses of Eryri, and, as the season was the middle of May,[114] the host found itself, when it reached Degannwy, unable to feed at the expense of the country, and, in default of other provision, exposed to the danger of famine. Eggs commanded the price of fowls[115] and horseflesh did duty for beef and mutton. For the moment John was baffled by the special difficulties of Welsh warfare and was forced to beat a retreat, returning to England at the end of the month.[116] But he was by no means diverted from his purpose; fresh preparations were made, on an ampler and more provident scale, and on 8th July he was on the border again.[117] He set out this time from Oswestry[118] and made rapidly for the mouth of the Conway, driving Llywelyn before him into the wilds of Arllechwedd. Arrived at Aber, he was able to humble another magnate who had ventured to defy his irresistible power. Bishop Robert of Bangor[119] had refused to meet an excommunicated king; John's answer was to send a troop of Brabançons to the episcopal city, who, after setting fire to it, seized the bishop as he stood in his robes at the high altar of his cathedral and forcibly carried him off to the king's camp. The payment of a fine of two hundred hawks secured him his liberty, but lost honour and peace of mind were not so easily retrieved, and it is hardly fanciful to suppose that it was as the result of this outrage that Robert died in the following year.

Llywelyn was now in a dangerous plight, and it was well for him that he had in his wife Joan an advocate who could plead his cause with the king. Vicious though he was, John was not without affection for his children, and he agreed to terms which, though severe and crushing, yet left to the prince of Gwynedd life, liberty, and a sufficient, if contracted, realm. He took possession of those four cantrefs of the "Perfeddwlad" or Middle Country,[120] which, lying as they did next to England and outside the limits of Snowdonia, were always first seized upon by an English king desiring to curtail the power of a prince of Gwynedd, and thus restricted Llywelyn to the lands beyond the Conway. He took from him in addition some thirty hostages,[121] and imposed upon the country an enormous tribute of cattle, with a smaller render of horses, dogs, and birds. Having thus, as he supposed, settled the affairs of Wales as triumphantly as those of Ireland, John returned to Oswestry in the middle of August.[122] In South Wales, too, all opposition was swept aside. Falkes of Breauté, with the aid of the knights of Dyfed and Glamorgan and the support of Maelgwn and Rhys Gryg, attacked Northern Ceredigion and reduced Rhys and Owain ap Gruffydd to submission. The two young princes were sent to England to make their peace with the king in person, and Falkes took possession of their territory for the crown, building in it at Aberystwyth a new castle which was no doubt designed to be an effective check upon future movements of the Welsh of Mid Wales.[123]

But in his overweening pride John had gone too far; the erection of the castle at Aberystwyth proved to be a serious error in tactics. What had secured him his easy victory was his success in isolating Llywelyn, whose pre-eminence had aroused the envy and jealousy of so many of his fellow-princes. By continuing the policy of balancing one prince against the other, the king might have retained a real control over Welsh affairs, but he chose to embark instead upon a scheme of conquest and settlement which was to cover the whole of Wales. Not only at Aberystwyth, but also in the Middle Country and in Powys, castles began to rise, symbols of a power which would ere long leave no substantial foothold for that of any Welsh chief. Maelgwn and Rhys Gryg soon came to the conclusion that it was not for this they had fought; suddenly passing from the royalist to the patriotic side, they forced the garrison at Aberystwyth to capitulate and burnt the new fortress to the ground. At the same time another Welsh prince who had done battle for John in his foreign wars, Cadwallon ab Ifor Bach of Senghenydd, broke out into revolt and ravaged the lowlands of Glamorgan.[124] Before the end of this year 1211, it was evident that the victory won in the summer was of the showy rather than of the solid and enduring type.

For a little while it might seem as if the king and Llywelyn were to resume the former footing of friendship, for the latter, accompanied, no doubt, by Joan, was induced to spend the Easter of 1212 with John at Cambridge.[125] But this visit to the English court can hardly have failed to disclose to the two the crazy foundations on which rested the imposing superstructure of the king's power. His lawless and insolent tyranny had created among the great men of his realm such an atmosphere of fiery resentment and hate as needed but a spark of opportunity to make it flare out in open revolt. Llywelyn thus learnt that he had no reason to fear a second invasion of his territories, and in the summer threw in his lot without hesitation with the new league which was being formed in Wales for the destruction of the recently built castles.[126] The combination included not only Llywelyn, Maelgwn, and Rhys Gryg, but also Gwenwynwyn, who was being edged out of his possessions by Robert of Vieuxpont, the king's lieutenant in Powys, and it revealed itself in a sudden revolt at the end of June, while John was in the north, giving help to King William of Scotland.[127] Fuel was added to the flame by the action of the pope, who, in his resolve to exhaust every available means of reducing the king to submission, released the insurgents from their allegiance, encouraged them to resist to the utmost of their power, and rewarded them by freeing their country from the burden of the interdict.[128] With such approval and countenance, it is no wonder that the movement proved highly successful; Llywelyn recovered the whole of the Perfeddwlad, except the castles of Rhuddlan and Degannwy, and captured a royal official, one Robert the Wolf, who had long been a thorn in the side of the Welsh.[129] Gwenwynwyn besieged Robert of Vieuxpont in his new castle at Mathrafal, and Rhys Gryg set fire to the town of Swansea.[130] Madog ap Gruffydd[131] in North Wales and Rhys and Owain ap Gruffydd[132] in the South held aloof from the rising, but their abstention was but as a featherweight in the balance compared to the advantage won by Llywelyn in shaking himself free from the dangerous isolation of the previous year and regaining his natural position as leader of the Welsh people.

John had intended this summer to invade France, but the news of the revolt brought about a sudden change of plans. He resolved instead upon a Welsh expedition, which was to crush Llywelyn once for all. Throughout July and well into the middle of August, he was directing the organisation of a host which was to assemble at Chester on the 19th of the latter month, amply furnished with provisions and other requisites for a Welsh campaign.[133] In the meantime he paid a hurried visit to the border, and about 1st August carried off Robert of Vieuxpont from his perilous position at Mathrafal.[134] A few days before the proposed muster, he arrived at Nottingham and struck the keynote of what was to be a war of pitiless vengeance by wreaking his wrath upon certain of the Welsh hostages, refusing, the chronicler tells us, to taste food or drink until they had been despatched.[135] But it was not long ere his schemes suffered a complete and final overthrow. Letters from more than one quarter, including one written by his daughter Joan, who had, no doubt, the safety of her husband, as well as of her father, in mind, disclosed to him the existence of a conspiracy among his barons to betray him to his foes or make him a prisoner during this Welsh campaign by which he set such store.[136] He saw that the plot was feasible, and, on the 16th, countermanded all the preparations for the muster.[137] The great onslaught upon Llywelyn resolved itself into an order to the fleet assembled at Chester to sail around the North-Welsh coast and inflict as much damage as was possible.[138] Later in the year the baffled king had recourse to another expedient;[139] he sought out two rivals of the prince of Gwynedd, namely, Owain ap Dafydd, who lived in England with his mother, Emma,[140] and Gruffydd ap Rhodri, and invested these cousins of Llywelyn's with the three cantrefs of Rhos,[141] Rhufoniog, and Dyffryn Clwyd, promising them Arfon, Arllechwedd, and Lleyn, if they could win them also. It does not appear that this grant had any practical effect; Llywelyn, as the champion of Welsh liberty, was too firmly fixed in the affections of his people to be thus dislodged, and the close of the year saw him more securely established than ever.[142]

Early in 1213 the capture of the two castles which still held out for the king in Gwynedd, namely, Rhuddlan and Degannwy,[143] filled to the full Llywelyn's cup of triumph. His alliance with Maelgwn and Gwenwynwyn still held good, and the latter prince was able to keep Robert of Vieuxpont at bay at Carreghofa on the Tanat.[144] It was only in South Wales that the family feuds of the house of Deheubarth enabled John to win some successes. Rhys and Owain ap Gruffydd had had the misfortune always to espouse the losing cause; they had fruitlessly supported Llywelyn in 1211 and the king in 1212, and they now demanded help from the crown to recover their standing in the country. Falkes of Breauté[145] was sent from Glamorgan and Engelard of Cigogné[146] from Hereford to their assistance, and a determined attack was made upon the possessions of Rhys Gryg, who had refused to share with his nephews. Late in the January of 1213 the army set out from Brecknock, now in the king's hands, encamped at Trallwng Elgan[147] in Cantref Mawr, and thence marched against Rhys, who was defeated in the field, not far from Llandeilo. There followed in quick succession the capture of Dinefwr, the flight of Rhys, with his family and his retainers, to Ceredigion to seek the protection of his brother Maelgwn, and the capitulation of his fortress of Llandovery—disasters which brought the fortunes of this prince to the lowest ebb and gave the Great and the Little Cantref to his nephews. As though this were not enough, he fell later in the year into the hands of the king's men and was promptly imprisoned in the royal castle of Carmarthen.

The point has now been reached when John sought relief from the difficulties which beset him by absolute submission to the pope and acceptance of Stephen Langton as Archbishop of Canterbury. On 15th May, 1213, he made over his realms of England and Ireland to the holy see and received them again as fiefs from the papal legate. Certain immediate advantages were bought by this act of self-abasement; the dreaded French invasion was warded off, the friendship of Innocent was secured, the plotting of the barons came to an end. Among other results of the political transformation, the Welsh revolt lost its character of a holy war and became once more simple rebellion, to the manifest disadvantage of Llywelyn and his allies. But Innocent showed some appreciation of the service rendered to him by the mountaineers of Wales, whose romantic story he had no doubt often heard from the lips of Giraldus. He instructed his legate, Pandulf, to negotiate a truce between them and the king, and on 3rd June it was signified to the custodians of the marches that they were to arrange for a two months' cessation of strife.[148] Archbishop Stephen took an active share in the work of pacification,[149] with the result that the truce was prolonged throughout the year 1214[150] and that Wales remained quiet while John was prosecuting in that year his campaign for the recovery of Normandy. Llywelyn had won all he desired in Gwynedd; his allies, Maelgwn and Gwenwynwyn, were secure in their territories of Ceredigion and Southern Powys; so that it needed no great effort on his part to comply with the terms of the truce.

John had hitherto staved off, by the display of force or by skilful change of policy, the outburst of angry rebellion which his unbridled tyranny made sooner or later inevitable. His failure to achieve success abroad brought the domestic trouble to a head; the defeat of the coalition he had formed against Philip Augustus of France at the battle of Bouvines on 27th July, 1214, was a blow from which he never recovered. When he returned to England in October, he found a large section of the baronage, who had with them the sympathy of Langton, in open opposition; from his fruitless interview with the malcontents at Bury St. Edmunds in November may be dated the beginning of the movement which led to the sealing of Magna Carta.[151] His first thought was, as usual, to divide his enemies, and during the next few months he made diligent efforts to detach certain powerful interests — the church, the primate, the citizens of London — from the baronial cause. In pursuance of this policy, he began to angle for the support of the Welsh, having, perhaps, in his mind the example of his father, who had derived valuable help from Wales in suppressing the feudal rebellion of 1173.[152] On 18th December, being at Monmouth on a short visit to the Herefordshire marches, he ordered Engelard of Cigogné to deliver to Llywelyn four of his hostages, in response, as he said, to the petition of his daughter Joan.[153] At the beginning of March, 1215, he went a step further and commissioned four men who were in his confidence, including William of Cornhill, the new bishop of Lichfield, to interview Llywelyn,

Maelgwn, Gwenwynwyn, and Madog ap Gruffydd on the border and make such offers as would secure their support in the coming struggle.[154] In April Gwenwynwyn was gratified by the release of a hostage who had been confined in the distant castle of Richmond.[155] It is impossible to mistake the purpose of these overtures, made at a time when the resistance of the barons was daily growing stronger and pointing unmistakably to civil war.

But the net was spread in vain in the sight of men who now saw their opportunity of profiting by the discords of the English realm. John found that his belated show of friendship made as slight an impression upon the Welsh as upon the other powers which he was striving to lure from the baronial cause. The situation had now arisen which was to repeat itself more than once in the constitutional conflicts of this century; the barons of the march, Walter Lacy, John of Monmouth, Hugh Mortimer, Walter Clifford, Peter fitz Herbert, ranged themselves on the side of the king and of royal authority;[156] the Welsh, led by the prince of Gwynedd, threw in their lot with the advocates of reform. For the people of Wales, as for the English folk, the time had come when there was greater reason to fear the central power, grown incredibly strong, than the little tyrants of the countryside, whose feudal pride and insolence had been sorely humbled. Thus it was that Llywelyn, rejecting the offers of the king, entered into a close alliance with the northern insurgents, and when they had on 17th May made their position secure by the seizure of London, marched upon Shrewsbury, where town and castle were surrendered to him without a blow.[157]

The link which connected Llywelyn with the baronial organisation was forged, there is good reason to believe, by Giles de Breos, bishop of Hereford.[158] Like most of the English bishops, Giles had been in exile during the interdict period, but his was a private rather than a public quarrel, and, though on his return in 1213 he had taken his place in the royal counsels,[159] he had not forgotten the cruel persecution of his house, the death of his father in poverty abroad, the wasting end of his mother and eldest brother in a Windsor dungeon. John had at first shown a disposition to treat him well and had granted him the Breos lands in England and in Wales, but had then delayed the fulfilment of his promise until the bishop's heart was ripe for rebellion.[160] About the middle of May, Giles sent his brother Reginald [161] to the marches, with orders to join the Welsh in an attack upon the constables who held the Breos castles for the king; in this way Pencelli,[162] Abergavenny, White Castle, and Skenfrith[163] were won, and when the bishop himself appeared upon the scene, the still more important strongholds of Brecon, Hay, Radnor, Builth, and Blaen Llyfni were regained for the family which had held them for so many years. Throughout there was a close cooperation between the house of Breos and the Welsh, erstwhile the most obstinate of foes: Reginald sealed the alliance by marrying Llywelyn's daughter, the dark-eyed Gwladus,[164] and Elfael, once the theatre of bloody strife between the two races, was left, with its castles of Painscastle and Colwyn, to be occupied by the Welsh under Gwallter ab Einion Clud.

Meanwhile the princes of South Wales, it may be readily believed, were not idle. The sons of Gruffydd ap Rhys, fickle as ever in their allegiance and yet never separated from each other, cut themselves adrift from the royal cause and came to terms with their uncle Maelgwn. On the 27th of May[165] Maelgwn and Rhys invaded Dyfed and were well received by the Welsh inhabitants of Emlyn and Elfed; resistance was offered in Cemais, so that they ravaged the province, burning the vill of Maenclochog, and then retired to seek reinforcements. The representative of the royal power in South-west Wales was the Earl Marshall, who had the custody of the castles of Cardigan and Carmarthen,[166] as well as his own fortresses of Pembroke and Cilgerran, but he had at the moment a more important office to discharge as the king's chief lay counsellor in the negotiations with the insurgent barons, so that he was forced to let the Welsh rising run its course. It occurred to someone that it might be advantageous to give Rhys Gryg his liberty, and the order was accordingly issued two days before the famous meeting at Runnymead;[167] its sole effect was, however, to add another to the list of Welsh chieftains in revolt. Maelgwn and Owain ap Gruffydd went north to secure the aid of Llywelyn, while the younger Rhys swept the coast of the Bristol Channel from Swansea to Carmarthen.[168]

Magna Carta has often been described as a treaty of peace between the king and his subjects. So far as the Welsh were concerned, this was its sole significance. What they desired from the king was, not the redress of constitutional grievances, the Welsh legal system being independent of the English and wholly under Welsh control, but the reversal of certain acts arising out of the state of war between the two countries—the restoration of lands and castles seized by the crown, the freeing of hostages, the return of charters deposited in pledge of good behaviour. These demands were included by the barons in the articles which they submitted to John on 15th June, and were accepted by him.[169] The charter provides that all lands, liberties and the like, in England and in Wales,[170] of which the Welsh have been deprived without legal warrant since the king's accession, shall be forthwith restored to them; in cases of dispute, there shall be a proper trial on the march, the law invoked to be English, Welsh, or marcher law, according to the situation of the land which is claimed. The Welsh are to reciprocate as to any unlawful seizures made upon their side.[171] Seizures of the period 1154 to 1199 are to stand over, unless already the subject of a legal process, until the king has performed, or been released from, his vow to go on crusade. All Welsh hostages, including Llywelyn's son Gruffydd,[172] are to be released and all charters returned to their owners.

The charter, however, was no sooner sealed than suspicion began to grow up on both sides and to blight the hopes which had been founded upon it. At first the work of reconciliation seemed to be making good progress; the Archbishop of Canterbury arranged at the end of July to escort Llywelyn and his allies to the royal presence,[173] hostages were set free,[174] and John made a grant to the prince of Gwynedd of the manors of Bidford in Warwickshire and Suckley in Worcestershire.[175] But, as the summer wore on into autumn, it became clear that the peace between king and baronage would not stand, and the power of the church to act as mediator was crippled by the action of the pope, who denounced the charter and the whole movement for reform. Bishop Giles, who had hitherto held aloof from all negotiations,[176] now felt compelled to yield obedience;[177] he made his peace with John on 21st October,[178] but at Gloucester on the return journey fell sick and died.[179] By this time war had broken out and the barons had taken the decisive step of inviting Louis, the eldest son of Philip Augustus, to bring a French army to their aid and thus win for himself the English crown. The first contingent of troops sent in response to this call landed at the end of November.

The moment had now come for the renewal of the Welsh campaign. Early in December, Llywelyn appeared in South Wales at the head of an army gathered from every Welsh state which retained its independence; with him were Hywel ap Gruffydd ap Cynan,[180] Llywelyn ap Maredudd ap Cynan,[181] Gwenwynwyn, Maredudd ap Rhotpert,[182] Rhys Gryg, Maelgwn, the sons of Gruffydd ap Rhys, those of Maelgwn ap Cadwallon (of Maelienydd), and, as representing their lord, the household troops of Madog ap Gruffydd. It was a decisive epoch in the career of the prince of Aberffraw—the first occasion on which he had led the whole chieftaincy of Wales to battle, his first appearance as a war-leader in South Wales. He won such victories as secured to him the unquestioned primacy of his race until the end of his life. On the 8th he attacked Carmarthen, for seventy years the centre of royal power in the valley of the Towy;[183] in five days it was surrendered to him, after which with little ado he made himself master of the castles of Kidwelly, Llanstephan, St. Clear's, Laugharne, Narberth,[184] and Newport.[185] Christmas was now approaching, but the mildness of the season encouraged the princes to persist in their campaign and they were rewarded on the 26th by the capture of Cardigan and of Cilgerran.[186] Thereupon, as the patriotic chronicler tells us with triumph and pride, "the Welsh returned joyfully to their homes, but the French, driven out of all their holds, wandered hither and thither like birds in melancholy wise".[187]

These successes left the crown no foothold in South Wales save around Pembroke and Haverfordwest. The Breos lands were in the possession of Reginald, Llywelyn's son-in-law and ally, who had seized them on the death of his brother the bishop.[188] Glamorgan was ruled by the insurgent Earl of Essex, in right of his wife Isabella. Llywelyn resolved to establish his influence in the south on a still firmer footing by a formal partition of the Welsh districts, a partition in which he wisely took no share for himself, but which gave him the more valuable status of overlord over the sons and grandsons of the Lord Rhys. It was made at Aberdovey early in 1216, in the presence of an assembly of magnates, which may be regarded as virtually a Welsh parliament, the first of its kind, though not, it is true, assembled together under the provisions of any Welsh law. The justice and moderation with which the delicate task of division was performed are evinced by the permanence of the results, which were not substantially affected during the lifetime of Llywelyn. Maelgwn received in Dyfed the Uppermost Cantref[189] (with Carmarthen), Cemais and Emlyn (with Cilgerran), in Ystrad Tywi the two commotes of Mallaen and Hirfryn (with Llandovery),[190] and in Ceredigion the two commotes of Gwinionydd and Mabwnion. To Rhys Gryg were assigned Cantref Mawr and Cantref Bychan (except the two commotes allotted to Maelgwn), and therewith Cydweli and Carnwyllion. Ceredigion, with the castle of Cardigan,[191] was made over to the sons of Gruffydd ap Rhys, with the exception of Maelgwn's commotes, which lay along the river Teifi.

Not long after this South-Welsh triumph, Llywelyn won a final victory over his old enemy Gwenwynwyn. The prince of Powys had, in the fervour of the late movement, done him homage, given him hostages, recorded his loyal submission in formal documents. But he could not reconcile himself to the defeat of all his ambitions, and early in 1216 he lent an ear to the persuasions of John, who, well pleased at the prospect of a renewal of the old dissensions, gave him his forfeited land in Derbyshire[192] once more, and added the important manor of Montgomery.[193] Llywelyn was strong enough to take immediate action; marching upon Southern Powys, he seized his defiant vassal's dominions and drove him before him into Cheshire. This was the closing chapter in the history of the hapless heir of Owain Cyfeiliog, for before the end of the year he died,[194] leaving an infant son named Gruffydd, who could not for many years make good his claim to his father's inheritance. Such was the pitiful end of a career that once bade fair to be illustrious and noble—a gray and sullen sunset, whose leaden clouds quenched the bright beams which once had illumined the whole of Mid Wales. Gwenwynwyn had in him the making of a patriot, but fate decreed that he should rule over Powys, the weakest of the three realms of Wales, and that he should be pitted against Llywelyn, whom he could not overcome and whose ascendancy he could not endure.

The prince of Gwynedd had now little to fear but the possible recovery by John of his old authority and despotic power, and the king's death on 19th October, 1216, relieved him ere long of all anxiety upon this account. The baffled tyrant had spent the last few months of his life in destructive raids upon those parts of his realm which he thought not to be well affected to him, and in July and August he was on the Welsh border, where, failing to secure the submission of Reginald de Breos, he burnt his castles of Hay and Radnor and also the Fitz Alan castle of Oswestry.[195] But he could not touch Llywelyn, and his death created an entirely new situation, which was for the Welsh leader a hopeful and auspicious one. Even if, as proved to be the case, the French pretender should fail in his enterprise, and the house of Anjou, represented no longer by the hated John but by his nine year-old son, should regain the allegiance of the English people, the power of the crown could not, on its new basis, be for many years as menacing as it had been during the past reign. Llywelyn awaited the result of the war with equanimity, confident that, whatever its issue, he would be able at its close to dictate his own terms of peace.

The young Henry III. had not only the advantage of birth and of wise counsels around him—for his regent was the prudent and just Earl Marshall—but he was also supported by the whole weight of the ecclesiastical power. Innocent had been succeeded by a new pontiff,[196] but Honorius III. was no less ardent in his devotion to the interests of the reigning house, and his legate Guala joined in the coronation of Henry, concurred in the reissue of the charter which formed the political platform of the new government, and excommunicated all the barons of the opposite party. The attitude of the pope naturally governed that of the bishops, and among the prelates who were in attendance at Henry's court at Bristol on 12th November were Iorwerth of St. David's, Henry of Llandaff, Cadwgan of Bangor, and Reiner of St. Asaph.[197] They no doubt gave their countenance to the interdict pronounced by Guala at this time upon the whole of Wales as a punishment for its support of Louis,[198] and left Llywelyn with no shadow of ecclesiastical support. Of greater practical importance to him at this moment was the gradual crumbling away of the French or baronial party, as the issue came to be more and more clearly denned as that of English versus foreign rule. The barons of the march, it has been already remarked, for the most part took the royalist side in this struggle, but at the death of John there were gaps in this section of the party, which the year 1217 saw step by step filled. The knights of Glamorgan,[199] Peter fitz Herbert,[200] Isabel of Gloucester,[201] Thomas Corbet of Cause,[202] John fitz Alan,[203] and Foulk fitz Warren[204] successively made their peace and received their lands again, each one an ally lost to Llywelyn in his contest with the crown.

The most serious defection of this kind was that of Reginald de Breos. Many efforts had been made by John[205] and by the Earl Marshall[206] to win him over, and at last, on 23rd June, 1217, it was announced that he had submitted and had been restored to all the possessions of his house.[207] His Welsh relatives were much displeased at this desertion of their cause; his nephews, Rhys and Owain,[208] at once crossed the moors of Tregaron and fell upon the province of Builth, while his father-in-law Llywelyn invaded Brecknock and threatened destruction to the town of Aberhonddu. Through the intervention of Rhys, the burgesses were allowed to offer hostages for the payment of 100 marks and thus escaped fire and pillage, while Llywelyn pushed on for Gower. His march across the bleak morasses of the Black Mountains and down the valley of the Tawe was an arduous one, but his purpose of conquest seemed almost achieved when Reginald, with six other knights, came to meet him and by the surrender of Swansea[209] averted the further ruin of his lands. Leaving Rhys Gryg to guard the mouth of the Tawe, Llywelyn set off in a fresh direction, and the news was soon spread that it was his intention to subjugate Rhos. A deputation of Flemings who met him at Cefn Cynfarchan,[210] near Whitland, could not turn him from the enterprise, and, having forded the Western Cleddau at Wolfsdale,[211] he was preparing to assault Haverford, when Iorwerth, the canon of Talley who had been made bishop of St. David's, intervened in the interests of peace and induced him to retire on receiving twenty-four hostages from the burgesses as a pledge of their willingness to submit to his rule, or, in the alternative, to pay him a fine of 1,000 marks before Michaelmas.

Meanwhile the cause of Louis and the insurgent barons had reached a desperate pass, and on 11th September, 1217, the Treaty of Lambeth was concluded, which ensured the withdrawal of the foreign claimant and the union of all England under the young Henry III. A clause in the treaty extended its benefits to Llywelyn and the Welsh, if they wished to be included,[212] but, as the terms offered to them involved the surrender of all their late conquests, it is no marvel that they were rejected. The prince of Gwynedd knew that he had but to bide his time to obtain peace on very different conditions. His ally, Morgan ap Hywel, was attacked by the Earl Marshall and deprived of his ancestral seat of Caerleon,[213] but he himself was not so vulnerable, and in March, 1218, after long negotiations,[214] terms were granted to him which no doubt realised his highest expectations. Having been absolved by the authority of the legate from the excommunication he had incurred by his resistance to the pope's ward, he did homage to the king at Worcester in the presence of Guala, the Earl Marshall, and all the magnates of the realm, and was confirmed in the possession of all his conquests.[215] The royal castles of Cardigan and Carmarthen, to which he could lay no hereditary claim, were formally placed in his custody, to be maintained at his own charges until the king was of age[216] and could dispose of them as he pleased. The lands of Gwenwynwyn, including Montgomery, were similarly vested in him as custodian until the heirs of his old rival attained their majority. He did not succeed in obtaining the restoration of Caerleon,[217] but in all other respects the peace was greatly to the advantage of Wales, and Llywelyn had no difficulty in persuading the lesser princes to follow his example and render homage to a king whose counsellors showed so pacific a spirit.[218]

The Earl Marshall, pattern of chivalry as he was, nowhere appears in a more unselfish and patriotic light than in this surrender, for the sake of the security of Henry's trembling throne, of two castles in the future of which he was, as lord of Pembroke, most intimately concerned. It was certainly not to his private advantage that Cardigan and

Carmarthen should be held by the powerful prince of North Wales, but he waived this consideration in view of the urgent necessity of a general pacification which would give England time to recover from the wounds of civil war. The desire to put an end to strife was general; Earl Ranulf of Chester came to terms with Llywelyn,[219] leaving to him his acquisition of Mold, and then set out for the East, with other great English lords who wished to draw the sword in nobler quarrels than had of late engaged them. The year 1218 closed in profounder peace between English and Welsh than had been seen for many a long year, and yet the struggle had not exhausted the energy of Llywelyn, who had merely completed the first stage in his victorious career, the period of growth, of youthful triumph, of ascendancy achieved. He had still before him many years of strenuous and successful work, of assured supremacy, of good fortune which scarcely knew a rebuff.

CHAPTER VIII

LLYWELYN THE GREAT: MATURITY

(In addition to the Close and Patent Rolls and Rymer's Foedera, Shirley's Letters of the Reign of Henry III. supplies much useful record material. Chronicles are represented by Wendover and the Annales Monastici. Of modern works I have used Tout's History of England from 1216 to 1377.)

I. FROM THE PEACE OF WORCESTER TO THE KERRY CAMPAIGN.

THE history of Llywelyn, from the Peace of Worcester until his death in 1240, is that of a prince who was supreme beyond challenge in his hereditary dominions and who could therefore pursue a bold and independent policy in matters external, unfettered by the fear of trouble at home. An attempt will first be made to outline the course and development of this policy down to the time when advancing years moderated the ambition and checked the energy of Llywelyn, and thereafter a brief sketch will be given of the background of domestic security, disturbed only by family discords, which was the basis of the power of the strongest ruler Wales had known since the Norman Conquest.[1]

If the Peace of Worcester be carefully considered, it will be seen to rest upon the assumption that Llywelyn was to be humoured and pacified rather than coerced, to be won to loyalty to the young king by the fullest recognition of his predominance in Wales and not driven into rebellion by irksome restrictions upon his power. This was the liberal and statesmanlike policy adopted by Guala and by the Earl Marshall, and, though the return of the legate to Italy in November, 1218, and the death of the earl in May, 1219, ere long removed from the scene the two men chiefly responsible for it, it was not sensibly modified during the next few years. The new legate, Pandulf, who exercised the chief control over English affairs until July, 1221, was no less friendly to Llywelyn than his predecessor had been, nor did the justiciar, Hubert de Burgh, who, after the departure of Pandulf, stepped into the position of chief minister of the crown, think it at all necessary to depart from the old footing of confidence and goodwill. Though there was much negotiation and conference about matters in dispute, nothing like a breach between the government and Llywelyn took place until 1223. On 10th July, 1219, Pandulf had an amicable meeting with the prince at Shrewsbury.[2] Early in May, 1220, there was at the same place an important border council, attended by the legate, the justiciar and the Archbishop of Canterbury,[3] when Llywelyn was gratified by two concessions, the grant of a market to his Warwickshire manor of Bidford[4] and the recognition of his son David as his heir.[5] At the beginning of July, 1221, he was once more at Shrewsbury, whither the court had come to settle a dispute between him and Rhys Ieuanc.[6] The latter complained that, although Maelgwn, his uncle, had received Carmarthen in accordance with the partition of 1216, he had not been established in Cardigan, as that compact had provided. Llywelyn, who had at first resented the demand and seized Rhys's castle of Aberystwyth, yielded the point at Shrewsbury, but the grant of a market to Ellesmere[7] and other favours [8] he received show that his prestige had not suffered. In January, 1222, he was specially protected in the enjoyment of his manors of Suckley and Bidford,[9] and, when Rhys Ieuanc died in the August of this year,[10] it was with the royal authority that he took charge of the lands of the deceased,[11] and, in default of a direct heir, divided them between Maelgwn and Owain ap Gruffydd. He was still treated by the crown as its best friend and supporter in all dealings with the princes of Wales.

Yet the situation was none the less made difficult and precarious by the inevitable feuds between the Welsh and the marcher lords. There were unsettled questions, such as the ownership of Maelienydd, claimed by Hugh Mortimer from its Welsh lords, relatives and vassals of Llywelyn.[12] Petty local quarrels were certain to draw the great men into their toils and ultimately to involve the king and the prince in a conflict on the grand scale. With one of the border magnates Llywelyn, indeed, maintained throughout the most cordial relations, amounting to a veritable alliance. Earl Ranulf of Chester had a fellow-feeling for a great territorial lord whose franchises were threatened by the activity of the central government, and his warm support of Llywelyn relieved the prince from all fear of hostilities along the Cheshire border. On the day of Ranulf's return to Chester from the crusade, namely, 16th August, 1220, the two magnates met in that city,[13] and in 1222 the bond was drawn closer by the marriage of the earl's nephew and heir, John the Scot, to Llywelyn's daughter Helen.[14] With other marcher lords there were not the same ties of friendship; Hugh Mortimer and Llywelyn were often at odds,[15] and after the desertion of 1217 Reginald de Breos was also suspect. It was probably with the idea of harassing Reginald that the Welsh prince in 1219 gave his daughter Margaret to the young John de Breos, son of the younger William of that name, who had just been released from a long captivity, and was seeking, with a very substantial title, to oust his uncle from the family estates.[16] Llywelyn took Gower from Rhys Gryg to bestow it upon John,[17] and in December, 1221, encouraged him to repair the demolished castle of Swansea.[18]

But Llywelyn's chief enemy was the new Earl of Pembroke. William Marshall the younger had succeeded to his father's wide domains in England, Ireland, and Wales, but not to his high office in the state. It was but to be expected, therefore, that he should regard Welsh affairs, not with the broad outlook of a statesman, but as a mere marcher lord, regretting dangerous concessions to the dominant power in Wales. The maintenance of the peace between Llywelyn and the Earl Marshall was a problem which gave Pandulf and the justiciar no ordinary trouble, and it was well for the prince that William, as a prominent member of the baronial opposition under John, was for a time by no means in good standing at court, and received little more than the bare minimum of support.[19] It was perhaps the knowledge of this mistrust of the earl which encouraged Llywelyn in 1220 to venture upon an attack, crowned at the moment with success, but ultimately followed by a bitter retribution.[20] He had more than once complained to the legate of the conduct of the earl's tenants in Pembrokeshire, who, regardless of the truce, made inroads upon the Welsh inhabitants of Dyfed, lifted their cattle, burned their churches, and carried off captives.[21] In the August of this year he resolved to take measures of reprisal; neglecting a promise he had made to appear at Oxford on the second of the month for the settlement of all outstanding matters of dispute, he gathered a great host and marched southward, to the alarm of the government, who at first suspected a design upon Reginald de Breos.[22] Authority had been given to Llywelyn, probably at Shrewsbury in the preceding May, to eject by force such Welsh princes as were still holding baronial lands,[23] and, on arriving in the valley of the Towy on the 29th, he had, after a skirmish at Carmarthen, persuaded Rhys Gryg to give up Kidwelly, Carnwyllion, Widigada, and Gower.[24] But he soon turned to more congenial work. In the first few days of September, he destroyed the two castles of Narberth[25] and Wiston, set fire to the town of Haverford[26] (the castle was not in this case attacked) and mercilessly ravaged the cantref of Rhos. From his quarters at the priory of Pill on Milford Haven,[27] he threatened the head of the lordship itself, that fortress which had never yet been the prize of a Welsh victory, but the men of Pembroke bought off the attack by promising a payment of £100 to the redoubtable lord of Gwynedd. Llywelyn then returned to the north, having inflicted enormous damage upon the Earl Marshall[28] and made of him an implacable foe.

It was not, of course, to be expected that the legate and the justiciar would countenance these proceedings, and the appeals of the Earl Marshall for protection[29] were in due course, though not with any extraordinary haste, answered by the declaration of 5th October,[30] that the king had not authorised the doings of Llywelyn and that his name had been used without warrant in the affair. At the same time, the men of Pembroke were released from payment of the promised tribute, and Llywelyn was ordered to transfer to the bishop of London and another the custody of the lands he had taken from Welsh princes in virtue of the recent commission.[31] But at the time there was no further development; the prince of North Wales was soon restored to full favour, and the feud between him and the earl, like a hidden volcanic fire, slept a guileful slumber. The hot and naming outburst which was the true sequel to the great Pembrokeshire raid did not break forth until 1223, when the Earl Marshall seized his opportunity for a most signal revenge.

In the beginning of this year,[32] for some unexplained reason, Llywelyn crossed the Shropshire border and took the castle of Kinnerley, near Knockin,[33] and, not long afterwards, the more important fortress of Whittington, which stood not far from his manor of Ellesmere and was the property of Foulk fitz Warren.[34] The king and the justiciar, who were in the valley of the Trent, moved westward to Shrewsbury, which they reached on 7th March,[35] in the hope of composing the quarrel. But, though Earl Ranulf appeared to plead the cause of his friend Llywelyn,[36] no settlement was arrived at. At this juncture the Earl Marshall landed on 15th April in the neighbourhood of St. David's with an army he had collected in Ireland; on the 24th he took Cardigan and on the 26th Carmarthen, in both cases without opposition.[37] He also regained Emlyn and fortified its castle of Cilgerran. Llywelyn sent his son Gruffydd with an army to block the earl's progress towards England, but the latter took the sea route and was in his lordship of Nether Went by the middle of May.[38] Vain attempts at reconciliation occupied the summer, which, as they were based on the assumption that the earl had done a service to the crown in snatching the two royal castles from the grasp of Llywelyn, only embittered the quarrel,[39] and thus it came about that early in September the prince of Gwynedd laid siege to the Breos fortress of Builth.[40] Hubert de Burgh, the king's chief counsellor, now realised that a serious situation had arisen; the knighthood of the realm was summoned to a formal campaign against the Welsh, and on the 19th assembled at Hereford for the relief of the beleaguered castle. A hasty march up the valley of the Wye compelled Llywelyn to relinquish his prey and the royal host then made its way north to Montgomery.[41] It was resolved that this important strategic point should no longer be held by so formidable a personage as the ruler of Southern Powys,[42] but should be taken over by the crown and converted into a border stronghold of the first rank. Ere long the walls and towers of New Montgomery began to crown the narrow, precipitous ridge, admirably suited for defence, which here juts out into the vale of Camlad.[43]

It was now time for Llywelyn to draw rein and consider his position. His hereditary dominions were in no real danger, but his authority and influence in South Wales and in Powys were in serious jeopardy. He had forfeited, of the gains of the civil war, Cardigan, Carmarthen, and Montgomery, and his South Welsh allies, Rhys Gryg, Owain ap Gruffydd, and Maelgwn ap Rhys[44] ran the risk of losing everything in his cause. Confronted by the united strength of the English realm, he resolved to safeguard the substantial power he still retained by a timely submission, and found no difficulty in securing tolerable terms. On 7th October Langton absolved him from the sentence of excommunication which, according to the regular Canterbury practice, had been launched against him;[45] on the 8th, he made his peace with Henry at Montgomery, accompanied by his allies, Rhys Gryg, Maelgwn, Maredudd ap Rhotpert, Madog ap Gruffydd and others of less note.[46] The basis of the agreement was that Llywelyn should resign his Shropshire conquests, while the South Welsh princes who acted with him were in return to receive again the lands of which they had been deprived by the Earl

Marshall.[47] For his own losses there was to be no reparation, and Cardigan and Carmarthen were soon formally transferred to the custody of their conqueror.[48]

This was the only serious check sustained by Llywelyn during the reign of Henry, and it was due to the fact that for the moment unity reigned in England, so that the justiciar could act promptly and without hesitation. Old parties were breaking up; the Earl Marshall, now fully established in favour, received the king's sister, Eleanor, in marriage,[49] and in May, 1224, was sent to rule Ireland as justiciar.[50] But, while the government was making new friends, it was losing old ones, and thus the general concord was no sooner set on foot than it was again broken up by the defection of supporters of long standing. Immediately after the peace with Llywelyn, the first formidable movement against Hubert de Burgh took shape; the Earl of Chester, Bishop Peter of Winchester, Falkes of Breauté, Engelard of Cigogné, and many others who had served the royalist cause under John and during the minority resented the power of the justiciar, which appeared to grow rather than decline as the king reached years of discretion. A renewal of civil war seemed imminent. As it chanced, the storm cloud passed by, with no more momentous result than the fall of Falkes, who carried his opposition a step too far, and, finding no support in his deeds of insolent violence, was forced to quit the realm, after the king's successful siege of his castle of Bedford. But, though Falkes failed to enlist the help of Llywelyn and of the Earl of Chester,[51] the breach between the justiciar and his enemies was not healed, and Llywelyn was emboldened to tell the king that his liberties were as large as those of the king of Scotland, and gave him the right, if he chose, to harbour fugitives from English justice. His language, though not wanting in dignified courtesy towards a suzerain and near relative, bespeaks the consciousness of power; with a divided England against him, he resumes the tone of confidence and independence.

Years of comparative quiet followed, during which conflict was avoided both by Llywelyn and the English government. The former thought it prudent to risk nothing by further acts of aggression; the latter was content to see the prince of Gwynedd powerful, as long as his power led to no disturbance on the march. In January, 1227, Henry declared himself of age, but the end of the minority by no means involved the withdrawal of Hubert de Burgh from the active control of affairs; rather, it enabled him to enhance his authority by dispensing with the aid of other counsellors, and the justiciar was, after this declaration even more than before it, the real governor of the realm. His friendly disposition towards Llywelyn is evinced in many ways. The agreement of October, 1223, was to be followed by a more elaborate and permanent settlement, and, after many delays, due not to any reluctance on the Welsh side, but to the king's other more pressing engagements,[52] a meeting for the purpose took place at Shrewsbury at the end of September, 1224.[53] All appears to have gone off well, and Joan, who had prepared the way for the conference by an interview with the king at Worcester,[54] was rewarded in February, 1225, by the gift of the royal manor of Rothley, in Leicestershire.[55] Llywelyn, in turn, showed his goodwill in the following summer by sending Henry a present of goshawks, falcons, and sparrow hawks [56] — a fit compliment from the lord of the crags of Eryri. Another meeting was now planned, but successive postponements[57] pushed it on until the end of August, 1226, when the king was once more at Shrewsbury, and Joan and Llywelyn, with their son David, came thither to meet him.[58] In the April of this year Honorius III., acting, no doubt, on a suggestion from the English court, had granted to Joan a dispensation which declared her of lawful birth,[59] and advantage was taken of the Shrewsbury interview of this year to bestow upon her yet another manor, that of Condover in Shropshire.[60] Husband and wife stood well with the government and received many marks of its friendly favour.[61]

In Wales itself there were few changes, and such as there were increased rather than diminished the power of Llywelyn. Death removed two of his old enemies about this time; in November, 1227, Hugh Mortimer was succeeded at Wigmore by his brother Ralph,[62] and in the following June Reginald de Breos died,[63] to be succeeded by his son William.[64] William Marshall turned his attention from South Wales to Ireland, and in August, 1226, the king took from him the custody of the castles of Cardigan and Carmarthen, which he entrusted to his own officers.[65] There was now less danger that the Marshall influence might overshadow the whole of the South and reduce to insignificance Llywelyn's authority over the princes of that region. That authority was still vigilantly exercised and justified itself in the protection which the lord of Gwynedd was able to afford to his allies of Deheubarth. In February, 1225, the appearance of two envoys of Llywelyn at Westminster[66] was followed by a warning to the Earl Marshall's bailiff to respect the rights of Maelgwn,[67] whose lands lay in Dyfed and Southern Ceredigion, while in April of the same year he obtained the appointment of a commission of ten, five representing himself and five the earl, to meet at Pont Rheidol, near

Aberystwyth, for the purpose of making a proper partition between Maelgwn and his nephews, Cynan ap Hywel and Owain ap Gruffydd.[68] Cynan had been on the earl's side in the conflict of 1223,[69] and Owain was in temporary opposition to Llywelyn.

The second break in the good relations between Llywelyn and the government came in 1228, and, as it was not provoked by any aggression on the part of the Welsh leader, so it came to an end without diminishing his power and prestige, which indeed were greatly augmented. Early in the year the resumption by the king of the manors of Rothley and Condover[70] seems to indicate a less friendly attitude towards Llywelyn, but the event which directly led to hostilities was the grant to Hubert de Burgh, on 27th April, of the castle and lordship of Montgomery, which had been in the king's hands since 1223.[71] Not only did a very strong border fortress thus come under the direct control of the energetic justiciar, but, from the orders given for the clearing of the forest which lay to the south-west of it and protected the Welsh commote of Kerry, it appeared likely that the new lord had a scheme of conquest afoot.[72] Welsh levies gathered in haste around the spot, and in August the castle was so closely beset that Henry and the justiciar hurried to its relief.[73] As yet Llywelyn had not himself taken the field, but hoped for a peaceful settlement; his wife met the king at Shrewsbury and arranged a truce, and early in September polite letters passed between Henry and his brother-in-law, in which the latter apologised for the way in which his men had interfered with the royal commissariat, and the former accepted the apology and expressed the desire to receive more substantial proofs of Llywelyn's professed goodwill.[74] But war was nevertheless inevitable; already the leading men of the march, the Earls of Gloucester and Pembroke, William de Breos, Roger Clifford and others, had been summoned to Montgomery,[75] and, when the royal host invaded Kerry and Hubert began to build there another strong castle, to threaten Llywelyn's lands in Arwystli, the prince of Gwynedd plunged without hesitation into the fray. The Welsh had much in their favour in this campaign, the help of the country folk, including the men of the grange of Cwm Hir at Gwern y Gof, who had their house burnt to the ground by the English for their pains,[76] the rough, wooded character of the country, the difficulty of provisioning Henry's great army and the jealousies and dissensions of the host, who threw little zeal into this enterprise for making the justiciar still richer and greater. Thus everything went badly for the king; there were many losses, the most conspicuous being the capture, of William de Breos, while engaged in a foraging expedition; food ran short, and at last Hubert was forced to conclude that the conquest of Kerry was impossible. In October there was a humiliating retreat; the commote was restored to Welsh rule,[77] and Henry undertook to raze to the foundations the half-built castle,[78] a concession for which Llywelyn was glad to pay a sum of £2,000. As its walls were rising, the justiciar had playfully christened it "Hubert's Folly"; his foes, as they watched its demolition, turned the jest with pitiless irony against him and said that here indeed was a prophet, and more than a prophet.

The failure of the Kerry campaign was a serious blow to the authority of Hubert and showed Llywelyn that henceforth he had little to fear from the English government. Increasing boldness marks his attitude as he realises that England is divided against itself and that the opportunities which he found so profitable at the time of the Great Charter struggle are recurring in another form.

II. FROM THE KERRY CAMPAIGN TO THE PACT OF MIDDLE.

Llywelyn had come through the troubles of 1228 with flying colours. His restoration to good standing at court was marked by the re-establishment of Joan in her manors of Condover and Rothley in November,[79] while early in the following year the king gave his sanction to the terms upon which William de Breos obtained his liberty.[80] Important steps followed for the recognition of David as Llywelyn's successor; after negotiations carried on through the abbot of Vaudey,[81] the young man went up to London at Michaelmas, did homage for all lands and rights that would accrue to him on the death of his father, and was promised a grant out of the royal lands of the value of £40 a year.[82] Henry was now engaged in the preparations for that French expedition which, after some delay, set sail from Portsmouth on 1st May, 1230, and it was his desire to leave Wales at peace and its prince contented, a purpose to which Llywelyn lent himself with great readiness. The "prince of Aberffraw and lord of Snowdon," as he had now begun to style himself, was fully conscious of the improvement in his position, but he had at the time no adventurous designs and wished only quietly to reap the fruits of his victory. If the year 1230 was signalised by a dramatic act of vengeance upon an English baron, so ruthless and bold as to startle the whole English realm, the deed finds its explanation in a cruel domestic crisis, which shook Llywelyn through and through, and not in any political scheme of aggression. It was the outraged husband, not the astute politician, who hanged William de Breos.

William had been set free at the beginning of 1229 upon promise of a ransom of £2,000[83] a sum corresponding so precisely to that which Llywelyn had engaged to pay to the king that it is reasonable to conjecture that the prince meant the one liability to discharge the other.[84] He had also undertaken never again to bear arms against Llywelyn, and, as a further pledge of amity, had agreed to bestow upon David the hand of his daughter, Isabella, with the lordship and castle of Builth as her marriage portion. The two magnates seemed to be about to enter into a close alliance when the tie was suddenly snapped by Llywelyn's discovery of an intrigue, no doubt set on foot during the period of captivity, between William and his wife.[85] It was during a visit paid by the rash lover to Llywelyn's court at Eastertide that the storm broke; the prince's suspicion was aroused, and he burst in upon the pair at dead of night, to find full confirmation of all he had feared. The confidence he had placed in Joan as his best friend and faithful supporter throughout many years was the measure of his wrath; both she and her paramour were forthwith imprisoned,[86] together with the knights brought by the latter in his train, and in a few days William paid the penalty of his folly. All Wales had heard the news of his capture, and the enemies of his house hastened from every quarter to see this scion of a hated stock brought to his account; even had Llywelyn been in the mood to resist the tide of popular passion, he might have found it hard to withstand the demand that William should die. "On 2nd May," reports the abbot of Vaudey[87] a few days later, "at a certain manor called 'Crokein,'[88] he was made 'Crogyn,'[89] *i.e.*, hanged on a tree, and this not privily or in the night time, but openly and in broad daylight, in the presence of more than 800 men assembled to behold the piteous and melancholy spectacle."

It was a lamentable affair, but in no sense a declaration of war against England. Llywelyn treated the matter as one affecting William only and wrote to the widow[90] and to her brother, the Earl Marshall,[91] to say that, notwithstanding the action of his enraged subjects, he still wished the alliance between David and Isabella to stand. This view was apparently shared by the Breos family, for no separation took place. The very envoy who gave to the chancellor (ruling the land during Henry's absence) the news of the sad event was at the time arranging for a conference between his master and Llywelyn, which, there is reason to think, was held near Shrewsbury about 12th June and issued in a friendly agreement.[92] In August the government and the Welsh leader were on the best of terms, and the former discreetly alluded to the execution of William as the "mischance which befell him".[93] The

renewal of strife was due to quite other causes and may with good reason be chiefly ascribed to the ill-will with which Llywelyn saw the justiciar attempt to build up for himself a mighty power in South Wales.
Hubert had been since the beginning of the reign a Welsh marcher
lord in virtue of his tenure of the three castles of Grosmont, Skenfrith
and White Castle in Upper Gwent,[94] and in 1223 he had added to
these the castle and honour of Montgomery. He now began to extend
these Welsh possessions largely and on such a scale as to show that his
aim was to wield in South Wales the authority held by Llywelyn in the
North. In 1227 he obtained a grant of the region of Archenfield[95] in
Herefordshire; in 1229 he was invested with the lordships of
Cardigan and Carmarthen, which were erected into a new marcher
holding, held by the service of five knights.[96] At the end of 1230 the
lordship of Gower was subordinated to this new fief, and John de
Breos was told no longer to regard himself as a tenant of the crown.[97]
About the same time the death of Earl Gilbert of Gloucester in
Britanny, leaving his wide possessions to an heir of eight, opened up a
fresh opportunity;[98] Hubert obtained the custody of lands and heir
and thus became virtual lord of Glamorgan, with the right to command the service of the minor chieftains of the hill-country of
Morgannwg.[99] Early in April, 1231, another windfall added to the jus-
ticiary gains; the Earl Marshall died suddenly, a week after his sister's
wedding to Earl Richard of Cornwall, the king's brother,[100] and the
custody of the Breos lands which the dead earl had received from the
crown was thus set free and in a little while bestowed upon Hubert.[101]
In the early summer of this year there was hardly a corner of South
Wales where the enterprising justiciar had not planted his banner.

Trouble had already been brewing on the border before this last
grant to Hubert.[102] The death of the Earl Marshall had encouraged
the Welsh to attack the Breos territories, and the king had sent his
brother Richard to the disturbed area, promising soon to follow in
person.[103] On the 20th of May he was at Hereford, where he issued
orders forbidding the dwellers in the march to furnish the Welsh
with provisions while the disturbance lasted.[104] But negotiations with
Llywelyn were proceeding, as it seemed, favourably,[105] and the king
had returned to the Thames valley when at the beginning of June
the prince of Gwynedd suddenly resolved upon war and kindled the
flames of revolt throughout the length and breadth of South Wales.
He is said to have been stung into rebellion by the beheading of
certain prisoners taken by the garrison of Montgomery,[106] but this
step, for which Hubert de Burgh was responsible, was no doubt but

the final item in the growing burden of the justiciar's offences. Gathering his warriors about him, Llywelyn swept southward and burnt the new settlement at Montgomery; Radnor, with its castle, and the towns of Hay and Brecon were likewise involved in fiery ruin, and in his rage of battle the prince did not spare the churches, in which the women and the clergy had taken refuge from the hurricane of war.[107] Next, he made his way to Caerleon, a Marshall stronghold defended by Morgan ap Hywel, who hoped by the king's favour to recover it for his house; the town was destroyed, but the castle resisted the onslaught, and Llywelyn then crossed the mountains to Neath, imposing by the way a levy of sixty marks on the terrified convent of Margam.[108] He had the help of the Welsh princes of Glamorgan, Rhys ap Gruffydd, Hywel ap Maredudd, and Morgan Gam,[109] and at the end of June with their aid took and razed to the ground the castle of Neath, a success soon followed by the capture of Kidwelly. He closed the campaign with an achievement which gave him peculiar pleasure. Maelgwn the Younger, who had just succeeded to the lands of his father Maelgwn in Ceredigion,[110] had, with Rhys Gryg and Owain ap Gruffydd, thrown himself with zeal into the great uprising and had burnt the town of Cardigan to the castle gates. In a few days the castle itself was battered into surrender, and Llywelyn snatched from the grasp of the justiciar the proud fortress at the mouth of the Teifi the loss of which eight years previously had been so mortifying a blow to his authority in South Wales.

Llywelyn's resonant challenge was at once taken up by the crown, but the wheels of Hubert's administration moved somewhat slowly. Ecclesiastical weapons were first invoked, and for his offences against the church Llywelyn, with twelve of his allies, was excommunicated by an assembly of the bishops of the province of Canterbury and the sentence promulgated throughout England.[111] Steps were taken on 2nd July for the relief of the castle of Newport, which was said to be hard pressed,[112] and on the 7th Llywelyn was deprived of his wife's manor of Rothley.[113] It was not, however, until the month of July was far advanced that Henry met at Gloucester and at Hereford the military forces of the West which he had summoned thither for a great campaign against the Welsh.[114] Deliberate as these preparations were, they did not lead to much fighting; instead of marching upon Llywelyn, the king's advisers settled down, as in 1223 and 1228, to the building of a fortress, and chose Painscastle, in Lower Elfael, a spot continually in debate between the Welsh and the house of Breos,[115] as the point of vantage upon which to concentrate their strength. It was, no doubt, chosen with reference to its nearness to Llywelyn's recent acquisition of Builth, and here the army remained from 30th July to 22nd September, while the old timber defences of "Matilda's Castle" were "elegantly rebuilt in stone and mortar". How Llywelyn was meanwhile employed there is little to show, but one skirmish is recorded, fought probably on the Wye near Hay,[116] in which, with the help of a trick played upon the English by a monk of Cwm Hir, he scored a signal success. Henry avenged his defeat upon the abbey by burning one of its granges and forcing the abbot to pay a fine of 300 marks.

When, with the approach of winter, the king withdrew from Painscastle, he had done little to humble the pride of Llywelyn. His brand-new fortress was imposing, but it did not prevent the Welsh prince from harrying the lands of the priory of Leominster, until the prior was ready to pay handsomely for freedom from disturbance.[117] Henry had nothing better in view than a renewal of the struggle in the following summer, with the prospect of help from Ireland in an attack upon Anglesey,[118] when he learnt that Llywelyn was prepared to agree to a suspension of hostilities.[119] The power of Hubert de Burgh was now being shaken to its base; his old enemy, Bishop Peter of Winchester, had returned from crusade and was seeking to supplant him; it was to his interest to rid himself of the Welsh entanglement, while Llywelyn desired nothing better than to be allowed to keep what he had won. Accordingly, on 30th November, 1231, a truce was concluded for a year, on the basis of the actual situation and with the hope that the year's respite might be employed in negotiating more permanent terms of peace.[120]

Negotiations went on throughout the year 1232, but, though the border remained fairly peaceful, little progress was made with them.[121] England was, in this year, in the throes of an internal conflict, as the result of which the great edifice of the justiciar's power came toppling down, and Bishop Peter rose to the chief position in the realm. The bishop's nephew (or son), Peter of Rivaux, received large grants in consequence of the change, and, in particular, succeeded to nearly all Hubert's possessions in Wales.[122] The new government, jealously watched by the great lords and in its foreign complexion disagreeably recalling the despotic days of John, was not formidable to Llywelyn, who kept up cordial but distant relations with it. At the end of the year, he lost his firm friend and ally, Earl Ranulf of Chester,[123] who had championed his cause at Painscastle in the king's councils, and, effecting nothing, had withdrawn from the siege in high dudgeon.[124] But the earl, though he left no peer in the king's

dominions in territorial dignity and in weight of influence, was succeeded at Chester by Llywelyn's son-in-law, John the Scot,[125] so that
there was no break in the friendly relations between Gwynedd and
the great border earldom. In this year another son-in-law of Llywelyn
disappears from the scene; John de Breos was killed at Bramber by a
fall from his horse, and, as his son and heir, William, was under age,
Gower and Swansea came into the king's hands, to be added for the
time being to the piled up wealth of the insatiable Peter of Rivaux.[126]

Its rapacity and tyranny were fast making the new government
impossible, and in the summer of 1233 a crisis came which, by rekin-
dling the fires of civil strife, relieved Llywelyn from all present anxiety as to the doings of the English crown. William Marshall had been
succeeded as Earl of Pembroke[127] by his brother Richard, a gallant
and high-minded knight, recalling in many respects his distinguished father, who had hitherto lived in France and taken no part
in English politics. It was not long ere Richard and the foreign clique
in power were openly at odds, and in August, Henry, abandoning a
scheme for an expedition to Ireland, established himself in the west
country with the intention of bringing the recalcitrant earl to subjection.[128] After measures against the earl's ally, Walter Clifford,[129] the
king laid siege on 6th September to the castle of Usk. His failure to
take it put him for a time into a wiser frame of mind; he offered, if
Richard would consult the royal dignity by a *pro forma* surrender of
the place, to remit all his hostility against him and summon a council
of reform.[130] On this basis there was a brief pacification, seeming for
the moment to promise a general peace, but being in fact but an
interlude in the struggle, which broke out with renewed violence in
the middle of October.

Llywelyn was meanwhile watching the conflict as an interested
spectator. Except for a transient quarrel in March, when he had
attacked the Breos lands and the earls of Cornwall and Pembroke had
restored for their protection the broken defences of Radnor,[131] he
had maintained during 1233 the attitude of willingness to negotiate
which he had taken up in the previous year.[132] As late as 14th October
the grant of the manor of Purleigh in Essex to David testified to the
good relations between him and the English court.[133] But when Earl
Richard, impatient at the delay in the restoration of Usk, forcibly
retook the castle from the royal garrison,[134] and his friends in
Glamorgan carried Cardiff Castle by assault,[135] Llywelyn ranged himself on the side of the baronial opposition and a war broke out along
the march in which the Welsh acted with the Marshall interest and

the knights of Glamorgan against the forces of the crown, backed by the Shropshire and the Herefordshire marchers.[136] The struggle at first raged chiefly in the valleys of the Usk and the Wye, where the earl obtained possession of Abergavenny, Newport, and Monmouth, in addition to his own castles of Usk, Caerleon, and Chepstow,[137] forced the king to retire from Grosmont after raiding his camp at dawn on 11th November[138] and defeated John of Monmouth in a pitched battle fought near that town on 26th December. Llywelyn was meanwhile employed in the siege of Brecon, with the result that, after a month's battering of the walls with warlike engines, he reduced the town to ashes, but failed in taking the castle.[139] In January, 1234, Richard and he devastated the border far and wide, making their power felt as far as Shrewsbury.[140] The princes of South Wales, Rhys Gryg, Owain ap Gruffydd, and Maelgwn Fychan, threw all their strength into an attack upon the town and castle of Carmarthen,[141] which they cut off from all succour on the seaward side by building a bridge across the Towy. It was not a successful enterprise; in March the experienced warrior, Henry of Turbeville, was sent with a fleet from Bristol to raise the siege;[142] the bridge was broken and the Welsh army scattered with much slaughter. Among men of less note, the veteran Rhys Gryg was mortally wounded and died not long afterwards at Llandeilo Fawr.[143]

Early in February Earl Richard left Wales for Ireland, where the conflict was also being carried on. It was, however, reaching its natural close, as the king realised the impotence of the foreign party and gradually yielded to the pressure brought to bear upon him by the bishops in the interests of reform. Foremost among the peacemakers was the primate elect, Edmund Rich, who sent the bishops of Lichfield and Rochester to the border to see what they could do with Llywelyn. The prince of Gwynedd had no strong reason for continuing the struggle, and accordingly he agreed to a truce on 6th March at Brockton, near Bishop's Castle,[144] and sent envoys to the king, who confirmed the arrangement for a respite of fighting on the 28th.[145] In this way the ground was cleared for the much desired revolution at court; on 9th April the newly consecrated archbishop won a complete victory over Peter of Winchester and his train, and matters were ripe for the restoration of the Earl Marshall to his due position of honour and authority in the realm. On the 15th, however, the earl died in Ireland,[146] as the result of hostile measures long before set on foot by his enemies, and it was now but a question of reconciling his brothers and his adherents to the king and of securing a permanent peace with Llywelyn. In June there was a general pacification; Gilbert

Marshall became Earl of Pembroke, the insurgents in England and South Wales were received again into favour, and Peter of Rivaux was stripped of all his Welsh possessions. Upon learning that his allies had received satisfactory terms, Llywelyn also accepted conditions of peace;[147] on 21st June the archbishop and the two bishops who had negotiated the armistice of Brockton met him at Middle, half-way between Ellesmere and Shrewsbury, and concluded a truce for two years, which was ratified by the king on 7th July.[148] The basis of the agreement was adherence to the state of things which obtained at the outbreak of the war; no new castle was to be built, no ruined one restored, on either side, but all conquests of earlier date than the outbreak of the quarrel with Earl Richard were to be retained, so that Llywelyn kept his hold upon Cardigan and Builth. In form the settlement was merely temporary and determined no questions of right, but, on the expiration of the prescribed two years, the truce was renewed from year to year until Llywelyn's death,[149] so that in substance the Pact of Middle was a treaty of peace, the crowning achievement of the prince's long and victorious career. He fought no more battles with the English; he had won for himself and for his people a secure and well-guarded independence, and henceforth his chief concern was to make sure that the edifice of national power and prosperity he had erected would survive his removal from the scene.

III. WALES UNDER THE RULE OF LLYWELYN.

While the Welsh leader was thus fighting and parleying and bargaining with the king and the barons of the march, the realms of Gwynedd and Powys lay in profoundest peace. Hardly a ripple disturbed the face of the waters, and the domestic history of the period is almost a blank. The question of the succession, no doubt, gave Llywelyn some anxiety from time to time, but, apart from this, there was no internal problem to harass him. The age was one in which, under the powerful protection of the lord of Gwynedd, Welsh society followed the lines of its natural development, and Welsh literature, law and religion quietly prospered.

Wide as was the scope of his authority, stretching from Cardigan to Mold and from Builth to Anglesey, Llywelyn never claimed the title of prince of Wales. He used the official designation of "princeps Norwalliæ," i.e., prince of Gwynedd, until the spring of 1230, when he began to style himself "prince of Aberffraw and lord of Snowdon," a title ere long recognised by the English government.[150] It can hardly be supposed that the longer and more sonorous style was adopted for mere reasons of euphony; a serious purpose lay behind it. Llywelyn wished to emphasise his primacy in Wales as the holder of that "principal seat" to which tradition assigned the pre-eminence; the prince of Aberffraw held himself to be the natural lord of the prince of Dinefwr, and thus found a justification in traditional lore for the actual supremacy which he exercised.[151] "Lord of Snowdon" was perhaps added for greater effect, the humble Aberffraw conveying to English ears no such suggestion of ancient greatness as to the Welshman steeped in the history of bygone days.

But, though Llywelyn. did not formally style himself prince of Wales, he had much of the power which such a title might imply.

The South — dost thou not rule it as rightful lord?

triumphantly sings his bard, Llywarch ap Llywelyn,[152] and he let no opportunity escape him of winning authority even in distant Gwent and Glamorgan.[153] It may be said, however, that his prestige in the South, though always great, was a variable quantity, depending on the fortune of war; in the North it was at all times unquestioned and involved the complete subjection of the other ruling princes. Among these were Maredudd ap Rhotpert of Cydewain,[154] Llywelyn ab Owain and Owain Fychan of Mechain,[155] the stock of Owain Brogyntyn in Edeyrnion,[156] and Llywelyn ap Maredudd in Meirionydd.[157] Chief of Llywelyn's Northern vassals was Madog ap Gruffydd, whose lands stretched from the Tanat to the outskirts of Chester, the founder of Valle Crucis, the lord of Overton Castle, towering on its cliff above the beautiful, sinuous course of the Dee.[158] From the Peace of Worcester until his death in 1236, when he was laid to rest in the abbey he had endowed,[159] Madog was unswervingly faithful to his great chief,[160] and his fidelity, with the friendship of the Earls of Chester, put Llywelyn at his ease as to the security of his eastern border as far south as the rock of Carreghofa. After Madog's death, his domains were divided among his sons, Gruffydd Maelor, Gruffydd Ial, Hywel, Maredudd, and Madog, and the too familiar tale of fraternal jealousy and strife was once more repeated. In 1238 Maredudd brought about the death of Gruffydd Ial, whereupon Llywelyn intervened as overlord and deprived the fratricide of his lands.[161]

Not only vassals, but also able ministers, both clerical and lay, seconded the efforts of the prince of Gwynedd. Chief among them was Ednyfed Fychan, who succeeded Gwyn ab Ednywain[162] about 1215 as "distain" or seneschal, and henceforward takes the first place among the counsellors and envoys of Llywelyn. Tradition would have us believe that he first won fame as a warrior, fighting against Earl Ranulf of Chester and cutting off the heads of three Englishmen, which were thereafter figured upon his escutcheon.[163] But his true glory is the place he filled and the services he rendered until his death in 1246[164] as the prudent adviser and skilful agent of two successive lords of Aberffraw. He first appears in connection with the Peace of Worcester in 1218,[165] and next as a witness to the compact between Llywelyn and the Earl of Chester on the occasion of the marriage of John the Scot in 1222.[166] From 1229 onwards he is constantly engaged in the business of the prince,[167] and it cannot be doubted that the part he played in shaping the policy of Gwynedd was substantial. Of his private history little is certainly known;[168] the death of his wife Gwenllian, a daughter of the Lord Rhys, is recorded in 1236,[169] and he would seem in the previous year to have made a pilgrimage to the Holy Land.[170] He had estates at Rhos Fyneich[171] (near Colwyn Bay), at Llansadwrn and Llanrhystyd in South Wales,[172] and, no doubt, also in Anglesey, where his descendants were mighty folk for many generations. Not the least of his claims to respectful notice from the historian is that from him sprang, by direct male descent, the puissant House of Tudor, so that his stock might have used, with even greater propriety than the Mortimers, the boastful motto —"Not we from kings, but kings from us".

The greatness of Ednyfed cast a shade over the lesser agents of Llywelyn's purposes, men such as Einion Fychan,[173] David, archdeacon of St. Asaph,[174] and the clerical envoys, Ystrwyth,[175] Adam,[176] David[177] and Philip ab Ifor.[178] But the prince had one emissary whose diplomatic services far outran those of the seneschal and who helped him in this capacity for the greater part of his reign. To the assistance of his wife Joan, both as advocate and counsellor, there can be no doubt he was much indebted. Reference has already been made to the part which she played as mediator between Wales and England up to 1230; the tragedy of that year brought about a sudden suspension of her diplomatic activity, but it was not long ere it was resumed. In the following year she was forgiven and released from prison,[179] and in 1232 she appears once more in the accustomed role of representative of her husband.[180] She died at Aber, the royal seat of the commote of Arllechwedd Uchaf, now becoming a favourite residence of the princes of Gwynedd,[181] on 2nd February, 1237,[182] and the best proof of her complete restoration to the old footing of trust and affection is to be found in the honour paid by Llywelyn to her memory.

Her body was borne across the sands of Lafan and ferried to the Anglesey shore, where, not far from the prince's manor of Llanfaes, a new burying-ground had been consecrated by Bishop Hugh of St. Asaph. Here she was laid to rest, while for monument Llywelyn built on the spot a house for Franciscan friars, so that the most saintly of the religious, as they were then accounted, might pray for her soul.[183] Her coffin of stone, with its graceful carving and comely present-ment of the diademed head in bas-relief, was torn from its place at the dissolution, but has recently found fitting shelter and protection in Baron Hill Park.[184]

Joan had one son, David, the indubitable heir to Llywelyn's great position, as heirship was reckoned in feudal and Christian Europe. But the position was complicated by the fact that the prince had an older son, Gruffydd, born to him before his marriage, and that under Welsh law this youth might fairly claim, though not born in wedlock, to share his father's dominions with his younger brother.[185] Gruffydd was the son of a Welsh mother, Tangwystl, daughter of Llywarch the Red of Rhos,[186] and both this circumstance and his fiery and enter-prising spirit—for he was an Ishmael by disposition no less than in respect of his birth—made him a popular hero and counterbalanced the disadvantage he suffered in the public recognition of David as sole heir. Thus a conflict arose which outlasted the life of Llywelyn, and which, while he lived, was a constant source of trouble to him. He never wavered in his determination that David should succeed to the whole of his territories; apart from his attachment to Joan and the recollection that his own accession to full power was a triumph for legitimacy, there was the certainty that only David, strong in his rela-tionship to the English king and in the possession of an unassailable title, could hold together what had become a virtual principality of Wales. In 1220 he secured the recognition of David by the English Government,[187] in 1222 by the pope,[188] and in 1226 by the magnates of Wales;[189] in 1229 followed the homage of the heir to Henry III., and in 1230 his marriage to Isabella de Breos.[190] Meanwhile, Llywelyn's treatment of Gruffydd had varied; he had sometimes indulged him, and then again, moved by his reckless violence, had turned upon him and punished him. He had at first given him Meirionydd and Ardudwy, but the ravages committed by Gruffydd upon his own territories led him in 1221 to recall his gift.[191] In 1223 Gruffydd was so far in favour again as to be in command of forces which acted for Llywelyn in Ystrad Tywi,[192] but in 1228 his father imprisoned him in Degannwy as the only method of ensuring his good behaviour, and he, remained a prisoner for the next six years.[193] With Gruffydd under lock and key, David's path was clear of difficulties, and the rivalry between the two brothers was suspended until it burst forth again at the close of the reign.

Turning from the circle of Llywelyn's personal relations to the land over which he bore sway, one observes that, after the great struggle at St. David's, the Welsh Church enjoyed quiet during the rest of his period of rule. The successful movement against the tyranny of John enabled him in 1215 to carry, without serious opposition, in the case of the two most important Welsh sees, the point for which he had contended earlier in the reign, namely, the election of Welsh bishops. Geoffrey of St. David's died in 1214,[194] and thereupon negotiations were set on foot by the court for the appointment of a successor acceptable to the king.[195] But John found it impossible to achieve his purpose, and he was forced, a few days after accepting the Great Charter, to agree to the elevation of Iorwerth, abbot of Talley, unanimously chosen by the chapter, no doubt with the concurrence of Llywelyn.[196] Giraldus, whose claims were on this occasion with one consent ignored, avenges himself by suggesting that Iorwerth's election was not quite free from the taint of simony, but he admits that the new bishop was a good, simple man,[197] and he would seem to have filled his office well, mediating between Welsh and English in time of strife,[198] reforming the services of his cathedral,[199] and, probably, continuing the building work of Bishop Peter.[200] With Iorwerth, Archbishop Langton consecrated to the vacant see of Bangor Cadwgan, abbot of Whitland, who was the son of a priest famed for his Welsh preaching and was himself in high favour with Llywelyn.[201] It was a choice which was undoubtedly due to the predominance of the prince of Gwynedd at this time, though Giraldus, in the disappointment of his declining years, sneers at it and paints the new bishop in the most unpleasing colours, as an unfilial son and a wicked schemer. But what history has to tell of him is to his credit; avarice cannot be laid to the charge of a prelate who in 1234 bought a shipload of corn in Ireland to feed the poor of his diocese,[202] nor yet love of power to the account of a man who in 1236 resigned his episcopal dignity and found shelter for his aged bones as a humble monk in the Cistercian house of Dore.[203] Under the gentle sway of Iorwerth and Cadwgan and of the undistinguished bishops of St. Asaph,[204] the ecclesiastical air was untroubled, even if there hung about it a suggestion of drowsy content which one might have looked for in vain if the ambitions of the fiery reformer of Manorbier had been realised.

It was in the monastic sphere that enterprise and energy came to light in the Welsh Church of this period, and here Llywelyn showed himself the enlightened friend of reform, with no narrow suspicion of new religious movements. His sympathies in this respect were as broad as those of Rhys ap Gruffydd. He befriended the canons of Priestholm or Ynys Lannog, who were members of no recognised monastic order, but a company of anchorites of the old Welsh pattern,[205] and secured them in the possession of the church and manor of Penmon.[206] But he was no less favourable to the Cistercian fraternity, now firmly rooted both in North and South Wales; he issued to Cymer and to Aberconwy charters confirming to those houses their extensive lands in Gwynedd,[207] and he maintained the most amicable relations with Strata Florida [208] and Cwm Hir. It was probably under his patronage that the Knights Hospitallers found a home at Dolgynwal, or Yspyty Ifan, on the banks of the Conway,[209] and mention has already been made of the welcome he gave to the Franciscans, representing the newest type of religious devotee, who, at the time of their settlement at Llanfaes, had only been some thirteen years in these islands. In the realm of religion, as in that of politics, Llywelyn was accessible to new impulses and ideas.

There is reason to think that the prince's care for the welfare of his people exhibited itself in yet another channel, namely, that of law. The Venedotian Code, that edition of the laws of Hywel the Good which embodies the special usages of Gwynedd, would seem to have been compiled by one Iorwerth ap Madog about the beginning of the thirteenth century.[210] If this be the case, it can hardly be doubted that the moving influence in the matter was the Venedotian lord, whose interest it was that all his subjects should be under the authority of one body of law. His privileges are naturally asserted to the full: "gold," as satisfaction for an insult, "is paid only," we are informed, "to the king of Aberffraw,"[211] but a beneficent purpose may also be traced in the reform, for this was one of the ways in which, as the annalist puts it, "he showed good justice to all, according to their deserts, in the love and fear of God."[212] Iorwerth ap Madog was apparently a man of Arfon, and he records prominently the special rights of the warriors of that cantref, the men of the black-headed shafts, who had earned them, tradition alleged, in the tribal wars of far distant days.[213]

The age of Llywelyn, it scarcely needs to be said, was one of brilliant literary achievement in Wales. Ten bards are mentioned by Stephens in *The Literature of the Kymry*[214] as having written during this period poetry which survives, and included in the list are the honoured names of Cynddelw the Great Maker (Y Prydydd Mawr) and Llywarch ap Llywelyn, the Poet of the Swine (Prydydd y Moch). Most of them confess, in rapturous odes to the prince of Gwynedd, the debt which poesy owed him as the doer of noble deeds and the begetter of heroic strains. He is, says Cynddelw,

> The proud lord whom God made without a fault.[215]

Prydydd y Moch declares —

> Well known it is that thy long hand never falters
> As it bestows the red and the yellow gold:
> God made thee braver than any man that breathes —
> Most liberal, too, as far as the sun's course extends:
> It is thy father's kindly instinct that to thee clings,
> And in thee the generous dead is reborn.[216]

Dafydd Benfras almost declines the impossible task of adequate eulogy —

> Had I the skill of a wizard
> In the primitive, eloquent bardic strain,
> I could not for the life of me paint his prowess in battle,
> Nor could Taliesin.[217]

While the simple lines of Einion ap Gwgon, his loyal kinsman and retainer, set forth what, it may well be believed, were in general the relations between the prince and his subjects —

> He to me as the crystal mind,
> I to him as the hand and the eye.[218]

Besides the work of known authors, there is much anonymous literature, both in verse and in prose, which undoubtedly came into being during this age of fruitful growth. To it may be assigned not a few of the predictive poems, in which national history is unfolded, as in the case of Cowper's "Boadicea" and Gray's "Bard," by a prophetic figure of the past who tells the story by way of prognostication. The "Hoianau," a celebrated specimen of the type, contains a reference to the struggle of Llywelyn and John and the vengeance inflicted on the foreigner by the outraged saint of Bangor —

> When Daniel, son of Dunod Deinwyn, is kindled to wrath,
> The Frank shall return in flight — he shall not ask the road![219]

The *Mabinogion,* too, the famous romantic tales of the Welsh, though there is little to fix the date of their composition, cannot be moved far from the age of Llywelyn, in whose lifetime the earliest known manuscript of the Four Branches was penned.[220] It was the luxuriant and free flowering springtime of the Welsh genius, when fancy and patriotic fervour and wistful love of the past took a hundred different shapes—the ode, the stanza, the triad, the romance, the legend of saintly life, the mystic prophecy. And foremost figure of the race, its pride and its delight, was the lord of Aberffraw —

Great chief of our fair, white land and its adornment![221]

IV. CLOSING SCENES.

Llywelyn was now growing old and a slight paralytic stroke added to the burden of his sixty-five years.[222] Having secured peace with England on the basis of the *status quo,* he devoted his fast-ebbing energies to the task of making sure of the succession of David. In 1234 Gruffydd had been released from captivity and had received the half of Lleyn;[223] his behaviour giving satisfaction, this provision had been in later years very greatly increased, until in 1238 he is found holding, in addition to the whole of this westernmost cantref of Gwynedd, a substantial share of Powys, where his father apparently designed to establish him as successor to Gwenwynwyn.[224] But the feud between the two brothers did not admit of so easy a solution, and in this year it came to a violent issue. On 19th October an assembly of all the princes of Wales took place at Strata Florida Abbey, which was friendly, as ever, to the power of Llywelyn, and each one swore fealty to David as next heir.[225] Armed with this new authority, the young prince stripped his rival of all his lands in Powys, leaving him only Lleyn, and in the following year, whether provoked by some fresh act of hostility or taking advantage of a more secure footing in the realm, he imprisoned Gruffydd and his son Owain in Criccieth,[226] and thus made himself undisputed master of North Wales.

It was thus, with every object of his life achieved, with a strong and prosperous principality ready to be handed on to the son of Joan, that Llywelyn died on 11th April, 1240.[227] He spent his last hours in the abbey of Aberconwy, where he took the monastic habit and where his body was honourably entombed. Bard and chronicler sang his praises with unanimous voice. "Thus died," writes the Cistercian annalist, "that great Achilles the Second, the lord Llywelyn. . . whose deeds I am unworthy to recount. For with lance and shield did he tame his foes; he kept peace for the men of religion; to the needy he gave food and raiment. With a warlike chain he extended his boundaries; he showed justice to all. . . and by meet bonds of fear or love bound all men to him."[228] In the like strain of eulogy did Einion the Weak mourn the loss of his prince, marvelling at the low estate of one who had a few short hours before been so great: —

> True lord of the land — how strange that to-day
> He rules not o'er Gwynedd!
> Lord of nought but the piled up stones of his tomb,
> Of the seven-foot grave in which he lies.[229]

Among the chieftains who battled against the Anglo-Norman power his place will always be high, if not indeed the highest of all, for no man ever made better or more judicious use of the native force of the Welsh people for adequate national ends; his patriotic statesmanship will always entitle him to wear the proud style of Llywelyn the Great.

CHAPTER IX

BETWEEN TWO TIDES

I. THE STRUGGLE OF DAVID FOR INDEPENDENCE.

THE six short years of David's rule have the interest of an unfinished experiment. Llywelyn had done all that foresight could achieve to ensure the continuance of his own power unbroken in the hands of his youngest son; time alone would show whether the scheme would be successful. But David's early death put an end to the experiment in its most crucial stage, and the fact that he left no heir cleared the board even more thoroughly than would otherwise have been the case—nothing remained of the edifice so laboriously built by Llywelyn. Nor must it be supposed that, before the removal of David, the English crown had virtually won its victory; the prince had, in point of fact, surmounted his early difficulties, and there is no reason to suppose that, had he lived, he might not have achieved a decisive triumph.

His first steps were easily taken, so carefully had the way been prepared. He had the powerful support of Ednyfed Fychan, of the bishop of St. Asaph, and of Einion Fychan,[1] and his accession to the principality of North Wales was taken for granted at the English court. Gruffydd was in close confinement, and for the moment no one, save, perhaps, Bishop Richard of Bangor, was disposed to make much of his claims.[2] Accordingly, on 15th May, 1240, little more than a month after his father's death, David attended a royal council at Gloucester, was knighted, did homage for Gwynedd, and wore the "talaith" or coronet which was the special symbol of his rank.[3] The other magnates of Wales did homage in his company, and his rule seemed to have begun auspiciously in peace and security.[4] But fair as was the aspect of the heavens, there was inevitable trouble brewing; the English government, while fully prepared to recognise David as his father's lawful successor, did not intend that he should retain Llywelyn's conquests. To abstain from robbing the redoubtable lion of Gwynedd of his prey was one thing; to allow it to pass, with no effort at recovery, into the jaws of the lion-whelp was quite another. The chief territories in dispute were Cardigan, claimed by Earl Gilbert of Pembroke under a royal grant,[5] Mold, out of which the barons of Montalt had been kept for more than forty years,[6] Southern Powys, the inheritance of Gruffydd ap Gwenwynwyn,[7] and Builth, which David alleged to be the dowry of his wife, Isabella de Breos.[8] Gilbert proceeded at once to make good his claim by despatching an army under his brother Walter to the mouth of the Teifi, where the keep of Cardigan was rebuilt and English ascendancy restored, in spite of the resistance of Maelgwn Fychan, the Welsh lord of Southern Ceredigion.[9] Elsewhere, matters were not so easily adjusted, and an attempt was made to recover the lost lands by negotiation with David, who fenced with the question as long as he was able.

He was by no means so well placed for maintaining a struggle of this kind as his father had been. On the death of John the Scot in June, 1237, leaving no heir, the earldom of Chester had reverted to the crown,[10] and the city on the Dee, which had hitherto been, under Earl Ranulf and his nephew, an outpost of the Welsh power, became and permanently remained an aggressive centre of royal influence. The justiciar of Chester was now a royal official, and from 1240 to 1245 the post was held by John Lestrange, a Shropshire baron who was ever active in the king's service.[11] There was another respect in which David was at a disadvantage; he had not the confidence of all his fellow-princes, and a little later a number of them openly espoused the cause of Gruffydd. Nevertheless, he did his best to postpone the day of reckoning. In his anxiety to secure the recognition of his title by the king, he had agreed at Gloucester to submit the matter of the disputed lands to a body of arbitrators, partly English and partly Welsh, with the pope's legate, Otto, at their head.[12] He had thus furnished his opponents with a weapon of which they were not slow to avail themselves, and for twelve months the burden of the English letters is the difficulty of inducing David to carry out the arbitration proposal. A meeting of the arbitrators was perhaps held at London on 7th December,[13] but, if so, it did not complete its work, and an effort was made to secure another meeting at Worcester in February, 1241, when it was proposed to fill the places of two members of the body who had gone abroad. David ignored this proposal and was then cited to appear at Shrewsbury on 17th March.[14] When this day arrived, he was again absent and unrepresented, and the government were emboldened to set up judicial proceedings, hearing the complaints of the dispossessed lords and declaring the case settled against David by default.[15] This was a false move, for the prince made haste to point out that it substituted law for the promised arbitration, and on 28th April his envoys succeeded in replacing the matter on its original basis.[16] None the less did he prove a defaulter on the new day fixed for the trial of the issue, namely, 16th June, when the parties were to meet at Montford on the Severn.[17]

The king's patience was now exhausted,[18] and at the beginning of August he appeared in the western counties with a force for the subjugation of David.[19] That prince was almost wholly bereft of allies, for he had against him, not only the claimants whom he was keeping out of possession, Roger of Montalt, Gruffydd ap Gwenwynwyn, and Ralph Mortimer,[20] but also Gruffydd ap Madog of Northern Powys, Maredudd ap Rhotpert, and Maelgwn Fychan. On 12th August, at Shrewsbury, Henry granted the petition of the wife of the imprisoned Gruffydd that, if the release of her husband could be brought about, he should have his due share of Gwynedd, and the other princes gave their cordial support to this proposal for the diminution of the territories of David.[21] The army moved on to Chester,[22] invaded Tegeingl, and by the end of the month was at Rhuddlan, having encountered no resistance. Some preparations, such as the razing to the ground of Degannwy,[23] were made to receive the onslaught, but the prince of Gwynedd was placed at the king's mercy by the defection of an ally which had rarely failed a Welsh chief in the hour of his need, namely, the Welsh climate. The summer was one of remarkable drought; marshes were dried up, rivers became fordable, lakes shrank into shallow pools, and the ordinary natural obstacles to a Welsh expedition almost wholly disappeared.[24] The royal troops moved so easily across the great marsh of Rhuddlan that David was in danger of being cut off from his Snowdonian base;[25] on the 29th he made a complete surrender to the king at Gwern Eigron on the river Elwy[26] and the bloodless campaign was at an end.[27]

Henry had no wish to deprive his obstinate nephew of his position as prince, but in other respects the terms were hard. Hardest of all was the requirement that Gruffydd, with his son Owain and the other companions of his captivity, should be delivered to the king, with the prospect of his establishment as independent ruler of some portion of North Wales. All the conquests of Llywelyn, including Mold, Southern Powys, and Meirionydd,[28] were to be restored to their rightful owners, and all homages of Welsh chiefs who ought to hold directly from the crown were to be relinquished. As a penalty for his resistance, David was to pay the expenses of the war and to lose Ellesmere and Tegeingl. The peace was ratified in London soon after Michaelmas, when the defeated prince attended a gathering of magnates and agreed to a further sacrifice, giving up Degannwy in discharge of the claim for expenses;[29] in the course of a few months the new order of things, rightly regarded by Henry as a great triumph for the royal authority,[30] was firmly established in Wales. Roger of Montalt was in possession of his fortress of Mold;[31] Gruffydd ap Gwenwynwyn, married to a daughter of John Lestrange, ruled peacefully in Southern Powys;[32] Degannwy had been placed in charge of the justiciar of Ireland;[33] Gruffydd ap Madog had been rewarded with an exchequer pension;[34] in Tegeingl a new castle, to take the place of Rhuddlan, was built by the king's orders on the rock of Maelan above the church of Diserth.[35] South Wales was no less completely subdued; the death of Earl Gilbert from injuries received in a tournament in June, 1241, enabled Henry to resume possession of Cardigan and Carmarthen;[36] John of Monmouth, the royal lieutenant in the southern march, made himself master of Builth,[37] and Maredudd ap Rhys Gryg was ordered to withdraw from the commotes of Kidwelly and Widigada.[38]

David's first bid for greatness and power had thus been unsuccessful, and he had to content himself with a narrower platform than the one he had at first marked out for the exercise of his authority. Henry, having secured his main objects, spared him the last humiliation of having to divide his shrunken realm with Gruffydd, who only exchanged a Welsh for an English prison, being still kept in confinement. But the possession of Gruffydd was an element in the contest of which David could not overlook the decisive importance; the king had at his disposal a popular rival who could at any time be sent to Wales to dislodge his brother, and accordingly the policy of the prince of Gwynedd for the next two years is one of prudence and self-restraint. Wales is at peace and its chronicles are uneventful; the princes of Powys are friendly to the English authority, while those of Deheubarth, Maelgwn of Is Aeron, Maredudd ab Owain of Uwch Aeron, and Rhys Mechyll ap Rhys Gryg of Dinefwr, not strong enough to stand alone, are reduced to inaction by the want of a leader.[39] In

Glamorgan, there is a new lord, the young Earl Richard of Gloucester, who sets himself to compose the feuds between the Welsh chiefs and the barons of his lordship.[40]

An unhappy accident in the Tower of London, early on the morning of St. David's Day, 1244, at once altered the aspect of affairs and threw Wales again into confusion.[41] Gruffydd grew weary of his long confinement, lightened though it was by a liberal royal allowance and the companionship of his wife, and resolved to make a dash for freedom. His chamber was high in the great keep, which, then as now, was the central feature of the capital fortress of the realm, and his plan was to let himself down from his window, under cover of night, by means of an improvised rope fashioned out of torn sheets, tablecloths and hangings. Unfortunately, he did not allow for the weight of a particularly bulky body, made unwieldy by the torpor of a comfortable captivity; the rope gave way and he fell to the ground from a height which meant instant death. The break of day disclosed his shattered corpse and told the story of the tragedy to the negligent warders of the Tower.[42]

Before many weeks had elapsed, the effect of this removal of Gruffydd from the scene was apparent in the renewed activity of David, who entered into an alliance with all the Welsh chiefs except the two Gruffydds of Powys and Morgan ap Hywel of Gwynllwg and reopened the conflict with the English.[43] According to the Welsh chronicles, he was stirred to indignation at the lamentable fate of his brother, but it needs little shrewd-ness to see that the calamity in the Tower was in truth a great deliverance for him and removed the one obstacle to a bold and enterprising policy. There could not be, in short, an apter illustration of the saying of Giraldus, that the Welsh princes showed far more affection for their brothers when they were dead than when they were alive.[44] Before the beginning of June, David was in the field, stirring up war throughout the length and breadth of Wales, and the summer was one of unrest and strife; there were nightly raids upon English territory,[45] Diserth was almost cut off from its base at Chester, and the English leanings of Gruffydd ap Gwenwynwyn were punished by an invasion of Cyfeiliog.[46] By a bold stroke of policy which bespeaks a mind of some originality and resource, the prince of Gwynedd brought a new power into the arena and successfully appealed to Innocent IV. for support against the English king.[47] It was with no small surprise that in the autumn Henry received a summons from the abbots of Cymer and Aberconwy, duly appointed as papal commissioners, which cited him to the border

church of Caerwys, there to defend himself against the charge of having in 1241 wantonly cast aside arbitration in favour of war. He had
no thought of obeying the citation, but he could not entirely ignore
it; his envoy to the pope was forthwith primed with the royal version
of the facts, and in 1245 came back with a new document, transferring the case from Welsh into English hands and revealing not
obscurely the influence of the weightier purse.

At first Henry does not seem to have taken the Welsh revolt very
seriously. His easy victory over David in 1241 had misled him; he
failed to realise how fortuitous it was. Being much engrossed this year
in a design upon the Scottish king, he left the border warfare to the
Earls of Gloucester and of Hereford (the latter's son was now lord of
Brecknock) and the two wardens of the march, John of Monmouth
and John Lestrange.[48] Even when, in August, a peace with Scotland
set him and his army free for other business, he did not attack Wales,
as was expected,[49] but despatched instead a small force of knights
under Herbert fitz Mathew. Another expedient adopted by him,
which proved altogether ineffective, was to release Owain the Red,
the eldest son of the dead Gruffydd, and send him to Wales in the
hope he might win adherents from the revolted David.[50] With the
turn of the year, however, Henry began to see that a really formidable
movement was on foot, such as no half measures could quell, for it
had the active backing of nearly all the magnates of Wales,[51] and
David as their leader made his presence felt in every quarter of the
country. The king resolved to undertake a regular campaign against
the Welsh as soon as the season allowed, and ordered the justiciar of
Ireland to accumulate provisions for the purpose.[52]

The Welsh continued to win successes during the spring. On 5th
February Herbert fitz Mathew was struck by a stone as he was thread-
ing a pass between Margam and Aberavan and fell a victim to the fury
of the warriors of Rhwng Nedd ac Afan.[53] A victory of the English
near Montgomery, where 300 Welshmen were drawn into an ambush
and slain,[54] was more than counterbalanced by the loss of Mold, taken
by David from Roger of Montalt on 28th March.[55] These disasters
quickened the resolve of Henry to undertake a set campaign against
the Welsh; in June the knighthood of the realm was summoned to the
border,[56] and the imminent danger of Diserth[57] led the king to plan
an expedition to Degannwy, which he proposed so to fortify as effectually to shield the northern coast from the attacks of the men of
Gwynedd. He arrived at Chester with a strong force on 13th August,
and, after a week's delay, pushed on for the banks of the Conway,

where he pitched his camp on the 26th.[58] Here he remained for two months, occupying his energies, as in earlier campaigns, in the building of a great fortress and exposing his troops to the weakening and demoralising influence of a persistent and harassing succession of attacks from the Welsh side of the river. A letter written from the king's camp about a month after the arrival at Degannwy has been preserved in the pages of Matthew Paris,[59] and it reveals to us, as in the cold, clear photography of the lightning flash, the weird scene on the shores of "old Conway's foaming flood"—the desperate valour of the Welsh, the fears, hopes, and hardships of the invaders, the rough chances of battle. "We dwell here," says the writer, "in watchings and fastings, in prayer, in cold and nakedness. In watchings, for fear of the Welsh, with their sudden raids upon us by night. In fastings, for lack of victuals, since the halfpenny loaf cannot be got for less than fivepence. In prayer, that we may quickly return safe and sound to our homes. In cold and nakedness, for we live in houses of linen and have no winter clothes." With a hostile country all around, the army was dependent for its supplies upon what could be borne by sea, from Chester and from Ireland,[60] and this was a precarious method of provisioning, liable to break down in the hour of need. Our correspondent tells how an Irish vessel with a cargo of wine was clumsily steered, as it entered the estuary, into a sandbank on the Welsh side of the Conway, where, on the retreat of the tide, it lay at the mercy of the enemy. Welsh and English fought over the stranded ship for some twenty-four hours, but ultimately the former carried off most of the sixty casks of precious liquor and burnt half of the vessel itself. Such accidents explain how at one time there was but a single cask of wine in the whole camp, while a load of corn cost twenty shillings, a fat ox three or four marks, and a hen eight pence.

The war was waged on both sides with ruthless severity. No respect was paid by the English to the sanctity of Aberconwy, the Cistercian house which stood near the rock now occupied by Conway Castle, almost opposite to Degannwy; its church was rifled of all it contained and the outbuildings set on fire. The English slaughter of noble prisoners, including a young son of Ednyfed Fychan,[61] led to cruel reprisals; captive knights were hanged, beheaded, and torn asunder. Heads of Welshmen were brought in to the camp as trophies after every English victory. Anglesey was ravaged and despoiled of its crops of corn by an Irish force.[62] Yet David, protected by the mighty barriers of the Snowdonian range, still obstinately refused to yield, and on the 26th of October[63] the king, seeing that the impending winter must ere long add enormously to his losses, already sufficiently great, resolved to withdraw and leave the final conquest of Gwynedd to be achieved another year. It was a confession of failure,[64] but yet no outright triumph for David, for whom the new castle of Degannwy was, as Paris phrases it, a "thorn in the eye"[65] and a pledge of the speedy renewal of the struggle. Ere he left the border, Henry set a new justiciar over Cheshire in the person of John de Gray,[66] and gave orders for a strict embargo on all trade with Wales, especially upon the carriage thither of the corn, salt, iron, steel, and cloth which the country itself could not supply.[67]

Ere the conflict could be reopened, death intervened and closed it by the removal of the Welsh protagonist. On Sunday, 25th February, 1246, David died at his court of Aber in Arllechwedd,[68] leaving by his wife Isabella no son or daughter to transmit his claims.[69] He was buried with his father in Aberconwy, the house which had suffered such loss as the penalty of loyalty to his cause. Whether he could have permanently maintained his position against the power of Henry must remain an open question; this, at any rate, may be said of him, that during his brief reign he showed himself, in courage, prudence, and leadership, no unworthy son of the great Llywelyn. The chronicler mourned the loss of the "buckler of Wales"[70] and Dafydd Benfras set his harp to plaintive strains in honour of the fallen chief —

> He was a man who sowed the seed of joy for his people,
> Of the right royal lineage of kings.
> So lordly his gifts, 'twas strange
> He gave not the moon in heaven!
> Ashen of hue this day is the hand of bounty,
> The hand that last year kept the pass of Aberconwy.[71]

II. WALES AGAIN IN SUBJECTION.

The gallant effort of David at independence was succeeded in Wales by a period of depression and subjection to which no parallel is to be found without going back to the days of Henry I. Henry III. might well suppose he had repeated the achievement of his namesake and reduced the country to complete dependence upon the power of the crown. Half of Gwynedd was in the hands of the king, the other half divided between two (as yet) insignificant princes. Powys was ruled by two lords who gave little trouble to their neighbours; the remnants of the kingdom of Deheubarth belonged to various descendants of the Lord Rhys, of whom the most enterprising, Maelgwn Fychan, had been humbled to the dust. Such was the plight of Wales for some ten years, from the death of David to the appearance of Llywelyn ap Gruffydd as a national leader. It was a time during which the sense of national solidarity was for the moment lost, and what remains to tell is but the good and evil hap of each individual prince and each separate province.

In Gwynedd a succession question at once arose. The only male descendant of Llywelyn ab Iorwerth on the spot was the young bearer of that great name, the second son of Gruffydd,[72] but his elder brother Owain, who had latterly been living under the king's protection at Shotwick, near Chester,[73] no sooner heard of the death of his uncle than he fled like a hare, in the picturesque phrase of Paris, into the recesses of Wales and made ready to push his claim.[74] Wise counsellors, among whom may perhaps be reckoned Ednyfed Fychan, rendering to his country a last service ere his death,[75] averted the impending conflict and persuaded the two young men to divide Gwynedd between them.[76] The domestic problem having been thus settled, there remained the question of relations with the crown. Owain and Llywelyn inherited with their new honours the burden of the struggle with the English king, and during the year 1246 the war went on without intermission. No royal host repeated the somewhat hazardous experiment of the previous autumn, but Nicholas of Meules, seneschal of Cardigan and Carmarthen, having conducted a successful campaign in South Wales, led his army across the Dovey and appeared in regions which had not seen an English host in battle array for more than a hundred and twenty years.[77] The Welsh retreated before him into the wilds of Eryri; he passed through Meirionydd, Ardudwy, and the Conway valley without opposition, and finally reached his goal at Degannwy. His operations from this centre against Owain and Llywelyn were unsuccessful, but his unobstructed march, upon which he was accompanied by Gruffydd ap Gwenwynwyn, showed that the king had Gwynedd below Conway in his grip, and thus paved the way for the agreement of the following spring.

After concluding a truce with John de Gray, the royal representative at Chester,[78] the young princes met the king at Woodstock, and on 30th April, 1247, agreed to terms which remained in force for the next eight years.[79] They were recognised as the rightful rulers of Gwynedd above Conway and duly rendered homage for their territories, but were forced to abandon all claim to the four cantrefs of the Middle Country,[80] namely, Rhos, Rhufoniog, Tegeingl, and Dyffryn

Clwyd; Mold, too, was finally resigned and the homages of all the minor chieftains of North Wales. The rights of certain Welsh supporters of Henry were safeguarded, and among these appears later a mysterious Maredudd ap Rhicert, of unknown descent, who set up a claim to be heir to the cantref of Lleyn and was upheld for many years in this district by the royal power.[81] The Peace of Woodstock was a painful humiliation for Gwynedd, after the proud ascendancy she had enjoyed for so many years, but the sacrifice of the Middle Country was necessary, if the main body of the province was to retain its independent life, and the ruthless surgery was ultimately followed by a complete recovery of strength. Meanwhile the tide of affairs ran a somewhat sluggish course, and the only change to record is the appearance on the stage of a third son of Gruffydd, named David,[82] who in 1252 was lord of the commote of Cymydmaen in Lleyn and in the following year was summoned to do homage for his possessions.[83]

Elsewhere in North Wales there was the weakness which comes from division and lack of leadership. Henry retained a firm hold of the Middle Country, with its strong castles of Diserth and Degannwy, and in 1252 made the latter of these two places a chartered borough, thereby signifying that the royal power was to be regarded as a fixture in the Creuddyn peninsula.[84] There was no thought of creating a new Earl of Chester;[85] on the contrary, the crown was bent upon making the most out of this valuable bit of territory, and in 1251 John de Grey was replaced as justiciar by Alan la Zuche, who promised to make the Welsh portion of his charge considerably more profitable to the exchequer.[86] "Unhappy Wales!" is the not inappropriate comment of Matthew Paris upon this transaction. Northern Powys was held by the sons of Madog ap Gruffydd,[87] of whom Gruffydd, who had married Emma, a daughter of Henry Audley,[88] was the senior, ruling over the two Maelors, east and west of the Dee.[89] Southern Powys belonged to Gruffydd ap Gwenwynwyn, who was also married to an English wife, namely, Hawise Lestrange, and was lord of Cyfeiliog, Mawddwy, Arwystli, Caereinion, Llannerch Hudol, Ystrad Marchell, Deuddwr, and Mochnant above the Rhaeadr.[90] Cydewain had been restored in 1248 to Owain ap Maredudd, the son of its former lord.[91] Meirionydd was in the hands of Maredudd ap Llywelyn, of the line of Cynan ab Owain Gwynedd.[92] Mechain was divided between three brothers, Llywelyn, Owain, and Maredudd ap Llywelyn.[93]

"Divide and rule" was also the policy of the king's advisers in South Wales. The united front opposed to the English power by the princes of Deheubarth did not survive the death of David; in the following

April, Maredudd ap Rhys Gryg and Maredudd ab Owain made their peace with Henry and were forthwith sent to help Nicholas of Meules in the task of reducing to obedience the recalcitrant Maelgwn Fychan.[94] Maelgwn was a prince of some energy and was allied by marriage with the chieftains of Meirionydd and Cydewain. But the coalition against him was too strong to be withstood; he was forced to seek refuge in North Wales[95] and, later in the year, to surrender himself to the king's mercy. In November, he was allowed to return to Ceredigion, there to keep a sadly diminished state as lord of the two commotes of Geneu'r Glyn and Iscoed.[96] His men consoled themselves with the thought that, though Maelgwn's day was over, his son Rhys was daily growing into the likeness of the ideal deliverer whom they hoped to see hurl back ere long the tide of English conquest. But their hopes were blasted by Rhys's early death in 1255; he and his two sisters were, within the space of a few months, laid to rest together in the chapter house of Strata Florida.[97] Another South Wales chief came to terms with the king in the summer of 1246. By the death of Rhys Mechyll in 1244,[98] his son Rhys Fychan had become the heir to Dinefwr, but his path was beset with many hindrances—the rivalry of his uncle, Maredudd,[99] the hostility of his mother, Matilda de Breos,[100] and the overshadowing menace of the castle of Carmarthen. He did homage in the August of this year[101] and contrived to retain his position as ruler of the ancestral seat of Deheubarth notwithstanding all opposition.

Royal and baronial authority asserted themselves at almost every point of vantage in South Wales. In Northern Ceredigion the king retained a considerable part of the territory of Maelgwn, lying around Llanbadarn Fawr, which he administered through a Welsh bailiff, one Gwilym ap Gwrwared[102] of Cemais. Cemais itself had been recovered for English rule by Nicholas fitz Martin.[103] The great inheritance of the Earls Marshalls had, on the death of Anselm, the last of the line, in December, 1245,[104] been divided among the numerous coheirs who represented the daughters of the house, but the English hold upon South Wales was not thereby seriously weakened. The king's half-brother, William of Valence, became lord of the castle and county of Pembroke;[105] Earl Roger of Norfolk succeeded, in right of his mother, to Chepstow and Nether Went;[106] Earl Richard of Gloucester obtained Caerleon and Usk;[107] Emlyn, with the castle of Cilgerran, passed to William Cantilupe.[108] Cardigan and Carmarthen, with their respective districts, the king continued to keep in his own possession.[109] Kidwelly was still in the hands of its former mistress,

Hawise of London, but her first husband, Walter de Breos, was dead, and in 1244 she had married a second time, carrying her inheritance, which included the lordship of Ogmore in Glamorgan, to Patrick of Chaworth.[110] William de Breos, having attained his majority, now ruled Gower in place of his father John.

Passing from West Wales to the marchland, one notes the strength of the lordship of Glamorgan, ruled since 1240 by the vigorous Richard de Clare, Earl of Gloucester and Hertford, no unworthy scion of that ancient line. He proved his ability to hold the Welsh chieftains of his domain in subjection by expelling Hywel ap Maredudd from Miskin in 1246, so that he was forced to take refuge in Gwynedd and abandon his territory to the chief lord.[111] It was perhaps a result of this energetic action that no trouble henceforth arose in the other mountain fiefs; Morgan Crookback was succeeded at Baglan by his son Morgan,[112] Morgan of Caerleon at Machen by his grandson, Maredudd ap Gruffydd,[113] and Rhys ap Gruffydd in Senghenydd by his son Gruffydd.[114] Time was transforming these turbulent raiders into feudal barons, scarcely to be distinguished from the Turbevilles of Coety, the Sumerys of Dinas Powis, and the Umfravilles of Penmark, among whom they lived.

Like the Marshall estates, the Breos group of lordships had been divided among daughters, of whom William de Breos had in 1230 left four. Isabella, the widow of David, received Haverford;[115] Eleanor, the wife of Humphrey de Bohun, took Brecknock as her portion; Eva, married to William Cantilupe, had Upper Gwent and Abergavenny assigned to her;[116] Matilda enriched her husband, Roger Mortimer, with Radnor.[117] Builth alone was retained by the king in his own hands. It was in 1246 that Roger, son of Ralph Mortimer, came by his father's death into possession of those border manors[118] which, with Maelienydd, Gwerthrynion, and Radnor, were gradually raising the family into a position of high importance and qualifying its head for the title of Earl of March. Other changes which fall to be recorded among the lesser baronial houses of the border are the succession in 1248 of a new John of Monmouth, son of the old bearer of the name,[119] the marriage of Matilda Lacy, heiress of Ewias and Ludlow, first to Peter of Geneva and then to Geoffrey of Genville,[120] and the entry upon his lands at Oswestry and Clun of John fitz Alan, whose father John died in 1241.[121] The generation which had witnessed the struggle against the tyranny of John and preserved its memories was quitting the scene, to be replaced by the actors in the great drama of the Barons' War.

Two of these actors, the interweaving of whose fortunes in the web of destiny forms the concluding episode of the present narrative, step forward at the close of this period into the forefront of the stage. In 1254 the young Edward was invested by his father the king with all the crown possessions in Wales; in 1255 Llywelyn ap Gruffydd became ruler of the whole of Gwynedd above Conway. The time was still far distant when they were to be the protagonists in a decisive struggle between England and Wales, but fate had already in a sense pitted them against each other. Born in 1239, the heir to the English throne was now being carefully provided for; a marriage was arranged for him with a princess of the royal house of Castile, and, in order that he might have a suitable appanage, Henry bestowed upon him Ireland, Gascony, Cheshire, and Wales, the last mentioned including the Middle Country, with Diserth and Degannwy, the lordships of Cardigan, Carmarthen, Montgomery, and Builth, and the three castles of the famous trilateral of Upper Gwent, Grosmont, Skenfrith, and White Castle.[122] This action betokened a purpose of drawing the reins still tighter than had yet been the case; it was not enough that the country should be, as Alan la Zuche alleged, thoroughly pacified and brought under English control;[123] it must yield a larger revenue, and, with this end in view, the Middle Country was entrusted to Geoffrey Langley, a royal officer whose experience had hitherto lain chiefly in the administration of the bugh and masterful justice of the Forest.[124] It was at this juncture that the prince of Gwynedd came to the enjoyment of that full and undivided authority for which his talents so eminently fitted him. A quarrel had arisen between him and his brother Owain, which, as it concerned the partition of Gwynedd,[125] probably arose out of some demand made on behalf of David, and in the summer of 1255[126] the matter was referred to the arbitrament of war. Llywelyn awaited the armies of his brothers at Bryn Derwin,[127] in the mountain pass which leads from Arfon to Eifionydd, not far from the battlefield of Bron yr Erw, and there in the space of one hour inflicted upon them a signal defeat, taking both Owain and David prisoners.[128] His triumph was complete and secured for him that lordship of Anglesey and Snowdonia which was only wrested from him with life itself. He was now ready to play his part on the wider platform of South and Mid Wales.

CHAPTER X

LLYWELYN AP GRUFFYDD

I. THE CONQUEST OF POWYS AND THE SOUTH.

(The age of Llywelyn ap Gruffydd fares better at the hand of the English historian than most epochs of Welsh history, and has been fully treated by Tout in Wales and the March in the Barons' War (Owens College Essays, 1902) and Edward I. (English Statesmen Series) and by J. E. Morris in The Welsh Wars of Edward I. I have also used Bémont's Simon de Montfort.)

THE last stage has now been reached in the history of Wales under native rule. And at no period is the interest of the story more personal; for from beginning to end the tale of these twenty-six years centres in the doings of Llywelyn ap Gruffydd, who is not only the foremost of the princes of Wales, but also the single force which is of any account in Welsh politics. Rivalry with him is out of the question; he dominates the country with as genuine a mastery as that of Llywelyn the Great, and at last attains a wider territorial influence, as he boasts a prouder title, than was enjoyed even by his grandfather. The ruinous end of his career may justly qualify one's admiration and suggest that he had not, with all his merits, the statesmanlike insight and prudence of the elder Llywelyn, but it invests the whole with the light of romance, touches it with a most poignant pathos, and closes the narrative in a vein of dignified tragedy, as who should tell the vain struggle of weak human will against the resistless forces of Nature.

The victory of Bryn Derwin had placed Llywelyn in a commanding position in North Wales, and it was not long ere he obtained the opportunity of playing the part of national leader against the English.[1] At the end of 1256 there was a revolution in the Middle

Country. Edward had during the summer paid his first visit to the county and city of Chester, from which he drew his title of earl, had been taken thence to Wales, to see his castles of Diserth and Degannwy, and had received the homages due to him in the district.[2] All had passed off smoothly, without untoward incident, but, when the Welshmen of the four cantrefs realised after his departure that no improvement in their lot was to be looked for from their young lord, beset as he was with a train of foolish, roystering cavaliers,[3] and that they were left as before to the tyrannous exactions of Geoffrey Langley, who was seeking to extend the English shire system to these border regions,[4] they broke out into revolt and summoned the prince of Gwynedd to their aid. Llywelyn was nothing loth; releasing his young brother David, who, he thought, would be a useful ally,[5] and taking with him Maredudd ap Rhys Gryg, whom Rhys Fychan and the English had ejected from South Wales, he crossed the Conway[6] and within one week had extended Gwynedd to its old bounds. The castles of Diserth and Degannwy, still held by the foreigner, were left enisled in the midst of what was now purely Welsh country,[7] and Llywelyn carried his victorious arms almost as far as Chester itself.[8]

He had chosen a most favourable opportunity for his enterprise. The winter was a wet and stormy one, such as always served the Welsh well in resisting an English attack.[9] Geoffrey Langley was in England and did not hear until it was too late to retrieve the disaster of the losses his rapacious policy had entailed upon his master.[10] Edward himself was powerless; he had no money for measures of retaliation, nor had his thriftless father, now drawing near the great crisis of the reign; even when a loan was obtained from the king's brother, Earl Richard of Cornwall, it proved useless, so serious were the hindrances to a campaign against Llywelyn. Obstacles of will and temper seconded those created by nature; the great men of the realm, angered by continual misgovernment, were in no mood to oblige the crown and relieve it of its embarrassments—rather, they sympathised with the insurgents as victims of a common tyranny, and the very barons of the march, hereditary foes of the Welsh, viewed their rebellion with toleration, if not actual friendliness.[11] The attitude of the magnates is reflected in that of the chroniclers; Matthew Paris, who was moved to such righteous indignation by the revolt of David in 1244,[12] now holds up the Welsh as a noble example to the timorous English, and tells with evident zest and appreciation the story of the valiant fight for their ancestral laws and liberties fought by these brave descendants of the famous champions of Troy.[13]

The easy triumph won by Llywelyn in the Middle Country set his ambition afire and led him to dream of still greater successes. His quick imagination showed him that the hour was ripe for the restoration of the supremacy of Gwynedd over the rest of Wales, and he set out at once upon the path trodden to such good purpose by his grandfather. At the beginning of December, with a great host of warriors which included very many well-equipped knights,[14] he invaded Meirionydd, driving out Llywelyn ap Maredudd, who had just succeeded his father as lord of this cantref.[15] Thence he moved on to Ceredigion, conquered what was held for Edward around Llanbadarn, and bestowed it upon Maredudd ab Owain, who gladly acknowledged the suzerainty of Llywelyn in return for this grant and that of the cantref of Buellt, won from the grasp of the crown at the same time.[16] Ystrad Tywi witnessed the next assertion of Llywelyn's power; here Rhys Fychan was ejected from Dinefwr and Carreg Cennen,[17] and his uncle Maredudd, restored by the strong arm of his northern protecter, gained possession of the whole of the Great and the Little Cantref.[18] The last conquest of the year was Gwerthrynion, taken from Roger Mortimer and retained by Llywelyn for himself, who elsewhere had followed the judicious policy of his grandfather and used his acquisitions to reward his allies.

After a Christmas which was certainly not wanting in elements of festivity, the prince of Gwynedd took the field once more in January, 1257, and turned his attention to Powys. Gruffydd ap Madog had already been put to flight and his territories ravaged as part of the movement of the previous year.[19] Gruffydd ap Gwenwynwyn was now made to suffer for his adherence to the cause of the crown; Llywelyn invaded the valley of the Severn, occupied the country as far as Pool and burnt the little town which clustered round Gruffydd's castle at that place. Gruffydd himself withdrew beyond the Severn and sought the help of John Lestrange and John fitz Alan, who could do nothing, however, but hold Montgomery.[20] Flushed with this victory, the Northern army then transferred itself to a new district, and in February and March was busy in the region between the Towy and the Tawe, winning the Welsh of Gower, Kidwelly and Carnwyllion to Llywelyn's obedience, and undermining the power of Patrick of Chaworth and William de Breos. The distracted king sought to bring the influence of his brother Richard, just elected emperor, to bear upon the situation, but, though Llywelyn replied courteously, and even amicably, to the great man's representations, he would yield no jot of his conquests, and, short of peace on his own terms, was only

prepared to agree to a long truce, such as would enable him to consolidate his gains.[21] He returned to Gwynedd before Easter, and in
May won a minor success in Mechain Uwchcoed, where he took the
castle of Bodyddon, not far from Llanfyllin.[22]

There followed, at the beginning of June, so crushing a defeat of
the English in the valley of the Towy that Henry was at last stung out
of his attitude of helpless protest.[23] Rhys Fychan had persuaded the
king's representatives in South Wales to attempt his reinstatement,
and with this object the experienced royal official, Stephen
Bauzan,[24] set out on 31st May from Carmarthen with a considerable
force. The day was a Thursday, and, upon the arrival of the host
before Dinefwr, they found the surrounding hills occupied by a still
larger force under Maredudd ap Rhys and Maredudd ab Owain,
who, having their enemies thus at their mercy, harassed them with
darts and arrows throughout the Friday. On Saturday, while matters
were in this critical position, Rhys suddenly changed sides, and, fleeing with a few of his men to the shelter of Dinefwr, left his allies in
the lurch. There was nothing for it but to beat a retreat, and a retreat
under these circumstances soon became a rout; first, the baggage
and sumpter horses were lost; then, about midday, at a place called
Cymerau, a general attack was made by the Welsh, and the expedition, with its leader, was overwhelmed. No such disaster as this had
befallen the royal authority in South Wales for a generation, and the
king showed his sense of its gravity by calling together the feudal
array to meet him at Chester on 1st August for a campaign against
the dauntless Llywelyn and his confederates.[25]

Meanwhile, the Welsh made haste to reap the fruits of their victory.[26] The castles of Laugharne,[27] Llanstephan, and Narberth were
carried by storm, and at midsummer[28] the Northern leader again
came south to direct operations. With the aid of the Maredudds and
Rhys Fychan, all for the moment in alliance with him, he ravaged
Cemais and seized its castle of Newport, raided Rhos and threatened
Haverford, and finally, in the middle of July, attacked Glamorgan and
destroyed Earl Richard's castle of Llangynwyd.[29] It was now time to
return north to meet the expedition which the king was bringing to
North Wales. Great preparations were made to repel it; women, children, cattle and other belongings were moved from the low-lying
hamlets into the rocky security of Snowdon, meadows were ploughed,
mills destroyed, bridges broken, and fords made impassable by the
digging of holes in their midst.[30] But the attack proved to be a much
less formidable affair than had been expected. Henry set out from

Chester with a great host on 19th August,[31] and, with the help of a naval contingent from the Cinque Forts,[32] raised the siege of Diserth and of Degannwy. But beyond the latter fortress he did not venture to penetrate; after waiting in vain for assistance which had been requisitioned from Ireland,[33] he abandoned the struggle and withdrew ingloriously to Chester, with Llywelyn hanging upon the skirts of his army and cutting off all who fell behind in the retreat.[34] This was the king's last invasion of Wales and the most unprofitable.

Llywelyn's star was now fairly in the ascendant, and, shortly after the king's withdrawal, Gruffydd ap Madog resolved to throw in his lot with the winning interest and to desert the English for the Welsh side.[35] With this accession of strength, the prince of Gwynedd was able to complete his conquest of Southern Powys and to expel Gruffydd ap Gwenwynwyn from all his territories, so as to bring the whole of North Wales under his power. Having arranged to tide over the winter months by means of a short truce,[36] the king was preparing to renew the conflict in 1258,[37] when the uprising of the barons against his misgovernment, so long threatened and so long delayed, at last burst irresistibly upon him and changed the whole current of affairs in the English state. The Welsh question was now quite overshadowed by the gravity of the constitutional crisis; it sank into a subordinate place, and the reforming party gladly accepted a solution of it which freed them for more serious business. They came armed, indeed, to the famous assembly which met at Oxford on 11th June,[38] in apparent readiness for the muster of the knighthood of the realm at Chester on the 17th, but it was with no intention of actually taking the field in another Welsh expedition. They were firmly convinced that the need of the hour was to limit the authority, not of Llywelyn, but of the king, and accordingly the abbot of Aberconwy had no difficulty in securing for his master a truce for thirteen months which allowed him to retain all his conquests and only conceded to Henry the right to revictual the hard-beset castles of Diserth and Degannwy.[39] In their fierce opposition to the king's misrule in England, many of the barons overlooked, or made light of, their substantial interests in Wales, for it has been pointed out that among the reformers were nearly all the lords of the March, men who stood to lose heavily by any policy of concession to Llywelyn.[40] It is true that the last to suffer at the hands of the Welsh had been the bitterly hated William of Valence, whose Pembrokeshire lands had been attacked by the men of Cemais and Peuliniog, and who had angrily denounced the leaders of reform as responsible through their lukewarm conduct for his loss.[41] But this was a mere chance; the revived patriotic fervour of Wales was equally dangerous to all foreign lords, and men like Earl Richard of Gloucester, Roger Mortimer, Humphrey de Bohun, risked much when they allowed Llywelyn to grow strong in order that they might have leisure to work out the problem of the regeneration of the English realm.

How strong Llywelyn had now become appears from a notable step which he took in the early part of this year 1258. Every Welsh prince except Gruffydd ap Gwenwynwyn was now on his side, and he resolved to turn these allies into feudal vassals and to cement their union under his sway by the assumption of a new title. At an assembly of the magnates of all Wales, he received the homage and fealty of the minor chieftains of the land,[42] and it was, no doubt, with the assent of this gathering that he now began to style himself "prince of Wales".[43] His grandfather's "prince of Aberffraw and lord of Snowdon," sonorous though it was and implying much, was not sufficiently clear cut for his ends; he desired a title which would justify the furthest stretch of his ambition. Nor did he mean this sovereignty of all Wales to be a form merely, without practical effect. Not long after the meeting of the princes the inevitable defection took place; Maredudd ap Rhys, whom the crown had been seeking for some time to detach from his connection with Llywelyn,[44] made his peace with the English,[45] who saw in him a convenient instrument for the punishment of the treacherous Rhys Fychan. At once the allies bore down upon him, and, led by Llywelyn, ravaged his lands in the upper valley of the Towy. He retained his castles, but, even with the aid of Patrick of Chaworth, the king's seneschal in the district, could make no headway against the hostile forces arrayed against him, and was severely wounded in a battle fought near the bridge of Carmarthen. He was to find later that the vengeance of Llywelyn had not exhausted its means of punishing the betrayer of the common cause.

The union of all Wales under his leadership led Llywelyn to look abroad and form schemes for foreign alliances. He saw that he might add much to the strength of his position by allying himself with the national party in Scotland, which was vigorously opposing the influence of Henry III. in that kingdom. His overtures were well received, and on 18th March, 1258, the Earl of Menteith and his associates put in the hands of the Welsh envoy, Gwion of Bangor, a document[46] in which they bound themselves to make no separate peace with the king of England, to give him no aid against the Welsh and to encourage trade intercourse between Scotland and Wales. Henry's difficulties at home soon deprived the compact of its importance by relieving both Scotch and Welsh of the fear of invasion, but it has great interest as revealing the width of Llywelyn's outlook and the extent of the support which he now enjoyed, as shown by the list of princes who joined him in his appeal to the sister nation in the north.[47]

Good fortune seemed to wait upon every movement of the Welsh, until it was not strange that they believed their arms to be under the special blessing of heaven. Early in September[48] David ap Gruffydd, Maredudd ab Owain, and Rhys Fychan were together in Emlyn,[49] where a conference was proposed between them and Maredudd ap Rhys, who, with Patrick of Chaworth, was at Cardigan with a large force, assembled from all the marcher lordships of West Wales. The meeting was to have come off at Cilgerran, but Patrick, unhappily for himself, was persuaded to deal treacherously[50] with his foes, and on the evening of 4th September attacked them with all his host. Notwithstanding the surprise and their inferior numbers, the Welsh successfully met the onslaught, and in the rout which followed the lord of Kidwelly was slain.

The year 1259 saw no diminution of Llywelyn's greatness. He signalised it, indeed, by a new assertion of his authority as prince of Wales. On 28th May Maredudd ap Rhys, who had fallen into his hands, was formally tried by his peers and fellow-vassals in a council held in Arwystli, convicted of treason to his lord and imprisoned. He languished in Cricieth Castle until Christmas, when Llywelyn released him on receiving as pledges of future obedience his eldest son and his two castles of Dinefwr and Newcastle, with the commotes of Maenor Deilo and Emlyn above Cuch in which they stood.[51] Thus did the man who five years before had been but the obscure lord of a few cantrefs in the north prove his claim to have established that entirely new thing—a veritable principality of all Wales, and the English government, immersed in other business, had no alternative but to stand aside and let Llywelyn take his course. The usual summons went out this year for a campaign in the summer against the Welsh,[52] but largely as a matter of form; it was to France, where the king made his way in November, that all eyes were turned, and what was desired from Llywelyn was a renewal of the truce. This was arranged with him by royal commissioners on 25th June, at Rhyd Chwima, the "ford of Montgomery," which witnessed so many compacts of the kind, and a month later was confirmed by the king.[53] Peace was thus secured on the border for another twelvemonth, from 1st August, 1259, to the same date in 1260. Llywelyn, not knowing how soon a reunion of the

English forces might snatch his hard-won acquisitions from his grasp, would gladly have gone further and negotiated a peace, but his envoy to the court, Bishop Richard of Bangor, got no satisfaction on this head, though ready to offer a sum of 16,000 marks for terms acceptable to his lord.[54]

Llywelyn's overtures might be rejected, but his progress was not thereby stayed. While the king and the baronial leaders jealously watched each other, he was adding to his gains. The castle and lordship of Builth had been entrusted by the government to Roger Mortimer, who had driven out the Welsh tenants of Maredudd ab Owain. On the 10th of January, 1260, the prince of Wales appeared with an army in the district, restored the balance in favour of the Welsh and took the lordship into his own hands. Leaving a body of troops to besiege the castle, he then made his way, with a goodly company of mail-clad horsemen, westward to Dyfed and burnt the town of Tenby.[55] In April, his allies from Kerry and Cydewain poured into the valley of the Teme and set fire to Knighton.[56] On 17th July the resistance of the garrison at Builth suddenly collapsed; three of the men who manned the castle walls let in the Welsh besiegers under cover of night, out of ill-will, it is said, towards a clerk or notary set in authority over them.[57] Forthwith, Rhys Fychan and his followers were upon the scene and made sure of the advantage won for the Welsh by razing the castle to the very foundations. Elfael was now exposed to the inroads of the followers of Llywelyn, and the submission of the Welsh chieftain[58] who had hitherto been unfriendly and kept in check by the holding of his son as a hostage, was at once ensured. He did homage to the prince and received in return his son's release, with a handsome gift of money.

Meanwhile, the party struggles which had arisen out of the constitutional movement paralysed the English defence. The king, busy with the French negotiations, wrote from the neighbourhood of Paris when he heard of Llywelyn's attack upon Builth to urge the barons to drop their plans for a February parliament and concentrate on the Welsh question.[59] But no heed was paid to his words; domestic problems were still all-absorbing, and the party conflict was at its height when the news arrived of the fall of the castle. It chanced that its owner, prince Edward, and its custodian, Roger Mortimer, were on opposite sides, for the former was in temporary alliance with the Earl of Leicester, while the latter was one of the following of the Earl of Gloucester, which had at the moment the support of the king. Hence the easy capture of this important fortress became a subject of recrimination, until Mortimer found it necessary to obtain from Henry and the royal council a formal statement that he was entirely free from blame in the matter.[60] All parties agreed in thinking that the crisis called for action, and the king, with the assent of the barons, summoned the feudal array for 8th September, upon which day the Earl of Gloucester and a part of the force were to assemble at Shrewsbury, while the rest, under the Earl of Leicester, was to meet at Chester.[61] There was, as yet, no thought of Earl Simon as a possible ally of the prince of Wales, although the time was approaching when hard necessity was to bring this about. But there was enough distrust in the air to incline all, when the first gust of military enthusiasm was over, to negotiation rather than war; Llywelyn was, as usual, ready to treat, and on the 22nd of August a meeting took place at the ford of Montgomery between his commissioners, the bishop of Bangor and the abbot of Aberconwy, and those of the king, which resulted in the renewal of the truce for another period, not of one but of two years.[62]

This lengthened period points to a desire on both sides for peace, which, though not formally and finally proclaimed, was to be attained in substance, as in the closing years of Llywelyn the Great, by a succession of truces. The compact of 1260 was better kept than any of its predecessors and the two years which it covered are among the quietest in Welsh history. In England, events were slowly ripening for the fatal breach between the king and the reformers; in Wales, Llywelyn was resting on his oars and moving gently with the auspicious current which made for his triumph.

II. LLYWELYN AND EARL SIMON.

Llywelyn maintained his attitude of judicious neutrality throughout the year 1261 and almost to the close of 1262. Invitations to throw in his lot with the reformers were not wanting to him, but he deemed it prudent to set them aside.[63] Even the opportunity afforded by the sudden death of the great Earl of Gloucester in July, 1262, was allowed to pass by;[64] the Earl of Hereford, to whom the custody of the Gloucester inheritance was given, had some natural alarm for the safety of Glamorgan,[65] but no army from the north disturbed the peace of its borders. Breaches of the truce occurred, sufficient to afford a pretext for the renewal of the border warfare, but Llywelyn was content to await the working, which was none too expeditious, of the machinery provided for the peaceable settlement of disputes.[66] A rumour reached Henry at Amiens in the summer of 1262 that he was dead, giving occasion for a very interesting letter in which the king discloses his plans for such an emergency.[67] The prince had no son to succeed him, and what was to be feared, therefore, was the advent of his brother David to the full and undiminished measure of his power. David, it appears, was to be checkmated by the release from captivity of his elder brother, Owain, the king was to recover the homages of the minor Welsh chieftains, and the barons of the march were to assemble at Shrewsbury to carry out this programme by force. Help was looked for from Gruffydd ap Madog, his brother Hywel, and the Southern dissident, Maredudd ap Rhys. As it chanced, these ingenious schemes were rendered vain by the circumstance of Llywelyn being alive; they prove, however, how much there was which it was deemed hopeless to accomplish in his lifetime. His authority was paramount in Wales, and for the moment he exercised it in the interests of peace and good neighbourhood.

At the end of 1262 the air once more grew thunderous and the march was speedily involved in a conflagration which set the whole realm alight.[68] On 29th November the men of Maelienydd took Roger Mortimer's new castle at Cefnllys by stratagem and proceeded to dismantle it; when Roger and young Humphrey de Bohun came with an army to repair the broken walls, Llywelyn swooped upon them with a still larger force, closely beset them in the ruined fortress, and then induced them to accept the offer of a free passage through his lines across the border. Their undignified retreat led many to suspect an understanding, although, in point of fact there was none;[69] Llywelyn merely wished to facilitate the conquest of Maelienydd, and before Christmas had reduced the castles of Bleddfa, Knucklas, Knighton, Norton, and Presteign, and added an extensive region to the area under his rule. His men ravaged the Herefordshire lowlands as far as Weobley and Eardisley, and Bishop Peter of Hereford, a royal partisan who between the Welsh and the barons was betwixt two fires, left his episcopal seat in a panic and betook himself to Gloucester.[70] Llywelyn then pushed on for Brecknock[71] and soon had the whole lordship at his feet; even in its furthest corner of Ystrad Yw his banner was triumphant, until his border was but a few miles from Abergavenny.[72]

The king, who had just returned from France in very feeble health, wearily set about the defence of the borders. Appealing to the marcher lords to forget their quarrels, he arranged that troops should assemble in February, 1263, at Ludlow and at Hereford to withstand the threatened inroads of the jubilant men of the hills.[73]

Peter of Montfort, a supporter of Earl Simon's but not a relative, played his part well, if his own account is to be believed,[74] and at the end of the month offered a stout resistance at Abergavenny to a Welsh host, led by Gronw ab Ednyfed[75] and the princes of South Wales, which but for this would have swept over the fair fields of Gwent. Nevertheless, a genuine campaign against the Welsh was more than ever impossible; the real desire of the great men of the realm was to fight out the domestic quarrel. Edward, who had shown little interest in the fate of his Welsh possessions,[76] crossed over from France and in April led a force into North Wales.[77] But he did nothing beyond giving a little temporary relief to the hard-pressed garrisons of Diserth and Degannwy,[78] and was soon recalled by his father, who had begun to perceive, after despatching his son to the border, that the real crisis was in the heart of his own realm. David, dissatisfied for some reason with his brother's treatment of him, chose this moment, with singular lack of insight, for transferring himself from the side of Llywelyn to that of the king, and was promised the cantrefs of Rhufoniog and Dyffryn Clwyd, but this ill-timed abandonment of a rising cause had no effect upon the situation.[79]

The landing of Earl Simon at the end of April, after a short absence abroad, marks the beginning of the civil war. With no such rival as the late Earl of Gloucester to contest his right to leadership, Simon now placed himself at the head of the party of reform and organised it for war. The Welsh march was still the stronghold of the baronial interest, and it was here the struggle broke out. About the end of June an attack was made upon the bishop of Hereford, who had been persuaded to return to his diocese, by a coalition which included Roger Clifford, John fitz Alan, Humphrey de Bohun, the young Earl Gilbert of Gloucester, and Hamo Lestrange; Peter and his Savoyard canons were captured in their cathedral and shut up in the Clifford castle of Eardisley.[80] The allies next took possession of Gloucester, Worcester, and Bridgenorth, until they had made themselves supreme in the West. Two powers can hardly wage war simultaneously against a third without entering, however divergent their ultimate aims, into a working alliance, and thus it was inevitable that Llywelyn and the barons should draw together and forget age-long enmities and feuds in the excitement of the conflict with the crown. It was, no doubt, with the goodwill of the reformers that the prince of Wales, aided by Gruffydd ap Madog, laid siege about 1st July to the long threatened castle of Diserth; he took it by storm on 4th

August and utterly destroyed it, thus closing its brief history of twenty-two years.[81] Welshmen were besieging Bridgenorth on the one side as the barons attacked it on the other, and thus, though as yet there was no formal treaty, the understanding between Earl Simon and Llywelyn, so fruitful of results in later years, had virtually come into existence.[82]

This first stage of the civil war ended as abruptly as it had begun; the king and Edward yielded to the forces which the Earl of Leicester had marshalled against them, and in the autumn both parties were pressing Llywelyn to agree to a truce, with the object of saving Degannwy.[83] It was agreed that the place should be revictualled, but the compact was not carried out; on the 28th September the garrison, reduced to the direst straits by famine, threw their gates open to the besiegers, and not a foot of land remained to Edward any longer in North Wales.[84] It was almost immediately afterwards that a very important change took place in the balance of parties in England, and the fall of Degannwy, following upon that of Diserth, had no doubt its share in bringing about this result. Edward, whose policy had hitherto been neither steadfast nor clear, saw in the alliance between the barons and the Welsh great possibilities of mischief to the realm, and in the parliament which met in October used all the arts of diplomacy to break up the baronial coalition and to detach as many of its members as possible from their allegiance to Earl Simon.[85] He was remarkably successful, and, in particular, contrived to win over to the royalist cause almost all the men of the march, who had hitherto been zealous champions of reform. Not only the Earl of Hereford and Roger Mortimer, who had for some time withdrawn from the active reformers, but also John fitz Alan, Hamo Lestrange, and Roger Clifford, the very men to whose initiative the war was due, now espoused the cause of the king, who also had the support of James of Audley, Reginald fitz Peter, and William de Breos. It was this defection of quite one-half the baronial party which induced Earl Simon, at the close of the year, to agree to submit the dispute to the arbitration of St. Louis.[86]

Meanwhile, Llywelyn secured the allegiance of the last Welsh prince who held out against his authority as prince of Wales. On 12th December, 1263, he came to an agreement with Gruffydd ap Gwenwynwyn, who, true to the policy of his house, had hitherto resolutely opposed the claims of Gwynedd.[87] Gruffydd submitted to Llywelyn as suzerain and lord, and in return received those of his territories which the northern prince had occupied. He had probably contrived to hold his castle at Pool through all vicissitudes, but the western uplands of Cyfeiliog, Arwystli, Caereinion, and Mochnant had for several years been lost to him and were now regained as the price paid to him for his homage. The two princes entered into an alliance against their enemies along the border, and it was stipulated that Gruffydd should have all conquests north of the Camlad,[88] while Llywelyn, as lord of Kerry and Cydewain,[89] should keep those made to the south of that river. The former at once took advantage of the bargain to wipe off an old score against Thomas Corbet of Cause, whose lands in the "Gorddwr," or country "beyond the water" of Severn he annexed to his own.[90]

The French arbitration, with its uncompromising verdict for the king, brought no peace to the land, and at the beginning of 1264 Earl Simon reopened the conflict. He was now in acknowledged confederacy with Llywelyn, and the border war dropped into its more familiar aspect of a contest between the Welsh and the lords marchers, though the Earl of Gloucester and Humphrey de Bohun were still on the baronial side. In February a baronial army, led by Henry of Montfort, went west to wreak the vengeance of the party upon Roger Mortimer, whose castle and town of Radnor were destroyed, with the help of an army brought by Llywelyn to South Wales.[91] Reprisals soon followed; Edward and the marchers captured the Bohun castles of Huntington and Hay, and thence penetrated into Brecknock, which was taken from Humphrey and bestowed upon Mortimer.[92] Such was the prelude of the campaign which reached its crisis in the battle of Lewes (14th May), a victory for Earl Simon as brilliant as it was unexpected, which placed the king in his hands and made him the real ruler of England for more than a twelvemonth. The marchers escaped from the field without serious loss, and henceforward their compact resistance in the West was one of the most serious military problems with which Simon had to deal. In the task of their reduction Llywelyn gave substantial assistance; he co-operated with the earl in an expedition in the summer which won for the government the castles of Hereford, Hay, Ludlow, and Richard's Castle, and ended in a temporary submission of the marchers at Montgomery.[93] When they again took to arms in the autumn and were again attacked by Earl Simon, the prince of Wales set upon them in the rear and thus helped to bring about a second capitulation at Worcester in December.[94] On neither occasion was there any real settlement, for the policy of the marchers was merely to gain time, but Llywelyn undoubtedly played his part well and the barons had no reason to regret their choice of him as an ally.

Llywelyn, on his part, regarded the recognition of his conquests as the price to be paid for his alliance, and at the end of 1264 Earl Simon was able to meet his wishes in the matter of the Cheshire border. The justiciar of Chester, Alan la Zuche, with the renegade David, had held Chester for Edward throughout the greater part of the year, but in November the royalist defence broke down, and the county, with all its appurtenances, was taken from the heir to the crown and bestowed upon the Earl of Leicester.[95] On 5th January, 1265, Henry of Montfort, acting for his father, met Llywelyn and Gruffydd ap Madog at Hawarden and secured peace along the line of the Dee by abandoning all claim to the lands and castles which had fallen into Welsh hands. Could the great earl have been as sure of his hold upon the mouth of the Severn, all might have been well with him; with Llywelyn as his good friend, he might have contrived to hold the barons of the middle march in check. But this was the weak spot in the impressive edifice of his power; he could not, or, it may be, in foolish confidence he neglected to retain the slippery loyalty of the young Earl of Gloucester, with the result that Gilbert passed over to the marcher party and gave it the solid basis of strength which it needed. On the 28th of May Edward escaped from his captivity at Hereford and a new war began, in which the odds were all against Earl Simon and his ruin all but inevitable.

The earl, with his puppet king, was in the heart of a hostile country, which the vigour of Edward and his followers was making more hostile every day. By the loss of Worcester his road to London and the friendly east was barred against him. It was natural, therefore, he should turn to Llywelyn and offer him better terms than any yet suggested on the English side, in return for a thorough-going alliance. The bargain was struck at Pipton, near Glasbury on the Wye,[96] where, on 19th June, the prince of Wales was encamped with a great company of his vassals, including the two Gruffydds of Powys, Rhys Fychan of Dinefwr, and Owain ap Bleddyn of Edeyrnion. Simon promised, in the king's name, the recognition of the title of prince of Wales, with the suzerainty of the other Welsh chieftains which this implied, the restoration of all lands (including Montgomery and, no doubt, Carmarthen) taken at any time from the first Llywelyn or his son David, and the cession of Painscastle,[97] Hawarden, and Whittington. For these ample concessions, which were deemed by the ordinary Englishman a great blot upon the fair fame of the reformer,[98] Llywelyn agreed to pay thirty thousand marks, in ten annual instalments, and to render willing obedience to the king, but, chiefly and above all, to support the existing government, as controlled by the earl, against all its enemies.[99] Fortified by this alliance, Simon moved southward, hoping to cross the Severn from Newport and so reach Bristol; he took Monmouth, Usk, and Newport itself, all Gloucester castles at the time, without much difficulty, and let Llywelyn loose upon the plains of Gwent.[100] But Edward's army successfully barred the passage of the river and turned the earl, dragging the captive king in his train, back into the Welsh uplands. Here he was safe, under the protection of the prince of Wales, but could make no long stay; the diet of the hardy folk of the hillsides, reflecting in its abundance of milk and meat and its meagre supply of bread the pastoral habits of the country, was repulsive to the corn-fed warriors of the lowlands,[101] and at the beginning of August he was in Hereford once more.[102]

On 4th August at Evesham was fought the fateful day which not only reversed the verdict of Lewes, but closed for ever the eventful career of the Earl of Leicester. In the army at the head of which he fell, there was a large contingent of Welsh foot, as the result of the treaty with Llywelyn, but it proved of little service, taking to flight at the outset of the battle and vainly seeking refuge in corn-fields and gardens.[103] Welsh troops, accustomed only to the methods of fighting which were a tradition in their forest-clad hills, were not as yet of much value in the pitched battles of feudal warfare, and the absence of all the Welsh leaders is enough to show that no great result was expected from their participation in this campaign. It may be that, as has been maintained,[104] Llywelyn missed a great opportunity in not embarking more heartily and unreservedly in the cause of Earl Simon, but, while a capable warrior and skilful in the management of his own people, he had not the keen understanding of foreign conditions and the power to adapt himself to them which distinguished his greater namesake. It was, for him at least, the safer and surer course to keep to the limits of Wales, and in the next few years the policy of caution was fully justified.

Evesham made the march once more a solid mass of resistance to the Welsh.[105] Ten days after the battle Edward regained possession of his county and city of Chester,[106] and it seemed likely that Llywelyn might have a hard struggle to maintain his position. In the event he did so without difficulty, and even succeeded in breaking new ground. In September he aroused general alarm by capturing the castle of Hawarden, which he forthwith, for the protection of the Mold valley, completely destroyed.[107] The army sent against him under Hamo Lestrange and Maurice fitz Gerald was scattered in flight. His position was so strong that the old talk of concluding a truce with him was revived,[108] and Cardinal Ottobon, the papal legate who arrived in England on 29th October to lend his aid in the general restoration of royal authority, showed especial interest in the matter, hoping that as an outsider and as representing the most exalted power in Christendom he might effectively arbitrate between the two peoples.[109] For the present, however, peace was not attainable, and the year 1266 was spent in conflict, in which Llywelyn continued to have the advantage. On 15th May Roger Mortimer, the most formidable of the lords of the middle march, was signally defeated in an attempt to occupy Brycheiniog, barely escaping with his life in the overwhelming slaughter of his men.[110] Llywelyn's cause, in short, was unaffected by the overthrow of the Montfort party; he had built up for himself a power which could stand alone, and it became clear to the government, after the lapse of a couple of years, that no ordinary terms would satisfy a prince who had achieved successes so remarkable.

In England the aftermath of the sweeping victory over the Montfort party had been a long struggle with the defeated remnant, ending in the concession of reasonable terms. It was a struggle which developed opposing interests among the triumphant royalists, Roger Mortimer holding out against any compromise, while the Earl of Gloucester exerted himself to save his former associates from irremediable ruin.[111] These differences, sharp enough to be a serious menace to the hard-won peace of the realm, aided Llywelyn in maintaining his ground[112] and formed an additional reason for agreeing to his demands. In the autumn of 1267, the eleven years' war was at last closed by a formal pacification. Henry and the cardinal took up their quarters at Shrewsbury, and, after a month's negotiation, agreed on 25th September to terms which met the wishes of Llywelyn.[113] On the 29th the prince of Wales did homage and swore fealty at Rhyd Chwima, the ford of Montgomery, and Ottobon, greatly rejoicing at the reconciliation of the king and this "great and puissant member of the English realm," issued a document embodying the particulars of the compact.[114]

The Treaty of Montgomery was a remarkable triumph for Llywelyn, in the completeness with which it recognised his claims. In the extent of its concessions it did not fall far short of the Treaty of Pipton, so that almost as much was obtained from the restored king of a united England as had been wrung from the leader of a discredited party tottering to its fall. The foremost concession was the acknowledgment by the crown of Llywelyn's right to bear the title of prince of Wales, which was now confirmed to him and to his heirs; the title carried with it feudal overlordship over the other chieftains of the Welsh race, with the exception of Maredudd ap Rhys, whose devotion to the English cause was rewarded by permission to remain a direct vassal of the king. Hardly less important were the territorial gains which Llywelyn secured. The four cantrefs of the Perfeddwlad are resigned to him by the crown. Robert of Montalt is to be released,[115] and Hawarden is to be restored to him, but he is to build no castle there for thirty years. Gruffydd ap Gwenwynwyn is to have all the land he held as the king's ally, but to give up later conquests. Llywelyn is to have Whittington (with due regard to existing interests),[116] Kerry, Cydewain,[117] Builth,[118] Gwerthrynion, and Brycheiniog;[119] even Maelienydd, if he can demonstrate his right to it, though in the meantime Roger Mortimer may build a castle there. As against these concessions, Llywelyn is required to make suitable provision for his brother David, either by giving him what he had at the time of his secession in 1263, or, if this be now deemed insufficient, by such augmented grant as may be approved by the two Gruffydds of Powys, Hywel ap Madog, Owain ap Bleddyn, and Tudur ab Ednyfed. He is further to pay for his privileges the substantial sum of 25,000 marks, being 5,000 less than in 1265, and careful provision is made for the payment year by year of the instalments of this amount, until the whole has been wiped off.

Since the coming of the Normans no Welsh prince had attained to such a height of authority and landed influence. Llywelyn the Great had, indeed, held some important places, such as Cardigan and Montgomery, not included in the grant to Llywelyn ap Gruffydd, but he had no such position along the southern march, from Kerry to Crickhowel, as in 1267 enabled the younger prince to present a firm front to Roger Mortimer at every point of the border. Moreover, he was but prince of North Wales and his claim to lordship in the South, despite its substantial basis of fact, was never formally recognised by the crown. The son of Gruffydd might well be pardoned for thinking that he had raised his country to a state of security and well-being unknown before, and founded a principality that would stand the test of time and of many a futile English attack. If his hopes were belied, it was because the circumstances of the hour disguised alike the inherent weakness of his own position and the latent strength of that of the English king.

III. PEACE AND SUPREMACY.

From the coming of the Normans to the Peace of Montgomery, Wales had never been under the rule of a single prince, and the nine years of Llywelyn's tenure of unchallenged power are, therefore, full of interest as a picture of what might have been the history of the country for generations had the fates looked with a kindlier eye upon Welsh independence. Gilbert of Gloucester was, until the ire of King Edward was aroused, the only formidable enemy with whom the prince of Wales had to contend, and thus he had leisure to work out the salvation of his people. That he was not able to build up in these years an enduring structure must be, at any rate in part, ascribed to his lack of foresight and penetration. Well able to lead his folk in time of war and to guide them along familiar and well-trodden paths, he had not the instinct which scents danger from afar, is beguiled by no facile victory, and draws its forces together for the coming battle, while the unseeing eye has not as yet discerned the rising of its shadow above the horizon.

Little light is thrown by contemporary authorities upon the home policy of Llywelyn during this period. He was unmarried and had, apparently, no plans for the succession. He continued to keep his elder brother, Owain the Red, in captivity, despite the protests of the bards, with whom the imprisoned prince was popular, and who did not shrink from telling Llywelyn that brother should forgive brother, as both hoped for Divine mercy, and that it was God's prerogative alone to deprive a man of his lawful inheritance.[120] Another brother, Rhodri, was also kept in prison as a difficult person, although in 1272 an effort was made to dispose of him respectably by giving him money to marry an Irish heiress.[121] The match did not come off, and Rhodri ultimately solved the difficulty by escaping to England.[122] David had been specially provided for in the peace, and, although difficulties arose as to the execution of its terms, was at last settled in 1269[123] upon land of his own, through the mediation of the bishops of Bangor and St. Asaph.[124] He was with his brother at the siege of Caerphilly in November, 1271,[125] and is mentioned as of his council in September, 1273.[126] Nevertheless David, the restless, discontented, shifty schemer, true neither to the Welsh nor to the English side, was Llywelyn's evil genius; first by conspiring against him he was the means of bringing about the disastrous war of 1277, and then, by luring him into the ill-judged outbreak of 1282, he achieved his final overthrow.

Trusty counsellors of other than royal blood were not wanting to Llywelyn. Two sons of the great Ednyfed Fychan were much engaged in his affairs; the elder, Goronwy, succeeded his father as seneschal or "distain" of Gwynedd, and was constantly with the prince, attesting the Scottish agreement, the compact with Gruffydd ap Gwenwynwyn, the Treaty of Pipton, and the Peace of Montgomery.[127] He died on 17th October, 1268,[128] mourned by Bleddyn Fardd and the Little Poet as "the buttress of Gwynedd," the loss of whom made all men sad —

Hard it is to learn to be without him.[129]

His brother, Tudur, who had been no less active in Llywelyn's service,[130] followed him as "steward of Wales" [131] and was the prince's chief adviser in the stormy year 1277. Both Goronwy and Tudur would seem to have worthily upheld the traditions of their office, which made them guardians of the dignity of the court in the absence of their lord.[132] Another "uchelwr" often found engaged in Llywelyn's business was Einion ap Caradog, who seems to have been lord of Penychen in Eifionydd.[133] Of a younger generation was Goronwy ap Heilyn of Rhos, prominent in the events of the disastrous close of the prince's career.[134]

Llywelyn's relations with the Church were, upon the whole, friendly and free from serious strain, although he was not, like the Lord Rhys and Llywelyn the Great, conspicuous as a monastic founder and benefactor. The age for the establishment of new religious houses was, in fact, passing by, and the reaction was setting in which is well typified by Edward I.'s Statute of Mortmain. Two bishops occupied the see of Bangor in the latter half of this century, whose successive episcopates cover the unusually long period of seventy years. Richard, consecrated about 1237,[135] supported Gruffydd in the conflict with David,[136] but was at first no friend of Gruffydd's son; he took refuge, after the settlement of 1247, in the abbey of St. Alban's and made this his home, with occasional visits to Wales, for the next ten years.[137] About 1258, possibly as the result of the truce of that year, he ranged himself on Llywelyn's side and he acted as envoy for him in 1259 and 1260.[138] Then came a quarrel about a matter which was a fruitful subject of discord in this age in Wales, the limits of royal and of episcopal jurisdiction. The laws of Hywel the Good, dating from a time when the bishop often o'ertopped the local chieftain in dignity and power, conceded much in the way of ecclesiastical immunity which Llywelyn, here following in the footsteps of his grandfather, was unwilling to allow. A settlement was patched up in 1261 by the efforts of the bishop of St. Asaph, the sons of Ednyfed, and other clerical and lay mediators,[139] but the dispute flared up again in 1265, when Richard interdicted the performance of Divine worship in the prince's chapel.[140] At last, in 1267, after the conclusion of the Peace of Montgomery, he abandoned the struggle, begging the pope to relieve him of a charge which old age, increasing weakness, and the malignity of his flock made too heavy for him to bear.[141] He was succeeded by Anian, or Einion,[142] a cleric of a more accommodating temper, who kept on good terms with Llywelyn until the final crash, and was afterwards no less acceptable to Edward I.[143] In 1278 bishop and prince, it is true, were at variance,[144] but in 1280 their differences were composed.[145] The Pontifical or service-book of Anian, containing the words and music of the many liturgical functions in which he had to bear a part, is still among the treasured possessions of his cathedral.[146]

At St. Asaph two bishops bearing the popular name of Anian were the contemporaries of Llywelyn ap Gruffydd. Anian I. was appointed in 1249, when the English were in full control of the valley of the Clwyd, and accordingly acknowledged without reserve the authority of the crown in all matters touching his election.[147] He found no difficulty, however, in working with Llywelyn after the conquest of 1256, and acted in 1261 as one of the arbitrators in the dispute between the prince and his brother prelate of Bangor.[148] Anian II. succeeded to the bishopric in 1268,[149] having previously, it is said, been prior of the Dominican convent at Rhuddlan, not far from the cathedral. "The black friar of Nannau," as he was familiarly styled, was a highly combative ecclesiastic and engaged in more than the usual number of lengthy lawsuits on behalf of the privileges of his see. He fought the abbey of Shrewsbury over the patronage of Oswestry, that of Valle Crucis over the churches of Llangollen and Wrexham, Isabella, widow of John fitz Alan III., over the advowson of Llanymynech, and the bishop of Hereford over the diocesan rights of Gorddwr.[150] It is not surprising that this "foremost champion and assertor of the rights of his bishopric" should come into conflict with Llywelyn. At first, their relations were amicable; the bishop assented to the submission of doubtful church claims to the verdict of a jury,[151] helped the prince to a settlement with his brother David,[152] and acted as his envoy at the court of Henry III.[153] But in 1273 Anian began to accuse his lord of hostility to the church, and especially to the monks, and, although the Welsh Cistercian abbots, assembled at Strata Florida, strongly protested to the pope against this attempt to blacken the fame of a most just and pious ruler,[154] he did not relax his opposition, but carried on the quarrel persistently,[155] until the Peace of Conway brought it to an end by removing almost the whole of his diocese from Llywelyn's control.

While Llywelyn was thus frequently embroiled with his bishops, he was on the best of terms with the members of all religious orders. In 1274 the abbots of Whitland, Strata Florida, Cwm Hir, Ystrad Marchell, Aberconwy, Cymer, and Valle Crucis joined in his defence against the charges of the bishop of St. Asaph, and assured the pope that he was a prominent and vigorous champion of their order. He gave Aberconwy the royal chapels of Llanbadrig and Llanbeblig, attached to his courts of Cemais and Carnarvon respectively,[156] and was often aided by Cistercian abbots in the transaction of business of state.[157] The new orders of friars nourished under his protection; in addition to the Franciscan convent of Llanfaes, founded by his grandfather, Dominican priories came into existence at Bangor and at Rhuddlan, the former before 1251,[158] and the latter before 1268,[159] and the favour shown to this latest development of ascetic zeal by Llywelyn may readily be guessed from the appearance in his train of friars so unmistakably Welsh as Jonas of Bangor and Ieuan Goch and Iorwerth ap Cadwgan of Llanfaes.[160]

In passing to the consideration of Llywelyn's relations with his brother princes, the "barons" whose homage formed the solid foundation of his titular dignity of "prince of Wales," one is tempted to look for signs of internal weakness, such as might help to explain the collapse of 1277. But it is difficult to find them; the principality never wore so flourishing an aspect as in the year or two which preceded its reduction by Edward I. to the limits of Gwynedd above Conway. If anything, its weakness was geographical; its interests in the middle march, constantly inviting attack from England, proved a snare to Llywelyn, who spent his energies at Caerphilly and Dolforwyn, instead of securing his position in Ceredigion and Ystrad Tywi, which history had shown to be the true strongholds of the independent South.

His hold upon Powys was complete until the outbreak of the war. Gruffydd ap Madog of Maelor, who, true to the policy of his house, had adhered to the cause of Gwynedd from an early stage in the struggle with Henry III., died in December, 1269, and was buried in his father's foundation of Valle Crucis.[161] His brothers Hywel and Madog quitted the scene about the same time, leaving no male issue,[162] and thus Powys Fadog came into the hands of the four sons of Gruffydd, with the exception of Maelor Saesneg and its castle of

Overton, which were reserved for the dowager, Emma Audley, and did not again come under Welsh rule.[163] Of the four co-heirs, Madog, the eldest, had Welsh Maelor, or Bromfield,[164] Gruffydd received Ial,[165] to Llywelyn was assigned the region south of the Dee,[166] and to Owain, Bangor Iscoed;[167] and it is significant of the subordinate position of all four that the provision they made for their mother in 1270, by a deed executed at Dinas Bran Castle, was submitted to Llywelyn for his approval.[168] South of the Tanat the political aspect of Powys was very different; except for the small holdings of Madog ap Gwenwynwyn in Mawddwy[169] and of the posterity of Llywelyn ab Owain Fychan in Mechain below the Forest,[170] the whole country was in the hands of one prince, who from his castle of Pool ruled over almost the whole of the modern Montgomeryshire. But the power of Gruffydd ap Gwenwynwyn was no menace to Llywelyn, for until 1274 he was his cordial supporter and ally, joining, for instance, in the campaign of 1271 against Caerphilly,[171] and, when he turned traitor and cast off his allegiance, he was easily driven out of his territories by his overlord, who for the moment was stronger than ever. Moreover, Llywelyn commanded the southern border of Powys by his hold upon Kerry and Cydewain, a hold which he strengthened in 1273 by building in the latter district, on a rock which frowns above the Severn, the castle of Dolforwyn, a challenge flung out to the royal walls of Montgomery.[172]

It was in 1274 that the conspiracy was hatched which Llywelyn avenged by the conquest of Southern Powys.[173] The moving spirits were Gruffydd's wife, Hawise Lestrange, who kept the incriminating documents in a strongbox in Pool Castle, and her eldest son, Owain, but Gruffydd was undoubtedly in the secret. The plan was to work upon the jealousy of David, secure his aid in the assassination of Llywelyn, and then raise him to the vacant throne; in return, David promised Owain his daughter in marriage and the cession to Powys of Kerry and Cydewain. All this was to be carried out in February, but storms and floods of more than common violence threw the schemes of the conspirators into confusion and nothing was done. Soon the story oozed out and its echoes reached the ears of Llywelyn, but at first his information was only enough to create a strong suspicion and was not so precise as to justify extreme action. David was cited before the prince's council at Rhuddlan and questioned about his proceedings, while Gruffydd was summoned to meet his overlord at Dolforwyn and required to give up Owain as a hostage for his loyalty and good behaviour, the cantref of Arwystli and a part of Cyfeiliog

being in addition taken from him as a warning of the dangers of treason.[174] It was not long, however, ere the whole design was laid bare;
David fled to England, without waiting for the further examination
which was to take place at Llanfor in Penllyn, and Owain, under what
pressure it is impossible to say, unburdened himself of the details of
the plot to the bishop of Bangor. Again Llywelyn sent messengers to
Gruffydd, who upon their arrival at Pool were well received. But that
very night the prince of Powys, with his wife, children, and household
goods, made his escape to Shrewsbury;[175] the Northern envoys were
clapped into the castle dungeon, the walls were manned and the banner of Powys set defiantly streaming from the height of the topmost
tower. This was an invitation to battle which Llywelyn met with
alacrity; he captured and destroyed the castle and forthwith occupied
the whole of Gruffydd's lands.[176]

With West Wales, the ancient kingdom of Deheubarth, Llywelyn
during this period concerned himself but slightly. The suggestion has
already been made that his neglect of this region, in which his grandfather had achieved some of his greatest successes, was a political
error. But it is to be remembered that there was no serious challenge
here to his position as lord paramount of the Welsh race. Ceredigion
and Ystrad Tywi were divided among puny chiefs, who could not stand
for a moment against the power of the ruler of Gwynedd. In the former region Maelgwn Fychan was represented by his grandson, Rhys
Ieuanc, who, just before the war of 1277, held the land north of the
Ystwyth,[177] while the place of Maredudd ab Owain was filled by his
three sons, Owain, Gruffydd, and Cynan, sharers of a none too ample
domain to the south of that river.[178] In Ystrad Tywi, the two prominent
figures of the previous generation, Maredudd ap Rhys and Rhys
Fychan, disappear within three weeks of each other; Maredudd, who
at the close of his life had been obliged to submit to the overlordship
of Llywelyn, died at his castle of Dryslwyn on 27th July, 1271, and
Rhys Fychan (or Ieuanc) at Dinefwr on 17th August, in the same
year.[179] Their representatives and heirs were Rhys ap Maredudd and
Rhys Wyndod, the latter tracing his descent through three other
chiefs of the name of Rhys to the great bearer of that name whose
broad patrimony was now so broken and dismembered.

Nothing was done during this period to weaken the English hold
upon West Wales. Edward had transferred his lordships of Cardigan
and Carmarthen to his younger brother, Edmund, some little time
before the conclusion of the Peace of Montgomery,[180] and the Earl of
Lancaster continued to bear rule over them until 1279. A survey of

Carmarthen and its appurtenances made in 1275 [181] shows us this
ancient centre of royal authority in a state of indifferent repair and
bringing but a poor revenue to its owner, but at the same time little
troubled by fear of attack from the Prince of Wales. The five-towered
donjon, the great tower, the hall, chapel, stable and kitchen, the castle gate and the castle wall were all in a state of great dilapidation, and
the whole value of the lordship was under £50 per annum. But in the
three commotes of Elfed, Derllys, and Widigada, attached to the castle, there was a great multitude of Welshmen who rendered kine and
did suit at their lord's court; in the borough there were 181
burgesses, and in the country around knights who did feudal service
to the lordship for holdings at St. dear's, Laugharne, Llanstephan,
and Abercywyn.[182] The shadow of Llywelyn's power did not, apparently, darken the sky at Carmarthen, which on the west joined hands
with William of Valence, lord of Pembroke, and on the east with Pain
of Chaworth, lord of Kidwelly.[183]

It was in Eastern South Wales that Llywelyn was at this time busy,
guarding his conquests and even extending them. He kept his hold
upon Builth, Gwerthrynion, and Elfael[184] without much difficulty,
though he had no title to the last-mentioned district under the
Treaty of Montgomery. But in Brecknock his task was more difficult.
The young Humphrey de Bohun, grandson of the Earl of
Hereford,[185] was by no means disposed to acquiesce in the abandonment to the Welsh of his mother's inheritance in the valley of the
Usk, which had been under the rule of Anglo-Norman masters since
the days of William Rufus. He took up arms to assert his rights and
hostilities followed, in which the crown, mindful of its obligations
under the peace, at first strove to play a mediating part. In 1272
Henry declared his readiness to see that redress was given for any act
of violence on the part of Humphrey,[186] and in the following year
Reginald fitz Peter, of Dinas and Blaenllyfni, and his vassal, Hugh
Turbeville of Crickhowel, were rebuked by the king for gratuitously
throwing themselves into the fray.[187] In 1274 again, the king's envoys
to Llywelyn were specially charged with the duty of arranging a truce
between him and Humphrey de Bohun.[188] The zeal of the government in this matter cooled with the development of its own quarrel
with the prince, and in 1275 it begins to treat Humphrey as the
rightful Lord of Brecknock.[189] But Llywelyn held his ground at
Brecon, nevertheless, until the general movement against him two
years later forced him to relinquish a prize of which he was, no
doubt, pardonably proud.

The stiffest encounter of these years was between Llywelyn and Earl Gilbert of Gloucester. Not only did the former's tenure of Brecknock bring him into touch with the lordship of Glamorgan, but it would even appear that during the baronial struggle he had encroached considerably upon its borders and attached to his cause the chieftains whose lands lay round the upper waters of the river Taff. It was, perhaps, for undue favour to Llywelyn that Gruffydd ap Rhys, last of the ruling house of Senghenydd, was taken prisoner at Cardiff at the beginning of 1267 and despatched for safe keeping across the sea to Kilkenny.[190] The Peace of Montgomery included no settlement between the two great western magnates, and early in 1268 Gilbert began the building of that elaborate fortress at Caerphilly which was to stand sentinel at the entrance of the Rhymney valley and guard the lowlands around Cardiff from the inroads of their dangerous new neighbour. About the same time Llywelyn fought a battle with the knights of Glamorgan, in which a son of the lord of Penmark was slain.[191] In the September of this year, after a conference with royal commissioners sent to Montgomery to bring about a general settlement of grievances, the two antagonists agreed at Gwenddwr in Cantref Selyf to lay their claims before four Welsh and four English arbiters, and in the meantime Llywelyn was allowed to retain Senghenydd north of the Caeach and Miskin north of Pontypridd.[192] There was, however, no finality about this settlement; in October, 1270, war blazed out again, and Llywelyn took advantage of the renewal of the conflict to destroy the castle at Caerphilly, the rising towers of which he had watched with so jealous an eye.[193] Next year Gilbert, with undaunted resolution, addressed himself once more to the building of this stronghold, which represented the last word in the science of fortification.[194] The prince of Wales brought a formidable army to the spot, and was on the point of repeating his exploit of the previous year, when the bishops of Lichfield and Worcester appeared upon the scene, and on 2nd November induced him to desist from his operations by giving a pledge that the castle would be taken into royal custody and no further building allowed. The pledge was honestly given, but the government were not strong enough to carry it out; by some carelessness or treachery, the place in a little while fell again into the hands of the earl, and the duel between him and Llywelyn thus ended in his favour.[195]

If in this particular, however, the prince of Wales failed to realise the utmost stretch of his ambition, he was, without Caerphilly, a most potent lord. As his poet Bleddyn intimates, his power extended without a break from the banks of the Taff to the furthest coasts of the isle of Anglesey.[196] Pope Gregory X. recognised his exceptional position in the English realm and excused his officers and subjects from the necessity of answering citations to England issued by the Archbishop of Canterbury; their cases were to be dealt with by means of commissioners sent to Wales.[197] Ere the sun of Welsh independence set for ever, it shone with a refulgent evening glow, pleasant to look upon in its wealth of golden pageantry, but changing, even as the eye rested upon it, into the dull pallor of nightfall.

IV. THE DOWNFALL.

With the war of 1277 begins the story of the Edwardian Conquest of Wales—a long story, crowded with interest and, as an episode in English military history, already told in some detail by Mr. J. E. Morris. Though it has other aspects than the military, it is no part of the design of the present work to embark upon it and to describe the fundamental changes which created the Wales of the fourteenth and fifteenth centuries. This would be to enter upon a new subject, more fitly reserved for separate treatment: It will be enough for the present to complete the narrative of the period of independence by briefly tracing the personal fortunes of the last native ruler of Gwynedd to the day of his inglorious death.

Llywelyn's relations with the crown during the closing years of Henry III. were thoroughly cordial. He paid the annual render of 3,000 marks prescribed in 1267 with regularity,[198] and both sides showed great anxiety to maintain the terms of peace agreed upon in that year. As the government continued to be in the same hands for some time after the old king's death in November, 1272, while Edward's return was awaited, the prince's attitude underwent no marked change at this time, and in September, 1273, he can write an amicable letter from Rhyd Lanfair to his "particular friend, Reginald de Gray, justiciar of Chester," acknowledging the receipt of an invitation to the coronation and promising to send venison for the royal larder.[199] But from the moment of Edward's accession, while there was as yet nothing like a breach, Llywelyn begins to eye the king with suspicion, and distrust, born of the old baronial struggles, silently takes the place of the former confidence and goodwill. The payment of the yearly tribute ceases;[200] moreover, another obligation is persistently evaded, and Llywelyn cannot be got to swear fealty to the new sovereign.[201] Nor are matters mended when the king himself makes his appearance in the realm; the prince of Wales was absent from the great crowning ceremony of 19th August, 1274, and, though later in the year he sent messengers to treat with Edward at Northampton,[202] no progress had been made towards an understanding when the abortive conspiracy of David and the house of Powys darkened the current of Llywelyn's thoughts and hardened his suspicion into unfeigned hostility. Both David and Gruffydd ap Gwenwynwyn fled to England, and it was when Llywelyn learnt that they had been sheltered there and received into the royal favour that he cast off all show of friendliness and prepared for a struggle.[203]

Meanwhile, Edward was beginning to show natural irritation at the virtual refusal of homage and fealty. In September, 1275, he visited Chester, where Llywelyn was duly warned to present himself, but with no result.[204] At the very moment he was laying his grievances before the pope, accusing the king of infringing the peace and, in particular, of harbouring his fugitive barons; he would do homage, he explained, if any safe place were proposed; as it was, he declined to risk his liberty and his princely power.[205] Against such deep-seated suspicion, argument and remonstrance were of no avail, and it was, no doubt, a satisfaction to Edward when fortune placed in his hands a weapon of a different kind, which he hoped would at once end the dispute. A little before his fall Earl Simon had planned a marriage between his only daughter Eleanor and the Prince of Wales;[206] the scheme had then been abandoned, but in 1275, the parties being still unmarried, and the lady twenty-three,[207] it was revived. By whom the initiative was taken at this time is not apparent, but the revival of the proposal may be connected with the death of the Countess of Leicester in the spring of this year,[208] leaving her daughter without protection, and with Llywelyn's growing determination to thwart the king by all means in his power. Whether the prince really hoped to revive the Montfort party in England one can scarcely tell, but there is no doubt that Edward regarded the alliance as a menace and took steps to prevent its being carried out until, at any rate, Llywelyn's submission had made it harmless. After a marriage by proxy in her French home,[209] the bride, whose beauty was such as befitted the consort of a prince,[210] sailed, in the heart of the winter of 1275–6, for the Welsh coast, escorted by her brother Amaury (who was a cleric) and a number of knights and friars. But off the Scilly Isles the ship was waylaid by vessels from Bristol,[211] and its light-hearted company brought in dejection to that city, whence Eleanor was soon carried off for safe custody to Windsor, and Amaury to the royal prison of Corfe.[212]

Llywelyn, notwithstanding this mischance, had still no thought of submission, and at the end of 1276 Edward began to make ready for a Welsh campaign on an unprecedented scale. The prince of Wales had not misjudged the military strength of his position, for it cost the king £23,000[213] and twelve months' labour to bring him to terms; it was in his judgment of the political situation that he went astray. Throughout the baronage were unanimous in their support of the crown, and no trace appears of the cleavage of the Montfort period. To this result Llywelyn, there can be no doubt, had himself contributed by his endeavour to build up a power in the marches; no sooner was the signal given for a general attack upon him than Ralph Tony won for himself Elfael,[214] the Earl of Hereford Brecknock,[215] Peter Corbet Gorddwr,[216] and many another baron realised that the hour had now come to enforce claims upon Welsh soil which had long been in abeyance. This unity on the English side was not matched by any like spectacle on the side of the Welsh. David was with the king, and it was proposed, at one stage of the war, to make him and Owain Goch princes of Gwynedd in Llywelyn's stead.[217] Gruffydd ap Gwenwynwyn was one of the earliest to profit by the general uprising against the prince of Wales and soon recovered his patrimony in Southern Powys.[218] The princes of South Wales, as was to be expected from so divided a group of insignificant chieftains, offered no united front to the invader. First, Rhys ap Maredudd of Dryslwyn, inheriting his father's enmity towards Llywelyn, made his peace with the captain of Edward's forces in South Wales;[219] next, Rhys Wyndod surrendered Dinefwr and Llandovery,[220] which thus passed finally from the line of Rhys ap Tewdwr; lastly, the minor chiefs of Ceredigion, Rhys Fychan and the house of Maredudd ab Owain, bowed to the storm and did homage to the king at Worcester.[221] In this way Edward deftly cut away the props which supported the power of the prince of Wales before he aimed a single blow at Llywelyn himself.

The operations of 1276-7 fall, in fact, into two parts. From November to July, Edward was engaged in clearing the ground by means of expeditions working from Chester, Montgomery, and Carmarthen. The force which set out from Chester recovered Mold and Northern Powys; the Montgomery contingent won Southern Powys for Gruffydd ap Gwenwynwyn, and Cydewain, Kerry, Builth, and Gwerthrynion for the king; while it was the Carmarthen section which removed all obstacles to the restoration of royal authority in Ystrad Tywi and Ceredigion.[222] In the summer the second stage of the war began; Edward himself took the field and, taking his start from

Chester, moved upon Snowdonia by the familiar coast road. As he passed on, he secured his communications by building strongholds at Flint and Rhuddlan, which at a later time grew into formidable castles; a fleet from the Cinque Ports beset Anglesey and not only harassed Llywelyn's rear, but also, by burning the harvest of that fruitful isle, threatened him with famine in his rock-hewn citadel. Edward had, in fact, learned the secret of successful warfare against Gwynedd, which was, to treat the inaccessible wilderness of Snowdon as a natural fortress, capable, by a skilful combination of naval and military power, of being starved into surrender. Llywelyn found it impossible to shake himself free from the grip of his adversary, and on 7th November, 1277, he finally agreed to the terms proposed to him on behalf of the king.

The Treaty of Conway[223] humbled Llywelyn as signally as that of Montgomery had exalted him. By it he lost all his conquests in South and Mid Wales and even that Middle Country between the Conway and the Dee which no strong ruler of Gwynedd had ever let slip, and which he had held from the beginning of his victorious career. His territory was confined within the comparatively narrow bounds of Gwynedd above Conway. His feudal authority fared no better; all the homages of his barons, the princely vassals whose obedience made him venerable and great, were taken from him save five; he was left lord of four chiefs in the vale of Edeyrnion[224] and of Rhys Fychan, who had been driven from Geneu'r Glyn across the Dovey to Meirionydd.[225] He was further forced to release his brother Owain, whom he had held so long a captive, and to provide him with land, which he did by establishing him in the cantref of Lleyn.[226] For David the king himself made provision, giving him the landward two of the Four Cantrefs, namely, Rhufoniog and Dyffryn Clwyd, with the lordship of Hope,[227] and therewith the hand of his kinswoman Elizabeth, daughter of the Earl of Derby and widow of William Marshall of Norfolk.[228] Llywelyn was reduced to the position he had held in early life, before his triumphant spear had swept all before it; he was but one of a group of princes who divided Gwynedd between them.

Yet, despite his humiliation, he was not crushed and still held a position which many an English earl might envy. Edward made no ungenerous use of his victory, and indeed always treated Llywelyn as a dangerous opponent whom he was bound to keep under, but for whom he had a high personal regard. Some of the harsher conditions of the treaty were there as matters of form merely and were afterwards waived;[229] moreover, the prince was not deprived of his title, and, according to one authority,[230] the motive for leaving him five of his old feudatories was that it might not be altogether shorn of its former dignity and honour. Thus the storm of 1277 was followed by a calm which lasted for four years. Llywelyn accepted his defeat and the lower rank to which fortune had once again assigned him with resignation and with no treacherous hinderthought in his heart; convinced of the solid strength of Edward's power, he set himself to fill the dignified place in the realm which was still reserved for him. At Christmas he went to London and rendered the long deferred homage,[231] and in return received a promise that his bride should be released and given to him.[232] The king was at first somewhat doubtful of the sincerity of Llywelyn's conversion to the policy of peace and good neighbourhood, but the quiet lapse of the summer months of 1278 and a meeting with the prince near Rhuddlan in September showed him that he had nothing to fear.[233] On 13th October the marriage of the prince of Wales and Eleanor of Montfort at last took place, in Worcester Cathedral, in the presence of the king and the queen and a brilliant assemblage of English magnates.[234] Thus, as the Annals of Osney say, with a romantic enthusiasm not usual in the recording of mediæval weddings, did Llywelyn win, "with a heart that leapt for joy, his beloved spouse, for whose loving embraces he had so long yearned".

The final breach between Llywelyn and the king came suddenly and there is little in the history of the preceding three years to suggest that it was impending. No doubt, the prince had his grievances, but they were not of the first order, and Edward was taken completely by surprise when news was brought to him at Devizes of the outbreak of March, 1282. The cause of the war was the oppressive rule of the royal officials, now as of old doing their master grave disservice, in the districts which had been taken from Llywelyn, and the prince was drawn into the field, not so much by his own wrongs as by those endured by his former subjects. The situation recalled that of 1256, but whereas in that year he had made his political fortune by lending a willing ear to the cries of the men of the Four Cantrefs, the same course of action followed in 1282 wrought his irretrievable ruin.

It was David, hitherto the friend and the favourite of the English, who, deeply dissatisfied with the position of affairs in his lordships of Denbigh and Hope, first threw down the gage of battle, and on the eve of Palm Sunday took the castle of Hawarden by assault. In the week ensuing, and, no doubt, as the result of previous arrangement, the chieftains of the South attacked the royal castles of Aberystwyth,

Llandovery, and Carreg Cennen. The revolt had now become general in South and Mid Wales, and, when Llywelyn resolved to make common cause with the insurgents and once more to challenge the might of Edward, the whole country was aflame and the king had the entire Welsh problem upon his hands. In the measures which he adopted, he repeated to a large extent the expedients which had proved so successful in 1277. A force of knights was sent as before to clear the way, Edward himself came down to North Wales and the conquest of Anglesey was undertaken, with the aid of the sailors of the Cinque Ports, as a preliminary to the shutting up of Llywelyn and David in their stronghold of Eryri. These were steps well calculated in the course of time to bring the conflict to an end, but the process was slow and the Welsh were in the meantime encouraged to resist by more than one serious check to the designs of the English king. On June 16th a force led by the Earl of Gloucester was defeated near Llandeilo Fawr. On November 6th a still graver disaster befell the troops operating in Anglesey; attempting to cross the bridge of boats which had been thrown across the Menai Straits near Bangor,[235] some sixteen knights, with their followers, were set upon by the Welsh and overwhelmed. It is not surprising that Llywelyn brushed aside the well-meant but clumsy efforts of Archbishop Peckham at mediation, rejecting his offer of an English estate worth £1000 a year, and cast about him for new methods of defence.

What he had especially to fear was that Edward, undeterred by his reverses, would at length reproduce the situation which had forced upon the Welsh the Peace of Conway and effectively blockade the region of Snowdonia. To meet this danger, Llywelyn resolved to make his way to the South, where resistance to the foreigner had somewhat nagged, and there create a diversion which would relieve the pressure upon Gwynedd. In the month of November he appeared in the highlands of Builth. The lordship was in the hands of the king, and the castle, standing on the south side of the Irfon where it falls into the Wye, had lately been rebuilt at considerable cost. To win over the Welsh tenants of the district was an easy matter, but to capture the castle, defended by John Giffard and a body of Shropshire levies, was a serious military undertaking, and it was in the endeavour to accomplish it that the last Prince of Wales of the native line came to his melancholy end.

He died, not at the head of his army in a well-fought fray, but almost alone, in an unregarded corner of the field, as he was hastening from some private errand to rejoin the troops who were holding the north bank of the Irfon against a determined English attack. The man who struck him down with his lance, one Stephen Frankton, knew not what he had done, and it was only afterwards that the body was recognized. It is probable that the true story of that fateful 11th of December will never be rightly known and, in particular, why Llywelyn, with dangers on every side, had thus allowed himself to be separated from his faithful troops. But, mysterious accident though it was, the prince's death was decisive for the struggle between the two races; without him, the Welsh could not continue the conflict, and, though Edward had still much to do to secure the fruits of victory, the turning point had been reached in the contest between Welsh independence and the English crown. Only Llywelyn ap Gruffydd could give life to the cause which must eventually succumb to the centralising tendencies of English politics.

Upon recognition of the fallen hero, his head was cut off and sent to Edward, who exhibited it to the army in Anglesey and then despatched it to London, so as to gratify the citizens with concrete evidence of his triumph. The body, when some ecclesiastical scruples had been satisfied, was buried in the abbey of Cwm Hir,[236] where, however, nothing remains to mark the site of the grave. Llywelyn's wife, Eleanor, had died in childbirth in June in the midst of the conflict and had been buried in the friary at Llanfaes. The little Gwenllian, their only child, soon fell into the hands of the king, and spent her days as a nun of Sempringham. No heir, therefore, carried on the traditions of the lost leader, and his followers felt there was nothing more to live for —

> O God! that the sea might engulf the land!
> Why are we left to long-drawn weariness?

was the lament of the desperate Gruffydd ab yr Ynad Coch, who read the tragedy of the hour in the beating of the wind and of the rain, the sullen wash of the waves upon the grey beach, the roar of the wind-whipt oaks that miserable and more than wintry December. It was for a far distant generation to see that the last Prince had not lived in vain, but by his life-work had helped to build solidly the enduring fabric of Welsh nationality.

GENEALOGICAL TABLES.

1. THE LINE OF GWYNEDD.

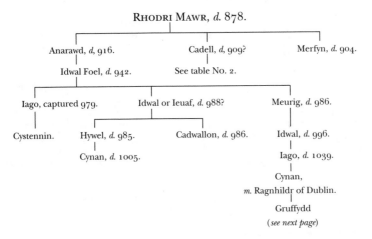

RHODRI MAWR, *d.* 878.

Anarawd, *d,* 916.

Idwal Foel, *d.* 942.

Cadell, *d,* 909?

See table No. 2.

Merfyn, *d.* 904.

Iago, captured 979.

Idwal or Ieuaf, *d.* 988?

Meurig, *d.* 986.

Cystennin.

Hywel, *d.* 985.

Cadwallon, *d.* 986.

Idwal, *d.* 996.

Cynan, *d.* 1005.

Iago, *d.* 1039.

Cynan,
m. Ragnhildr of Dublin.

Gruffydd
(*see next page*)

THE LINE OF GWYNEDD (*continued*).

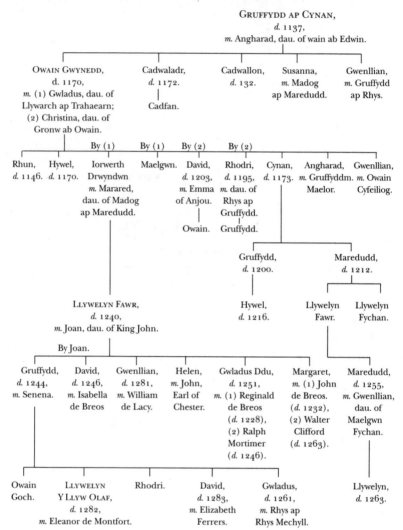

GRUFFYDD AP CYNAN,
d. 1137,
m. Angharad, dau. of wain ab Edwin.

OWAIN GWYNEDD,	Cadwaladr,	Cadwallon,	Susanna,	Gwenllian,
d. 1170,	*d.* 1172.	*d.* 132.	*m.* Madog	*m.* Gruffydd
m. (1) Gwladus, dau. of			ap Maredudd.	ap Rhys.
Llywarch ap Trahaearn;	Cadfan.			
(2) Christina, dau. of				
Gronw ab Owain.				

	By (1)	By (1)	By (2)	By (2)		
Rhun,	Hywel,	Iorwerth	Maelgwn.	David,	Rhodri,	Cynan,	Angharad,	Gwenllian,

Rhun, *d.* 1146.   Hywel, *d.* 1170.   Iorwerth Drwyndwn *m.* Marared, dau. of Madog ap Maredudd.   Maelgwn.   David, *d.* 1203, *m.* Emma of Anjou.   Rhodri, *d.* 1195, *m.* dau. of Rhys ap Gruffydd.   Cynan, *d.* 1173.   Angharad, *m.* Gruffyddm. Maelor.   Gwenllian, *m.* Owain Cyfeiliog.

Owain.   Gruffydd.

Gruffydd, *d.* 1200.   Maredudd, *d.* 1212.

LLYWELYN FAWR, *d.* 1240, *m.* Joan, dau. of King John.   Hywel, *d.* 1216.   Llywelyn Fawr.   Llywelyn Fychan.

By Joan.

Gruffydd,	David,	Gwenllian,	Helen,	Gwladus Ddu,	Margaret,	Maredudd,
d. 1244,	*d.* 1246,	*d.* 1281,	*m.* John,	*d.* 1251,	*m.* (1) John	*d.* 1255,
m. Senena.	*m.* Isabella	*m.* William	Earl of	*m.* (1) Reginald	de Breos.	*m.* Gwenllian,
	de Breos	de Lacy.	Chester.	de Breos	(*d.* 1232),	dau. of
				(*d.* 1228),	(2) Walter	Maelgwn
				(2) Ralph	Clifford	Fychan.
				Mortimer	(*d.* 1263).	
				(*d.* 1246).		

| Owain Goch. | LLYWELYN Y LLYW OLAF, *d.* 1282, *m.* Eleanor de Montfort. | Rhodri. | David, *d.* 1283, *m.* Elizabeth Ferrers. | Gwladus, *d.* 1261, *m.* Rhys ap Rhys Mechyll. | Llywelyn, *d.* 1263. |

2. THE LINE OF DEHEUBARTH.

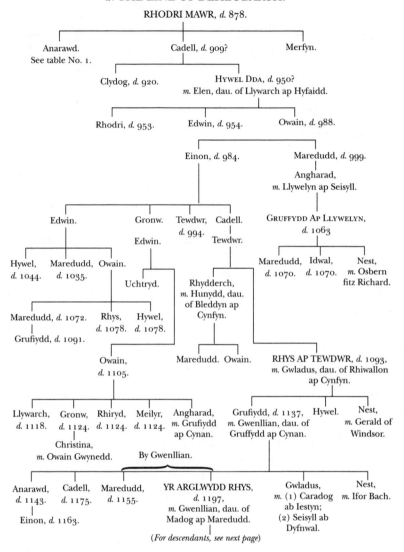

RHODRI MAWR, *d.* 878.

Anarawd.
See table No. 1.

Cadell, *d.* 909?

Merfyn.

Clydog, *d.* 920.

HYWEL DDA, *d.* 950?
m. Elen, dau. of Llywarch ap Hyfaidd.

Rhodri, *d.* 953.

Edwin, *d.* 954.

Owain, *d.* 988.

Einon, *d.* 984.

Maredudd, *d.* 999.

Angharad,
m. Llywelyn ap Seisyll.

Edwin.

Gronw.

Tewdwr,
d. 994.

Cadell.

GRUFFYDD AP LLYWELYN,
d. 1063

Edwin.

Tewdwr.

Hywel,
d. 1044.

Maredudd,
d. 1035.

Owain.

Uchtryd.

Rhydderch,
m. Hunydd, dau.
of Bleddyn ap
Cynfyn.

Maredudd,
d. 1070.

Idwal,
d. 1070.

Nest,
m. Osbern
fitz Richard.

Maredudd, *d.* 1072.

Rhys,
d. 1078.

Hywel,
d. 1078.

Grufiydd, *d.* 1091.

Owain,
d. 1105.

Maredudd.

Owain.

RHYS AP TEWDWR, *d.* 1093,
m. Gwladus, dau. of Rhiwallon
ap Cynfyn.

Llywarch,
d. 1118.

Gronw,
d. 1124.

Rhiryd,
d. 1124.

Meilyr,
d. 1124.

Angharad,
m. Grufiydd
ap Cynan.

Grufiydd, *d.* 1137,
m. Gwenllian, dau. of
Gruffydd ap Cynan.

Hywel.

Nest,
m. Gerald of
Windsor.

Christina,
m. Owain Gwynedd.

By Gwenllian.

Anarawd,
d. 1143.

Cadell,
d. 1175.

Maredudd,
d. 1155.

YR ARGLWYDD RHYS,
d. 1197,
m. Gwenllian, dau. of
Madog ap Maredudd.

Gwladus,
m. (1) Caradog
ab Iestyn;
(2) Seisyll ab
Dyfnwal.

Nest,
m. Ifor Bach.

Einon, *d.* 1163.

(*For descendants, see next page*)

THE LINE OF DEHEUBARTH (*continued*).

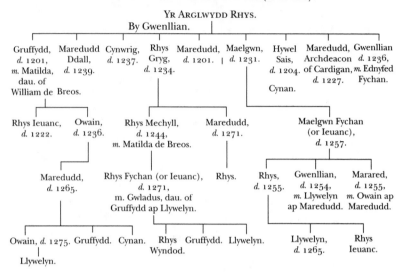

YR ARGLWYDD RHYS.
By Gwenllian.

Gruffydd, *d.* 1201, *m.* Matilda, dau. of William de Breos.

Maredudd Ddall, *d.* 1239.

Cynwrig, *d.* 1237.

Rhys Gryg, *d.* 1234.

Maredudd, *d.* 1201.

Maelgwn, *d.* 1231.

Hywel Sais, *d.* 1204.

Maredudd, Archdeacon of Cardigan, *d.* 1227. Cynan.

Gwenllian *d.* 1236, *m.* Ednyfed Fychan.

Rhys Ieuanc, *d.* 1222.

Owain, *d.* 1236.

Rhys Mechyll, *d.* 1244, *m.* Matilda de Breos.

Maredudd, *d.* 1271.

Maelgwn Fychan (or Ieuanc), *d.* 1257.

Maredudd, *d.* 1265.

Rhys Fychan (or Ieuanc), *d.* 1271, *m.* Gwladus, dau. of Gruffydd ap Llywelyn.

Rhys.

Rhys, *d.* 1255.

Gwenllian, *d.* 1254, *m.* Llywelyn ap Maredudd.

Marared, *d.* 1255, *m.* Owain ap Maredudd.

Owain, *d.* 1275. Llywelyn.

Gruffydd. Cynan.

Rhys Wyndod. Gruffydd. Llywelyn.

Llywelyn, *d.* 1265.

Rhys Ieuanc.

3. THE LINE OF POWYS.

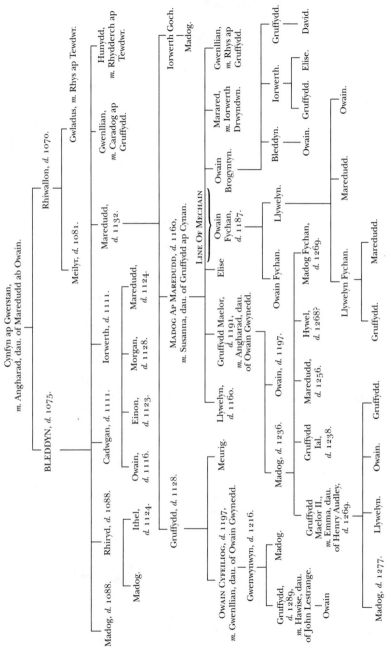

4. THE LESSER DYNASTIES.

ARWYSTLI AND CYDEWAIN.

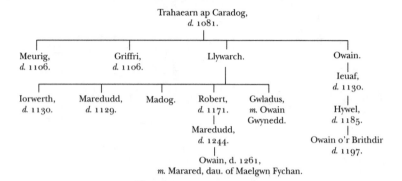

Trahaearn ap Caradog,
d. 1081.

Meurig,
d. 1106.

Griffri,
d. 1106.

Llywarch.

Owain.

Ieuaf,
d. 1130.

Iorwerth,
d. 1130.

Maredudd,
d. 1129.

Madog.

Robert,
d. 1171.

Gwladus,
m. Owain
Gwynedd.

Hywel,
d. 1185.

Maredudd,
d. 1244.

Owain o'r Brithdir
d. 1197.

Owain, d. 1261,
m. Marared, dau. of Maelgwn Fychan.

RHWNG GWY A HAFREN.

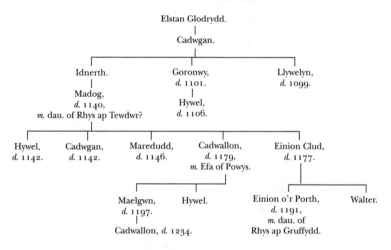

Elstan Glodrydd.

Cadwgan.

Idnerth.

Goronwy,
d. 1101.

Llywelyn,
d. 1099.

Madog,
d. 1140,
m. dau. of Rhys ap Tewdwr?

Hywel,
d. 1106.

Hywel,
d. 1142.

Cadwgan,
d. 1142.

Maredudd,
d. 1146.

Cadwallon,
d. 1179,
m. Efa of Powys.

Einion Clud,
d. 1177.

Maelgwn,
d. 1197.

Hywel.

Einion o'r Porth,
d. 1191,
m. dau. of
Rhys ap Gruffydd.

Walter.

Cadwallon, *d.* 1234.

SENGHENYDD.

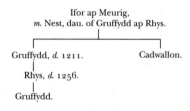

Ifor ap Meurig,
m. Nest, dau. of Gruffydd ap Rhys.

Gruffydd, *d.* 1211.

Cadwallon.

Rhys, *d.* 1256.

Gruffydd.

GWYNLLWG.

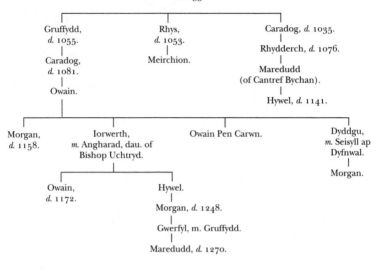

Rhydderch ab Iestyn,
d. 1033.

Gruffydd, *d.* 1055.	Rhys, *d.* 1053.	Caradog, *d.* 1035.
Caradog, *d.* 1081.	Meirchion.	Rhydderch, *d.* 1076.
Owain.		Maredudd (of Cantref Bychan).
		Hywel, *d.* 1141.

Morgan, *d.* 1158.

Iorwerth, *m.* Angharad, dau. of Bishop Uchtryd.

Owain Pen Carwn.

Dyddgu, *m.* Seisyll ap Dyfnwal.

Morgan.

Owain, *d.* 1172.

Hywel.
Morgan, *d.* 1248.
Gwerfyl, m. Gruffydd.
Maredudd, *d.* 1270.

MORGANNWG.

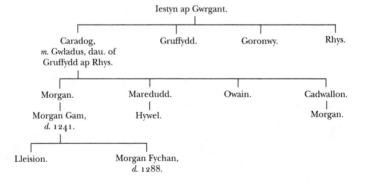

Iestyn ap Gwrgant.

Caradog, *m.* Gwladus, dau. of Gruffydd ap Rhys.	Gruffydd.	Goronwy.	Rhys.
Morgan.	Maredudd.	Owain.	Cadwallon.
Morgan Gam, *d.* 1241.	Hywel.		Morgan.

Lleision.

Morgan Fychan, *d.* 1288.

ENDNOTES

CHAPTER I

[1] "Cum sis unicus et haeres regis" (*De Nugis*, 97). For Map's evidence see *Trans. Cymr.* 1899–1900, 127.

[2] "Iaco ri bretan a suis occisus est," say Tighernach (*Rev. Celt.* xvii. p. 378), *Ann. Ult. s.a.* 1039 and *Chron. Scot.* 1037 (= 1039). Only *B. Saes.* (a late translation, be it remembered) asserts the complicity of Gruffydd.

[3] "Nocte ante circumcisionem," says Map (*De Nugis, ut supra*), but he probably confounded the Celtic and English New Year's Day. The former was 1st November, and its eve was a recognised time for seeking omens (*Trans. Cymr.* 1899–1900, 128).

[4] *Cf.* with the Welsh notices *A.S. Chr.* MS. C. *s.a.* 1039, Fl. Wig. *s.a.* 1052 (where "per insidias" is important), and Heming's Cartulary (Oxford, 1723), 278. For the reasons which make it impossible to locate this battle at Upton on Severn (*Norm. Conq.* i. (3), p. 506), see my paper, 129–30. Rhyd y Groes was near Gungrog and Cefn Digoll (*Mab.* 146, 148); the fact that it was on the Severn at once excludes the place of this name east of Forden (*Mont. Coll.* vii. (1874), 163–72), and 1 cannot find any good authority for the view that it was the ford to the west of that village.

[5] For the chronology of this reign see *Ann. C.* as printed in *Trans. Cymr.* 1899–1900, 166–71, and the notes thereto. *B. Saes.* is two years in arrear.

[6] "A thyna'r unig weithred, o'r holl weithredoedd a wnaeth Ruffydd, a beris anfoddlondeb i'r doethion " (s.a. 1038).

[7] *Lib. Land.* 264–5 shows "Riderch rex filius gistin" as witness to a grant of land "iuxta lannbocha" (St. Maughan's, nr. Monmouth) made to Bishop Joseph of Llandaff. His son "Grifud rex morcanhuc filius riderch" attests another grant to Joseph of land "super ripam mingui (the Monnow) ex alia parte lanncintall (Rockfield)" (*ibid.* 264).

[8] *A.S. Chr.* MS. C. **s.a.** 1046.

[9] The "uchelwr" or "breyr " is regularly "optimas " in the Latin versions of the laws.

[10] See pp. 316–7.

[11] So I interpret the notices of *Ann. C.* MSS. B. and C. The latter has; "Hoc anno tota dextralis patria (*i.e.*, Deheubarth) deserta est metu gentilium".

[12] For the incidents of this campaign see *A.S. Chr.* MS. D. *s.a.* 1050 (=1049; Plummer, i. 165; ii. 228–9) and Fl. Wig. i. 203, with the comments in *Trans. Cymr.* 1899–1900, 133. Freeman's discussion of it in *Norm. Conq.* ii. (3), 612–5 suffers from the attempt to connect it with the mishap to the Danish fleet in 1052, which *B. Saes.*, hereabouts two years in arrear, dates 1050. There is nothing to support his view that Gwent was at this time in English hands.

[13] *Trans. Cymr.* 1899–1900, 145–6. *Lib. Land.* 255–7, our authority for this incident, shows that it took place before the death of Hywel ("De laicis mouricus rex et hiugel pater suus").

[14] *A.S. Chr.* MS. C. *s.a.* 1052 (really 1053, since C.'s year ends at Easter (Plummer, ii. cxl), MS. D. *s.a.* 1053; Fl. Wig. i. 211 (*s.a.* 1053) Fl. says definitely that Rhys was "Griffini regis *Australium* Walensium frater," and this is supported by *Lib. Land.* 278 ("grifudi filii riderch, caratoci fratris ejus, et ris similiter") and by the mention of a Meirchion ap Rhys ap Rhydderch in *B.T.* and *B. Saes. s.a.* 1074 (= 1076). *GW. BRUT* (*s.a.* 1056) talks of "Rhys ap Llywelyn ap Seisyllt"; the author had probably nothing but Powel's "brother of Gruffyth king of Wales" (p. 72) to guide him and made one of his usual unlucky guesses. Wm. Malm. *G.R.* 237 (330) had made the same mistake.

[15] *A.S. Chr.* MS, C. *s.a.* 1053.

[16] *A.S. Chr.* MS. D. *s.a.* 1052 (second and correctly dated notice); Fl. Wig. i. 207. Ralph's parentage may be learnt from Ord. Vit. vii. 14; tor the Norman settlement in Herefordshire see Round, *Feudal England* (London, 1895), pp. 317–26.

[17] For this dating see *Trans. Cymr.* 1899–1900, 170, note.

[18] The events of this year are narrated in *A.S. Chr.* MSS. C. D. E. and Fl. Wig. i. 212–4. Fl. Wig. has the fullest account, which is only marred by the disposition to make the most of Harold's achievements. C. is, as usual, hostile to the house of Godwine, E. is friendly and D. trims.

[19] The sources imply that Ælfgar and Gruffydd did not come to terms until the former had returned from Ireland, and so the view of *Conq. Eng.* pp. 563–4 that their earlier relations had provoked the attack upon Ælfgar, is to be rejected.

[20] *B.T.* and *B. Saes.* (*s.a.* 1054) speak of the capture of the "gaer," and the latter adds that it was done "tra uuant ar ev bwyt ".

[21] "Ultra Straddele" (Fl. Wig.); *cf. Trans. Cymr.* 1899–1900, 134, note 2.

[22] *Trans. Cymr.* 1899–1900, 134. Billingsley may be found in the old one-inch Ordnance map (sheet 43).

[23] This paragraph is based upon an examination of the Domesday evidence as to border vills T.R.E. which will be found in *Trans. Cymr.* 1899–1900, 138–46.

[24] *Cart. Sax.* iii. 245–6 (No. 1041). "Odeslei" was in the possession of the abbey T.R.E. and T.R.W. (Domesd. 263*a*, 2).

[25] Meurig was still in power at the time of the election of Bishop Herwald of Llandaff (*Lib. Land.* 266), but this n;ay have been several years earlier than his consecration in 1056 (*Reg. Sacr.* (2), 36), since the previous bishop, Joseph, had died in 1045 (*Ann. C. MS. B.*). The "Grifido monarchia britonum prepollente" of this election may for the same reason be either Grulfydd ap Rhydderch (so index to *Lib. Land.* 400) or Gruffydd ap Llywelyn.

[26] To this period no doubt belongs the document in *Lib. Land.* 269–70, for I cannot accept the view of the editor (index, 400) that this Gruffydd is also Gruffydd ap Rhydderch.

[27] *A.S. Chr.* MSS. C. D. *s.a.* 1056; Fl. Wig. i. 214–5.

[28] Plummer, ii. 246.

[29] For the site of the battle see *Trans. Cymr.* 1899–1900, 135.

[30] Fl. Wig. and Plummer, ii. cxlix.

[31] William of Jumieges, vii. 31; Ord. Vit. iii. ix (II. 119), iv. 4 (II. 183). Ord. is of course wrong in making Bleddyn (Blidenum) a son of Gruffydd's, but, as Gruffydd certainly left a daughter Nest (Gir. Camb. vi. 28–9 (*Itin.* i. 2)), he is probably right in his account of her parentage.

[32] *A.S. Chr.* MS. D. *s.a.* 1058; Fl. Wig. i. 217. Doubt has naturally been raised with regard to this second banishment and return of Ælfgar, which is mentioned in one only of the Anglo-Saxon Chronicles, and that very summarily (*Norm. Conq.* ii. (3), 443). But the Chronicle, Fl. Wig., *Ann. C.* MSS. B. C., *B.T.* and *B. Saes.* 1056 (= 1058), and Tighernach (*Rev. Celt.* xvii. p. 399) furnish the outlines of a consistent story, though each has a special point of view.

[33] See William of Malmesbury's life of Wulfstan of Worcester in *Anglia Sacra*, ii. 251.

[34] *A.S. Chr.* MS. D. *s.a.* 1063; Fl. Wig. i. 221. For the later events of 1063 see also *B.T.*, *B. Saes.*, *Ann. C.*, Gir. Camb. vi. 217 (*Descr.* ii. 7), Gaimar, vv. 5071–84, John of Salisbury's *Polycraticus*, vi. 6, with the notes in *Trans. Cymr.* 1899–1900, 137–8.

[35] Fl. Wig. and *Ann. Ult.* place the death of Gruffydd in 1064, and John of Salisbury's "expeditione in biennium prorogata" points in the same direction. But I prefer to follow the explicit statement of the English Chronicle D. ("on ðissan ilcan geare"), supported as it is by *B. Saes.* (1061 = 1063) and *Ann. C.*

[36] *Bruts*, 267 (*B.T.* 45).

[37] Gaimar, v. 5084 ("Vnc puis de Waleis nout reguard").

[38] VI. 217 (*Descr.* ii. 7). No trace of any inscription of this kind has ever been found. The notion perhaps took its rise from the discovery of some early inscription running: "Hic iacit Victor. . . ," Victor (= Gwythur, *Mots Latins*, 215) being a name which occurs in this type of monument (at Clydai in Pembrokeshire, *W. Ph.* (2), 275; *Inscr. Chr.* vi. No. 110; *Lap. W.* 123).

[39] *Polycraticus*, lib. vi. c. 6.

[40] *A.S. Chr.* MS. D. *s.a.* 1063. "Blethgente" and "Rigwatlan " represent the old Welsh forms Bledgint and Riguallaun.

[41] *B.T.* gives his ancestry s.a. 1068.

[42] For Cadwgan see *Trans. Cymr,* 1899–1900, 147, note.

[43] Lti.LaKd.278.

[44] *A.S. Chr.* MSS. C. D. *s.a.* 1065. D. probably derives its account from C. (Plummer, ii. 251). "Portascihð" is the "Porth Ysgewin " of mediæval Welsh literature, the southern limit of Wales (Gir. Camb. vi. 165 (*Descr.* i. 1); Triad i. 5 = iii. 65; *Myv, Arch.* i. 270 (193)). The Domesday form is Poteschiuet (i. 162*a,* 1). There were still four vills in Gwent in 1086 which had not recovered from the devastation "per regem Caraduech ".

[45] *Dict. Nat. Biog.* xix. 188; *Trans. Cymr.* 1899–1900, 148–50; *Eng. Hist. Rev.* xv. (1900), pp. 76–7.

[46] *A.S. Chr.* MS. D. *s.a.* 1067; Fl. Wig. ii. 1–2.

[47] Ord. Vit. iv. 4. In his account of the years 1066–71, Orderic follows the contemporary narrative of William of Poitiers (see iv. 7).

[48] Ord. Vit. iv. 5.

[49] Fl. Wig. ii. 7.

[50] Wm. Malm. *G.R.* 314 (431).

[51] *Trans. Cymr.* 1899–1900, 148–9.

[52] *Eng. Hist. Rev.* xv. (1900), pp. 302–3.

[53] "Guallorum reges Risen et Caducan ac Mariadoth aliosque plures prostravit" (Ord. Vit. iv. 7 (ii. 219)).

[54] *Lib. Land.* 274 speaks of "Rogerii filii Willelmi filii Osberni" as "domini Guenti,' and the title is implied in what is said in Domesday of the doings of William in this region.

[55] In a grant of land at Llangwm Isaf ade in 1071–5, the lay witnesses include (*Lib. Land.* 274) "elinui filius idnerth," "ithail filii teudus," and "guassuith," who are clearly the "prepositi" called "Elmui," "Idhel," and "Wasuuic" in Domesd. ("Castellum de Estrighoiel," i. 162*a* 1). "Elinui" also occurs in a grant made by Caradog ap Gruffydd (273), and Ithel not only in this, but also in one of Gruffydd ap Llywelyn's (270).

[56] Domesd. i. 187*b,* 1 (Terra Grifin filii Mariadoc; Lege).

[57] *Ibid.* 187*a,* 1 (Terra Hugonis Lasne; Chenecestre).

[58] "Illi tres cum multis aliis exhereditati sunt" (*Lib. Land.* 278). It should, however, be noted that what Powel (82) says of the share of the Welsh in the "Bridal of Norwich" rests on a misunderstanding of the "Bryttas" (= Bretons) of the A.S. Chr.

[59] For the date see *Trans. Cymr.* 1899–1900, 148, note (2), and the texts printed as an appendix to the paper.

[60] *Ann. C.*

[61] *Trans. Cymr.* 1899–1900, 147, note.

[62] So I understand the "Caratocvs rex morcannuc" of *Lib. Land.* 272. The names of the witnesses show that the grant is of this period.

[63] *B.T. s.a.* 1076 (=1078, battle of Goodwick); *Bruts,* 269.

[64] *LL.* i. 166, 252; ii. 198, 678.

[65] Mostyn MS. 117, written in the last quarter of the thirteenth century, traces the lineage of Cynfyn through mythical ancestors to Beli Mawr (Evans, *Rep.* i. p. 63), but *B.T.* merely calls him "cynuyn ab gwerstan" (*Bruts,* 303). Cynfyn had, however, married the widow of Llywelyn ap Seisyll, King Maredudd's daughter Angharad, and thus Bleddyn and Rhiwallon were uterine brothers of Gruffydd ap Llywelyn (*Bruts,* 281, 296–7, 303).

[66] "Consobrinus" (*Ann. C.* MS. C.); "y gefynderw" (*Bruts,* 268).

[67] See chapter viii. p. 249.

[68] Palmer, *Ancient Tenures of Land in the Marches of North Wales* (Wrexham, 1885), pp. 87–8.

[69] "Grifud. . . nepos Iacob" (*Ann. C.* MS. C.). See *Trans. Cymr.* 1899–1900,. 154.

[70] For the text and a translation of this life, with historical notes, see *The History of Gruffydd ap Cynan,* by Arthur Jones (Manchester, 1910).

[71] See note in *Trans. Cymr.* 1899–1900,153. "Ragnell" (Evans, *Rep.* i. p. 339) no doubt represents the well-known form, Ragnhildr.

[72] *Ibid.* note 2.

[73] *Ibid.* 154, note 1. Gruffydd's foster-father, "Cerit," was at Bron yr Erw.

[74] Eachmarcach son of Ragnall, a cousin of Gruffydd's grandfather, was driven out in 1052 by Diarmaid Mac Maelnambo, who held Dublin until his death in 1072 (*War of G. and G.* p. 291; Tighernach in *Rev. Celt.* xvii. p. 410).

[75] For the events of this year *Bitch. Gr. ap C.* is relied on. *Ann. C., B.T.* and *B. Saes.* merely mention Gruffydd's seizure of Anglesey, the death of Cynwrig, and the battle of Bron yr Erw.

[76] There was a mill of "Kevyng" in this neighbourhood (*Rec. Carn.* 275).

[77] Ord. Vit. iv. 7; vi. 2.

[78] Given him by the Welsh ("Hugo Crassus," *Ann. C. s.a.* 1101; "hu vras," *Bruts,* 275) and the Danes ("Hugoni Dirgane (from Norse "drjugr"?) id est Grosso," Ord. Vit. x. 6). There is no ancient authority for the epithet "Lupus".

[79] Ord. Vit. viii. 3.

[80] This is the date implied in the "per xv annos" of Ord. Vit. viii. 3 (III. 284, first line) and it is in harmony with *Buck. Gr. ap C.* and with the reference to "Blideno" in Robert's epitaph.

[81] "Praecipuam, pulchro Blideno rege fugato, Praedam cum paucis cepit in insidias" (Epitaph in Ord. Vit. viii. 3).

[82] *Buch. Gr. ap C.* clearly distinguishes "y baili" from "e twr" (38 (725)).

[83] The native line of Eifionydd had become extinct about 930; see chap. viii. note 57.

[84] He was slain in 1081 (*Ann. C.* MS. B.; *B.T. s.a.* 1079). Nothing is known of his ancestry or local connections.

[85] *Cyff Beuno* (Tremadog, 1863), by Eben Fardd, 32.

[86] "Guallter yarll henford" (*Buch. Gr. ap C.* 42 (726)) is, of course, a misdescription.

[87] "Duxit captivum, lorisque ligavit Hoellum,
    Qui tunc Wallensi rex praeerat manui" (Epitaph in Ord. Vit. viii. 3). I take tfiis to be the Hywel ab Ithel *of Ann. C. s.a.* 1099 (= *B.T. s.a.* 1097) and 118 (= *B.T. s.a.* 1115); the Hywel ab Owain of South Wales who was killed in 1078 is not likely to have had any relations with Robert of Rhuddlan. Ord. Vit. mentions (viii. 3) the building of "Dagaunoth " and (in the epitaph) Robert's success against "Trehellum ".

[88] The authorities for the battle of Mynydd Carn are *Ann. C. s.a.* 1079 (for the true readings see *Trans. Cymr.* 1899–900, 176–7), *B.T., B. Saes., Buch. Gr. ap C.*, and the poem by Meilyr Brydydd in *Myv. Arch.* I. 192 (142). The latter is the earliest piece of Welsh verse of which the date can be fixed by means of its historical allusions; its references to Gruffydd's transmarine allies —"Irish black devils; savage Scots" — are explicit. Stephens' translation (*Lit. Kym.* (2), 11) obscures the fact that the poet chooses to speak as a prophet of what is to come. As to the site of the battle, Carno (Powel, 85; *GW. BRUT. S.A.* 1080; Penn. iii. 194) does not suit the conditions, nor is this form to be found in any ancient authority for Mynydd Carn. Phillimore (*Cymr.* xi. 167) cites a passage from L. G. Cothi (215) which seems to connect Mynydd Cam with southern Ceredigion, but it is not clear that the reference is more than a bit of rhetoric, to be coupled with the mention of Camlan a little later.

[89] *Buck. Gr. ap C.* 112 (728). "Hu" did not become "iarll amwythic" until 1093, so that his father Roger is probably intended.

[90] i. 262*b* (2).

[91] i. 268*b* (2). For Atiscross or "Croes Ati" see Harl. MS. 473, cited in Owen, *Catalogue,* 152, and Penn. i. 71.

[92] i. 269*a.*

[93] "Ipsis burgensibus annuerunt leges et consuetudines que sunt in hereford et in bretuill" (269*a* (2)). *Cf.* note 52 above and *Eng. Hist. Rev.* xv. (1900), pp. 306–7.

[94] i. 269*a* (2), (Biscopestrev).

[95] i. 267*a* (1).

[96] i. 268*a* (1), (Gretford. In Extan hd.).

[97] i. 269*a.* See *Trans. Cymr.* 1899–1900, 156–7.

[98] "Hic annotantur tenentes terram de rege in Sciropescire. . . . Comes Rogerius quod reliquum est tenet cum suis hominibus" (i. 252*a* (1)). The manors held of the king are separately entered on pp. 260*a* and *b.*

[99] See Stubbs, *Const. Hist.* i. (3), pp. 271, 364.

[100] Ord. Vit. iv. 7.

[101] See entries under "Dodefort" (i. 254*a* (2)) and "Etbritone" (255*b* (1)), with Ord. Vit. v. 13 (II. 414) and *Mon. Angl.* iii. 518.

[102] "Ipse comes Rogerius tenet de rege ciuitatem Sciropesberie et totum comitatum et totum dominium quod rex Edwardus ibi habebat" (254*a* (1)).

[103] Eyton, *Shrops.* x. 320–1.

[104] *Ibid.* vii. 5.

[105] *Trans. Cymr.* 1899–1900, 160, note.

[106] Mr. Tait's objection (*Historical Atlas of Modern Europe*, ed. R. L. Poole, introd. to map 17) to Eyton's identification of this "finem terrae Walensis" with Maelor Saesneg (x. 315) is based on good grounds. Nanheudwy, on the other hand, is not otherwise accounted for, and, as Mr. Palmer points out (*Cymr.* x. 44), most of the old Welsh families of the Chirk district traced their descent from Tudur ap Rhys Sais.

[107] It is the mother church of Churchstoke, Forden, Hyssington, Snead and Montgomery (*Welsh SS.* 345).

[108] *A.S. Chr.* MS. E, *s.a.* 1087 (Plummer, i. 224).

[109] Ord. Vit. viii. 3 is our authority for the circumstances of the death of Robert. The topographical questions involved are discussed in *Trans. Cymr.* 1899–1900, 157–8. The mention of "Grithfridus rex Guallorum" as the leader of this raid has naturally led to its being regarded as an exploit on the part of Gruffydd ap Cynan. But to this view there are weighty objections. *Buch. Gr. ap C.* makes Gruffydd a prisoner for twelve (or, according to another passage, sixteen) years after 1081, and, if it be rejoined that a mistake in the figure may easily have been made, there is the more serious difficulty of the absence of any reference to this incident of 1088 in the "Buchedd". Had Gruffydd really won this triumph, it is scarcely conceivable that the affair could have escaped the notice of his official panegyrist, writing in the reign of his son Owain. As Orderic is the sole authority for the story, it seems most likely that he had been misinformed as to the chief who led the Welsh on this occasion.

[110] Gaimar (v. 6043) says Rufus gave Hugh "Nort Wales".

[111] *Buch. Gr. ap C.* 114 (728). "Hen gaer Custennin" is said of Carnarvon on the authority of *Hist. Britt.* c, 25.

[112] See p. 448.

[113] *Mon. Angl.* ii. 386.

[114] Fenton's identification of "Pullgudic" (*Ann. C.*) with Goodwick in Pembrokeshire (second ed. p. 7) is made certain by the fact that Mostyn MS. 116, the probable original of the Red Book copy of *B.T.*, calls this battle "urwydyr Llan wnda" (Evans, *Rep.* i. p. 57).

[115] *B.T. s.a.* 1076 (= 1078).

[116] For the correct pedigree, Rhys ap Tewdwr *ap Cadell* ab Einon ab Owain ap Hywel Dda see Gir. Camb. vi. 167 (*Descr.* i. 3), Mostyn MS. 117 (Evans, *Rep.* i. p. 63), and Jesus Coll. MS. 20 in *Cymr.* viii. 88 (No. xxiv.). The omission of Cadell, as in Powel (85) and Dwnn (ii. 16), led to Rhys being regarded as the son of the Tewdwr ab Einon who died in 994 and as performing, therefore, the achievements of his reign between the ages of eighty-five and one hundred!

[117] *Gw. Brut, s.a.* 1077 says he came from Brittany (*cf.*, however, "Brut Ieuan Brechfa," in *Myv. Arch.* II. 520 (719), which brings him from Ireland), and in *Iolo MSS.* 215, it is added that he brought with him the "System of the Round Table". Notwithstanding the reliance placed upon these statements by Stephens (*Lit. Kym.* (2) 322, 405–6) and others, it will be seen that they come from thoroughly untrustworthy sources.

[118] "Causa orationis" (*Ann. C.* MS. B., with which MS. C. agrees).

[119] *A.S. Chr.* MS. E. *s.a.* 1081.

[120] Domesd. i. 179*a* (2), (Herefordscire). *Cf. Trans. Cymr.* 1899–1900, 163.

[121] Raddrenove (1810 (2)), Chenistetone (2606 (2)), Nortune (*ibid.*), and Cascop (260*a* (1) and 186*b* (2)) were all waste in 1086. The first three were claimed by Hugh the Ass (Lasne), the last by Osbern fitz Richard.

[122] i. 1866 (2), 2600 (1). Richard's Castle is "Avretone" (*i.e.*, Overton).

[123] Osbern held most of his lands T.R.E. as well as in 1086, and Old. Vit. viii. 2 (III. 270–1) calls him "Osbernus Ricardi cognomento Scrop filius". For the marriage see note 135 below.

[124] *Dict. Nat. Biog.* xxxix. pp. 130–1.

[125] i. 183*b*, 260*a, b*. Pilleth is "Pelelei," with which *cf.* "Mair o bilale" in Pen. MS. 147 (Evans, *Rep.* i. p. 915) and "Pylaley" in Dwnn, i. 258.

[126] i. 258*a*.

[127] i. 183*a* (2).

[128] Ord. Vit. iv. 7. Walter died on 27th March, 1085 (*Dict. Nat. Biog.* xxxi. p. 389).

[129] Weobley is the "Wibelai" of 184*b* (2); the "terram Ewias dictam" is carefully distinguished (1840 (1)) from the "castellaria de Ewias," which was at Ewias Harold.

[130] i. 186*a* (1). *Cf.* Round, *Feudal England*, p. 324.

[131] The early history of Monmouth is outlined in *Lib. Land.* 276–8, where it is said that the castle was built by Earl William, and, on the fall of the house of Breteuil and its adherents, given to "gueithenauc," who became a monk and was succeeded, first by "Randulf de Coliuil" and then by "Willelmus filius Batrun". The charters of Monmouth Priory corroborate this account in several particulars, showing that "Wihenocus" became "sancti Florentii monachus" and was succeeded by his nephew, William fitz Baderon (*Cal. Doc. Fr.* 406–7). William was the castellan and local magnate in 1086 (i. 180*b* (2)).

[132] There are two notices of this holding, one under Herefordshire (Terra Willelmi de Scohies, 1856 (1)) and another under Gloucestershire (Isdem Turstinus habet sex carucatas terrae ultra Huscham, 1620 (2)). They differ somewhat in detail, but neither betokens a settlement of any importance. Hence the view, founded on *Ann. Marg. s.a.* 1081 (Et aedificata est villa Cardiviae, sub Willelmo primo rege), that the Normans had already reached the Taff appears very questionable. See *Trans. Cymr.* 1899–1900, 162.

[133] *A.S. Chr.* MS. E. *s.a.* 1087; Fl. Wig. *s.a.* 1088 (ii. 24–6); Ord. Vit. viii. 2 (III. 270–1).

[134] *Cart. Glouc.* i. 80. For the importance of the church see chap. viii. note 249.

[135] Some account of Bernard will be found in Ord. Vit. vi. 8; the statement that he served *three* kings of England is confirmed by the fact that he is one of the witnesses (Bernardus de novo mercato) to a charter executed by William I. in 1086–7 in favour of Battle Abbey (*Mon. Angl.* iii. 245). He does not seem to have held any English lands in 1086. As to his marriage, there is, in addition to the fact that Fl. Wig. calls him son-in-law of Osbern fitz Richard, the evidence of the charters of Brecon Priory, which show that his wife Agnes gave to the priory the manor of Berrington, near Tenbury, held by Osbern in 1086 (Domesd. i. 176b). See *Arch. Camb.* III. xiv. (1883), 141–2; *Mon. Angl.* iii. 244, 264. Gir. Camb. vi. 28–9 (*Itin.* i. 2) further shows that Agnes was also called Nest and that she was the daughter of another Nest, a daughter of Gruffydd ap Llywelyn, whose marriage to Osbern is thus established.

[136] The name of the place at which the battle was fought is not to be recognised in the corrupt forms which have come down to us, *viz.*, "penllecheru" (*Ann. C.* MS. B. in *Trans. Cymr.* 1899–1900, 176), "penlethereu" (MS. C. 177) and "llych crei" (*Bruts*, 270); "llech ryt" (B. *Saes. s.a.* 1087), though adopted by Powel (88) and others, does not seem to me a happy conjecture.

[137] Domesd. i. 187b (1).

[138] FL. wig. *s.a.* 1093; *Ann. C.* and *Bruts*.

[139] Fl. Wig. says "inpugna," Gir. Camb. "dolo suorum" (vi. 89; *Itin.* i. 12).

[140] "Ac yna y dygwydawd teyrnas y brytanyeit" (*Bruts*, 270). B. *Saes.* (*s.a.* 1091) has: "ac yna y syrthws brenhiniaeth kymre" — obviously another translation of the same Latin sentence.

CHAPTER II

[1] On 30th April. "Pridie Kal. May" (*Ann. C.* MS. B.) is rendered wrongly in *B.T.* ("yr eildydo vei"), but with fair accuracy in B. *Saes.* ("ychydic kyn kalan mei") — one of the many proofs of their independence.

[2] "Geir Haw aber teifi (the river-mouth, not the town) yny lle aelwir dingereint. y lle y grwndwalassei roger iarll kyn no hynny (*i.e.*, before 1110) gastell" (*Bruts*, 289; *B.T.* 105, where Robert is Ab Ithel's mistake for Roger). In spite of the delusive similarity of the names (Cilgerran is from *Cerran*, with the feminine inflexion, not from *Geraint; cf.* "castell cerran" in *Lib. Land.* 126, and the note on names of this type in Owen, *Pemb.* i. 422), Dingereint cannot be, as maintained by J. R. Phillips (*History of Cilgerran*, London, 1867, p. 84), the modern Cilgerran, for this is not in Ceredigion, nor is it "close to the fall of the Teifi into the sea". Cardigan is a corruption of Ceredigion, formed on the analogy of Carnarvon and Carmarthen; as the name of the town, it first occurs, in the form "Caradigan," in Cont. Fl. Wig. *s.a.* 1136.

[3] *Bruts*, 295; *B.T.* 121. For Arnulf see Ord. Vit. v. 13, 14; viii. 16, 25; *Cal. Doc. Fr.* i. 165.

[4] *Gir.* Camb. vi. 89 (*Itin.* i. 12).

[5] For William fitz Baldwin see J. H. Round, *Feudal England*, pp. 329–30 (note).

[6] Their early history is to be gleaned from *B.T.* 119, 121 (*Bruts*, 294–5), where it is told in connection with their appearance in arms in 1115.

[7] See chap. xi. note 132.

[8] *Trans. Cymr.* 1899–1900, 145 (note), 162.

[9] The legend of the conquest of Glamorgan is given diversely by each of the following four authorities, none of them of older date than the sixteenth century: Humphrey Llwyd in *Powel's Historie*, 89–90; Sir Edward Stradling in the same, 90–107; *Gw. Brut, s.a.* 1088; *Iolo MSS.* 15–16. There is only one point at which it comes into contact with contemporary records, and this is its account of the death of Rhys ap Tewdwr. Here it is demonstrably wrong, since Rhys fell in battle with the Normans of Brecknock, and not with the followers of Fitz Hamon.

[10] *Dict. Nat. Biog.* xix. pp. 159–62 (Prof. Tout).

[11] *Cal. Doc. Fr.* i. 401 (No. 1120). No. 1118 (p. 400) shows that William of Briouze was still living at the end of 1093; in 1096 Philip, who had meanwhile succeeded his father, seems to have joined the First Crusade (No. 1119). *Cart. Glouc.* ii. 103 affords evidence of the existence of a borough at Radnor, of which Philip was lord.

[12] Gir. Camb. vi. 16 (*Itin.* i. 1).

[13] A letter of Anselm's addresses and enjoins obedience to the Welsh Bishop Wilfrid upon "Roberto Comiti (*i.e.*, Robert of Bellême, now Earl of Shrewsbury) et fratri ejus Ernulfo comiti et Radulfo de Mortuo Mari et Philippo de Braiosa et Bernardo de Novo Mercato" (H. and St. i. 300; Migne, clix. 214). The districts involved were probably Ceredigion, Dyfed, Maelienydd, Buellt and Brycheiniog respectively. As to the date, H. and St., in suggesting 1095, overlooked Robert's title, which imposes the limits 1098–1102. It will be observed that the letter gives Arnulf also the title of "comes," supporting the testimony of Eadmer (Rolls ed. 419) and Ord. Vit. (v. 14; viii. 25). But that he was Earl of Pembroke is a mere conjecture.

[14] At Mid-Lent (*A.S. Chr.* MS. E. *s.a.* 1094).

[15] This is stated by Fl. Wig. s.a. 1094 ("primitus North-Walani," ii. 35) and confirmed by *Ann. C.*, MS. C., *B.T.* and *B. Saes.*

[16] "Koet yspwys" (*Bruts*, 271) or "koet yspes" (*B. Saes. s.a.* 1092) has not yet been identified.

[17] See *A.S. Chr.* MS. E. *s.a.* 1094.

[18] But whether in 1093 or 1094 is uncertain. The former date is given for Earl Roger's death by Fl. Wig. and derives support from the statement of Ord. Vit. (v. 14; see Le Prevost, II. 422, where the date 1094 is said to be an interpolation in the text) that Roger survived the Conqueror six years. On the other hand, as the day was certainly 27h July (*ibid.*), very little time is left for the earl's operations in Ceredigion in that month, and one inclines to the later year, which fits in with another passage of Ord. Vit. (x.6) giving four years (*i.e.*, 1094–8) as the length of Hugh's tenure of the earldom.

[19] *A.S. Chr. ut supra.*

[20] "Caduugaun," says *A.S. Chr.* MS. E. *s.a.* 1097, was the worthiest of the Welsh elders; he was the son of Gruftydd's (half) brother.

[21] See chap. xi. note log.

[22] "Gothrei vrenhin," who rules "enyssed denmarc" (*Buch. Gr. ap C.* 116; Grothrei in *Myv. Arch.* 729), can hardly be any one else. Godred died in 1095 (*Orkneyinga Saga*, ed. for the Rolls Series, vol. i. (1887), pp. xliv. 413).

[23] Until Michaelmas, 1095. The "dwy vlyned" of *Buch. Gr. ap C.* is an overstatement.

[24] Dec. 29 (Fl. Wig.).

[25] Ord. Vit. viii. 23, where it is said that the king also fined Earl Hugh of Shrewsbury £3000 for his part in the revolt.

[26] *A.S. Chr.* MS. E. *s.a.* 1095.

[27] Details are supplied by *A.S. Chr.* MS. E. *s.a.* 1095 and *Buch. Gr. ap C.* 118–20 (730–1). The latter allows the spirit of panegyric to carry it so far as gravely to assert that it was only the magnanimity of Gruffydd which saved the life of Rufus, as David had spared that of Saul!

[28] *B.T.* and *B. Saes.* (both *s.a.* 1094) have different renderings of the passage about the castles and the men of the country, but they agree that the castles were not taken.

[29] That the armies which in 1096 invaded Gwent and Brecknock came from Glamorgan is an inference, but one which seems to fit in well with the facts of the case.

[30] The forms of the name (Cellidarnant, *Ann. C.* MS. B.; Kellitaruant MS. C.; Kelli carnant, *Bruts,* 272; Kelli carnawc, *B. Saes.*) vary so widely that it is difficult to fix the spot.

[31] Cadwgan was the son of Elstan Glodrydd (*Bruts,* 302, and Mostyn MS. 117, as cited by Evans, *Rep.* i. p. 63. II. *d*), who is well known as the founder of the fifth of the "Royal Tribes" of Wales, but of whom nothing is recorded on any good authority. Besides Idnerth, Cadwgan had two other sons, Goronwy and Llywelyn (Jesus Coll. MS. 20 in *Cymr.* viii. 88, Nos. xxx. and xxxii.), who appear in 1075 and 1077 as opponents of Rhys ab Owain (*Trans. Cymr.* 1899–1900, 174, note). Goronwy, or Gronw (d. 1101), was the father of the Hywel ap Gronw mentioned in the text of the above paragraph (d. 1106); Llywelyn was slain in 1099 by the men of Brycheiniog. The sphere of influence of the family was Buellt and Rhwng Gwy a Hafren; from it, through Madog ab Idnerth (d. 1140), sprang the later princes of Maelienydd and of Elfael.

[32] For the river Llech see *Breconsh.* (a), p. 490.

[33] Hywel's ancestry is given in note 31 above; Uchtryd and his brother Owain are said to have been the sons of Edwin ap Gronw ab Einon ab Owain ap Hywel Dda, an unattested but not an impossible pedigree. Edwin married Iwerydd, a half-sister (on the father's side) of Bleddyn ap Cynfyn (*Bruts,* 303); it has been conjectured that he was the freeman of the name who held "Coleselt" (= Coleshill, near Flint) both under the Confessor and in 1086 (Domesd. i. 268*b* (2); Taylor, *Historic Notices of Flint*, London, 1883, p. 10).

[34] Gir. Camb., who relates these anecdotes (vi. 89–90 (*Itin.* i. 12)), does not supply a precise date, but the siege of 1096 is the event with which it is most natural to connect them. Wilfrid's "hospitium" is also not indicated, but, as it was clearly not far off, there is little risk in supplying the name of Lamphey.

[35] According to Eadmer (77–9, 377), the Welsh expedition came between William's return from Normandy (just before Easter, *A.S. Chr.*) and the Whitsuntide court, held this year at Windsor. *A.S. Chr.* MS. E. and Fl. Wig. also place it after Easter, but the former has a further note of time, pointing to the month of July. For this reason, Freeman (*William Rufus*, i. pp. 572, 583; ii. pp. 110–11) suggested a double campaign, divided by Whitsuntide. But it is strange that no Welsh or English authority should mention such a break in the operations, and I adopt the simpler solution of supposing that an error has crept into the *A.S. Chr.* There is a further doubt as to whether the king in this year visited South or North Wales, a point as to which no direct evidence is available. It is in favour of the South that *Buch. Gr. ap C.* only speaks, of one invasion of Gwynedd by Rufus and that Gir. Camb. (vi. 109–10 (*Itin.* ii. 1)) has a story which brings the king to the neighbourhood of St. David's.

[36] For the events of this memorable year see *Ann. C.* MSS. B.C. *s.a.*, *B.T.* and *B. Saes. s.a.* 1096, *Buch. Gr. ap C.* 120–4 (731–2), Fl. Wig. *s.a.*, Ord. Vit. x. 6, Gir. Camb. vi. 129 (*Itin.* ii. 7), *Corpus Poeticum Boreale*, ed. Vigfusson and York Powell (Oxford, 1883), ii. 242, and *Orkneyinga Saga* (ed. Vigfusson for the Rolls series), i. 69–70. Ord. Vit. gives the date of Earl Hugh's death ("circa finem Julii mensis"), but his account of the campaign is coloured by his desire to represent the earl's action in the best possible light; the expedition to North Wales was, according to him, designed to prevent Magnus from invading the realm. Wm. Malm. ("Angliam per Anglesiam obstinatus petebat" — *G.R.* ii. 376 (ii. 506)) has the same story, but it is most improbable and reads like an afterthought.

[37] Fl. Wig. says Hugh fell on the seventh day after the outrage upon "Cenred" the priest; Gir. Camb. dates the event "infra mensem" from the desecration of Llandyfrydog.

[38] The passage about Owain does not occur in either MS. of *Ann. C.* and is differently rendered by *B.T.* and *B. Saes.* Hence it is not easy to define his position after the withdrawal of the Normans.

[39] For the home of the writer of *B.T.* at this time, see that work, pp. 130–4.

[40] Ord. Vit. says (x. 7 (IV. 32)) "per quatuor annos immania super Gualos exercuit," but gives no details.

[41] "Coepit etiam in Walonia aedificare aliam (arcem), in loco qui Caroclove dicitur" (Fl. Wig. *s.a.* 1101). Carreghofa is a township in the parish of Llanymynech. For the history of the castle see *Mont. Coll.* vii. 377–88.

[42] For the fall of Robert and his brother Arnulf see Ord. Vit. xi. 3; Fl. Wig. *s.a.* 1102; *B.T.* and *B. Saes. s.a.* 1100.

[43] Domesd. i. 257*a* (2), *b* (1).

[44] The account of the *Bruts* as to the relations between Arnulf, Murkertagh, and Magnus appears to be fairly accurate, except that Arnulf married one daughter (called "Lafracoth" by Ord. Vit.) and Sigurd Magnusson another (whom the *Orkneyinga Saga* calls "Bjadmunja"). On the other hand, the story of Ord. Vit. (xi. 8) is difficult to accept, especially when it is remembered that Magnus fell in a chance skirmish near Downpatrick, which was not within the territory of Murkertagh. At the same time, it is right to say that the difficulties have been needlessly enhanced by the general assumption (Freeman, *William Rufus*, ii. p. 624; *Dict. Nat. Biog.* xlix. p. 103) that the "regi " to whom Arnulf was finally reconciled was Murkertagh, and not Henry I.

[45] "A gwedy torri llawer o wyd defnyd" (*Bruts*, 277). According to the *Chronicle of Man* (ed. Goss for the Manx Society (vol. xxii. of series), Douglas, 1874, p. 58), Magnus had in 1098 similarly obtained timber from Galloway for the building of his Manx forts.

[46] "Genero meo Ernulfo auxilio et interventione. . . succurristi" (Letter of Murkertagh to Anselm in Migne, clix. 243 (IV. 85)).

[47] For Arnulf's later life see Eadmer, 419–20; Ord. Vit. xi. 3, 8; xii. 8.

[48] Eyton, *Shrops.* ii. pp. 193–201.

[49] Nothing is known of this knight, though the name as given in the *Bruts* is clearly genuine.

[50] Between 1102 (fall of Earl Robert) and 1114 (Henry's first Welsh expedition) MSS. B. and C. of *Ann. Camb.* disagree in their chronology, and at first sight it is difficult to say which has preserved the true dating. But it is to be observed that, while B. has correct dates for several of its entries hereabouts which can be checked, *e.g.*, the notices of the conquest of Normandy (1106), the foundation of St. Mary's, Southwark (1106), the council of London (1107), the plague of 1112, and the admission of St. Bernard to Citeaux (1113), none of these are to be found in C. or the *Bruts, so* that it is clear they were inserted at some time in the original chronicle and afford no guarantee of the correctness of the dating in other respects. On the other hand C. is correct in the dating of three events which also appear in the *Bruts* and in two cases in B. also, *viz.*: (1) Capture of Duke Robert in 1106 (first notice *s.a.* 1105 in B., in which there is through confusion a double entry). (2) Death of King Edgar of Scotland in 1107 (*B.T.* only). (3) Capture of Robert of Bellême in 1112 (B. has 1113). *It is to be concluded, therefore, that C. is the MS. which preserves the order of the original compiler, and I have followed it in the text. As B. Saes.* has omitted the blank year 1104, its dates, in and after 1102 = 1105, are three, instead of two, years in arrear up to 1118 = 1121. These, it is to be remembered, are the dates printed by Ab Ithel in his edition of *B.T.*

[51] Richard succeeded his brother as sheriff of Devon and died in 1136. References to him will be found in Round, *Feudal England*, pp. 330, 472–3, 486, and *Peerage and Family History* (1901), p. 214.

[52] Gir. Camb. vi. 91 (*Itin.* i. 12).

[53] This appears from an observation made by the writer of the original of *B.T.* and *B. Saes.* in narrating the events of 1116; see *Bruts*, 303, *B.T.* 140, *Myv. Arch.* II. 552 (674, col. 2).

[54] *Ann. C.* and *Bruts.* See chap. xi., note 87.

[55] "Kanys oe hamdiffyn wynteu (Maredudd and the sons of Cadwgan) ae kanhaledigaeth yd oed ef yn kynnal y gyfran or wlat a dathoed yn ran idaw" (*Bruts*, 303; *B.T.* 142 (1115 = 1118)).

[56] *Buch. Gr. ap C.* 124 (732–3). The account of Gruffydd's progress is not quite clear, but it is implied that he reached in a few years the position indicated in the text.

[57] The *Bruts* (*Bruts*, 302; *B.T.* 138–40; *B. Saes. s.a.* 1113 (= 1116) in *Myv. Arch.* II. 552 (674)) have a list of the sons of Cadwgan. Besides Owain, whose mother is not named (the "Iweryd verch Edwin" of *B. Saes.* is clearly a misunderstanding of a passage about Uchtryd ab Edwin given fully by *B.T.*), they were: (1) Madog, by Gwenllian, daughter of Gruffyddap Cynan. This connection is confirmed by *Buch. Gr. ap C.* 120 (731), where Cadwgan is described in 1098 as Gruffydd's son-in-law ("ei ddaw"), but the Gwenllian intended is not the daughter of Angharad who bore that name (*ibid.* 118 (730)), since Angharad, who died in 1162 (*Bruts*), cannot have had a marriageable daughter at this time, and indeed had only just been married to Gruffydd. This Gwenllian was probably illegitimate and born about 1080. (2) Einon (d. 1123), by Sanan, daughter of Dyfnwal. (3) Morgan (d. 1128), by Ellyw, daughter of Cydifor ap Gollwyn. (4) Henry, and (5) Gruffydd by a daughter of Picot of Sai. (6) Maredudd (d. 1124), by Euron, daughter of Hoedlyw ap Cadwgan ab Elstan.

[58] It may well have been Aber Teifi, but the author of *Gw. Brut* (*s.a.* 1107), followed by Laws (*Lit. Eng.* p. 108), is only guessing when he says so, and guessing still more rashly when he makes the feast the occasion of a great Eisteddfod. Powel (122) says the place was in Dyfed (Amroth, acc. to Lewis, *Top. Dict. s.v.*), but there is no evidence that Cadwgan had any land in this region.

[59] The situation of Cenarth Bychan is still an unsolved problem, owing to the fact that the name ceased to be used soon after this event, and that no clue is to be found to its successor. Pembroke itself (*B. Saes. s.a.* 1105; Powel, 122), Carew (*Lit. Eng.* p. 105) and Cilgerran (*Ann. C.* MS. C.) have been suggested. Cenarth Bychan must in any case have been so called by contrast with Cenarth Mawr on the Teifi, and this seems to me to favour Cilgerran, which is in the same neighbourhood and upon the same river. It lies close to Ceredigion — a point of some weight in the argument — and is found at a later date in the possession of Gerald's descendants.

[60] *B. Saes.* (*s.a.* 1107) has "primas o flandrys" — a form which obviously comes from the original Latin text.

[61] "Heb allel godef andynolyon voesseu y gwydyl" (*Bruts*, 289).

[62] See chap. viii. note 111.

[63] *Bruts*, 292; *B.T.* 112. *B. Saes.* is in agreement.

[64] This affords the most natural explanation of Maredudd's action in 1113, as described in *B.T. s.a.* 1110. For the position of the "penteulu" see p. 316 above.

[65] The expedition is mentioned in *A.S. Chr.*, Fl. Wig. and Hen. Hunt., and supplies a fixed point in chronology. The dating of *Ann. C.* MS. B. is henceforth correct to the end of the reign, while *B. Saes.* (followed by Ab Ithel in *B.T.*) continues to be three years in arrear until 1132.

[66] *B.T.* 139. The Red Book text has, incorrectly, "Kereinawc" (*Bruts*, 302).

[67] The *Bruts* do not indicate the scene of the encounter, though they suggest it was not far from Carmarthen. *Ann. C.* MS. C. has, however, "Owein a Flandrensibus in Estrat Brunus occiditur," and thus recalls the "lann teliau mainaur brunus" of *Lib. Land.* 254 (*cf.* 62, 125, 287), which was Llandeilo Rwnws (for Frwnws), an extinct chapel in the parish of Llanegwad (Rees, *Welsh SS.* pp. 247, 330), formerly standing near the bridge over the Towy at Dolybont (Spurrell, *Carm.* 96). The name Ystrad still survives in the immediate neighbourhood.

[68] "Owinus rex Walanorum occiditur" (*s.a.* 1116).

[69] Y gwr nys dichawn neb ymoscryn ac ef eithyr duw e hun. y neb a rodes y medyant idaw" (*Bruts*, 298).

[70] Gerald is last mentioned in connection with the death of Owain ap Cadwgan in 1116. "Filii Geraldi" first appear in *Ann. C.* MS. B. *s.a.* 1136. "Odo de kerreu" (Gir. Camb. i. 26) was the son of William fitz Gerald; from him issued the Carew family, for whom see Fenton (2), 138–9. The Welsh form of the name appears to be, not Caerau, but Caer Rhiw; see *Bruts*, 374 (gaer riw) and 384 (idem).

[71] Pipe Roll, 31 Hen. I. 137, shows that in 1130 "Willelmus filius Odonis de Barri" paid, through the sheriff of Pembroke, £4 out of a sum of £10 due from him "pro terra patris sui". Gir. recounts his parentage in the first sentences of "De Rebus a Se Gestis" (*Wks.* i. 21). The family took its name from Barry Island on the coast of Glamorgan.

[72] Pipe Roll as above, 136–7.

[73] Mention is made in the account of a "Godebertus Flandrensis de Ros," and it includes payments made by Walter fitz Wizo of Deugleddyf.

[74] For the Flemish settlement see *Ann. Camb. s.a.* 1107; *B.T.* and *B. Saes. s.a.* 1105; Fl. Wig. *s.a.* 1111 (the date 1108 is preferred in the text as that of the local chroniclers); Ord. Vit. xiii. 16; Gir. Camb. vi. 83–4 (*Itin.* i. 11); Cunningham, *Growth of English Industry and Commerce*, fourth edition (1905), i. p. 641 (Appendix E.). The importance of sheep and wool in the economy of the settlement is illustrated by Gir. Camb. i. 24–5; vi. 87–8. A marginal note in Cott. MS. Domitian i. fo. 1450 (= *Ann. Camb.* MS. C.), which may be assigned to the sixteenth century, says that the Flemings of the district were even then distinguishable as "male Anglice loquentes".

[75] These are "Villa Lamberti," "Villa Huberti" and "Villa Jordahi" in *Tax. Nich.* 275, and it is interesting to observe that Pipe Roll, 31 Hen. I. mentions among the men of the shire a "Hubertus," a "Lambertus Echeners " and a "Jordanus filius Alwini".

[76] Haverford became on Welsh lips successively Hawrffordd ("hawrfort" in "Y Canu Bychan" in *Myv. Arch.* I. 303 (214)), Hawlffordd ("hawlfford" in *Bruts,* 359) and Hwlffordd.

[77] Gir. Camb. vi. 85–7 (*Itin.* i. 11) gives some account of the family, which was connected by marriage with his own (*Wks.* i. 26). Tancard survived the monk Caradog, who died in 1124, but I suspect that he is the "Tanchelinus" whose son and land were in 1130 in custody in consequence of the father's death (Pipe Roll, 31 Hen. I. 137).

[78] In 1130"Walterus filius Witsonis" was in possession of his father's lands, while "Aluredus filius Wihenoc" had married the widow of "Witsonis Flandrensis" and obtained her dower (Pipe Roll as above, 136). That these lands lay in Deugleddyf is known from *Cart. Glouc.* i. 228, 264–6. "Castellum Wiz" (*Ann. C.* MS. B. *s.a.* 1148; *B.T.* has "castell gwiss " — see *Brutts,* 314) is first mentioned by that name in 1147.

[79] Camden, *Britannia,* 583; Owen, *Pemb.* i. 437. Martin of Tours appears to have succeeded to the Devonshire manors of William of Falaise, as entered in Domesd. i. 111*a* (*cf.* Owen, *Pemb.* i. 430–2), but there is nothing which clearly connects him with Cemais. His foundation of St. Dogmael's rests only on the: authority of Thomas Lloyd, precentor of St. David's from 1534 to 1547 (*MON. ANGL.* iv. 129), and there is no hint of it in the early charters of the monastery.

[80] If Cilgerran was the site of the castle of Cenarth Bychan, it may be supposed that it was not reoccupied for some years after the attack of 1109, and hence, it may be, the change of name.

[81] For the Clare family see *Dict. Nat. Biog.* x. p. 375 (articles by J. H. Round) *Feudal England,* pp. 472, 574–5.

[82] *B.T.* 104; *Bruts,* 289.

[83] Note 2.

[84] The bridge was already in existence in 1136 (Cont. Fl. Wig. *s.a.*).

[85] *B.T.* describes the castle as on a hill which sloped to the river Ystwyth and which faced Ystrad Antarron (*Bruts,* 299). The Tanycastell height exactly fulfils these conditions; there is the further evidence of the name and of the earthworks still visible on the summit.

[86] *Ann. Camb.* MS. B. *s.a.* 1136 mentions "castello Walteri de Bek. . . et castello Ricardi de la Mare". The situation of the former is indicated by the alternative name of Llanfihangel Castell Gwallter for Llanfihangel Geneu'r Glyn (Carlisle); that of the latter is uncertain, but it seems to have stood between Aberystwyth and Caerwedros, if one may judge from the narrative cited above.

"Walterus de Beco" (who is confused by Powel (p. 138) with Walter Espec, the founder of Rivaux Abbey) appears in Pipe Roll, 31 Hen. I. 102 (Bucks); according to *Lib. Nig.* 221, he was a tenant ("Walterus del Bec") of Earl Ferrers in this reign.

[87] "Castellum hunfredi" (*Ann. Camb.* MS. B. *s.a.* 1137) was in 1151 rebuilt by Hywel ab Owain Gwynedd and thus acquired its more familiar name of Castell Hywel (*B.T.* 180).

[88] "Castellum Stephani" (*Ann. Camb. ut supra*) is not likely to have been Llanstephan, which is always described in the chronicles by that name (= St. Stephen's). The guess in *GW. BRUT, S.A.* 1137, may for once be right, though the connection with *King* Stephen is, of course, imaginary.

[89] *Ann. C. s.a. B.T.* (MSS. B. and C.) and B. Sacs. (s.a. 1114) say he died of a lingering complaint.

[90] "Ef adamweinawd dyuot Gwallter ucheluaer kaer loyw y gwr a orchymynassei y brenhin idaw llywodraeth (kaer loyw) ac amddiffyn lloeger hyt yg kaer vyrdin" (*Brunts*, 283; *B.T.* 88). *B. Saes.* calls him "escob caer loyw," and otherwise mangles the passage. For the position and history of Walter see *Feudal England*, p. 313; Round, *Anc. Charters*, pp. 4, 18, 19–20; *Cal. Doc. Fr.* 167.

[91] See chapter viii. note 218. "Veterem civitatem de kermerdyn" was held by the priory (*Carm. Cart.* p. 28).

[92] There is no evidence of the existence of a bridge at Carmarthen in the early Middle Ages. Giraldus crossed the ferry at Llanstephan (vi. 80 —"transeuntes. . . navigio") and the bridge of 1233 was a temporary one, set up to block the waterway.

[93] "Alur. filius Anschet. Driue debet lx. s. pro terra patris sui" (Pipe Roll, 31 Hen. I. 90). *Cf.* No. 34 in *Carm. Cart.* p. 10, in which "Alfredus Drue" gives to Carmarthen priory the chapel of St. "Keyn" ("Egluyskeyne" in No. 78 on p. 28) "que est in feudo meo," with land in the vicinity.

[94] "Homines de Cat (for *Cantre*) maur debent xl. s. pro homine Episcopi saresburiensis quem occiderunt" (Pipe Roll 90). The bishop was lord of Kidwelly, which at Abergwili was only separated from Cantref Mawr by the Towy.

[95] "Blehien de Mabuderi et fratres sui debent vii m. argenti pro filia Bleheri quam vi rapuerunt" (Pipe Roll 90).

[96] "Bledri uab Kediuor" had charge in 1116 of a Norman castle near Carmarthen (*Bruts*, 297; *B.T.* 126). There is no evidence to show that he was the son of Cydifor ap Gollwyn, the Demetian magnate who died in 1091.

[97] Pipe Roll 89.

[98] No. 33 in *Carm. Cart.* (p. 10) is a confirmation by Henry I. of the gift to Carmarthen priory of four carucates in "Eglusnewit" by "Bledericus Latemeni" ("Latemeni" in No. 78). The attestations show that the document belongs to 1129–1134.

[99] *Bruts*, 296; *B.T.* 125.

[100] For Richard fitz Pons see Round, *Anc. Charters*, p. 24. The evidence for his tenure of Cantref Bychan will be found *ibid.* 8, 21; *Mon. Angl.* iii. 448 (grant of church to Great Malvern Priory); *Bruts*, 296 (rickert pwnswn); *B.T.* 123; *B. Saes. s.a.* 1113 = 1116 (Ricardvab Pvnson). Llanamddyfri, as in *Ann.* C., appears to be the original form, in which case "amddyfri" is to be taken as a variant of "amddyfrwys" — see Evans, *Dict. s.v.*

[101] *Mon. Angl.* iv. 64–5. *Cf.* the mention of "homine episcopi saresburiensis" in connection with Cantref Mawr in Pipe Roll, 31 Hen. I. 90. The date is based upon the mention of Bishop Wilffre, who died in 1115; the grant was also made while Turstin was still prior of Sherborne and before his consecration as abbot in 1122.

[102] *Mon. Angl.* iv. 65 suggests that Bishop Roger was followed by a Richard fitz William and that Maurice of London came next, at the very end of Henry's reign. There is nothing to connect William of London, Maurice's father, who died before 1126 (see *Lib. Land.* 29), with Kidwelly.

[103] The *Bruts* (*Bruts*, 296; "aber tawy. . . bioed iarll aelwit henri bemwnd"; *B.T.* 123; *B. Saes. s.a.* 1113 = 1116) are supported by *Cal. Doc. Fr.* i. 106.

[104] *Ann. Wint.* The date usually given, *viz.*, 20th June, 1123 (*Dict. Nat. Biog.* xl. p. 317), is inconsistent with the fact that Roger witnesses as Earl of Warwick a charter belonging to the early part of 1123 (*Feudal England*, pp. 482–4).

[105] *Mon. Angl.* vi. 999; *Cal. Doc. Fr.* i. 237–9. The statement that the church was within the castle ("in eodem Castro positam") has caused some difficulty, but it is simpler to suppose an inaccuracy in the charter than to assume that Arnulf's castle was at Monkton and embraced the church.

[106] *Welsh SS.* p. 349.

[107] The earliest charters of St. Dogmael's are those contained in the cartulary of the mother abbey of Tiron (Eure et Loir — see *Cal. Doc. Fr.* i. 352–4). After these, which belong to 1116–1120, comes that printed in *Mon. Angl.* iv. 130 (in an "inspeximus"), which maybe assigned to the autumn of 1121.

[108] The early history of Carmarthen Priory is told in the Chronicle of Battle Abbey (*Chronicon de Bella*, 1846, pp. 55–6, 61–2), where it is said that the king gave Battle "quandam ecclesiam in honorem Sancti Petri apostoli fundatam apud Walliam in civitate quae Chaermerdi dicitur" and also "aliam ecclesiam antiquissimis temporibus in honore sancti Theodori martiris (a bold endeavour to make respectable the unknown and uncouth Teulyddog!) ibidem fundatam". A document printed in Round, *Anc. Charters*, p. 27, throws further light upon the withdrawal of Battle. The cartulary of the priory was privately printed from a seventeenth-century transcript (Hengwert MS. 440) in 1865 by Sir Thomas Phillips; it contains grants by Bernard (No. 26) and Alfred Drue (No. 34), and a confirmation by Henry 1. of the grant of Bledri (No. 33).

[109] See note 101 above.

[110] *Cal. Doc. Fr.* i. 106.

[111] The documents bearing on the history of this cell are in *Cart. Glouc.* ii. 73–9. *Cf.* Gir. Camb. vi. 121 (*Itin.* ii. 4). *Cart. Glouc.* i. 106 (*i.e.*, the "historia" dates the foundation of the priory in 1111, the year after Gilbert's acquisition of Ceredigion, but the foundation charter in ii. 73–4 is witnessed by Bishop Bernard, and is, therefore, not earlier than September, 1115.

[112] *Bruts*, 294–6; *B.T.* and *B. Saes. s.a.* 1112 = 1115. On p. 118 of *B.T.* (third line from the bottom), MS. B. supplies the correct reading, *viz.*, "ebryfygu" = to forget (Davies, *Dict. s.v.*).

[113] *B.T.* carefully distinguishes the "rac castell" or bailey from the "twwr" or keep.

[114] Later in the year Rhydderch and his sons joined the movement and took part in the siege of Aberystwyth.

[115] *B.T.* and *B. Saes.* translate very differently here, but it is evident that in the original a protest against the invasion was uttered from the point of view of the prudent Welshmen still in undisturbed possession of Llanbadarn. That MS. B. of *B.T.* (p. 128) is right in reading "kyghor" and not "kediuor," as in the Red Book text (*Bruts*, 298, line 10) and its original, Mostyn MS. 116 (Evans, *Rep.* i. pp. 56, 59), is clear from the agreement of *B. Saes.*

[116] Now Blaen Porth simply. The river is called the Howni, for an older Hoddni (*cf.* "porth hodni," *i.e.*, Aberporth, in *Buch.* Gr. ap C. 114 (729)), whence Hoddnant and Hodnant. Earthworks mark the site of the castle.

[117] P. 422.

[118] *Ann. C. s.a.; B.T.* and *B. Saes. s.a.* 1124.

[119] Gir. Camb. i. 34 (*Itin.* i. 2). It may be added that "quartae partis" is due to the erroneous idea that every cantref contained four commotes and that the editor, when he sets out here and in the index (p. 248) to correct the topography of his author, merely gives currency to a blunder which has crept into Pen. MS. 163 and texts derived from it.

[120] *Cymr.* viii. 88 (Jesus Coll. MS. 20, No. xxv.).

[121] There are four references to Philip in Pipe Roll, 31 Hen. I. (72, 103, 126, 157). He lost his lands in 1110, but recovered them in 1112 (*A.S. Chr.* MS. E.).

[122] See the reference in *B.T. s.a.* 1143 (= 1144) to the reconquest of Elfael and Maelienydd by Hugh, son of Ralph.

[123] Bernard appears in the list of magnates of the diocese of Llandaff (which was held to include Ystrad Yw) addressed by Calixtus II. in 1119 (*Lib. Land.* 93), but in the corresponding list of 1128 his place is taken by Miles of Gloucester (*ibid.* 37).

[124] See the "secunda (really the first) carta" of Bernard in the Brecon cartulary (*Arch. Camb.* IV. xiv. (1883), 142–3), which gives "quinque burgenses". The limit of date is fixed by the appearance among the witnesses of "Valdrici cancellarii" — see *Feudal England*, pp. 480–1.

[125] *Chronicon de Bella* (= Cott. MS. Domitian ii.), ed. 1846, 34–5.

[126] "Vetus villa" appears in the charters as "vastam civitatem que vocatur Carnois" (141) and "Chaer" (146); the latter passage gives bounds, which seem to be those of the township of Fenni Fach.

[127] See chap. xi. note 135.

[128] The cartulary of Brecon Priory was printed by R. W. Banks in *Arch. Camb.* IV. xiii. (1882), 275–308, xiv. (1883), 18–49, 137–68, 221–36, 274–311, from a transcript made about 1710. In the notes following this it is cited as *Cart. Brec.* by reference to the page, vol. xiv. being understood when xiii. is not specified.

[129] *Cart. Brec.* 143 ("Quidam ex meis hominibus nomine Picardus").

[130] *Ibid.* 167–8, 221.

[131] *Med. Mil. Arch.* ii. 499–503; *Breconsh.* (2), p. 418.

[132] Robert "de Turbertuulla." was not a donor to Brecon, but he appears as a principal tenant of Bernard's in 1121 (Round, *Anc. Charters*, p. 8; *cf.* p. 24). Jones appears to be right in maintaining that there is no historical evidence for the common statement that the Burghills preceded the Turbevilles at Crickhowel (*Breconsh.* (2), pp. 387–8).

[133] Haja taillata" in Round, *Anc. Charters*, p. 8, clearly represents, as the editor points out, "la haie taillée" (the article was long retained, though not the adjective — see Leland, *Wales*, pp. 10, 42, 104, 108, no, 111). Walter Map's "Sepes Inscisa (for Incisa)" (*De Nugis*, 103) is an attempt at a more elegant translation. For Y Gelli Gandryll, see *Breconsh.* (2), p. 360.

[134] Round, *Anc. Charters*, p. 8, mentions "feodum. . . Willelmi reuelli" in 1121, and *Cart. Brec.* 48, of about the same date, shows it was Hay.

[135] Round, *Anc. Charters*, pp. 8, 24; *Cart. Brec.* 142 (for the situation of the Baskerville lands see 162–6).

[136] For the strange form "cymwd cantref Selyf" see Domitian viii. *fo.* 120A (com. Cantreselif) and Pen. MS. 147 (kwmwd kantre sely — Evans).

[137] Judging from *Lib. Land.* 134, the old cantref extended to the neighbourhood of Llandeilo'r Fân.

[138] *Mon. Angl.* v. 555, No. vii. (Charters of Dore Abbey.)

[139] Gir. Camb. (vi. 29 — *Itin.* i. 2) is the authority for this story.

[140] See the king's charter in Round, *Anc. Charters*, pp. 8–9.

[141] Gir. Camb. vi. 34–5 (*Itin.* i. 2).

[142] Caer Dyf (whence the English Cardiff) is the older form (*cf. Bruts*, 330, 348, 349, 350, 367; Fl. Wig. *s.a.* 1134); the modern Welsh Caer Dydd is a derivative of it; *cf.* cam*dd*a for camfa. For the Roman fort see p. 77.

[143] Clark's account (*Med. Mil. Arch.* i. 336–50) is full, but needs to be supplemented by that of Ward in *Archæologia*, lvii. (1901), 335–52.

[144] A charter of Robert fitz Hamon speaks of the "burgum" at Cardiff (*Cartae Glam.* i. 1) and another grants the two churches to Tewkesbury Abbey (*MON. ANGL.* ii. 67).

[145] There was a "comitatus" of Glamorgan (*Cart. Glouc.* ii. 20) or Cardiff (*ibid.* i. 347) and a "vicecomes" of Glamorganshire (*ibid.*) or Cardiff (*Cartae Glam.* i. 2; *Lib. Land.* 93, 29), but no "comes," the earldom being merged in that of Gloucester.

[146] For the places of the knights in Cardiff Castle see Leland, *Wales*, pp. 34–5; Powel, 95; *Med. Mil. Arch.* i. 349.

[147] After the extensive donations made to the Cistercian convent of Margam, the region around Llangynwyd became isolated from the rest of the lord's demesne and came to be specially known as "Tir yr Iaril" or "The Earl's Land". See the lists of commotes; Leland, *Wales*, pp. 28, 33, 34; *Arch. Camb.* IV. ix. (1878), 124.

[148] See the foundation charter of Neath Abbey (1130) in *Mon. Angl.* v. 259. Richard de "Greinuilla" (Grainville on the west coast of Normandy?) appears in the Pipe Roll, 31 Hen. I. (Dorset, p. 15) and among the witnesses to a treaty between the Earls of Gloucester and Hereford which has been assigned to June, 1142 (*Geoff. Mand.* 381–3).

[149] *Gw. Brut, s.a.* 1088 (Llangenys).

[150] Caradog first appears in *Ann. Marg. s.a.* 1127. He married Gwladus, a daughter of Gruffydd ap Rhys (Gir. Camb. vi. 69 (*Itin.* i. 7); *B.T. s.a.* 1175 (p. 227; *Bruts*, 333)).

[151] For the limits of the lordship of Coety see *Arch. Camb.* IV. ix. (1878), 114–5. "Pagano de Turbertiuilla" witnesses the agreement made between Earl Robert and Bishop Urban of Llandaff in 1126 (*Lib. Land.* 29); *cf.* also the foundation charter of Neath ("Torbivilla" — *Mon. Angl.* v. 259). It is not clear how the family were connected (if at all) with the Turbevilles of Crickhowel in Brecknock.

[152] This is asserted by dark in his account of Rhuthyn (*Arch. Camb.* IV. ix. (1878), 12) and is confirmed by the fact that Rhys gave to Neath Abbey the church and land of "Saint Ilith," *i.e.*, Llanilid (*MON. ANGL.* v. 259).

[153] Herbert "de S. Quintino" and Robert "le Sor" witness a charter which was drawn up in the time of Robert fitz Hamon (*Cartae Glam.* i. 2). See also the *History of the Monastery of Abingdon* (Rolls ed. 1858), ii. 96, 106. William "de lundriis" is mentioned as the father of Maurice in *Lib. Land.* 37, and *B.T. s.a.* 1113 (p. 126) shows that "gwilim o lundein" (*Bruts*, 297) held a castle in South Wales in 1116. Robert "de Umfranvilla" appears in the Neath charter of 1130 (*Mon. Angl. v.* 259). In 1126 most of the knightly families of Glamorgan were in the second generation; Maurice had succeeded William, Richard Herbert of St. Quintin and Odo Robert le Sor. dark (*Land of Morgan*, p. 31) also includes the houses of Siward and Sully among the early settlers, but the evidence seems weak. The Flemings, the St. Johns and the Stradlings were undoubtedly later arrivals, notwithstanding the attempts (Powel, 90–4) to connect them with the conquest.

[154] Wm. Malm. *G.R.* 475 (625); Fl. Wig.; *Ann. Marg.* and *Ann. Theokesb. s.a.* 1107; *Mon. Angl.* ii. 60; *Dict. Nat. Biog.* xix. p. 159.

[155] Probably for ten or fifteen years (*Land of Morgan*, pp. 44–5).

[156] Between April, 1121, and June, 1123 (*Geoff. Mand.* 420–34).

[157] *A.S. Chr. s.a.* 1126; Cont. Fl. Wig. *s.a.* 1134; Ord. Vit. xii. 46, xiii. 9; Wm. Malm. *G.R.* 463 (611).

[158] *Gesta St.* 96–7 (94). The silence of all the authorities, including Giraldus Cambrensis, whose interest in his mother's kindred is so well known, makes it very improbable that Robert was, as has been alleged (*Gw. Brut, s.a.* 1110), the son of Nest. He was born before 1100 ("quem ante regnum susceperat" — Wm. Malm. *H.N.* 529 (692)). See *Norm. Conq.* v. p. 852.

[159] "Robertus de Haia," with the consent of Robert fitz Hamon, gave Basaleg and other churches in this district to Glastonbury (*Cartae Glam.* i. 2) and St. Woollo's to St. Peter's, Gloucester (*Cart. Glouc.* ii. 51). The latter grant was said to have been made before the death of Herwald of Llandaff in 1104.

[160] "Y castell newyd ar wysc" may be found in *B.T.* 218 (where the editor's "*Newcastle* upon Usk" is a pleasant invention of his own) and *Bruts*, 330. "Cas" in such forms as Cas Gwent (Chepstow), Cas Llychwr (Loughor), etc., is explained in Owen, *Pemb.* i. 210, 410. For "port" in the sense of town, borough, see *A.S. Chr.* MS. C. *s.a.* 1055, where it is used of Hereford, and Plummer's note (ii. 245). The Latin rendering was "Novura Burgum".

[161] For Walter fitz Richard see the table in *Feudal England*, p. 473, and Round, *Peerage and Family History* (Westminster, 1901), p. 212.

[162] For a full account of the Ballon family see Round, *ut supra*, chap. iv.

[163] In the letter of Calixtus II. addressed to the magnates of the diocese of Llandaff in 1119 (*Lib. Land.* 93), we have "Willelmo filio badrun," but in that of Honorius II. belonging to 1128 (*ibid.* 37), "Batrun filio Willelmi".

[164] Ord. Vit. viii. 23; *Feudal England*, pp. 176, 312.

[165] "Pagano filio Johannis" was a magnate of the diocese of Llandaff as early as 1119 (*Lib. Land.* 93).

[166] Tradition ascribes the foundation to Robert of Gloucester (Tanner, 715), but the charter of Robert fitz Hamon printed in *Cartae Glam.* i. 1, implies that there were in his time monks settled at Cardiff and holding St. Mary's for Tewkesbury.

[167] The foundation charter is printed in *Mon. Angl.* v. 259 and *Cartae Glam.* i. 6–7. For the date see *Ann. Marg.* and *Ann. Camb. s.a.* 1130. Ord. Vit. (viii. 27) tells the story of the beginnings of Savigny (on the borders of Normandy, Maine and Brittany); *cf.* the charter of Hen. I. in *Cal. Doc. Fr.* 287–8.

[168] *Eng. Hist. Rev.* viii. (1893), pp. 668–70. "Not" on p. 669 is Neath.

[169] *Cartae Glam.* i. 2; *Mon. Angl.* iv. 633–4.

[170] *Lib. Land.* 30, 53; *Mon. Angl.* v. 173–4; Round, *Peerage and Family History*, p. 197.

[171] *Mon. Angl.* vi. 1022; Charter Rolls, ii. 361–3. Gir. Camb. vi. 56 (*Itin.* i. 5) explains the name; *cf.* Coxe (2), 60–1. The Welsh called the place Gallt Eurin (Rees, *Welsh SS.* p. 342).

[172] *Mon. Angl.* iv. 652–4.

[173] *Cat. Doc. Fr.* i. 367–8; Round, *ut supra*, 192.

[174] The early charters of Monmouth were printed by Marchegay in *Chartes du Prieuré de Monmouth* (Paris, 1879 — a reprint from the *Bibliothèque de l'Ecole des Chartes*, vol. xl.). Their contents are summarised in *Cat. Doc. Fr.* i. 406–14, so far as they are preserved in the departmental archives at Angers.

[175] The early history of Llanthony is told by Gir. Camb. vi. 37–41 (*Itin.* i. 3) and in Cott. MS. Julius D. x., the contents of which are summarised in *Arch. Camb*, I. i. (1846), 201–28. *Cf.* also *Angl. Sac.* ii. 299–305, 321–2; *Lib. Land.* 63.

[176] "Llantony" is an English corruption of the true name in its shorter form "Llan Nant Honddu".

[177] The MS. has apparently "Ramelino". Urban and Reinelm were consecrated together on 11th August, 1107 (*Reg. Sacr.* (2), 41).

[178] "In episcopatu Menevensi habitum suscepit canonici et ibi sepultus est" (*Cart. Glouc.* i. lxxvi-vii).

[179] Synods of the British Church are often mentioned in connection with the sixth and seventh centuries; *cf.* Bede, *H.E.* ii. 2 (ut secundo synodus pluribus aduenientibus fieret); H. and St. i. 1166–8, 121. But nothing of the kind appears in later times. The "sened" of the laws (*LL.* i. 18, 52, 356, 476, 478, 638) is clearly the ecclesiastical court for the trial of offences by or against clerics.

[180] H. and St. i. 308, note to Wm. Malm. See pp. 287–8 for alleged consecrations of Bishops of Llandaff and St. David's before 1066 by Archbishops of Canterbury; the Llandaff cases may be genuine, since the evidence comes from *Lib. Land.*, but the St. David's instances from R. de Diceto carry no conviction.

[181] "Hervé Britonis" (Ord. Vit. xii. I (IV. 312)).

[182] H. and St. i. 299 (from Arundel MS. 220).

[183] *Hist. Ch. York*, ii. 104; H, and St. i. 299; *Reg. Sacr.* (2), 40.

[184] No profession of Hervé's is to be found in the Canterbury rolls (H. and St. i. 299).

[185] Inter barbaros barbarice et stolide promotus est" (Letter of 12th Dec., 1102, addressed to Anselm — see Eadmer, 139).

[186] *Angl. Sacr.* i. 678–80; H. and St. i. 303–6. *Cf.* Wm. Malm. *O.P.* 325–6.

[187] To the foregoing references, add *Angl. Sacr.* i. 615–6; Eadmer, 210–1; Migne, clix. 162–3 (Letter of Anselm to Henry I.); Wm. Malm. *G.R.* 517–8 (680).

[188] "Propter Anglorum vicinia(m), a quibus in ecclesiastico quidem ministerio nichil discrepabant, quia apud eosdem fuerant tarn nutriti quam eruditi" (Letter of Bishop Urban to Calixtus II. — *Lib. Land.* 88).

[189] According to *Lib. Land.* 246, Gwgon was consecrated by Dunstan, at a date which may be fixed between 963 (consecration of Æthelwold of Winchester) and 971 (death of Æltheah "dux" — see Fl. Wig. *s.a.*). The figure DCCCCL-XXXII is to be taken with "migrauit ad dominum" and gives the year of Gwgon's death. Bledri was similarly consecrated by Elfric (995–1005), though elected in 983 (*Lib. Land.* 252), and Joseph by Æthelnoth (1020–1038). The

year in the latter case cannot be 1022, as in the MS. (*ibid.*), for Æthelnoth was
then at Rome (*A.S. Chr.* MS. D. *s.a.*); Stubbs suggests 1027 (*Reg. Sacr.* (2), 34),
when 1st October fell upon a Sunday.

[190] *Lib. Land.* 265–6. P. 280 shows that for 1059,1056 is to be read (so *Reg. Sacr.*
(2), 36), a date which explains the part played by Kinsige, since Stigand did
not receive the pall or consecrate bishops until 1058.

[191] *Lib. Land.* 280.

[192] *Ibid.* 88.

[193] Migne, clix. 52–3; H. and St. i. 299–300.

[194] *Lib. Land.* 280; Eadmer, 187; Fl. Wig. *s.a.*

[195] Urban had a brother who bore the Norman name of "Galfridus" (*Lib. Land.* 360,
from Cott. MS. Vesp. A. xiv.) and another called "Esni" (*ibid.* 85), which is apparently English (there was an Esne, bishop of Hereford, in 786 — *Reg. Sacr.* (2),
15). No inference can be drawn from his own name, and the forms "Worgan" (*B.
Saes. s.a.* 1104) and "Gwrfan" (*Gw. Brut, s.a.* 1103) are of no authority.

[196] See the profession in H. and St. i. 303.

[197] Eadmer, 255; *Lib. Land.* 89.

[198] This may be inferred from the fact that the summons received by Urban and
the acts of the Council have been copied into *Lib. Land.* 49–51. The copyist
seems, however, to be wrong when he states that Urban revived his claim
against the bishops of Hereford and St. David's in this Council. See Cont. Fl.
Wig. *s.a.* 1128.

[199] Cont. Fl. Wig. *s.a.*

[200] *Lib. Land.* 86.

[201] *Ibid.* 48.

[202] See the account by Freeman of the Norman church in *Arch. Camb.* II. i.
(1850), 113–9.

[203] *Lib. Land.* 27–9.

[204] *Eng. Hist. Rev.* ix. (1894), pp. 531–2. Hen. Hunt. enters the death of Urban
under the thirty-fourth year of Henry I. (253), which, in the case of an event
between 5th August and 31st December, means 1133. Roger of Wendover's
unauthorised 1134 has misled many later writers.

[205] On this question see H. and St. i. 148–50.

[206] FOR Sulien and his descendants see note appended to this chapter.

[207] This is implied in the statements of Fl. Wig. *s.a.* 1115 (usque ad illum episcopi extitere Brytonici) and Gir. Camb. vi. 105 (Bernardus. . . primus
Francorum apud Meneviam episcopus). The best attested forms of the name
are Wilfre (*Ann. C.* MS. B. *s.a.* 1115; Gir. Camb. vi. 104), Wilfridus (MS. C.;
Fl. Wig.; Eadmer; Gir. Camb. iii. 152) and Wilfredus (Gir. Camb. vi. 90).
Only *B.T.* has Ieffrei (p. 118 — *Bruts*, 294), and only *Gw. Brut* Griffri (*s.a.*
1112), which are to be rejected, together with the conjecture Gruffydd (H.
and St. i. 301).

[208] The idea that Sulien was succeeded by his son Rhygyfarch is due to a slip of the copyist *of Ann. C.* MS. C., who wrote epē (episcop*us*) for epi (episcopi) in the notice "Rikewarth. f. Sulien epē moī". *Cf.* also the true text of *Ann. C.* MS. B. *s.a.* 1085 (*Trans. Cymr.* 1899–1900, 176), which has "fre" (for Wilfre), not "frater" (Ab Ithel's text, p. 28), assumed in H. and St. i. 297 to be an error for "filius". The "Rhyddmarch Escob Dewi" of *Gw. Brut, s.a.* 1098 is of no authority, and the form "Rhyddmarch" is not elsewhere found.

[209] See pp. 407–8 above.

[210] Gir. Camb. iii. 57 (*Invect.* ii. 6).

[211] Eadmer, 72. The meeting took place at the end of May on the road between Windsor and Canterbury.

[212] See note 13 above.

[213] *Cart. Glouc.* i. 265–6.

[214] P. 235.

[215] "O anuod holl ys(c)olheigon y brytanyeit gan eu tremygu" (*Bruts*, 294; *B.T.* 118). *B.T.* here represents the view of the contemporary Llanbadarn chronicler.

[216] *B.T. s.a.* 1124 (= 1127). That he was actually elected (Jones and Freem. 270) is an unwarranted assumption, founded upon a misunderstanding of *B.T.*'s description of him as "Daniel uab Sulyen escob Mynyw," which translates the "Daniel filius Sulgeni episcopi" of *Ann. Camb.* MS. C. *s.a.* 1127.

[217] Eadmer, *ut supra. Cf.* Fl. Wig. *s.a.* 1115.

[218] H. and St. i. 307.

[219] "Vir curialis atque facetus et copiose litteratus" (Gir. Camb. iii. 152–3 (*Men. Eccl.* ii.)).

[220] Eadmer, 255; Cont. Fl. Wig. *s.a.* 1119.

[221] Cont. Fl. Wig. *s.a.*

[222] Eadmer, 295.

[223] *Feudal England*, p. 483.

[224] Cont. Fl. Wig. *s.a.*; H. and St. print (i. 315–6), from Harl. MS. 1249 (see Owen, *Catalogue*, p. 236), a confirmation of the rights of the see obtained by Bernard on 25th May, 1123, from Calixtus II.

[225] *Lib. Land.* 53.

[226] Hen. Hunt. 251.

[227] *Lib. Land.* 66.

[228] Hen. Hunt. 253.

[229] See *Ann. C. s.a.* 1131 —"Dedicatio Menevensis ecclesiae." Jones and Freem. do not, however, regard this notice as conclusive (140).

[230] Gir. Camb. iii. 153–4 (*Men. Eccl.* ii.). Jones and Freem. discuss (310–14) the questions raised by this passage. No deanery was constituted and St. David's was without this officer until 1840 (Gir, Camb. i. 41; iii. 184; Jones and Freem. 355).

[231] See p. 432.

[232] The letter of Gruffydd printed in Eadmer, 259–60, suggests that there had been no bishop (in quibus nec chrisma habuimus nec aliquid Christianitatis vere), but the threat to go to Ireland (quaeremus aliquem de Hibernia insula), if the primate will not consecrate David, is of some significance in this connection.

[233] *G.R.* 498–9 (655–6). Ord. Vit. (x. 1) also refers to the work of the "Irensis scholasticus".

[234] See the objections of Prof. Tout in *Dict. Nat. Biog.* xiv. pp. 115–17.

[235] According to *Ann. Wigorn. s.a.* 1120, he was a Welshman, which, with the *Scottus* of Wm. Malm., may be taken to show that he was known to come from the non-Teutonic part of the British Isles.

[236] Eadmer, 260; Cont. Fl, Wig. *s.a.* 1120.

[237] H. and St. i. 314.

[238] The first date is that of the establishment of Robert at Rhuddlan (see p. 382 above); the second is suggested by Owain Gwynedd's capture of Mold in 1146 and appearance at Coleshill in 1150. Evidence as to the continued predominance of the foreign element in Tegeingl under Henry I. is to be found in the charters of St. Werburgh's Abbey. In 1119 William of "Punterleya" gives the church and manor of Bodffari (Buttanari) and "Burell" the church of Holywell; under Earl Ranulf I. (1121–8), his brother William gives the church of Diserth (*Mon. Angl.* ii. 387).

[239] Hen. Hunt. recognises only three Welsh bishoprics (10).

[240] There is clear evidence that it was founded before 1147 (*Eng. Hist. Rev.* viii. (1893), p. 669) and by Earl Ranulf (II.) — see Charter Rolls ii. 289–91; *Mon. Angl.* v. 262–3. The precise year is taken from Dugdale.

[241] See § ii. of this chapter.

[242] P. 461.

[243] *Hist. Ch. York*, ii. 211 (Hugh the Chantor).

[244] See pp. 431–2 above.

[245] *Mon. Angl.* II. 66, 67; *Cartae Glam.* iii. 40. The form used is "Landiltuit".

[246] *Cart. Glou.* i. 93.

[247] See p. 397.

[248] See especially Migne, clix. 214 (Anselm); *Lib. Land.* 93 (Calixtus II.); *ibid.* 37 (Honorius II.).

[249] Gir. Camb. iii. 152–3 (*Men. Eccl.* ii.); i. 309 (*Sym. El.* i. 31). For the identification of "Ucketune" see Owen, *Pemb.* i. 294.

[250] *Lib. Land.* 88.

[251] See Ruestoch (= Meliden, Thomas, *St. Asaph*, p. 295), Calstan, Brenuuen, Chiluen, and Bodugan in Domesd. i. 269o. For an early list of the possessions of the see, see Thomas, *ut supra*, 180.

[252] See Eadmer, 235 (sub patrocinio Beati Andreae et Sancti David); H. and St. i. 315; Gir. Camb. vi. 107 (*Itin.* ii. 1).

[253] *Lib. Land. passim.* The forms "episcopus teiliav," "sacerdos teiliav," and "tota familia teliaui" in the Book of St. Chad show that anciently only Teilo was recognised.

[254] See *Carm. Cart.*, in which "ecclesia sancti Johannis Evangelistae et sancti Theulaci de Kermerdyn" is a common form, but not nearly so common as the Church of St. John the Evangelist *simpliciter.*

[255] See chap. viii. note 249.

[256] J. R. Phillips, *History of Cilgerran.* (London, 1867), pp. 50-2.

[257] The Church of St. "Kinephaut" of "Rokevilla" is mentioned in a bull of Urban III. (28th December, 1186) as belonging to St. Florent of Saumur (*Cal. Doc. Fr.* i. 405; Marchegay, 14). It is the "aecclesiam Sancti Cenfaldi" of William fitz Baderon's grant (*Cal. Doc. Fr.* i. 407; Marchegay, 18) to Monmouth Priory (a cell of St. Florent) and, no doubt, the "merthir (or lann) cinfall" of *Lib. Land.* 171, 173, 264. Round (*Cal. Doc. Fr.* i. li.) is in error as to the present dedication of Rockfield (see *Welsh SS.* pp. 322, 344), and his "Cennfaeladh" (p. 407) is an Irish and not a Welsh form.

[258] The "lann tiuoi" of *Lib. Land.* 275 is clearly Foy, now dedicated to the virgin St. Fides.

CHAPTER III

[1] See note 56 to chap. xii.

[2] *Ann. Cest.* and *Ann. C. s.a.* 1101; *B.T.* p. 66. Ord. Vit. x. 18 (IV. 111) gives the day as 27th July, and says he died in his own abbey of St. Werburgh's, Chester.

[3] "Puer vii annorum" (*Ann. Cest. s.a.* 1101). The Welsh authorities (*Ann. C.* MS. C., *B.T., B. Saes.*) all call him Roger, a mistake which clearly goes back to the original Llanbadarn record.

[4] *Ann. C. s.a.* 1114; *B.T.* pp. 112–18; *B. Saes. s.a,* 1111; *Buch. Gr. ap C.* 124 (733a); *A.S. Chr.* MS. E. *s.a.* 1114 (*cf.* also MS. H. in Plummer, i. 245); Fl. Wig. s.a. 1114.

[5] I cannot identify the "Gilbert tywyssawc o gernyw" of *B.T.* (*B. Saes.* calls him "Gilbert iarll holl dehev lloegyr a chyrnyw").

[6] The statement that Alexander and the earl came to "Pennant Bachwy" (*B.T.* MS. C., *B. Saes.* — the Red Book has "Pennaeth," *Bruts,* 293) raises serious difficulties. For Pennant Bachwy or Bacho is in the Plinlimmon region (L. G. Cothi, 468), a little east of Dylife, and very far from any line which we can suppose the Earl of Chester to have taken in his march against Gruffydd. Either the original chronicler substituted for an unfamiliar name one with which he was acquainted or the meeting-place of the southern contingent has been accidentally assigned to the northern.

[7] *Buch. Gr. ap C.* 118 (730), where Angharad is described as "walltwen"; *B.T.* 152 (*s.a.* 1122). The daughters were Gwenllian (not the wife of Cadwgan ap Bleddyn — see note 57 to chap. xii. — but of Gruffydd ap Rhys), Marared, Rannillt (the name of Gruffydd's mother), Susanna (who married Madog ap Maredudd) and Annest.

[8] "Dux Powisorum" (*Ann. C.* MS. B. *s.a.* 1132); "tegwch a diogelwch holl powys ae hamdifyn" (*B.T.* 156).

[9] For this expedition see *Ann. C. s.a.* 1121; *B.T.* 146–50; *B. Saes. s.a.* 1118; *A.S. Chr.* MS. E. *s.a.* 1121; Cont. Fl. Wig. *s.a.* 1121; Wm. Malm. *G.R.* 477 (628). *B. T.* tells how an arrow shot at random by one of Maredudd's skirmishers struck the king in the region of the heart, his coat of mail alone shielding him from instant death. It makes merry over his alarm, but a different complexion is put upon the affair by Wm. Malm., who says that Henry was firmly convinced that the shaft was sped by a traitor in the ranks of his own army.

[10] *Sim. Dun.* ii. 263. Earl Richard and his wife Matilda, sister of the future king Stephen, were drowned in the *White Ship* off Barfleur on 25th November, 1120 (*Ann. Cest. s.a.*; Ord. Vit. x. 18; xii. 26; Wm. Malm. *G.R.* 496–7 (654)). Richard's cousin, Ranulf of Bayeux, also known as "le Meschin" or "the younger," was raised to the earldom in 1121 (*Ann. Cest. s.a.*; Ord. Vit. xii. 28; *Rot. Norm.* ii. p. cliv). The "sons of the king of the Welsh" were probably Gruffydd and Hywel ap Maredudd, who died in 1128 and 1142 respectively; the two castles burnt would be not far from Maelor.

[11] So the *Bruts*; here, as throughout the reign of Henry I., they take the standpoint of Powys, but this testimony is to be preferred to the vague assertions of Gruffydd's panegyrist (*Buch. Gr. ap C.* 126 (733)) as to his resolute resistance in 1121.

[12] See p. 416.

[13] As the cantref contained three commotes (Dogfeiling or Rhuthyn, Llannerch and Coleion), it was easily divided between several lords.

[14] Maes Maen Cymro is a township in the parish of Llanynys and lies, I am informed by Mr. Ezra Roberts of Ruthin, in the neighbourhood of Rhewl railway station. The battleground was thus on the border between Dyffryn Clwyd and Cymeirch (a commote of Rhufoniog).

[15] It is to be borne in mind that the Llanbadarn chronicler is a partisan of Powys and records nothing which can redound to the credit of Gwynedd. Hence the story of the successes of the sons of Gruffydd has to be read into his narrative as an inevitable deduction from the plain facts.

[16] See p. 416.

[17] "Upon a little bank near the monastery, called Y Pentre, once stood Castell Cymmer" (Robert Vaughan *apud Camb. Reg.* i. 190 and *Arch. Camb.* II. i. (1850), 202). A tumulus marks the spot.

[18] He was with them in the battle of Maes Maen Cymro.

[19] First mentioned in this annal. "Kadwalladyr" (*Bruts*, 307) is a slip on the part of the scribe of the Red Book; all the other texts, including Mostyn MS. 116 (Evans, *Rep.* i. p. 59), have Cadwallon. The same mistake is made by this copyist in writing out the annal 1124. Cadwaladr was the youngest of the three brothers and does not appear until 1136.

[20] "Nanneudui" (*Ann. C.* MS. B.); "nanhevdwy" (*B. Saes. s.a.* 1129). *Ann. Cest.* mentions the death of "Cadwathlan" in battle s.a. 1132, but I cannot locate its "Wadiece".

[21] For the whitewashing of churches see North, *Old Churches of Arllechwedd* (Bangor, 1906), p. 83, and *cf. Myv. Arch.* I. 360 (249), where Llywelyn Fardd describes Towyn as

"Eglwys wenn wyngalch wynhaed".

[22] *Arch. Camb.* I. i. (1846), 62.

[23] The date comes from *Ann. C.* and the *Bruts*, the particulars from *Buch. Gr. ap C.* 128 (734).

[24] "Dwy flynedd a phetwar ugeint."

[25] "Symeon archdiagon gwr addfed o oed a doethineb." He died in 1152 (*B. Saes. s.a.* 1151, the "Kelynnawc" of which is to be preferred to the "Keueilawc" of *B.T.* 180). In Cont. Fl. Wig. *s.a.* 1139, he appears as the spiritual adviser of Bishop David's successor, Meurig, who urged the new prelate not to swear fealty to the king of England. In 1148 Bernard of St. David's invites him, as a known sympathiser with the claims of that see, to support them in the forthcoming Council of Rheims (Gir. Camb. iii. 59). As in St. Asaph, there was at this time but one archdeacon in the diocese.

[26] Besides Dublin, the list includes St. Werburgh's, St. Peter's, Shrewsbury, St. David's, Bangor, Holyhead, Penmon, Clynnog, Bardsey, Meifod, Llanarmon (in Yale?) and Dineirth (Llandrillo in Rhos). Most of the Welsh churches named are known to have been ancient mother churches having a "clas".

[27] Founded by Sitric of the Silken Beard, it is said, about 1040.

[28] See *B.T.* 196; *B. Saes. s.a.* 1161 = 1162.

[29] Gir. Camb. vi. 19 (*Itin.* i. 1). Hoare (*Itin.* i. 6) suggests that the lake was Llyn Bychllyn, near Llanbedr Painscastle.

[30] Gir. Camb. vi. 88 (*Itin.* i. 11).

[31] Cont. Fl. Wig. *s.a.* 1136, MS. G.; *Gesta St.* 11 (10); Gir. Camb. vi. 78 (*Itin.* i. 9), whose "Anglos de finibus illis" is evidence of the existence of an *English* colony. The *Bruts* carefully distinguish Hywel ap Maredudd of Brycheiniog from his namesake (grandson of Rhydderch ap Caradog) of Cantref Bychan.

[32] Gir. Camb. vi. 79 (*Itin.* i. 9). For Gwenllian and her children see Jesus Coll. MS. 20 in *Cymr.* viii. 88 (No. xxv.). The mention of "Gaufrido *praesulis* constabulario" would almost seem to imply that Bishop Roger had, while parting with the lordship, retained his hold of the castle. See p. 429.

[33] Hoare, *Itin.* i. 168.

[34] Cont. Fl.Wig. *s.a.* 1136, MS. G.; *Gesta St.* 12 (10–11); Gir. Camb. vi. 47–8 (*Itin.* i. 4), whose account, as it is the fullest, so also seems the most reasonable (except for the fiddling incident, which may be an embellishment of oral tradition). *Ann. C.* MS. B. and the *Bruts* make Morgan ab Owain, Iorwerth's elder brother, the doer of the deed; he probably laid the plan which his brother exe-

cuted. For the ancestry of both see *B.T. 210*. The "evil pass" of "Coit Wroneu" must have been near the point where the Grwyne crosses the direct route from Brecon to Abergavenny; for it seems clear that Giraldus and Baldwin followed this road. Hoare's assumption (*Itin.* i. 93) that they went round by Talgarth is unsupported by any evidence. His "Coed Dias" is, therefore, too far to the north; moreover "dias" = vengeance is not Welsh, and the true name of the spot is Coed Euas = the Wood of Ewias (Owen, *Pemb.* i. 199).

[35] See p. 467.

[36] See note 86 to chap. xii.

[37] *Bruts*, 309.

[38] See p. 432.

[39] See note 31 to chap. xii.

[40] Meyrick, *Card.* (2), 262.

[41] *Ibid.* p. 233.

[42] *Ann. C.* and *Bruts*; Cont. Fl. Wig. *s.a.* 1136; *Gesta St.* 12–13 (11–12); Gir. Camb. vi. 118 (*Itin.* ii. 3).

[43] "Gens haec. . . armis. . . et equis a Normannis et Anglis. . . edocta paulatim et assueta" (Gir. Camb. vi. 218 (*Descr.* ii. 7)).

[44] This "great mound" is a knoll, now commonly called Banc y Warren, close to the road from Aberaeron to Cardigan. "Cruc maur" in "Cereticiaun" is one of the *mirabilia* of Nennius (*Hist. Britt.* c. 74).

[45] MS. B. of *B.T.* adds "Gwilym ap Orc" (p. 158 — *cf. B. Saes.* "William vab. . . " and Powel, 138, "William Fitziohn"), which may possibly be for "Willelmus filius Odonis," *i.e.*, William de Barri of Manorbier.

[46] See *Gesta St.* for the burning of "templa". According to *Cart. Glouc.* ii. 74, 76, Gilbert fitz Richard gave the church "sanctae Trinitatis de Kardigan" to St. Peter's, Gloucester, and the donation was confirmed by Henry II. The dedication points to a Norman foundation, the old church of the district being probably Llangoedmor. Meyrick's statement (176) that a son of Brychan named Mathaiarn was buried at Cardigan rests on a mistranslation of the "Ceredigion" of *Iolo MSS.* 119.

[47] This is expressly stated by *Ann. C.* MS. B. ("castello Francis rernanente") and explains the account in *Gesta St.*

[48] For Baldwin see *Geoff. Mand.* 148; *Feudal England*, p. 474.

[49] "Robertus filius Heraldi" (*Gesta St.* 14 (13)) is, no doubt, as suggested by dark (*Med. Mil. Arch.* ii. 43), Robert of Ewias, the founder in 1147 of the Cistercian abbey of Dore and the benefactor of his father's foundation of Ewias Harold (*Cart. Glouc.* i. 287). He was the son of Harold of Ewias, who may be safely identified with the "Heraldus filius Radulfi comitis (of Hereford)" of Domesd. i. 169*a* (2). On the death of Alfred of Marlborough, Harold had obtained his castle and lordship in South-western Herefordshire (see page 396 above), which thus came to be called Ewias Harold by way of distinction from the more westerly Ewias Lacy.

[50] Besides *Ann. C.* MS. B., this raid is also mentioned by *Ann. Marg. s.a.*

[51] Letterston (which is in Pebidiog) appears as "Lettardistoune" in *Blk. Bk. of St. David's,* 137 (*cf.* 95, 97, 139), as "Villa Becard" (for Letard) in *Tax. Nich.* 2750, and as "Tre Letert" in Pen. MS. 147 (Evans, *Rep.* i. p. 917). Ivo "filius Letardi" gave the church of Letterston to the preceptory of Slebech (Owen, *Pemb.* i. 353; Fenton (2), 347).

[52] Cont. Fl. Wig. says "dolo conjugis suae circumventus"; *Ann. C.* and the *Bruts* give no details.

[53] Maredudd was in his twenty-fifth year when he died in 1155 (*B.T.* 182) and was, therefore, born in 1130 or 1131, while Rhys was still younger ("Resus. . . junior" — *Ann. C.* MS. B. *s.a.* 1156 = 1155).

[54] See notes 87 and 88 to chap. xii.

[55] Only MS. C. of *Ann. C.* has this notice; the *Bruts* have dropped the year altogether, and accordingly *B. Saes*, which is a year behind in its dating of the events of 1135-7, is *two* years in arrear from 1138 to 1140, which it divides into two (1138 and 1139), thus returning to the old position. The eclipse of 20th March, 1140, is perhaps assigned to 1137 (=1139) because the chronicler's year did not end until 25th March.

[56] *Ann. Cest.* Marford and Wrexham (which appear as "merfort" and "Vnknan" in Dom. viii. fo. 119*a*) were the heads of the two commotes into which Bromfield or Maelor was divided when it came under Welsh rule.

[57] Ord. Vit. xiii. 16 (V. 43). The event appears to be assigned to 1134, but it is far more likely that the author is describing what took place after Henry's death than that he should be recording an otherwise unknown revolt of that king's last days. The castle of "Caus," the "Alretone" of Domesd. i. 253*b*, belonged to the Corbet family and could only have been held temporarily by Payn (Eyton, *Shrops.* vii. pp. 5, 10).

[58] Cont. Fl. Wig. *s.a.* 1137; *Gesta St.* 16-17 (15), with editor's note. His possessions passed to Roger, eldest son of Miles of Hereford, who had married his eldest daughter, Cecilia (Round, *Anc. Charters,* pp. 35-8).

[59] Madog ab Idnerth died in 1140. Two of his sons, *viz.,* Hywel and Cadwgan, were slain in 1142 by Helias of Say (*Ann. C.* MS. C. *s.a.*), who was lord of Clun (Eyton, *Shrops.* xi. p. 228). A third, Maredudd, was killed by Hugh Mortimer in 1146. The remaining two, Cadwallon and Einion, lived to rule over Maelienydd and Elfael respectively.

[60] Gir. Camb. vi. 21 (*Itin.* i. 2). This Hywel ap Maredudd (unless he be H. ap M. ap Bleddyn, slain in 1142) is not heard of after 1136, though his sons Maredudd (d. 1140) and Rhys (see *Ann. C. s.a.* 1145 and 1148 = 1147) are several times mentioned.

[61] H. ap M. of Cantref Bychan (for his father see pp. 429 and 434 above) was killed in 1141 by Rhys ap Hywel of Brycheiniog, and with him ended, so far as is known, this branch of the posterity of Rhydderch ab Iestyn. Richard fitz Pons

is last heard of in 1128 (*Lib. Land.* 37). For his son Walter, who took the surname of Clifford from the home of the family, see *Dict. Nat. Biog.* xi. p. 81;
Round, *Anc. Charters*, pp. 21, 24.

[62] Ord. Vit. xiii. 37 (V. 110), where Le Prevost reads "Morgan Gualus (*i.e.,*
Wallensis) Ucham (tenuit)". For Morgan's connections see note 34.

[63] He is found in this position at the accession of Henry II., when the sheriff of
Gloucester is allowed an annual deduction of 40s. for crown lands granted to
"Morgan" in "Carliun" (Pipe Roll, 2 Hen. II. 49). "Morganus filius Oweni et
Jorwerd frater ejus" were donors to Goldcliff Priory about 1140 (Charter
Rolls, ii. 363).

[64] *Geoff. Mand.* 278–83.

[65] Rymer, i. 14; *Geoff. Mand.* 123–4.

[66] *Gesta St.* 73 (74), 80 (81).

[67] Wm. Malm. *H.N.* 556 (725), 573 (743); *Geoff. Mand.* 82.

[68] *Geoff. Mand.* 94, 135.

[69] Ord. Vit. xiii. 37 (V. 112–13); *Geoff. Mand.* 123, 125, 418.

[70] *Geoff. Mand.* 82–3.

[71] See note 58 above.

[72] *Gesta St.* 97 (94 "umbra quaedam pacis").

[73] Ord. Vit. xiii. 37 (V. 112).

[74] *Geoff. Mand.* 178.

[75] *Ann. Cest. s.a.* According to John of Hexham (*Sim. Dun.* ii. 287), Ranulf had
narrowly escaped capture by the Welsh in 1137.

[76] *Gesta St.* 123–5 (121–3), where the story is told from the court point of view.
Cf. Hen. Hunt. 279; *Ann. Cest. s.a.* 1146.

[77] Almost all that is known of the history of Bernard's suit is derived from the
works of Gir. Camb., who carried on the struggle a couple of generations later.
Gerald was an unscrupulous combatant, but there is no reason to think that this
part of his narrative is untrustworthy, and I have in the main adhered to it. The
view of H. and St. (i. 317; *cf.* also 344), that Bernard "held his peace. . . until
the death of his patron Henry I.," is based on too rigid an interpretation of
"post annos. . . circiter viginti, defuncto rege" in Gir. Camb. iii. 49 (*Invect.* ii. 1).
In the earliest account given by Giraldus of the matter, it is stated in the clearest
terms that Bernard first moved in the time of Henry; see vi. 106 (*Itin.* ii. 1). The
passage was written in 1191 (editor's pref. pp. xxxiii-vi) and is repeated in iii.
152–3 (*Men. Eccl.* ii), in a work composed a quarter of a century later.

[78] Gir. Camb. iii. 59–60 (*Invect.* ii. 10). *Cf.* the life of David fitz Gerald, in which it
is said that Bernard prosecuted his claim "temporibus Honorii, Lucii, et
Innocentii paparum" (*ibid.* iii. 431). I know of no evidence that the matter was
raised under Calixtus II. (Jones and Freem. 278).

[79] For an analysis of the St. David's claim see note appended to this chapter.

[80] Gir. Camb. iii. 58 (*Invect.* ii. 7).

[81] *Ibid.* 59 (ii. 9). For the circumstances see p. 483.

[82] *Ibid.* 52–3 (ii. 3), 187 (*Men. Eccl.* iii.).

[83] *Ibid.* 56–8 (ii. 6).

[84] According to Hen. Hunt. (10), "tempore. . . nostro recepit episcopus S. David pallium a papa, quod scilicet fuerat olim apud Kairtegion, sed statim tamen amisit".

[85] Gir. Camb. iii. 50, 51–2, (*Invect.* ii. 1, 2,), 180–1 (*Men. Eccl.* ii.). Jaffé is clearly right (ii. 45), as against H. and St. (i. 354–5), in assigning the pope's letter to 1147, since in June, 1148, Eugenius was passing through Burgundy on his way back to Italy. The letter to Simeon (Gir. iii. 59) is evidence, at the same time, of Bernard's intention to raise the matter at the Council of Rheims in March, 1148. For the testimony of the bishop of Bath see H. and St. i. 353–4; as he had been a monk (Cont. Fl. Wig. *s.a.* 1134), he is no doubt the "monachus falsus" of the life of David fitz Gerald (Gir. Camb. iii. 431).

[86] The chronology of *Ann. C.* is here in disorder, but the 1147 of *B. Saes.* and *B.T.* 176 clearly = 1148, which is also the year given by *Ann. Theokesb.*

[87] *B.T.* 176; Gir. Camb. iii. 50 (*Invect.* ii. 1), 154–5 (*Men. Eccl.* ii.), 431; H. and St. i. 355–6; *Reg. Sacr.* (2), 47.

[88] See p. 416.

[89] The "Vita Davidis II. episcopi Menevensis" is printed from Domitian i. in *Ang. Sac.* ii. 652–3 and Gir. Camb. iii. 431–4. Brewer thought it might be by Gir. (Pref. to vol. iii. p. xlvii), but Wharton well brings out the difference of attitude (Pref. to *Ang. Sac.* ii. p. xxvi).

[90] He is last mentioned in connection with Gruffydd's death — see p. 468.

[91] "Meuruc" (*Bruts,* 322) may, of course, be an attempt to give a Welsh dress to a foreign "Mauricius". But a Welsh origin is strongly suggested by the relations with Archdeacon Simeon.

[92] Cont. Fl. Wig. *s.a.* 1139.

[93] See note 25 above. The chronicler mentions no name, but "vir magnae religionis. . . et praedecessoris mei David archidiaconus" can hardly be any one else. The idea that Meurig had himself been archdeacon (B. Willis, *Bangor,* pp. 61, 131) probably arose out of a confused recollection of this passage.

[94] H. and St. i. 345–6.

[95] Cont. Fl. Wig. *s.a.*

[96] Gir. Camb. iii. 59 (*Invect.* ii. 9).

[97] *Dict. Nat. Biog.* lviii. p. 3. Uchtryd appears as archdeacon in 1126 (*Lib. Land.* 29), in 1131 (*ibid.* 60, 64), and in 1133 (*Eng. Hist. Rev.* ix. (1894), p. 532).

[98] Cont. Fl. Wig. *s.a.*

[99] H. and St. i. 346, note *a.*"

[100] See, for instance, the correspondence printed by H. and St. (i. 346–7).

[101] He is, presumably, the "Henricum (for Huctritum). . . Landavensem" of the letter (possibly spurious) of the chapter of St. David's to Eugenius III. printed in Gir. Camb. iii. 56–8 (*Invect.* ii. 6).

[102] *B.T.* 212 (*Bruts*, 328); *B. Saes. s.a.* 1171.

[103] This is also suggested by the praise of the *Bruts* (*B.T.* 176; *B.* Sacs. s.a. 1147).

[104] He died in the same year as Bernard — see note 86 above.

[105] "AC yny ol ynteu y bu escob nicol uab gwrgant" (*Bruts*, 315; *B.T.* 176 — *cf. B. Saes. s.a.* 1147 = 1148).

[106] See his letter of 1173-4 to Alexander III. in *Cart. Glouc.* ii. 173-4.

[107] "Opus enim manuum vestrarum ipse est et plantatio vestra," says Gilbert Foliot in a letter to Theobald (H. and St. i. 356). He was consecrated at Canterbury on 14th March, 1148 (*Reg. Sacr.* (2), 46).

[108] Not, of course, of the father of Iestyn ap Gwrgant (*Camb. Biog.* 266), who cannot have nourished much later than 1050, nor yet of Bishop Urban (H. and St. i. 303, 387), for the form "uab gwrgant *escob*" appears to be a slip of MS. B. (*B.T.* 176, note 1) and Mostyn MS. 116 (Evans, *Ref.* i. p. 60).

[109] H. and St. i. 347-8.

[110] Gir. Camb. iii. 58 (*Invect.* ii. 6). Not only is the name wrongly given as "Ricardum," but the dates of Stephen's captivity (1141) and of Gilbert's consecration (1143) do not run so closely together as to warrant the idea of a connection.

[111] See p. 525.

CHAPTER IV

[1] From 1143 to 1154 the chronology of both MSS. of *Ann. Camb.* is in disorder. Nor is this surprising when it is understood that their common original had omitted the year 1152 and attached the end of 1153 to the beginning of 1151, as may clearly be seen from a comparison with the *Bruts* for the same period. *B.T.* and *B. Saes.* seem to have the right arrangement of years, and I follow the chronology of the latter, adding as before (see chap. xiii. note 55) one year.

[2] "Oeni magni" (Gir. Camb. vi. 143).

[3] See his letter to Owain in H. and St. i. 373-4, and *Mat. Hist. Beket.* v. 236-8.

[4] vi. 143-5 (*Itin.* ii. 12).

[5] "Virum... discretum" (Abp. Thomas); "vir in gente sua moderantiae magnae et sapientiae" (Gir. Camb.). *B.T.* (p. 206) speaks of his "brudder".

[6] Gir. Camb. (vi. 145) mentions him as one of three princes distinguished by "justitia, prudentia, principalisque modestia regiminis".

[7] I follow *B. Saes.* (*s.a.* 1161: "am varw y vam") in preference to *B.T.* (p. 197: "o achaws hynny," *i.e.*, the loss of Tafolwern).

[8] This is suggested by the "si cognatam tuam diligis" of the archbishop's letter (H. and St. i. 374).

[9] Gir. Camb. vi. 145 (*Itin.* ii. 12).

[10] *Gesta St.* 69 (70), Hen. Hunt. 268, 273, and Ord. Vit. xiii. 43 (V. 126, 127) agree that the Welsh contingent had been raised by Earl Ranulf. Ord. Vit. gives the names of the leaders as "duo fratres Mariadoth et Kaladrius"; the former I take to be Madog ap Maredudd, who had married Cadwaladr's sister, Susanna.

[11] *B.T.* and *B. Saes.* differ on this point. In the text of the former (*Bruts*, 311), "nas" is to be supplied before "ofynhaei" ("so that he did not fear" — see Mostyn MS. 116 in Evans, *Rep.* i. p. 60) and some such word as "digyfoethi" after "mynnu".

[12] The *Bruts* (B.T. 164; *B. Saes. s.a.* 1143) mention as leaders of the Danes Otter son of Otter (d. 1148? see *Chron. Scot. s.a.*), a MacTurcaill (perhaps Ragnall, who d. 1146) and a Mac "Cherulf".

[13] Remains of entrenchments are still to be seen behind the farm of Bryn Castell, which is not far from the Cynfal of to-day.

[14] "Y ty gwyn" (*Bruts*, 315; so also *B. Saes. s.a.* 1146) is always taken to be Whitland (Y ty gwyn ar Daf) — see *Gw. Brut. s.a.* 1146; Carnh. 547; Gw. ap Rhys, ii. 46; Hoare, *Itin.* i. 184; *B.T.* 175 (trans.). But it is a wildly improbable assumption that a Cistercian abbot, in the early days of that order's austerity, should have held a castle for a Welsh prince sixty miles from the monastery he ruled. The difficulty is solved if we suppose the true form to be "y tywyn" and Morfran to be the head of the "clas" at that place.

[15] Powel (147) and others following him were misled by a slip in *B. Saes.*, or a MS. nearly allied to it, into supposing that Cadwaladr was imprisoned by his nephew, Hywel ab Owain Gwynedd, in 1150. It was his son Cadfan to whom this befell, as may be seen from a careful comparison of the notices for this and the previous year in *Ann. C.* and the *Bruts*.

[16] Powel, 148; *Gwydir Fam.* 14.

[17] See the Haughmond charter cited in *Gwydir Fam.* 14, note 3 (from an unknown source), and Owen, *Catalogue*, ii. p. 451 (from Harl. MS. 6068).

[18] So Sir John Wynne, and Eyton, *Shrops.* x. p. 257. Powel's "Gilbert Earle of Clare" is certainly wrong, for, though Gilbert fitz Richard had a daughter named Alice, she married Aubrey de Vere and on his death in 1141 entered the monastery of St. Osyth's (*Geoff. Mand.* 389–92).

[19] *Geoff. Mand. 160.* Earls Ranulf and Gilbert and Cadwaladr are in fact shown to have been at Chester together in 1151 or 1152 by a Shrewsbury Abbey Charter (Eyton, *Shrops.* x. p. 257).

[20] *Ann. Cest. s.a.* 1146. For Wich, Fulwich, Droitwich or Dritewich, on the borders of Cheshire and the Maelor district of Flintshire, see *Arch, Camb.* IV. vii. (1876), 91–3. Nantwich, suggested by Christie, is too far east.

[21] For the pedigree of the Norman lords of Mold see Helsby's edition of Ormerod's *History of Cheshire*, i. p. 58. Robert, hereditary steward of the earldom of Chester, was nephew of the Hugh fitz Norman who held half of Bistre and other lands in the Mold district in 1086 (Domesd. i. 269*a* (2)). Mold is "Mons Altus," which, like the Welsh "Y Wyddgrug" (The Burial Mound), refers to the great barrow known as the Bailey Hill, the site of the keep of the mediæval castle. There is nothing to support Powel's view (115) that under Rufus one "Eustace Cruer" did homage for Mold and Hopedale.

[22] His grandfather, Gruffydd ap Cynan, had "gwallt melyn" (*Buch. Gr. ap C.* 114 [728]).

²³ This was the well-known Castell (or Tomen) y Rhodwydd, in the township of Bodigre'r Iarll and the parish of Llanarmon. The identification will be found in Powel (147, marginal note) and was adopted by Pennant (ii. 13). In Leland's day (*Wales*, pp. 70–1) the place was used as a sheepfold; he knew it as Castell Cefn Du and had heard it belonged to Owain Glyndwr — no doubt a popular mistake for Owain Gwynedd. The Rev. John Lloyd of Ruthin visited it in 1693 and gave Edward Llwyd an account of it (*Arch. Camb.* II. ii. [1851], 57). "Y Rhodwydd" is explained as "The Mound" (*Goss. Guide*, pp. 134–5; *cf. Arch. Camb.* V. xii. [1895], 19–20); if this be correct, the later form, *Tomen* y Rhodwydd, is an instance of unconscious tautology. There is no sort of authority for the "Castell yr *adwy*" of the recent Ordnance Survey maps. Buddugre (for the form see Evans, *Dict. s.v.* and Thomas, *St. Asaph*, p. 622) was at a later period divided between the lord of the commote and Valle Crucis Abbey (Bodigre'r Iarll and Bodigre'r Abbot).

²⁴ Llywarch ap Trahaearn is last heard of in 1123 (see p. 467) and the strife among the members of his house which marked the years 1129 and 1130 was no doubt due to his death. Ultimately, Hywel ab Ieuaf ab Owain ap Trahaearn (for the pedigree see Dwnn, ii. 15) succeeded, holding the district until his death in xi85. That he acknowledged Madog ap Maredudd as his overlord maybe seen from the Trefeglwys charter ("Notum sit omnibus quod Madawc Rex Powissentium") printed (from a lost Wynnstay MS.) in *Arch. Camb.* III. vi. (1860), 330–1.

²⁵ The romance entitled *Breuddwyd Rhonabwy* begins: "Madawc uab maredud a oed idaw powys yny theruyneu. Sef yw hynny o porford hyt yg gwauan yg gwarthaf arwystli" (*Mab.* 144). There is a Nant Bryn Gwanon near the source of the Ystwyth, in the extreme south-west of Arwystli.

²⁶ *Myv. Arch.* i. 202 (148). The poet's Bangor is, of course, Bangor Iscoed. It may be noted that Madog, as the lord of the whole of Powys, could not, as has so often been asserted (Powel, 153; Carnh. 565; Yorke (2), 45), have given his name to Powys Fadog. The distinction between Powys Fadog and Powys Wenwynwyn obviously arose about 1200.

²⁷ For William fitz Alan and his family see Eyton, *Shrops.* vii. 211–62, and Round, *Peerage and Family History*, chap. ii.

²⁸ "Alanus filius Fladaldi qui honorem vicecomitis Warini post filium eius [a mistake] suscepit" (*Mon. Angl.* iii. 519). For Rainald see page 388.

²⁹ Ord. Vit. xiii. 37 (V. 112–3); Cont. Fl. Wig. *s.a.* 1138 (p. 110).

³⁰ See *Cymr.* x. 43, note (A. N. Palmer). It may be added that *Ann. Camb.* MS. C. has (*s.a.* 1151) the correct form "*ræ*dificavit".

³¹ For Owain Brogyntyn see *Dict. Nat. Biog.* xlii. p. 395. It may be added that "Oenus de Porchinton" appears frequently in the Pipe Rolls from 1160 to 1169 as receiving money by the king's orders from the sheriff of Shropshire.

[32] In 1152 Madog's son Llywelyn slew Stephen, son of Baldwin (*B.T.* 180; *B. Saes. s.a.* 1151). This was the lord of Montgomery, a castle which Henry I. had given to Baldwin de Bollers before 1121 (Eyton, *Shrops.* xi. p. 120) and which thus obtained its Welsh name of Castell Baldwyn (*Bruts*, 260, 295, 365, 376; *Myv. Arch.* I. 303 [214]). Tre Faldwyn, which is properly the vill and not the castle, came into use later.

[33] *Mab.* 144–5.

[34] See p. 244.

[35] This is suggested by the fact that Geoffrey of Monmouth, who was bishop of St. Asaph from 1152 to 1155, died without having visited his see.

[36] In 1093; see *Mon. Angl.* ii. 386.

[37] According to *Ann. Cest.* "comes Hugo ii" was born in 1147.

[38] Stephen died on 25th October, but Henry was not crowned until 19th December.

[39] *Ann. Camb. s.a.; Gesta St.* 16–17 (16), 95–6 (93), 103 (101). The day was 24th December; for the contention between Llantony and St. Peter's, Gloucester, for his body, see *Carl. Glouc.* i. lxxv. Roger afterwards raised, on the scene of the tragedy at Flaxley, a Cistercian abbey in memory of his father (Gir. Camb. iv. 219; *Mon. Angl.* v. 590).

[40] See page 438 above. In addition to Brecknock he had from his father the lordship of Upper Gwent, which Brian fitz Count had made over to Miles in 1141 or 1142. See the charter of the Empress Maud in Round, *Anc. Charters*, p. 43, and the notes following, in which the errors are exposed of the genealogical narrative in *Mon. Angl.* iv. 615.

[41] Gervase, i. 161–2; Eyton, *Itin.* 9.

[42] Gervase, i. 162; R. de Torigni, 184–5; Eyton, *Itin.* 10. Hugh is usually made out to be the son of the Ralph Mortimer of 1086 (see page 395 above), but a generation probably intervened. Wigmore and Cleobury were old Mortimer possessions, but Bridgenorth, then known as Brug, was a royal castle and was accordingly resumed by the king.

[43] For the events of this campaign see *Ann. Camb.; B.T.* and *B. Saes.* (*s.a.* 1156); R. de Torigni, 193, 195; Wm. Newb. ii. 5; *Ann. Cest.*; Gir. Camb. vi. 130–1 (*Itin.* ii. 7), 137–8 (ii. 10); Gervase, i. 165.

[44] In the second and third years of Henry II. the sheriff of Shropshire was allowed a deduction of £7 in respect of crown lands of that annual value given by the king to Cadwaladr (Pipe Rolls 43, 88). After Michaelmas, 1157, the grant appears in the name of John Lestrange (with 10s. added), to whom it was no doubt transferred when Cadwaladr recovered his Welsh possessions, and the entry in the Pipe Roll of the sixth as of succeeding years shows that it lay in Ness, in the hundred of Baschurch. *Cf.* Eyton, *Shrops.* x. p. 255.

[45] See Pipe Roll, 3 Hen. II. (1156–7), 89, for payments as follows made by the king's writ in that year through the sheriff of Shropshire: to "Maddoch," £8 10s., to "Geruetto," 40s., to "Hoelo filio Joaf," 40s. *B.T.*

186 has a curious passage about the conduct of Madog in this struggle, while *B. Saes.* (followed by Powel and others) sends him to Anglesey in command of the fleet! *Cf.*, however, *Ann. Camb.* MS. C. (*s.a.* 1158 = 1157) — "Henricus rex Anglorum movit exercitum versus Nortwalliam, adjuvante Madauc filio Maredut". Iorwerth Goch was the son of Maredudd of Powys (*B.T.* 188; *Mab.* 144); according to *The Dream of Rhonabwy*, he had no territory in the time of his brother Madog and had to be content with the office of captain of the guard (penteulu).

[46] Stubbs, *Const. Hist.* i. (3), p. 589.

[47] "Et in liberatione archiariorum regis in exercitu, 47s." (Pipe Roll, 3 Hen. II. 89 — Salopescire).

[48] This is suggested by the names of the leaders and by the following entry in Pipe Roll, 3 Hen. II. 108 (civitas Wintonie) —"Et in locanda una navi ad portandum corredium regis usque Pembroc, Rogero constabulario, £4".

[49] According to Gir. Camb., *Ann. Cest.* and Jocelyn of Brakelond, the fight took place near Coleshill. MS. C. of *B.T.* has "Koet Kennadlaoc," a name which probably stands for Pennardd Alâog, *i.e.*, Hawarden, now known to the Welsh as Penarlâg (Owen, *Pemb.* i. 419; *cf.* also the forms of the name in MS. E. of *B.T.* 372, and Pen. MS. 131, as cited in Evans, *Rep.* i. p. 821). Powel (150–1) and *Gw. Brut, s.a.* (1156) have "Coed Eulo," which may be a guess or from some unknown source. No precise indication of the site seems at present possible.

[50] Jocelyn of Brakelond gives this detail, his ultimate authority being Henry of Essex himself; see *Memorials of St. Edmund's Abbey*, edited by T. Arnold for the Rolls Series, i. 273–4.

[51] Henry was subsequently accused by Robert of Montfort of having had a traitorous design in this flight, and, after long delay, the matter was brought to the arbitrament of the judicial duel in 1163, when Henry was defeated. Much to the regret of the king, who believed his protestations of sincerity, he was forced to retire from secular life and became a monk of Reading (R. de Torigni, 218; Wm. Newb. ii. 5; Jocelyn, *ut supra*; Eyton, *Itin.* 61–2).

[52] To Cil Owain, *i.e.*, Owain's Retreat, says *B.T.* If, however, the chronicler wishes to suggest that the place, which is a mile south-east of St. Asaph, got its name from this incident, he is easily refuted, for "Chiluen" appears in Domesd. i. 269a (1) as a berewick of Rhuddlan.

[53] "Tal llwyn pina" (*B.T., Bruts,* 319), or "Tal llwyn pennant" (B. Saes.), is identified by Powel with Bryn y pin (151), above Kinmel, a spot which certainly fits in well with the geography of the campaign. There are no remains of entrenchments.

[54] The tract "O Oes Gwrtheyrn" (*Bruts,* 405; *Comment.* (2), 155) and the poet Gwalchmai (*Myv. Arch.* I. 197 [145]) both fix this battle at "Tal Moelfre," and I know of no Moelfre in Anglesey save the one on the east coast. The two

churches mentioned in the text are not far off; Llandyfrydog, which was also despoiled, according to Giraldus, is in the same district. On the other hand, it is noteworthy that *B. Saes.* mentions Aber Menai as the landing place, and, if this be correct, Gwalchmai's line —

"A menai heb drai o drallanw gwaedryar"
(And Menai ebbed not, for the inflowing of the streams of blood)

is much more to the point. "Eglwys ueir ac eglwys bedyr" can also be found at Llanfair yn y cymwd and Newborough, though it is doubtful whether the old church of Rhosyr was not Llananno, rather than Llanbedr.

[55] "Henricus filius Geraldi. . . velut alii volunt, filius fuit Henrici regis" (*Ann. Camb.* MS. B.); "Henricus. . . regis Henrici primi filius. . . ex nobili Nesta, Resi filii Theodori filia, in australi Kambria Demetiae finibus oriundus" (Gir. Camb. vi. 130 [*Itin.* ii. 7.]). Henry fitz Henry's lands were in Narberth and Pebidiog (i. 59 [De Rebus, i. 9]). There is no evidence as to the date of his birth, except that it befell while Nest was the wife of Gerald. The order of names in Gir. Camb. i. 59 seems to me geographical and not chronological.

[56] Robert was the son of Stephen, constable of Cardigan in 1136, by Nest, whom the constable may well have married after the death of Gerald. He succeeded his father at Cardigan and also had lands in Cemais (Gir. Camb. i. 59; *cf.* his gift of Llanfyrnach on the Taf to Slebech [Fenton (2), 347]).

[57] The sheriffs of London paid in the financial year 1157-8 72s. for wearing apparel for the use of Owain's hostages (Pipe Roll, 4 Hen. II. 114).

[58] Henceforth Rhuddlan is a royal fortress and not dependent upon the earldom of Chester.

[59] The authority for the year of the foundation is Dugdale (*Mon. Angl.* v. 261), who quotes from a chronicle of St. Werburgh's, Chester, not yet identified. The house was certainly in existence in 1147 (*Eng. Hist. Rev.* viii. p. 669) and the charters of Earl Ranulf are summarised in Charter Rolls, ii. 289–90 from an inspeximus of 1285.

[60] *Mon. Angl.* v. 262-3. Pipe Roll, 4 Hen. II. (1157–8) is the first which contains the allowance to the fermor (terra Willelmi Peurelli) of 20s. for lands in "Langedenedale" given to the monks of Basingwerk. All trace of the house of Templars which Henry at the same time set up between Rhuddlan and Basingwerk (R. de Torigni) has long since disappeared.

[61] "Gobeith a chedernyt a gogonyat y deheuwyr" (*Bruts*, 311).

[62] "Achastell arall ym mab udrut" (*Bruts*, 312; *B.T.* 166). For the situation of Mabudryd see p. 267; Spurrell's "Castell Moel," or Green Castle (*Carm.* 84), is in the wrong direction.

[63] The identity is assumed of the castle in Mabudryd and "gastell dinweileir yr hwnn awnathoed gilbert Iarll" (*Bruts*, 312), in the absence of any other indication of the situation of "Dinweilir".

[64] "Meibon Geralt ystiwert a Gwilim ab Aed" (*B.T.* 168); "meibion Gerald a William or hay" (*B. Saes. s.a.* 1145). "Willelmus filius Hay" was a son of the famous Nest (perhaps by "Hait," sheriff of Pembroke in 1130), who held St. Clears (Gir. Camb. i. 28, 59).

[65] *B. Saes.* treats William and Hywel as defenders of the castle against Cadell, but its authority as a translation is inferior to that of *B.T.*, which in this case is supported by the evidence of *Ann. Camb.* MS. B. For Walter fitz Wizo see chap. xii. note 78.

[66] The conjecture is due to Laws (*Lit. Eng.* p. 115). For Coed Rhath see Owen, *Pemb.* i. 49, 86, 315–6. Leland notices it (*Wales*, p. 117), though not by name ("a wood not veri greate"). It gave its name to one of the three commotes of Cantref Penfro.

[67] This is the date implied by *B.T.* and *B. Saes.* Both MSS. of *Ann. Camb.* assign the event to the year before Henry's first expedition, *i.e.*, to 1156.

[68] *De Rebus*, i. 1 (i. 22). He was about seven years old in 1153.

[69] See above, p. 440.

[70] The documents given (in English) in *Card. Priory*, 133–4, from the muniments of Gloucester Cathedral show that Gilbert Earl of Hertford (not Hereford) about 1145, with the consent of Bishop Bernard, confirmed to St. Peter's, Gloucester, the church of Holy Trinity at Cardigan, then held by Edward the priest.

[71] "Castell aoed ympenn gwern yn llan vihangel" (*Bruts*, 316). Pen y wern is close to the village of Llanfihangel Geneu'r Glyn.

[72] It is not easy to understand how Hywel was able at the end of this campaign of 1151, fought in North Cardiganshire, to fortify "gastell hwmfre yn dyffryn clettwr" (*Bruts*, 317; *cf. B. Saes. s.a.* 1150), though the name of Castell Hywel, still borne by the spot, points to a real connection. Possibly the notice has got out of its right place.

[73] Maredudd is praised, not only by *B.T.* (182–4), but also by Gir. Camb. (vi. 145 [*Itin.* ii. 12]), who further notices the singular fortune of Rhys, comparing it with the parallel case of Richard fitz Tancard, castellan of Haverford (vi. 85 [*Itin.* i. 11]).

[74] Roger was the second son of the Richard fitz Gilbert who was killed in 1136; his elder brother, Gilbert, the first Earl of Hertford, died without issue in 1152 and never held Ceredigion (*Geoff. Mand.* 271).

[75] For this castle see chap. xiii. note 40.

[76] There is no direct evidence of this, but an earlier date than 1158 seems unlikely.

[77] The statement of the *Bruts* (*B. Saes.* having here, it would seem, the better translation) is confirmed by *Ann. Theokesb. s.a.* 1158: "Rex, facta pace cum Reso, transfetavit".

[78] 14th August (Eyton, *Itin.* 40).

[79] For the story of this exploit see Gir. Camb. vi. 63–4 (*Itin.* i. 6); the date is supplied by *Ann. Marg. s.a.* 1158. *B. Saes. s.a.* 1175, preserving a notice which has dropped out of the Red Book text of (*B.T.*, explains the connections of Ifor Bach. The sheriff of Worcestershire paid "Iuori paruo" four marks in 1160–1 (Pipe Roll, 7 Henry II. 55).

[80] *B.T.* 188 (where the "Gwynedd" of MS. E. is a late blunder); *B. Saes. s.a.* 1157 (= 1158). The "trydyd" of the Red Book (*Bruts*, 320) is a scribal error; *cf.* Mostyn MS. 116 in Evans, *Rep.* i. p. 60. For Morgan and Iorwerth ab Owain see pp. 471 and 478 above. The Pipe Roll 3 Hen. II. (1156–7) is the last in which Morgan's name appears; in and after Michaelmas, 1158, the entry under "terrae datae" (Gloucestershire) is "Et filio [for fratri] Morgani xl. s̃. bl. in Carliun".

[81] He died in 1166 (*Ann. Marg.*), leaving only sisters to inherit.

[82] Eyton, *Shrops.* i. pp. 250–1.

[83] I can find no authority for the statement of Powel (153) that Madog died at Winchester, except the narrative of Rhys Cain (Cae Cyriog MS. in *Powys Fadog*, i. 119–120), which tells an impossible story and confuses John Fitzalan II. (the real son-in-law of Rohese of Verdun) with his great grandfather, the contemporary of Madog. See Eyton, *Shrops.* vii. p. 252. Gwalchmai's elegy gives the season of the year as "dechreu garawys," *i.e.*, about 9th February (*Myv. Arch.* I. 202 [149]). The churchyard of Meifod anciently included three churches, dedicated to Gwyddfarch, Tysilio and the Virgin (Thomas, *St. Asaph*, pp. 777–9); of these the last had been consecrated as recently as 1156 (*B.T.* 184).

[84] *Myv. Arch.* I. 212 (155).

[85] *Ibid.* 201 (148).

[86] *B. Saes. s.a.* 1162 has the correct reading, "Owein ap Grufud *ac* (not ap) Owein ap Madoc". The Maredudd ap Hywel who acted with them was probably the lord of Edeyrnion who in 1176 gave "Esgen gaynauc" (Esgair Gaenog, near Gwyddelwern) to the monks of Ystrad Marchell (*Mont. Coll.* iv. [1871], 21). "Kaer offa" (*Bruts*, 323) is a fancy form found in the Red Book, but not in the other texts of *B.T.* — see Ab Ithel's note, p. 197. The Pipe Rolls for the 5th, 6th, 7th, 8th and 9th years of Henry II., *i.e.*, from 1158 to 1163, regularly contain entries (62, 26, 38, 15, 3) of payments made by the sheriff of Shropshire for the maintenance of the castle and garrison of "Carrecoel," but, in conformity with the statement of the *Bruts*, the castle is not mentioned after Michaelmas, 1163.

[87] *Myv. Arch.* I. 212 (155). It is possible that the references in Pipe Roll, 6 Hen. II. p. 26, to the repair and custody of the Castle of "Dernio" or "Dermant" on behalf of the crown may have to do with an attempt made by the English king in 1160 to protect Edeyrnion from the attacks of Owain.

[88] For Hywel ab Ieuaf see note 24 above. *Ann. C.*, MSS. B. and C., and *B. Saes.* have the form "Walwern," but this appears to be inferred from "castellum dewalwern," or, as the Red Book has it, "daualuern" (*Bruts*, 322, 325), which in modern parlance becomes "Tafolwern". Possibly the true form is the "dywalwern" of Cynddelw (*Myv. Arch.* I. 241 [175]).

[89] Pipe Roll, 5 Hen. II. 21 shows that during 1158–9 the sheriff of Somerset paid 20 marks (due from him to the crown) towards the cost of the defences of Carmarthen.

[90] *Ann. Camb.* MS. B. and the *Bruts* furnish the names of three of the earls, *viz.*, those of Cornwall, "Bristol" (*cf.* "comes Bricstowensis Robertus" in Cont. Fl. Wig. 134) and Clare. The complete list is given by the poet Seisyll Bryffwrch in his reference to the repulse of the "pumieirll taer"; he styles them "iarll cernyw," "iarll brysteu," "iaril gwent" (Earl Richard was lord of Striguil)," iarll padrig" and "iarll clar" (*Myv. Arch.* I. 340 [237]).

[91] See chap. xiii. note 59.

[92] He was imprisoned in Worcester Castle, but contrived to escape.

[93] In Pipe Roll, 6 Hen. II. (1159–60), payments of £41 (23), £35 3s. 6d. (28), and £18 5s. (30) appear in respect of the castle of "Canter bohhan"; in the next roll (1160–1) the amounts are £63 (22), £82 12s. and £44 12s. 6d. (54), and in that of 8 Hen. II. (1161–2), £21 (56).

[94] According to Herbert of Bosham (*Mat. Hist. Becicet*, iii. 180), the mission of Thomas of London (then chancellor) to England in May, 1162, partly arose out of the disturbances in Wales.

[95] For this expedition and its incidents see *Ann. Camb., B.T., B. Saes., Ann. Marg.*, Gir. Camb. v. 374 (*Exp. Hib.* ii. 31); vi. 62–3 (*Itin.* i. 6), 81–2 (i. 10), 138 (ii. 10).

[96] Attributed to Merlin, but not in any known collection of prophecies bearing his name.

[97] Believed by Hoare (i. 130) to be the old ford across the Ebbw. The name Pencarn is still preserved in the neighbourhood.

[98] "Interventu Oeni avunculi sui" (Gir. Camb. v. 374).

[99] "Ad deditionem dolose magis quam virtuose compulso" (*ibid.* vi. 81).

[100] "Per Elennyth ac Mailennyth usque Radenoram" (Gir. Camb. vi. 138). Elenydd is the Plinlimmon region; see Gir. Camb. i. 117; vi. 119, 170, 171, 173; *Mab.* 62; Owen, *Pemb.* i. 203 (where it is derived from the river Elan and identified with Cymwd Deuddwr).

[101] "Decani [*i.e.*, rural dean] de Cantrefmaur." The canttef was included in 1291 in the deanery of Ystrad Tywi, but it may well have been a separate deanery at this date.

[102] Diceto, i. 311.

[103] This may be inferred from the position of the notice in the record of the year's doings in *B.T.* and *B. Saes.*

[104] I follow *Ann. Camb.* MS. B. *B.T.* and *B. Saes.* both mistranslate.

[105] For the situation of Mabwnion see p. 259.

[106] "Castell aber reidawl" (*Bruts*, 323) only appears here under this name. It would seem as if, after the destruction of the last Aberystwyth Castle of the older situation (for this see p. 426) in 1143, the chief stronghold of the district had been moved to the mouth of the Rheidol, a position which it ever afterwards retained, though people still insisted upon calling it Aberystwyth.

[107] *Mat. Hist. Becket*, iii. 70.

[108] *Ann. Camb.* MS. B.

[109] For the events of this campaign see *Ann. Camb.*, *B.T.*, *B. Saes.*, Gir. Camb. vi. 138 (*Itin.* ii. 10), 143-4 (ii. 12); R. de Torigni, *s.a.* 1164, 1165.

[110] So Wm. Newb. ii, 18 —"immenso tam ex regno quam ex transmarinis provinciis exercitu adunato". The "prydein" of *B.T.* (*Bruts*, 324) is more correctly "prydyn," as in *B. Saes.*, *i.e.*, Scotland (*Celt. Br.* (3) p. 241).

[111] "Et pro uestiendis coterellis, £137 9s. 8d. per breve regis. . . . Et pro ccc targis coterellorum Ernulfo scutario, £30 per breve regis" (Pipe Roll, 11 Hen. II. 31).

[112] *Feudal England*, pp. 265-6, 282-4. With the "promissio servientium" *cf.* the "promissa multitude" of the Council of Northampton.

[113] Pipe Roll, 11 Hen. II. 31, 68, 73.

[114] Eyton, *Itin.* 77-9. For Henry's fears see *Mat. Hist. Becket*, v. 174.

[115] This hasty visit to Rhuddlan is only mentioned in the *Bruts*, but, as pointed out in *Feudal England*, p. 284, it is implied in the reference in Pipe Roll, 11 Hen. II. 109 to "ii exercitibus".

[116] Henry granted a charter to the abbey of Préaux in Normandy "apud Album Monasterium in Valliis" (*Cat. Doc. Fr.* i. 116).

[117] Probably at Tregeiriog. Tradition locates the skirmish between Henry and the Welsh at Adwy'r Beddau, near Chirk Castle (Powel, 186-7; Penn. i. 363-4), but this spot is off the natural line of the king's march.

[118] *Arch. Camb.* IV. xiii. (1882), 102.

[119] Gir. Camb. (vi. 143 [*Itin.* ii. 12]) agrees with the *Bruts* that Henry was turned back "subita et inopinata pluvialium aquarum inundatione". Wm. Newb. (ii. 18) blames the "inextricabiles locorum difficultates".

[120] *Cf. Ann. Waverl. s.a.* 1165: "rex. . . perdidit obsides regis Audoeni". Rhys had three sons named Maredudd, but this was no doubt the "Maredudd Ddall (the Blind)" who died in 1239 (*B.T.*).

[121] For this visit see Eyton, *Itin.* 83.

[122] *Ann. Ult. s.a.* 1165 refer to this campaign and the aid given by the foreigners of Dublin.

[123] R. de Torigni, *s.a.* 1166 (p. 226). For the efforts made to retain the castles of Rhuddlan, Basingwerk, and Prestatyn see Pipe Roll, 12 Hen. II. p. 67; 13 do. pp. 77, 140, 160; 14 do. p. 199.

[124] The incident is recorded in Gir. Camb. vi. 143-4 (*Itin.* ii. 12), in a passage added by the author in the second edition of the *Itinerary*.

[125] With the accounts in *Ann. C.* and the *Bruts cf. git.* Camb. v. 229 (*Exp. Hib.* i. 2) and *B.T. s.a.* 1171 (p. 212). His name suggests that Rhygyfarch may have been a member of the famous clerical family descended from Bishop Sulien — see note appended to chap. xii.

[126] See a letter from "frater Nicolaus" of Rouen to Archbishop Thomas in *Mat. Hist. Becket*, vi. 77. Its date is clearly November, 1166. *Cf.* also Eyton, *Itin.* 99.

[127] One result of the victory of 1165 was that Godfrey, the Norman bishop of St. Asaph, who had been consecrated to that see in 1160 (Gervase, ii. 385; *Reg. Sacr.* (2), 48), was forced to retire from the district. The king

gave him a position as administrator of the abbey of Abingdon (*Chronicon Monasterii de Abingdon*, 1858, ii. 234–5, 293; H. and St. i. 362–4; Eyton, *Itin.* 88–9).

[128] Eyton, *Shrops.* ii. p. 109.

[129] *Cf.* the entries as to Chirk in Pipe Roll, 11 Hen. II. p. 90; 12 do. p. 59, and 14, p. 110.

[130] Pipe Roll, 12 Hen. II. 59, records a payment of 100s., "nuntiis Oeni de Chiuiliac" in the year 1165–6.

[131] The correspondence is to be found in H. and St. i. 364–75; *Mat. Hist. Becket*, v. 225–38.

[132] "De Bardsey," according to B. Willis, *Bangor*, p. 121. The surname, as given in the MSS. of the letters, is not to be identified.

[133] *Mat. Hist. Becket*, vi. 458, where the reference to "regum Gualliae" no doubt covers Owain.

[134] H. and St. i. 371–4; *Mat. Hist. Becket*, v. 236–9. *Cf.* also Gir. Camb. vi. 133–4 (*Itin.* ii. 8).

[135] Dwnn, ii. 107.

[136] R. of Torigni, *s.a.* 1171 (p. 251), and *Ann. Cest. s.a.* 1170, give the year; for the month see *B.T.*, and for the day, the reference in *Bruts*, 405 (O Oes Gwrtheyrn), to "wyl clemens". *B. Saes.*, which is one year in arrear from 1140 to 1170, divides the latter year into two (1169 and 1170) and thus gets its chronology right. *Ann. C. MS. B.* is one year in advance in its dating from 1154 to 1180.

[137] Gir. Camb. vi. 133 (*Itin.* ii. 8).

[138] His first appearance is in 1123 — see p. 466 — when he can hardly have been under fourteen years of age.

[139] For the subject-matter of section iv. the reader is referred to Stephens, *Literature of the Kymry.*

[140] See, especially, Prof. W. Lewis Jones's treatment of the subject in *Trans. Cymr.* 1898–9, 52–95; *Quarterly Review*, July, 1906.

[141] "Gaufrid[us] Monemutensis" in the Berne MS. (*Hist. Reg.* i. 1).

[142] No weight can be attached to the statements in *Gw. Brut. s.a.* 1152 as to his connection with Llandaff. Bishop Uchtryd seems, indeed, to have had a nephew named Geoffrey; see Cart. *Glouc.* ii. 55 for "Galfrido sacerdote nepote episcopi". But Geoff. Mon. was not ordained priest until a week before his consecration as bishop.

[143] So R. de Torigni, 75, 168; Gir. Camb. vi. 58, 179; Wm. Newb. p. 4.

[144] The "Galffrai ab Arthur" of *Gw. Brut* cannot, of course, be relied upon as evidence. See, however, Giry, *Manuel de Diplomatique* (Paris, 1894), p. 361, for patronymics of this form.

[145] See p. 396. Arthur is a very unusual personal name among the early Welsh (*cf.*, however, p. 521 and *Cymr.* ix. 171).

[146] *Hist. Reg.* xii. 5.

[147] *Mon. Angl.* vi. 251, where the comma is to be deleted in "Gaufrido, Arturo".

[148] *Hist. Reg.* i. 1.

[149] R. de Torigni, 64, 75.

[150] *Trans. Cymr.* 1898-9, 64-5.

[151] A difficulty is raised by the use of the imperfect tense in *Hist. Reg.* vii. 1, where mention is made of the stately retinue of Bishop Alexander of Lincoln ("non erat alter. . . alliciebat"), who did not die until 1148, in the year following the death of Earl Robert. It is best met by supposing Geoffrey to refer to a greatness brought to an end by the king's attack in 1139; no doubt, the words are to be found in the same form in the Berne MS., but it is not certain that the text of this MS. dates from 1136-8, as the dedication apparently does.

[152] H. and St. i. 360; R. de Torigni, *s.a.* 1152; *Ann. Waverl.* For the position of the see at this time see pp. 485, 494; the foreign origin of its first bishops is sufficiently shown by their names — i. Gilbert, 1143-?; 2. Geoffrey, 1152-5; 3. Richard (Gervase, ii. 385); 4. Godfrey, 1160-75.

[153] Rymer, i. 18.

[154] *B. SAES. S.A.* 1154 (= 1155); *B.T.* 184. Both have Llandaff for Llanelwy, a slip of the original chronicler, for Nicholas was bishop of Llandaff from 1148 to 1183. The phrase "ar offeren" (at mass) of the Red Book (*Bruts*, 318) is merely a misreading of "a rosser" — see Mostyn MS. 116 in Evans, *Rep.* i. p. 60.

[155] For Britannia = Wales see Asser, 7, 79, 80. Welsh is called "lingua Britannica" in *Hist. Reg.* ii. 1.

[156] Gir. Camb. (vi. 58, 179) and Wm. Newb. (pro œmium) were unbelievers, but from the time of Roger of Wendover until the Renaissance Geoffrey was in high repute as a historian. Polydore Vergil was among the first to cast doubt upon his trustworthiness and was answered by Sir John Prise in *Historiae Brytannicae Defensio* (London, 1573).

[157] *Myv. Arch.* II. 81 (432); Peter Roberts, *Chronicle of the Kings of Britain* (London, 1811), preface, xi.

[158] *Bruts*, xvi.-xx.; Evans, *Rep.* ii. pp. 39, 90.

[159] Geoff. mentions both Bede and Gildas (i. 1) and draws largely upon them, taking from the former, for instance, the substance of xi. 12,13, and from the latter that of i. 2; xi. 4, 5, 6. But he is silent as to his third and principal source, the *Historia Brittonum*, and it has been pointed out that his references to Gildas are very far from agreeing with what we know of that author's work (*Gildas*, ed. Mommsen, 23).

[160] The Berne MS. reads as follows (viii. 2): "oppidumque genoreu [Gannerew] petivit. . . . Erat autem oppidum illud in natione hergign [Erging or Archenfield] super fluvium guaie [the Wye] in monte qui cloartius [for 'doartius': Doward seems to be from Dougarth — *cf. Lib. Land.* 164, 408] nuncupatur". *Cf. Bruts*, 157; Usher, *Britannicarum Ecclesiarum Antiquitates* (Dublin, 1639), 62, 386.

¹⁶¹ The forms given are those of the Berne MS., which in its spelling of Welsh proper names is more accurate than the printed texts. They appear in the genealogies in Harl. MS. 3859 as "Dumngual moilmut" (*Cymr.* ix. 174), "Guurgint bar(m)b truch" (178), "Garbaniaun" (174) and "Cursalen" (173). Sometimes Geoffrey made a mistake, as when he was misled by the appearance of Guendoleu into taking it for a female name and bestowed it (ii. 4), as "Guendoloena," on the jealous wife of Locrinus. It thus happens that there is no Welsh equivalent for the English Gwendoline.

¹⁶² "Ipse [Allectus] post eum Britannias triennio tenuit; qui ductu Asclepiodoti praefecti praetorio oppressus est" (Eutropius, ix. 22, followed by Orosius, *adv. Paganos*, vii. 25). For the fuller accounts see Sextus Aurelius Victor, 39; *Panegyrici Latini*, ed. Baehrens, 132–48.

¹⁶³ V. 4, 5.

¹⁶⁴ XI. 3–7.

¹⁶⁵ "Karadoco Lancarbanensi contemporaneo meo" (xii. 20).

¹⁶⁶ "Nancarbanensis (for the form, see chap. vii. note 52) dictamina sunt Caratoci" (*Gildas*, ed. Mommsen, 3–4, 110; ed. Williams, 412).

¹⁶⁷ The original of *B.T.* and *B. Saes.* Caradog of Llancarfan, who is only known from Geoffrey's reference to him, has often been confused (*e.g.*, by Ab Ithel — see *B.T.* pref. xxiii-xxv) with Caradog the hermit, whose history has been handed down in detail and who died in 1124 (see p. 591).

¹⁶⁸ There is reason to think that not only the original of *B.T.* but also that of *Buch. Gr. ap C.* was written in Latin.

¹⁶⁹ The oldest extant Welsh MS. is the Black Book of Carmarthen, a collection of poetry put together in the latter half of the twelfth century. See *Blk. Bk.* pref. and Evans, *Rep.* i. p. 297.

¹⁷⁰ For the exceptional case of a story which was too elaborate to be recited without a book see the close of "Breuddwyd Rhonabwy" (*Mab.* 161).

¹⁷¹ See pp. 86, 130, 169–71.

¹⁷² *IV. Anc. Bks.* ii. pp. 1–2, 311–14.

¹⁷³ *LL.* i. 78, 436; ii. 18.

¹⁷⁴ Hence such local names as Pentref y beirdd and Tre'r beirdd (the bard's hamlet). The former is found in the township of Broniarth, near Meifod; of the latter there are several instances, *e.g.*, in mid-Anglesey (Llanfihangel T. B.), near Mold and near Llanidan. There was a "Wele Predythion" (Poets' holding) in the vill of Gest in Eifionydd (*Rec. Carn.* 40).

¹⁷⁵ *Myv. Arch.* I. 210 (154).

¹⁷⁶ Ven. I. xli. 6; Gw. I. xxxvii. 12, 13; *LL.* ii. 18.

¹⁷⁷ Ven. I. xiv.; Dim. I. xviii.; Gw. I. xix.; Lat. A. I. xxii.; Lat. B. I. xxi. 9. For the meaning of "Prydein" or "Prydyn" see *W. People*, p. 76.

¹⁷⁸ He had a "swyd" (i. 388), "penkeirdaeth" (i. 678) or "provintia" (ii. 833). A "bardd gorwlad," *i.e.*, one who came from another principality, was not subject to his authority.

[179] This appears from Ven. I. xiv. 5 (guedy ebart kadeyryauc ebard teulu).

[180] This is suggested by the fact that the "ynad llys," at the conclusion of the ceremony, got the buffalo horn, the gold ring, and the cushion used for it (Dim. I.
xiv. 7; Gw. I. xiii. 25).

[181] Ven. I. vi. 1; xiv. 5. *Cf.* Dim. I. xxv. 8; Gw. I. xxxvii. 8.

[182] Gw. I. xxxvii. ii. *LL.* ii. 18 (§ 28) amplifies the old rule to suit changed conditions.

[183] *LL.* ii. 18 (§ 26).

[184] For an early holder of the office see *Buch. Gr. ap C.* 118 (730), where it
is recorded that "Gellan telynyaur," Gruffydd ap Cynan's "penkerd," fell
in the retreat from Aberlleiniog in 1094. For the name Gellan *cf. Lib.
Land.* 146, 154.

[185] *Cambro-Br. SS.* 151. For the date assigned to the life see *Cymr.* xi. 128. The
poem is of a well-known class; in the *Myv. Arch.* there are poems to St. David, St.
Tysilio, and St. Cadfan.

[186] See note 88 to chap. xi. The mythical and traditional poetry associated with
the names of Aneirin, Taliesin, etc., is here left out of account, as yielding no
certain evidence of its date.

[187] *Dict. Nat. Biog.* xxxvii. p. 215.

[188] *Myv. Arch.* I. 190 (140). The reference is probably to the campaign of 1114.

[189] *Myv. Arch.* I. 193 (142). For "marw-ysgafyn" see *Mots Latins,* p. 215.

[190] In the fourteenth century Trefwalchmai (now Gwalchmai), in the commote of
Malldraeth, was shared between three kins who claimed descent from three
sons of Gwalchmai, named Meilyr, Dafydd, and Elidyr (*Rec. Carn.* 48).

[191] *Myv. Arch.* I. 194 (143).

[192] *Myv. Arch.* I. 200 (147).

[193] *Ibid.* 213 (156).

[194] *Ibid.* 214 (156).

[195] "Try anhebkor gwrda y telyn ay ureckan ay kallaur" (*LL.* i. 76).

[196] "Omnes quoque de curia seu familia viri citra doctrinam omnem citharizandi
per se peritiam tenent" (Gir. Camb. vi. 183 [*Descr.* i. 10]).

[197] *Myv. Arch.* I. 265 (190).

[198] The word is said to be of French origin (*Mots Latins,* p. 186); in the *Laws* it is
represented by "trulliad" (*LL.* i. 44).

[199] See Cynddelw's reference (*Myv. Arch.* I. 259 [187]): —

> "Twr kynuael yn kwytaw
> A flameu odrum yn edrinaw."
> ("Cynfael's keep topples over and flames roar above it.")

[200] *Myv. Arch.* I. 277 (198). "Kymer deu dyfyr" is the full name of Cymer on the
Mawddach — see p. 466.

[201] vi. 189 (*Descr.* i. 13).

[202] *Ibid.* 187 (i. 12).

[203] *Ibid.* 202 (i. 17), where a specially famous story-teller, Bledri, is mentioned, who nourished in the early part of the twelfth century. It has been supposed that he was one of the early disseminators of stories about Arthur — see *Arth. Legend*, pp. 373–4.

[204] Gir. Camb. vi. 167–8 (*Descr.* i. 3), where reference is made to such an early collection of royal pedigrees as may be found in Harl. MS. 3859.

[205] *Ibid.* 194–5 (*Descr.* i. 16). "Awen," whence the form "awennithion," has lost its special meaning of "oracular frenzy" and now denotes the poet's inspiration.

CHAPTER V

[1] *B. Saes.*, hitherto one year in arrear in its dating, divides the year 1170 into two ("Anno ix°." and "Anno dom. M°. c°. lxx°.") and is henceforth correct. Both *B.T.* and *B. Saes.* assign the murder of St. Thomas to the beginning of 1171, which shows that their original dated its years from the Nativity (25th Dec.).

[2] The chief authorities for the story of the conquest of Ireland are Gir. Camb. v. (*Top.* and *Exp. Hib.*) and the French poem entitled by its latest editor, G. H. Orpen, "The Song of Dermot and the Earl" (Oxford, 1892), but formerly cited by the name of its supposed author, Morice Regan. I have usually followed Orpen's chronology (xxxix-xli).

[3] *Ann. C., B.T.* and *B. Saes.* agree in assigning Dermot's exile to the year following the Berwyn victory, *i.e.*, 1166. This is also the date in *Ann. Ult.* For the visit to Henry see Gir. Camb. v. 227 (*Exp. Hib.* i. 1), "Song of Dermot," p. 262.

[4] Earl Gilbert died in 1147 (the year to be inferred from *Ann. C.* and *B.T.*) or 1148 (*Mon. Angl.* v. 270). The Welsh authorities (*Ann. C.* MS. B. *s.a.* 1149; *Bruts*, 326; *B. Saes. s.a.* 1171) call him "strangboga" and "vwa kadarn," but do not apply the title to his son. Netherwent, with its castle of Chepstow or Striguil, was held under Henry I. by Earl Gilbert's uncle, Walter fitz Richard, the founder of Tintern, who died without issue in 1138 (*Mon. Angl.* v. 270 — so also *B. Saes. s.a.* in an entry not belonging to the original chronicle). The lordship seems to have passed, through Gilbert, to his son, who is called "comes Strigulensis" (Gir. Camb. v. 228; *cf.* R. de Torigni, *s.a.* 1176) quite as often as Earl of Pembroke. The "Tristig" of *Bruts*, 326, is for the "stristig" of Mostyn MS. 116 (Evans, *Rep.* i. p. 60) and this for "striguil".

[5] Gir. and the "Song of Dermot" agree that there was an interview with the earl at this stage, but three years passed ere it bore any substantial fruit.

[6] Again Gir. and the poet agree as to the meeting, but the former obscures the fact that it led to no immediate result.

[7] "Le fiz godoberd ricard" ("Song of Dermot," v. 410). "Godebert," a Fleming of Rhos, is mentioned in Pipe Roll, 31 Hen. I. 137, as a landowner in the Pembroke district. Robert son of Godebert was one of three barons who joined in the gift of Rhosmarket to Slebech (Fenton (2), 347); both he and his brother Richard took part in the Irish invasion ("Song of Dermot," p. 264).

[8] "Per triennium in vinculis et careere tentus" (Gir. Camb. v. 229 [*Exp. Hib.* i. 2]).

[9] Son of the Henry fitz Henry who fell in 1157 (see p. 499). Meilyr's name points to a Welsh upbringing.

[10] The "Milo Menevensis" of Gir. Camb., expressly called in the "Song of Dermot" "le fiz leuesque de sein daui" (v. 450), *i.e.*, of David fitz Gerald. "M. filius episcopi" witnesses a charter of Bishop David's granted to Carmarthen Priory (*Carm. Cart.* No. 32).

[11] Son of William of Barry and brother of Giraldus. See *Exp. Hib.* i. 4.

[12] A prominent figure in the "Song of Dermot," but only once mentioned by Gir. (v. 230–1).

[13] For the true pedigree of Hervé see *Feudal England,* p. 523.

[14] See Gir. Camb. v. 259 (*Exp. Hib.* i. 19) for measures taken at the end of 1170. According to Gir., the earl had received some sort of a permission, but it was "ironica magis quam vera" (p. 248 — *Exp.* i. 13).

[15] "Mense Julio, rex congregavit barones sues apud Argentonium et cum ibi tractaretur de profectione sua in Hiberniam, legati comitis Ricardi venerunt ad eum" (R. de Torigni, p. 252).

[16] Eyton, *Itin.* 160.

[17] Gir. Camb. v. 273 (*Exp. Hib.* i. 28). The "Penbroc" of the "Song of Dermot," v. 2230, is clearly a guess.

[18] "Ris, rex Walensium, pacificatus est cum rege Anglorum," says R. de Torigni, *s.a.* 1171 (p. 251), apparently referring to an early period of the year. But perhaps the notice is out of its proper place.

[19] "Ac yna y deuth attaw yr arglwyd rys or (*read* ir) lle ydoed yn llwyn danet" (*Bruts,* 327; *B.T.* 210). "Llwyn danef occurs in *Bruts,* 149, as a translation of the "Daneium (Daneum in the Berne MS.) nemus" of Geoff. Mon. (*Hist. Reg.* vii. 4), which is no doubt the Forest of Dean. The forest is variously styled "Fforest y Ddena" (*Mab.* 245; *cf.* "y ddena" in *Cymr.* ix. 331), "silva Danubiae" (Gir. Camb. vi. 55), "Dena" (*De Nugis,* p. 76), and "Dene" (*Lib. Land.* 333; Domesd. i. 167*b*, 1).

[20] See p. 478. The fulness with which *B.T.* and *B. Saes.* give the history of this family suggests that their original had incorporated some local annals, perhaps those of the Cistercian abbey of Caerleon.

[21] See Pipe Roll, 18 Hen. II. (1171–2), p. 119.

[22] Gir. Camb. v. 274 (*Exp. Hib.* i. 29).

[23] He reached Pembroke on 21st September (*B.T.*).

[24] At Pembroke he granted a general confirmation of the rights of St. David's (Charter Rolls, i. 258).

[25] For the devotion of the invaders of Ireland to "Sein Daui" see the "Song of Dermot," vv. 987, 1938, 3442–55.

[26] Earl Roger of Hertford was with Henry and witnessed a royal charter at Pembroke on 7th October (Round, *Commune of London,* p. 152).

[27] The reading of *B.T.* is, of course, to be preferred to the "arwistli ac alvael" of *B. Saes.* Ystrad Tywi must in this instance be taken not to include the third cantref (Cantref Eginog). For the situation of Ystlwyf or Oisterlaph see Owen, *Pemb.* i. pp. 206, 213.

[28] William apparently received no compensation, but on his death in 1174 (Gir. Camb. v. 310 —"ob patris quern audierat obitum") his eldest son Odo received twenty librates of land in Braunton in North Devon "in escambium Castelli et terrae de Emelin quamdiu Resus filius Griffini ea habuerit" (Pipe Roll, 20 Hen. II. 89).

[29] *B.T.*, if we read "tachwed" for the obvious slip "racuyr," agrees with Ben. Abb. (i. 25) as to these dates.

[30] Eyton, *Itin.* 164–7.

[31] Suggested by the editor (G. H. Orpen) as really meant by the "portƒinan" of the "Song of Dermot," v. 2758. It lies, "a demi lui de sein daui" (v. 2761), opposite Ramsey Island — see Jones and Freem. 13.

[32] Ben. Abb. i. 30; Diceto, i. 351; Gir. Camb. v. 286–92 (*Exp. Hib.* i. 38, 40). For the "Alba Porta" or "Porth Gwyn" see Jones and Freem. 208.

[33] "Iustus yn holl deheubarth" (*Bruts*, 330; *B.T.* 218); "vstvs ar deheubarth kymre" (*B. Saes. s.a.* 1172). The position of the notice implies that the writ or other formal instrument was issued after the king's return to England.

[34] *B.T.* first uses the title in its account of 1165 and thereafter has it regularly. *B. Saes.* and *Ann. C.* are without it. We probably owe it in the first instance to the poets.

[35] Gir. Camb. vi. 64–5 (*Itin.* i. 6). St. Piran was a Cornish saint (H. and St. i. 157); his chapel, according to Leland (*Wales*, 35), was in Shoemaker Street (now Duke Street) — a description which does not suggest it was part of the castle buildings.

[36] *B.T.* p. 222; *B. Saes. s.a.* 1173.

[37] Diceto, *s.a.* 1174 (i. 384). The Pipe Roll, 20 Hen. II. (1173–4) records allowances made to the sheriffs of Gloucester, Oxford, and Hereford for food and drink supplied to Rhys and his men in this campaign (21, 77, 121).

[38] Ben. Abb. i. 73.

[39] *Ibid.* i. 74 ("duxit secum. . . mille Walenses"). This force must have been that of Rhys, since between 31st July and 8th August there was no time to collect a new one.

[40] "Y gwr aoed garedickaf gyfeillt gan y brenhin yn yr amser hwnnw" (*Bruts*, 333; *B.T.* 226).

[41] Ben. Abb. i. 92, whose date I adopt in preference to that of *B. Saes.* ("Duw gwyl Iago apostol," *i.e.*, 25th July). *B.T.* and *B. Saes.* give the particulars as to the "aliis regibus Walliae".

[42] For Cadwallon's ancestry see chap. xiii. note 59. "Y gefynderw" implies that Madog ab Idnerth had married a daughter of Gruffydd ap Cynan or of Rhys ap Tewdwr. As Gir. Camb. (i, 31) claimed kinship with Cadwallon, the latter is the more likely explanation.

[43] According to Gir. Camb.vi. 14 (*Itin.* i. 1), it was Einion *ab* Einion Clud who had a daughter of Rhys to wife, and this is for reasons of chronology more likely.

[44] Of unknown parentage. Gir. Camb. vi. 17 (*Itin.* i. 1) says he was a mighty hunter, but lost his right eye and became paralysed after shooting a marvellous doe which had horns like a buck's.

[45] For Caradog see chap. xii. note 150.

[46] This name has dropped out of *B.T.* For Ifor see page 507. *B. Saes.* makes Gruffydd a brother of Ifor, but from *Cartae Glam.* iii. 112–3 it appears that he was the son of Ifor and Nest.

[47] Gir. Camb. (vi. 49, note 2 — the passage only occurs in the first edition) confirms this statement as to the connection of Seisyll and Rhys. Seisyll had been previously married to Dyddgu, sister of Iorwerth ab Owain (*B. Saes. s.a.* 1171 — the "agharat" of the Red Book [*Bruts*, 328] is a slip due to the occurrence of the name in the previous line).

[48] *B.T.* and *B. Saes.* "Iarll bristaw" is Earl William of Gloucester, who was lord of Glamorgan from 1147–83.

[49] *B.T.* (222) is precise in its dates, and, if "yr eildyd (arbymthec — MSS. B. C.) o vis Medi" be taken to mean xvii. *Kal.* Sept., will be found correct in its mention of the days of the week. Gir. Camb. vi. 60 (*Itin.* i. 5) refers to the raid; it was foretold, he says, by Meilyr, a famous Welsh seer of these parts.

[50] This, too, was predicted by Meilyr (Gir. as above). The capture of Usk from the Welsh by the men of Earl Richard is recorded in Pipe Roll, 20 Hen. II. 22, and also in Gir. Camb. vi. 60–1, where it is said that the seer was thereat mortally wounded.

[51] "Idem vicecomes [Wm. of Briouze, sheriff of Herefordshire] reddit compotum de £333 6s. 8d. [= 500 marks] de fine Cadewallan et Enial Clut quem fecerunt cum Rege de animalibus, quisque de mille. In thesauro £59 12s. Et in Camera Curie per manum Rannulfi Poherii £63 per breve regis" (Pipe Roll, 21 Hen. II. 88–9). The balance of £210 14s. 8d. was never paid, though, in accordance with the system of the Exchequer, it appeared regularly in the rolls, being found as late as Michaelmas, 1189 (Pipe Roll, i Rd. I. 142).

[52] *Ann. Theokesb., B.T.* (see Mostyn MS. 116 in Evans, *Rep.* i. p. 60, for the true reading —"a rosser iarll henford"), R. de Torigni, p. 185. For charters granted by Roger to Brecon Priory see *Arch. Camb.* III. xiv. (1883), 143–51.

[53] Walter ceased to be sheriff of Herefordshire in the autumn of 1159, and is not heard of afterwards. For his charters to Brecon see *Arch. Camb.* as above, 152–4. Gir. Camb. vi. 51, note 3 (text of first ed.), appears to say he died a sudden death after a deed of treachery against the Welsh at Abergavenny. Upper Gwent had been acquired by Earl Miles in 1141 or 1142 (chap. xiv. note 40).

[54] Gir. Camb. vi. 29–30 (*Itin.* i. 2). There was a fifth son, William, placed by Gir. between Henry and Mahel, who did not live to succeed.

[55] According to a document of the time of Edward I. printed in *Mon. Angl.* iv. 615, Henry was slain "a quodam satellite nomine Senell filio Donwaldi iuxta castrum Arnaldi," i.e., Arnold's Castle, S.E. of Abergavenny.

[56] Gir. Camb. vi. 30–1 (*Itin.* i. 2). For a charter of "Maihelus de Herefordia" to Brecon, see *Arch. Camb.* III. xiv. (1883), 154–5. He had been given by his father as a hostage to Robert of Gloucester in 1142 (*Geoff. Mand.* 382). As "Matthaeo de Herefordia" he was a witness to the Constitutions of Clarendon in 1164 (Stubbs, *Select Charters*). For the Clifford lordship of Cantref Selyf in Brecknock see p. 438.

[57] The date of Mahel's death is not recorded, but it must clearly have been earlier than that of the massacre.

[58] The common account, drawn from *Mon. Angl.* iv. 615, makes Bertha the consort of Philip of Briouze, but for the true genealogy see *Dict. Nat. Biog.* vi. p. 229 (J. H. Round). For the Briouze family see pp. 402, 436.

[59] *Ann. C.; B.T.* 226; *B. Saes. s.a.* 1175; Diceto, i. 401; Gir. Camb. vi. 49–53 (*Itin.* i. 4).

[60] The original of *B.T.* and *B. Saes.*, a contemporary chronicle, is the authority for this event. *Gw. Brut* is the sole authority for the eisteddfodau of 1107 (= 1109) and 1135 (= 1136).

[61] "Phrydyn" (*B. Saes.*), "Phrydein" (*Bruts*, 334). See chap. xiv. note

[62] Only in *B.T.*, but *B. Saes.* is much given to omitting details. Gir. Camb. (vi. 187 [*Descr.* i. 12]) says: "tribus autem utuntur instrumentis; cithara, tibiis, et choro," and the same trio is found in *LL.* ii. 18: "telyn yhun a crud yarall a pybeu yr tredyt". The "crotta" (whence "crwth" and crowd) was a British musical instrument in the sixth century (Venantius Fortunatus, *Carmina*, ed. Leo, VII. viii. 64).

[63] P. 530.

[64] In ddition to the sons who died before him, *viz.*, Rhun (d. 1146) and Llywelyn (d. 1165), and the two hostages, Cadwallon and Cynwrig, blinded by Henry II., Owain had the following sons who survived him: (1) Hywel, by Pyfog, an Irishwoman. By Gwladus, daughter of Llywarch ap Trahaearn of Arwystli, (2) Iorwerth and (3) Maelgwn. By Christina, (4) Dafydd and (5) Rhodri. By an unknown woman, (6) Cynan.

[65] *Ann. C.* MS. B.; *B.T.* 206; *B. Saes. s.a.* 1170; poems in *Myv. Arch.* I. 418, 524 (281, 346). Graves discovered in 1903 on the farm of Rhos y Gad (Battle Moor), near Pentraeth, are supposed to be those of warriors who fell in this fray (*Arch. Camb.* VI. iv. [1904], 82–4).

[66] *Cf.* Gir. Camb. vi. 212 (*Descr.* ii. 4).

[67] "O wyl clemens hyt yn nos ynyt [Shrove Tuesday night] a blwydyn y bu varw cadwaladyr wedy owein" ("O Oes Gwrtheyrn," *Bruts*, 405). *B.T.* says "vis Mawrth" He was buried in Bangor Cathedral, by the side of his brother (Gir. Camb. vi. 133 [*Itin.* ii. 8]).

[68] "Ierverdum Troyndun, quod Kambrice simus sonat" (Gir. Camb. vi. 134).

[69] Powel, 166, followed by many others. The blemishes which excluded an heir under Welsh law were only those which incapacitated for judicial or military duties (Dim. II. xxiii. 9). Penn. (iii. 174–5), relying on local tradition, pointed out Iorwerth's tombstone in the churchyard of Pennant Melangell in

Montgomeryshire. But the effigy in question is of much later date than 1175 and seems to commemorate a thirteenth-century descendant of Rhiryd Flaidd (*Arch. Camb.* IV. viii. [1877], 321).

[70] *Myv. Arch.* I. 338 (235–6). For Tudclud see chap. viii. note 38.

[71] North (*Old Churches of Arllechwedd*, Bangor, 1906, p. 131) believes that the existing ruins may be in part of the age of Iorwerth.

[72] So far as is known, Dafydd had in 1174 no "ewythred" (*B.T.*) or "gevynderiw" (*B. Saes.*) on the male side. No doubt the chronicler meant to say "nephews".

[73] Ben. Abb. i. 51.

[74] Pipe Roll, 20 Hen. II. 7, 133, records two payments made to this messenger.

[75] Diceto, i. 397–8.

[76] So thinks Eyton, *Itin.* 85, note 5.

[77] "*Vix* obtinuit," says Diceto.

[78] *B.T.* and *B. Saes.* assign it to 1175, Diceto to 1174; the entries in Pipe Roll, 20 Hen. II. 9, 16, 94, show conclusively that it was celebrated before Michaelmas in the latter year. The sheriffs of London provided the lady's wedding outfit at a cost of £28 17s.

[79] *Myv. Arch.* I. 274 (196–7). "Vreyenhin Kemeis" points to the two years (1173–5) during which Dafydd held Anglesey.

[80] "Awdl. . . i Dafyd mab Owain" in *Myv. Arch.* I. 198–9 (146).

[81] "Canu. . . i Rodri fab Owain" in *Myv. Arch.* I. 199–200 (146–7). For "Rodri mawr mur ciwdodoed" see v. 16.

[82] Ben. Abb. i. 159.

[83] Ben. Abb. i. 162.

[84] Gir. Camb. vi. 144–5 (*Itin.* ii. 12). He is mentioned, with Dafydd, as one of the supporters of the king in 1173 (Ben. Abb. i. 51).

[85] Cynddelw in his elegy (*Myv. Arch.* I. 216 [157]) calls him "arglwyt. . . mochnant," "rwyf mechein," and "keinllyw kynlleith" For the division of Mochnant in 1166 see p. 520.

[86] Eyton, *Itin.* 214.

[87] I would thus explain the "rex de *Delwain*" of Ben. Abb.

[88] The lordship of Ellesmere was given by Henry I. to William Peverel of Dover, from whom it passed to his son, William, and his nephew, Walkelin Maminot.

[89] Gir. Camb. vi. 227 (*Descr.* ii. 10).

[90] He is not mentioned in *Ann. C., B.T.* or *B. Saes.* Gervase (ii. 411) has a short account, strongly hostile to Gir., of the struggle of 1198–1203.

[91] *De Rebus*, i. 1 (i. 21). Manorbier ("natale solum genialeque territorium") is described in *Itin.* i. 12 (vi. 92–3). For the year *cf.* i. 41 (*De Rebus*, i. 9), where it is said that Giraldus was not 30 (or 29?) at the time of his election in the summer of 1176, and viii. 292 (*Princ. Instr.* iii.), where it is said he was about completing his twentieth year at the time of the birth of Philip Augustus in August, 1165.

[92] See p. 538.

[93] Gir. v. 351.

[94] "Ex utraque gente originem duximus" (*Descr.* ii. 10 [vi. 226]).

[95] Pref. prima to *Descr.*

[96] *Invect.* v. 21 (i. 150); i. 4 (iii. 27).

[97] *Descr.* i. 15 (vi. 192–3).

[98] For his translations of place-names see vi. 36, 37, 92, 127, 131, 165, 169, 171, 172. His explanation of Ynys Lannog (see chap. vii. note iii) suggests that he made independent guesses and did not always follow local information. Nevertheless, there is no record of his preaching in Welsh; the interpreter in 1188 was Archdeacon Alexander of Bangor.

[99] See p. 482.

[100] "Tresque status annorum plurium" (*De Rebus*, i. 2 [i. 23]) means far more than "three years" (Brewer *in loco*). He was in Paris in 1165 — see note 91 above.

[101] Wharton (*Ang. Sacr.* ii. 374) suggested 1172 and this is accepted by Brewer (vol. i. pref. xv). But the first known event in the history of Giraldus after his return connects him with Archbishop Richard, who was consecrated at Anagni on 7th April, 1174 (*Reg. Sacr.* (2), 49).

[102] See, especially, *Spec.* ii., iii. and *Itin.* i. 3.

[103] "Monachus. . . sui solius curam agit. Clericus vero circa multorum curam solicitari tenetur" (*Top. Hib.* i. 30 [v. 176]).

[104] For the prevalence of a married clergy in Wales, see pp. 215–6.

[105] Gir. Camb. vi. 203 (*Descr.* i. 18).

[106] Son of William fitz Gerald. See note 28 above.

[107] See chap. xiv. note 64.

[108] "Veteranmn quendam archidiaconum terrae illius concubinam suam secum in domo publice tenentem" (De Rebus, i. 4 [i. 27]). Gir. does not name him, but "Jordano archidiacono" attests charters of Bishop Bernard (*Carm. Cart.* Nos. 26, 35), of Earl Roger of Hereford (*Arch. Camb.* III. xiv. [1883], 147) and of Henry of Hereford (*ibid.* 151, 152). From his name one would infer that he was not a Welshman.

[109] Probably obtained at the time of the Council of Westminster (May, 1175), for Bishop David was present (Ben. Abb. i. 84).

[110] *Itin.* i. 2 (vi. 20), 3 (47).

[111] i. 32, 56; iii. 73, 227, 325; Jones and Freem. 314.

[112] iii. 73, 227.

[113] i. 29.

[114] iii. 352.

[115] They were separate deaneries in 1291 (*Tax. Nich.* 274), and, no doubt, in 1175. It is possible that the division of the diocese of St. David's into four archdeaconries was of Norman origin and that the system had not been fully accepted by the Welsh. The Archdeacons of Carmarthen and Brecon first appear about 1120 (*Arch. Camb.* III. xiv. [1883], 49). For the dioceses of Bangor and St. Asaph see chap. xiii. note 25.

[116] The "ecclesia partium de Melenith" (i. 31) can be no other. See page 256.

[117] "Cui sanguine junctus fuerat." Probably his mother was first cousin to Cadwallon — see note 42 above.

[118] Ben. Abb. i. 90. For Godfrey's withdrawal from St. Asaph see chap. xiv. note 127.

[119] He was known as Adam de Parvo Ponte. See *Dict. Nat. Biog.* i. pp. 75–6, H. and St. i. 387, and the Benedictine *Histoire Littéraire de la France,* ix. (1750), 62, 64, 70, 73; xiv. (1817). 189–90. Hoveden (ii. 78) calls him "Adae *Walensi*". Gir. knew him well: "Parisius olim socii fuerant et conscolares" (i. 34).

[120] See p. 252.

[121] "Ecclesiam S. Michaelis de Keri" (i. 33). The parish included Mochdref (All Saints), which is not mentioned in *Tax. Nich.*, and it was therefore coextensive with the commote (Pen. MS. 147 in Evans, *Rep.* i. p. 915). Several of the old lists include Ceri in Maelienydd — see *Bruts,* 409; *Cymr.* ix. 328.

[122] "Quasi xv diebus ante Pentecosten [23rd May]" (i. 41).

[123] It was in the deanery of Maelienydd (*Tax. Nich.* 274).

[124] It was united to Cydewain and so became part of the lordship of the Mortimers and, ultimately, of the county of Montgomery.

[125] It was transferred to St. Asaph in 1849 (Thomas, *St. Asaph,* p. 310). At the Lateran Council of 1179 Adam gained a temporary victory over Bishop Peter, but the latter afterwards regained the church (i. 323).

[126] De Rebus, i. 8 (i. 40). The bishop held aloof, in view of the oath he had taken in 1148 (p. 482).

[127] De Rebus, i. 11 (i. 43–4). The place, "Wintoniam," suggests the time (Eyton, *Itin.* 205). Peter, who had a larger income as prior than as bishop (iii. 344), had been put at the head of Wenlock, which was a cell of La Charité sur Loire, after 1170 (Eyton, *Shrops.* iii. p. 249).

[128] Diceto, i. 415; H. and St. i. 384–5; *Reg. Sacr.* (2), 49. B.T. gives the bishop his French name of "Pyrs" (*Bruts,* 334), *i.e.,* Piers.

[129] He was there at the time of the Lateran Council (March, 1179) — see *De Rebus,* ii. 2 (i. 48).

[130] *Exp. Hib.* ii. 30 (v. 351). This visit, which may have lasted a year (Dimock, pref. to Gir. vol. v. p. xlviii), is not mentioned in *De Rebus.*

[131] No date is given in *De Rebus,* ii. 8 (i. 57), but it is natural to connect this appearance "in Marchiae finibus ad Walliam pacificandam" with the negotiations carried on with Rhys in July, 1184, at Worcester (Ben. Abb. i. 314).

[132] Giraldus was known to him and about this time visited him at his manor of Blockley (iv. 104).

[133] The first edition was ready in March, 1188 (*Itin.* i. 2 [vi. 20]).

[134] Fully described in *Itin.*

[135] At Geddington on 11th February. *Ann. Cest.* says it was at "Briexcoc," *i.e.,* at Bristol, a little later.

[136] See note 39 above and the statement in Ben. Abb. i. 355–6 that at the end of 1186 Henry was anxious to have "servientes" from Wales for foreign service.

[137] *Itin.* i. 5 (vi. 55); ii. 7 (126). His native name was Cuhelyn and he had been a faithful follower of Archbishop Thomas in his exile. Like a true Welshman, he was of ready tongue and much given to jesting (*Mat. Hist. Becket,* iii. 56, 528; Gir. Camb. vii. 68, viii. 83).

[138] See, especially, *Itin.* ii. 1 (vi. 105) —"in singulis cathedralibus ecclesiis, tanquam investiturae cujusdam signum, missam celebravit".

[139] *Itin.* i. 1 (vi. 15–16).

[140] At Radnor Rhys had resolved to join in the movement and he spent a fortnight in preparations. But he was then dissuaded from his purpose by his wife, Gwenllian, daughter of Madog ap Maredudd (*Itin.* i. 1 [vi. 15]).

[141] "Circa jejunii caput" (2nd March), says Gir. But the actual day must have been about a week later — see Stubbs, pref. to *Epistolae Cantuarienses* (Rolls Series, 1865), p. lxiv.

[142] *Itin.* ii. 13 (vi. 147).

[143] There is some doubt as to the real name of this bishop, which variously appears as "gwiawn" (*Bruts,* 337), "Gwion," (*B. Saes. s.a.* 1191), "Guianus" (Gir. vi. 125), "Wiano" (i. 85), "Guido" (Diceto, i. 420), "Gwido" (Ben. Abb. i. 165), "Guydo" (profession rolls — see H. and St. i. 385). The emphatic praise of *B.T.* (p. 236; *Bruts,* as above), his attitude in 1188, and the silence of the English chroniclers with regard to him after his appointment, all suggest, however, that he was a Welshman, and that Guido, or Guy, was a Latinised form of his Welsh name, which, in this case, was no doubt Gwion (see *Rec. Carn.* index, 317, for its occurrence in Gwynedd). The election of Gwion ended the long conflict between the Bangor authorities and the crown as to the filling of this see; he was consecrated at Amesbury by Archbishop Richard, after the usual profession of obedience, on 22nd May, 1177 (Ben. Abb. i. 165–6; *Reg. Sacr.* (2), 49).

[144] De Rebus, ii. 19 (i. 77). The "croesan" or jester was a familiar figure in Welsh courts (*LL.* i. 28, 30, 376, 650; ii. 760, 821, 899; Evans, *Dict. s.v.*).

[145] So Dimock in pref. to Gir. vi. pp. xxxiii-vi. A second edition was issued in 1197 and a third after 1213.

[146] Dimock, as above, p. xxxix. The second edition appeared about the beginning of 1215 (pp. xli-ii).

[147] *Itin.* ii. 5 (vi. 122–3). It is not quite clear which of the two brothers held Ardudwy, but if, as is likely, the "pontis cujusdam" of Gir. was at or near Aberglaslyn, the division was no doubt as above.

[148] "Y ulwydyn rac wyneb y ryfelawd meibon kynan yn erbyn yr arglwyd rys" (*Bruts,* 335; *B.T.* 230; *cf. B. Saes. s.a.* 1178).

[149] *Itin.* ii. 7 (vi. 126–7).

[150] *Ibid.* ii. 10 (137), 12 (145).

[151] *Ann. Cest. s.a.* 1177. Earl Hugh, who had been a principal rebel in 1173, had only just been restored to full possession of his lands (Ben. Abb. i. 135). He died on 30th June, 1181, and was succeeded by his son Ranulf (born 1170), who was knighted and married Constance, heiress of Brittany, early in 1188 or 1189 (*Ann. Cest.*). It is difficult to accept the statement of Powel (212) that Hugh was born in Cyfeiliog and thence derived his surname; in 1147 the commote was beyond a doubt in the hands of the Welsh.

[152] For Owain's possessions see p. 553. Carreg Hofa, a royal stronghold, had been taken by the Welsh in 1163.

[153] *B.T.* 233; *B. Saes. s.a.* 1187; Gir. Camb. vi. 142-3 (*Itin.* ii. 12). "O Oes Gwrtheyrn" says (*Bruts*, 405) Owain was killed at "gwern y vinogyl".

[154] *Itin.* ii. 12 (vi. 142).

[155] *B.T.*, 236; *B. Saes. s.a.* The year is made certain by the mention of the notable eclipse of 23rd June.

[156] "Yr haelaf o holl tywyssogyon kymry" (*B.T.*); "yr haylaf or kymre" (*B. Saes.*); distinguished for "largitas," says Gir. (vi. 145).

[157] The marriage of Madog ap Maredudd and Susanna, daughter of Gruffydd ap Cynan (for whom see *Buch. Gr. ap C.* . 118 [730]), is not directly attested by any ancient authority, but it is certainly made very probable by this allusion of Gir. ("consobrina sua. . . Oeni principis filia" — vi. 142).

[158] For Owain Brogyntyn see note 31 to chap. xiv. He is not mentioned in *B.T.* or *B. Saes.* or by Gir., but he is known to have given Gwernhefin and Llyn Tegid in Penllyn to Basingwerk Abbey, the latter during the episcopate of Reyner of St. Asaph (1186–1224). See Charter Rolls, ii. 290–1; *Mon. Angl.* v. 263. His descendants held Edeyrnion.

[159] The "Elisset" of Gir. vi. 142 (*Itin.* ii. 12). He succeeded Owain Brogyntyn in Penllyn; see *Mon. Angl.* v. 263 ("Helyso") and *B.T.* 258 (year 1202).

[160] *B.T.* 233; *B. Saes. s.a.* For Hywel's ancestry see note 24 to chap. xiv. Cynddelw celebrates him as "tarw talgarth" (*Myv. Arch.* I. 254 [184]), referring, no doubt, to the place of that name near Trefeglwys.

[161] Brithdir is a township in the parish of Llanidloes (Carlisle, *Top. Dict.*).

[162] For Robert fitz Martin see pp. 425, 431. The pedigree of the family will be found in Owen, *Pemb.* i. p. 491, but there is some uncertainty as to the earlier links. Robert appears in *Lib. Land.* 37 [1128], Pipe Roll, 31 Hen. I. 15 [1130], *B.T.* 158 [1136], *Geoff. Mand.* 94 [1141], and *Cal. Doc. Fr.* i. 290. William is not traceable, at least in Wales, before 1191; hence he may have been a grandson of Robert.

[163] See notes 43 and 87 above. The death of Einion o'r Porth is recorded in *B.T. s.a.* 1191; he is clearly the same as the donor to Cwm Hir called Einion "de Porta" in *Mon. Angl.* v. 459.

[164] For this affair see *B.T.* and *B. Saes. s.a.* 1179; Diceto, i. 437; Pipe Roll, 25 Hen. II. 39; Eyton, *Shrops.* iv. pp. 205–6. In Powel, 173, and *Gwydir Fam.* 15, there is confusion between Cadwallon and Cadwaladr ap Gruffydd.

[165] Gir. Camb. vi. 50–1 (*Itin.* i. 4).

[166] Ben. Abb. i. 288–9; Gir. Camb. vi. 51–2 (*Itin.* i. 4); Eyton, *Itin.* 248. The site of the castle was still pointed out at the beginning of the nineteenth century — see Hoare, *Itin.* i. 90.

[167] Gir. Camb. vi. 119 (*Itin.* ii. 4).

[168] Ben. Abb. i. 314; Eyton, *Itin.* 256. *Ann. Cest. s.a.* 1184 combines in one notice the events of 1182–4; its "vice comitem *Wigorniae*" must be meant for Ranulf Poer.

[169] Ben. Abb. i. 317.

[170] Ben. Abb. (i. 355–6) describes the business of the envoys; the account of the dinner is from Gir. Camb. (i. 57–8 [De Rebus, ii. 9]), who was present. It may be remarked that Brewer's marginal date, 1184, is impossible, since William did not become bishop of Hereford until the summer of 1186.

[171] Walter fitz Robert was a grandson of Richard fitz Gilbert, the first Norman lord of Clare (*Feudal England*, p. 475). Bishop William was either the son or the grandson of Aubrey de Vere (d. 1141) and his wife Adeliza, daughter of Gilbert fitz Richard (*Geoff. Mand.* 390–2).

[172] In the summer of 1188 Glanville obtained a large force of Welsh mercenaries tor Henry, who took part in the operations against Philip Augustus and returned in October (Ben. Abb. ii. 40, 46, 50).

[173] Earl Hugh died on 30th June, 1181 (*Ann. Cest.*). Ben. Abb. i. 277, agrees as to the year and *Mon. Angl.* iii. 218 as to the day. Ranulf was born in 1170 (*Ann. Cest.*).

[174] Ormerod's *History of Cheshire*, ed. Helsby, i. p. 58.

[175] See p. 553.

[176] Eyton, *Shrops*, xi. 229.

[177] *Ibid.* xi. 120–7.

[178] Pp. 547–8.

[179] Gir. Camb. vi. 23 (*Itin.* i. 2).

[180] Ben. Abb. i. 125; Diceto, i. 407; R. de Torigni, 270; Gir. Camb. v. 332–4 (*Exp, Hib.* ii. 14); *Ann. Camb.* MSS. B. and C.; *Ann. Ult. s.a.* 1176.

[181] Ben. Abb. ii. 73. For William's career see *Dict. Nat. Biog.* xxxvi. p. 225.

[182] *Ann. Marg.* See p. 508 above.

[183] Diceto, i. 415.

[184] *Ann. Marg., Ann. Theokesb.*, R. de Torigni (308). When the latter closed his chronicle, the future of Hawise was still uncertain; he says that the king "cui voluerit dabit eam".

[185] *Ann. Marg.*, illustrated by Pipe Roll, 31 Hen. I. (1184–5), as cited in *Cartae Glam.*, i. 27–31.

[186] *Cartae Glam. ut supra.*

[187] Gir. Camb. vi. 72 (*Itin.* i. 8). For the family see p. 440. Besides Morgan, Caradog left three other sons, Maredudd, Owain, and Cadwallon, of whom Owain was killed by Cadwallon sometime before 1183 and Cadwallon was struck down soon afterwards at the siege of a castle (Gir. Camb. vi. 69 [*Itin.* i. 7]).

[188] He appears in the Pipe Roll (*Cartae Glam.* i. 29) as one of six who during 1184-5 kept the castles of Glamorgan and Gwynllwg for the king.

[189] Gir. Camb. (vi. 145 [*Itin.* ii. 12]) couples him with Dafydd ab Owain as having won the confidence and respect of both nations by a judicious impartiality of attitude.

[190] See note 140 above.

CHAPTER VI

[1] 6th July.

[2] Gir. Camb. i. 80-4 (*De Rebus*, ii. 21).

[3] "Tabulas grandes Itinerarium suum et laborem annuum nusquam adhuc alibi scriptum continentes" (p. 82).

[4] *Ann. C.*, MS. B. *s.a.* 1189, Gir. Camb. vi. 80 [*Itin.* i. 10]. "Abercorran" is the ancient name of the town at the mouth of the river Corran now known as Laugharne; "Talacharn" is properly the commote in which it stands, Laugharne being a shortened form of "Castell Talacharn" — *cf.* Builth, Kidwelly, Cardigan (Owen, *Pemb.* i. 46, 206; Gir. Camb. vi. 172, 239; Carlisle, *Top. Dict. s.v.* Llacharn). Gir. treats the devastation of Rhos on this occasion as a judgment upon the inhabitants for their refusal to pay tithes of their wool (i. 24 [*De Rebus*, i. 3]).

[5] "Patriam prae morte regis valde turbatam plurimum adventu et interventu suo pacificavit" (p. 84).

[6] Gervase, i. 457; ii. 86.

[7] "Episcopo de Asfath in Wallia, episcopo de Pangor in Wallia" (Ben. Abb. ii. 79).

[8] Ben. Abb. ii. 78.

[9] *Ibid*, 87-8. It was, no doubt, at this time that the Welsh princes made the promise, recorded by Richard of Devizes (ed. Stevenson, 1838, pp. 8-9), not to attack England while the king was on crusade.

[10] Ben. Abb. ii. 97. *Ann. C.* MS. B. lays stress on the tact that the peace between Rhys and John was "privata".

[11] "Sicut rex pater suus solebat" is added by Hoveden (iii. 23) to the narrative of Ben. Abb.

[12] *Ann. C.* MS. B. St. Clear's is mentioned in the *Itinerary* (i. 10) as a castle held in 1188 by enemies of the Welsh. Its archers killed a young Welshman who was hastening to the archbishop to take the cross.

[13] *B.T.* 236; *B. Saes. s.a.* 1190. For William's father Maurice see pp. 430, 470. William had succeeded to the lordships of Ogmore and Kidwelly about 1160; see his "carta" in *Lib. Nig.* i. 113, showing that in 1166 he held one knight's fee in Wiltshire.

[14] *Ann. C.* MS. B. *s.a.* 1191; *B.T.* 236. *Ann. C.* MS. C. has "Kemer" by mistake, and the "dyneinir" of *B. Saes. s.a.* 1191 represents the "de newer" of the Latin original. Gir. Camb. vi. 111-12 (*Itin.* ii. 2) accuses Rhys of breaking solemn oaths in thus attacking William.

[15] For the family see p. 425. Philip son of "Wiz" and his son Henry gave lands in "Dungledi," *i.e.*, Deugleddyf, to the commandery of Slebech (Fenton (2), 347).

[16] See *Ann. C.* MS. B. *s.a.* 1189 —"Willelmoque de breusa *socero* suo". Matilda died in 1210 (*B.T.* 266).

[17] Rhys is known to have been the son of Gwenllian of Powys—see Jesus Coll. MS. 20 in *Cymr.* viii. 88 (No. 27). For his epithets see the poem of Prydydd y Moch in *Myv. Arch. I.* 293 (207).

> "Rys uychan y galwant—ys geu!
> Rys uawr ualch yg calch yg cadeu!
> Rys gryc y galwant golofyn peu —
> Nyd Rys gryc yn kynnyc kameu!"

[18] "Hominique sub sole quern magis exosum habebat, Mailgoni scilicet fratri suo," says Gir. Camb. (vi. 112 [*Itin.* ii. 2]).

[19] *B.T.* 234; *B. Saes. s.a.* 1187.

[20] Gir. calls Gruffydd "viri versipellis et versuti" (vi. 111). It was, perhaps, an instance of his adroit manoeuvring that, while professing great anxiety to join the crusade (so I understand "altercantibus de crucis susceptione fratribus"), he contrived that the impetuous Maelgwn should actually go with the archbishop (vi. 119, 122).

[21] One may thus explain the fervid adulation of the author of *B.T.* (pp. 234 234–6).

[22] "Kyt bei kymhedrawl y ueint" (*Bruts*, 336; *B.T.* 234).

[23] P. 568.

[24] He died in 1237 (*Ann. C.* MS. B.; *B.T.* 326).

[25] The "*madawc* uab rys" of *Bruts*, 337 (*B.T.* 236) is an error of the Red Book text.

[26] The account in *Ann. C.* and the *Bruts* is supplemented by Gir. Camb. vi. 112 (*Itin.* ii.2).

[27] Richard was out of England from 11th December, 1189, to 13th March, 1194.

[28] Richard of Devizes, p. 30.

[29] *Ibid.* p. 32.

[30] *Ann. Waverl. s.a.* 1193; Gervase, i. 515.

[31] *Sym. El.* i. ep. xxviii. (i. 295). Gir. does not specify his errand, but it laid him open to the charge of being too friendly with his Welsh relatives (p. 296).

[32] He sailed from Portsmouth on 12th May.

[33] He was sheriff of Herefordshire from 1192 to 1199 and a justice itinerant in Staffordshire in 1196 (*Dict. Nat. Biog.* vi. p. 229).

[34] He was still "inclitus adolescens" (*Ann. C.* MS. B.) and "gwas ieuanc" (*B.T.* 256) when he died in 1201. Two other sons of the Lord Rhys bore this name, *viz.*, Maredudd Ddall (the Blind), blinded by Henry II. in 1165, who became a monk of Whitland and died there in 1239 (*B.T.* 326), and Maredudd, Archdeacon of Cardigan (*B.T.* 316), who died in 1227. The indices of *Bruts* and *B.T. do* not properly distinguish the chieftain, the Cistercian monk, and the secular cleric.

[35] I follow *B. Saes.* in connecting the imprisonment, and not the capture, with Ystrad Meurig.

[36] "Hu dysai" (*Bruts,* 338); "Hvgyn o Say" (*B. Saes. s.a.* 1196). Osbern fitz Richard (for whom see p. 395) had been succeeded by his son Hugh and his grandson Osbert (*Feudal England,* pp. 176, 179; *Lib. Nig.* i. 217), but shortly before 1189 Richard's Castle came into the possession of "Hugo de Say" (Pipe Roll, i Rd. I. 143).

[37] *Ann. C.* MSS. B. and C., *B. Saes.* and MS. C. of *B.T.* (p. 244) all give the day as iv Kal. Maii, whence Powel's "fourth daie of Maie" (181).

[38] He was born about 1132 (chap. xiii. note 53).

[39] *Ann. C.* MSS. B. and C.; *cf. B.T. s.a.* 1233 (p. 322 — burial of Rhys Gryg). The tomb and effigy ascribed to him by tradition (Fenton (2), 45; Hoare, *Itin.* ii. 25) are of the fourteenth century (Jones and Freem. 113–5). For elegiac verse composed in his honour see *Ann. C.* 61; *B.T.* 246–8; Fenton (2), 47.

[40] The story is told in *Ann. Wint. s.a.* 1197.

[41] The Register of Aberconwy printed in vol. i. (1847) of the *Camden Miscellany* cites his epitaph and says he was buried near the high altar (p. 7).

[42] Gervase (i.543) and *Ann. Cest.* (*s.a.* 1196) confirm the account of the *Bruts.* The "Henri" of the Welsh accounts is probably due to a perfunctory extension of an original "H".

[43] For the early history of the place see pp. 248, 421. The assumption very generally made since the time of Camden, that the site of the early castle of Trallwng is marked by the present Powis Castle, appears to be without foundation. "Y Castell Coch," as the Welsh style it, is not in either of the old townships of Pool (Pool town and Welsh town), but in that of Trallwm *Gollen.*

[44] Owain held Maelor Saesneg; see *Mon. Angl.* v. 325, for his grant (as "Owynus filius Griffini de Bromfeld") to Combermere Abbey in 1195 of tithes accruing from his lordship of "Overtone et Bumfeld". This district, which in 1086 was reckoned a part of Cheshire (see "Beddesfeld" and "Hurdingberie" in Domesd. i. 2640, 2) was held in 1138 by William Peverel (who fortified "Obretonam" — Ord. Vit. xiii. 37) and under Henry II. by Roger and Jonas of Powis.

[45] In a Valle Crucis charter of 1202, printed in *Arch. Camb.* III. xii. (1866), 414, Madog grants "omnem pasturam tocius terre mee scilicet Malaur Saisnec et provincie de Maylaur et Yayl et Nanhendu et Kenylleid".

[46] In all the lists of commotes Mochnant above Rhaeadr is separated from Mochnant below Rhaeadr, and the one appears in Powys Wenwynwyn, the other in Powys Fadog. The division of 1166 (see p. 520) must, therefore, have been permanent. It is perhaps hardly necessary to say that the common account of Powys Fadog as owing its name to Madog ap Maredudd (Powel, 153; Penn. i. 277) is a quite impossible one. The elder Madog had the whole of the province, and the two names clearly could not have arisen before 1195.

[47] *B. Saes.* is right in reading "Owein or brithtir *vab* Howel ap Ieuaf"; *cf. B.T.* 250, notes *a* and 3, and the notice of the death of Hywel in 1185 (*B.T.* 233).

[48] The "curiam regis adivit" of *Ann. C.* MS. B. is to be interpreted in the light of Hoveden, iv. 21 ("Hubertus. . . fines Gwalliae adiit").

[49] "Regi pro Carrec Huwa dedit" (*Ann. C.* MS. B.). The castle was in Welsh hands in 1187—see p. 565.

[50] *Ann. Wint. s.a.* 1198.

[51] "Talu y hen deilygdawt yr kymry ae hen briodolder ae teruyneu" (*Bruts,* 341; *B.T.* 252). From this point on the evidence of *B. Saes.* is no longer available, owing to the loss of the latter portion of the MS., Cleopatra B. v. Fo. 1620 is the last which is quite legible; 1626 is filled to the last line, but was for so long a time an outside page that it is now most difficult to read.

[52] *Ann. Camb. s.a.* 1195; *B.T.* 240; *B.Saes. s.a.* 1195. There had been an earlier Mortimer conquest of Cymaron in 1144, and in 1181 it apparently came into the king's hands on the death of Roger's father Hugh (Eyton, *Shrofs.* iv. p. 206). For the sons of Cadwallon see Gir. Camb. i. 32 (*De Rebus,* i. 5).

[53] *B.T.* 250; *B. Saes. s.a.* 1197.

[54] He was slain by his brother (*B.T.,* 236; *B. Saes. s.a.* 1191), and the allusion of Gir. Camb. (vi. 19) in the later editions of the *Itinerary* (i. 1) to terrible crimes committed "in his inter Waiam et Sabrinam. . . finibus his nostris diebus" by kinsfolk jealous of each other's power may be taken to show that the incident was one of a series. The culprit was possibly Gwallter ab Einion Clud, who appears in 1215.

[55] The two commotes are known to this day as the hundreds of Colwyn and Painscastle.

[56] *Ann. Wigorn.* Camden (*Britannia,* 568) identified "Matildis castrum" with "Colewent," *i.e.,* Colwyn, but a careful collation of the English and Welsh authorities for the events of 1198 and 1231 will make it clear that Painscastle is really the fortress intended. Breconshire tradition preserved a lively image of "Moll Walbee," who was believed to have built Hay Castle in a single night (*Breconsh.* (2), p. 57), while a legend was current among the Welsh which gave "Mallt Walbri" the part of Gessler in a doublet of the story of Tell and the apple (Pen. MS. 131 in Evans, *Rep.* i. p. 819).

[57] *Ann. Camb.* MS. B.; *B.T.* 252; *Ann. Cest. s.a.* 1198 (for "Paui," which misled the editor, read "Pain"); Hoveden, iv. 53; Gervase, i. 572; Diceto, ii. 163; Gir. Camb. i. 91, 95 (*De Rebus,* iii. 2, 4). In the first of his two references, Gir. has antedated the battle.

[58] Gervase makes the archbishop leader on this occasion. But the king had already on 11th July transferred the justiciarship to Geoffrey (Rymer, i. 71), who accordingly appears as the general in Hoveden, and this agrees with the statement of Gir. Camb. (iii. 25) that Hubert heard the news of the victory at Bridgenorth (castrum Brugense).

[59] "Die festo sancti martyris Ypoliti" (Diceto). *Ann. Cest.* has "ije idus [12th] Augusti". Either date fits in with the statement of MSS. C. E. of *B.T.* that the siege began about 22nd July ("ar ael gwyl Vair Vadlen") and lasted three weeks.

[60] See p. 550.

[61] "Or pan vu varw owein [November, 1170], yny anet llywelyn vab Iorwerth dwy vlyned a hanner. Or pan anet llywelyn yny las owein vab Madawc ar ymlad gwern y vinogyl [1187 — see p. 565]: pedeir biyned ardec" (O Oes Gwrtheyrn in *Bruts,* 405).

[62] "Llewelyn. M. marereda. Mereh madawc. M. maredud," says Jesus Coll. MS. 20 (*Cymr.* viii. 88), and this is confirmed by Prydydd y Moch, who calls Llewelyn not only "wyr ywein," but also "wyr madawc" (*Myv. Arch.* I. 301 [213]). In view of this evidence, the suggestion of Eyton (*Shrops.* vi. p. 160), founded upon *Mon. Angl.* vi. 497, that Llywelyn's mother was of the Corbet family, can hardly stand; it may be that on her widowhood she married a Corbet and that it was thus Llywelyn came to call William Corbet "avunculi mei".

[63] That he was born there (Penn. ii. 303) is merely a conjecture ("it is thought credible," says Sir John Wynne in *Gwydir Fam.* 15).

[64] Gir. Camb. vi. 134 (*Itin.* ii. 8), in a passage added to the *Itinerary* about 1197. Yet it would appear that Iorwerth had, like his father and his brother-in-law, Gruffydd Maelor (see p. 566), married his first cousin.

[65] See p. 522.

[66] Powel, 165.

[67] See p. 286.

[68] Gir. *ut supra.* "Puer tune duodennis" overstates the case; Llywelyn was fifteen. The "quasi" of the third edition shows that the author became aware that he had been too positive.

[69] Soon after 1188 ("in brevi postmodum"), says Gir. Camb. (vi. 126-7 [*Itin.* ii. 7]), but not in 1193, as Dymock suggests in his note, for the passage is found in the first edition, issued in 1191.

[70] "Drwy nerth gwrthrych urenhin manaw," says *B.T.* 238 (*Bruts,* 337), but *B. Saes.* (*s.a,* 1193) has more correctly "*meibion* Godrich". Godred of Man died in 1187, leaving a lawful son, Olaf, under age, and a natural son, Reginald, who at once assumed power and ruled the island at this period. For Rhodri's marriage, see p. 617.

[71] "O Oes Gwrtheyrn" assigns "haf y gwydyl" (*Bruts,* 405) to a year which is clearly 1193. For the explanation *cf. Comment.* (2), 156-7 (Moses Williams).

[72] The authorities for this revolution in Gwynedd are Gir. Camb. vi. 134 (added to *Itin.* ii. 8 in the second edition, *i.e.* in 1197); *B.T.* 240; *B. Saes. s.a.* 1194; *Ann. C.* MS. B.; and the following poems — Cynddelw to Llywelyn (*Myv. Arch.* I. 262-3 [189]), Prydydd y Moch to Llywelyn (*ibid.* 297-300 [210-2]) and to Rhodri (*ibid.* 284 [202]). Gir. draws no distinction between the fate of

Rhodri and that of David, while the *Bruts* place Rhodri among the victorious allies. The poets do not furnish a clear solution of the problem, for, in one poem Prydydd y Moch speaks of "plygu rodri rwyd esgar ymon," while in another he seems to leave Rhodri victor, even after the battle of Aberconwy. "O Oes Gwrtheyrn" confirms the mention by the poets of a battle of "Coettaneu" (*Bruts*, 406 — *cf.* "Coytdanew" in *Rec. Carn.* 57) and assigns it to 1194.

[73] *Ann. C. s.a.* and *Bruts*, 406. He is said to have been buried at Holyhead (*Gwydir Fam.* 19).

[74] Prydydd y Moch calls him "vt mwynbell mon," "rwyf kemeis," and "rwy dygannwy" (*Myv. Arch.* I. 288–9 [204–5]). He died in 1200, and was buried at Aberconwy (*B.T.* 254).

[75] See *B.T.* and *B. Saes.* Gir. also says that something was left to David (vi. 134).

[76] The Red Book text has an "a" before "dauyd ab owein gwyned" (*Bruts*, 341) which is not in *B. Saes.* or in MS. C. (*B.T.* 250, note 1) and gives a different and much less likely meaning to the passage. The justiciar came to the Welsh frontier in January, 1198, and arranged for Dafydd's release — see note in Feet of Fines, 9 Rd. I. (Pipe Roll Society's vol. 23), p. 79.

[77] See pp. 551, 553.

[78] "Precipue homines Lewelini interempti sunt" (*Ann. Cest. s.a.* 1198).

[79] *Ann. Cest. s.a.* 1198 (read "by" instead of "from" in the translation) and "O Oes Gwrtheyrn" in *Bruts*, 406.

[80] For Robert see Helsby's edition of Ormerod's *History of Cheshire,* i. p. 58.

[81] See p. 492. Owain had, no doubt, given up Mold in 1157.

[82] "Pryder Lloegr ai cythrudd. . . Alun rac hil run bu rudd" (*Myv, Arch.* I. 263 [189]).

[83] P. 430 *et seq.*

[84] The Cluniac priory of St. dear's, a cell of St. Martin des Champs in Paris, had in 1279 but two monks, who had shaken off all monastic obligations, and Gir. Camb. (i. 324) speaks of a time when there was but one. See *Mon. Angl.* vi. 1056; *Visitations*, Sir G. Duckett (1890), p. 26; *Tax. Nich.* 277.

[85] See p. 216.

[86] The life of Caradog was written by Gir. Camb. (i. 416 — *cf.* 395), of whose work, now lost, the account in Capgrave's *Nova Legenda Angliae* (ed. Horstman, Oxford, 1901, pp. 174–6) and *Acta Sanctorum*, 13th April, ii. 151, is probably a digest.

[87] "Resi Soutwallie principis."

[88] Caradog was perhaps "pencynydd" (chief huntsman). The "leporarii," as royal "milgwn," were worth 10s. each (*LL.* i. 498), *i.e.*, aa much as a horse.

[89] *Cf. Lib. Land.* 279, where it is said that Bishop Herwald (1056–1104) "in lann Cinith. . . ordinauit. . . caratocum uirum sanctum et religiosum in monachum". For the priory afterwards established here see p. 432.

[90] "Insula nomine Ary" is thus explained in Owen, *Pemb.* i. 114.

[91] Both Capgrave and Gir. Camb. vi. 85–6 (*Itin.* i. 11) describe the place of Caradog's sojourn as "Sanctum Hysmaelum in Rosensi provincia". But St. Ishmael's at the mouth of Milford Haven, though favoured by Phillimore (Owen, *Pemb.* i. 307), is too far from Haverfordwest to suit the story told of the young Richard fitz Tancard by Giraldus, whereas Haroldston East is close to the town, is dedicated to St. Ismael (Rees, *W. SS.* p. 252), and could until recently show "Caradog's Well," around which was held an annual fair (Hoare, *Itin.* i. 198; *Lit. Eng.* p. 139).

[92] The life confuses Tancard with his son Richard, but Gir. shows us that Tancard (for whom see p. 425) survived the saint and that Richard was then but a boy.

[93] "O Oes Gwrtheyrn" so far concurs (*Bruts*, 405) as to place the death of "caradawc vynach" eight years before that of Cadwallon ap Gruffydd and Maredudd ap Bleddyn (in 1132).

[94] See the account in *Lib. Land.* 2–5 of a visit paid by him about 1115 to the hermit Elgar of Bardsey.

[95] Jones and Freem. (106–7) think the grave can be identified.

[96] Gir. Camb. iii. 63–4 (*Invect.* iii. 6, 7), 182–3 (*Angl. Sac.* ii. 547).

[97] Nowhere, says Gir. (vi. 204 [*Descr.* i. 18]), will you find hermits and anchorites of greater austerity and spirituality than in Wales.

[98] *Cart. Glouc.* i. 75–6; *cf.* ii. 14–15, 135–6. The date is supported by an added passage in *Ann. Marg.* — see the facsimile in *Margam Abb.* p. 277. No account need be taken of Leland's statement that the founder was "Syr Jo: Loudres" (*Wales*, pp. 50–1), or of that of *Gw. Brut*, that the year was 1111. The priory was sometimes known as that of Ogmore (Vggemore), from the lordship in which it stood; hence it is confused with Wigmore in the index to *Cart. Glouc.*

[99] Gir. calls it "cellulam de Ewennith" (vi. 67 [*Itin.* i. 7]). For the church see Hoare, *Itin.* i. 147–51, and *Arch. Camb.* III. iii. (1857), 114–28 (E. A. Freeman).

[100] *Orig. Cist.* i. 62. I leave Tintern (founded in 1131) out of account, as a house which had no real connection with the Welsh.

[101] *Ann. C.* MS. C. *s.a.* 1144. The date is due to the editor, but is probably right and to be preferred to Wharton's 1143 (*Angl. Sac.* ii. 649). The MS. reads: "Ducti sunt monachi ordinis cysterciensis qui modo sunt apud albam landam in Westwalliam per bernardum episcopum qui dedit eis locum apud trefgarn in deuglethef" (Cott. MS. Dom. i. 147a (2)). Neither Trefgarn Owain nor Great Trefgarn can be described as in Deugleddyf, but Little Trefgarn is locally within the hundred, though reckoned a detached portion of the parish of St. Dogwell's. For its relation to St. David's see Fenton (2), 181–2.

[102] So Janauschek (*Orig. Cist.*).

[103] P. 339.

[104] Possibly translating a Welsh "Waun Wen". There was a Præmonstratensian Blanchland in Northumberland and another in the Cotentin. "Alba Domus," often used by Gir., is a translation of Ty Gwyn.

[105] King John, in his confirmation charter of 27th December, 1214 (*Rot. Chart.* 206), confirms to the church of St. Mary of "Alba Landa" and its monks "terram in qua abbatia de Alba Landa sita est, quam habent de dono Johannis de Thorynton". *Cf. Royal Charters*, 73.

[106] According to *Orig. Cist.* i. 74–5, the Cistercian lists give 22nd July, 1143, as the date of the first foundation. For "Marreduch f. Maylgon" as donor of the capital endowment, see John's charter of 1214 in *Rot. Chart.* i. 205, and that of Henry III. 1st June, 1232, in *Mon. Angl. v.* 459.

[107] Possibly Maredudd ap *Madog* is meant, who ruled Maelienydd from 1140 to 1146.

[108] This is the view of Janauschek.

[109] *Eng. Hist. Rev.* viii. (1893), 669.

[110] The history of this abbey is very fully told, with the aid of its rich collection of muniments (now the property of Miss Talbot), in Birch, *Margam Abbey* (London, 1897).

[111] *Eng. Hist. Rev.* viii. p. 648.

[112] *Wales*, p. 115.

[113] Accounts of the Cistercians as they appeared to English observers will be found in Wm. Malm. *G.R.* 382–3 (514); Ord. Vit. viii. 26; Gir. Camb. iv. 111–15.

[114] Rhys's charter, which is not dated, will be found in *Card. Priory*, 144–5, where it is printed from an inspeximus of 3 Hen. VI. Documents of which there are translations in this book (pp. 135–6) show that the church of Holy Trinity at Cardigan was in dispute about 1160 between Chertsey and Gloucester. Earl Roger of Hertford then decided in favour of the latter, but Chertsey seems to have won at a later date.

[115] See Gir. Camb. iv. 100–1 (*Spec. Eccl.* ii. 32), where the tale is told how the cell was broken up about 1185 as the result of the scandalous misconduct of the monks. The church had been given to Great Malvern by Richard fitz Pons before 1126 (*MON. ANGL.* iii. 448).

[116] He gave the churches and vills of Llanrhystud and Llansantffraid in Ceredigion, with land at Ystrad Meurig (Fenton (2), 347–8).

[117] "Conano abbate Albe Terre" witnesses a grant made to Margam by Earl William of Gloucester before the death of his son Robert in 1166 — see *Cartae Glam.* iii. 101. *B.T.* 226 and *B. Saes. s.a.* 1176 (the true year) record the death of "Kynan abat y ty gwynn". He is praised by Gir. Camb. (vi. 59 [*Itin.* i. 5]) as "viro probo et religioso".

[118] For the gifts of Rhys see John's charter to the abbey in *Rot. Chart.* 206. They include Blaen Gwyddno, near Lampeter Velffrey, Cilfargen, near Llandilo, Rhyd y Maengwyn, near Llanfyrnach, Crug y Chwil, Crug Eryr and Rhuddlan (near Llandysul) in South Cardiganshire.

[119] Gir. Camb. iv. 143–5; *Arch. Camb.* V. x. (1893), 120–4, 226.

[120] See note 120 to chap. xiv., *B.T. s.a.* 1239, and Evans, *Rep.* i. p. 824 (from Pen. MS. 132, of the sixteenth century).

[121] *Orig. Cist.* i. 151. *B.T.* 202 and *B. Saes. s.a.* 1164 appear to assign the event to 1165, but their evidence is outweighed by that cited by Janauschek.

[122] I agree with the late Mr. Stephen Williams that the first site of the abbey must have been at "Yr Hên Fynachlog" (The Old Monastery), on the stream still known as the Fflur, but much better authority than that of Leland is needed to prove that this first foundation was due to Rhys ap Tewdwr. See *Str. Flor.* 19–23.

[123] Newell (*History of the Welsh Church*, 1895, p. 303) was the first to point out the significance in this connection of Gir. Camb. iv. 152 ("domus Cisterciensis ordinis. . . sub montanis Elennith a. . . Roberto Stephani filio. . . primum fundata").

[124] The only extant charter bestowed by Rhys upon the abbey is a confirmation of earlier gifts granted in 1184 at Llansantffraid Cwm Toyddwr (*Mon. Angl.* v. 632–3; *Str. Flor.* Appendix, x-xiii). A charter of Henry II. confirming the donations of Rhys (*Mon. Angl.* v. 633; *Str. Flor.* Appendix, xiii-xiv). is assigned by Eyton (*Itin.* 246) to December, 1181.

[125] See map in *Str. Flor.* 107. The grant of these pastures only gave the abbey common rights and did not shut out the older inhabitants; this was so even in Leland's time — see *Wales*, p. 123.

[126] Excavations on the site were commenced in 1886 and the results are fully described in *Str. Flor.* chap. v. by the prime mover in the matter, Mr. Stephen W. Williams of Rhayader.

[127] "Y vlwydyn honno ybu uarw dauyd abat ystrat fflur" (*Bruts,* 335; *cf. B.T.* 233, and *B.* Sacs. *s.a.* 1185, which is correct). The new church was ready for use on 12th May, 1201 (*B.T.* 256).

[128] Gir. Camb. vi. 119, 126 (*Itin.* ii. 4, 7).

[129] *B.T.* 226; *B. Saes. s.a.* 1175. For Cadell see p. 503.

[130] *B.T.* 233; *B. Saes. s.a.* 1185. Hywel may well have been, as is suggested in *Str. Flor.* 111, the donor to the abbey of the church of Llangurig.

[131] *Orig. Cist.* i. 160. Janauschek thinks there may have been a removal from the first site to the present one on 1oth July, 1172, and thus explains the appearance in the lists under that date of an abbey of "Pola," clearly identical with Ystrad Marchell.

[132] See Owain's grant in an inspeximus of 13 Edw. II. (*Mon. Angl.* v. 637). The manor of Ystrad Marchell includes the whole of the parish of Guilsfield (except Tir y Myneich) and an adjacent part of that of Meifod. Tir y Myneich represents the portion assigned to the abbey, and therefore reckoned a separate manor (*App. Land. Com.* 451). The abbey ruins actually stand in the township of Gungrog Fawr and the parish of Welshpool, but there is evidence that in the thirteenth century "Hergyngroyk" was in "Soyr stradmarghel" (*Mont. Coll.* i. 124–5). A large number of charters of Ystrad Marchell are printed (some in translations only) in *Mont. Coll.* iv. (1871), but there is a difficulty in accepting them all as genuine records. Not only do they come into conflict with other well-known sources, but it may be noted as most suspicious that two assigned to 1183 and 1198 have precisely the same witnesses and in the same order, notwithstanding the interval of fifteen years.

[133] We owe the story to Gir. Camb., who three times refers to it (ii. 248; iv. 168–9; vi. 59). Meilyr of Caerleon is said to have had supernatural intelligence of the abbot's fall immediately it took place; this would place it earlier than 1174, when the wizard was killed at the siege of Usk — see note 50 to chap. xv.

[134] *Orig. Cist.* i. 74. There is a full account of the abbey by S. W. Williams in *Trans. Cymr.* 1894–5, pp. 61–98.

[135] Leland (*Wales*, p. 52) makes him the founder, though he is not mentioned in the charters of the abbey.

[136] He gave Carnaff in Lower Elfael, now known as Tir y Myneich in the parish of Clyro. See *Rot. Chart.* 206; *Radnorsh.* (2), 334 and 250.

[137] *B.T.* 233; *B. Saes. s.a.* 1184.

[138] Caerleon is the earlier, Lantarnam the later form; although separately noticed by Tanner (327, 331) and Dugdale (*Mon. Angl.* v. 727–8), they are shown to be the same by the passages in *B.T.* (p. 230) and *B. Saes.* (*s.a.* 1179) as to the foundation and by a reference in a document of 1465 to "Karelyon alias Lanternan" (*Arch. Camb.* II. iii. [1852] 70). Nant Teyrnon perhaps took its name from the "arglwyd ar went is coet teirnyon twryf vliant" of Mob. 20; for the corruption "Lantarnam" *cf.* Lancarfan (chap. vii. note 52).

[139] The date is yielded by *B.T.* and *B. Saes.* It is from a Bassaleg charter granted by "Hoelus filius Ioruorthi filii Oeni" that we incidentally learn that Hywel, in the lifetime of his father, had given "Emsanternon," *i.e.,* Ynys Nant Teyrnon, to white monks (*Mon. Angl.* iv. 634), and, in accordance with this, the convent of "Karlyon" some years later refer to "Dominus H. de Karliun" as their "patronus" (*Mon. Angl.* v. 728).

[140] For the lands of the house see *Tax. Nich.* 281 and *Valor Eccl.* iv. 365; during the thirteenth century it was often at odds with Margam as to the great common of Hirwaen Wrgan, near Aberdare — see *Margam Abb.* pp. 174–5, 266–8; *Cartae Glam.* i. 101–3, 104–6; iii. 236–7; *Str. Flor.* xxx-xxxi. There seems no good ground for believing that the convent was ever housed in Caerleon itself.

[141] *B.T.* 233; *B. Saes. s.a.* 1186. The day was 24th July, according to *Reg. Conway.* Rhedynog Felen (parish of Llanwnda) continued to be a possession of the abbey — see Llywelyn's charter in *Mon. Angl.* v. 672 (Redenocuelen); *Tax. Nich.* 292 (Reddenaut); *Reg. Conway,* 8 (Redinoc Velyn).

[142] They were there in the spring of 1188, if we may accept the statement of Gir. in *Itin.* ii. 10 (vi. 136–7). One notes, however, that the passage was added in the second edition (1197).

[143] *Reff. Conway,* 7–8. The blank may safely be filled with the name of Gruffydd, who was buried (in 1200) at Aberconwy (*B.T.*) and was certainly lord of Anglesey — see note 74 above. Gelliniog is near Dwyran in the parish of Llangeinwen.

[144] Printed in *Mon. Angl.* v. 672–4 and thence in Williams' *Aberconwy,* 163–71. The date 1198 must be wrong, for Llywelyn was not at that time "totius Norwalliae princeps," or in a position to make many of the grants included in the charter.

[145] Aberconwy and Beddgelert are clearly the houses indicated by Gir. Camb. in the story told in *Spec. Eccl.* iii. 8 (iv. 167–8), and so manifest are the allusions that the keeping back of the names is a mere affectation of reticence. The former of the two had the grange of Nanhwynain (the modern Nant Gwynant), with lands extending from Beddgelert church to Penygwryd and "ad caput Wedduavaur" (*Aberconwy*, p. 168).

[146] *B.T.* 252 gives the former date; Janauschek, relying on the old lists, prefers the latter (*Orig. Cist.* i. 202)

[147] Seep. 466. Maredudd was lord of Meirionydd in 1202 (*B.T.* 256) and probably received it from his brother in 1194—see p. 589.

[148] The earliest known charter is that of Llywelyn ab Iorwerth, confirming in 1209 the gifts of Maredudd and Gruffydd ap Cynan and Hywel ap Gruffydd (*Mon. Angl.* v. 458–9 [wrongly assigned to Cwm Hir]; *Rec. Carn.* 199–201). The lands lay chiefly in the parishes of Llanfachreth, Llanelltyd, Llanegryn, and Trawsfynydd, but the abbey had also an important grange at Neigwl in Lleyn.

[149] *Orig. Cist.* i. 205. *B.T.* notices the foundation of "manachlawc lenegwestyl yn ial" (pp. 254–6; *Bruts,* 342) at the end of 1200.

[150] See the foundation charter in *Mon. Angl.* v. 637 (wrongly assigned to Ystrad Marchell) and *Arch. Camb.* III. xii. (1866), 412–13. That Llyn—not Glyn or Llan—Egwestl is the true form appears to be established by a line of Einion Wan —"Gwyrwawryn llawrllynn egwestl" (*Myv. Arch.* I. 333 [233]). For the pillar of Elisedd (not Eliseg) see p. 244.

[151] Halton in the parish of Chirk and the commote of Nanheudwy was given by Madog in 1218 (*Arch. Camb.* IV. xi. [1880], 149).

[152] Llanllyr is, beyond a doubt, the "domus monialium pauperum" of Gir. Camb. iv. 152 (*Spec.* iii. 5), where its early history is told. For other references see Gervase, ii. 443 (A. Lanter); *Tax. Nich.* 276; *Valor,* iv. 397; Leland, *Wales,* p. 51.

[153] For Maredudd, see p. 648.

[154] The foundation charter will be found in *Mont. Coll.* ii. (1869), 305–6. *Cf.* also *Mont. Coll.* xxi. (1887), 332 (under "Llanveyr"); *Tax. Nich.* 289; *Valor,* iv. 456; *Arch. Camb.* III. xiv. (1868), 162.

[155] For a full account of Tal y Llychau see *Arch. Camb.* V. x. (1893) xi., (1894). It is, no doubt, the "A. Premustre" of Gervase, ii. 443.

[156] Gir. Camb. iii. 361, where he is called "purum Walensem".

[157] Note 116. Slebech claimed Wizo as a benefactor ("ex dono Wiz"—Fenton (2), 347), but, inasmuch as he died before 1130 (chap. xii. note 78), when the order had as yet no footing in the island, his son would seem to have been the true founder.

[158] The earliest reference to Dolgynwal belongs to 1225, when Llywelyn bestowed upon it the tithes of Ellesmere (Eyton, *Shrops.* x. p. 247). It may be assumed that it had already existed for some years.

[159] "Agris igitur plurimum utuntur pascuis, paium cultis, floridis parce, consitis parcissime" (vi. 201 [*Descr.* i. 17]).

[160] Gir. vi. 179–80 (*Descr.* i. 8).

[161] *De Nugis*, p. 52.

[162] Wm. Newb. ii. 5.

[163] App. Land Com., 262.

[164] See p. 230.

[165] See Williams, *Observations on the Snowdon Mountains* (Oxford, 1802), p. 19.

[166] For the imports into Wales see Gir. vi. 218 (mercimonia ferri, panni, salis et bladi); Rymer i. 264 (terrum vel acerum vel pannum); Matt. Paris, *Hist. Major,* v. 675, 677.

[167] Gir. vi. 184 (*Descr.* i. 10), where mention is made of "panno. . . duro et aspero, quern patria parit, qui et vulgari vocabulo brachan dicitur". It is clear from this passage and from *Mab.* 146 and *De Nugis,* p. 102, that the "brychan" was not a "cloak" (*LL.* i. 77, 723) or "bed coverlet" (*ibid.* 83), but a bed or mattress upon which the sleeper lay.

[168] *Chronicon Monasterii de Abingdon,* ed. Stevenson (Rolls Series, 1858), ii. 150.

[169] "Non mercimoniis, non navigiis, non mechanicis artibus. . . vexantur" (vi. 180 [*Descr.* i. 8]).

[170] There were "burgenses" in Cardigan in 1199, when Maelgwn sold the place to King John (*Rot. Chart.* 63*b*), and it was no doubt to oblige this foreign colony that Rhys had allowed the priory to maintain its position. About 1185 Rhys had "burgenses" attached to his castle of "Lananeveri," who threatened to leave the place and go back to England if a stop were not put to the excesses of the monks of the adjacent cell of Malvern (Gir. Camb. iv. 101).

[171] See pp. 406, 463, 465, 506.

[172] See p. 634.

[173] For the construction of Welsh houses see p. 314. It may be added that Dim. II. viii. 67 shows that the evidences of the former existence of a Welsh homestead would be, not ruined walls or a garden run wild, but "the place of a drying-kiln, a hearthstone or a horse-block".

[174] Gir. Camb. vi. 179, 182, 181 (*Descr.* i. 8, 9).

[175] For this story see *De Nugis*, pp. 101–2. The owner of the mare is called "Cadolanus filius *Vther,*" but the mention of "Gesligair" as his home affords a strong presumption that Cadwallon ab Ifor Bach, for whom see p. 637, is really meant. There is a moated moundat Gelligaer (besides the Roman fort), pointing to the existence here of a "llys" of the lords of Senghenydd (*Arch. Camb.* VI. i. [1901], 59).

[176] vi. 180 (*Descr.* i. 8).

[177] *Cf. De Nugis*, p. 100 (Fit ut pauci canescant).

[178] *Ibid.* pp. 209–10 (ii. 3).

[179] *Ibid.* p. 177 (*Descr.* i. 6); 54 (*Itin.* i. 4).

[180] *Ibid.* pp. 220–1 (*Descr.* ii. 8).

[181] With Gir. Camb. vi. 182–4 (*Descr.* i. 10) *cf. De Nugis*, pp. 94–5.

[182] Gir. vi. 181 (nudis autem pedibus ambulant), 184, 182 (*Descr.* i. 8, 10, 9). The dress of the ordinary Welshman consisted of a linen shirt ("crys," the "interula" of Gir.) and drawers ("llawdyr"), over which was worn a woollen coat or tunic ("pais," "pallium"), reaching the knees or the calves and secured by a girdle ("gwregys"). Sometimes a "mantell" or cloak was added. Women wore the "crys," the "llenlliein," which was a long robe reaching the feet, and the "ffunen," a white headband, compared by Gir. to the turban of the East. See *LL.* i. 56, 64, 94, 238, 308, 380, 392, 676, and the rough drawings in Lat. A. (dating from about 1200). Map remarks that the Welsh wore little wool and no fur and went barefoot (*De Nugis*, p. 52).

[183] Gir. Camb. vi. 192–3 (*Descr.* i. 15).

[184] The charge of perfidy is made by Gir. (vi. 206 [*Descr.* ii. 1]), Wm. Newb. ii. 5) and Map (*De Nugis*, p. 94).

[185] Chap. xiv. §4.

[186] Gir. Camb. vi. 203–4 (*Descr.* i. 18). *Cf. De Nugis*, p. 75.

CHAPTER VII

[1] *B.T.* 254. Gruffydd had been a benefactor to the abbey (see p. 601), and the eulogy of him in MS. C. of *B.T.* probably came therefore from a monk of the house. For Prydydd y Moch's lament see chap. xvi. note 74.

[2] This is to be inferred, notwithstanding the silence of *B.T.*, from Llywelyn's action in 1201.

[3] Degannwy was in Creuddyn, a commote of Rhos, and therefore in Gwynedd *below* Conway, but it seems to have been held at his death by Gruffydd — see the elegy of Prydydd y Moch.

[4] *B.T.* 256.

[5] In 1188 Lleyn "erat filiorum Oenei" (Gir. Camb. vi. 123), *i.e.*, of Rhodri. At some time or other between that year and 1200, probably in 1194 or 1195, it passed to Gruffydd ap Cynan, as is shown by that prince's grant of three acres and three tenants in Nevin to the canons of Haughmond (*Arch. Camb.* III. vi. [1860], 332, from a lost Wynnstay MS.). It may be added that the common ascription of this grant to the elder Gruffydd ap Cynan (d. 1137) is obviously wrong; Cadwaladr was the first to bestow upon Haughmond the church of Nevin, no doubt during his residence at Ness (chap. xiv. notes 17 and 44), and the gift was confirmed by Dafydd ab Owain, his wife Emma, and Llywelyn ab Iorwerth (*Arch. Camb. ibid.*).

[6] *B.T.* 256. Hywel is mentioned in the Cymer charter of 1209 as one of the benefactors of the abbey (*Rec. Carn.* 199).

[7] *B.T.* 256–8. For Elise see p. 566.

[8] When Giraldus visited Gwenwynwyn in the latter half of August, 1202, he found him "in expeditione contra Lewelinum, cui tunc concordatus fuerat" (iii. 226).

[9] The well-known "Tomen y Bala" is, no doubt, the castle mound.

[10] A township in the eastern part of the parish of Llandderfel.

[11] *Rot. Chart.* 23 (Le Mans, 28th Sept.).

[12] *Ibid.* 63 (Poitiers, 4th Dec.).

[13] *Rot. Chart.* (Poitiers, 3rd Dec.).

[14] *Ibid.* 44 (Worcester, 11th April).

[15] *Ibid.* 100 (Stow, 13th Jan.).

[16] *Ibid.* 103 (Westminster, 3rd April). The safe-conduct was to hold good until 6th May.

[17] *Ibid.* 103–4 (Cirencester, 2nd May).

[18] Rymer, i. 84; *Rot. Pat.* i. 8–9.

[19] Gir. Camb. iii. 196, 200, 206.

[20] *Ibid.* 226.

[21] *Rot. Pat.* i. 23 (Alençon, 18th Jan. [1203]).

[22] See *Rot. Pat.* i. 39 (Worcester, 16th March), 40.

[23] Llywelyn, Madog ap Gruffydd (of Northern Powys) and their companions were expected to meet John at Worcester about 1st September (*Rot. Pat.* i. 44 — Windsor, 20th July) and probably did so. There is no trustworthy evidence as to Joan's mother, but one may accept the statement of *Ann. Cest. s.a.* 1204, that she was "filiam. . . nocham," *i.e.,* noiham. The promise of her hand had been made by the king before 15th October, 1204 (*Rot. Claus.* i. 12).

[24] See p. 551.

[25] *B.T.* 258. *Cf.* "O Oes Gwrtheyrn" (*Bruts,* 406; *Comment.* (2), 158), where the event is (wrongly) dated one year after 1200 and (rightly) five years before 1208.

[26] On 10th April, 1200, John had taken "Emmam uxorem David filii Oeni" under his protection, especially in respect of proceedings touching her manors of Ellesmere and Hales[owen] (*Rot. Chart.* i. 44). In May, 1203, he bids the justiciar find for David's widow an equivalent as far as possible from the marches for the castle of Ellesmere (*Rot. regn. Joh.* 36). On and August John repeats his wish to have the castle in his own hands, and says other provision must be made for David's son Owen (Audoeñ) — see *ibid.* 56. In Oct. 1204 he proposes to give him thirteen librates in Elmdon, Warwickshire (*Rot. Claus.* i. 12) and in Nov. 1205 fifteen in Waltham, near Grimsby (*ibid.* 56). Emma still held Hales in 1212 (*Testa de Nevill,* 56).

[27] *Ann. Cest.* date it 1204, but assign to the same year the Portsmouth assembly of June, 1205. *Ann. Wigorn.* and *Reg. Conway* mention it under 1206, which is less likely to be the true year.

[28] On 23rd March, 1205, the keeper of Ellesmere Castle was ordered to hand it over to Llywelyn (*Rot. Pat.* i. 51). *Cf. Rot. Claus.* i. 23. The formal gift in frank marriage followed on 16th April (*Rot. Chart.* i. 147).

[29] The three letters of Innocent III. which deal with this business will be found in Migne's *Patrologia* (series Latina, ccxiv. 791 [25th Nov. 1199]; ccxv. 49 [20th April, 1203], 534 [17th Feb. 1205]. *Cf. Papal Letters,* i. 8, 13, 19). The patruus is not named, but must clearly be Rhodri, whose alliance with the sons

of Godred of Man is mentioned by *B. Saes. s.a.* 1193. He was married in 1188 to a daughter of the Lord Rhys (Gir. Camb. vi. 126–7), but may have put her away or lost her by death before 1193. With equal certainty the "princeps insularum" may be taken to be Reginald, who had become king of Man in 1188.

[30] On 22nd Jan. 1198 Maelgwn had confirmed to Strata Florida all his father's donations. Rhys Gryg was at the time with him (*Str. Fior.* xiv.).

[31] *Rot. Chart.* i. 63. The name of the "camao" (commote) is given in the letter of 1200 as "Bisbirwern," for "Hishirwern". Strictly speaking, Is Hirwen was a half-commote, the river Hirwen, which flows into the Teifi at Pont Ystrad, dividing the commote of Iscoed into two parts.

[32] *Rot. Chart.* i. 44 (11th April, Worcester) probably marks the completion of the transaction.

[33] *Ann. Camb.* MS. B. *s.a.* 1200.

[34] "Allwed holl Kymry" is the true reading of *B.T.* — see Mostyn MS. 116, as cited by Evans, *Rep.* i. p. 61.

[35] *Ann. Camb.* (B. gives the day); *B.T.* 256. Maredudd was buried at Kidwelly.

[36] Gruffydd was buried at Strata Florida; so also Matilda, who died on 29th December, 1210, at Llanbadarn Fawr (*B.T.* 266).

[37] The death of Hywel Sais furnishes one of the few cases in which there is an irreconcilable divergence between *Ann. C.* and *B.T.* One can but adopt the account which seems most probable, and in this case I have rejected the testimony of the former (MS. B. *s.a.* 1199) for that of the latter, on the ground that the reference to a visit to the court of King John "erga Pascha" in this year creates suspicion. John did not reach England until Ascensiontide, when he was crowned.

[38] In 1202 Rhys had confirmed to Strata Florida all earlier donations in a charter stated to be his first, when as yet he had no seal, and witnessed by his mother, Matilda (*Str. Flor.* xv). He had at the end of this year Llandovery, if not Dinefwr (*B.T.*).

[39] In August, 1204, when Gwenwynwyn was asked to meet the king at Woodstock, it was requested that he should, if possible, bring Maelgwn with him "ad loquendum nobiscum" (*Rot. Pat.* i. 45). In December the Earl of Chester incurred the king's displeasure by giving his countenance to Gwenwynwyn (*Rot. Claus.* i. 16) and about this time the prince of Powys was for a while deprived of his manor of Ashford (*ibid.* 24).

[40] Under Henry II. Emlyn had been regarded as belonging to the Carew family (see p. 542), but on 16th April, 1200, John granted to Earl William "Wilfrey" and "Oistrelef," *i.e.,* Efelffre and Ystlwyf (for which see *ibid.*), "donec ei deliberaverimus terram suam de Emelin" (*Rot. Chart.* 47). William arrived in England in May, 1204.

[41] This is the date given by *Ann. C.* MS. C. and *Ann. Marg.* Other authorities mention Monday, the 24th. An undated letter in the Papal Registers specially orders that Wales shall not be regarded as exempt (*Papal Letters,* i. 30).

[42] *Rot. Chart.* i. 66 (Caen, 3rd June, 1200); *Cartae Glam.* iii. 177 (from a late transcript).

[43] *Rot. Pat.* i. 19 (Domfront, 23rd Oct. 1202). When John had secured in 1200 the dissolution of his marriage with Isabella of Gloucester, he had not resigned the lands he held in virtue of the union. When, however, in 1214 she married Geoffrey de Mandeville, Earl of Essex, he relaxed his hold, and on 26th January ordered his bailiff, Falkes of Breauté, to give the earl possession of the honour of Glamorgan (*Rot. Pat.* i. 109).

[44] The charter, dated Rouen, 24th February, 1203, is printed by dark (*Cartae Glam.* iii. 234–5) from the Breviate of Domesday (K.R. miscellaneous books i.), p. 475.

[45] *Rot. Pat.* i. 68; *Cartae Glam.* i. 52.

[46] A full account of the circumstances which led to the fall of William is given by John in the document printed in Rymer, i. 107–8. *Cf.* also Norgate, *John Lackland*, pp. 146–52, 287–8.

[47] Peter appears frequently in the Charter, Patent, and Close Rolls from 1204 to the end of the reign, and Wendover mentions him (iii. 238) among the evil counsellors of John. He was the son of Herbert fitz Herbert (Madox, *Baronia Anglica*, 232–3) and Lucy of Hereford (*Rot. Claus.* i. 296).

[48] *Rot. Pat.* i. 86 (Gillingham, 29th Sept.).

[49] For the terms of the "conventio" see Rymer, i. 101. B.T. has dropped the year 1207 and is accordingly a year behindhand from this point to 1212.

[50] So *B.T.* 262. According to *Ann. C.* MS. B. the castle taken was that of "luchewein," and the deed had been done before, in 1206 (the entry follows the notice as to John's expedition to Poitou). These two notices possibly refer to a castle at Llwch (or Llech) Owain (the llwchewin of *Mab.* 139), a lake in the southern part of the parish of Llanarthney (commote of Iscennen). There is an entrenchment here known as Castell y Garreg.

[51] *Rot. Pat.* i. 88 (Bristol, 25th Dec.); Rymer, i. 102. On 21st January 1209, the knights of the Earl of Chester were told they must serve the earl in the campaign he was organising "super inimicos nostros de Wallia pro excessibus Lewelini" (*Rot. Pat. ibid.*), but this was probably a mere measure of precaution, for on 29th January, at Shrewsbury, a safe-conduct was issued to Llywelyn (91).

[52] See the safe-conduct of 16th March (*Rot. Pat.* i. 89), which proposes a meeting at Northampton on the 29th.

[53] This is asserted by "O Oes Gwrtheyrn" (*Comment.* (2), 159; in *Bruts,* 406 "ruuein" is for "prydein"), and the statement is confirmed by entries in the Misae Roll of 11 John (*Trans. Cymr.* 1899–1900, 136).

[54] "Weno senescallo suo" (*Rot. regn. Joh.* 126). "Gwyn filius Eduyweyn senescallus noster," witnesses Llywelyn's charter to Cymer, dated in this year 1209 (*Rec. Carn.* 201). He was of Eifionydd (*Rec. Carn.* 39, 40) and also appears in 1198 (*ibid.* 148). The "distain" or steward was the chief officer of the royal household (Ven. I. vii. 1) and held his position by hereditary right (Ven. II. xi. 33, "tir ebo suyd ohonau mal. . . disteiniat").

[55] "Magister Ostrucius" appears as an envoy of Llywelyn as early as August, 1204. He received from the king, first a pension of £5 (*Rot. Claus.* i. 10, 11, 43), then a prebend in Ellesmere Church (60), and finally in February, 1209, the crown living of Salkeld in the diocese of Carlisle (*Rot. Pat.* i. 89). He had been in December the bearer of a letter from Llywelyn to the king (*ibid.* 88), and at Norham he transacted the prince's business for him (*Rot. regn. Joh.* 125, 126), He was a witness to the Cymer charter as "magister Strwyth" (*Rec. Carn.* 201), and was still alive in 1222 (Owen, *Cat.* 357 —"magistro Estruit").

[56] See *Rot. regn. Joh.* 111, 116, 129, 133, 136, 141, 142, 152 (May, 1209–Jan. 1210).

[57] The incident is mentioned in *Ann. S. Edm. s.a.* and Wendover, iii. 227. There is nothing in the statement of the latter as to its novelty; homage had been done by the Welsh at this very place in 1163 (p. 513) and fealty sworn at Geddington in Northamptonshire in 1177 (p. 552). John was at Woodstock from 16th to 19th October; he also passed through it on his way westward on 25th November, but the circumstances of the earlier visit are much more suggestive of a fixed meeting.

[58] *Rot. regn. Joh.* 145.

[59] For this date see Gir. v. pref. liii, note 2.

[60] He speaks in *De Rebus,* iii. 1 (i. 89) of "indignas nec iuxta merita promotiones".

[61] i. 93. The second edition of the *Itinerary,* with the dedication to Bishop Hugh, belongs to the period of residence at Lincoln.

[62] Gir. speaks vaguely ("quasi in principio autumni"), but see *Ann. Theokesb.* for the precise day.

[63] In iv. 147 it is estimated at two-thirds. On another occasion (iii. 19) Gir. makes it out to be little more than a bare majority.

[64] iii. 312. Robert son of Jonas was very old at the time of the dispute (i. 164), having a son Henry among the canons (iii. 214), so that Jonas must have nourished about 1150. "Magister Johannes iuvenis" was a canon in 1176 (i. 158) and was probably the son of the "magister Johannes canonicus de Sancto David "who witnessed a Brecon charter of 1148–55 (*Arch. Camb.,* IV. xiv. [1883], 44).

[65] For the connections of Peter see iii. 34, 219–20, 299. He was said to be illegitimate, being perhaps the fruit of a clerical marriage (iii. 299–300).

[66] i. 87, 139. The see was vacant through the death of William of Saltmarsh in 1191 and was filled by the consecration of Henry, prior of Abergavenny, on 12th December, 1193.

[67] i. 111; iii. 191.

[68] For this question see pp. 480–2 and note to chap. xiii. § 3.

[69] According to Gir. iii. 133, 344, the fixed income was no more than twenty marks. In *Tax. Nich.* 274, the bishop's prebend is valued at £20, but he had also temporal possessions yielding £104 17s. per annum (277).

[70] In i. 139, Gir. says he refused two bishoprics (i.e., Bangor and Llandaff) in Wales and four in Ireland.

[71] See the letter of the Welsh princes, no doubt drafted by Giraldus himself, in iii. 244–6.

[72] iii. 15.

[73] The names prefixed to the letter are those of Llywelyn, Gwenwynwyn, Madog [ap Gruffydd], and the four sons of Rhys, Gruffydd, Maelgwn, Maredudd and Rhys (iii. 244). Though connected by Gir. with his third visit to Rome, the document must have been prepared before July, 1201, when Maredudd and Gruffydd died. Probably it belongs to the first visit, since Innocent's letter of 5th May, 1200 (iii. 62–3) looks like an answer to it.

[74] See his views as expressed at a banquet of his magnates in iii. 209.

[75] Giraldus reported him to be "quasi penitus idiota," and there was enough substance in the allegation to induce Innocent to order an examination into his qualifications (iii. 68–9). Walter significantly declined the test (iii. 234).

[76] The situation is explained in iii. 198.

[77] On 13th January, 1201, John sent two messengers to signify to the chapter and to the clergy of the diocese that lie had not assented and did not then assent to the election of the Archdeacon of Brecknock (*Rot. Chart.* i. 100). For other expressions of the king's displeasure see *Rot. Pat.* i. 3 (17th Dec. 1201), *ibid.* 7 (8th March, 1202), *ibid.* 9 (10th April, 1202), *ibid.* 34 (11th Sept. 1203).

[78] iii. 259. Before Hubert's change of policy, they had been held by the prior of Llantony.

[79] iii. 197.

[80] Giraldus was in Gwynedd at Christmastide, 1201 (see heads of lost chapters of *De Rebus* in i. 10), and was followed to St. David's by the special envoy of Llywelyn, Laurence, prior of Bardsey (iii. 197). Llywelyn also saw him in August and, "ut erat vir liberalis et lenis," afforded him every help (iii. 226).

[81] iii. 226.

[82] The party of Giraldus included in April, 1202, Pontius, Archdeacon of St. David's, Robert son of Jonas, his son Henry (the one resident canon who was loyal to the end — iii. 316), and Meilyr (iii. 214).

[83] Eustace, bishop of Ely from 1198 to 1215, had known Giraldus in his student days at Paris (iii. 232). He was much in request as a papal commissioner. Mauger, bishop of Worcester from 1200 to 1212, was also a friend of the archdeacon's (*ibid.*), perhaps for the same reason.

[84] iii. 227.

[85] This letter is to be found in the Papal Registers, which fix the date as 26th May (*Papal Letters*, i. p. 14).

[86] See *Papal Letters*, i. p. 14.

[87] Gir. says that among the laity of Wales he found much loyalty, among the clergy scarcely any (iii. 287).

[88] *Ann. C.* MS. C.; *Ann. Waverl.; Reg. Sacr.* (2), 53. *Ann. C.* MS. B. has 6th December by mistake.

[89] For the form of profession see H. and St. i. 451.

[90] In a letter of 5th January, 1204 (*Rot. Pat.* i. 37), John announces the reconciliation.

[91] Two Brecon charters of 1204–14 and 1204–8 are attested by "magistro Giraldo de Barri et G[iraldo] archidiacono de Breconia nepote suo" (*Arch. Camb.* III. xiii. [1882], 307; xiv. [1883], 156).

[92] The closing paragraph of *Men. Eccl.* (iii. 373) shows he was still writing at the age of seventy.

[93] The likeliest date is 1223; for in that year his death was signified to the bishop of Lincoln and his Oxfordshire living of Chesterton was filled (Register of Bishop Hugh of Lincoln, vol. ii. pp. 9–10). There is no evidence that he was buried at St. David's; the tomb now shown as his is of the fourteenth century (Jones and Freem. 122–3).

[94] iii. 209.

[95] According to the document in Rymer, i. 107–8, in which the king justifies his proceedings against the family, William was in Herefordshire about May, at Pembroke (where he met the king) in June, and in Herefordshire again in July or August.

[96] This would be certain if the "Walensium nonnulli" of the Barnwell chronicle (Walt. Cov. ii. 202, *s.a.* 1210) included Llywelyn.

[97] See Norgate, *John Lackland*, p. 288. William died in exile in France in 1211 (*Ann. Marg.*: Wendover, iii. 237).

[98] *Ann. Dunst.*

[99] *B.T.* 264. "O Oes Gwrtheyrn" adds the detail "ac a'i cadarnhaodd o waith [Cardiff MS. 50 reads "wydh" = timber] Ysgubor y Creuddyn" (*Comment.* (2), 159).

[100] He was at Cardiff on 25th May (*Rot. regn. Joh.* 170), at Margam on the 28th (*ibid.* 172), where the monks entertained him (*Ann. Marg.*), at Swansea on the same day (*Rot.* 172) and at Haverford on the 31st (*ibid.*).

[101] See an entry in Rot. de Prestito (*Rot. regn. Joh.* 172) of £8 6s. 9d. advanced to Falkes for the king's accommodation "dum fuit in baillivia sua". Falkes had been appointed in February, 1207 (*Rot. Pat.* i. 68).

[102] From that day to the 16th the king was at "Crucem subter Penbroc" (*Rot. regn. Joh.* 172–7). The situation of this spot is discussed in Owen, *Pemb.* i. 318–19.

[103] *Rot. r. J.* 228. *Ann. C.* MS. C. agrees as to the place, but its date (17th August) is too early.

[104] For Richard see chap. xvi. notes 91, 92. The pedigree is established by the charter (5 Edw. III.) printed in *Mon. Angl.* vi. 444–5.

[105] i. 179, 315. He was an adversary of the archdeacon's (iii. 313–4).

[106] *Mon. Angl. ut supra.*

[107] *Rot. Pat.* i. 85 (Higham, 23rd July, 1208). On 17th November, 1207, the king had granted Robert his port of Milford at Haverford, a Sunday market, and an annual fair at the beginning of May (*Rot. Chart.* i. 173).

[108] *Ann. C.* MS. C. *s.a.* 1210, 1211; Gir. Camb. i. 179–80.

[109] "Griffino fili(o) Cadugan" witnessed a charter of Maelgwn to Strata Florida in January, 1198 (*Str. Flor.* appendix xiv.). The "kynan" of the Red Book of Hergest (*Bruts*, 346) is a slip for "kadwgan" — see Mostyn MS. 116 in Evans, *Rep.* i. p. 61 and *B.T.* 266, note 2.

[110] Described by *B.T.* (p. 266) as "Gelart (MSS. C. E.) synyscal kaer loyw". Engelard, one of John's group of foreign captains and officials, appears as sheriff of Gloucester on 26th February, 1210 (*Rot. regn. Joh.* 152). For his origin and history see *Trans. Roy. Hist. Sue.* 1904, p. 250. Builth had come into the possession of the crown with the fall of William de Breos, and Engelard was apparently custos of the Breos estates in Wales — see *Rot. Claus.* i. 135, 137, 148, 149.

[111] For John's Welsh expedition see *Ann. C.* MSS. B. and C.; *B.T.*; "O Oes Gwrtheyrn" in *Comment.* (2), 160, and Cardiff Public Library MS. 50; Wendover, iii. 235; Walt. Cov. ii. 203; *Ann. Marg., Theokesb. and Wigorn. s.a.* It is unfortunate that no Chancery roll of any description for the thirteenth year of John (1211–12) is now extant.

[112] In *B.T.* 267 "Kaer lleon" is absurdly translated "Caerleon"!

[113] Hywel, it has been shown, went with Llywelyn to the Scottish border in 1209. Madog and Llywelyn are coupled together in a royal letter of 29th July, 1204 (note 23 above), and the former was in the king's good graces in the spring of 1205, when the latter was cementing his alliance with the crown (*Rot. Claus.* i. 23).

[114] "Cito post pascha [3rd April]" — says *Ann. C.* MS. B. But John did not reach Chester until 16th May — see Hardy's *Itinerary* and *cf. Annales S. Albani* in Liebermann, *Ungedruckte Anglo-Normanische Geschichtsquellen*, p. 169.

[115] "Yar keynyauc atal" (Ven. III. xiii. 1).

[116] "Amgylch y sulgwyn" [22nd May] — *B.T.*

[117] *Ann. S. Albani, ut supra,* and Wendover.

[118] "Album Monasterium" is rendered Whitchurch by Coxe (Wendover, iii. 235) and also by Hardy in the entries for 6th to 10th August, 1216, in his *Itinerary*. But, though Whitchurch occasionally appears under this name, as in Gir. Camb. vi. 142 (*Itin.* ii. 12) and *Tax. Nich.* 247, it was indubitably borne also by Oswestry — see Gir. Camb. v. 375 (*Exp. Hib.* ii. 31); *Ann. C.* MS. B. *s.a.* 1233; *Cal. Doc. Fr.* i. 116 — and there was no comparison between the two towns as a suitable starting-point for a Welsh expedition.

[119] Robert had been consecrated by Archbishop Hubert at Westminster on 16th March, 1197 (H. and St. i. 391; *Reg. Sacr.* (2), 52). It would seem, however, that he had never been elected (Gir. Camb. i. 114), and interwoven with the story of the St. David's suit is that of the efforts of a certain "R.," subprior of Aberconwy, to obtain recognition as the true bishop-elect of Bangor (Gir. iii. 38–40, 66–7, 193, 195, 240–2, 287–8). He was at first supported by

Llywelyn, but his cause was afterwards given up, probably as part of the agreement with John in 1204. For Robert's death in 1212 see *B.T.* 272 (1211 = 1212); *Ann. Theokesb.* and *Wigorn. s.a.*

[120] "Y berued wlat" (*B.T.*) included Rhos, Rhufoniog, Tegeingl, and Dyffryn Clwyd (Rymer, i. 267).

[121] Thirty, according to *Ann. C.* MS. C. Wendover says twenty-eight, *Ann. Marg.* thirty-two, "O Oes Gwrtheyrn" twenty-five, including Llywelyn's son, Gruffydd, of whom this is the earliest mention.

[122] 15th August, according to Wendover.

[123] *B.T.* and *Ann. Marg.* For "Ffawcwn" as "synyscal kaer dyf" see note 101 above.

[124] "Catwalo in glamorgan predas et combustiones fecit" (*Ann. C.* MS. B. *s.a.* 1211). Cadwallon ab Ifor appears with other leading Welshmen of Morgannwg in a Margam charter of 1199 (*Cartae Glam.* iii. 175). In the summer of 1203 he was with the king in Normandy and helped Giraldus in his money difficulties (Gir. iii. 303), and in the following March John was anxious to take him abroad with him once more (*Rot. regn. Joh.* 85 — Westminster, 27th March). Giraldus calls him "cognatum suum" — he and the archdeacon were second cousins (p. 507). *Ann. Marg.* records the vengeance taken by John upon the two sons of Cadwallon whom he held as hostages.

[125] "Qui in Pascha cum rege Anglie fuerat, dicto rege apud Kanteberge Pascha celebrante" (*Ann. S. Edm. s.a.*). Miss Norgate's account of the relations of John with the Welsh during this year (*John Lackland,* pp. 167 9) overlooks this fact and is inexact in several other respects.

[126] The 1211 and 1212 of *B.T.* (pp. 270–2) are really the same year (the battle in Spain is that of Las Navas de Tolosa, fought on 16th July, 1212) Through this repetition, the error due to the omission of the year 1207 is righted, and the chronology of the Rolls edition becomes correct.

[127] *Ann. S. Edm.* John was at Durham on 28th June. He had on 26th May transferred Ceredigion from Maelgwn to Rhys ap Gruffydd (*Rot. Pat.* i. 93), but this was a consequence of the attack upon Aberystwyth in the previous year. The first indication in the rolls of fresh trouble in Wales is to be found on 6th July, when the king asked Falkes of Breauté what force he needed to repel an attack and ordered the replenishing of the stock of provisions kept at Oswestry (*Rot. Claus.* i. 119).

[128] *B.T., Ann. Waverl.*

[129] *Ann. S. Edm.* "Robertus Lupus" was made a custos of the vacant see of Lichfield (or Chester) on 9th October, 1208 (*Rot. Pat.* i. 86–7), and he was still acting in that capacity in May, 1212 (*Rot. Claus.* i. 116). He had also in June, 1212, the manor of Ellesmere (*Testa de Nevill,* 56). For the negotiations for his release see Pat. Rolls, Hen. III. i. 8.

[130] *Ann. Marg.*

[131] On 3rd August, the Earl of Chester was warned to treat him as a friend and ally (*Rot. Claus.* i. 121); a little later he is found in John's pay (123). Thus *B.T.* is clearly wrong in including him in the Welsh confederation, and the same remark applies to Maredudd ap Rhotpert of Cydewain — see *Rot. Claus.* i. 123. Neither name appears in the corresponding passage in *Ann. C.* MS. B.

[132] About 1st September Falkes was ordered to supply their needs (*Rot. Claus,* i. 123).

[133] *Rot. Claus.* i. 131.

[134] *B.T.* and *Ann. S. Edm.* relate the incident; the date is furnished by the Misae Roll of 14 John — see the edition of Henry Cole (1844), pp. 236, 237.

[135] Wendover says that all the hostages given up in 1211 were put to death, but this is an exaggeration; Gruffydd ap Llywelyn, in particular, was spared.

[136] Wendover, iii. 239; *Ann. S. Edm.*

[137] *Rot. Pat.* i. 94 (letters to the sheriffs and to the baronage); *Rot. Claus.* i. 121 (letters as to cattle). Miss Norgate assumes that there was only a temporary change of tactics on 16th August, and that the incident of the letters, followed by the final abandonment of the expedition, is to be connected with the September visit to Nottingham (*John Lackland,* pp. 168–9). But there is nothing in the rolls to warrant this view; on the contrary, they show that on 16th August all preparations for the Welsh war came suddenly, and for no specified reason, to an end — see especially the letter of the 18th written to the Mayor of Angoulême (*Rot. Claus,* i. 132).

[138] Rot. Claus. i. 121–2. Two galleys were to take surplus stores to Bristol.

[139] *Rot. Chart.* i. 188 (Southwark, 30th Oct.) — *cf. Gwydir Fam.* 17.

[140] See note 26 above.

[141] The king, however, retained the commote of Creuddyn in this cantref, with the castle of Degannwy.

[142] Gruffydd ap Rhodri appears a little later as a captain of Welshmen in the king's service (*Rot. Claus.* i. 210 — 14th Aug. 1214).

[143] *B.T.* 278.

[144] On 10th June, 1213, Robert was ordered to transfer "Carrecou" to the care of John Lestrange (*Rot. Pat.* i. 100). Other border castles held by him at this time were Chirk, Oswestry, Shrawardine and "Eggelawe" (*ibid.* and *Rot. Claus.* i. 132).

[145] "Ffawcwn synysgal kaerdyf" (*Bruts,* 349; *B.T.* 274).

[146] "Synysgal henford" (*ibid.*). Engelard appears as sheriff of Herefordshire in November, 1212 (*Rot. Claus.* i. 127). Cf. *Trans. Roy. Hist. Soc.* 1904, p. 250.

[147] Trallwng Elgan is a township in the north of the parish of Talley; it belonged to the canons of that place (*Mon. Angl.* iv. 164; *Arch. Camb.* V. x. [1893] 323).

[148] *Rot. Pat.* i. 100 (Wingham).

[149] *Ibid.* 103 (Northampton).

[150] On 18th August, 1214, the king wrote from Angoulême, ratifying the truce concluded between the justiciar, Bishop Peter of Winchester, and Llywelyn, Maelgwn, Gwenwynwyn and Madog ap Gruffydd (*Rot. Pat.* i. 120). Madog had clearly returned to his old allegiance in the course of the year.

[151] *Ann. C.* MS. B. aptly quotes, in reference to this movement, the prophecy of Merlin —"nam discidium alienigenarum orietur" (*Hist. Reg.* vii. 3).

[152] See page 544.

[153] *Rot. Pat.* i. 125; Rymer, i. 126. See also *Rot. Claus.* i. 181, for a letter of the same date to the sheriff of Gloucester, asking him to see that the hostages pay all charges incurred on their behalf before they depart. In January, 1215, William of Cantilupe was ordered to deliver another of Llywelyn's hostages to his clerk Ystrwyth (Rot. Pat. i. 126).

[154] *Rot. Claus.* i. 203; Rymer, i. 127. For William see *Dict. Nat. Biog.* xii. p. 228. The suggested place of meeting ("Ruth vel Crucem Griffin") was possibly Rhyd y Groes, near Welshpool, the scene of the victory of Gruffydd ap Llywelyn in 1039. The letter to the Welsh princes in *Rot. Pat.* i. 131 (Nottingham, 25th March) was probably given to the commissioners to take with them as their authority to the conference.

[155] *Rot. Pat.* i. 132.

[156] The first four were at the head of a force assembled at Gloucester for the king's defence at the end of April, 1215 (*Rot. Pat.* i. 134 — Marlborough, 30th April). Walter Lacy had been reinstated in his lands, except Ludlow, in July, 1213 (*Rot. Claus.* i. 147), and Ludlow was added in October, 1214 (*ibid.* 175). Peter was with the king when the Charter was sealed.

[157] *B.T.* 282. Letters despatched by John on 15th, 16th, and 24th May (*Rot. Pat.* i. 136, 138) show that he was anxious about the safety of the great Shropshire fortress of Bridgenorth ("Bruges").

[158] The alliance with the barons is proved by the Welsh articles in Magna Carta, no less than by the statements in *B.T.* and *Ann. C.* MS. B., while the latter source adds the special league with Bishop Giles.

[159] He witnesses royal charters dated 15th December, 1213, 28th October, 22nd November, 27th December, 1214, 9th and 15th January, 1215 (*Rot. Cart.* i. 195, 202, 203, 204, 206).

[160] For the "fine" see *Rot. Claus.* i. 189 (5th March, 1215); on 10th May (*Rot. Pat.* i. 141) John made a concession with regard to it, but it was too late. By 15th May Giles was in open hostility — see the order for the seizure of his Gloucestershire estates in *Rot. Claus.* i. 200.

[161] *B.T.* has "robert" (*Bruts*, 352), but no Robert de Breos of this age is otherwise known. Probably the author of this chronicle wrongly extended an R of his Latin original, which stood for Reginaldus. Powel (196) has, in fact, "Reynold".

[162] On the Usk, below Brecon. See *Breconsh.* (2), pp. 458–9; *Arch. Camb.* IV. iii. (1872), 386.

[163] The three castles of Grosmont, White Castle (or Llantilio — it stands in the parish of that name), and Skenfrith (from the Welsh "ynys gynwreid" — see *Bruts*, 352–3 and *Lib. Land.* 419 [index]), forming a triangle in Upper Gwent, nearly always went together. In the reign of Henry II. they were royal castles, for which the sheriff of Hereford was responsible — see Pipe Roll, 7 Hen. II. 19–20; 8, p. 58; 9, p. 7; 10, p. 6; 11, p. 100. John gave them on 26th July, 1201, to Hubert de Burgh (*Rot. regn. Joh.* 19), but on 16th December, 1205, transferred them to William de Breos (*Rot. Cart.* i. 160; *Rot. Pat.* i. 57). There are considerable remains of all three — see Coxe (2), 264–72.

[164] *B.T.* 286; *Ann. Wigorn.* and *Dunst.* (p. 52). She survived Reginald and in 1230 married Ralph Mortimer (*Ann. Wigorn. s.a.*); widowed the second time in 1246, she died in 1251 (*B.T.* 336 —"y bu uarw Gwladus Du").

[165] "In vigilia assencionis" (*Ann. C.* MS. B.).

[166] On 29th Jan. 1214, John ordered Falkes of Breauté to deliver to the Earl Marshall the castles of "Kaermerdin, Cardinan et Goher" (*Rot. Pat.* i. 109).

[167] *Rot. Pat.* i. 143 (Windsor, 13th June). "Resus Boscan" = Rhys Fychan; for the epithet see chap. xvi. note 17.

[168] Four castles in Gower were captured by Rhys, namely, those of Loughor, "Castell Hu" (possibly at Talybont — see Powel, 196; Morgan, *Survey of West Gower*, London, 1899, pp. 5–8), Oystermouth (= Ystum Llwynarth — see *Arch. Camb.* IV. xi. [1880], 155), and "Seinhenyd". The last named cannot have been in Senghenydd, which is many miles from Gower; it has been variously fixed at Llangenydd (*Arch. Camb.* II. ii. [1851], 67–8; Owen, *Pemb.* 1.258) and at Swansea (Morgan *ut supra*, 221–50; *W. People*, p. 248).

[169] FOR chapters 56, 57, and 58 of M. Carta (text, translation and commentary) see McKechnie, *Magna Carta* (Glasgow, 1905), pp. 533–7. The Articles of the Barons, §§ 44, 45, will be found on p. 574.

[170] Cases in point were 1: Ashford, which was in the king's hands in January, 1215 (*Rot. Claus.* i. 185–6); 2. Ellesmere, in John's possession in August, 1214 (*ibid.* 171); 3. the church of Salkeld, given by the king to Thomas of Argenteuil in September, 1214 (*Rot. Pat.* i. 122).

[171] McKechnie is surely wrong in classing this among instances of the action of the barons in securing their own rights, since the marcher interests of the insurgents were very small. The Earl of Essex (lord of Glamorgan — see note 43 above) is, of course, a notable exception, and one may add Foulk fitz Warren, who since 1204 had been lord of Whittington (*Rot. Pat.* i. 46 — *cf. Rot. Claus.* i. 126 and *Testa de Nevill*, 56 (inquest of 1212)).

[172] The "filium Lewelini" is not named, but can hardly be other than Gruffydd, who was handed over to the king in 1211 (see note 121), was still in captivity on 30th August, 1213 (*Rot. Pat.* i. 103), and, according to "O Oes Gwrtheyrn" (*Comment.* (2), 160–1), was released at the instance of Archbishop Stephen about 1215.

[173] *Rot. Pat.* i. 150 (Oxford, 22nd July).

[174] *Ibid.* 151 (Bridgenorth, 31st July).

[175] *Rot. Claus,* i. 226 (Downton, 19th Aug.).

[176] He was not at Runnymead, and on and July John invited him, with any friends he might choose, to an amicable conference (*Rot. Pat.* i. 146).

[177] "Rac ofyn y pab," says *B.T.* expressly. A reference in *Papal Letters* i. 41 shows he was threatened with suspension.

[178] A safe-conduct was issued to him on 9th Oct. (*Rot. Pat.* i. 156) and on the 21st John announces the agreement, made at the siege of Rochester (*ibid.* 157; *Rot. Claus.* i. 232).

[179] 17th November (*Reg. Sacr.* (2), 53). In *B.T.* 284 the reading of MSS. B. and C. (note *b*) is to be preferred to that of the Red Book.

[180] Hywel died in 1216 and was buried at Aberconwy (*Ann. C.* MS. B.; *B.T.* 294). Prydydd y Moch mourned his early death (*Myv. Arch.* I. 295 [208]; with "huysgwr yn oed gwas" *cf.* "was ieuanc" of MS. C. of *B.T.*). The "i ewythr" of the Book of Basingwerk (*B.T.* 288) is one of the inept additions of Gutyn Owain.

[181] Maredudd ap Cynan died in 1212 ("O Oes Gwrtheyrn" in *Comment.* (2), 160). His elegy was sung by Prydydd y Moch, who deplores (*Myv. Arch.* I. 297 [210])

> Dwyn meibyon kynan kyn bu llwyd yr un.

[182] Of Cydewain — see note 131. Maredudd was the son of Robert ap Llywarch ap Trahaearn (Dwnn, i. 107), who died in 1171 (*B.T.* 208; *B. Saes. s.a.*). He founded (before 1236) the Cistercian nunnery of Llanllugan (*Mont. Coll.* ii. [1869], 305–6).

[183] It had been in English hands since 1145 — see p. 501.

[184] Narberth is included in MS. B. of *B.T.* and also in Mostyn MS. 116; *cf.* also *B.T.* 306.

[185] The Welsh "Trefdraeth" (Strand Hamlet), which had since 1195 taken the place of Nevern as the seat of the lords of Cemais. The new "port," or borough, was founded by William fitz Martin.

[186] *B.T.* assigns the surrender of Cilgerran to the 27th (p. 286).

[187] *Ann. C.* MS. B.

[188] *B.T.*

[189] The "[p]elunyawc" of *B.T.* (*Bruts,* 355), *i.e.,* Peuliniog, was included in Cantref Gwarthaf — see p. 265.

[190] He had also the "maenor" of Myddfai in the Middle commote (Perfedd) of Cantref Bychan.

[191] "Castell Nant yr Arian," added in *B.T.,* was near Goginan, in the commote of Perfedd.

[192] On 13th April, 1216, at Reading, John ordered Brian de l'Isle to deliver to Gwenwynwyn his land "in Pecco" (*Rot. Pat.* i. 175).

[193] As early as 28th January John mentions in a letter to William Cantilupe that "terra de Mongumery" has been promised to Gwenwynwyn and must be reserved for him (*Rot. Claus.* i. 246).

[194] *Ann. C.* MS. B. is the sole authority for the date (its 1215 = 1216), but no reference to Gwenwynwyn as alive is to be found after 27th June, 1216 (*Rot. Pat.* i. 189 — Corfe).

[195] His itinerary is as follows: July 24–27, Hereford; 27, 28, Hay (= y Gelli of *B.T.* 292 — see p. 437 of this book); 29–31, Hereford; 31, Aug. 1, Leominster; 2, Radnor (= maes hyfeid of *B.T.*) and "Kingeshemed"; 3, "Kingeshemed" and Clun; 4, Shrewsbury; 6–10, Oswestry (not Whitchurch — see note 118 to this chapter); 11–14, Shrewsbury.

[196] Consecrated 24th July, 1316.

[197] See the preamble to the charter of 1216.

[198] *Ann. Waverl. s.a.*

[199] Raymond of Sully, Herbert of St. Quintin, Robert le Sor, Henry of Umfraville and Gilbert of Turbeville submitted on 28th June (*Rot. Claus.* i. 312–13).

[200] Peter was on the king's side as late as May, 1216 (*Rot. Pat.* i. 184; *Rot. Claus.* i. 272, 273), but by 6th August he had gone over to the opposition (*Rot. Claus.* i. 280). He returned to his allegiance on 13th July, 1217 (*Rot. Claus.* i. 314).

[201] Her second husband, the Earl of Essex (see note 43 to this chapter), died in February, 1216 (Coggeshall). At the time other submission (17th Sept. — Pat. Rolls, Hen. III. i. 92; *Rot. Claus.* i. 322) a third marriage, to Hubert de Burgh, was contemplated or had been effected (*Rot. Claus.* i. 319), but she died before 15th October (Pat. Rolls, Hen. III. i. 105), leaving no issue.

[202] His father, Robert Corbet, had been disseised on his account (Pat. Rolls, Hen. III. i. 127).

[203] William fitz Alan II. of Oswestry and Clun died in 1210 (*Ann. Dunst.*), leaving his heir, William fitz Alan III., under age. Thomas of Erdington had the custody of the lands in August, 1214 (*Rot. Claus.* i. 170) and married his daughter Mary to the young William (*ibid.* 330, 356), who, however, died without issue not long afterwards. The younger brother John then came into the property, but, being on the baronial side, did not enter into full possession until his submission on 14th November, 1217 (*Rot. Claus.* i. 343).

[204] He was "manifestus inimicus noster" as late as September, 1217 (*Rot. Claus.* i. 321), but had submitted before 11th February, 1218 (*ibid.* 352).

[205] *Rot. Pat.* i. 184, 192.

[206] *Rot. Claus.* i. 335.

[207] *Ibid.* 312; Pat. Rolls, Hen. III. i. 72–3.

[208] Sons of Matilda de Breos.

[209] A comparison of *B.T.* and *Ann. C.* MS. B. at this point will certainly confirm the supposition that the "Sein Henydd" of the former is Swansea. For the establishment of the Breos family in Gower see note 44 above.

[210] See MS. C. of *B.T.* Cefn Cynfarchan formed part of the original endowment of Whitland Abbey (*Rot. Chart.* i. 206); it lies a little eastward of Llanfallteg.

[211] "Lewelinus fait [apud] Woluedale [*sic* MS.] in Ros" — *Ann. C.* MS. C. in the same year as its notice of Henry's coronation.

[212] Rymer, i. 148.

[213] *B.T.* 302; *L'Hisfoire de Guillaume le Maréchal*, ed. Paul Meyer (Paris, 1894), ii. 277–9. Morgan had succeeded his father Hywel (for whom see p. 572) about 1210; he attests a Bassaleg charter of 1214–6 (*Mon. Angl.* iv. 634) as "Morgan de Karlion".

[214] A settlement was expected in November, 1217 — see Rymer, i. 149.

[215] The documents will be found in Rymer, i. 150; *Rot. Claus,* i. 378–9; Pat. Rolls, Hen. III. i. 143. The date was 16th March.

[216] This term, which is definitely mentioned in the crown missive to the men of the castelries of Cardigan and Carmarthen, was a common one at the time, it being held that no valid grant in perpetuity could be made while the king was a minor — see *Trans. Roy. Hist. Soc.* II. xviii. (1904), 280.

[217] According to the author of the metrical life of the Earl Marshall, there was a debate on the question at Worcester (ii. 279–82).

[218] *B.T.* 304; Rymer, i. 151 (*Rot. Claus.* i. 362); Pat. Rolls, Hen. III. i. 155.

[219] *Ann. Cest. s.a.*

CHAPTER VIII

[1] The chronology of *B.T.* is correct from 1218 to 1240, but there is much confusion in both MSS. of *Ann. Camb.*

[2] Letters, Hen. III. i. 136. Shirley assigns the letter to 1220, but it cannot be separated from another despatched by Pandulf from the same place on 11th July, which most certainly belongs to 1219. See H. and St. i. 457–8.

[3] Rymer, i. 159. Worcester and 7th January had originally been fixed for this meeting (*Rot. Claus.* i. 434), but at Llywelyn's request the day had been put off to 9th February (Letters, Hen. III. i. 58–9; 76). This arrangement, again, was upset by the need for Pandulf's presence in London (Rymer, i. 158). For the letter in which Llywelyn expresses, his readiness to come to Shrewsbury see Letters, Hen. III. i. 113–14.

[4] *Rot. Claus.* i. 417, 419.

[5] Rymer, i. 159. This is the earliest allusion to David.

[6] *B.T.* is the authority for this dispute and its settlement. Independent evidence as to the Shrewsbury meeting is afforded by Pat. Rolls, H. III. i. 294 (safe-conduct for Llywelyn, 23rd June) and *Rot. Claus.* i. 463 (letters dated from Shrewsbury, 28th June to and July).

[7] *Rot. Claus.* i. 463.

[8] On 3rd July (Bridgenorth), an annual pension of ten marks was granted to Llywelyn's clerk, Ystrwyth (*ibid.* 464).

[9] *Rot. Claus.* i. 486, 487.

[10] *B.T.* 310. He was buried in Strata Florida.

[11] See the writ of 11th August in *Rot. Fin.* i. 91.

[12] See Llywelyn's case in Letters, Hen. III. i. 122–3, which is clearly a reply to the demand of 10th May, 1220 (Worcester — *Rot. Claus.* i. 418). Hugh Mortimer II. had succeeded to the Wigmore barony on the death of his father Roger in June, 1214 (*Rot. Norm.* II. cxxi.).

[13] *Ann. Cestr. s.a.*

[14] *Ibid.* In Owen, *Catalogue*, 357, will be found an abstract of the marriage settlement (from Harl. MS. 2044), which shows that Llywelyn gave his daughter Bidford, Suckley, and Willington (in Shropshire) in frank marriage. The witnesses include Reiner, bishop of St. Asaph, Hugh, abbot of St. Werburgh's (d. 1226), Philip of Orreby, justice of Chester, Ednyfed Fychan, his son Goronwy, Master Ystrwyth and Master Adam. The original agreement, with Llywelyn's seal attached, is also in the British Museum, being Cotton Charter, xxiv. 17 — see Owen, 526.

[15] In addition to Maelienydd, there was a dispute about the manors of Knighton and Norton (Letters, Hen. III. i. 59–60) in the same region, which John had given to Thomas of Erdington in March, 1207 (Charter Rolls, i. 229) and which had afterwards passed to Llywelyn.

[16] For the marriage see *B.T.* 304. The four sons of the younger William de Breos (d. 1210), John, Giles, Philip, and Walter, were set at liberty in January, 1218 (Pat. Rolls, H. III. i. 134) — *cf. Rot. Pat.* i. 108 (21st January, 1214) and *Rot. Claus.* i. 168 (16th July, 1214). In the following year John and his mother, Matilda, who was a daughter of Earl Richard of Clare, sued Reginald de Breos for their rights (*Rot. Claus.* i. 405; Letters, H. III. i. 136). Except in Gower, however, Reginald was in possession and thus excluded his nephew in virtue of "casus regis" — see Pollock and Maitland, *History of English Law,* ii. p. 283.

[17] The ejection of Rhys from Gower is mentioned by Llywelyn himself in a letter which I am inclined to assign to the end of August, 1220. See Letters, Hen. III. i. 176 (the date July, 1221, rests on no substantial basis).

[18] *B.T.* 310. The date (about 6th December) comes from MS. C., and "sein henyd" is assumed to be Swansea.

[19] William was one of the twenty-five executors of Magna Carta. He took a leading part in the movement on behalf of Louis, and, notwithstanding his father's position, did not join the young king until March, 1217 (*Trans, Roy. Hist. Soc.* II. xviii. 263). At the time of Llywelyn's raid, there was a question at issue between him and the Government, *viz.,* his retention of Fotheringay Castle — see Patent Rolls, H. III. i. 236, 257, 272; *Rot. Claus.* i. 429; Letters, H. III. i. 150. He was, as he complained, not asked to join in the expedition of January, 1221, against the Count of Aumale (Letters, i. 170–1). *Cf.* as to his position, Letters, i. 244–6.

[20] For this raid see *Ann. Camb.* MSS. B. and C.; *B.T.* 306; *Ann. Dunst. s.a.* 1220; Rymer, i. 164.

²¹ See the letter in Letters, H. III. i. 141–2, which I am inclined to assign to 1219 rather than to 1220, as being of the nature of an appeal from one who had no design of immediate vengeance.

²² *Rot. Claus.* i. 428 (Striguil, 21st August).

²³ This authority is mentioned by *Ann. Dunst.* and also in the royal letter to Llywelyn of 5th October, 1220 (Rymer, i. 164).

²⁴ Letters, H. III. i. 176. "Die Veneris ante decollationem S. Johannis Baptistae" is to be compared with the "gwyl Ievan y kols" of *B.T.* Rhys Gryg had received Kidwelly and Carnwyllion in 1216; they were now restored to Hawise, the heiress of Thomas of London (Pat. Rolls, H. III. i. 291–2). The. . . gada of Shirley's text is, no doubt, Widigada, the part of Cantref Mawr between the Gwili and the Cothi, which had come to be regarded as an appurtenance of the castle of Carmarthen (*Royal Charters of Carmarthen*, Alcwyn Evans, 1878, 43, 46). An ode of Prydydd y Moch shows that Rhys afterwards took part in the raid upon Pembrokeshire. See *Myv. Arch.* I. 293 (207): *Kastell gwis* kystyngeist yn gleu. Ac *arberth* gosymerth goleu.

²⁵ Restored since its capture by the Welsh in 1215.

²⁶ On 5th September (*Ann. Camb.* MS. C.). The lordship of Haverford had been granted to the elder William Marshall in October, 1213 (*Rot. Pat.* i. 105; *cf. Rot. Claus.* i. 158–9).

²⁷ "Deinde apud pil (*sic* MS.) in ros pernoctauit" (*Ann. Camb.* MS. B). The priory of Pill, which stood a little to the north of the modern town of Milford Haven, was a cell of St. Dogmael's, founded by Adam of Roch, a knight of Rhos, about the year 1200 (*Mon. Angl.* iv. 502–5; Fenton (2), 100, 327).

²⁸ According to *Ann. Dunst.* the amount of the loss was greater than that of King Richard's ransom (£100,000) — a wild exaggeration which shows that the injury done was very substantial.

²⁹ See Letters, H. III. i. 143–4, 144–5, 150.

³⁰ Rymer, i. 164.

³¹ *Rot. Claus.* i. 431.

³² The story of this year must be pieced together from the following sources: *Ann. Camb.* MSS. B. C.; *B.T. s.a.; Ann. Dunst.*; Wendover, iv, 71–2 (wrongly inserted *s.a.* 1221) and 84–5 (where the events of 1220 and 1223 are run together); Rymer, i. 168, 169, 170; Pat. Rolls, H. III. i. 413, 481.

³³ The "dies captionis castri de Kinardesle" is often mentioned (Rymer, i. 170; Pat. Rolls, i. 481) as the day of the outbreak of war. The place was then held by Baldwin of Hodnet (*Rot. Claus.* i. 554), but the vill really belonged to Madog (ap Gruffydd ab Iorwerth Goch) of Sutton (Eyton, *Shrops*, xi. pp. 23–8).

³⁴ Foulk had been established at Whittington, in succession to the Welsh lords of Maelor Saesneg, in October, 1204 (*Rot. Pat.* i. 46). He was allowed to fortify his castle in June, 1221, but the concession was, in view of his record as a rebel baron, somewhat grudgingly made (*Rot. Claus.* i. 460 — *cf.* 520).

[35] *Rot. Claus.* i. 536.

[36] *Ann. Dunst.*

[37] For the dates see *Ann. Camb.* MS. C. and *B.T.* MS. B.

[38] On 16th May, at Westminster, the expenses were paid in advance of a royal messenger going to Usk with a letter for the earl (*Rot. Claus.* i. 546).

[39] It is said in *B.T.* that Llywelyn and the earl met before the king's council at Ludlow. A meeting at this place was certainly projected, to be held on 12th July (Pat. Rolls, H. III. i. 376), but there is no direct evidence that the purpose was fulfilled. One may note, however, after that date a distinct stiffening in the attitude of the government, as shown by ostentatious patronage of the sons of Gwenwynwyn (Pat. Rolls, i. 378) and cordial acknowledgment of the services of the Earl Marshall (*Rot. Claus.* i. 571).

[40] Rymer, i. 170. Reginald had in 1219 been aided by the crown to put the castle in a state of defence (*Rot. Claus.* i. 409).

[41] The following dates are supplied by the Close and Patent Rolls: Hereford, 19th September; Brenles (= Bronllys), 20th; Hereford, 24th; Leominster, 25th, 26th; Shrewsbury, 29th; Montgomery, 30th–11th October; Shrewsbury, 12th.

[42] See p. 649.

[43] The rolls are full for the next few months of references to building operations, etc., at Montgomery. The emphasis laid on the fact that this was *New* Montgomery (see especially Charter Rolls, i. 101) leaves no doubt that the former castle and town stood elsewhere, probably at Hên Domen.

[44] The three are mentioned as "inprisii" of Llywelyn in Pat. Rolls, H. III. i. 413, 481. On the other side was Cynan ap Hywel (see p. 634), who seized Is Aeron during this war, but ultimately received Emlyn and Ystlwyf from his patron, the Earl Marshall (*Ann. Camb.* MS. C.; Letters, H. III. i. 427).

[45] There was also a "generale interdictum in Wallia" (*Ann. Cest. s.a.*).

[46] Rhys and Maelgwn had set out to make their submission on 21st September and duly rendered it on 7th October (*Rot. Claus.* i. 564–5; Patent Rolls, i. 386).

[47] A commission, consisting of six supporters of Llywelyn and six of the earl, was appointed to determine by inquest what each prince held before the outbreak of hostilities (Pat. Rolls, i. 481). A document cited by Bridgeman (*Pces. S. Wales,* 100–2) shows that in 1222 Maelgwn still held Llandovery, Emlyn, Cemais, Ystlwyf, Gwinionydd, and Mabwnion, assigned to him in 1216.

[48] Pat. Rolls, i. 413–4 (7th November); *Rot. Claus.* i. 574 (6th and 8th November). The pope's letters of 5th October, 1223 (Rymer, i. 180 has 1225, incorrectly) to the Archbishop of Canterbury (*Papal Letters,* i. 93), and the Archbishop of York (Letters, H. III. i. 212–4) arrived, of course, too late to affect the situation.

[49] *Ann. Theokesb., Winton., Waverl. Cf.* Pat. Rolls, i. 426.

[50] Pat. Rolls, i. 437.

51 When Falkes fled before the royal attack upon him to Wales (Wendover, iv. 96), the king, at the suggestion of the bishop of Lichfield (Rymer, i. 175), wrote to Llywelyn, urging him not to receive or give encouragement to the fugitive. Llywelyn's reply will be found in Letters, i. 229–30. Falkes had, in fact, come and gone (by way of Chester) on the same day, and by 10th July was secretly making his way back across the border (*Rot. Claus.* i. 632). On 4th August the bishop of Lichfield brought the Earl of Chester a letter from the king, asking him to safeguard the peace of the marches, whereupon the earl met Llywelyn and arranged a month's truce (Letters, i. 233–5). Both magnates seek in their letters to exonerate Falkes, but the earl nevertheless joined in the siege of Bedford.

52 3rd February (*Rot. Claus.* i. 574), 5th, 12th May (Rymer, i. 172), 19th, 28th July (*Rot. Claus.* i. 631), and 8th September (Pat. Rolls, i. 489) were successively proposed by the king.

53 See the safe-conduct of 23rd September in Pat. Rolls, i. 471.

54 On 24th September, at Shrewsbury, the king orders the exchequer to allow the sheriff of Salop £8 7s. 4d. paid by him towards the expenses of Joan's journey to Worcester (*Rot. Claus.* i. 622). Henry was at Worcester on 19th September (*ibid.* 621).

55 *Rot. Claus.* ii. 18 (de manerio de Roel). Its annual value was £25.

56 *Ibid.* 47.

57 The dates proposed were 27th April, 8th July (Rymer, i. 178), 15th August (*Rot. Claus.* ii. 72), 3rd November, 1225, 29th March, 1226 (*ibid.* 83).

58 The general safe-conduct of 28th July (Patent Rolls, ii. 56) was supplemented by the more precise document of 27th August (*ibid.* 59). Henry's itinerary at this time is as follows: Hereford, 15th–21st August; Leominster, 22nd; Lydbury North, 23rd; Shrewsbury, 27th–29th; Wenlock, 29th; Bridgenorth, 30th.

59 *Papal Letters*, i. 109.

60 *Rot. Claus.* ii. 135 (29th August).

61 See especially, Pat. Rolls, ii. 110–11 (13th February, 1227), 112 (18th March, 1227).

62 Hugh was reported to be on his death-bed on 8th November (Pat. Rolls, ii. 169); on the 23rd, Ralph, having paid a relief of £100, was put in possession of his lands (*ibid.* 171).

63 There was a false report of his death in June, 1222 (Pat. Rolls, i. 334; *Rot. Claus.* i. 500). From *Rot. Fin.* i. 172 it is clear that it took place early in June, 1228. His son William succeeded to his lands on 13th July, 1228 (Pat. Rolls, ii. 194; *Rot. Fin.* i. 174).

64 William was of mature years, for as early as August, 1218, his father handed over to him his Sussex honours of Knap and Bramber (Pat. Rolls, i. 165). Hence he was not the son of Gwladus, Llywelyn's daughter (see p. 645) but of an earlier marriage.

[65] Pat. Rolls, ii. 80–1 (Rymer, i. 182); ii. 58 (Hereford, 18th August). Henry Audley was succeeded as keeper by John de Breos (25th October, 1226 — Pat. Rolls, ii. 66) and he in turn by Walter Clifford (25th April, 1228 — *ibid.* 184).

[66] Two marks were paid on 16th February to Master Philip and "Wrenno," envoys of Llywelyn, for their home-going expenses (*Rot. Claus.* ii. 18).

[67] *Ibid.* ii. 17 (15th February). The same envoys obtained a writ in favour of the widow of Robert ap Madog, who had nursed one of Llywelyn's daughters. Robert was a Welsh tenant of the honour of Montgomery and had fought for Llywelyn in 1223 (Rymer, i. 170; *Rot. Claus.* i. 611, 623; ii. 8, 16, 17).

[68] The appointment of the commission (perhaps because that of November, 1223 — see note 47 above — had proved abortive) was asked for by Llywelyn, through his messenger David, and granted on 14th April (Rymer, i. 178). David came back on 3rd June (see the order for payment of his expenses on the 4th — *Rot. Claus.* ii. 43) to say that Owain ap Gruffydd, who now held Northern Ceredigion, would not give up the commote of Creuddyn to Maelgwn, to whom the commissioners had awarded it (*ibid.* 73).

[69] Note 44.

[70] *Rot. Fin.* i. 169 (27th March); Close Rolls, Hen. III. i. 50 (16th May).

[71] Charter Rolls, i. 74. *Cf.* Pat. Rolls, H. III. ii. 186.

[72] Wendover (iv. 172–4) is the principal authority for the campaign. The names of Cefn y Coed, Bron y Coed and Goetre still preserve the memory of the "silvam quae spatiosa erat nimis habens quinque leucarum longitudinis".

[73] Henry's itinerary, as extracted from the rolls, is as follows: Bridgenorth, 28th August; Shrewsbury, 29th–31st; Montgomery, 3rd–23rd September; Shrewsbury, 24th; Kerry, 25th–4th October.

[74] The king's letter, dated 8th September, is in Close Rolls, i. 116, and Letters, i. 335–6. It refers to the truce, which was no doubt arranged by Joan under protection of the safe-conduct granted to her on 13th August (Pat. Rolls, ii. 201). At that time Henry thought it possible Llywelyn might come also, and the marchers were warned not to molest him (Close Rolls, i. 114, and Letters, i. 334–5).

[75] Close Rolls, i. 115.

[76] There is no evidence that a Cistercian abbey ever stood in the vale of Kerry, and the "habitaculum albi ordinis" must, therefore, have been a grange. Cwm Hir possessed, as part of its original endowment, lands at Gwern y gof, Caeliber, Gwenrhiw and Bahaithlon (*Rot. Chart.* 206; *Mon. Angl.* v. 459), which formed the grange of Gwern y gof in the lordship of Kerry (*Valor Eccl.* iv. 407), and, after the dissolution, the manor of Hopton (*App. Land Com.* 452). Whence the name "Cridia" comes is not apparent; I hesitate to accept the conjecture, adopted by Mr. Richard Williams in his article on this campaign, that it is a corruption of "Crefydd-dy" (*Arch. Camb.* IV. x. (1879), 249), for the term does not seem to have been in common use in mediæval times. It may, indeed, be a mere misreading of Cuira (Cumira), which is found in Wendover, iv. 222.

[77] According to *Ann. Dunst.* "Justus haeres" got "terram de Keri "in return for a fine of 1,000 cows.

[78] Its site cannot be fixed with certainty, but Mr. Williams's view that it was at Pen y Castell has much to recommend it.

[79] Close Rolls, i. 123 (8th November, Westminster).

[80] Pat. Rolls, ii. 239 (12th February, Westminster).

[81] Nicholas, "abbas de Valle Dei" in Lincolnshire, received a safe-conduct for the purpose of visiting Llywelyn about 15th July (Pat. Rolls, ii. 257).

[82] The safe-conduct for the purpose was issued at Windsor on 5th September (*ibid.* 263), and Henry announces the result of the visit on 3rd October, (*ibid.* 269–70 and Rymer, i. 196). The sister who came with David and is afterwards found in the care of Segrave (Close Rolls, i. 259) was perhaps Gwladus Ddu — see Pat. Rolls, ii. 248.

[83] For the terms of release see *Ann. Dunst.* (p. 117).

[84] This was what actually happened as to the instalment of 250 marks due from Llywelyn at Easter, 1229 (Pat. Rolls, ii. 241).

[85] Brief accounts of this tragedy will be found in *Ann. C.; B.T.*; Wendover (iv. 209); *Ann. Cest., Marg., Theokesb., Waverl., Wigorn;* Letters, i. 366–7. All agree as to the charge against William, but some of the annalists treat it as false and Llywelyn's action as a mere plot to justify murder. This is unlikely for many reasons; against it may be urged, in particular, the fact of the imprisonment of Joan (*Ann. Cest.*), and the circumspect attitude of the government. Hubert de Burgh was accused at the time of his fall of having given the information which brought about the crisis (Wendover, iv. 247), which shows that Llywelyn was not supposed to have acted without good grounds.

[86] The news of William's imprisonment reached the king at Portsmouth on 20th April, and he forthwith made arrangements for the custody of his castles of Radnor, Brecon, Hay, Huntington, Abergavenny, and St. Clear's (Pat. Rolls, ii. 336; *cf.* 339).

[87] Letters, i. 366–7. William's death was known to the chancellor as a certainty on 25th May, when he gave the custody of his lands to the Earl Marshall (Close Rolls, i. 353). The king did not hear of it until 31st May (Pat. Rolls, i. 377).

[88] "Crokein" cannot, unfortunately, be located with any certainty. The traditional scene of the execution is Aber (Pennant, iii. 111–12), where Gwern y Grog (Gallows Marsh) and Cae Gwilym Ddu (Black William's Field) are popularly associated with it. But there is reason to think that this arose from the notion that Llywelyn's court was always at Aber. On 15th May, he was at "Tynbey," *i.e.*, Denbigh (Letters, i. 366).

[89] For "Crogyn" = hangdog, see Evans, *Dict. s.v.*

[90] Letters, i. 368. She was Eva, daughter of the elder William Marshall.

[91] *Ibid.* 369. "*Fratri* carissimo" is explained by the fact that the earl was married to Joan's half-sister, Eleanor.

[92] *Ibid.* 366. The letters printed by Shirley in ii. 3–8 clearly refer to difficulties which arose between Llywelyn as lord of Buellt (for his son David) and William of Christchurch, seneschal of the Earl Marshall (Close Rolls, i. 355, 489), at the time when the latter had the custody of the Breos lordship of Brecknock (Close Rolls, i. 353; Patent Rolls, ii. 427). Further, since William writes to the chancellor, the letters belong to the period of Henry's absence in 1230, while the reference to the harvesting of crops (ii. 5) points to the September of that year. Now there is in them definite mention of a "colloquium" recently held between Llywelyn and the chancellor at "Nokesbure" (a place not yet identified) which resulted in an agreement, and which must surely be connected with the plans of Letters, i. 366 and the presence of the chancellor and Segrave at Shrewsbury on 11th, 12th, and 13th June (*Rot. Fin.* i. 198; Pat. Rolls, ii. 346; Close Rolls, i. 355).

[93] Close Rolls, i. 368.

[94] See chap. xvii. note 163. The "tria castra domini justiciarii" (*Arch. Camb.* IV. x. (1879), 304) were declared to have been adjudged to Hubert by the king's court in a letter to the sheriff of Hereford dated 26th January, 1219 (*Rot. Claus.* i. 386). They were claimed by the Breos family, and in 1228 John was for a short time allowed to hold them (Charter Rolls, i. 74), but before the end of the year they were recovered by the justiciar (*ibid.* 83), who held them at his fall.

[95] Originally made on 25th August, 1227 (Charter Rolls, i. 57); for later confirmations see *ibid,* 58, 83. *Cf.* also Pat. Rolls, ii. 145.

[96] Charter Rolls, i. 100; Pat. Rolls, ii. 276. The grant was confirmed in 1231 — see Pat. Rolls, ii. 424.

[97] Pat. Rolls, ii. 417 (20th November, 1230); Charter Rolls, i. 127.

[98] Gilbert died at "Penros" (Perros Guirec?) on 25th October, on the way home from the French expedition. His eldest son, Richard, was born on 4th August, 1222 (*Ann. Theokesb.*).

[99] Pat. Rolls, ii. 412 (1st November, 1230).

[100] *Ann. Camb.* MSS. B. and C.; Wendover, iv. 220; *Ann. Theokesb.*

[101] They had at first been committed to the Earl of Cornwall (Pat. Rolls, ii. 428 — 11th April), but were afterwards transferred to Hubert (*ibid.* 434 — 20th May).

[102] The fullest account of the war of 1231 is that given by Wendover (iv. 220–7), but it requires to be checked by comparison with *Ann. C.* MS. B.; *B.T.*; *Ann. Cest., Marg., Theokesb., Dunst,, Wigorn.*, and the Charter, Patent and Close Rolls.

[103] Close Rolls, i. 585 (Windsor, 27th "Octobris" — a slip for "Aprilis").

[104] *Ibid.* 588. This was a favourite method of applying pressure to the Welsh; see Wm. Newb. ii. 5 and Gir. Camb. vi. 218 (*Descr.* ii. 8).

[105] Llywelyn's envoys met the king at Worcester on 27th May and plans were laid for a further conference of delegates at Shrewsbury on 3rd June (Rymer, i. 200; Pat. Rolls, ii. 436).

[106] Wendover.

[107] *B. T.* suggests that all four castles ("Y kestyll") were taken, but *Ann. Marg.* says of "Aberotheny" (Aberhonddu, *i.e.*, Brecon) "castellum non cepit," and *Ann. C.* MS. B. has "mungumriam brechoniam et haiam cum radenor castello".

[108] *Ann. Marg. Ann. ad* 1198 says Llywelyn took "castrum de Neth" about 29th June. For Morgan see chap. xvii. note 213; he sued the Ear) Marshall for Caerleon in the king's court in 1220 (*Rot. Claus.* i. 436), but, notwithstanding some threatening proceedings on the part of the crown (Pat. Rolls, i. 352, 363; ii. 82–3), "Kaerlyon" was in the earl's possession at his death (*ibid.* ii. 427).

[109] For the first two see Pat. Rolls, ii. 412. Rhys was the son of Gruffydd ab Ifor (*Cartae Glam.* iii. 542), who died in 1211 (*B. T.* MS. C.), and he was, no doubt, like his father (*Cartae*, iii. 112–13), lord of Senghenydd. Hywel was the son of Maredudd ap Caradog ab Iestyn and his portion of Morgannwg was Miskin, to which he seems in 1228 to have added Glyn Rhondda, held by his cousin, Morgan ap Cadwallon (*Ann. Marg. s.a.* 1228, 1229; *Ann. Theokesb. s.a.* 1242; *Cartae Glam.* iii. 262; *Arch. Camb.* VI. i. (1901), 2). Morgan Gam (the Crooked) inherited Rhwng Nedd ac Afan from his father, Morgan ap Caradog ab Iestyn.

[110] Maelgwn ap Rhys last appears on 20th November, 1230 (Close Rolls, i. 458); by 14th February, 1231, his place has been taken by Maelgwn Fychan (Pat. Rolls, ii. 424). *B. T.* assigns his death to 1231, but *Ann. C.* MS. C. has "Mailgun f. resi obiit," in a passage omitted from the printed text, under an "annus" which is clearly 1230. Maelgwn died at Llannerch Aeron and was buried in the chapter house of Strata Florida (B.T.); his lands were chiefly in Ceredigion below Aeron.

[111] *Ann. Dunst.*; Letters, i. 400–1. The assembly was no doubt held, as arranged, at Oxford on 13th July. Anselm of St. David's and Elias of Llandaff, being Englishmen, were summoned, but not, it will be observed, Martin of Bangor and Abraham of St. Asaph. The archbishop was at the time in Italy.

[112] Close Rolls, i. 592 (castrum de Novo Burgo).

[113] *Ibid.* 523; Pat. Rolls, ii. 440.

[114] The king was at Gloucester on the 19th and at Hereford on the 22nd. For the summons to the host see Close Rolls, i. 592 (end of June), and for Henry's apologies for delay, *ibid.* 594–5.

[115] See p. 586. The "castrum Matildis" of the rolls ("castellum Matildis" in Wendover, "castellum Maud" in *Ann. Theokesb.*) is "(k)astell paen" in *B. T.* and "castellum payn" in *Ann. Cest. Ann. C.* MS. B., in ignorance of the identity, duplicates the entry, having first "castellum paen" and then "castrum matildis".

[116] Wendover, whose account is circumstantial, says "non longe a castello Mentis Gomerii" (iv. 222), but the Tewkesbury annalist, who knew the district better, has "non longe ab Haya," and Walter of Godarville, who was sent to Abergavenny on 12th May (Pat. Rolls, ii. 434), is more likely to have been moved to Hay than to Montgomery. The abbey had made its peace before 22nd August, when special protection was accorded to its granges of Cabalva and Carnaff (= Tirymyneich, near Clyro; see *Radnorsh.* (2), pp. 250, 334), not far from Hay.

[117] *Ann. Theokesb.* p. 80. In *Mon. Angl.* iv. 56 is a letter, probably belonging to this period, in which Llywelyn warns his bailiffs of Maelienydd not to interfere with the priory.

[118] Letters, i. 402–3 (= Close Rolls, i. 600). An organised attack by sea would have placed Llywelyn in great straits, but there is no indication that this policy was ever taken up in good earnest by the crown.

[119] A safe-conduct was issued to the Welsh envoys on 24th November (Pat. Rolls, ii. 452) and they appear to have come to London.

[120] Rymer, i. 201 = Pat. Rolls, ii. 453.

[121] Philip and "Instructus," received a safe-conduct to visit the king in February, 1232 (Pat. Rolls, ii. 460) and Philip was at Westminster on 12th March (*ibid.* 466). Correspondence had meanwhile passed as to breaches of the truce (Close Rolls, ii. 127, 132, 139). The king was at Shrewsbury on 27th May, on 7th August, and on 4th December, but apparently did not meet Llywelyn, who was represented by his wife, his son David, and Ednyfed Fychan (Pat. Rolls, ii. 476; Cal. Pat. R. i. 4).

[122] On 19th September, 1232, the tenants of Cardiff, Newport, Glamorgan, Cardigan, and Carmarthen were notified that they were to obey Peter as "custos" (Pat. Rolls, ii. 500–1), and on the 28th a similar notice was sent to the constable of the "three castles" in Upper Gwent (*ibid.* 502 — Blancchastel == Llantilio).

[123] The earl died at Wallingford on 26th October (*Ann. Cest., Theokesb.*), a date confirmed by Close Rolls, ii. 123 (De manerio de Lech), 123 (Pro dementia).

[124] *Ann. Theokesb.* (p. 79) and *Ann. Cest.* (pp. 56–8) mention the quarrel, but not its cause; according to *Ann. Dunst.* (p. 127), the earl "nimis fovit partes Lewelini".

[125] Acc. to *Ann. Cest.*, he received the earldom at Northampton on 21st November.

[126] *B.T.* 320; Pat. Rolls, ii. 490 (Lambeth, 16th July), 491; Close Rolls, i. 86. John's widow, Margaret, was promised on 7th June, 1233, that her hand should not be disposed of against her will (Cal. Pat. Rolls, i. 18), a concession obtained, it is clear, by the envoys of her father (see the previous entry in the roll).

[127] On 22nd June, 1231, Henry promised Richard his brother's possessions (Close Rolls, i. 590–1) and on 8th August it was announced that he had received them (*ibid.* 541). Grave doubt is thus thrown upon Wendover's story (iv. 225) as to Richard's extorting recognition by force from an unfriendly sovereign.

[128] For the Irish scheme see Close Rolls, ii. 315–9. Its abandonment was announced on 28th August (*ibid.* 322). Henry was at Hereford from the 19th of this month until the 29th, at Hay from the 31st until 3rd September, at Ewyas on the 3rd, at Abergavenny on the 5th, and again on the 7th and 8th, at Usk on the 6th and 7th, and again at Hereford on the 10th.

[129] Walter's lands were seized before 23rd August (Close Rolls, ii. 251), and before the end of the month the king was in possession of his castles of Bronllys (Brenles) and Glasbury (Cal. Pat. Rolls, i. 25). At the same time, his knight,

Hugh of Kinnersley, lost Aberllyfni (Close Rolls, ii. 257). He made his peace on 17th September at Shrewsbury (*ibid.* 267 — *cf.* Cal. Pat. Rolls, i. 25 (16th Sept.)) and was with the king in the war at the end of the year.

[130] Wendover (iv. 275); *Ann. Theokesb,;* Close Rolls, ii. 259, 323.

[131] *Ann. C.* MS. B.; *B.T.; Ann. Theokesb.*

[132] Rymer, i. 210 (Close Rolls, ii. 322, 323–4); Letters, i. 423 (*ibid.* 324–5).

[133] Close Rolls, ii. 280. *Cf.* 327 (order to sheriff of Salop on 15th Oct.). Purleigh was transferred to another grantee on 25th December (*ibid.* 356).

[134] Richard had not declared himself on 14th October — see Close Rolls, ii. 280 — but on the 28th preparations were in full swing for a campaign against him and the Welsh (*ibid.* 542–3). Usk was held for the king by Henry de Turbeville (*ibid.* 353–4).

[135] *Ann. Theokesb.* dates this event 15th October and says that Warin Basset fell in the assault. Earl Richard was at Cardiff on the 21st.

[136] With the Marshalls were Gilbert Turbeville, Raymond Sully, Gilbert Umfraville, John le Sor, John of St. Quintin, and Roger Berkrolles. The king's adherents included John of Monmouth, John fitz Alan, Walter Clifford, Walter Lacy, and Thomas Corbet.

[137] Hubert de Burgh was carried off to Chepstow, by way of Aust ferry, on his release from captivity at the end of October (Wykes).

[138] Wendover, iv. 278–9. Henry was at Grosmont on 11th, 12th, and 13th November (Close Rolls, ii. 338; Cal. Pat. Rolls, i. 32).

[139] *B.T.*

[140] Wendover, iv. 291. *B.T.* and *Ann. C.* MS. B. mention the burning of Clun, Oswestry, and the Teme valley, and the capture of an unknown "castell hithoet". The last-named appears as "Castell Coch" (*i.e.* Powis Castle) in *B.T.*, but this castle was in Llywelyn's own territory of Powys Wenwynwyn.

[141] *Ann. C.* MS. C.; *B.T.; Ann. Theokesb.*

[142] Henry was appointed constable of Carmarthen on 17th March, 1234 (Cal. Pat. Rolls, i. 41), and ten days later the men of Bristol were ordered to supply him with corn, beans, pease, bacon, salt, and wine for the provisioning of the castle (Close Rolls, ii. 394).

[143] *Ann. Theokesb.; B.T.; Ann. C.* MS. B. Rhys was buried in St. David's Cathedral and his elegy was sung by Dewi Mynyw (*Myv. Arch.* I. 543 (357)), or, it may be, Y Prydydd Bychan (*ibid.* 384 (262)).

[144] Or, perhaps, near Worthen, where there is also a place of this name.

[145] The truce of Brockton is referred to in Letters, i. 433 (Cal. Pat. Rolls, i. 43). A safe-conduct was issued to Llywelyn's envoys on 11th March (*ibid.* 41), and on the 28th the king informed his captains at Monmouth that he had agreed to a truce, though for a shorter period than that proposed by the two bishops (Close Rolls, ii. 555).

[146] *Ann. Theokesb.; Mon. Angl.* v. 266.

[147] Immediately after the council of 9th April, Henry had confirmed the truce of Brockton, securing peace until 25th July, and it was arranged that the archbishop should see Llywelyn on 2nd May as to a permanent agreement. See Letters, i. 433–5. But, on hearing of the death of Earl Richard, Llywelyn apparently declined to proceed until there had been complete reparation to the earl's injured followers. Hence the letter of the king dispatched early in June and printed in Rymer, i. 212 (Close Rolls, ii. 564–5).

[148] Cal. Pat. Rolls, i. 59. *Cf.* Rymer, i. 213 (Close Rolls, ii. 568–9).

[149] It was prolonged on 11th July, 1236 (Rymer, i. 229; Cal. Pat. Rolls, i. 153), on 14th June, 1237 (Rymer, i. 232; C.P.R. i. 186), and on 8th July, 1238 (Rymer, i. 236; C.P.R. i. 225). The Patent Roll for 1238–9 is not extant.

[150] The earliest occurrence of the title which I have been able to trace is on 1st May, 1230 — see Evans, *Rep.* ii. p. 859 (copy by Ieuan Brydydd Hir of Rhos Fyneich charter). In English documents it first appears on 27th May, 1231 (Rymer, i. 200; Pat. Rolls, ii. 436).

[151] The supremacy of Aberffraw is involved in the statement of Ven. I. ii. 3 that "gold is not paid (as sarhad) to any other than the king of Aberffraw," and is explicitly asserted in Lat. C. I. v. 1 (ii. 894–5). Both authorities, it should be added, are Venedotian and not older than the thirteenth century.

[152] *Myv. Arch.* I. 304 (215) ("Y deheu neud teu ual teithyawc").

[153] See Letters, i. 452–5 (Close Rolls, ii. 590–1,595) for an attempt in August, 1234, to obtain suzerainty over Morgan Gam, Rhys ap Gruffydd, Hywel ap Maredudd, and Morgan of Caerleon.

[154] See chap. xvii. note 182.

[155] Sons of the Owain Fychan who was slain in 1187 (p. 565). Llywelyn obtained protection from John on 30th August, 1204 (*Rot. Pat.* 45). He was dead in 1241, but his son Llywelyn and his brother Owain appear in that year in *Rot. Fin.* i. 342. Owain, known like his father as Owain Fychan, appears as a magnate in May, 1218 (Rymer, i. 151; *Rot. Claus.* i. 362).

[156] Represented in 1245 by Gruffydd ab Owain, Owain ap Bleddyn ab Owain (for Bleddyn see Rymer, i. 151), and Elise ab Iorwerth ab Owain (Rymer, i. 258).

[157] *B.T. s.a.* 1215.

[158] Madog appears as lord of Maelor Saesneg in 1212 (*Arch. Camb.* III. xii. (1866), 414) and in 1229 (Close Rolls, i. 250), and, no doubt, Overton Madog took its name from him, since there is no evidence that it was ever held by Madog ap Maredudd.

[159] *Ann. C.* MS. B. and *B.T.*

[160] Madog appears in association with Llywelyn in 1218 (*Rot. Claus.* i. 379), 1223 (Pat. Rolls, i. 411), 1229 (Close Rolls, i. 250), and 1232 (*ibid.* ii. 139).

[161] *Ann. C.* MS. B. and *B.T.*

[162] See note 54 to chap. xvii.

[163] The story comes from the report of the commission as to Henry VII.'s ancestry (Wynne, 331–2). It may be a genuine reminiscence of the campaign of 1210 — see p. 632.

[164] "Item obiit Ideneueth Justiciarius Walliae" (*Ann. Cest. s.a.*)

[165] *Rot. Claus.* i. 379 (Etuenech Bachan).

[166] Owen, *Catalogue*, i. p. 357. In 1223 he was nominated as one of the six representatives of Llywelyn upon the commission of inquiry as to South Wales lands (Pat. Rolls, i. 413, 481).

[167] Pat. Rolls, ii. 271 (Edeneuet senescallus Lewelini), 453, 471, 475, 476 Cal. Pat. Rolls, i. 3, 4, 17, 225, 237; Close Rolls, ii. 139.

[168] The usual meaning of the epithet "Fychan" (Little) at this time, *viz.*, Junior, would make him a son of Ednyfed, but the pedigrees do not show this.

[169] *Ann. C.* MS. B.

[170] Cal. Pat. Rolls, i. 108. The journey talked of in December, 1232 (*ibid.* 6), was clearly not carried out at the time.

[171] A charter copied by Ieuan Brydydd Hir from the original contains Llywelyn's confirmation at "Estrad" (near Denbigh), on 1st May, 1230, of the purchase by "Idneved Vachan Senescallus noster" of "Ros Veneych" from the heirs of Dineirth of the tribe of Marchudd (ap Cynan). See Evans, *Rep.* ii. p. 859 (Panton MSS.).

[172] Pat. Rolls, ii. 271.

[173] Pat. Rolls, ii. 471, 476; Cal. Pat. Rolls, i. 3; Rymer, i. 236.

[174] Pat. Rolls, ii. 436; Rymer, i. 235, 236.

[175] See chap. xvi. note 53. The "Instructus" of Pat. Rolls, ii. 452, 460, and Close Rolls, ii. 132, was perhaps a younger man.

[176] Pat. Rolls, ii. 436; Owen, *Catalogue*, p. 357; Cal. Pat. Rolls, i. 3.

[177] *Rot. Claus.* ii. 43; Rymer, i. 178, 208; Pat. Rolls, ii. 436.

[178] Pat. Rolls, ii. 452, 460, 466; Close Rolls, ii. 132; Cal. Pat. Rolls, i. 225; Rymer, i. 236.

[179] "Lewelinus princeps Wallye recepit uxorem suam. . . quam antea incarceravit" (*Ann. Cest. s.a.* 1231).

[180] Pat. Rolls, ii. 476.

[181] Other royal residences of this period were Carnarvon, Rhosyr, Cemais, and Llanfaes — see *Mon. Angl.* iv. 582.

[182] "In Purificationis" (*Ann. Cest.*); "vis whefrawr yn llys Aber" (*B.T.*).

[183] *B.T.* Llanfaes was the royal manor of Tindaethwy, with a port and ferry — see *Trib. System*, App. 3–4. Its church (St. Catherine's) was in 1254 the most valuable in the deanery (*Arch. Camb.* V. xi. (1894), 32) and was quite distinct from the friary. Bangor was vacant; hence the appearance of the bishop of St. Asaph.

[184] *Arch. Camb.* I. ii. (1847), 316; IV. vi. (1875), 142–3 (Bloxam).

[185] The first mention of Gruffydd is as a hostage in the hands of King John from 1211 to 1215 — see chap. xvii. notes 121 and 172. That he was illegitimate is clear from the language of the papal letter of 26th May, 1222 (*Papal Letters*, i. p. 87), language, it is to be noted, which was dictated by Llywelyn himself.

[186] Dwnn, ii. 107.

[187] See p. 656.

[188] *Papal Letters*, i. p. 87.

[189] *Ibid.* p. 109.

[190] See pp. 670, 671.

[191] *B.T.* It was, no doubt, after this that Llywelyn ap Maredudd (see note 157) obtained his patrimony of Meirionydd.

[192] *Ibid.*

[193] *Ann. Cest. s.a.* 1228 and 1234, confirmed by *B.T. s.a.* 1234.

[194] *B.T.* The appointment of the Earl Marshall as custos was signified on 11th January, 1215 (*Rot. Pat.* i. 126; *Rot. Claus.* i. 182).

[195] *Rot. Claus.* i. 191, 203. John's candidate was Hugh Foliot, Archdeacon of Salop.

[196] *Rot. Pat.* 143 (Windsor, 18th June). Iorwerth was consecrated at Staines on 21st June (*Reg. Sacr.* (2), 54).

[197] *Men. Eccl.* vii. (*Works*, iii. 361–4).

[198] See p. 653.

[199] Jones and Freem. 321.

[200] The new tower collapsed in 1220 (*Ann. C. MS. C.*), and important building was done between this date and 1248 (Jones and Freem. 147).

[201] Bishop Robert had died in 1212 (chap. xvii. note 119). On 13th March, 1215, John granted the request of the chapter for freedom of election, but asked them (was it to save his face?) to elect the abbot of Alba Landa (*Rot. Pat.* 130). By 13th April this had been done and the royal assent was given on that day (*ibid.* 132 — read *C* for *O*). For his consecration see *Ann. Wigorn.*, H. and St. i. 455, *Reg. Sacr.* (2), 54. *B.T.* calls him "Kadwgawn llan dyffei" (*Bruts*, 353), *i.e.*, of Llandyfeisant (near Llandeilo) or Lamphey. The "Martinus" of *Ann. Wigorn.* and *Ann. Theokesb.* (which are clearly not independent in this notice) is probably a slip; the latter has the right name *s.a.* 1241. The unnamed bishop who is pilloried by Gir. Camb. in *Spec.* iii. 7 (*Works*, iv. 161–7) is beyond doubt Cadwgan, and the abuse, exaggerated as it no doubt is, would be pointless if Llywelyn had not favoured his election.

[202] Close Rolls, ii. 417.

[203] Gregory IX. gave his consent on 1st March, 1236 (*Papal Letters*, i. p. 151), and about 6th June Master Guy, dean of Bangor, obtained the leave of the crown for a new election (Cal. Pat. Rolls, i. 149). The submission of "Caducanus" to the abbot of Dore will be found in B. Willis, *Bangor*, pp. 186–7. He died in the abbey on 11th April, 1241 (*Ann. Theokesb.*).

[204] Bishop Reiner (there were perhaps two of the name) died in 1224 (*Ann. Theokesb.*) and was succeeded by Abraham, probably a Welshman, who was consecrated on 20th June, 1225 (*Reg. Sacr.* (2), 56), and died in 1232 (*B.T.*). Permission to elect was granted to the chapter on 4th February, 1233 (Cal. Pat. Rolls, i. 10), and on nth April, 1234, the king assented to the election of Hugh, a Dominican friar (*ibid.* 42), who was consecrated on 17th June, 1235 (*Reg. Sacr.* (2), 58).

[205] Gir. Camb. (*Itin.* ii. 7 (vi. 131)) describes the life of the "eremitae" of "Enislannach". They puzzled Gervase of Canterbury, who calls them "monachi albi per se" (ii. 444). But they were certainly not Cistercians, nor yet Benedictines (Dugdale and Tanner); as in the cases of Aberdaron, Enlli and Beddgelert, their usual designation of "canons" was an attempt to interpret their real position as members of an ancient "clas". See chap. vii. § 2.

[206] See Llywelyn's charters of 15th October, 1221, and 10th April, 1237 (with confirmations by David as heir in 1229 and 1238) in *MON. ANGL.* iv. 581–2. It is not clear whether the prior and canons of "Insula Glannauc" (for the name see chap. vii. note in) possessed the "abbadaeth," *i.e.*, the ecclesiastical and territorial rights, of the "clas" of Penmon before 1237, but this seems most likely. There was a church on the island, of the same age as that on the mainland.

[207] Chap xvi. notes 144, 148.

[208] Gir. records visits paid by Llywelyn to Strata Florida about 1214 (iv. 162–3) and it was at the abbey that the important assembly of 1238 took place.

[209] P. 604.

[210] See chap. x. extra note B.

[211] See note 151.

[212] *Ann. C.* MS. B. *s.a.* 1240.

[213] *LL.* i. 104–6. According to Dr. Gwenogvryn Evans, "Breinieu Arfon" is not in the same hand as the text of MS. A. before and after (*Rep.* i. pref. to pt. ii. note on p. viii), but it so refers to Iorwerth as to make it clear that he is the author of the section.

[214] *Lit. Kym.* (2), p. 118.

[215] "Niwnaeth Duw fwlch ar falchnaf" (*Myv. Arch.* I. 262 (189)).

[216] *Myv. Arch.* I. 301 (213).

[217] *Ibid.* 308 (218).

[218] *Ibid.* 322 (226).

[219] Blk. Bk. fo. 28*b*, vv. 1, 2; *IV. Anc. Bks.* ii. p. 23; *Lit. Kym.* (2), pp. 244–5, where the allusion is not rightly understood. The poet sees in John's later defeats a punishment for the burning of Bangor in 1211.

[220] Of this only a few fragments survive in Pen. MS. 6 (Evans, *Rep.* i. p. 316). Dr. Evans dates them "*circa* 1225".

[221] "Mawr benn Cymru wenn ai chymmhenrwydd" (*Myv. Arch.* I. 311 (219)).

[222] M. Paris, *Chron.* iii. 385. The evidence of the records (see note 149 above) shows that no important change of policy took place in or about 1237.

[223] *Ann. C.* MS. B.

[224] According to *B.T.* 326, Arwystli, Kerry, Cyfeiliog, Mawddwy, Mochnant, and Caereinion were in Gruffydd's hands.

[225] It appears from letters of 8th March, 1238, in Rymer, i. 235, that an attempt had been made to bring off this ceremony earlier in the year and that the English government had entered a protest against it.

[226] *B.T.*

[227] M. Pans, *Chron.* iv. 8.

[228] *Ann. C.* MS. B. The following corrections must be made in the text of Ab Ithel; for "dominabat" read "domabat"; omit "Christ;" (top of p. 83); for "tenore" read "terrore".

[229] *Myv. Arch.* I. 335 (233).

CHAPTER IX

[1] Rymer i. 239. The chronology of *B.T.* continues to be correct from 1240 to 1256, but, owing to a slip in the Rolls edition, two years are there included under 1252 (see p. 339) and the printed dates are therefore a year behind the true reckoning from 1253 to 1256 inclusive.

[2] I follow in the text the statement of *Ann. C.* MS. B. and *B.T.* that Gruffydd was imprisoned in 1239. According to M. Paris, however (*Chron.* iv. 8, 47–8), the imprisonment followed the death of Llywelyn, and the matter remains in some doubt. Paris is probably right in his account of the attitude of the bishop of Bangor (*ibid.* 148–9), but there is no record evidence showing that the king concerned himself about Gruffydd before August, 1241.

[3] *Ann. C.* MS. B.; *B.T.; Ann. Theokesb.; Ann. Wigorn.* For the text of the agreement then entered into between David and the king see Rymer i. 239–40.

[4] He granted a charter as "princeps Northwalliæ" to Basingwerk at Coleshill on 25th July, 1240, when he was accompanied by the bishop of St. Asaph, Ednyfed Fychan and Einion Fychan (*Mon. Angl.* v. 263).

[5] See p. 674 for its capture by Llywelyn.

[6] See p. 590. Robert of Montalt had meanwhile been succeeded by his brother, Roger (d. 1232), and he by his son, Roger. The family at this time lived at Hawarden (*Ann. Cest. s.a.*).

[7] See p. 650.

[8] See p. 670.

[9] *Ann. C.* MSS. B. C.; *B.T.* Earl Gilbert, already lord of Pembroke and Nether Went, received on 9th December, 1234, a grant of the castles of Cardigan and Carmarthen (Charter Rolls, i. 189), and on 28th February, 1235, the custody of the honour of Glamorgan (Cal. Pat. Rolls, i. 96), "ita ut totam maritimam possideret usque Sancti David" (*Ann. Theokesb.*). It appears from the proceedings recorded in Harl. MS. 6068, *f.* 8–9*b* (printed in *Str. Flor.,*

appendix xx-xxiv. — the true year is 24, not 25 Hen. III.) that he not only seized Cardigan in May, 1240, but also attempted, without success, to make Maelgwn Fychan his vassal.

[10] *Ann. Cest.*; Cal. Pat. Rolls, i. 184, 185.

[11] He was appointed on 6th December, 1240 (Cal. Pat. Rolls, i. 240) and replaced by John de Gray at the end of October, 1245 (*Ann. Cest.*).

[12] Rymer i. 239. The arbitrators appointed were the legate, the bishops of Worcester, Norwich and St. Asaph, Earl Richard of Cornwall, John of Monmouth, Ednyfed Fychan and Einion Fychan.

[13] *Ibid.* i. 240 (letter of 30th November, 1240).

[14] *Ibid.* (letter of 19th February). The king was at Worcester on 10th–14th February. The Earl of Cornwall had gone on crusade in the previous summer and the legate left England in January, 1241. For David's safe-conduct to Worcester see Cal. Pat. Rolls, i. 242, and for that to Shrewsbury, *ibid.* 246.

[15] The judges were the Bishop of Lichfield, Segrave, William Cantilupe and John Lestrange, appointed on 5th March (*ibid.* 246). An entry in *Rot. Fin.* i. 342 shows that, among other business, the court upheld the claim of Llywelyn Fychan and Owain Fychan of Mechain (see p. 683) to Mochnant Uch Rhaeadr, held by David (see the reference in Rymer, i. 242) with the bulk of Powys Wenwynwyn.

[16] Rymer, i. 241.

[17] For the safe-conduct granted on this occasion see Cal. Pat. Rolls, i. 252.

[18] An ultimatum was sent on 14th July (Rymer i. 242).

[19] The men of the counties controlled by John Lestrange, *viz.,* Cheshire, Shropshire, and Staffordshire, were warned on 13th July to be in readiness, and on 6th August Henry was at Shrewsbury (Cal. Pat. Rolls, i. 254, 255).

[20] The lands of Ralph were being harassed by certain Welsh chiefs of Kerry and Maelienydd in alliance with David — see M. Paris, *Chron.* iv. 319–20.

[21] M. Paris, *Chron.* iv. 316–18 and Charter Rolls, i. 262–3.

[22] According to *Ann. Cest.* the king reached Chester about 15th August. He was certainly there from the 19th to the 24th (Cal. Pat. Rolls, i. 257–8). His stay at Rhuddlan lasted eight days (*Ann. Cest.*), *i.e.,* no doubt, from 25th August to 1st September. On 2nd September he was again in Chester.

[23] *Ann. C.* MS. C.

[24] M. Paris, *Chron.* iv. 150; *cf.* 176–7.

[25] "David. . . exclusus ab exercitu regis a Snaudonia subdidit se" (*Ann. Wigorn. s.a.*).

[26] M. Paris, *Chron.* iv. 321–3; Rymer, i. 242–3, and Cal. Pat. Rolls, i. 264. "Alnetum" translates the Welsh "gwern" (alder grove) and no doubt stands for Gwern Eigron (so Cal. Pat. Rolls), now a couple of miles south of Rhuddlan. The alders formerly stretched as far north as Pengwern.

[27] "Sine sanguinis effusione" (Paris).

[28] Restored, according to *Ann. C.* MS. B. and *B.T.*, to the sons of Maredudd ap Cynan, who died in 1212. *Rot. Fin.* i. 371 shows that the two brothers, both called Llywelyn, agreed to pay £80 for the restoration of the cantref. They were distinguished as Llywelyn Fawr and Llywelyn Fychan (*Mont. Coll.* i. 255). Both supported David in 1245 (Rymer, i. 258).

[29] The undated document in Rymer, i. 243, seems to belong to the visit to London in October mentioned by *Ann. Camb.* MS. B., *B.T.*, and Paris, *Chron.* iv. 150-1.

[30] "Exemplum de Wallia. . . ubi nuper feliciter triumphavimus" (Paris, iv. 183).

[31] It was at first taken over by the crown, but on 6th May, 1242, Roger of Montalt was made its keeper (Cal. Pat. Rolls, i, 288), and on 25th May, 1244, the actual holder (*ibid.* 426).

[32] In August, 1241, he agreed to pay 300 marks for his father's lands (*Rot. Fin.* i. 350-1). On 24th February, 1242, he was allowed to give his wife dower in the manor of Ashford in the Peak (Charter Rolls, i. 266), which had been given to him, as the son of Gwenwynwyn, in 1232 (Close Rolls, ii. 70).

[33] Cal. Pat. Rolls, i. 265 (29th October, 1241).

[34] *Ibid.* 268.

[35] The site is described as "forti rupe iuxta disserth" (*Ann. C.* MS. B.) and "(k)astell y garrec yn ymyi y Disserth" (B.T.). It is clearly the "new place" near Rhuddlan provided as a gift by Lestrange — see letter of 3rd September, 1241, in Cal. Pat. Rolls, i. 258, and appears for a while as "Castellum de Rupe" — see *ibid.* 267, 278, 279, where the identification with Beeston is a mistake. The rock, still crowned with the ruins of Henry's fortress, bore the names of Dincolin (Penn. ii. 117 — see Domesd. i. 269a (2)) and Carreg Faelan (*B.T. s.a.* 1263, MS. E.; for the name Maelan see *W. Phil* (2), 202, 380).

[36] The earl held at his death the castles of Chepstow (Striguil), Usk, Caerleon, Pembroke, Cilgerran, Cardigan and Carmarthen (Cal. Pat. Rolls, i. 254), but the last two were not regranted to his successor (M. Paris, *Chron.* iv. 158 and Cal. Pat. Rolls, i. 265).

[37] *B.T.* and *Ann. C.*, MS. B. In the latter the words "a domino Johanne de monemu in buelth et" have slipped out of the printed text.

[38] Cal. Pat. Rolls, i. 289; Carmarthen Charters (Carmarthen, 1878), p. 43. Widigada was regarded as a parcel of the lordship of Carmarthen; it lay east of the Gwili.

[39] For mention of these princes see Cal. Pat. Rolls, i. 242, 243, 279. Maelgwn in 1242 built the castle of Garth Grugyn, which was certainly in Ceredigion (*Mab.* 140) and perhaps near Llanilar (Evans, *Rep.* i. p. 724, in a list of castles by Dr. J. D. Rhys). The distribution of commotes between him and Maredudd is not easily ascertained, but about 1240 he seems to have held Mefenydd (*Ann. C.* MS. B. *s.a.* 1236), Perfedd (Cal. Pat. Rolls, i. 488 — Llanbadarn Fawr was in this commote), and probably Creuddyn (Rot. Claus. ii. 73), while Maredudd

had Geneu'r Glyn and Iscoed (Cal. Pat. Rolls, i. 493), Gwinionydd and Mabwnion (*ibid.* 487 and Charter Rolls, i. 475), and Pennardd (*Ann. C. ut supra*). Rhys Mechyll had succeeded his father at Dinefwr in 1234; he married Maud de Breos (of the line of Gower?) and died early in 1244 (*Ann. C.* MS. B. and *B.T.*), leaving a son Rhys and other children (Cal. Pat. Rolls, i. 422).

40 Richard, who married Maud, daughter of the Earl of Lincoln, in January, 1238 (Cal. Pat. Rolls, i. 208), came of age in 1243 and on 28th September received his lands (*Ann. Theskesb.*). For quarrels between Hywel ap Maredudd, lord of Miskin, Rhys ap Gruffydd, lord of Senghenydd, and Gilbert Turbeville, lord of Coety, see *Ann. Theokesb. s.a.* 1242.

41 M. Paris, *Chron.* iv. 295–6, whose account is confirmed by *Ann. C.* MS. B., *B.T.* and Cal. Pat. Rolls, i. 424. *Ann. C.* MS. C. is suspicious —"sive dolo seu aliter ignoratur," but, as the event showed, Henry stood to lose, and not to gain, by the death of Gruffydd.

42 In 1248 Gruffydd's body was taken by the abbots of Strata Florida and of Aberconwy from London and reinterred in the latter abbey (*B.T. s.a.*).

43 M. Paris, *Chron.* iv. 358 ("tempore vernali"). The war was general as early as 3rd June — see Cal. Pat. Rolls, i. 427. For the dissident princes see *Ann. C.* MS. B. and *B.T.*, and *cf.* Cal. Pat. Rolls, i. 430 (concessions for Gruffydd ap Madog), and Letters, H. III. ii. 38. "Morgan de Karliun" (Cal. Pat. Rolls, i. 447) was still kept out of the castle which gave him his name by the power of the Marshalls; his castle of Machen was also seized by Gilbert Marshall in 1236, but subsequently restored (*B.T.*; Rymer i. 223, 229, 230; Cal. Pat. Rolls, i. 160).

44 *Descr.* ii. 4 (vi. 212).

45 M. Paris, *Chron.* iv. 385 ("praecipue noctibus").

46 Letters, H. III. ii. 38–40. "Walwar" is Tafolwern, for which see p. 510.

47 See the documents in M. Paris, *Chron.* iv. 398–9 (Genoa, 26th July, 1244), and Rymer, i. 255 (Lyons, 8th April, 1245 (not 1244)). I cannot explain the "Gustefend" of Luard's text. It should be observed that the letter of 1244 will scarcely sustain the edifice Paris seeks to build upon it, though it is possible that David attempted, as he alleges, to do far more than recover lost lands.

48 M. Paris, *Chron.* iv. 358; Cal. Pat. Rolls, i. 431–2.

49 Paris, iv. 385–6.

50 Cal. Pat. Rolls, i. 446, 462. Owain Goch was the eldest son (*Ann. Cest. s.a.* 1255; M. Paris, iv. 321 —"filio suo primogenito").

51 The list of David's allies at the beginning of 1245 (Rymer, i. 258) includes the following; the two Llywelyns of Meirionydd; Owain ap Bleddyn, Elise ab Iorwerth, and Gruffydd ab Owain, of the line of Owain Brogyntyn; Llywelyn ap Gruffydd (the future prince of Wales); Maredudd and Iorwerth ap Madog of Maelor and their brother Madog Fychan; Madog ap Gwenwynwyn; Llywelyn Fychan and the sons of Owain Fychan of Mechain; Owain ap Hywel of Kerry; Maelgwn Fychan, Maredudd ab Owain, Maredudd ap Rhys Gryg and the sons of

Rhys Mechyll in Deheubarth; Rhys ap Gruffydd, Hywel ap Maredudd and the son of Morgan Crookback in Glamorgan. In Harl. MS. 6068, by George Owen of Henllys this list is disguised as one of "barons of North and South Wales who did homage to the king" (Owen, *Cat.* 450).

[52] Rymer, i. 258 (Westminster, 10th January).

[53] *Ann. Camb.* MS. C.; *Ann. ad* 1298 ("prope Margan in die beatae Agathae virginis"); Paris, *Chron.* iv. 408–9; *Rot. Fin.* i. 430 (order of 12th February).

[54] Paris, *Chron.* iv. 407, 409.

[55] *Ibid.* 409; *Ann. Cest. s.a.*

[56] Rymer, i. 260; Paris, iv. 423.

[57] Cal. Pat. Rolls, i. 456.

[58] *Ann. Cest.* has the following itinerary — Chester, 13th–20th August; Coleshill, 21st; Whitford, 22nd and 23rd; Rhuddlan, 24th; Abergele, 25th Degannwy, 26th.

[59] iv. 481–4.

[60] For the use made of the resources of Ireland see Cal. Pat. Rolls, i. 461, (21st October); *Historic and Municipal Documents of Ireland* (Rolls Series, 1870) i. 103–4.

[61] So I understand the "filium Odonis Naveth" of Paris (iv. 482), a learned embellishment, no doubt, of the original "f. Odonaveth".

[62] Paris, iv. 486; *Ann. Wigorn, s.a. Cf.* the lines of Dafydd Benfras —"Dyfod hyd attaw dyhedd Iwerddon

I farchogaeth Mon dirion diredd" (*Myv. Arch.* I. 316 (223)).

[63] *Ann. Cest.* The king re-entered Chester on the 27th.

[64] The somewhat complacent tone of M. Paris (iv. 486 —"securus enim erat," etc.) needs the correction supplied by *Ann. Cest.* ("parum proficiens") and *Ann. Dunst.* ("pertaesus. . . rediit").

[65] "Quasi spina in oculo" (iv. 486).

[66] *Ann. Cest.; Ann. Dunst.*

[67] Paris, *ut supra*; Rymer, i. 264. *Cf.* Gir. Camb. vi. 218 (*Descr.* ii. 8).

[68] *Ann. C.* MS. B.; *B.T.; Ann. Cest.* (whence the date); *Ann. Wigorn.* (read "dominica" for "die").

[69] Isabella's claim to Builth as her dowry was never conceded by the crown, but after her husband's death she received out of the Marshall estates, in right of her mother Eva, the castle of Haverfordwest, with lands in Caerleon and Glamorgan (*Rot. Fin.* i. 458–9). On 18th August, 1246, arrangements were made for bringing the stock which fell to her as a widow under Welsh law from Wales to the land of the Earl of Gloucester (Cal. Pat. Rolls, i. 485).

[70] "Ille clipeus Wallie" (*Ann. C.* MS. B.).

[71] *Myv. Arch.* I. 316–7 (222–3). I have altered the order of the lines.

[72] Mentioned as a magnate of North Wales in 1245 ("Lewelino f. Griffini" — Rymer, i. 258).

[73] Cal. Pat. Rolls, i. 465.

[74] Paris, iv. 518; *Ann. Cest.*

[75] According to *Ann. Cest.* "Ideneueth Justiciarius Wallie" died in 1246, and this is confirmed by entries in Cal. Pat. Rolls, i. 461, 496, showing he was an envoy for David in October, 1245, but had died before January, 1247.

[76] *Ann. C.* MS. B.; *B.T.; Ann. Cest.* The distribution of commotes between the two brothers cannot be ascertained, except that Llywelyn had Penllyn — see his charter to Basingwerk, dated 8th April, 1247, in Charter Rolls, ii. 291 — and Tindaethwy — see his charter to Penmon, dated 6th January, 1247, in *Mon. Angl.* iv. 582.

[77] *Ann. C.* MSS. B. C.; *B.T.* Nicholas "de Molis," who had been seneschal of Gascony, was made custos of the castles of Cardigan and Carmarthen, in succession to John of Monmouth, on 17th August, 1245 (Cal. Pat. Rolls, i. 459).

[78] Cal. Pat. Rolls, i. 498.

[79] Rymer, i. 267. For a footnote to the treaty see Cal. Pat. Rolls, i. 501.

[80] The "Pernechelad" of Rymer represents the Welsh "Perfeddwlad".

[81] "Mereduc Abricard" was with David in October, 1245 (Cal. Pat. Rolls, i. 461), but on 27th January, 1247, "Mereduk son of Res" received a grant of the land of "Thlen" in consideration of loyal service (*ibid.* 496), and the letter of Owain and Llywelyn to the king printed in Letters, H. III., ii. 64–6, shows that about 1250 "Maredud filius Ricardi de Heyn," a king's man, held great estates of the two princes without rendering anything to them. The documents cited in *Pces. S. Wales*, p. 126, appear to refer to this potentate, and not to Maredudd ap Rhys of Deheubarth.

[82] *Rec. Carn.* 252 (domino de Kemedmaen). David, who is first mentioned (as a hostage) in 1241 (M. Paris, *Chron.* iv. 317), had with him on this occasion (11th July, 1252) his mother Senena and Bishop Richard of Bangor.

[83] Rymer, i. 291 (Portsmouth, 8th July).

[84] Charter Rolls, i. 378–9; *cf. Eng. Hist. Rev.* xvii. (1902), pp. 284, 287–8.

[85] See the notification of 10th May, 1247 (Cal. Pat. Rolls, i. 501).

[86] M. Paris, *Chron.* v. 227; *cf. Ann. Cest. s.a.*

[87] The four brothers, Gruffydd, Maredudd, Hywel, and Madog, join in executing a document in favour of Valle Crucis in December, 1247, which is witnessed by their men of Maelor, Ial, Cynllaith, and Mochnant (Is Rhaeadr). See *Arch. Camb.* I. iii. (1848), 228–9, and III. x. (1864), 100–1.

[88] *Trib. System*, app. p. 103. She was the widow of Henry Tuschet of Lee Cumbray, who died in 1242 (Eyton, *Shrops.* vii. pp. 343–5).

[89] He gave to Valle Crucis in 1254 land in Stansty, near Wrexham (*Arch. Camb.* I. i. (1846), 151–2; *cf.* Palmer, *Country Townships of Wrexham*, 1903, p. 183).

[90] Gruffydd's possessions in 1277–8 are set forth in the deed printed in *Mont. Coll.* i. 124–8. For his wife see note 32.

[91] *Rot. Fin.* ii. 37. *B.T.* has O. "ab Rotbert" by mistake.

[92] He died in 1255 (*Ann. C.* MS. B.; *B.T.*), and was, probably, the son of the elder "Lewelino f. Mereduc" who recovered Meirionydd in 1241 and was with David in 1245 (Rymer, i. 258).

[93] Bridgman discusses the difficult question of the family history in *Mont. Coll.* i. 197–203. The true key is supplied by Cal. Close R. Ed. I. i. 399, 434, whence it appears that Llywelyn ab Owain Fychan (*Rot. Pat.*, 45) had three sons: (1) Llywelyn Fychan (*Rot. Fin.* i. 342; Rymer, i. 258); (2) Owain; (3) Maredudd (these three appear in Rymer, i. 370 *s.a.* 1258) and that Llywelyn Fychan left two sons, Gruffydd and Maredudd, who shared Mechain Iscoed with their uncles in 1277.

[94] *B.T.*; M. Paris, *Chron.* iv. 551; Cal. Pat. Rolls, i. 479 (27th April).

[95] According to *Ann. C.* MS. B., in Meirionydd; it appears from Cal. Pat. Rolls, i. 486 (30th August) that he afterwards passed to Southern Powys.

[96] *Ann. C.* MS. B.; Cal. Pat. Rolls, i. 493 (25th November). He lived to see the revival of Welsh power under Llywelyn ap Gruffydd, but took no part in the movement and died in 1257.

[97] *Ann. C.* MS. B.; *B.T.* Rhys died at the end of June, 1255, Gwenllian, wife of Maredudd ap Llywelyn of Meirionydd, at Llanfihangel y Creuddyn (for the form "gelynrot" see Meyrick, *Card.* 286) on 25th November, 1254, and Margaret, wife of Owain ap Maredudd of Cydewain, on 25th September, 1255.

[98] *Ann. C.* MS. B.; *B.T.* On 6th April, 1244, the king gave his protection to Matilda de Brausa, widow of Res, son of Res, until her children came of age (Cal. Pat. Rolls, i. 422). Matilda was, no doubt, of the house of Gower.

[99] Maredudd was invested by Gilbert Marshall, about 1240, with the commotes of Emlyn above Cuch and Ystlwyf, probably in succession to Cynan ap Hywel — see Cole, *Docts.* 47–8, and chap. xviii. note 44. He began to claim his hereditary due in 1244 (Cal. Pat. Rolls, i. 447 — 27th December), and had apparently succeeded in getting four commotes before February, 1246, when further offers were made to him (*ibid.* 474). In 1250 his lands included the commote of Catheiniog in Cantref Mawr and the castle of Llandovery in Cantref Bychan (H. and St. i. 476–8).

[100] See B.T. *s.a.* 1248, which records the recovery by Rhys of his castle of Carreg Cennen (in Iscennen), treacherously handed over by his mother to the "French".

[101] Cal. Pat. Rolls, i. 485 (20th August).

[102] *Ann. C.* MS. B. and *B.T. s.a.* 1252. For William, see Letters, Hen. III. i. 426, where he appears in 1244 (the true date) as a Pembrokeshire tenant of the Earl Marshall; Charter Rolls, i. 347; Meyrick, *Card.* (2), 206 (pedigree of the lords of Tywyn, near Cardigan).

[103] Nicholas, son of William fitz Martin and Angharad, daughter of the Lord Rhys (*Rot. Fin.* i. 144–5), after being in wardship for many years, came to his own about 1230.

[104] Earl Gilbert had been succeeded by his brother Walter, who died at Goodrich Castle towards the end of November, 1245 (M. Paris, *Chron.* iv. 491; Ann. C. MSS. B. C.; *Rot. Fin.* i. 444). The death of Anselm at Chepstow a month later,

before he had been invested as earl (Paris, *ut supra; Ann. C.* MS. B.; *Ann. Wigorn.*), removed the fifth and last of the sons of the great Earl Marshall, none of them, by a singular fatality, leaving any issue.

105 Pembroke had at first been assigned, in the general partition, to John, son of Warin of Montchensy and Joan, fifth daughter of the first Earl Marshall. But he died shortly afterwards, in June, 1247, and his portion passed to his sister Joan (*Rot. Fin.* ii. 14), who in the August of the same year was married to William of Valence (M. Paris, *Chron.* iv. 627–9; Cal. Pat. Rolls, i. 506; Sweetman, i. 433) William was the fourth son of Count Hugh of La Marche and Isabella of Angoulême (whose first husband was King John). According to Tout (*Dict. Nat. Biog.* lxi. p. 373), it is probable he was never formally created earl.

106 He was the son of the eldest daughter, Matilda.

107 Through his mother, Isabella Marshall.

108 Cal. Pat. Rolls, Ed. I. i. 9. William Cantilupe, third in succession of that name, married Eva de Breos, whose mother, Eva, was the fourth of the Marshall daughters. He died in 1254 (M. Paris, *Chron.* v. 463), leaving his son and heir, George, under age.

109 Robert Waleran had the custody of Cardigan and Carmarthen and of the former possessions of Maelgwn Fychan on 26th September, 1250 (*Rot. Fin.* ii. 87).

110 Walter de Breos married Hawise and obtained the honour of Kidwelly and Carnwyllion in July, 1223 (Pat. Rolls, i. 376–7). He died, apparently, during the war of 1233–4; *cf.* Cal. Pat. Rolls, i. 17 and Close Rolls, ii. 447. The second marriage took place early in 1244 (*Ann. Theokesb.* p. 133), and in the December of that year Patrick and his wife fined one hundred marks for the possession of Kidwelly (*Rot. Fin.* i. 410). For Hawise's position in Ogmore see *Cart. Glouc.* i. 284–5; *Cartae Glam.* i. 108.

111 *B.T.* For Hywel see chapter xviii. note 109. The conquest of Miskin was final, and the earl built there the castle of Llantrisant (*Arch. Camb.* VI. i. (1901), 1–7).

112 For a list of the fiefs of Glamorgan and their value in the middle of this century see *Cartae Glam.* i. 107–9. Morgan Gam died in February, 1241 (*Ann. Theokesb.*), leaving two sons, *viz.,* Lleision ap Morgan (see *Cartae Glam.* iii. 429–30; *Margam Abb.* pp. 256–8) and Morgan Fychan (*ob.* 1288), who followed him in this order in the Welsh lordship of Avan (*Margam Abb.* pp. 312–13).

113 Morgan of Caerleon, holding the commotes of Edlygion in Gwynllwg and Llebenydd in Gwent, but not Caerleon itself, died a little before 15th March, 1248 (*Rot. Fin.* ii. 31). There was doubt, at first, as to the legitimacy of Maredudd ap Gruffydd (Inq. p. mortem, Hen. III. p. 36), but the bishop of Llandaff certified in 1251 in his favour (H. and St. i. 478–9) and later he is found holding one commote (*i.e.* Edlygion) of the Earl of Gloucester at "Machhein" (*Cartae Glam.* i. 109).

114 "Griffid ab Rees tenet ii cummod (*i.e.* Uwch Caeach and Is Caeach) in Seingeniht" (*ibid.*). Rhys died in July, 1256 (*Ann. ad* 1298).

[115] See note 69 above. After her death, the manor of Haverford (*i.e.*, Rhos) passed to Humphrey de Bohun the younger, who had married her sister Eleanor (Madox, *Baronia Anglica*, pp. 45–6, note; Cal. Pat. R. Ed. I. 54).

[116] Charter Rolls, ii. 41.

[117] See p. 734.

[118] For Ralph's death see *Ann. C. MS. B.*, *B.T.* The castles of Wigmore, Cefnllys and Knucklas (Y Cnwc Glas = the Green Hillock) were in the king's hands on 2nd October, 1246 (Cal. Pat. Rolls, i. 489). Roger fined 2,000 marks for his father's lands on 26th February, 1247 (*Rot. Fin.* ii. 7–8).

[119] *Rot. Fin.* ii. 41–2.

[120] On the death of Walter Lacy in 1241 (M. Paris, *Chron.* iv. 174), his grand-daughters, Matilda and Margaret, succeeded to his estates. Matilda married Peter in 1244 (*Rot. Fin.* i. 413–14) and was a widow in September, 1249 (*ibid.*, ii. 61).

[121] See *Rot. Fin.* i. 360–1, 384, 417.

[122] The grant was first made on 14th February (Rymer, i. 297) and renewed on 11th October (*ibid.* 309). "Alium castrum" is, of course, a mistake for "Album Castrum". Edward was formally invested with the earldom of Chester, in the person of his representative, Bartholomew of the Peak, on 26th March (*Ann. Cest. s.a.* 1254).

[123] M. Paris, *Chron.* v. 288.

[124] *Rot. Fin.* ii. 87, 91, etc.

[125] "Super terrarum participacione" (*Ann. Cest. s.a.* 1255).

[126] *B.T.* 1254 = 1255 (see note 1 above), the year given by *Ann. Cest.* and *Ann. C. MS. B.* According to the latter, the battle was fought "hisdem diebus " as an event ascribed to the neighbourhood of 24th June, and another occurrence dated 25th September was "non multum post".

[127] Llygad Gwr (*Myv. Arch.* I. 344 (239–40)) refers to the battle of "Brynn der-win" as fought "yg gymysc aruon ac eityonyt" and "ger drws deuvynyt," so that it is beyond a doubt to be located near the modern Bwlch Derwyn and Derwyn Fawr (corruptly "Derwydd" and "Derwen" in the maps), on the borders of the parishes of Clynnog and Dolbenmaen. Bwlch Dau Fynydd is a little to the west. See *Cyff Beuno*, 31.

[128] *B.T.* makes David escape, but *Ann. Cest.* confirms the account of *Ann. C. MS. B.*

CHAPTER X

[1] *Ann. C.* and *B.T.* continue to be the most valuable sources for the internal history of Wales during this period. The 1255 of the latter = 1256, the 1256 = the first half of 1257; thenceforward the printed dates are correct.

[2] According to *Ann. Cest.* he arrived at Chester on 17th July and left it, after the visit to Wales, on 3rd August.

[3] M. Paris, *Chron.* v. 598.

[4] *Ann. Dunst.* p. 200.

[5] *Ann. Cest.*

[6] About 1st November (*Ann. Cest.* and Paris, v. 592).

[7] *Ann. Cest.* says that "vallem Moaldie" (*i.e.*, Ystrad Alun) was occupied, and probably the castle was taken at this time. See notes 90 and 115.

[8] Paris, v. 594.

[9] *Ibid.* 593.

[10] On 6th November, 1256, he was with Edward at Windsor (Charter Rolls, i. 454).

[11] Paris, v. 593, 597–8.

[12] *Ibid.* iv. 324.

[13] *Ibid.* v. 639.

[14] The numbers given by Paris (*Chron.* v. 597, 614) are, no doubt, much exaggerated, but the army was clearly a formidable one.

[15] For his father see chap. xix. note 92. In Letters, Hen. III. ii. 123–4, is a petition from Llywelyn, asking the king to provide for him, since he has lost Meirionydd through his loyalty.

[16] Llywelyn was at Llanbadarn on 4th December and was met by Maredudd at Morfa Mawr, near Llannon, a grange of Strata Florida (*Str. Flor.* 179, app. xcvi.), on the 6th (*Ann. C. MS. B.*).

[17] He was married to Llywelyn's sister Gwladus, who died in 1261 (*B.T.*), but such ties counted for little in Welsh warfare.

[18] The particulars given in Charter Rolls, i. 475, seem to show that, before his expulsion and flight to the North, Maredudd had Hirfryn and Perfedd in Cantref Bychan, Mallaen, Caeo, and Catheiniog in Cantref Mawr, and Emlyn uwch Cuch and Ystlwyf in Dyfed, while Rhys had Is Cennen in Cantref Bychan, and Maenor Deilo, Mabudryd, and Mabelfyw in Cantref Mawr. I transpose Catheiniog and Is Cennen, assuming a clerical error in this respect on the strength of the references to Dryslwyn and Carreg Cennen and of H. and St. i. 476–8.

[19] Paris, *Chron.* v. 597, 613. As nothing is said on the subject in *Ann. C.* or *B.T.*, it is possible that Paris has here made a mistake, as he has undoubtedly done on p. 646.

[20] See *Ann. C. MS. B.* for the details. After "filius Grifini" (top of p. 92) supply "terram Grifini," dropped by the scribe as a result of "like ending". The name "Trwst Llywelyn" (near Berriew) may perhaps preserve the memory of the stampede "in campo magno inter Hafren et Eberriw". Montgomery itself was attacked before the end of March, and in the sack of the town a prominent burgess named Baldwin, for whom see *Str. Flor.* app. xxix. and Charter Rolls, i. 404, was killed.

[21] The letter printed by Shirley and by him tentatively assigned to the summer of 1267 (ii. 312–14) is clearly an answer to the expostulations made by Richard in 1257 (Paris, v. 613), and was probably sent in the March of that year, when he was in England (*ibid.* 622), under the cover of safe-conduct to be found in

Rymer, i. 354. The offer to give up the commotes of Creuddyn and Prestatyn meant nothing, for they were dominated by the castles of Degannwy and Diserth, which Llywelyn did not win until 1263.

[22] Bodyddon, locally known as "Bydyfon," is a township in the parish of Llanfyllin, and within it is Tomen yr Allt, near Abernaint, which may well be the castle mound.

[23] For a full account see *Ann. C.* MS. B. The place called Cymerau, out of which Ab Ithel evolved his "mutual engagement" (p. 343), is apparently not now known by that name, but it was probably at the confluence (cymer) of the Towy and the Cothi.

[24] He had been seneschal of Gascony (Letters, Hen. III. ii. 400) and was "regi carissimus" (M. Paris, *Chron.* v. 646).

[25] The terms of the writ are given in a St. Alban's memorandum printed in M. Paris, *Chron.* vi. 372–3. It was afterwards resolved to assign a number of the knights to a South Welsh expedition (Rymer, i. 361).

[26] *Ann. C.* MS. B. wants all the events of 1257 after the middle of June, but they are supplied by *B.T.* under the fresh year 1257 (p. 344), and, as it was previously a year in arrear, this error puts its chronology right again.

[27] For the "aber *toran*" of *B.T.* (*Bruts*, 374) read "aber *coran*" as *s.a.* 1189, and see chap. xvi. note 4.

[28] MS. C.of *B.T.*

[29] Paris, v. 642; *B.T.* The latter has "llan geneu" (*Bruts*, 375), but there is no place of this name in Glamorgan, while Llangynwyd, in the lordship of Tir yr Iarll (The Earl's Land), was the seat of a castle in 1246 (*Cartae Glam.* iv. 592) and is mentioned about 1262 as a manor of the chief lord, much injured by war (*ibid.* i. 113).

[30] Paris, v. 639.

[31] *Ann. Cest.*, which says that the king arrived in Chester on the 5th. *Cf.* Charter Rolls, i. 472.

[32] *Ann. Osen.* p. 117.

[33] *Antt. Legg.* p. 29. A note cited in Sweetman, ii. 91, shows the king was at Degannwy from 26th August to 4th September.

[34] Paris, v. 651.

[35] "Circa festum Sancti Michaelis" (*Ann. Cest.*). *Cf. B.T.*

[36] It expired in April (Paris, v. 676).

[37] On 14th March the knights were summoned to Chester for a Welsh campaign, to open on 17th June (Stubbs, *Const. Hist.* ii. p. 76). This was reluctantly agreed to at the "Hoketide" Parliament (Paris, v. 677).

[38] Paris, v. 696.

[39] Rymer, i. 372. A safe-conduct had been issued on and June to Llywelyn's envoys, who were coming under the escort of Peter of Montfort (*ibid.*), and, therefore, it may be presumed, by arrangement with the barons. According to Paris (v. 727), Llywelyn would have paid at this time 4,500 marks for a peace recognising his conquests, but the king would not hear of it.

[40] See Tout in *Owens College Essays*, pp. 88–91.

[41] Paris, v. 676. *Ann. C.* MS. B. records a raid upon Cemais on Monday, 1st April, by men of Pembroke and Rhos, avenged not long afterwards by the Welsh of Cemais and "Plumauc" (read "Pluwauc").

[42] The only direct mention of this assembly is in *B.T.*, but something of the kind is implied in the account of the trial of Maredudd ap Rhys in 1259. Indeed, the names given in the Scotch document of 18th March (see note 47 below) may well be regarded as forming a list of those present, and the document itself as an immediate result of the assembly.

[43] The earliest use of the title by Llywelyn which I can date is in the Scotch agreement. The letters assigned in Rymer, i. 336, 339, 340, 341 to 1256 (in which it occurs) belong, not to that year, but to 1262 and 1263. It was, of course, not recognised by the English government.

[44] On 18th October, 1257, Henry announced that he had received Maredudd into his favour and had given him his own land, that of Rhys Fychan (see note 18 above) and two commotes, *viz.*, Mabwnion and Gwinionydd, of the land of Maredudd ab Owain (Charter Rolls, i. 475).

[45] This was not long after 1st April (*Ann. C.* MS. B.).

[46] Rymer, i. 370. Bain (*Calendar of Documents relating to Scotland*, i. 421 — *cf.* Pref. p. xliii) understands the 1258 of this document to be 1258–9. But the Earl of Menteith died in November, 1258 (Paris, v. 724), and "Maredud fil. Ris" ceased to be an ally of Llywelyn in the April of that year.

[47] They are his brother David (Owain Goch was still in prison — see Paris, v. 718), Gruffydd ap Madog of Maelor, Maredudd ap Rhys, Maredudd ab Owain, Rhys Fychan, Owain ap Maredudd of Cydewain (see p. 709), Madog ap Gwenwynwyn (of Mawddwy — see *Mont. Coll.* i. 118), Maredudd ap Llywelyn of Mechain, Madog Fychan (brother of Gruffydd ap Madog — see *B.T. s.a.* 1269), Owain ap Bleddyn and Elise and Gruffydd, sons of Iorwerth — the last three grandsons of Owain Brogyntyn. The list may be usefully compared with that of David's allies in 1245 (Rymer, i. 258).

[48] *Ann. C.* MS. B. dates the battle of Cilgerran 4th September, *Ann. Theokesb.* (p. 166, where "Keyrmerdin" is, of course, used very vaguely) 7th September.

[49] *B.T.* p. 346, where the cantref is meant and not (as implied in Lewis, *Top. Dict.*) the present Newcastle Emlyn. The "Maynour" of *Ann. C.* MS. B. is Maenor Deifi.

[50] The assertion of *B.T.* that there was "torri kygreir" (breaking of a compact) on the English side is fully confirmed by Paris (v. 717), and must, therefore, outweigh the "seducti" of *Ann. Theokesb.*

[51] *Ann. C.* MS. B. How Maredudd had become possessed of Dinefwr is not clear. "Castelh Nowid" (*cf.* Charter Rolls, 475) here makes its first appearance in the Welsh annals. It was built by Maredudd ("Novum Castrum de Emlyn supra Cuth") about 1240 (Cole, *Docts.* 47–8), and its name suggests that the site was a new one. The "old" castle of Emlyn was Cilgerran. Maredudd held the commote, first of Gilbert Marshall and then of the Cantilupes.

[52] *Flores*, ii. 429. On the death of Matthew Paris in 1259, his post as chronicler at St. Alban's was taken up by an unknown monk, who continued it until 1265. His work, long known by the name of "Matthew of Westminster," forms the basis of what Rishanger and Trevet have to say of the Barons' War.

[53] Rymer, i. 387.

[54] *Flores*, ii. 435.

[55] *Ann. C.* MS. B. *s.a.* 1259; *B.T. s.a.* 1260 ("heb wneuthur drwc y neb" refers to the Welsh of Deheubarth); Letters, Hen. III. ii. 149.

[56] *Ann. C.* MS. B. *s.a.* 1260, where "Trefetland" is for "Trefeclaud," *i.e.*, Tref y Clawdd.

[57] *Ann. C.* MS. B. Rymer, i. 398 gives the same date. MS. C. of *B.T.* (p. 346, note c.) has a different explanation of the affair; Llywelyn's men, it alleges, got in by a lucky, accident. No doubt this was the wardmen's story!

[58] I cannot trace the connections of "Owein ab Maredud o Eluael" (*B.T.*).

[59] The letter was written from Luzarches on 26th January, 1260 (the 16th of the roll is an obvious slip — see Bémont, 186, note), and three copies were sent to Richard of Cornwall, Edward, and the justiciar (Letters, Hen. III. ii. 148–50).

[60] Rymer, i. 398. For the political situation see Bémont, 188. It is significant that Edward afterwards repudiated the document.

[61] Rymer, i. 398–9; *Flores*, ii. 454.

[62] Power to conclude a peace or a truce was given to the royal commissioners on 10th August (Rymer, i. 400). For the instrument actually drawn up see Rymer, i. 404.

[63] See the king's letter of 8th January, 1262, in Rymer, i. 414.

[64] The earl died on 15th July (*Ann. Theokesb., Osen.; Rot. Fin.* ii. 378). His son Gilbert, born and September, 1243 (*Ann. Theokesb.*), received seisin of his father's lands in July, 1263 (*Rot. Fin.* ii. 402–3).

[65] Letters, H. III. ii. 217–18.

[66] Redress was promised in June, 1262, for certain injuries done to Gruffydd ap Madog (Rymer, i. 420), but the matter was still pending in the following September (Letters, ii. 214–17).

[67] Rymer, i. 420.

[68] *Ann. C.* MS. B.; *B.T.; Ann. Cest.; Flores*, ii. 476. For letters of Henry in regard to this campaign in Maelienydd see Letters, ii. 227, 228, 229, and for Llywelyn's defence, *ibid.* 232, 233.

[69] So Bishop Peter (Rymer, i. 423) and the king himself, in a letter to Edward (*ibid.*).

[70] *Ibid.*

[71] *B.T.*

[72] Letter of Peter of Montfort in Letters, ii. 230–1, which clearly belongs to the beginning of 1263. Reginald fitz Peter was lord of Dinas and Blaenllyfni, in succession to his brother, Herbert, and his father, Peter fitz Herbert. Roger Pichard was lord of Ystrad Yw, with a castle at Tretower, Roger Tony of Elfael Is Mynydd, and Robert le Wafre and Robert Turbeville of mesne lordships in Brecknock.

[73] Letters, i. 236, 237–8.

[74] See his French letter in Rymer, i. 339–40 and Letters, ii. 219–21 (translation, 367–9). This is not only wrongly assigned by Rymer to 1256, but even by Shirley is antedated 2nd October, 1262, at a time when there is no other evidence of commotion on the border. Hardy has pointed out (*Syllabus to Foedera*, vol. iii. p. xvi) that "le feste Seint Math*ie* lapostle" is the day of St. Matthias (24th February), not that of St. Matthew (21st September), and thus a date is arrived at, *viz.*, 5th March, 1263, which well suits the position described in the letter.

[75] For "W(r)enoch ab Edenavet seneschal Lewelin" see p. 743.

[76] See the king's letter of expostulation (December, 1262) in Rymer, i. 423.

[77] He was at Shrewsbury on 15th April (*ibid.* 425).

[78] The campaign is noticed in *B.T.*; Wykes, 133; *Flores*, ii. 478.

[79] *B.T.; Ann. Cest.*; Cal. Pat. R., Edw. I. i. 231–3 (patent of 10th October, 1277, confirming one of 8th July, 1263). According to *Ann. Cest.*, David was anxious to bring about the liberation of his brother Owain.

[80] *Ann. Dunst.* pp. 221–2; *Flores*, ii. 479–80; *Papal Letters*, i. p. 411. For John fitz Alan's seizure of Bishop's Castle on 12th July see *Roll of Bishop Swinfield*, ed. J. Webb for the Camden Society, vol. ii. Introd. p. xxii.

[81] *Ann. C. MS. B.; B.T.* ("a chaer faelan"); *Ann. Cest.* For the foundation of the castle and its various names see chap. xix. note 35.

[82] To the evidence adduced by Tout (*Owens College Essays*, 99, note 73) may be added the express statement of *Ann. Cest.*, that the siege of Diserth was undertaken "de mandate baronum".

[83] Rymer, i. 430, 433.

[84] *Ann. C. MS. B.; B.T.; Ann. Cest.*

[85] For the revolution effected by Edward see *Flores*, ii. 484; *Ann. Dunst.* p. 225; Wykes, p. 137. The first two speak of bribery ("terris amplis," "maneria"), but the "callidis allectionibus" of the third — the persuasive reasonings of a statesman — had probably more weight.

[86] For the state of parties in December, 1263, see the letters of the king and of the barons in the award of King Louis (Rymer, i. 433).

[87] *Ann. C. MS. B.; B.T.* For the terms of the agreement see *Mont. Coll.* i. 117–19 (from a Peniarth MS.).

[88] "A Keymynardo inferius versus Slosub (Salop)."

[89] He had probably taken possession of Cydewain on the death of Owain ap Maredudd in 1261.

[90] For the relations between Gruffydd and Thomas at this time see *Mont. Coll.* i. 26–32. Tout is no doubt right in locating the Gwyddgrug of *Ann. C. MS. B.* and *B.T.*, not at Mold, which was out of Gruffydd's reach, but in Gorddwr, where there was a castle of the name, of which the site is unknown (*Owens College Essays*, p. 101, note 75).

[91] *Ann. C.* MS. B. (end of annal 1263); *Flores*, ii. 486; *Ann. Dunst.* p. 227. On 4th February the king wrote to the sheriffs of Gloucester, Salop and Worcester, bidding them bar the passage of the rebels across the Severn (Letters, ii. 253–4).

[92] *Ann. C.* and *Flores*, as in foregoing note.

[93] For this expedition see *Flores*, ii. 498–9. It maybe assigned to June or July. Richard's Castle belonged to Hugh (son of Robert) Mortimer, who had succeeded to the inheritance of his mother, Margaret de Say, in 1259 (*Rot. Fin.* ii. 302–3). For a reference to the capture of "La Haye" in this campaign see Letters, ii. 280 (2nd March, 1265).

[94] *Flores*, ii. 502–4.

[95] See *Ann. Cest.* pp. 86–90; *Ann. Dunst.* p. 235 (expedition of the Earl of Derby). The grant of Cheshire to the earl is assigned by *Ann. Cest.* to November ("post festum omnium sanctorum"); the charter of 20th March, 1265 (Charter Rolls, ii. 54 — *cf.* Rymer, i. 454), probably embodies a somewhat fuller grant than the first.

[96] The document executed by Llywelyn will be found in Letters, Hen. III. ii. 284–6 (dated 19th June, 1265, "in castris juxta Pyperton"); the king's letter is in Rymer, i. 457 (Hereford, 22nd June). Pipton is a hamlet in the parish of Glasbury, which once had its own church — see *Arch. Camb.* IV. xiv. 223 for a "capellanus de Piperton".

[97] Henry gave Painscastle in 1233 to Ralph Tony as his lawful inheritance (Wendover, iv. 279; Close Rolls, ii. 268). In 1239 Ralph died at sea (Paris, *Chron.* iii. 638), leaving his heir, Roger, under age; Painscastle was subsequently entrusted to the keeping of the Earl of Hereford (*Rot. Fin.* ii. 108 — 20th June, 1251). Roger died in 1264, in possession of the castle and its appurtenances (Inq. p. mortem, Hen. III. p. 188).

[98] See especially *Antt. Legg.* pp. 73–4.

[99] Peter of Montfort was one of the two knights who carried the king's charter to Llywelyn.

[100] *Ann. C.* MS. B. ("Mori" for "Mon"); Wykes, 166–8 (for "Hulkes" read "Huske"); *Flores*, iii. 3–4. The king and the earl were at Monmouth on 28th June (Rymer, i. 457).

[101] Wykes. *Cf.* Gir. Camb. vi. 180 ("Carne plenius, pane parcius vesci solent").

[102] The account given in a Battle chronicle partially printed by Bémont (373–80) of the capture by Edward at this time of Brecon, Hay, and Huntington appears to me to be due to confusion with the events of February, 1264.

[103] *Flores*, iii. 5.

[104] By Prof. Tout in *Owens College Essays*, 115.

[105] The only notable marcher who fought on the losing side in this battle was Humphrey de Bohun (*Flores*, iii. 6). He was imprisoned in Beeston Castle (*Ann. Cest.*) and died there on 27th October, 1265 (*Mon. Angl.* vi. 135), leaving a son, Humphrey, aged seventeen (Inq. p. mortem, H. III. p. 205).

[106] On Edward's arrival at Beeston, Luke Tany surrendered Chester Castle to him on 13th August, and was succeeded by the royalist James Audley (*Ann. Cest.*).

[107] *Ann. Waverl.* 366 ("Hameclin" is, no doubt, for "Hawe(r)din"). The castle was in existence in June, 1265 (Rymer, i. 457), but had disappeared before September, 1267 (*ibid.* 474).

[108] On 28th November James Audley was empowered to conclude a truce until the following Lent (Rymer, i. 466).

[109] A safe-conduct was issued on 14th December to the messengers of Llywelyn coming to interview the cardinal (*ibid.* 467).

[110] *Ann. Waverl.* p. 370.

[111] *Owens College Essays*, 120–3.

[112] According to *B.T.*, Llywelyn and Earl Gilbert were allies at the beginning of 1267.

[113] Henry was at Shrewsbury as early as 28th August (Charter Rolls, ii. 79). By 6th September he was deep in the Welsh negotiations (Letters, ii. 314–6). The cardinal received authority on 21st September to arrange a peace (Rymer, i. 473), and the peace itself mentions the 25th as the day on which it was accepted by Henry and Edward and by the Welsh envoys, Einion ap Caradog and Dafydd ab Einion.

[114] Rymer, i. 474. The "duw gwyl galixte bab" of *B.T.* (*Bruts*, 378), *i.e.*, 14th October, perhaps has its origin in some confusion between "pridie *id.* Oct." and "pridie *Kal.* Oct." For a reference to this peace as made at "Rhydchwima" see Peckham, ii. 452, and for the cardinal's satisfaction with what he had done, *Eng. Hist. Rev.* xv. (1900), p. 118.

[115] *Cf. Ann. Cest. s.a.* It would appear that Llywelyn retained Mold, for he dates a letter from the place on 1st May, 1269 (H. and St. i. 497–8).

[116] See *Owens College Essays*, 125, note.

[117] Kerry and Cydewain, originally in no way connected and until 1849 in different dioceses, came into the hands of Llywelyn about 1262 (see note 89 above), and were thereafter usually coupled together in royal grants.

[118] So I interpret the "Burget" of Rymer. Builth, taken by Llywelyn in 1259–60, and not recovered (despite the grant to Edmund of Lancaster on 28th December, 1266 — Charter Rolls, ii. 67), was essential to the maintenance of the prince's position in Mid Wales, whereas Abergavenny (suggested in *Owens College Essays*, 124) was of little importance to him, even were there evidence that he had won it. Further, the king had no "right" ("jus quod habet in ea") in Upper Gwent, which belonged to the young George Cantilupe (Cal. Close R. Ed. I. i. 71, 114), while Builth had been treated since 1240 as the property of the crown.

[119] At his death Humphrey de Bohun held the lordships of Hay and Huntington, but the bulk of Brecknock was in the hands of Llywelyn. See Inq. p. mortem, Hen. III. p. 205. It is clear from Cal. Pat. R. Ed. I. i. 169, and Close R. i. 393, that Llywelyn also retained Elfael, of which the heir, Ralph Tony, was a minor.

[120] See the poems of Hywel Foel in *Myv. Arch.* I. 392–3 (266–7). According to Leland (*Wales*, p. 84), Owain's place of confinement was Dolbadarn Castle.

[121] See Cal. Close Rolls, Ed. I. i. 506 (11th September, 1278), whence it appears that on 12th April, 1272, at Carnarvon, Rhodri executed a deed renouncing all right to any share of Gwynedd on condition of receiving from Llywelyn 1,000 marks to enable him to marry the daughter of John le Botillier. For John and his daughter Edmunda, who afterwards married Thomas de Muleton, see Sweetman, ii. pp. 34, 189

[122] Trivet, 298. He was, perhaps, the "Roderic" son of "Griffin" who in January, 1275, went abroad with the queen mother (Cal. Pat. R. Ed. I. i. 76).

[123] Llyfr Coch Asaph, fo. 53*a*, in *Arch. Camb.* III. xiv. 161.

[124] See the papal confirmation (Lyons, 18th August, 1274) in Rymer, i. 515.

[125] *Cartae Glam.* i. 136.

[126] Rymer, i. 505.

[127] See Rymer, i. 370, 474; Letters, H. III. ii. 220, 286; H. and St. i. 489; *Mont. Coll.* i. (1868), 117.

[128] *B.T.* 356.

[129] *Myv. Arch.* I. 369–70 (254), 390 (265).

[130] See Rymer, i. 394, 474; H. and St. i. 489, 505; *Mont. Coll.* i. 117; *Cartae Glam.* i. 124.

[131] Cal. Close Rolls, Ed. I. i. 506.

[132] *LL.* i. 364 (§ 25).

[133] Rymer, i. 370, 474; H. and St. i. 489, 505; *Mont. Coll.* i. 117; *Gwydir Fam.* 25.

[134] Letters, Hen. III. ii. 351; Rymer, i. 548, Peckham, ii. 447–51, 458–60.

[135] *Reg. Sacr.* (2), 58. The date is approximately determined by the "plusquam triginta annis" of H. and St. i. 496.

[136] M. Paris, *Chron.* iv. 8, 148.

[137] *Ibid.* iv. 647; v. 288, 432, 608. He was with David ap Gruffydd in Lleyn in 1252 (*Rec. Carn.* 252).

[138] *Flores*, ii. 435; Rymer, i. 399.

[139] H. and St. i. 489–93 (from a Peniarth copy, taken from Llyfr Coch Asaph). The arbitrators say that "principem Lewelinum (ab Iorwerth) et suos successores" were the first to seize wreck and treasure-trove on church land (p. 490). See *LL.* i. 554; ii. 54 for a rule as to halving wreck in such cases.

[140] H. and St. i. 494. The royal order to withdraw or suspend the interdict comes, of course, from Earl Simon (15th May, 1265).

[141] *Ibid.* 496–7.

[142] The name Anianus was in use in the early Gallican Church and became popular in Wales at this time, no doubt as an ecclesiastical rendering of Einion.

[143] Leave to elect a successor to Richard was given on 8th November, 1267 and Anian received the temporalities on 12th December, 1267 (Godwin (2),

620). For his consecration see *Reg. Sacr.* (2), 63. He is found in close association with Llywelyn in 1268 (*Cartae Glam.* i. 124), in 1272 (Cal. Close Rolls,
Ed. I. i. 506) and in 1273 (Rymer, i. 505).

[144] Rymer, i. 559.

[145] Peckham, i. 125.

[146] For an account of this MS. see B. Willis, *Bangor*, pp. 70–2, 192–9.

[147] *Ann. Wigorn. s.a.* 1249; H. and St. i. 475–6.

[148] H. and St. i. 489.

[149] Anian I. died before Michaelmas, 1266, when the bishopric was in charge of a
"custos" named Maurice (H. and St. i. 495). In 1267 a certain John was consecrated, with Bishop Anian of Bangor (*Reg. Sacr.* (2), 63), but he died in a few
months, and on 21st October, 1268, Anian II. was consecrated in his stead (H.
and St. i. 498, note a).

[150] For details see Thomas, *St. Asaph*, pp. 41–5.

[151] See the convention of Mold, arrived at on 1st May, 1269 (H. and St. i. 497–8).

[152] See notes 123 and 124 above.

[153] In October, 1272 (*Cartae Glam.* i. 139, 140). On 12th April of that year he was
with Llywelyn at Carnarvon (Cal. Close R. Ed. I. i. 506).

[154] H. and St. i. 498–9.

[155] H. and St. i. 502–3, 503–5, 511–6.

[156] *Rcc. Carn.* 148.

[157] See Rymer, i. 372 (abbot of Aberconwy), 532 (abbot of Cymer).

[158] On 16th January, 1251, the justiciar of Chester was ordered to allow the friars
preachers of Bangor to carry victuals "per aquam de Gannoc et alibi" (Close
Rolls, 35 Hen. III., cited in *The Reliquary*, vol. xxiv. p. 225). The prior of the
preachers of Bangor was concerned in the agreement between Llywelyn and
Bishop Richard and also in that with Gruffydd ap Gwenwynwyn.

[159] The date of the appointment of Bishop Anian II, of St. Asaph. He was succeeded at Rhuddlan by a certain Cynwrig — see charter of 1270 in *Trib. System*,
App. 105 (Fr[atr]e Kenewrike Priore de Buthlan).

[160] In 1263 (*Mont. Coll.* i. 117). *Cf.* "frater Johannes Rufus" of H. and St. i.489.

[161] *B.T.* The Red Book text (*Bruts*, 379) is corrupt.

[162] For Madog Fychan see Rymer, i. 258 (Maddok f. Maddok), 370 (Madant
Parvo); Letters, Hen. III. ii. 286. He died in December, 1269 (*B.T.*). Hywel
appears in M. Paris, *Chron.* iv. 318; Charter Rolls, i. 309; Letters, H. III. ii. 286;
Rymer, i. 420. He was alive in September, 1267 (Rymer, i. 474), but died
before his brother Gruffydd, without heir to his manor of Eyton (*Trib. System*,
App. 102, 104).

[163] *Trib. System*, App. 101–3. For Emma see chap. xix. note 88. In 1278 she
resigned Maelor Saesneg to the king (Cal. Close R. i. 513).

[164] Cal. Close R. i. 399.

[165] He appears as "dominus de Yale" in February, 1278 (*Arch. Camb.* III. xiv.(1868), 329).

[166] In an ode addressed to him by the poet Llygad Gwr he is called "dreic y weun" (the Dragon of Chirk), and reference is made to his exploits in the Ceiriog Valley and against Whittington (y drewen) and Ellesmere (*Myv. Arch.* I. 341). He held Glyndyfrdwy also (Cal. Close R. i. 399 — Glenfridewe), and Llanarmon (Charter Rolls, ii. 213) and Lledrod (Peckham, ii. 463), the last two in Cynllaith.

[167] Charter Rolls, ii. 266. Bankerbur(y) is the "Bancornaburg" of Bede, *H.E.* ii. 2 — *cf.* Bankeburw of *Tax. Nich.* 248.

[168] "Cum confirmacione Lewelini tunc principis Walliae" (*Trib. S.* App. 102).

[169] For references to Madog see Rymer, i. 258, 370. By the convention of 1263 he was to retain Mawddwy for life as the vassal of his brother Gruffydd (*Mont. Coll.* i. 118).

[170] See chap. xix. note 93.

[171] *Cartae Glam.* i. 136.

[172] Dolforwyn ("The Maiden's Meadow" — see chap. viii. p. 249) is a township in the parish of Betws Cydewain. The castle is first mentioned by this name in *B.T. s.a.* 1274, but it would seem to be beyond a doubt the castle at "Abrunol," *i.e.*, Abermule, which Llywelyn was ordered on 23rd June, 1273, to desist from building (Rymer, i. 504). For an account of the ruins see *Med. Mil. Arch.* ii. 3.

[173] Our information comes from *B.T.* and the letter of the dean and chapter of Bangor to the Archbishop of Canterbury (18th April, 1276) in Rymer, i. 532.

[174] This was in April. The "thirteen trefs beyond the Dovey in Rhiw Helyg" taken out of Cyfeiliog would appear to be represented by the modern parish of Llanwrin (Owen, *Pemb.* i. 221), but one hesitates to accept the assertion of the jurors of 1375 and 1427 that this region "inter aquas de Dyvi et Dewlas" anciently formed part of Meinonydd and had been wrongfully transferred to Cyfeiliog about 1200 (*Mont. Coll.* i. 255–6). Their account of this matter and also of the position of Arwystli is full of obvious historical errors, and the Dulas was certainly the western boundary of the commote in 1201 (Penn. iii. 459 — charter of Gwenwynwyn).

[175] At the end of December the sheriff of Shropshire was told to allow Gruffydd and his "familiares" to dwell in Shrewsbury until further orders (Cal. Close R. i. 142).

[176] Among other territories Llywelyn occupied Gorddwr, taken by Gruffydd from Thomas Corbet, as far as Bausley (Cal. Close Rolls, i. 374).

[177] Rhys's brother Llywelyn died on 13th January, 1265 (*B.T.* 352). Rhys himself first appears in 1274, when he obtained Perfedd (the "Middle" commote of the cantref of Penweddig); see *B.T.* 360.

[178] For references to these three see *B.T. s.a.* 1273, 1274, 1275. Owain died in the last-mentioned year, leaving a young son, Llywelyn.

[179] *B.T.* 358, where "y whechet dyd wedy Awst" is obviously a mistake for "vi ante Kal. Aug." Maredudd was buried at Whitland and Rhys Ieuanc at Talley. For the concession of Maredudd's homage to Llywelyn see Bridgeman, *Princes of South Wales* (1876), p. 147.

[180] On 6th December, 1265 (*Eng. Hist. Rev.* x. (1895), p. 31).

[181] For text and translation see *Royal Charters*, 45–50. The commission given on 19th May, 1275, to master Henry of Bray (keeper of Abergavenny) and Hywel ap Meurig is in the Patent Rolls (Cal. Ed. I. i. 119).

[182] John Laundry, holder in 1275 of one knight's fee in the lordship, was "dominus de Lantelyo Abercowen" (*Carm. Cart.* No. 45). His ancestor Landric was in this region as early as the reign of Henry I. (Pipe Roll, 31 Hen. I. 89).

[183] On the death of Patrick of Chaworth in 1258, his widow, Hawise, lady of Kidwelly in her own right, obtained the custody of his land and heir (*Rot. Fin.* ii. 308; *cf.* Inq. p. m. Hen. III. p. 113). In due course Pain succeeded and in 1275 he appears as holder of the barony of Kidwelly and Carnwyllion. "Hawise of London" died in 1274 (Inq. p. m. Ed. I. p. 38).

[184] For Llywelyn's conquest of Elfael after the death of Roger Tony in 1264, and his power thereuntil dislodged in 1276, see Cal. Pat. Rolls, Ed. I. i. 169, and Cal. Close Rolls, i. 393.

[185] Humphrey became Earl of Hereford upon the death of his grandfather on 24th September, 1275 (*Mon. Angl.* vi. 135; *cf.* Inq. p. m. Ed. I. p. 70).

[186] Letter of 30th October in *Cartae Glam.* i. 138–40.

[187] Cal. Close Rolls, i. 56 (13th September, 1273). Peter fitz Herbert had been succeeded at Blaenllyfni in 1235 by his son Herbert (*Rot. Fin.* i. 282–3), who died in 1248 (*ibid.* ii. 35) and was followed by his brother Reginald. The lordship was reckoned a third of the barony of Brecknock and included Talgarth and Llangors. Reginald held it until his death in 1286 (Inq. p. m. Ed. I. 365). An entry in the Charter Rolls (ii. 248) shows that Hugh Turbeville held Crickhowel (or Ystrad Yw Isaf) of Reginald as a mesne lordship.

[188] Cal. Pat. R. i. 48.

[189] See the commission of 8th February, 1275, to determine whether the manor of Glasbury was (1) within the county of Hereford, (2) an independent marcher holding, or (3) parcel of the lordship of Brecknock (Cal. Pat. R. i. 116–7).

[190] *Ann. ad* 1298. For Gruffydd see *Cartae Glam.* i. 109.

[191] *Ann. ad* 1298.

[192] *Cartae Glam.* i. 123–5. The bishop of Exeter and other royal commissioners met at Montgomery on 14th September, 1268 (Rymer, i. 477), and this agreement followed on the 27th. "Pontem Monachorum in Cantref (s)ely" was, no doubt, near Gwenddwr, where the Cistercian abbey of Dore had property (*Mon. Angl.* v. 554).

[193] *Ann. ad* 1298 give the date as 13th October. I follow *B.T.* as to the year and connect the incident with the royal letter of 16th October, 1270 (Rymer, i. 486).

[194] *Ann. ad* 1298 (1st June). For an account of the extensive ruins see *Med. Mil. Arch.* i. 315–35.

[195] For the bishops' instructions (25th October, 1271), see *Cartae Glam.* i. 133–4, and for their convention with Llywelyn (and November), *ibid.* 134–6. A letter from Henry to his brother Richard tells us what happened (*ibid.* 136–8), and another to Llywelyn, dated 22nd February, 1272, is a lame attempt at an explanation (Letters, H. III. ii. 342–4).

[196] *Myv. Arch.* I. 368 (253). "Porth Wegyr" is Cemais harbour.

[197] H. and St. i. 500–1 (from Rymer, i. 515).

[198] At the death of Henry, the only sum in arrear was one of £2,000, due at Christmas, 1271, and assigned by the king, first to Alexander III. of Scotland and then to the London merchant, Poins of "Mora" (*Calendar of Documents relating to Scotland*, vol. i. No. 2580; Cal. Close R. Ed. I. i. 2, 57; Cal. Pat. R. i. 72).

[199] Rymer, i, 505. Reginald was justiciar from 1270 until Michaelmas, 1274 (*Ann. Cest.*). "Ryd Gastell" belonged to Aberconwy and adjoined its lands at Pentre Foelas (Williams, *Aberconwy*, pp. 166–7).

[200] For remonstrances on this head see Rymer, i. 505, 519; Cal. Close Rolls, i. 2, 57, 110.

[201] See Rymer, i. 499, for the fruitless mission of the abbots of Dore and Haughmond in January, 1273.

[202] Rymer, i. 519. Edward was at Northampton in the early part of November, 1274.

[203] About Christmas the sheriff of Shropshire was ordered to allow Gruffydd ap Gwenwynwyn and his companions to dwell in the town of Shrewsbury until further orders (Cal. Close R. i. 142). The result is seen in the events described in a letter of Llywelyn's, written from Aberyddon, which Shirley (Letters, H. III. ii. 328) assigns (with some doubt) to 1st May, 1269, but which should clearly, for the following reasons, be dated 22nd May, 1275: (1) The reference to "forma pacis" shows that the letter belongs to the period 1267–76. But there is nothing to suggest that Llywelyn and Gruffydd had any quarrel, or that the former occupied Ystrad Marchell, Llannerch Hudol, and Arwystli, between the peace of 1267 and the rupture of 1274. (2) Llywelyn is known to have been at Aberyddon on 25th May, 1275 (H. and St. i. 505), a date which in 1275 was only three days removed from "vigilia Ascensionis". (3) In May, 1275, the "parliamentum Londoniae," *i.e.*, of Westminster, the first of the reign, was just over. The new date proposed, of course, involves a slight change in the text of the letter, *viz.*, the substitution of "E" for "H" in the address.

[204] Rymer, i. 526, 528; Cal. Close R. i. 196, 241; *Ann. Cest.*

[205] Rymer, i. 528 (H. and St. i. 506–8). I cannot identify "Treschyn". At a later time John XXI. intervened with the king on behalf of Llywelyn — see *Papal Letters*, i. p. 452.

[206] This is asserted by Trevet (294) and *Ann. Winton* (121).

[207] She was born at Kenilworth in October, 1252 (*Dict. Nat. Biog.* xxxviii. p. 282).

[208] She died between 9th January (Cal. Close R. Ed. I. i. 224) and 3rd June, 1275 (Inq. p. mortem, Ed. I. p. 90). As she had been fully reconciled to her nephew, the king, and had received her dower lands (*Ann. Dunst.*, p. 258 and Cal. Pat. R. Ed. I. i. 59), it is not likely that the match was her work.

[209] *B.T.* says that Llywelyn wedded her "drwy eireu kyndrychawl," *i.e.*, per verba de praesenti. This is confirmed by *Ann. Dunst.* (266 —"per nuntios") and Llywelyn accordingly calls her his wife in 1276 (Rymer, i. 535).

[210] See especially the "juvencula elegantissima" of *Flores*, ii. 46.

[211] The accounts of the capture differ in detail. But it is certain that it was effected by sailors from Bristol — see Cal. Pat. R. Ed. I. i. 161. Further, Cont. Fl. Wig. refers to a certain knight named "Thomas Archidiaconus" as the man who laid the plot (216), and it is, therefore, significant to find that on 28th May, 1276, the sheriff of Cornwall was ordered to pay £20 to "Thomas le Ercedekne" for expenses incurred by him in carrying out a mysterious commission of the king's in that region (Cal. Close R. i. 292). This confirms the statement of Trevet that the capture took place "ad insulas Sillinas," on the direct route, and not, as other chroniclers allege, near Bristol, the vessel having accidentally got out of its course (Gervase ii. 283; Wykes, 267).

[212] *Ann. Osen.* 267. The order of 23rd January, 1276, as to prisoners whom the king is sending to Corfe, has reference, no doubt, to Amaury and his companions (Cal. Close R. i. 266) and enables us to assign the capture to the early weeks of the year.

[213] Morris, 140–1.

[214] Cal. Pat. R. i. 169 — *cf.* Cal. Close R. i. 393.

[215] *B.T.* 364.

[216] Cal. Close R. i. 374.

[217] Rymer, i. 544 (Flint, 16th August, 1277).

[218] *B.T.* 364.

[219] See the agreement of 11th April, 1277, in Rymer, i. 542.

[220] Peckham, ii. 451; Cal. Pat. R. Ed. I. i. 212.

[221] *B.T.* 366.

[222] Morris, 118–26.

[223] For its text see Rymer, i. 545.

[224] These were (1) Dafydd ap Gruffydd ab Owain Brogyntyn, whose elegy was sung by Bleddyn Fardd (*Myv. Arch.* I. 369 (253-4)); (2) Elise ab Iorwerth ab Owain; (3, 4) Two sons of Owain ap Bleddyn ab Owain. For the family see chap. xix. note 51.

[225] *B.T.* 368.

[226] *B.T.* 370.

[227] Cal. Pat. R. Ed. I. i. 231-2 (10th October, 1277); Peckham, ii. 445.

[228] The marriage had taken place before 2nd January, 1278 (Cal. Close R. i. 491). Trevet (298) is the authority for the lady's parentage and his account is confirmed by the statement of Hemingburgh that she was a relative of the king's (ii. 9), for Robert Ferrers, eighth Earl of Derby, married a daughter of Hugh XI. of Lusignan, half-brother of Henry III.

[229] Immediately after the conclusion of the treaty, Edward remitted the war indemnity of 50,000 marks and the prescribed annual render of 1,000 marks for Anglesey (Rymer, i. 546, 547).

[230] Trevet, 297.

[231] Cont. Fl. Wig. ii. 218–9; *Ann. Winton.* p. 125; *B.T.* 370. For the safe-conduct see Rymer, i. 548.

[232] On 4th January, 1278, the king was inquiring what dower Llywelyn proposed to allow to Eleanor (Rymer, i. 549).

[233] *Ann. Osen.* p. 276. Edward was at Rhuddlan from the 8th to the 12th of September.

[234] *B.T.; Ann. Osen.;* Cont. Fl. Wig.; Trevet (298). Edward bore the cost of the festivities and conveyed the bride's luggage as far as Oswestry — see Blaauw, *Barons' War,* second ed. p. 333, note, where "Whitchurch" is the usual mistranslation of "Album Monasterium".

[235] "Iuxta Bangoriam" (Trevet, 304). Powel (272) defines more precisely as "the place called Moel y donn" (near Portdinorwic), but upon what authority is not evident.

[236] So the contemporary Bury chronicler (Cont. Fl. Wig. ii. 227).

INDEX

The numbers refer to pages, bolder type indicating the principal reference.
n = note.

Abraham, Archdeacon of Gwent, 9.

—, Bp. of St. Asaph, 675 $n.^{111}$, 379 $n.^{204}$.

—, Bp. of St. David's, 72.

Accomplices, penalties against, 306.

Adam, Bp. of St. Asaph, **140-41 and 335 n.**^{119}.

— of Roch, 367 $n.^{27}$.

Ælfgar, Earl of Mercia, 6-7, 10 and 283 $n.^{32}$.

Agnes (Nest), wife of Bernard of Neufmarché, 289 $n.^{135}$, 58.

Alan Fergant.

— of Brittany, Count, 443.

Album Monasterium, places so called, 358 $n.^{118}$.

Alexander I., King of Scotland, 76 and 307 $n.^{6}$.

— III., Pope, 116.

—, Cistercian Abbot, 184.

— (Cuhelyn), Archdeacon of Bangor, 334 $n.^{98}$, 143 and 336 $n.^{137}$.

—, Bp. of Lincoln, 325 $n.^{151}$.

Alfred, King of England,

— of Marlborough, 30.

Alicia de Clare, wife of Cadwaladr, 96 and 315 $n.^{18}$.

Allectus, 119 and 326 $n.^{162}$.

Alretone. See Cause.

Amaury de Montfort, 267 and 401 $n.^{212}$.

Amwythig. See Shrewsbury.

Anarawd ap Gruffydd of S. Wales, 84, 89, **95**, 101.

Angharad, wife of Gruffydd ap Cynan, 294 $n.^{57}$, 76 and 307 $n.^{7}$, 80.

— — — Gruffydd ap Madog, 145.

— — — Iorwerth ab Owain, 90.

— — — Llywelyn ap Seisyll and later of Cynfyn, 12, 285 $n.^{65}$.

Angharad, wife of William fitz Martin, 286 $n.^{103}$.

— — — William of Barry, 138.

Angle (on Milford Haven), church, 140.

Anglesey (Mona, Môn) —

Aberconwy lands in, 168.

Arfon, Lleyn and Arllechwedd combined with, 162.

Cadwaladr ap Gruffydd driven from, 95.

Ednyfed's descendants in, 221.

Fertility of, 171.

Magnus Barefoot's rout of Normans in (1098), 39-40.

Manx troops in (1193), 161.

Render for, remitted (1277), 402 $n.^{229}$.

Anian (Einion), Bp. of Bangor, **260 and 396-97 n.**$^{142-6}$, 263.

— I., Bp. of St. Asaph, 260.

— II., Bp. of St. Asaph, 260–61 and 397 $nn.^{149, 153}$.

Annest dau. of Gruffydd ap Cynan, 307 $n.^{7}$.

Anselm, Abp. of Canterbury, 42, 66, **67**.

—, Bp. of St. David's, 373 $n.^{111}$.

Archenfield (Erging) —

de Burgh's grant of (1227), 214 and 372 $n.^{95}$.

Devastation of, by Gruffydd ap Llywelyn, 8.

Ardudwy, 95, 145 and 336$n.^{147}$, 222.

Arfon (see also Carnarvon and Segontium) —

Privileges of, 224.

otherwise mentioned, 162, 168.

Arllechwedd, 162, 168.

Armorican peninsula. See Brittany.

Arnulf. See Montgomery.

Arwystli —

Gruffydd deprived of, 262-63.

Gwenwynwyn's acquisition of (1197), 158-159.

INDEX

— ap Rhiwallon of Maelor, 18.

— ap Rhys ap Gruffydd, 147, **155 and 340 n.**[24].

— the Tall of Edeyrnion, 36.

DAFYDD. See David.

— ab Owain Gwynedd — repels Henry II., 99-100; kills Hywel at Pentraeth, 134 *and* 332 *n.*[64]; aggressions of, 135; marriage with Emma, 136 *and* 333 *n.*[78]; hostilities against Rhodri and sons of Cynan, 137; swears fealty to Henry II. (1177), 138; position of, in Rhuddlan, 145; defeated by Llywelyn, 161 *and* 344 *n.*[75]; closing years in England, 162; otherwise mentioned, 112, 152, 351 *n.*[5].

Danes —

Ireland, in. *See under* Ireland.

Pwll Dyfach defeat (1042), 4.

Welsh assistance to, against Wales, 5.

Daniel ap Sulien, Archdeacon of Powys, 68 *and* 305 *n.*[216], **74.**

David, St., status of, as archbishop, 91.

—, Archdeacon of Bangor, 116.

David, Archdeacon of St. Asaph, 225.

—, Bp. of Bangor, 69, 79-80, 89 *and* 313 *n.*[90].

— ab Owain Gwynedd. *See* Dafydd.

David ap Gruffydd ap Llywelyn, defeated and imprisoned by Llywelyn, 241 *and* 388 *n.*[128]; released by Llywelyn for 1256 campaign, 242; goes over to the English (1263), 251 *and* 393 *n.*[79]; provisions as to, in Treaty of Montgomery, 258; evil influence of, on Llywelyn, 259; conspiracy against Llywelyn and flight to England (1274), **263,** 267; Edward I.'s provision for, 269-70 *and* 402 *n.*[228]; hostilities of 1282,

270; otherwise mentioned, 237 *and* 385 *n.*[82], 247 *and* 391 *n.*[47], 250, 254.

— ap Llywelyn ab Iorwerth, recognition of, as heir — by English government (1220), **205 and 365 n.**[5], 222; by the Pope (1222), 222; by Welsh magnates (1226), 222; does homage (1229), **212,** 222; granted Purleigh Manor, 217 *and* 375 *n.*[133]; marriage to Isabella de Breos, **213,** 222; conflicts with his brother Gruffydd, 222, 226; receives fealty of Welsh princes (1238), 226; at Council of Gloucester, 227 *and* 380 *n.*[3]; negotiations with England as to lands in dispute, 227-28; English expeditions against, 228 *and* 381 *nn*.[19, 22]; formidable hostilities against English, 232-34; death of, 235; estimate of, 235; otherwise mentioned, 210, 372 *n.*[92], 216 *n.*[121].

De Bec, de Burgh, de Breos, etc. *See* Bec, Burgh, Breos, etc.

De la Mare, Richard, 51 *and* 296 *n.*[86], 82.

Degannwy —

Destruction of, by David (1241), 230.

English possession of, 231.

Llywelyn's acquisition of (1200), 177 *and* 351 *n.*[3].

Welsh raid on, against Robert of Rhuddlan, 26.

Degannwy castle —

Building of (1245), 234, 235.

Chartered borough, 236-37.

Creuddyn dominated by, 389 *n.*[21].

Destroyed and rebuilt (1210), 189.

Llywelyn ab Iorwerth's capture of (1213), 194.

— ap Gruffydd's hostilities against (1257), 245, 246; his acquisition of (1263), 252.

otherwise mentioned, 222, 240, 242.

Norton (Radnorshire), 28 *and* 288
n.[121], 366 n.[15]; castle, 250.
Nunneries, Cistercian, **170;** at
Llanllugan, **170,** 363 n.[182]; at
Llansantffraid, **167,** 170.

ODO of Barry, 49.
— of Carew, 295 n.[70], 140.
Offa, King of Mercia, 196 *and* n.[10],
197–201 *and nn.*[17, 19, 23].
Ogmore, 53, 238; castle, 60.
Olaf Godfreyson.
—, son of Godred, 343 n.[70].
Orreby, Philip of, Justice of Chester,
366 n.[14].
Osney Abbey, 118.
Oswestry —
Burning of (1234), 375 n.[140].
English recovery of (1155), 106.
Fitz Alan family at, 106, 148, 200, 240.
Henry II. at (1165), 112 *and* 346 n.[116].
John at (1211), 191 *and* 358 n.[118].
Madog's seizure of, 97.
Rainald the sheriff in possession of, 25.
Otto (Papal legate), 229 *and* 381 n.[12]
Ottobon, Card., 395 *and nn.*[109, 113, 114].
Overton (Avretone — Richard's Castle),
29 *and* 28 n.[122.]
— Madog, 220.
Overwent. *See* Gwent Uchcoed.
Owain ab Edwin, 291 n.[33], 38, **40, 44,** 76.
— ab Iorwerth of Caerleon, 129, 131.
—ap Bleddyn ab Owain Brogyntyn,
220 *and* 376 n.[156], 376 n.[51], 391
n.[47], 254, 257.
— ap Cadwgan, **44,** 75.
— ap Caradog, 52, **56.**
— ap Caradog ab Iestyn, 338 n.[187].
— ap Dafydd, 162, 194.
—ap Gruffydd ap Cynan. *See* Owain
Gwynedd.
— ap Gruffydd ap Gwenwynwyn, 263.

— ap Gruffydd ap Llywelyn. *See* Owain
Goch.
— ap Gruffydd ap Madog, 262.
— ap Gruffydd ap Maredudd. *See*
Owain Cyfeiliog.
— ap Gruffydd ap Rhys — with Rhys
acquires Cantref Bychan, 181; relations with Llywelyn, 182; success
against Maelgwn, 190; supports
Llywelyn (1211), 190; in submission to John, **191,** 193 *and* 360
n.[132]; routs Rhys with English aid,
194; in alliance with Maelgwn,
197; with Llywelyn (Dec. 1215),
199; territories assigned to (1216),
199; hostilities against Reginald de
Breos, 201; accession of territory
to, on death of Rhys, 205; submits
to Henry, 204; otherwise mentioned, 180, 209, 210 *and* 370 n.[68],
215, 218.
Owain ap Gruffydd Maelor, 158 *and*
341 n.[44].
— ap Hywel ab Ieuaf. *See* Owain o'r
Brithdir.
— ap Hywel of Kerry (1245), 383 n.[51].
— ap Llywelyn ab Owain Fychan, 237
and 386 n.[93].
— ap Madog ap Maredudd. *See* Owain
Brogyntyn *and* Owain Fychan.
— ap Maredudd of Cydewain, 237,
391 n.[47].
— ap Maredudd of Elfael, 248 *and* 392
n.[58].
— ap Maredudd ab Owain, 263 *and*
398 n.[178].
— Brogyntyn ap Madog ap Maredudd,
97 *and* 316 n.[31], 107, **145 and 337
n.**[158].
— Cyfeiliog ap Gruffydd ap Maredudd,
title of, 93; settled by his uncle
Madog, 93, 97; in the muster at

Corwen, 153; on English side, 115; poetic talent of, 124; opposed to Abp. Baldwin, 143; death and estimate of, 158 *and* 341 *n.*[41]; English estimate of, 137 *and* 333 *n.*[84]; otherwise mentioned, 107 *and* 321 *n.*[86], 145, 167.

— Fychan ab Owain Fychan, 220 *and* 376 *n.*[155], 381 *n.*[15].

— Fychan ap Madog ap Maredudd, 107 *and* 321 *n.*[86], 115, 116, 124, **137 and 373 n.**[85], **145 and 337 n.**[153], 376 *n.*[155].

— Goch (the Red) ap Gruffydd ap Llywelyn, imprisoned by David (1238), 226; delivered to the King 230; released (1244), 233; divides Gwynedd inheritance with Llywelyn, 236; defeated and imprisoned by Llywelyn, 240; kept imprisoned, 258 *and* 396 *n.*[120]; released and established in Lleyn, 269; otherwise mentioned, 391 *n.*[47], 249, 393 *n.*[79], 268.

Owain Gwynedd ap Gruffydd ap Cynan
— invades Ceredigion, 81, 84; opposition of, to Bp. Meurig, 87, 88; hostilities against Cadwaladr, 95; victorious progress of, 96; loss of his son Rhun, 26; capture of Mold, 306 *n.*[238], 78, 82, **96;** builds Castell of Rhodwydd, 96 *and* 316 *n.*[23]; secures Iâl and Tegeingi, 96, **97;** Henry II.'s expedition against (1175), 99; pacific attitude towards Henry II., 108, 108; rising of 1165, 111 ; attacks royal castles in Tegeingl, 114; controversy as to see of Bangor, 116; refusal of, to give up his wife Cristin, 94, **116;** death of, 116 *and* 324 *n.*[136]; estimate of, 94; sons of, 332 *n.*[64], oth-

erwise mentioned 76, 77 *and* 308 *n.*[19], 110.

— o'r Brithdir (ap Hywel), 146 *and* 337 *n.*[161], 159 *and* 342 *n.*[47].

Oystermouth (Ystum Llwynarth), castle, 362 *n.*[168].

PAINSCASTLE (Castle Maud) —
Cession of, to Llywelyn by Simon de Montfort, 254.
Maud's defence of, 160 *and* 342 *nn.*[55-6].
Rebuilding of (1231), 215 *and* 373 *n.*[115].
Rhys' success against (1196), 157.
Tony possession of, 394 *n.*[97].
Painscastle, battle of (1198), **160 and 342 nn.**[57-9], 162, 179.

Pandulf (Papal legate), 195, 204.
Pantulf, William, 24, 42.
Parliament, first Welsh, 199.
Pascal II., Pope, 65.
Pastoral basis of Welsh society in 12th cent., 171.
Pebidiog, 38.
Pembroke —
Henry II. at (1171), 129 *and* 329 *nn.*[23-4].
Priory at, 53.
Pembroke, Earls of —
Clare, Richard of, 109, **127,** 132, **149.**
Fitz Gilbert, Gilbert, 86, 102, 328 *n.*[4].
Marshall, Gilbert, 219, **231 and 380 n.**[9], **231,** 386 *n.*[99], 374 *n.*[104].
—, Richard, **217 and 374 n.**[127], 218, 681, **681.**
—, Walter, 386 *n.*[104].
—, William (the elder), **149 and 338 n.**[181], **181 and 353 n.**[40], 197, 201, **203,** 204, 367 *n.*[26]; end of male line of, 238 *and* 386 *n.*[104].
—, William (the younger), 206 *and* 366 *n.*[19], 368 *n.*[44], 210, 211, 213 *and* 371 *nn.*[87, 91], 214.

possession (1247), 237.

Gwynedd's acquisition of (1118), 77.

mentioned, 168.

Rhun ab Owain Gwynedd, 94, **96**, 332 *n.*[64].

Rhwng Gwy a Hafren, 112.

— Nedd ac Afan, 60, 373 *n.*[109].

Rbyd Chwima, 248, 256.

— y Groes, battle of (1039), **3 and 281 n.**[4].

Rhydderch ab Iestyn. King of S. Wales.

— ap Tewdwr, 52, 56 *and* 299 *n.*[114].

Rhydygors castle, **34,** 36, 37, 51.

Rhygylarch ap Sulien, **74.**

— of Cardigan, 155 *and* 347 *n.*[125].

Rhys ab Iestyn, 60 *and* 301 *n.*[152].

— ab Owain ab Edwin, King of Deheubarth, **16, 27,** 291 *n.*[31].

— ap Gruffydd ab Ifor, 215 *and* 373 *n.*[109], 383 *n.*[40], 383 *n.*[51], 239 *and* 387 *n.*[114].

— ap Gruffydd ap Rhys (Yr Arglwydd Rhys) — storms Mabudryd castle, 142; builds Tomen Las, 104; submits to Henry II., 105-6; attacks castles of Dyfed, 148; captures Llandovery (1162), 149; again submits to Henry (1163), 109-10; attacks Ceredigion, 111; rising of 1165, 111; reconquers Ceredigion, 113-4; aids Owain to capture Rhuddlan, 115; exceptional position of, 126; favoured by Henry, 127, 128-9; attitude towards Dermot's Irish invasion, 127; confirmed in his possessions, 129-30; appointed "Justice of S. Wales, 130 *and* 330 *n.*[33]; called "the Lord Rhys," 130 *and* 330 *n.*[34]; aids Henry (1173), 131 *and* 330 *nn.*[37-40]; organises first Eisteddfod, 133-34; claim of, to Meirionydd, 136, 145;

entertains Abp. Baldwin, 143, 145-6; difficulties with his sons, 147-8; close of reign of, 149; raids by, in S. Wales (1189), 152; hostility against King Richard, 152; attacks by, on Norman castles, 152-53; hostilities against Normans, 156; death of, 151, **157;** estimate of, 130; attitude of, towards monastic institutions, 166 *el seq.,* 169; family feuds among sons of, 154, 156; otherwise mentioned, 57, 84 *and* 311 *n.*[53], 115, 336 *n.*[140].

Rhys ap Gruffydd ap Rhys (son of Matilda de Breos). *See* Rhys Ieuanc.

— ap Hywel ap Maredudd, 311 *nn.*[60-1].

— ap Maelgwn Fychan, 238 *and* 386 *n.*[97].

— ap Maredudd of Dryslwyn, 263, 268.

— ap Rhydderch, 5 *and* 282 *n.*[14].

— ap Rhys ap Gruffydd. *See* Rhys Gryg.

— ap Rhys ap Maelgwn. *See* Rhys Ieuanc.

— ap Rhys Mechyll. *See* Rhys Fychan (of Dinefwr).

— ap Tewdwr, King of Deheubarth, pedigree of, 27 *and* 287 *n.*[116]; at Mynydd Cam, 21-22, 27; successes of, 31; death of, **31,** 289 *n.*[1], 34 *and* 290 *n.*[9]; otherwise mentioned, 44, 67, 163, 347 *n.*[122].

— Fychan (Ieuanc) ap Rhys Mechyll of Dinefwr, difficulties of, 238; ejected from Dinefwr and Carreg Cennen (1256), 242-3 *and* 389 *n.*[17]; possessions of, in Great and Little Cantrefs, 389 *n.*[18]; deserts from the English, 244; destroys Builth Castle, 248; death and burial of, 263 *and* 399 *n.*[179]; otherwise mentioned, 382 *n.*[39], 242, 247 *and* 391 *n.*[47], 254.

SAER (Norman knight), 43 *and* 293
n.[49], 44.

Sai, Robert of (Picot), 34, 29, 294 n.[57], 46.

St. Asaph —
Abeyance of See of, in 11th and 12th cents., 69-70.
Gilbert's consecration to (1143), 90 *and* 314 n.[110].
Spoliation of, by Normans, 71.

St. Clear's, 264; Cluniac Priory of, 344 n.[84].

— Clear's Castle, **153 and 339 n.**[12], 156, 199, 371 n.[86].

St. David's (Mynyw, Menevia) —
Archdeaconries of, 346 n.[115].
Fame and importance of, **67.**
Henry II.'s visit to (1171), 129 *and* 329 n.[24-5].
Independence of, 64-65 *and* 303 n.[180].
Metropolitanate controversy, **91;** under Bp. Bernard, **87-88 and 312-13 nn.**[77-85]; (1176), 141; (1188), 143; (1198–1203), 183 *et seq.*
Norman bishop of (1115), 50.
— re-dedication of 71-72.
— spoliation of, 71.
Rebuilding at cathedral of (13th cent.), 223 *and* 378 n.[200].
Rhys ap Gruffydd buried in, 157 *and* 341 n.[39].
Subordination of, to English Primate, 67, 68.
William the Conqueror's visit to (1081), 27-28.

St. Dogmael's Abbey, 53 *and* 298 n.[107].
— John family, 301 n.[153].
Re-dedication by Normans of churches founded by, 71-72.

Salisbury, Patrick, Earl of, 108.
Salkeld church, 362 n.[170].

Samson, Bp. of St. David's, 91.
—, St., Abp. of Dol, 87, **91.**
Sanan, dau. of Dyfnwal, 294 n.[57].
Say, Helias of, 311 n.[59].
—, Hugh de, 156 *and* 341 n.[36].
—, Margaret de, 394 n.[93].

Scotland —
Eisteddfod competitors invited from, 133.
Llywelyn's alliance with national party in (1258), 246 *and* 491 nn.[42-3, 46-7].
Troops from, with Henry II. against Welsh (1165), 152.

Segontium, (*See also* Carnarvon.)
Seinhenyd. *See* Swansea.
Seisyll, Abbot of Strata Florida, 167.
— ap Dyfnwal, 131 *and* 331 n.[47], **133, 134.**
— Brynwrch, 121, **124,** 135.
Selyf, 300 n.[137].
Senena, wife of Gruffydd ap Llywelyn, 385 n.[82].

Senghenydd —
Kidnapping of Earl William to (1158), 107.
Welsh possession of, in Norman times, 61.
mentioned, 373 n.[109], 239 *and* 387 n.[114].

Shrewsbury —
Henry II.'s army at (1165), 112.
Llywelyn's acquisition of, 196.

Shrewsbury, Earls of —
Montgomery, Hugh, 35 *and* 290 n.[18], 291 n.[25], **38.**
—, Roger, 22, **24-25, 33,** 290 n.[18].
Robert of Bellême, 290 n.[13], 40, **41.**

Shrewsbury castle, 97, 196.
Sigurd Magnusson, 293 n.[44].
Simeon of Clynnog, Archdeacon, 80 *and* 309 n.[25], 88 *and* 313 n.[93].
Simon de Montfort. *See* Leicester.